News for All the People

News for All the People

The Epic Story of Race and the American Media

Juan González and Joseph Torres

VERSO

London • New York

First published by Verso 2011
© Juan González and Joseph Torres 2011

1 3 5 7 9 10 8 6 4 2

Verso
UK: 6 Meard Street, London W1F 0EG
US: 20 Jay Street, Suite 1010, Brooklyn, NY 11201
www.versobooks.com

Verso is the imprint of New Left Books

ISBN-13: 978-1-84467-687-3

British Library Cataloguing in Publication Data
A catalogue record for this book is available from the British Library

Library of Congress Cataloging-in-Publication Data
A catalog record for this book is available from the Library of Congress

Typeset in Bembo by MJ Gavan, Cornwall
Printed in the US by Maple Vail

For
Gabriela González and Charis Torres

Contents

Introduction

> The ways in which information passes through a society are the key to that society's culture and are inseparable from its understanding of how to preserve itself and its internal group relationships. It is the silences that control a society and keep it "stable" much more than the conscious noise it generates.
>
> Anthony Smith, *The Geopolitics of Information*, 1980

In no place on earth has the daily production of news formed such an integral part of a people's image of themselves—of a national narrative—as in the United States. From the earliest decades of the Republic, Americans consumed more newspapers per capita than any people on earth. Today, we are literally drowning in news and information; we have 1,400 daily newspapers, 1,700 full-power television stations, 12,000 radio stations, 17,000 magazines, and hundreds of channels to choose from on our cable systems. We have news at five, at six, at ten and at eleven o'clock. We have a raft of twenty-four-hour cable news, sports and business networks, and hundreds of thousands of Internet news sites—from the Drudge Report, to the Huffington Post, to an endless stream of YouTube videos, all available at any hour of the day or night.

Access to instant news has become so indispensable to modern society that major media companies now wield unprecedented influence over public thought. The media amplify those events they wish to while exiling others to the shadows; they fashion political and popular heroes one day only to tear them down the next; they interpret the meaning of the most earth-shaking or insignificant incident before our morning coffee or commute back home.

Despite this incessant chatter, many Americans remain remarkably misinformed about the world around us, while the professional journalists who produce our news routinely engender fear and loathing from the mightiest politician or celebrity, as well as from the lowliest citizen. The believability of our nation's news organizations has plummeted sharply in recent decades. A 2005 survey by the Pew Research Center for the People and the Press found that only 19 percent of Americans believed the primary concern of news media was keeping them informed, while 75 percent thought they were more concerned with attracting the biggest audience.[1]

In the pages that follow we sketch the origin and spread of the system of news in the United States, retracing how the media came to exercise such enormous sway over public life. It is a fascinating and complex story, one that has been told in great detail many times before, but our account diverges from previous efforts in two basic ways. First, we offer an overall theory of *why* the American news media developed the way they did. That theory centers on the key political choices our leaders in Washington made about the role of the press in a democracy. We show how federal lawmakers and the courts repeatedly responded to technological breakthroughs in mass communications by rewriting the rules governing the media industry. And while those revisions were usually done at the behest of powerful corporate interests, the government was forced on several occasions to adopt important reforms that made the press more democratic and accountable to ordinary citizens, usually in an effort to placate incipient social movements or to quell civil strife, especially during times of war. At each new stage of our media system's evolution, however, furious debate has erupted over the same question: Are the information needs of a democracy best served by a centralized or decentralized system of news? The resolution of that key question, we conclude, is paramount for defending a free and diverse press.

Second, we focus on how newspapers, radio, and television depicted a fundamental fault-line of US society—that of race and ethnicity. You will find gathered in one place for the first time the details of a startling number of major news events in which press organizations consciously misled the public and inflamed racial bias. In compiling these examples, our aim was not merely to dredge up embarrassing media failures from the distant past or to indulge in some abstract content analysis of old news. Rather, we have utilized these various examples to chronicle the key historical battles over racial discrimination that took place inside the US media. In addition, we document how advances in communications technology affected the media's depiction of race, and we recount the roles played by scores of individual journalists and media executives—the famous and the obscure, the heroes and the villains, white and non-white—in the epic struggle to supply the American people with our daily news.

The News Media and Racial Bias

It is our contention that newspapers, radio, and television played a pivotal role in perpetuating racist views among the general population. They did so by routinely portraying non-white minorities as threats to white society and by reinforcing racial ignorance, group hatred, and discriminatory government policies. The news media thus assumed primary authorship of a deeply flawed national narrative: the creation myth of heroic European settlers battling an array of backward and violent non-white peoples to forge the world's greatest democratic republic. This first draft of America's racial history was not restricted to a particular geographical region or time period—to the pre–Civil War South, for example, or the western frontier during the Indian Wars; nor was it merely the product of the virulent prejudice of a few influential media barons or opinion writers or of a specific chain of newspapers or television stations. Rather, it has persisted as a constant theme of American news reporting from the days of *Publick Occurrences*, the first colonial newspaper, to the age of the Internet.

Stereotypes, of course, infuse the daily thinking of all human beings. Legendary newspaperman Walter Lippmann regarded them as essential tools for individuals to make sense of the complex world around us. Examining the origin and use of stereotypes in the media, Lippmann wrote in 1922:

> Of any public event that has wide effects we see at best only a phase and an aspect … Inevitably our opinions cover bigger space, a longer reach of time, a greater number of things, than we can directly observe. They have, therefore, to be pieced together out of what others have reported and what we imagine.[2]

It is the job of the modern journalist to witness events in the wider world and then convey those events and their meaning to the rest of us as quickly as possible. But such reports are fraught with weaknesses inherent to each reporter's own perception of reality—the subjectivity that so often springs from upbringing, education, class, race, religion and gender. The less the journalist knows about the event or the subject at hand, the more likely he or she is to produce a crude or blurred representation of it. Those reports are then further filtered by editors and publishers, who get to decide which portions of the reporter's dispatch are "newsworthy" and will survive, and which will disappear in the editing process. Lippmann warned of the substantial distortions that were inherent to such a process:

> For the most part we do not first see, and then define, we define first and then see. In the great blooming, buzzing confusion of the outer world we pick out what our culture has already defined for us, and we tend to perceive that which we have picked out in the form stereotyped for us by our culture.[3]

Unavoidable though they may be, media stereotypes can have a devastating effect. This is especially true given the double-edged function of news in modern industrial society—as both a means for the masses to hold their leaders accountable and a vehicle for a nation's rulers to control their own population. "He who molds public sentiment goes deeper than he who enacts statutes or pronounces decisions," Abe Lincoln once said. "He makes statutes and decisions possible or impossible to be executed."

Those stereotypes that achieved the most currency tended to mirror the worldview of media owners and editors, and their top writers. Exploiting racial fears became not only a reliable way to increase newspaper sales and broadcast ratings, but also served as a tool by which powerful groups in society could stir up public support for projects of territorial and imperial expansion, or by which to weaken opposition among the lower classes to unpopular government policies. "A sophisticated society controls its internal flows of information in ways more subtle than any government can duplicate or any legislature formulate," notes media historian Anthony Smith in an illuminating study of the mass communications battles between the West and the developing world.[4] Only by understanding the evolution of press ownership in America, and the close connection between major media companies and the nation's political and business circles, can we begin to understand the persistency of racial segregation and bigotry in the news.

The Origins of Our Media System

The birth of the United States owed much to its early rebel editors and their newspapers. As historian Arthur Schlesinger noted more than fifty years ago, "at every crisis the patriot prints fearlessly and loudly championed the American cause, never yielding ground as did some of the politicians," with several colonial-era editors participating "firsthand in subversive activities."[5]

Once the Revolution triumphed, American newspapers sprouted across the land with breathtaking speed, thanks largely to government support. Our entire media system, in fact, never depended entirely on the invisible hand of a free market. It developed as a direct result of media policies adopted by our political leaders at key junctures in the nation's history. Those "constitutive decisions," as one scholar has dubbed them, were often adopted with little public scrutiny.[6] Among the most important were:

- discounted postal rates for newspapers and magazines, and government-subsidized printing contracts, which made possible the mushrooming of thousands of local newspapers and magazines in virtually every town and rural area in the country;
- federally funded research into new communications technologies such as the telegraph, radio, satellite broadcasting and the Internet, which made possible an array of new delivery platforms and the diffusion of news and advertising into every corner of American life;
- direct government regulations, among them copyright and intellectual

property laws, the creation of the Federal Communications Commission to allocate and oversee the use of the public airwaves, and the development of municipally sanctioned cable monopolies—all of which assured order in the marketplace and uncommon financial rewards to those media owners who became most skillful at maneuvering through and manipulating federal regulation.

Each of those constitutive decisions was deeply influenced by the close relationship that developed between our media owners and the government, as the press—the only industry legally protected by the Constitution—gradually evolved from a hodgepodge of small, family-owned firms scattered in cities and hamlets throughout the country into a mature and increasingly centralized industry.

In the book's first few chapters, we examine the astonishing growth of a newspaper culture in early America. "Throughout the fifty years after 1776 newspapers were usually outrageously partisan [and] exacerbated all lines of cleavage in the early Republic," notes journalism historian Dave Paul Nord. The *New York Evening Post* was typical of the era. Founded by Alexander Hamilton in 1801, it became a platform for Hamilton's Federalists against Thomas Jefferson's Republicans. In their heyday, many such partisan papers flourished, and the overall effect on the society was a rich and vital clash of ideas and dissenting views, albeit within circumscribed limits.[7]

The US government's role in spawning this first communications revolution cannot be overstated. The Postal Act of 1792 and the roads the federal government built to transport the mail gave birth to America's first Internet. Thanks to the generous subsidies Congress provided for newspaper delivery through discounted second-class mail, the press assumed a fundamental role in nation-building, with the main job of our mail system throughout much of the nineteenth century being the delivery of newspapers.[8]

The emergence of the penny press during the Jacksonian era catapulted the media to an even more central role in public life. By the 1830s, white urban workers, having recently gained the right to vote, chafing from the horrid social conditions of the nation's industrial revolution, and inspired by revolutionary movements in France and England, had begun turning to radical street protests. The decade was marked by the nation's first major industrial strikes, by the rise of workingmen's parties and the abolitionist and women's movements, and by the emergence of a new and militant labor press.

In response to this growing activism from below, the commercial penny press emerged and became an instrument to channel urban workers away from radical action. It did not simply woo artisans and new immigrants as its readers—it propagated pro-slavery views and hunger for territorial expansion among them, and it became the purveyor of a narrow spectrum of "acceptable" news generally espoused by the Democratic Party. It also became a vehicle by which merchants of the expanding industrial revolution could sell their products to a larger market. Just as the urban working class gained the right to vote, in other words, the new penny press emerged to tie workers to the established political parties, thus shaping and controlling how they exercised that right.[9]

By the end of the nineteenth century, newspapers had come under the domination of wire services and newly formed publishing chains. Advertising surpassed circulation as the main revenue source for news organizations, and once it did, most papers moved steadily away from controversial coverage that might alienate big advertisers or particular demographic groups of readers. As chains became more prevalent, they sought to stamp out competitors, and by the second half of the twentieth century most US cities found themselves with only one newspaper. The chains, in turn, were gradually swallowed up into even bigger news and entertainment conglomerates.[10]

The development of radio soon brought with it a handful of national radio networks that rapidly established their control over the new medium. In recent years, commercial radio and television stations, and an increasing number of Internet news sites, have likewise become cloned subsidiaries of the big conglomerates, a half-dozen of which now exercise unparalleled influence over the dissemination of information.

The dominant companies in our nation's news industry today, Disney-ABC-ESPN, NBC-Universal-Telemundo, Time Warner-CNN, Rupert Murdoch's News Corp., the major cable and telecom companies, and a few slightly smaller newspaper-based conglomerates, function as what journalism historian Ben Bagdikian once labeled an interlocking Private Ministry of Information for the nation's political and economic elites. The executives of these companies strive to shape public opinion and defend the political status quo while at the same time assuring maximum market penetration for advertisers.[11]

This concentrated media ownership has become a major obstacle for those seeking to preserve a racially diverse and democratic system of news. Blacks, Latinos, Native Americans and Asian-Americans collectively comprised 33 percent of the US population in 2005, yet virtually none of the country's daily newspapers, only 7.7 percent of its commercial radio stations, and 3.2 percent of commercial television stations were owned by minority businesspeople, and recent studies indicate such ownership is decreasing even more.[12] Should those trends continue, we fear that minority media ownership could disappear in the United States, leaving the nation with a de facto apartheid media system. Given that people of color are expected to comprise a majority of the population by 2050, control of virtually all the principal news production and dissemination by a white minority would be inherently undemocratic.

There is a popular notion among many Americans, especially those who came of age after the Civil Rights movement, that the quest for racial diversity in any field is a manifestation of some outdated "identity politics"—a 1960s phenomena that is no longer relevant. But, as we document in this book, people of color have been protesting their exclusion from the mainstream media and false press portrayals of their communities since the early years of the Republic. And while their demand for full inclusion has ebbed and flowed depending on the era, it has always been at the heart of efforts to establish a truly democratic and free press in the United States.

In recent decades, the digital revolution has profoundly shaken the established media system. The rapid convergence of print, audio and video communication onto the Internet has created enormous upheaval and uncertainty. Traditional commercial models of delivering news and information are rapidly disintegrating, and even the major media conglomerates today fear potential new challengers. Daily newspaper circulation, broadcast television audiences, and telephone landline subscriptions have all shrunk dramatically. Old Media firms are straining to survive; some are disappearing altogether. Those that stay afloat keep slashing journalism staffs and reducing their expenditures on the gathering of original news.

Meanwhile, the newer delivery systems provided by wireless and cable companies over the Internet are exploding in size. They offer their customers combinations of all prior mediums: the "Triple Play" services of the major cable companies, for instance, or smart phones like Blackberry, iPhone, and Android, providing mobile access to an astonishing array of news, video, music, and consumer services. Internet and computer giants such as Microsoft, Google, Amazon, Yahoo, and Facebook are no longer mere producers of hardware or software services; they have become huge disseminators of news and information in their own right.

But while the Internet has opened up enormous opportunities for a return to the citizen journalism of our nation's early years, it is far from certain that people of color will share equally in those opportunities, or that the depictions of race in America will move substantially beyond repackaged stereotypes from prior eras.

As this book went to print, battles continued to rage in Congress, the Obama administration, and the federal courts over several critical aspects of national communications policy: the future of net neutrality, the principle that Internet service providers should not discriminate by blocking, speeding up or slowing down Web content based on its source, ownership or destination user; the government's role in assuring the availability of low-cost broadband service for all Americans; its role in assuring individual privacy protection in the digital era; its role, if any, in the preservation of local news-gathering as a function of the mass media; and finally, the kind of requirements our lawmakers will institute in the coming years for public-interest and educational programming, for diversity and affirmative action, especially given the changing landscape of converged media platforms. This new wave of constitutive decisions will determine the extent to which our news media serve to protect or undermine the democratic process. Those who hope to influence such decisions would do well to analyze how our nation confronted past revolutions in media technology—the rise of early newspapers, for instance, or the advent of the telegraph, of radio, of television, and of cable. Media advocates, professional journalists, people of color, and ordinary citizens frustrated with their local news organizations may find the lessons of prior battles that we have compiled here to be invaluable as they seek to understand and navigate the complex challenges to our nation's future media system.

The Limits of Press Freedom

Why have stereotypes been so persistent in American news, given the nation's founding commitment to freedom of the press and its many struggles over slavery, territorial expansion, and civil rights? For more than 250 years the nation's news media, no matter how politically liberal, conservative or radical, no matter what class they purported to represent, remained the press of its white population. Its key newspapers, magazines and broadcast stations were owned and operated by whites; the content they produced was aimed largely at white readers and listeners.

With a few exceptions, Native American, African-American, Latino, and Asian-American journalists were systematically excluded from the principal newsrooms of the country until the 1970s. Even today, four decades after the civil rights movement prompted top news media executives to concede their industry's past failures and to promise integration of their newsrooms, most media companies, even the most liberal and progressive ones, still employ minority journalists in numbers far below those reflecting the racial makeup of the communities they serve. The result has been an almost routine distortion of the lives and events of people of color by the press.

This occurred despite the fact that news coverage of non-white communities has always been a staple of the country's media industry. Indian barbarism, for example, was the overriding theme of numerous news accounts about Native Americans in our early media. "From Boston to Savannah newspapers reported atrocities inflicted upon innocent white settlers by the 'Sculking Indian Enemy,'" notes historian David Copeland. Late-nineteenth-century newspaper accounts about Indians, another study notes, were "more threatening and violent than actual Indians," thus "producing 'deviant' native identities that served the needs of a land-hungry nation."[13]

The systemic failures of our press on matters of race and ethnicity do not end merely with biased reporting and employment discrimination. The horrific record of the white press in fomenting mob violence and massacres against non-white communities is one of the lurid scandals of American journalism. We provide here enough examples—among them the anti-abolitionist riots of 1835; several anti-Chinese pogroms in the western states; the Camp Grant massacre of Apaches in 1871; the armed white overthrow of duly elected black leadership in Wilmington, North Carolina in 1898; the East St. Louis riot of 1917; the Los Angeles Zoot Suit riot of 1943; the violent eruption against the admission of James Meredith at Ole Miss in 1963—to suggest these were hardly aberrations of an otherwise fair and impartial press. What amazed us as we delved into the facts behind each incident is how often the white press portrayed the victims of such racial attacks as the instigators or perpetrators of violence.

We describe, in addition, how federal policies often aided the major press in perpetuating the white racial narrative. The Post Office, for instance—the critical mainstay of our early newspapers—eagerly bowed to Southern slaveholders and balked at delivering abolitionist or black newspapers to Southern readers. During both world wars, the federal government targeted the black press for special censorship and restrictions because of its continued calls for an end to Jim Crow. During the early years of radio, the Federal Communications Commission and its forerunner, the Federal Radio Commission, granted scarce broadcasting licenses to known racists or KKK-connected groups.[14]

Federal regulators did not simply ignore the white-supremacist views of some applicants—they refused to sanction racist broadcasts for violating the public-interest requirements of federal communications law. In 1931, for example, more than 700,000 African-Americans petitioned the Federal Radio Commission to complain about the racist stereotyping prevalent on the Amos 'n' Andy show, the black-face minstrel comedy that was hugely popular among white audiences. Robert Vann, publisher of the *Pittsburgh Courier*, then the nation's largest black newspaper, spearheaded the campaign and demanded the Commission cancel the show. In a sign of how little regard the Commission felt for the country's black population, officials never even bothered to respond.

Localism vs. Centralism—The Elephant in the Room

The vast reach of the Post Office, together with generous federal newspaper subsidies, produced something else that was critically important to the evolution of American democracy—a highly decentralized and autonomous news media system, one that placed a big premium on serving local communities. Thanks to a structure of locally based newspapers, our early media served as a bulwark against authoritarian or highly centralized political control, which explains why fierce battles have erupted throughout the nation's history pitting advocates of a decentralized information system against the forces of centralization.

Time and again, technological innovations in the collection of news and information subverted and transformed the older media structures and prompted political battles in Congress over new media rules. The rise of the electromagnetic telegraph in the late nineteenth century, for example, spurred a relentless campaign by America's business elite for private owner-ship of the new system of telegraph wires. The Western Union Company, which emerged as the first industrial monopoly in the US, then joined with news wire services such as the Associated Press to establish unprecedented control over the flow of news and information.

The advent of radio in the early twentieth century seemed at first to reverse that trend. Thousands of amateur radio enthusiasts ignited a new communications revolution with an exciting grassroots model of decen-tralized, non-commercial production of news and entertainment. But their vibrant effort was abruptly interrupted when the federal government shut down all private radio communications during World War I. Once the war ended, the US navy and the federal government under Secretary of Com-merce Herbert Hoover created a broadcasting system dominated by a new communications cartel, the Radio Corporation of America.

The cartel's domination endured for two generations, until new technolo-gies such as land-based cable TV systems and satellite broadcasting loosened the centralized control of the networks in the 1970s and 1980s. Once again, the spirit of localism surged: hundreds of community and municipal cable systems sprouted across the country, all of them promising a new age of diversity, democracy and richness in news and entertainment content. Unfortunately, cable TV's promise of a democratic renaissance ended with two companies, Comcast and Time Warner, devouring most of their com-petitors. Toward the end of the twentieth century, a handful of mega media firms emerged and successfully lobbied Washington lawmakers to deregulate the industry. Those companies achieved a major triumph with the passage of the Telecommunications Act of 1996. The new law, however, only signaled the start of another stage in America's media battles. In this newest period, technological innovation has once again shown itself to be a radical and destabilizing threat to the status quo.

We do not subscribe to the notion that new communication technolo-gies render Old Media obsolete, that newspapers will soon disappear, or that radio and television broadcasting belong to some prehistoric media era. In the real world, uneven development, coexistence, interpenetration and fusion of new and Old Media is much more prevalent than total obliteration of one form by another.[15] When television and FM radio arose, for example, AM radio broadcasting did not die. Media companies simply repurposed their stations to reach narrower segments of the public. The transition to those new technologies actually led to a spurt in minority ownership of radio stations, most of them AM stations.

And no matter what technology the media use to communicate to the people, the fundamental test of a truly free press remains the same: it is not simply the right to speak, but *the right to be heard by others*. As Justice Felix Frankfurter remarked in the pivotal 1945 Supreme Court decision that struck down the stranglehold of the Associated Press over wire-service news, freedom of the press is a public interest "essential to the vitality of our democratic government," but that freedom can be "defeated by private restraints no less than by public censorship."[16] Because of that threat from private as well as government interests, we believe the true linchpin of a democratic media system must be local and independent citizen access to mass communications.

The debate over centralism versus localism—between a news system that serves primarily the intelligence needs of national and transnational markets and one that serves first and foremost the educational and political needs of citizens in their local communities—has been constant throughout American history. How each generation resolved that debate was especially critical for racial and ethnic minorities in their long-running fight against the white racial narrative, for it was precisely in the periods when local autonomy in news media flourished that nonwhite journalists and their communities enjoyed the greatest freedom of expression. Likewise, periods of greater centralization of news ownership produced the greatest setbacks for journalists of color in their efforts to create their own independent news efforts. This is why tracing the evolution of that conflict over two centuries is a central theme of this book.

"We Wish to Plead Our Own Cause"

The alternative press was launched in the early nineteenth century by white editors and writers from marginalized political groups and nascent urban workers' organizations to champion dissident views. That press has been locked for more than two centuries in a war of words with the commercial media over the content and character of the nation's news. Unfortunately, our dissident press has long suffered from the same racial blind spot as our commercial press. Radical and labor editors have too often imitated commercial publishers by excluding people of color from their newsrooms and ignoring important stories in minority communities. This was equally true of the workingmen's or abolitionist newspapers of the 1830s, the populist muckraking or socialist press of the early 1900s, the New Left media of the 1970s, or the progressive bloggers of the Internet era.

Such racial exclusion gave rise to a separate, segregated wing of

America's opposition press, more commonly referred to today as the "minority" or "ethnic" media. The editors and journalists of this "other" press were often ignored, disdained or persecuted while they were alive; many of their newspapers and broadcasts were never archived for posterity in public and university libraries, and most have since been relegated to the footnotes of official journalism histories. Yet they waged heroic battles with their papers and over the airwaves to tell a different story—to assure fair and accurate news accounts of their communities; and they often proved to be more consistent defenders of press freedom and democratic values than the commonly celebrated titans of American journalism such as Greeley, Hearst, and Pulitzer.

Another major aim of this book is to unearth the saga of this "other" American journalism, to collect in one place and preserve for future generations some of the achievements of those editors and journalists of color who repeatedly challenged the worst racial aspects of our national narrative. "We wish to plead our own cause," John Russwurm and Samuel Cornish proclaimed in 1827 in their inaugural issue of New York's *Freedom's Journal*, the first black-owned newspaper in America. "Too long have others spoken for us."

In Chapters 4 to 8, we chronicle the rise of that minority press. Though the first Spanish-language newspaper in the United States, *El Misisipi*, was founded in New Orleans in 1808, a true press by journalists of color did not emerge in the country until the 1820s, when Rev. Felix Varela founded *El Habanero* in 1824 in Philadelphia, Russwurm and Cornish launched *Freedom's Journal*, and Elias Boudinot initiated the *Cherokee Phoenix* in 1828 in New Echota, Georgia. By 1854, the *Golden Hills News* became the first of dozens of Chinese-language newspapers that would be published in the United States during the nineteenth century.

Except for Russwurm, Frederick Douglass, Martin Delany, Ida B. Wells and a handful of others, the pioneering figures of the non-white press have been largely forgotten. Robert L. Vann, for example, served as the editor and publisher of the Pittsburgh *Courier* from 1910 until 1940. During that time his paper built a circulation of more than a quarter-million and Vann became the most influential black journalist of the twentieth century. Yet for white America it was as if Vann "had never really existed." His death in 1940 was barely mentioned in national publications, and even the press of his home city of Pittsburgh "gave him the most perfunctory recognition."[17]

Several immigrant journalists played major roles from this country in promoting press freedom and revolutionary movements in other parts of the world. Perhaps the finest example was José Martí, the poet and revolutionary who worked as a correspondent in the United States for Latin American newspapers for more than fifteen years. Then there is Sun Yat Sen, the founding father of modern China, who established the *Hawaiian*

Chinese News in 1896 in Honolulu; and Ricardo Flores Magon and Catarino Garza, both radical opponents of Mexican dictator Porfirio Díaz, who edited newspapers throughout the Southwest during the late nineteenth and early twentieth centuries.

We also recount the riveting personal stories of those nearly forgotten pioneer journalists who broke the color barrier in the commercial news media. They include Thomas Morris Chester, a war correspondent for the *Philadelphia Press* in the final years of the Civil War and one of the few nineteenth-century black writers to work in the commercial white press; Ted Poston, legendary staff writer for the *New York Post* in the 1940s and 1950s; John Rollin Ridge, the Cherokee poet and novelist who founded and published the *Sacramento Daily Bee* in 1857; Myrta Eddleman, who in 1897 became the first Native American woman to own a mainstream newspaper, Oklahoma's *Muskogee Daily Times*; Miguel Teurbe Tolón, a poet and publisher in his homeland of Cuba who worked in the 1850s as Latin affairs editor for the *New York Herald*; and fellow Cuban José Agustín Quintero, who founded *El Ranchero* in San Antonio in 1856, before embarking on a distinguished fifteen-year career as an editor at the New Orleans *Picayune*.[18]

In Chapters 9 to 16, we chart how the rise of giant newspaper chains, the news-wire services, and the radio and television networks sharply reduced opportunities for people of color to exercise real freedom of the press. By the end of the nineteenth century, our country was a growing world power with a new overseas empire. Rapid and reliable communications between parts of that empire became not simply an economic necessity but a requirement of imperial military strategy. Nonetheless, the first decades of the twentieth century witnessed more involvement by blacks and Hispanics in radio than is generally acknowledged. Scores of African-Americans were active in the amateur radio movement after World War I, and the Commerce Department issued the first commercial radio license to a Hispanic in 1922—more than twenty years earlier than commonly believed. But once the federal government moved to regulate access to the airwaves with the creation of the Federal Radio Commission in 1927, people of color were completely shut out of ownership in the growing industry; even their presence on the air was sharply reduced.

The massive entrance of blacks and Latinos into the military during World War II prompted some improvement in media portrayals of non-whites, as the government, responding to widespread social unrest and race riots during the war, pressured radio owners to provide more diversity in news and entertainment programming. On the heels of that effort, Raoul Cortéz became the first post-war Latino commercial radio owner when he launched KCOR-AM in San Antonio in 1946, and Jesse B. Blayton became the first African-American owner of a station license in 1949, with WERD in Atlanta.

It would take a new wave of urban riots twenty years later, and a pivotal battle in the federal courts to integrate Mississippi television, before the nation finally took significant steps toward the racial integration of our media system. In 1968, the US Commission on Civil Disorders strongly criticized the role played by the media in covering minority communities. "Along with the country as a whole, the press has too long basked in a white world, looking out of it, if at all, with white men's eyes and a white perspective," the Commission warned.

> That is no longer good enough. The painful process of readjustment that is required of the American news media must begin now. They must make a reality of integration—in both their product and personnel. They must insist on the highest standards of accuracy—not only reporting single events with care and skepticism, but placing each event into a meaningful perspective.[19]

The Commission urged immediate steps to increase the presence of minorities in the newspaper and broadcast industries. Its call led to sweeping media reforms by government leaders and press barons in the late 1970s. Thus began what we have called the new democratic revolution in the American press. That revolution included the adoption of federally mandated affirmative action programs to speed up minority employment and ownership in broadcasting, bold new programs by universities and associations of media executives to improve industry hiring practices, and the rise of Spanish-language television. The period also witnessed hundreds of challenges to local station licenses by minority communities—even some sit-ins and occupations of some stations. The unprecedented upsurge literally forced broadcast owners and publishers to hire and promote non-white journalists and to improve coverage of racial minorities.

Once that first generation of black, Latino, Asian and Native American journalists entered those newsrooms, they encountered such enormous hostility from white colleagues that they were forced to create their own professional associations as their only support networks. Those associations quickly grew in size, and assumed central roles as watchdogs and pressure groups within the industry to monitor news coverage and hiring practices.

All popular movements, however, provoke organized resistance from defenders of the status quo. By the 1980s and early 1990s, conservative politicians had begun rolling back several federal regulations aimed at assuring racial integration and diversity of ownership in newspapers and broadcasting. At the same time, the cable industry, which had initially ushered in a new era of diverse ownership and programming, became dominated by a few giant companies.

Some believe that the emergence of the Internet in the final decades of the twentieth century has offered hope for a return to a decentralized system of news dissemination. But cyberspace, as we show in the final chapter, has quickly evinced the same kind of unequal racial divide in ownership and content that has marked the rest of our media system.

The persistence of racial inequality in the news industry is part of a broader crisis facing American journalism. Thousands of professional journalists are today losing their jobs. The survivors find it increasingly difficult to produce the kinds of meaningful information the American people need. And while Internet blogs and websites run by citizen journalists are increasingly generating important news that the commercial media ignore, such sites have yet to provide an economic model for sustaining thousands of full-time journalists in the pursuit and production of news—a model that could replace what Old Media have done for 200 years.

The central role of the press in our society makes this industry-wide crisis a crucial problem for the entire nation. Thankfully, many citizens already understand this. In the first decade of the twenty-first century a new and powerful citizen movement for media reform came of age. That movement, which arose during a battle to prevent the FCC from deregulating broadcast ownership provisions, already counts millions of Americans from across the political spectrum in its ranks. The members of this new movement are deeply disturbed by the concentration of ownership in our news media. They are frustrated and angry over the endless hyper-commercialism, infotainment and obsession with violence and sex that dominate its content. They worry that despite the great potential of the Internet, the largest communications companies exercise too much control over news and entertainment. They fear that these big media firms, along with the cable, telecom, and satellite broadcast companies that control the "pipes" through which news, audio, video and Internet data reach every home, are displaying only disdain for the public-service responsibilities of the press, eliminating local voices, driving out diversity of viewpoints, undermining our democracy.

With each day that passes, with each new advance in mass communications technology, our biggest media companies feverishly race to readjust, to become bigger and more dominant in the marketplace. Only by clearly grasping the main conflicts and choices that shape our current media system can ordinary citizens successfully unite with the concerned journalists and workers within the system to bring about meaningful reform. The second democratic revolution of the US media has already begun. Those who hope to triumph in that revolution must first understand how our system of news reached its current state. It is an amazing saga, brimming with picturesque rascals and wide-eyed visionaries, with legendary big-city publishers and obscure immigrant editors, with writers of astonishing courage and legions of cowardly charlatans, with brilliant statesman and the worst of racial arsonists. We begin our story with the first newspaper on US soil.

I

The Age of Newspapers

"Barbarous Indians" and "Rebellious Negroes"

Nine of the Ethiopian Breed, belonging to this city, have been apprehended, committed, try'd and whipt at the whipping post for assembling
and meeting together in an Illegal manner, on Sunday.

New-York Weekly Post, 1755

On September 25, 1690, Benjamin Harris, a little-known Anabaptist Boston
bookseller and printer, launched *Publick Occurrences Both Forreign and Domestick*, a four-page, 6-by-9½-inch sheet commonly regarded as the first
newspaper in the New World. Harris vowed in his inaugural issue to counter
"the Spirit of Lying, which prevails among us," to report only "what we
have reason to believe is true." He then proceeded to publish several chilling accounts of the "Barbarous Indians" and "miserable savages" the white
settlers confronted. From then on, most colonial editors routinely crafted
similar images of Native Americans as threats to the peace and security of
white society.[1]

Before his arrival in Boston in 1686, the blunt-spoken Harris had been
a prosperous publisher in London, issuing strident anti-Catholic and anti-
Quaker pamphlets, which eventually landed him in jail on charges of sedition.
Shortly after his release, he published an edition of *English Liberties,* William
Penn's dissident polemic on individual freedom. British authorities promptly
confiscated 5,000 copies, whereupon Harris decided to head for America.
He moved to Boston and opened a bookstore that soon became popular as
a place to catch up on the latest gossip and indulge in lively political debate.
The store's success convinced Harris to try his hand once more at newspa-
per publishing. Unfortunately, his timing could not have been worse.

The Massachusetts colony was then locked in bitter conflict with French
settlers, racked by factional power struggles among its leaders, and embroiled
in a dispute with the king over control of colonial affairs. The first issue
of *Publick Occurences* drew the immediate wrath of the colony's Governing
Council for Safety, which condemned its "reflections of a very high nature"
and its "sundry doubtful and uncertain Reports." Governor Simon Brad-
street immediately suppressed the paper, and the Council decreed that only

printed material that was officially licensed could henceforth circulate in the colony.[2]

Until the seventeenth century, most European monarchs sought to stifle any challenge to their rule that might be spurred by the printing press. They required printers to be licensed, and routinely censored questionable literature. But the English Civil War (1642–48) propelled English society toward a markedly different information policy than in the rest of Europe. As part of his battle against King Charles I, parliament's leader Oliver Cromwell encouraged dissent in the nation's infant press. Thirty thousand news publications and pamphlets emerged in the streets and alleys of London in the two decades after 1640 in what historian Anthony Long called a flowering of mass communication that paved the way for modern popular journalism.[3] By the end of the century, English printers had largely broken free from licensing rules and other restrictions. The most successful printers became spokesmen for the country's rising merchant class. Their ascension signaled the birth of a new force in English public life: mass newspapers that monitored and even dared to question the actions of government leaders. Feisty sheets such as Harris's *Publick Occurrences* even began appearing in England's colonies, and the vital communication they provided for the settlers helped to sustain the colonizing effort. But this early association of printing "with the providential mission of a prospering expansive realm," notes historian Elizabeth Eisenstein, pointed the way to later trends among English Protestants —"to revolutionary messianism in the Old World and 'manifest destiny' in the New."[4]

After the squashing of *Publick Ocurrences*, no other editor attempted to produce a newspaper in the English colonies for the next fourteen years. That drought ended in1704, when Scottish-born bookseller John Campbell launched the *Boston News-Letter*. Campbell was Boston's postmaster at the time—a job that uniquely suited him to disseminate the latest intelligence to his fellow settlers. In the sparsely inhabited American colonies, where considerable distances often separated settler farms, every post office functioned as a vital nexus for the circulation of news and information.

The *News-Letter* extended Campbell's habit of composing periodic correspondence to friends with the latest information he'd gleaned as postmaster. Before long, other postmasters followed his example. Royal governors more often than not approved of these efforts. The postmaster/editors, after all, owed their main livelihood to a government appointment, and thus were unlikely to turn their sheets into platforms for criticizing the state. Campbell, for instance, carefully distinguished his paper from the earlier Harris sheet by prominently displaying the slogan "Published by Authority" on his masthead and by avoiding controversial issues within the colony. He filled it with drab items reprinted from London newspapers months after the fact, official proclamations, and death notices, and—unlike Harris—he even featured advertisements. In his first issue, Campbell made the following appeal:

> [A]ll Persons who have any Houses, Lands, Tenements, Farms, Ships, Vessels, Goods, Wares or Merchandise, etc. to be Sold or Let, or Servant Run away; or Goods Stole or Lose; may have the same Inserted at a Reasonable Rate; from Twelve Pence to Five Shillings…"[5]

At the height of its popularity, the paper barely had 300 subscribers in a city of 10,000 people. Still, Campbell's job of official postmaster guaranteed him a regular income, which enabled the *News-Letter* to survive as the first continuously published paper in the colonies. For the next several decades most newspapers operated as semi-official government organs, keeping controversy out of their pages.[6]

"Sculking Indians"—The Narrative Begins

Colonial printers, as we would expect, reported domestic events entirely from the perspective of the European settlers who were their only readers. They did, however, devote considerable space to two groups of non-Europeans who warily coexisted in the New World with the settlers: the Native American tribes and African slaves.

The lone edition of Benjamin Harris' *Publick Occurrences*, for example, contained five separate news items about the Native population in just three pages of text. In one entry, Harris wrote of two white children apparently kidnapped by "barbarous Indians" who were "lurking about" the town of Chelmsford. In another (the longest article in the newspaper), Harris gave an account of an expedition by the Massachusetts militia and their Mohawk allies against the French in Canada. The Mohawks killed some French prisoners "in a manner too barbarous for any English to approve," he wrote. In a related item on the same Canada campaign, Harris counseled his readers that they had "too much confided" in the Mohawks. "If Almighty God will have Canada to be subdu'd without the assistance of those miserable Savages … we shall be glad," he added. Only one of his reports did not associate the Natives with violence—an item on how the Christianized Indians of Plymouth "have newly appointed a day of Thanksgiving to God."[7]

Publick Occurrences thus created "the perfect prototype for news coverage of Native Americans by colonial newspapers," concludes David A. Copeland in an exhaustive analysis of the content of early American newspapers. Years of sporadic fighting over settler incursions on Native lands had already sparked the rise of anti-Indian captivity literature—outlandish tales of rape, infanticide, torture and dismemberment that both disgusted and fascinated the settlers.[8]

Descriptions of "Sculking" or "barbarous" Indians were commonplace then, much as today's news media use terms such as "wolf packs," "drug gangs," and "super-predators" as monikers for non-white criminals. Indian-white conflict, after all, engendered the highest level of fear and hysteria in colonial society. During a series of Indian wars that erupted throughout the 1700s along the Eastern Seaboard, the *News-Letter* and other colonial papers routinely stirred up settler outrage and dutifully reported govern-ment bounties for the killing of Indians. Massachusetts, for instance, urged its settlers in 1706 "to kill all male Indians over the age of twelve and capture women and children under the age of twelve for rewards," and when South Carolina declared war on the Tuscaroras in 1735, the colony's leaders offered "Fifty Pounds Current Money [for every Indian] who shall be taken alive." On more than one occasion, the papers reported scalps acceptable as proof that an Indian had been slain. Copeland's study found positive news items about Indians rare unless they "were involved in fighting for the colonists."[9]

Some news accounts even alleged cannibalism as a Native American practice. A 1745 article in the Boston *Evening Post* reported: "The Enemies had 2 kill'd and as many wounded in the Engagement, which being over, the Indians cut open Capt. Donahew's Breast, and suck'd his Blood, and hack'd and mangled his Body in a most inhuman and barbarous Manner, and then ate a great part of his Flesh." Once war with the Cherokees engulfed South Carolina in 1760, an astounding 30 percent of all stories in the *South Carolina Gazette* that year, 18 percent in the *Pennsylvania Gazette*, and more than 15 percent in the *New York Gazette* were about violence by Native Americans.[10]

Those early accounts thus established a voluminous and entirely one-sided newspaper narrative: Native Americas were depicted as cunning, barbaric, and evil—and certainly undeserving of the vast lands coveted by the European settlers.

Ben Franklin's Dissent

One of the few colonial editors who challenged the dominant narrative of Indian savagery was Benjamin Franklin. In early 1764, Franklin pub-lished a pamphlet that exposed a horrific incident of anti-Indian rioting by white frontiersmen in Lancaster County, Pennsylvania. In the pamphlet, he reported that on the previous December 14, a mob of whites had "mur-dered 20 Innocent Indians" who were living in peace among the Quakers. "These poor defenseless Creatures were immediately fired upon, stabbed and hatcheted to Death!" he wrote. "All of them were scalped, and otherwise horribly mangled. Then their Huts were set on Fire, and most of them burnt down ..."

His description of the massacre is one of the few in colonial-era journalism to portray Indians as victims. It also offered a rare glimpse into the deep divide among Pennsylvania's settlers over Indian policy, with the Moravians and Quakers urging humane treatment of the natives. As Franklin noted:

> The universal Concern of the neighbouring White People on Hearing of this Event, and the Lamentations of the younger Indians, when they returned and saw the Desolation, and the butchered half-burnt Bodies of their murdered Parents, and other Relations, cannot be well expressed.[11]

By the time he issued the pamphlet in early February, two months had passed since the massacre, yet neither of Philadelphia's papers—neither the *Pennsylvania Journal*, nor Franklin's former sheet, the *Pennsylvania Gazette*—had printed any account of the gruesome affair, other than proclamations by the governor condemning it and offering a reward for information about the killers. Franklin's rush to publish the details of the tragedy was undoubtedly his way of breaking the news blackout by the Philadelphia editors. His explicit condemnation of the bias and ignorance that fueled the massacre has a chilling resonance even today:

> The only Crime of these poor Wretches seems to have been, that they had a reddish brown Skin, and black Hair; and some People of that Sort, it seems, had murdered some of our Relations ... If an Indian injures me, does it follow that I may revenge that Injury on all Indians? It is well known that Indians are of different Tribes, Nations and Languages, as well as the White People. In Europe, if the French, who are White-People, should injure the Dutch, are they to revenge it on the English, because they too are White People?

Franklin rushed to publish his account after discovering that leaders of the massacre were threatening to march on Philadelphia to attack other peaceful Natives that Quaker Governor John Penn had placed under his protection. The impact of the pamphlet was so great that "1,000 of our Citizens took Arms to support the Government in the Protection of those poor Wretches," Franklin later reported. Those armed government supporters, who included the pamphleteer himself, confronted 500 of the anti-Indian rioters in Germantown and "the Fighting face we put on made them more willing to Reason."[12]

Unfortunately, no other colonial editor exhibited Franklin's extraordinary empathy for Indians or his courage in exposing abuses against them. The image of skulking Indians thus became firmly entrenched in the colonial press.

"Rebellious Negroes"

Early colonial newspapers disseminated similar stereotypes of the "rebel-lious Negro." Accounts of black life that did make it into print invariably focused on two main subjects: slave insurrections and common crimes. As early as 1706, Campbell's first full-fledged essay in the *Boston News-Letter* urged more importation of white indentured servants to reduce the colony's need for African slaves. The local black population, he warned, was "much addicted to Stealing, Lying and Purloining" and he urged the importing of more white servants because, unlike blacks, they could also be pressed into military service.[13]

In 1712 the *News-Letter* reported one of the earliest slave rebellions in the colonies. Seventy New York Negroes, it claimed, had been arrested for "their late Conspiracy to Murder the Christians," prompting authorities to execute the leaders of the plot and to punish their followers by breaking their bones on a wheel. Over the next sixty years, colonial newspapers chronicled fifty separate incidents of actual or suspected slave revolts.[14]

A similar obsession prevailed for violent crimes by individual slaves. After a slave in northern Massachusetts threw her owner's child down a well in anger, every newspaper between Boston and Annapolis reported the story. Such blanket news coverage revealed more about the anxieties of the editors and their readers than about the rage of a single slave. Fear of violence by blacks was rooted in the settlers' instinctual knowledge that slavery was not merely a highly profitable enterprise, but was indispensable to the very sur-vival of the British colonies. Africans comprised more than half of South Carolina's population in 1720, 8 percent of Boston's in 1755, and a third of all new immigrants entering New York at mid-century.[15]

That rapid growth of the black population only reinforced white fears of slave violence. In 1740, for example, the *Boston Evening-Post* published a letter from an angry resident who was seeking volunteers for a vigilante group to control slave conduct. "The great Disorders committed by Negroes, who are permitted by their imprudent Masters &c. to be out late at Night ... has determined several sober and substantial Housekeepers to walk about the Town in the sore part of the Night," the writer noted, adding, "[I]t is hoped that all lovers of Peace and good Order will join their endeavors for prevent-ing the like Disorders for the future." And in 1755 the *New-York Weekly Post Boy* reported that "nine of the Ethiopian Breed, belonging to this city, have been apprehended, committed, try'd and whipt at the whipping post for assembling and meeting together in an Illegal manner, on Sunday."[16]

As slave rebellions became more frequent and more violent, colonial editors adopted a new strategy: quashing all news about slaves. In South Carolina, suppression of such news started after the bloody Stono Rebellion near Charleston in 1739, in which twenty-one whites and forty-four blacks lost their lives. The *South-Carolina Gazette* printed no information about similar revolts in the colony in 1739 and 1740. It never mentioned the colony's newly enacted slave code that permitted any white person to stop and search a slave and kill him if he reacted violently.[17]

The depiction of blacks in those early colonial papers displayed a remarkable consistency. "African slaves revolted against their owners. Slaves murdered, robbed, raped, and burned out whites," Copeland notes of the coverage. As for any other aspect of black life, colonial newspapers "rarely printed a positive word," except to praise "slaves who warned their owners of impending slave revolts."[18]

One of the rare condemnations of slavery in the colonial press appeared in 1740 in the *Pennsylvania Gazette*, which published a letter from Rev. George Whitefield challenging the morality of holding others in bondage.[19] Ben Franklin was the paper's editor at the time. Even though he had owned slaves as a young man, and often published ads from slave-traffickers in his *Gazette*, Franklin was one of the few editors willing to provide space for abolitionist commentaries. He turned increasingly against slavery in his old age, and in his last public act in 1790 he petitioned Congress to put an end to the practice. By then, he was serving as president of the Pennsylvania Society for the Abolition of Slavery.

The Early Press and the Merchant Elite

The number of papers in the colonies grew from one in 1710—Campbell's *News-Letter*—to eighteen by 1750, far outstripping the four-fold growth of the settler population. But the average number of subscribers to those publications was only eight per 1,000 inhabitants—less than 1 percent of the population.[20] Newspaper readers were chiefly merchants, prosperous farmers, clergymen, and the political elite of the colonies, since only they could afford to pay a year's subscription of $10 in advance. In return, the printers meticulously geared their sheets to provide the latest "intelligence" to that elite.

Much of that early intelligence was actually commercial advertising. Before the Revolution, as much as 20 percent of all available space in colonial newspapers was devoted to ads, and even a good portion of the news was information about the arrival and departure of ships and the listing of cargo for sale. The percentage of overall space devoted to advertising grew steadily, until by 1784 it had reached 32 percent of the average newspaper. It continued to climb, so that that by the end of nineteenth century more than half the space in most US newspapers was taken up by advertisements.[21]

Legendary editor John Peter Zenger, for example, has long been celebrated for his legal victory for freedom of the press in 1735, but Zenger was as much a pioneer of commercialism as he was a voice of political dissent.

An immigrant from Germany, Zenger was only a child when his family settled in New York in 1710. He later served an eight-year apprenticeship in the shop of William Bradford, the colony's royal printer. Bradford launched New York's first news sheet, the *Gazette*, on November 8, 1725. By then, relations between the Council of the colony and a succession of royal governors had devolved into bitter discord. The most oppressive of the governors was William Cosby, who began feuding with the Council soon after his arrival in 1732. The following year Cosby summarily removed New York's popular Chief Justice Lewis Morris and replaced him with a royalist. Zenger, who was running his own print shop then, quickly issued a pamphlet defending Morris. He then started up his own paper, the *New-York Weekly Journal*, in November 1733, where he published sensational articles that accused "people in Exalted Stations" (Cosby and the "court" party) with election fraud, corruption, and tyranny. Morris and his supporters, the paper assured its readers, were defending the "rights and liberties" of the "industrious poor."[22]

Within a year, Cosby ordered copies of Zenger's newspaper burned, then had its thirty-seven-year-old editor arrested for "seditious libel." The bail slapped on Zenger was so high that he languished in jail until the start of his trial eight months later. Most experts gave him no chance of winning his case. But with his wife continuing to publish the paper, and with Zenger editing it from his cell, his supporters mounted a spirited public campaign on his behalf. One of the most illustrious lawyers in the colonies, Philadelphia's Andrew Hamilton, agreed to defend him for free. Hamilton, who was then nearly eighty years old, conceded to the jury that Zenger's articles were outrageous and defamatory according to existing law, but he argued instead that truth—the statement of facts that could be proved—was not libel. In his now legendary courtroom defense of free speech, Hamilton urged the jurors to nullify the existing law:

> Power may justly be compared to a great river which, while kept within its due bounds is both beautiful and useful; but when it overflows its banks, it is then too impetuous to be stemmed, it bears down all before it and brings destruction and desolation wherever it comes. If this then is the nature of power, let us at least do our duty, and like wise men use our utmost care to support liberty, the only bulwark against lawless power … the liberty both of exposing and opposing arbitrary power by speaking and writing Truth.[23]

The jury wasted little time in acquitting Zenger, touching off huge celebrations among the city's residents. The decision would embolden printers throughout the colonies to use their newspapers to voice dissent against English policies.

Unlike his celebrated fight for freedom of the press, Zenger's role in the commercialization of American newspapers has garnered scant attention. Following his release, the rebel editor and his paper enjoyed a surge in popularity, but he still found himself scrambling to meet his weekly costs. Meanwhile, Zenger's former employer and his chief competitor, William Bradford, editor of the *Gazette*, was prospering. The reason was simple: Bradford enjoyed the enviable perk of being the colony's official printer. To survive against the *Gazette*, Zenger was forced to resort to more private advertisements. To that end, he pioneered the use of half-page display ads, was the first to use broken-column rules to feature ads, and recruited a greater variety of types of customers than previous editors. Within a few years his paper boasted five times as much ad space as the *Gazette*; and by the late 1730s he had also won appointment as official printer for New York.[24]

Zenger thus established a whole new economic model for financing newspapers—paid advertising. "[I]t was largely through the development of profitable advertising," notes economist Steven Shaw, "that editors in England and the United States were able to free themselves from the subsidy and control of governors and political parties." Once they did so, they provided those papers with a greater financial cushion, freeing them to criticize government policies openly. The success of the Zenger model, however, also meant that editors would soon have to contend with economic pressures, at times subtle and at times vociferous, from their biggest advertisers.[25]

War and Revolution

The outbreak of the French and Indian War (1754–63) suddenly catapulted newspapers into a more important role in colonial society. The war, dubbed by one journalism historian "the great running story" of the colonial era, was a bitter and bloody conflict that engulfed the entire continent.[26] It spurred a new hunger among the settlers for timely intelligence on the progress of the fighting.

So great was the desire for information that the number of newspapers increased, and spine-tingling accounts of the rape and torture of innocent English families by the enemy and their Native allies became commonplace. Those accounts were often inaccurate, sparking a fear of both the French and their Indian allies "that was not entirely justified," according to David Copeland. They succeeded, however, in forging a new sense of unity among colonists along the Atlantic seaboard, propelling the inhabitants of the far-flung and disparate English colonies to regard themselves as a single people confronting common threats.[27]

Once the conflict ended, parliament faced the difficult task of paying off the massive debt the war had left behind. When it sought to do so, many of the same colonial printers objected to one of its key new revenue measures —the Stamp Act of 1765. The law struck directly at the livelihood of printers by imposing a halfpenny tax on each copy of a printed newspaper of a half-sheet or smaller, additional levies for each advertisement that appeared in the papers, and other taxes on pamphlets and business forms.[28]

"An unconstitutional restraint on the Liberty of the Press," declared Isaiah Thomas, one of the most prominent colonial editors.[29] Led by Benjamin Edes and John Gill of the *Boston Gazette* and Thomas and John Fleet of the *Boston Evening-Post*, the printers organized in every colony to defy the act. Their papers whipped up such popular resentment that riots erupted in several cities. These first outbreaks of mob violence in British North America—at least of violence by white settlers against fellow whites—were spearheaded by a newly organized secret society, the Sons of Liberty. The group counted among its members such prominent editors as Edes and William Bradford of the *Pennsylvania Journal*, and it soon formed what Arthur Schlesinger called an "interlocking directorate with the masters of the mob." Public clamor against the Stamp Act grew so loud that parliament was forced to rescind it within six months.[30]

The victorious printers suddenly found themselves at the forefront of opposition to British rule. "No longer were newspapers mere disseminators of information as in earlier colonial times," Schlesinger noted, "they had become makers and molders of opinion."[31] And they did not hesitate to use their new power, whether through the pages of their newspapers or in more extreme ways. Edes, for example, provided a regular forum in his *Boston Gazette* to patriot leaders Sam and John Adams. It was in the offices of the *Gazette* that the Sons of Liberty met on December 16, 1773, and donned their Mohawk outfits before heading out to the city's wharf to stage the historic Boston Tea Party.[32]

Once the Revolution erupted, newspapers proved essential to its victory. "It was by means of Newspapers that we receiv'd & spread the Notice of the tyrannical Designs formed against America, and kindled a Spirit that has been sufficient to repel them," boasted *New-York Journal* editor John Holt to Sam Adams.[33]

As with the French and Indian War coverage, however, printers and editors too often inflamed public sentiment through propaganda and outright distortions of news. Sam Adams became a chief practitioner of such sensationalism. His articles on alleged atrocities by British soldiers, many of them wildly exaggerated, described "blood-curdling incidents in which British soldiers brutally beat small boys in Boston's narrow streets" and their "violation of matrons and young girls."[34]

In their campaign for freedom, however, the patriot printers and editors never thought to include the huge population of African slaves. A lone and courageous exception was pamphleteer Tom Paine. "With what consistency, or decency," Paine wrote in 1775, could American colonists "complain so loudly of attempts to enslave them, while they hold so many hundred thousand in slavery?"[35]

By the time the war ended, the patriot printers were no longer a motley group of radicals using their small newspapers to give voice to a dissident movement. They had become an indispensable wing of the class of merchants, lawyers and farmers who would give shape to the new republic of white settlers. This remarkable transformation in the role of the press did not become fully apparent until the young government confronted its first major domestic threat: Shays' Rebellion on the western Massachusetts frontier. Disgruntled farmers driven into poverty by high taxes and mounting debts started meeting in 1786 in county conventions and appealing to government leaders to help save their land. When they received no reply, some 2,000 farmers under the leadership of Daniel Shays, a former Continental Army captain, launched an armed protest in early 1787, shutting down the local courts and preventing government officials from foreclosing on their land.

The same editors who only a few years before had urged rebellion against injustice, and even conspired to organize protests against British taxation, now recoiled in horror at this anti-tax revolt of the new nation's poor farmers. "Newspaper pieces attacked the rebellion participants for taking the law into their own hands. Essayists denounced the county conventions as 'unconstitutional ... because they weaken the government, which is feeble at best.'"[36] One printer, William Butler, even moved into the rebel area and quickly launched the *Hampshire Gazette*. He then proceeded to fill the paper each week with articles condemning the protest movement.

The unrest in Massachusetts prompted the country's elite to push for a stronger national government, a movement that culminated a few months later in the Constitutional Convention in Philadelphia. Most newspapers, especially those in New England, backed the results of the Convention and "freely attacked those who criticized the Constitution," notes historian Carol Sue Humphrey. They equated anti-federalists "with Tories and insurgents— 'enemies of good government' and 'the followers of Shay.'" According to a correspondent in the *Massachusetts Gazette*, "A more despicable junta than the herd of anti-federalist writers, were never leagued together."[37]

The biggest impact on the national debate over ratifying the Constitution came from a series of articles that initially appeared in five New York City newspapers as part of a massive propaganda campaign orchestrated by Alexander Hamilton, John Jay and other Founders. Those articles came to be known as the Federalist Papers.[38]

The early American press thus played a major role in promoting the Revolution, in suppressing Shays' Rebellion, and in securing ratification of the

Constitution. Printers chronicled the major events and seminal debates of the new society, and they helped shape a vision of the country's future. At the same time, they played a significant but disturbing role in fostering the white racial narrative that had begun with *Publick Occurences* and the *Boston News-Letter*. After 1776, hundreds of thousands of Indian and African inhabitants came under the sovereign power of the new nation, yet they enjoyed none of the legal rights granted to its white citizens. Only a few brave editors such as Ben Franklin and Tom Paine dared to question their treatment or challenge the prevailing bigotry. Blacks and Indians, meanwhile, lacked the means to tell their own story, to document the profound injustices they confronted, to chronicle the rich complexity of their daily lives. At the birth of American democracy, people of color possessed no press of their own.

2

In the Mail: The Post Office, the Press and the Mass Political Party

In Michigan forests there is not a cabin so isolated, not a valley so wild, that it does not receive letters and newspapers at least once a week.

Alexis de Tocqueville, 1832

No single policy of the federal government so shaped the creation and evolution of Americans' news media system as did the Postal Act of 1792. Its passage by Congress sparked a communications revolution that "transformed the role of newspapers in American life."[1] Over the next hundred years the Post Office methodically fashioned an elaborate system of post roads and delivery routes that connected virtually every citizen to a vast and unprecedented information network. As the territorial boundaries of the United States leaped at breathtaking speed across an entire continent, the Post Office, its legion of postmasters stationed in every town and village, became what historian Richard R. John has termed the "central administrative apparatus" of the United States.[2]

Their experience in the Revolutionary War had convinced the country's founders of the importance of a mail system for the general diffusion of knowledge to the average citizen, for binding together the far-flung and disparate colonies of the young Republic. They never forgot that when the Crown removed Ben Franklin as deputy postmaster of the primitive colonial-era post in 1774, the British army stepped up surveillance of private letters to keep track of dissident activities—thus one of the earliest acts of the delegates to the Continental Congress was to establish the Constitutional postal system, with Franklin as its head.[3]

After the Constitutional Convention, crucial debates arose over the structure and policies of a new federal postal system. Until that time, newspapers had been carried in the mails only when individual printers made their own arrangements with post riders. But Thomas Jefferson and others began advocating free delivery of papers. It is the "only means" of "conveying light and heat to every individual in the federal commonwealth," Benjamin Rush said in 1787. "Wherever information is freely circulated, there slavery cannot exist, or if it does, it will vanish as soon as information has been generally diffused," proclaimed Elbridge Gerry of Massachusetts, a delegate to the Constitutional Convention and future vice-president. George Washington reminded Congress in his annual address in 1790 of the "expediency ... of facilitating the intercourse between the distant parts of our country by a due attention to the post office and post roads." Like Rush and Jefferson, Washington backed free government delivery of newspapers.[4]

Those against free delivery included James Madison and John Fenno, editor of the *Gazette of the United States*. They warned that such papers would deluge the normal mail. Madison wanted a fee imposed that would restrict the number of publications the Post Office carried. Fenno, whose paper functioned as a semi-official organ of the federal government, urged selective admission at preferential rates, an option that would have benefited his and other publications closely tied to Congress. But Gerry and many Southerners in Congress feared that Northern big city papers, with their considerable resources, would drive small-town printers out of business, so they opposed selective admission. The debate over newspaper delivery thus became the first great battle over US media policy, pitting those who favored government intervention to protect local news and the diffusion of knowledge against the advocates of a more centralized and restricted means of disseminating information to the public.

The law Congress finally passed in 1792 was a compromise engineered by Madison. It authorized government delivery of newspapers to all subscribers at highly discounted rates compared to private correspondence; it mandated the free exchange of newspapers between printers; and it authorized the building of federal postal roads. The first provision assured all printers low-cost distribution of their product, a policy that still exists today in the second-class mail privilege; the second linked all newspapers in a nationwide news network by making it possible for editors to secure free news content from other papers around the country (this was before the era of copyright laws); and the third assured that collection of news and distribution of papers to all parts of the country would be as rapid as possible.[5]

Another provision of the new law—franking privileges for government officials—assured editors of even the smallest rural newspapers a free and steady flow of information about government activities, which they then reprinted to readers. And in a clear effort to prevent the type of government abuse practiced by the British, the Postal Act prohibited government surveillance of the mails or the denial of delivery to any newspaper, though this provision was to be repeatedly weakened by federal leaders during times of war, domestic unrest, or racial conflict.

The new law soon produced a mail delivery system of astonishing size. Postal roads, post offices and postal employees sprouted in so many cities, towns and rural districts that the agency soon dwarfed all other federal departments. Postmasters comprised three-quarters of the entire federal civilian workforce by 1831, surpassing even the US army in size. No mail system anywhere in the world was comparable. While France averaged four post offices per 100,000 inhabitants in 1828 and Great Britain seventeen, the United States averaged seventy-four.[6]

Cheap postal rates and the requirement for universal carriage unleashed a flood of new publications. A newspaper, after all, could travel any distance for only one and a half cents, while a one-page letter traveling 450 miles required postage of twenty-five cents. The federal government, in other words, subsidized the growth of newspapers through higher fees to other users of the system. Whenever costs exceeded revenue, Congress was ready to step in with direct public financing. As historian Wayne Fuller has said, federal postal policy meant

> that almost any ambitious young American with an old Franklin hand press, a printer's stone, some type, paper, roller, inking pan, and a bit of faith, hope, and the Post Office's charity thrown in, could set up shop in some prospective metropolis in the wilderness and begin printing a newspaper. And it made possible the greatest proliferation of newspapers the world had ever seen.[7]

Between 1790 and 1800 the number of US papers nearly tripled, from 92 to 234; it then mushroomed to more than 1,400 by 1840. The British Isles, in comparison, had only 369 newspapers in 1835. By then, the United States, with a population slightly smaller than Great Britian's, had three times the latter's total number of newspapers.[8]

The Rise of the Community Newspaper

American newspapers, moreover, were not confined to the big cities along the Atlantic seaboard. In a trend that would dramatically distinguish our media from that of other nations, countless papers sprouted in small towns and rural areas. The *Republic Ledger* in Portsmouth, New Hampshire, the *Vermont Gazette* in Bennington, Pittsburgh's *Tree of Liberty*, the *Virginia Argus* in Richmond, and the *Palladium* in Frankfort, Kentucky, were just some of the titles that flourished. By 1840, the town of Greenfield, Massachusetts, boasted two papers, the *Gazette* and the *Franklin Democrat*. The result was a highly decentralized and autonomous media system with a distinctly local and relatively diverse character.

Much of that rural proliferation of the press was due to the settler nature of American society. Each time a new western community took root, its inhabitants immediately sought their own local newspaper to inform them of faraway events, to bind together their fellow settlers who often lived miles outside of town, to spread news of their town's progress back through the postal network to the rest of the nation and the world. "[A] paper printed in a city some two, three, or five hundred miles distant cannot be expected to publish all the local news of every section of the country," admonished the Maine Farmer. "It would be impossible to do so before it became stale ... "[9] As each territory pressed Congress for statehood, more papers were needed in nearby towns to stir up the cause of annexation; and as political parties became a bigger part of American life, papers inevitably arose with competing political views.

The enormous influence of the nation's press was captured in this description by the editor of the *Michigan Expositor* in 1860:

> The Newspaper of today [is] an Educator of the people—Penetrating every corner of the land, found in every home, no matter how remote or how lowly, telling its tale of doings, good or ill, transpiring in this busy world of ours; having now a poem and now a gem of literature, expressing decided opinions upon current events with all the freedom and assurance of private conversation...[10]

When Frenchman Alexis de Tocqueville made his famous trek across America's heartland in the early 1830s he was amazed how there was "scarcely a hamlet that has not its newspaper." He marveled at the vitality of that press:

> [I]ts influence in America is immense. It causes political life to circulate through all the parts of that vast territory ... It rallies the interests of the community round certain principles and draws up the creed of every party; for it affords a means of intercourse between those who hear and address each other without ever coming into immediate contact.[11]

The town of Jacksonville, Illinois, was a classic example of what Tocqueville described. It was the largest town in that frontier state in 1830, with a total population of 446 residents. The following year, according to the records of the local post office, 486 Jacksonville residents received at least one periodical by mail, while eighty-nine of them received at least two. And that did not include any copies of the local newspaper which circulated by special delivery![12]

Early Battles to Preserve Local News Media

Back in Washington, debates over postal policy consumed an extraordinary amount of time in almost every session of Congress during the 1900s.

Lawmakers battled over the rates to charge for various classes of mail, over differential subsidies based on the distance the mail traveled, over where to build new roads and post offices, over appointments of top postal officials, over whether to treat newspapers differently from magazines and books, and later over how to respond to emerging technologies such as the telegraph. These were more than mundane squabbles over money and political patronage; they were disputes over the diffusion of knowledge to the public, over the degree of centralized vs. local control our news media system would exhibit, over the very nature of democracy and an informed citizenry.

The decisions that emerged from those debates transformed the Post Office into the engine of our media system, especially outside the big cities. Delivery of newspapers thus accounted for the bulk of postal deliveries throughout much of the nineteenth century, even though second-class periodical rates were so low that the federal government often lost money on them. In 1832, for example, newspapers comprised 95 percent of the weight of mail traffic but generated just 15 percent of postal revenue. Twenty years later, they accounted for 52 percent of all mail weight and less than 20 percent of revenues.[13] Even as late as 1901, President Roosevelt complained to Congress that second-class mail (newspapers and periodicals) then comprised three-fifths of the total weight of postal matter yet produced a mere 4 percent of the operating costs of the system.

Still, congressmen from rural areas fought to ensure that newspapers from the big cities would not drive out of business the small papers from their own districts. In the 1840s and 1850s, for instance, Congress approved free postal delivery of newspapers within each paper's local geographical area. "Regardless of its unequal regional benefits," notes historian Richard John,

> free circulation within 30 miles [in the Postal Reform Act of 1845] enhanced the competitive edge of local publications, protecting a community's outlets for news, opinion and culture ... Underwriting the long-distance circulation of newspapers thus was less important in diffusing information and, in fact, threatened the nation's burgeoning small-town press.[14]

Federal lawmakers intervened even more forcefully in the media marketplace toward the end of the century. In response to the growing strength of the populist movement among farmers, Congress approved an experiment with free rural delivery of mail in 1896, then extended it to the entire country in 1902, sparking a further explosion of rural weekly papers.[15]

Newspapers, Patronage and the Mass Political Party

The Post Office's central role in the nation's communications network also turned it into the center for federal patronage during the nineteenth century,

and the biggest beneficiaries of that patronage were newspaper editors. With
Andrew Jackson's election victory in 1828, both the press and the Post Office
emerged as critical building blocks for the Democratic Party, the world's
first mass political party. Old Hickory's victory was a result in no small
measure of the vast nationwide chain of newspapers his supporters established between 1824 and 1828 to spread the new party's message to voters.
In North Carolina, for example, nine new Jacksonian papers had appeared
by the middle of 1827, while in Ohio, eighteen arose in that four-year span.[16]
"Newspapers became essential ... as vehicles of intra-party communication,
as proselytizing agencies, as a kind of public address system to supporters,
and sometimes as forums for debating controversial issues," notes historian
Ronald Formisano.[17]

Tocqueville warned of a growing dark side to those newspapers that he
had witnessed in America:

> When many organs of the press adopt the same line of conduct, their
> influence in the long run becomes irresistible, and public opinion, per-
> petually assailed from the same side, eventually yields ... each separate
> journal exercises but little authority; but the power of the periodical press
> is second only to the people.[18]

Editors who supported Jackson were quickly rewarded with appointments
as postmasters—they were designated in each state to publish government
announcements, or they were apportioned printing contracts by various
federal agencies. Starting with Jackson's postmaster general, Amos Kendall,
all future Post Office heads became chief dispensers of patronage for
whichever party controlled the White House; and taking care of friendly
newspapers was a big part of that patronage.[19] Thus was formed the contours
of a grand alliance between newspapers, national political parties and the
Post Office, an arrangement that characterized American politics deep into
the twentieth century. "Usually newspapers did not reflect public opinion so
much as they reflected the determined efforts of inner circles within parties
to shape and direct opinion," Formisano notes.[20]

This transformation of newspapers into instruments of political parties
came just as popular unrest was sweeping the country. Successive financial
panics in 1819, 1827, and 1837 had combined to produce a deepening divide
between merchants, industrialists and rich landowners on the one hand, and
the mass of white artisans and factory workers on the other.[21] New York
City, for instance, was racked by several major riots in 1834 and 1835. One
erupted in April of 1834 during the city's first direct election for mayor,
when mobs of Whigs and Democrats, inflamed over the US Bank conflict,
fought in the streets for three days. In the midst of that disturbance, James
Watson Webb, editor of the *Morning Courier and Enquirer*, personally led a

group of 200 Nativist followers into pitched battle against Irish immigrants seeking to vote. In July, widespread violence erupted against prominent abolitionists and the city's black population (see Chapter 3). In September of the following year, stonecutters and masons angry over the city's decision to use inmate labor for construction of New York University rioted and occupied Washington Square for four days before the National Guard dispersed them.

Those urban disorders coincided with the rapid extension of the voting franchise to workingmen. Until the late 1820s, voting levels in America had been relatively low among the mass of white American males. Offices typically were filled either by appointment or by legislative bodies rather than through popular ballot; in some states there was no direct vote for president. But the removal of many state property and tax requirements for voting, coupled with rising labor discontent and the widespread availability of newspapers, sparked a stunning increase in both the number of voters and the frequency of local elections, thus dramatically altering how Americans conceived of the democratic process. All but three of the twenty-four states in the union had recognized the right of free white males to vote by 1826. "And accompanying that victory," notes historian Sean Wilenetz, "much of the old politics of deference still left over from the revolutionary era had collapsed."[22]

In 1824, for instance, only 27 percent of voting-age males cast ballots for president. The House of Representatives declared John Quincy Adams the winner even though Adams had lost the popular vote to Jackson. The resulting furor among Jackson supporters sparked a period of bitter turmoil, and led to the rise of new political parties—the Democrats and the National Republicans. Four years later, when Jackson ran a second time against Adams and steamrolled to victory, voter turnout zoomed to 56 percent. It then kept climbing, to 78 percent by 1840. In 1824, for example, just 250,000 white men had voted for president. Four years later, a million ballots were cast.[23]

The Rise of the Labor Press

The upsurge in newspaper influence was not just confined to the partisan sheets of the two big new parties. A new wave of dissident publishers soon gave voice to the hopes and discontent of ordinary urban workers. Those rebel editors and publishers traced their legacy to pamphleteer Tom Paine and to William Duane, the red-haired, radical editor a generation earlier of the *Aurora*, Philadelphia's Jeffersonian newspaper. They were inspired as well by the French Revolution of 1830 and by Britain's War of the Unstamped, an epic battle by working-class penny papers against parliament's onerous newspaper tax.

Protests against America's growing social inequality became common-place, and nothing drew greater anger than child labor in the textile and shoe industries. By the time the New England Association of Farmers, Mechanics and Other Workingmen was born in Boston in 1832, for instance, an esti-mated 40 percent of factory workers in Massachusetts were under the age of sixteen. In New York City, a mere 4 percent of the population had amassed 63 percent of the corporate and property wealth by 1828.[24]

Almost fifty labor papers were founded in the US between 1827 and 1832.[25] Leaders of the new dissident press included William Heighton with his *Mechanics' Free Press* (1828) in Philadelphia; the Scottish feminist orator and Owenite Fanny Wright, with her New York *Free Enquirer* (1829); George Henry Evans and Thomas Skidmore, with that city's *Workingman's Advocate* (1829); and Charles Douglas, with the *New England Artisan* (1832).

After Philadelphia's journeymen carpenters went out on strike in 1827 demanding a ten-hour day, they created the country's first citywide organi-zation of journeymen, the Mechanics' Union of Trade Associations (MUTA). The strike inspired the workers to launch the *Mechanics' Free Press*, the first labor newspaper in America, and soon afterward they created their own political organization, the Working Men's Party. In the pages of the new paper, Heighton railed against the country's privileged elite. He called for workingmen across the country to establish their own libraries and "poor man's press" for the "enlightenment of the working class."[26]

Associations of white mechanics started to spread to Boston and as far west as St. Louis. Those new groups, aided by the newspapers and politi-cal factions they founded, directly challenged the Democrats and National Republicans, and the coterie of partisan newspapers connected to each, for the allegiance of the new urban voters. In early 1829, 5,000 New York City workers marched to the Bowery to demand a ten-hour day. Labor leaders then founded their own new party, the Workies, and their own publication, the *Workingman's Advocate*. Among their leaders was Thomas Skidmore, a machinist, radical philosopher, and disciple of Thomas Paine and Robert Owen. Worky leaders also demanded free public schools, direct elections of local public officials, the abolition of imprisonment for debt and of inherit-ance of property, an end to tax exemption for churches, and the abolition of private banks and business monopolies. That same November, their movement stunned the city's political establishment by electing one labor candidate to the state assembly, placing a close second in six other races, and accumulating one-third of all votes cast.[27]

Similar electoral campaigns emerged in other cities. Jackson strategists skillfully courted the Workies, and they generally supported Old Hickory's program in Washington. But in local and state elections, the Workies and other radical labor groups often challenged both the Democrats and Whigs. As a result, the amorphous and fractious Workingmen's Party emerged for a short period as a decisive swing force in New York politics, and it even managed to secure several pro-labor reforms before suddenly disintegrating in 1831.

The Color of Mail

As the first truly national federal agency, the Post Office soon confronted the gathering sectional and racial storm over slavery. The first sign that mail delivery would not be color blind came with Jefferson's election to the presidency and the ascension to power of National Republicans over Federalists in Washington. Jefferson's postmaster general, Gideon Granger, spearheaded new postal regulations through Congress in 1803. Those regulations contained a provision that only "free white persons" could be employed to deliver mail. Although Granger hailed from Connecticut, he had turned increasingly sympathetic to Southern fears of slave insurrections in the wake of the Haitian Revolution, as had many white Americans.

Granger's aim was to prevent colored post riders from using mail delivery routes to organize their fellow slaves. Black mail carriers, he told one Georgia senator, were the most intelligent of the enslaved population:

> They are the most ready to learn and the most able to execute. By traveling from day to day, and hourly mixing with the people, they must, they will acquire information. They will learn that a man's rights do not depend on his color. They will, in time, become teachers to their brethren.[28]

The second, and more disturbing sign of racism's impact on the postal system came a generation later. On July 29, 1835, a group of prominent whites in Charleston, South Carolina broke into the town post office in the middle of the night and made off with a sack of mail. The intruders, who called themselves the Lynch Men, were led by South Carolina's former senator Robert Hayne. The pamphlets and newspapers they seized were part of a massive appeal that William Lloyd Garrison's newly formed American Anti-Slavery Society was sending to thousands of clergy and church members throughout the South to promote the cause of immediate abolition. The next night the Lynch Men built a huge bonfire on the grounds of the Citadel, the city's military academy, and brazenly burned the mail along with effigies of Garrison and fellow abolitionist Arthur Tappan in front of a cheering mob of more than 2,000 townspeople. With Nat Turner's 1831 slave uprising still fresh in their minds, town leaders from Mississippi to Virginia hastily established vigilante committees to censor their local mail.

Charleston touched off a controversy that raged for more than a year over use of the mails. Postmaster General Amos Kendall's first instinct was to appease Southern politicians and circumvent federal postal laws. A former editor of Kentucky's influential *Argus of Western America*, a close confidante and chief media strategist for President Jackson, Kendall also happened to be a slaveholder. He proposed allowing local postmasters to decide which outside newspapers to deliver in accord with the dictates of their local communities. But the president wanted even more direct action to suppress the abolitionist campaign. In December, he asked the House and Senate to allow the Post Office to ban incendiary literature from the mails entirely. Months of debate ensued over Jackson's proposal. Even some members of his own party denounced it as a clear violation of both the First Amendment and existing postal law.

Congress eventually rebuffed the president and barred any postmaster from "unlawfully" detaining mail. By then, however, many Southern states had passed their own laws authorizing interdiction of abolitionist mail, and they simply ignored Congress. As a result, says historian Sean Wilentz, "from the 1830s to the Civil War, a cotton curtain ... was drawn at the Mason-Dixon line" when it came to the mails.[29]

But the suppression of discussion of racial equality in the press was not confined to the South. As we shall see in the next chapter, it became the hallmark of most newspaper coverage throughout the nation.

Inciting to Riot: The Age of Jackson

They swell our list of paupers, they are indolent and uncivil, and yet if a black man commits a crime, we have more interest made for him than for a white.

New York Enquirer, November 21st, 1826

American newspapers gave passionate attention during the 1830s to two issues that would dramatically alter the evolution of the young republic: slavery and territorial expansion. They were not content, however, simply to chronicle public debate on those issues. A disturbing number of editors sowed racial hatred and clamored for wars of conquest, while several actually spearheaded bloody mob attacks against non-white communities and their abolitionist supporters.

This chapter traces the role played by many of the nation's most influential nineteenth-century editors in spreading bigoted views and instigating racial violence. It also examines how the commercial and labor press, by championing territorial conquest of Mexican and Latin American lands, helped to legitimize white-supremacist notions of Manifest Destiny in the public imagination.

Mordecai Noah and James Watson Webb

As previously noted, the decades after the Revolution gave rise to intense public debate over the extension of voting rights, with several northern states moving in the 1820s to adopt universal white male suffrage. New York's Constitutional Convention, for example, eliminated property qualifications for voting in 1821. But since the state legislature had previously decreed all slaves would be free by 1827, the Constitutional Convention was forced also to decide whether the state's large number of black residents would be allowed to vote. Influential papers like Mordecai Noah's *National Advocate* led fierce crusades against extending the franchise to free blacks and routinely lampooned black intelligence. "Africans—People of color generally, are very imitative, quick in their conceptions and rapid in their execution," Noah wrote, "but it is in the lighter pursuits requiring no intensity of thought or depth of reflection. It may be questioned whether they would succeed in the abstruse sciences though they have, neverthe-less, some fancy and humor."[1] Convention delegates eventually decided that only blacks who paid taxes on at least $350 of property could qualify as elec-tors, which assured that only sixteen of the 12,499 black residents of New York County could qualify to vote.[2]

Five years later, Noah wrote of blacks: "They swell our list of paupers, they are indolent and uncivil, and yet if a black man commits a crime, we have more interest made for him than for a white."[3] His newspapers often extolled the performances of "Jim Crow" Daniel Rice, the first white clown in black face.[4]

James Watson Webb was another prominent Jackson-era editor famous for his diatribes against blacks. A swashbuckling Indian fighter and veteran of the War of 1812, Webb purchased one of Noah's papers, the *Enquirer*, in 1829, then merged it with his *Morning Courier*. By the early 1830s, his *Courier and New York-Morning Enquirer* had become the largest and most powerful newspaper in the country. Webb kept Noah on his staff at first, along with an aggressive young writer who would later become one of the legen-dary figures of American journalism—James Gordon Bennett. Webb, Noah and other New York editors "frequently caricatured and parodied African Americans ... and denigrated their concerns," according to Jacqueline Bacon, noted historian of the black press.[5]

In a July 4, 1834 issue of his paper, for example, Webb published an article headlined "More Black Brutality," which recounted the gruesome assault by a black man on a white woman, an incident that had occurred not in New York City but in Philadelphia. The article's final sentence scornfully sur-mised that "abolition folks would interfere" once the culprit was captured.[6] In another issue, the paper warned: "Abolition is a miserable remedy for the mischief it leaves the colored population ... a poor degraded race." It urged instead the removal of all blacks to Liberia "under a government and laws of their own."[7]

Webb rejected any suggestion that the Negro might someday be a part of America and "opposed vehemently any plan that promised the eventual assimilation of 'inferior' breeds such as the Irish and the Latin American into the mainstream of American society," notes Leonard Richards in his study of anti-black violence in Jacksonian America.[8]

Press Fervor Against the Abolitionists

Webb and Noah's main competition in New York City was the staid *Journal of Commerce*, the mercantile paper that silk traders and evangelical reformers Arthur and Lewis Tappan launched in 1827.

Like Webb, Arthur Tappan had once been an active member of the

American Colonization Society, which promoted massive deportation of free blacks to Africa as the best way to preserve America for the white population.[9] Founded in 1816, the ACS represented an unusual alliance of prominent white leaders. Its program placated the concerns of Southern planters who feared that free blacks would stir up slave rebellion. At the same time, it attracted Northerners who were opposed to slavery but still believed that blacks were too inferior to be integrated into white society. ACS members and supporters included Henry Clay, Daniel Webster, Francis Scott Key, John Marshall, and for a time Abraham Lincoln. President Madison provided the Society with federal funds to establish the Republic of Liberia in 1822 as a colony of free American blacks.

The views of the ACS were not shared by educated free blacks or by a handful of radical evangelical white ministers, who favored instead a moral crusade for immediate abolition. William Lloyd Garrison, the most famous of the "immediatists," as they came to be known, routinely accused the ACS of duping the public and labeled it an obstacle to black freedom. In the pages of his paper the *Liberator*, and in a scathing pamphlet he authored in 1832, *Thoughts on African Colonization*, Garrison condemned the ACS's Liberia plans: "I am constrained to declare with the utmost sincerity, that I look upon the Colonization scheme as inadequate in its design, injurious in its operation, and contrary to sound principle; and the more scrupulously I examine its pretensions, the stronger is my conviction of its sinfulness." Garrison's polemic, in the words of his main biographer Henry Mayer, "captured the attention of the humanitarian public with a force unmatched in American journalism since Tom Paine's *Common Sense*."[10]

Journal of Commerce founder Arthur Tappan became gradually convinced that most free blacks wanted nothing to do with relocation to Liberia. Tappan then renounced the ACS and launched his own abolitionist publication, the *Emancipator*. In 1833—the same year England freed its slaves in the West Indies—Tappan joined with Garrison and other abolitionists to found the American Anti-Slavery Society.

Leaders of the ACS initially ignored the new group, but as they watched its ranks swell with converts, they turned increasingly hostile to Garrison and Tappan. On the night of October 1st, 1833, a group of New York ACS leaders met with Webb at the offices of the *Courier and Enquirer* to orchestrate the disruption of an abolitionist meeting scheduled for the following evening. Garrison was returning to America the next day from a much-publicized speaking tour in England, and Arthur Tappan had invited him to address New York's abolitionists the following night at Clinton Hall, the historic building at Nassau and Beekman streets that had only recently been rented as the site of the new City University of New York.[11]

"Are we to look tamely on and see this most dangerous species of fanaticism extending itself throughout society?" Webb asked in his paper on the morning of the event, urging his readers to nip "this many-headed Hydra in the bud."[12] An angry crowd of more than 1,500 whites responded to the call and assembled outside Clinton Hall that night. Webb himself showed up to lead the mob, along with James Gordon Bennett and other "men of property and standing" in the city. At one point the horde became so unruly that the building's owners summarily canceled the abolitionists' use of the hall. Word spread that Tappan's followers had quietly shifted their gathering to Chatham Street Chapel, whereupon the rabble rushed to the chapel and stormed it. Tappan and his small band narrowly escaped by slipping out through a back door.[13]

"We are pleased to perceive that the attention of the Daily Press has been at length roused to this subject," the *Courier and Enquirer* reported with obvious scorn in its October 4 issue, "and that in future we are to have able auxiliaries in frowning down the incendiary attempts of a few mischievous fanatics." Webb went on to quote excerpts from the reactions of his fellow New York editors to the mob action he had organized.

"The press, the unerring criterion of public opinion, took notice the matter and put a stop to the designs of Garrison and his followers," boasted the *New York Gazette*. "The opinion of an immense majority of the citizens of New York is decidedly opposed to any measure being taken in any shape on the subject of emancipation," said the *Mercantile Advertiser*.[14]

Webb proudly acknowledged his paper's role in fomenting the turmoil: "We have therefore solicited our fellow citizens to attend this meeting and by the legitimate republican exercise of the right of a vast and overwhelming majority, to protect us from the malignant designs of these mischievous incendiaries…"[15]

The Press and the New York Race Riot of 1834

The mob of 1833 visit was only the prelude to many that Webb and other New York editors would instigate. On July 4, 1834, another crowd broke up a gathering of whites and blacks at Chatham Street Chapel that was commemorating the seventh anniversary of Emancipation in the state.

Between July 1 and 15, the city's papers spread "ugly and fantastic rumors" about abolitionists conducting interracial marriages and adopting black children. Even the *Evening Post* joined in the hysteria by suggesting on July 8 that the Tappan brothers favored "promiscuous intermarriage of the two races."[16] According to William L. Stone's *Commercial Advertiser*, the July 4 incident erupted because the two races were "obnoxiously mixed" at Chatham Hall. That incident was followed by a second mob attack on a similar celebration held by black residents on July 7. But this time, several members of the audience fought back and tried to eject the intruders. A pitched brawl ensued in which several people were injured before police arrived to clear the building.

One of those beaten and arrested that night was a fugitive slave named Samuel Ringgold Ward. Only seventeen at the time, Ward would later become a Congregational minister, an agent for the American Anti-Slavery Society, and the influential editor of three black newspapers.[17]

The day after Ward's arrest, Stone's *Commercial Advertiser* claimed that "gangs of black fellows" had assembled on street corners during the night "threatening to burn the city." Mordecai Noah's *Evening Star* issued a dramatic call for white residents to act:

> When will the citizens of this city no longer submit to have their breth-ren attacked by the abetted mobs of Negroes: their ears harshly assailed with the vile and debased proposition of a general amalgamation of color? If they will not, let them fearlessly assert their determination, and show, though slow to move, when once aroused, their wrath will come with redoubled force.[18]

Webb's paper declared the July 7 events nothing less than a Negro riot. Innocent whites had been "beaten—yes, beaten, fellow-citizens, by the bludgeons of an infuriated and an encouraged Negro mob," reported his *Courier and Enquirer*. "How much more are we to submit? In the name of country, in the name of Heaven, how much more are we to bear from Arthur Tappan's impudence?"[19]

The outlandish press accounts only served to inflame further white anger. The extent of their inaccuracy can be gleaned from a July 9 article that appeared in the New York *Sun*. Benjamin Day's penny paper was one of the few that reported the violence objectively, even quoting the actual testi-mony that Samuel Ringgold Ward and the other blacks gave in court when they were arraigned:

> Samuel R. Ward, Abraham Lunyea, and John Hamilton, (colored), were brought up from the Chatham street Chapel.
>
> MAG.—what is the charge against these men?
>
> WATCHMAN—I don't know, sir. I brought them from the chapel.
>
> MAG. (To prisoners)—What were you doing in the chapel?
>
> PRIS.—We were holding a meeting there, sir. We hired the use of the chapel, and paid $15 for it.
>
> MAG.—Well, what then?
>
> PRIS.—When we were singing, Dr. Rockwell came in and said we must go out—and then they kicked up a row and the watchman came in and drove us out, and locked the doors.

Since none of the witnesses "could swear that the prisoners had been guilty of anything," the article said, the prisoners "were discharged."[20]

By the night of July 9, however, editors Webb, Stone and Noah had concocted and spread a frightening picture of black rebellion. Over the next
several days, bands of white thugs responded with a racial pogrom throughout Lower Manhattan. They destroyed sixty homes, six churches, and several
businesses belonging to black residents and white abolitionists. Among the
places targeted were Arthur Tappan's store, the stately home of Lewis Tappan,
and several brothels that employed black prostitutes. Before and during the
rioting, Webb's paper repeatedly denounced a white clergyman named
Samuel H. Cox for eliminating segregated pews in his church and for daring
to preach that Jesus was probably dark-skinned. Cox's Church ended up
among the buildings destroyed by the mob.[21]

Throughout the days of violence, Webb used his paper to openly cheer
the mob. In the July 14 issue of the *Courier and Enquirer*, he proclaimed:

> [W]E trust the immediate abolitionists and amalgamators will see in the
> proceedings of the last few days, sufficient proof that the people of New
> York, have determined to prevent the propagation amongst them of their
> wicked and absurd doctrines, much less to permit the practice of them.
> If we have been instrumental in producing this desirable state of public
> feeling, we take pride in it, let our political opponents make the most of
> the avowal.[22]

Mob Violence Spreads

New York's troubles were part of a wave of racial violence that swept the
country in the mid 1830s. More than 200 mob attacks by groups of white
men took place in the North alone between 1833 and 1838. The incidents
often erupted after articles appeared in local newspapers.[23]

The peak period for the nationwide unrest occurred in the months
after the Charleston postal mob incident of 1835 (see Chapter 2). It may be
difficult for today's reader to comprehend the enormous impact on both
Southern slaveholders and inhabitants of the Northern cities of the massive
postal propaganda campaign the abolitionists unleashed in the late spring
of that year. No one had ever seen anything like it. Garrison's Anti-Slavery
Society had disseminated some 122,000 pieces of literature the previous year,
but in 1835 its members distributed nearly ten times as many—1.1 million
newspapers and pamphlets. In the month of July alone, more than 20,000
pieces bound for the South passed through the Post Office. Those abolitionist publications often featured spine-tingling illustrations that depicted the
worst horrors of slavery. The cover of the May 1835 issue of the *Anti-Slavery
Record*, for example, portrayed a white slave-owner grabbing a black baby by
the wrist while he whipped the child's weeping mother.[24]

The campaign was a direct result of a decision made by Garrison and

Tappan to use the latest advances in printing technology to spread their message. The double cylinder Hoe press, for example, had just been perfected, and the first penny papers were using the new press in New York City. While older machines were capable of producing only 1,000 impressions per hour, a steam-powered Hoe press could churn out as many as 5,500. "Reduced costs and accessibility to steam presses enabled the Tappan group to take advantage of the cheap postal rates that newspapers had long enjoyed, and to flood the mail with tracts and papers," Richards notes, all of which made the abolitionists appear far stronger than they were.[25]

The abolitionists reflected in many ways the significant role that the evangelical press had begun to play in the mass media during the early 1800s. Bible and Tract societies had increasingly utilized low postal rates and highly organized industrial methods to perfect the massive dissemination of religious publications to the public. Many of the major national church publications of the day, the Methodists' *Christian Advocate and Journal*, the Presbyterians' *New York Observer*, and the Congregationalists' *Boston Recorder*, boasted circulations far bigger than any commercial newspaper.[26]

Since the wealthy Tappan brothers were in the forefront of bankrolling the efforts of the Tract societies, once they joined forces with Garrison the abolitionists moved to center-stage in the nation's political debates. They quickly infuriated both the open defenders of slavery and the gradualists of the American Colonization Society with the many startling images of abused blacks their press produced. "By mid August [of 1835], emotions had reached a high tide," Richards notes:

> Fiery speeches and torchlight parades became everyday news. Citizens formed vigilance committees to patrol Negro quarters, to question strangers, and to search post offices, ships and stages for antislavery literature. Southern vigilance committees offered rewards for leading abolitionists. In East Feliciana, Louisiana, citizens posted $50,000 for the delivery of Arthur Tappan ... dead or alive; in Mount Meigs, Alabama, $50,000 for Arthur Tappan or any other prominent abolitionist.[27]

Mobs in Utica, Boston and Cincinnati

Many commercial newspaper editors were openly hostile to the abolitionist press. In September 1835, Webb's *Courier and Enquirer* joined other state newspapers in calling for a mob attack in the town of Utica, where the Anti-Slavery Society was scheduled to meet on October 21st. Webb urged that the convention be "put down" either by the laws of New York, or by the "law of Judge Lynch." The Albany *Argus*, the Utica *Whig*, and the Utica *Observer* echoed Webb's call, as did Mayor Joseph Kirkland, Congressman Samuel Beardsley, and other prominent Utica citizens. "I will be here on that morning, and do my duty manfully to prevent the meeting, *peacefully if I can, forcibly if I must*," vowed Augustine G. Dauby, editor of the *Observer*, during a gathering of Utica leaders.[28]

But Utica's Common Council bravely resisted the pressure. It narrowly voted to uphold the right of free speech and allow the antislavery convention to proceed. Enraged opponents then decided to stop the meeting themselves. The morning of the convention, a mob stormed the church where the abolitionists had gathered. The intruders seized the podium, tore up antislavery literature, ripped the clothes off one delegate, and shouted down all other speakers, forcing the abolitionists to flee. That night, the mob ransacked the office of the *Oneida Standard and Democrat*, one of the few newspapers in town that had argued for allowing the convention to go forward.[29]

The same day of the turmoil in Utica, a mob assaulted Garrison in Boston as he was about to address a meeting of women abolitionists. Once again, newspaper editors directly incited the violence. Before the scheduled meeting, James Homer, publisher of Boston's *Commercial Gazette*, met with a group of merchants from the Central Wharf to plan their disruption. Flyers printed and distributed by Homer offered a $100 reward to anyone who first laid "violent hands on Thompson, so that he may be brought to the tar kettle before dark." The flyers were referring to George Thompson, the noted English abolitionist whom Garrison had invited to address the women's group that night. When he issued the flyers, Homer was unaware that Thompson had cancelled his appearance at the last minute.

The evening of the event, a hostile crowd assembled on Washington Street, broke into the women's meeting, then beat and chased Garrison from the building. A disheveled Garrison, his glasses broken, fled in terror to City Hall, where Mayor Theodore Lyman had to lock him up in a jail cell for the night to prevent the crowd from lynching him.

In its next issue, the Boston *Atlas* proclaimed that Garrison had been rightfully jailed as a "public agitator," while the *Patriot* described the whole incident as an unfortunate example of what happens "when women turn reformers." Homer's *Commercial Advertiser* claimed the protest had been merely "a meeting of gentlemen of property and standing from all parts of the city" who were determined to keep troublemakers like Garrison from disturbing the peace.[30]

That same summer, two of Cincinnati's newspapers, the *Daily Evening Post* and the *Cincinnati Whig*, published articles condemning Arthur Tappan and his "murderous tracts." They urged that any Tappan agent caught in the city be lynched. Local leaders were furious when James Birney, a former slaveholder turned abolitionist, launched his own antislavery newspaper, the *Philanthropist*, and moved the paper's offices into town in April. As soon as Birney set up shop, a mob set fire to a building that housed local Negroes.

The Cincinnati *Republican* jumped to defend the arsonists by labeling the site a gathering place for "rogues, thieves, and prostitutes—black and white."

Then, on July 12, a crowd of prominent city leaders attacked and wrecked the offices of Birney's newspaper. The members of the local Anti-Slavery Society immediately repaired the press and vowed to continue publishing the paper. The *Whig* responded with a letter that asked city residents if they were prepared to "permit a band of fanatics ... to make this city the theatre of their operations, from whence they may throw fire-brands in the slave states?" On the night of July 30, city residents gave their answer. A mob led by several key merchants once again attacked the press that printed the *Philanthropist*, then rampaged along Church Alley, a place where, according to the *Whig*, "black and white men and women, of infamous character ... huddled promiscuously in five or six small buildings."[31]

The Murder of Elijah Lovejoy

The wave of violence eventually produced a martyr. On November 7, 1837, abolitionist minister and newspaper editor Elijah Lovejoy was shot dead in Alton, Illinois, a small town on the Mississippi River, by a group of armed men who attacked and burned the offices of his newspaper. Lovejoy and a handful of his supporters tried at first to protect the new press he had just installed (a previous one having been destroyed by another mob), but raging flames eventually forced them to flee from the building. As he ran out, the abolitionist editor fired a gun at his attackers, but fell amidst a hail of bullets.

The publications that encouraged these attacks, we should keep in mind, were Northern papers, and they were owned by Whigs and Democrats alike. They thus reflected the pervasiveness of racial bigotry among the country's educated whites.

The press hysteria over racial amalgamation soon penetrated into the urban working class. That city's anti-abolitionist rioters of 1834 differed significantly in their class composition from anti-black mobs that would develop in other parts of the country. New York's rioters were more working-class in composition. Historian Leonard Richards examined 1834 court records for the worst days of the city's violence and found that half of the arrestees lived in the same lower Manhattan wards where the city's black population was concentrated, prompting him to conclude that whites in those neighborhoods were most stirred by press warnings that emancipation would inevitably lead to the "mongrelization" of the country.[32]

White workers were encouraged by Democratic Party leaders "to vent indignation upon the most visible scapegoats—free blacks—so that after 1830, racial segregation intensified ... and so did support for slavery," notes historian Anthony Gronowicz.[33]

The Rise of the Penny Press

On September 3rd, 1833, Benjamin Day, a twenty-two-year-old journeyman printer, launched the New York *Sun*, the nation's first penny newspaper. Day thus sparked a communications revolution by making newspapers accessible for the first time to the mass of urban workers. Unfortunately, the penny press also became a key instrument in the spread of racism among America's white working class. Until then, as we have mentioned, newspapers were prohibitively expensive for the average person. In a city like New York, for example, with its 200,000 inhabitants, Webb's *Courier and Enquirer* sold a mere 4,500 copies in the early 1830s—the largest circulation for any paper in the country. By comparison, the *London Times*, then the world's biggest newspaper, boasted 10,000 subscribers.[34]

Day was himself a product of the city's radical labor movement. A leader of the typographical workers union, he had been one of founders of the *New York Sentinel*, a labor sheet that arose in 1830 just as the Workingman's Party started splintering into factions (see Chapter 2). Once the *Sentinel* collapsed in 1832, he decided to start his own newspaper. But the young editor, having been chastened and disillusioned by the internal squabbling among radical leaders and by the vehement opposition to the Worky press from the city's elite, opted for a less confrontational style of journalism, one that was not tied to any particular political party. The new *Sun*, he promised in his prospectus for the newspaper, would be "deserving of the encouragement of all classes of society" and would provide "an advantageous medium for advertising."[35]

At one cent per issue, the *Sun* was far cheaper than the existing six-cent competition. To make it more accessible still, Day hired young newsboys to hawk single copies each day on the streets. He also made dramatic changes in style and content. Until then, most papers typically consisted of long polemics and letters printed on huge "blanket" pages of 24 by 35 inches—sheets so large that when they were fully unfolded the paper stretched to 4ft wide. Articles in the blanket sheets were written by the editor himself or by his acquaintances, and the content was then supplemented with countless reprints from other newspapers. Day designed a smaller, more manageable paper, consisting of four 8½-by-11-inch pages. More importantly, he hired actual writers to go out in the street and report on local events.

One of his best decisions was to hire George Wisner, an out-of-work printer, as a full-time reporter. Wisner quickly pioneered an entire new genre: crime reporting. He would rush to the local court early each morning and provide saucy, crisply written accounts on the myriad of daily hearings, trials and arraignments that took place there, providing the most specific and humorous details possible, as in this *Sun* issue of September 2nd, 1833:

William Luvoy got drunk because yesterday was so devilish warm, Drank 9 glasses of brandy and water and said he would be cursed if he wouldn't drink 9 more as quick as he could raise the money to buy it with. He would like to know what right the magistrate had to interfere with his private affairs. Fined $1—forgot his pocketbook, and was sent over to bridewell.[36]

Wisner's articles made the *Sun* an instant hit and soon landed him the job of co-editor. His conviction that "bad" news attracts more readers than "good" news has dominated much of commercial journalism ever since. A newspaper, Wisner once said,

> Must generally tell of wars and fighting, of deeds of death, and blood, of wounds and heresies, of broken heads, broken hearts, and broken bones, of accidents by fire or flood, a field of possessions ravaged, property purloined, wrongs inflicted … The abundance of news is generally an evidence of astounding misery, and even the disinterested deeds of benevolence and philanthropy which we occasionally hear of owe their existence to the wants or sorrows or sufferings of some of our fellow beings.[37]

With tantalizing and often humorous headlines such as, "Conjugal Fidelity," "The Hare Without Any Friends," "Knockdown Argument," and "A Treacherous Friend," the paper soon garnered a devout following. In one satirical article, headlined "Flea-ography," the *Sun* reported: "A learned professor of Philadelphia, anxious to promote the cultivation of good feelings, has advertised that he will teach the novel and sublime science of flea-ography, or the art and mystery of catching fleas."[38]

By November 1834, Day's paper was selling a torrid 10,000 copies a day, and after he installed the new Hoe version of the British Napier press the following year and added steam power, circulation shot up to more than 15,000.[39]

The *Sun* transformed American newspapers almost overnight from staid, somber intelligence sheets for the nation's elite into raucous reports for the masses. It was so successful that publishers in several cities, including several former underlings of Day, launched papers copying his formula. At least thirty-four new dailies started up in New York City alone between 1833 and 1837, though most did not survive for even one year.[40] By then, Day had sold the *Sun* to Moses Y. Beach, his brother-in-law and employee. Beach operated the paper until his retirement in 1848, and then passed it on to his two sons, Moses S. and Alfred Beach.[41]

James Gordon Bennett's Herald and the Respectable Working Class

The most successful of the *Sun's* imitators proved to be James Gordon Bennett's New York *Herald*. Born in Scotland, Bennett arrived in this country at the age of twenty-four and soon found himself drawn to journalism. A brilliant but fanciful writer, he spent years at a variety of newspapers, working at different times for both Mordecai Noah and James Watson Webb. In 1832 he tried to launch papers first in New York and later in Philadelphia, but both efforts failed.

By the age of forty, Bennett was out of work and heading nowhere when he made the shrewdest gamble of his life and ploughed his last $500 into starting a penny paper. The first edition of his New York *Herald* hit the streets on May 6, 1835, and it turned into a runaway success. Within a year, the paper boasted a circulation of 15,000 and had become the *Sun's* chief competitor.

Like Benjamin Day, Bennett claimed to be an advocate for the common man, but he consciously sought to distinguish his paper from the *Sun* by directing its appeal to the more upscale, financially secure and conservative sectors of the working and middle classes, even raising its price to two cents. Relying on his considerable knowledge of economics, Bennett pioneered the reporting of business news, so that the *Herald's* information on Wall Street affairs and machinations inside corporate America was soon unrivaled. He also initiated regular gossip items on another unique New York institution—the Broadway theater and its stars.

Even in crime reporting, the great staple of the penny papers, the *Herald* adopted a distinct class perspective. That outlook was best highlighted during the sensational Robinson-Jewett murder trial that dominated newspaper headlines in the late 1830s—much as the Lindbergh or O. J. Simpson cases did in the twentieth century. Helen Jewett, a beautiful twenty-three-year-old upscale prostitute, was found murdered in her elegant mahogany bed in the St. Thomas Hotel in New York City on the morning of April 10, 1836. Her attacker had used an ax to slash her face several times, and then set her body on fire. Police quickly arrested eighteen-year-old Richard Robinson, a well-educated merchant clerk and frequent client of Jewett's, who had spent the previous night with the woman and was apparently smitten with her. Every lurid detail of Jewett's life became daily fodder for the penny press. Both Day's *Sun* and the *Transcript*, a competing penny paper, immediately jumped to portray the accused Robinson as guilty.[42]

Bennett's *Herald*, on the other hand, declared Robinson innocent. The young clerk from a well-to-do New England family had lived "without a stain, except falling a victim to the fascination of Ellen [*sic*] Jewett," Bennett insisted. He could not have plummeted "at once from the heights of virtue to the depths of vice." The *Herald's* investigation showed that Robinson was the victim of a "bloody and unnatural conspiracy" concocted by the "licentious inmates of a fashionable brothel" and aided by a corrupt police department.[43]

Bennett knew precisely what he was doing with his extraordinary claim. The "respectable" citizens he wished to attract to his newspaper identified far more with Robinson than they ever could with Jewett. Let the *Sun* and the other penny papers defend the dead prostitute and the rabble around her; the *Herald* would stand with Robinson.

During the trial, all the city's penny papers fabricated information and embellished their stories in a tawdry effort to keep the public enthralled. When the jury astonished everyone by voting to acquit the young clerk, Bennett and the *Herald* emerged the biggest winners of all. His newspaper's circulation skyrocketed and his conservative bent now became ascendant in the world of penny papers.

Horace Greeley's Tribune and the Whigs

The other towering figure of American journalism who made his mark through the penny press was Horace Greeley. Born in 1811 on a New Hampshire farm, Greeley was a child prodigy, reading the entire Bible by the age of five and constantly devouring every book and newspaper he could find. Frail and blue-eyed, with a high-pitched voice and homespun clothes that never seemed to fit him properly, Greeley arrived in New York city at the age of twenty with $10 to his name—all the money he had been able to save after several years bouncing around upstate New York as an apprentice printer. He landed a job for a time at the *Evening Post*, but his dream was to run his own newspaper, so he soon embarked on a series of printing ventures by borrowing money and recruiting partners. First came a weekly whose main revenue was from lottery advertising, then a two-cent daily called the *Morning Post*, then a weekly literary sheet called the *New-Yorker*—all of which quickly failed.[44]

Greeley's luck turned when several editorials he wrote favoring Whig politicians caught the attention of Thurlow Weed, the publisher of a powerful Whig newspaper in Albany. Weed just happened to be a close confidant of William Seward, who was about to run for governor of New York. Weed recruited Greeley to run two Whig-sponsored newspapers in 1838, the *Jeffersonian* and the *Log Cabin*. Both papers supported Seward's run for governor, then backed the campaign of William Henry Harrison, the Whig candidate for president in 1840. When Seward and Harrison won their races, circulation of Greeley's papers zoomed. Thus was cemented a close friendship and political alliance between Weed, Greeley and Seward that would last for decades.[45]

Greeley eventually decided to launch a Whig-oriented penny paper to counter the Democratic leanings of the *Sun* and Bennett's *Herald*. His New York *Tribune* began publication on April 10, 1841. Within seven weeks it had reached a daily circulation of 11,000, and during the Civil War it sold up to 45,000 copies. By then, the *Tribune* was the most influential newspaper in America.[46]

Changing Views of Class and Race in the Penny Press

Unfortunately, the penny press contributed significantly to the spread of racist and imperialistic ideas among the American public. Penny papers developed an overall world-view that was "democratic in politics, expansionist in aspiration, and ferociously white egalitarian in identification."[47]

As they transitioned from radical labor journalists to successful commercial publishers, Day and his fellow artisan editors gradually abandoned their sense of a social mission or a moral cause. As historian Andie Tucher so perceptibly notes:

> Gone now was the aggressively rebellious tone of the Working Men's papers. The urgent calls for social justice and economic revolution had been almost entirely replaced by the low babble of the street, the theater and the police court. The reckless demands for equal rights had been elbowed aside by the piquancies of rampaging elephants and dissolute clergymen. Devoting their columns to the small tragedies and comedies of daily life, the editors recognized, was a safe choice as well as a practical one. Not only was reporting on such incidents cheap and easy; it also avoided the dangers of overt warfare against well-armed and seasoned opponents.[48]

Unlike the unstamped press in England, which used its strong appeal among the working class to expose and defy the policies of England's ruling circles, the penny press and other commercial newspapers in the United States confined themselves to news coverage that legitimized the state. True, papers like the *Sun* continued to provide editorial support for some of the major reform issues that affected workers—the ten-hour day, an end to imprisonment for debt, a ban on the use of prison labor—and they regularly defended workers' strikes, but they completely abandoned any dreams of an independent labor party that could transform the society. While the first penny papers did not openly endorse candidates or political parties, most gradually became closely associated with Jacksonian democracy. With so many American workers now exercising the right to vote, the penny press thus emerged as a key instrument in shaping the worldview of the urban working class. The more that workers turned to the papers for news, the more advertisers flocked to those same papers to sell products, and the more the ad revenues of the publishers grew. Transformed into captains of immensely profitable enterprises, those once-upstart radical publishers and editors gradually came to see the expansion of American capitalism as being in their basic self-interest.[49]

A hallmark of that expansionist outlook was the vision of the United States as an exclusively white nation. When it came to slavery and race, the *Sun* initially voiced a more humanistic and progressive view than other New York dailies. During the days of the 1834 race riots, for example, it generally condemned attacks by white mobs on blacks and abolitionists. As the racial violence intensified, the *Sun* directly denounced the *Courier and Enquirer* for backing the rioters. It even printed a heart-rending story of a dying slave, more than a hundred years old, who, after a lifetime of loyal service to the family that owned him, had been granted his final wish for freedom while on his deathbed.[50]

The *Sun*'s empathy for African-Americans, however, was hardly uniform. Earlier in 1834, the paper published an anecdote about a Captain Strickland who hated "these New York niggers" and who bested "two big greasy niggers" in a fight in the Five Points after the two men jostled him. That same summer, it published two front-page columns, "Cuffee's Lecture on Phrenology," that ridiculed black dialect.[51]

Many of the paper's sympathetic articles toward blacks were due not to Benjamin Day but to George Wisner, the police reporter who briefly became Day's partner and co-editor. As Day later revealed, the two men eventually "split on politics. You see, I was rather Democratic in my notions; Wisner, whenever he got a chance, was always sticking in his damned little Abolitionist articles. We quarreled … [I] kept the paper, paying him $5,000 for his share."[52] By 1847, the *Sun* under the Beach family had turned so openly racist that it proclaimed in one editorial: "The *Sun* shines for all white men and not for colored men."[53]

The paper's belittling of blacks, however, was mild compared to what Webb, Noah, and Bennett printed in their publications. Bennett, a fervent defender of the slaveholding South until the Civil War, commonly used the worst racial invectives in his writing, once calling the *Sun* a "decrepit, dying penny paper, owned and controlled by a set of woolly-headed and thick-lipped Negroes."[54] Such notions, of course, were common in nineteenth-century America, even among those journalists who otherwise were fierce opponents of slavery. Julia Ward Howe, for example, who penned the lyrics to the "Battle Hymn of the Republic," asserted in the *Atlantic Monthly* on the eve of the Civil War that northern Negroes had been "refined" and "elevated" by white culture and white blood. "The negro among negroes is a coarse, grinning, flat-footed, thick-skinned creature," she wrote, "ugly as Caliban, lazy as the laziest of brutes, chiefly ambitious to be of no use to any in the world."[55]

The Press and Manifest Destiny

In their views of territorial expansion, editors of the penny press were not much different from radical labor leaders such as George Henry Evans, who called for frontier land to be apportioned to workers as a means of solving the deepening social problems of the eastern cities. The *Sun* referred to western emigration in 1837 as "the means of securing welfare and safety ... The angel of relief and independent prosperity."[56] For that emigration to succeed, however, workers would have to join the seizure of western lands from the previous inhabitants—Native Americans and Mexicans. Western conquest "necessarily rested upon assertions of racial superiority," Saxton notes; thus it is not surprising that the penny papers "methodically propagated" such claims. From Boston to Philadelphia they periodically printed articles with headlines such as "More Indian Outrages in Florida." In an 1837 article about Crow Indians in the Black Hills, for example, the *Sun* warned its readers: "Trust to their honesty and they will steal the hair off your head."[57]

Under the Beach family, the *Sun* began to popularize the notion of Manifest Destiny, a term first coined by John O'Sullivan, editor of the *United States Magazine and Democratic Review*. O'Sullivan started the *Review* in 1837 to provide an intellectual center for followers of Jackson in their cultural battles against the Whig academics of the northeast. Largely a literary publication, it provided a venue for many of America's greatest writers, including Thoreau, Emerson, Edgar Allen Poe, Whitman and Hawthorne, while also crusading for the expansion of labor rights and political power for urban workers. O'Sullivan, also a New York City Tammany Hall assemblyman, fervently believed that territorial expansion would guarantee immigrant workers a greater future. He thus espoused the annexation of Texas and Oregon, the acquisition of Cuba, and war with Mexico. It was in the New York *Morning Star*, a short-lived paper he co-edited with future president Samuel Tilden, that O'Sullivan proclaimed in 1845 "[t]he right of manifest destiny to overspread and to possess the whole continent which providence has given us for the development of the great experiment of liberty and federated self government."[58]

Earlier that year, after Congress narrowly approved Texas annexation, O'Sullivan lauded the decision:

> Texas has been absorbed into the Union in the inevitable fulfillment of the general law which is rolling our population westward ... It was disintegrated from Mexico in the natural course of events, by a process perfectly legitimate on its own part, blameless on ours; and in which all the censures due to wrong, perfidy and folly, rest on Mexico alone.[59]

Whether the news concerned African slavery, Indian removal or the acquisition of more swaths of Mexico's land, both the penny press and old-line
newspapers spoke only to white Americans. An 1835 item from the Mobile
Chronicle, headlined "Horrid Massacre," for example, told of 112 men who
had been killed in a Seminole ambush and scalped. "We do not remember
the history of a butchery more horrid, and it stands without an example in
the annals of Indian warfare," claimed the article, a copy of which appeared
in the *United States Gazette*. The casualties, it turned out, were substantially
overstated, and the scalping had been committed not by the Seminoles but
by a band of former slaves who were allied with them and who arrived
after the men had been killed. As journalism historian John M. Coward
has pointed out in his study of nineteenth-century newspaper coverage of
Indians, "the story was wrong in both its particulars and its implications."[60]

Hezekiah Niles, editor of *Niles' Weekly Register* in Washington, DC, was
one of the few white journalists who repeatedly displayed sympathy in
his paper for the plight of Native Americans. In 1830, for example, Niles
reprinted a touching, though somewhat paternalistic, account of the progress
made by the Cherokees. The story was written by Colonel Benjamin Gold
of Connecticut, father-in-law of *Cherokee Phoenix* editor Elias Boudinot (see
Chapter 6). Describing his trip through the Cherokee nation, Gold wrote:

> Everything detailed to us, relative to the Cherokees, affords strong evi-
> dence that the wandering Indian has been converted into the industrious
> husbandman; and the tomahawk and rifle are exchanging for plough, the
> hoe, the wheel and the loom, and that they are rapidly acquiring domestic
> habits, and attaining a degree of civilization that was entirely unexpected,
> from the natural disposition of these children of the forest.[61]

Such attempts at more nuanced accounts of Indians remained rare. As
Coward has noted, "news-making practices of the 1830s defined Indian
news in an 'us-vs.-them' fashion, emphasizing Indian violence against whites
at the expense of other types of Indian news. When the papers were concerned about Indians at all, it was because Indian sympathizers took up the
cause."[62]

Even Horace Greeley, whose New York *Tribune* was the most consistent among the commercial press in opposing slavery, who exposed the
horrid slum conditions of New York's working class, who espoused for a
time Fourier's brand of utopian socialism and even employed Karl Marx as
a correspondent, evinced the same deep-seated racial biases that permeated
virtually all white-owned newspapers of that era. In his account of a trip
through the West in 1859, Greeley wrote:

I have learned to appreciate better than hitherto ... the dislike, aversion, contempt, wherewith Indians are usually regarded by their white neighbors, and have been since the days of the Puritans. [One] needs but little familiarity with the actual, palpable aborigines to convince any one that the poetic Indian—the Indian of Cooper and Longfellow—is only visible to the poet's eye."[63]

Greeley published equally abhorrent opinions toward the Chinese. An 1854 article in the *Tribune* warned of "grave fears" over the increase in Chinese immigration to California, and described the newcomers as "uncivilized, unclean and filthy beyond all conception, without any of the higher domestic or social relations ... Pagan in their religion, they know not the virtues of honesty, integrity or good faith."[64]

Like the Jacksonian Democrats, Greeley was an avid proponent of westward expansion, coining the legendary phrase, "Go west, young man; go west!"[65] His territorial ambitions, however, were inspired not by the Manifest Destiny ideology of the Democrats, but by classical Whig views, which favored government aid to the railways and telegraph companies and a homestead law for new settlers.

The outbreak of the Mexican-American War dramatically altered the trajectory of American democracy. Most Democrats, including the Northern labor radicals, initially backed the war. "Mexico must be thoroughly chastised," Walt Whitman declared in his *Brooklyn Daily Eagle*. "We have reached a point in our intercourse with that country, when prompt and effectual demonstrations of force are enjoined upon us by every dictate of right and policy." Bennett's *Herald* predicted the war would "lay the foundation of a new age, a new destiny, affecting both this continent and the old continent of Europe."[66]

It was indeed a new age. Our republic was rapidly stretching across an entire continent; its redrawn boundaries now contained a host of conquered peoples—mostly Mexicans and Native Americans. The newly acquired Western territories soon drew tens of thousands of settlers who flocked there from Europe and the eastern seaboard, but also from Asia and Latin America, thus assuring the country's transformation into a multi-racial, not simply multi-ethnic, state.

The Mexican acquisitions, in particular, presented a special challenge to the white settler narrative. Anglo editors who moved into the new Spanish-speaking territories after annexation lost no time in starting newspapers to disseminate their own views of events to both the old and newly arrived settlers. Atrocities such as lynching of Mexican settlers were often celebrated. A Corpus Christi correspondent for the *Galveston Weekly News*, for example, wrote this chilling account in 1855: "Eleven Mexicans, it is stated, have been found along the Nueces, in hung up condition. Better so than to be left on the ground for the howling lobos to tear in pieces, and then howl the more for the red peppers than burn his insides raw."[67] The Dallas *Herald* openly championed the Knights of the Golden Circle, a secret antebellum white group that sought to organize filibuster invasions into Mexico to expand Southern slavery. "Let these Texans range on the Mexican frontier and infuse some of the Anglo-Saxon ideas of progressiveness into the stupid, leaden souls of that people—and then the world will witness a change," noted the *Herald*.[68]

Historian and Civil Rights leader Carey McWilliams chronicled the widespread use of lynching in Southern California during the mid nineteenth century. According to McWilliams, throughout the 1860s "the lynching of Mexicans was such a common occurrence in Los Angeles that the newspapers scarcely bothered to report the details."[69]

Anglo-owned newspapers in the former Mexican territories almost never mentioned another crucial issue—land disputes between Mexicans and white settlers. Architect and landscaper Frederick Olmstead, who in the 1850s conducted a horseback trip through Texas, cited one of those few accounts in his memoir of that trip:

> MATATGORDA: The people of Matagorda county have held a meeting and ordered every Mexican to leave the county. To strangers this may seem wrong, but we hold it to be perfectly right and highly necessary; but a word of explanation should be given. In the first place, then, there are none but the lower class or "Peon" Mexicans in the county; secondly, they have no fixed domicile, but hang around the plantations, taking the likeliest negro girls for wives; and, thirdly, they often steal horses, and these girls, too, and endeavor to run them to Mexico. We should rather have anticipated an appeal to Lynch law, than the mild course which has been adopted.[70]

And so it was that US newspapers, whether the staid broadsheets or the ribald penny press, whether mainstream commercial publications or dissident sheets, kept spreading racial bias and justifying territorial expansion. So one-sided was the white press that it soon sparked an opposition press with a powerful counter-narrative. It is to those early opposition newspapers written and edited by journalists of color that we turn next.

II

Rebel Voices

4

A New Democratic Press

We wish to plead our own cause. Too long have others spoken for us ...
From the press and the pulpit we have suffered much by being incorrectly
represented.

Freedom's Journal, March 16th, 1827

A heavy snow was falling that frigid morning in December of 1823 when the merchant ship *Draper* unloaded three weary political refugees from Spain at the dock in bustling New York harbor. As the new arrivals stepped gingerly down the icy gang plank, their leader Félix Varela—a slender, thirty-five-year-old, bespectacled Cuban Catholic priest—suddenly slipped and stumbled. Only the quick action of a young disciple who had been waiting at the dock to greet them saved him from a nasty fall. "I'm holding up what Spain couldn't," the nimble disciple whispered as he steadied the fugitive priest.

A few weeks later, Varela, who was notorious in his homeland as an opponent of slavery and an advocate of Cuban liberty, moved to Philadelphia and began publishing a small pro-independence newspaper. He called it *El Habanero*, and his followers began smuggling copies onto ships bound for Cuba, then distributing it throughout the island.[1]

El Habanero was not the first Hispanic newspaper in the United States, but Varela was undoubtedly the most influential Latino journalist of the early nineteenth century, rivaled in his accomplishments only by fellow Cuban José Martí and Mexican-Americans Francisco Ramírez and Carlos Padilla toward the end of the century. All four embodied in their work the close connection between two distinct newspaper traditions—the Latin American and the North American—which have existed side-by-side in the New World since the early days of European colonialism.

Shortly after Varela settled in New York, a group of free black residents of that city started organizing their own response to the deplorable racist coverage of the city's black community by white newspaper editors like Moredchai Noah and James Watson Webb. John Brown Russwurm, born to a white father and a black mother in Jamaica, and a recent graduate of Bowdoin College in Maine, and the Rev. Samuel Cornish, the pastor of

New York's First Colored Presbyterian Church, gathered in late 1826 with a group of friends at 129 Leonard St., the home of M. Boston Crummell, one of the city's most prominent African-Americans.

Those who gathered at Crummell's house that day all agreed it was time for the black community to create its own newspaper, to challenge the endless stream of racial stereotypes in the white press. They chose dentist Thomas Jennings as chair of the stockholders' group for the new publication, and they appointed Cornish and Russwurm its editors. Backing for the new enterprise soon came from all over the northeast. David Walker, head of the Massachusetts General Colored Council and future author of *David Walker's Appeal*, volunteered to be an agent for the paper in Boston. Pennsylvania's Stephen Smith, a wealthy black lumber merchant and financier of the Underground Railroad, offered to donate money, and Thomas Hale of the New York Manumission Society recruited support from fellow white abolitionists.

Russwurm and Cornish began publishing *Freedom's Journal*, America's first black-owned newspaper, on March 16th, 1827. In its wake, some thirty black-owned papers would appear in the northern states in the period before the Civil War, while more than 1,100 would be published during the latter half of the nineteenth century.[2]

The same year that black leaders met to plan the launch of *Freedom's Journal*, a young Cherokee schoolteacher embarked on a speaking and fundraising tour among church and philanthropic groups in the northeastern United States. His name was Elias Boudinot, and on May 26th, 1826 he delivered an eloquent sermon at the First Presbyterian Church in Philadelphia on the paper he had been assigned to edit by the Cherokee Nation's tribal council in Georgia. The new publication, Boudinot said, would reflect "the feelings, dispositions, improvements and prospects of the Indians; their traditions, their true character, as it once was, as it is now." It would seek to "create much interest in the American Community, favorable to the aborigines, and to have a powerful influence on the advancement of the Indians themselves."[3] He then asked the congregation for its support.

Boudinot published the inaugural issue of the *Cherokee Phoenix* on February 21, 1828. The first Native American newspaper in history was a four-page weekly written in both English and Cherokee. Despite bitter opposition from white Georgians who were constantly encroaching into Cherokee territory, the *Phoenix* managed to appear regularly for the next six years.[4]

Thus, in the short period between 1824 and 1828, three of America's pioneer publications by people of color, *El Habanero*, *Freedom's Journal*, and the *Cherokee Phoenix*, quietly came into existence. They arose even as Jacksonian Democrats were methodically starting hundreds of partisan newspapers throughout the United States to help capture the presidency for their leader. The founding editors of the three publications did not know each other, though all had the same goal: to give voice to the moral and political struggle of a people who had long been denied their rights.

Few Americans realize that people of color published more than one hundred newspapers in this country before the Civil War. This new press, unlike the white-owned commercial publications of that era, or the foreign-language newspapers of the early European immigrants, or even the early radical labor newspapers, was forged in direct opposition to racism and colonial conquest. From the beginning, it spoke to its readers in Spanish and Cherokee as well as English, and later in Shawnee, Chinese, Japanese, and Korean as well—in so many different languages that its overall character as a separate wing of our nation's dissident press has not always been completely apparent. To the general public, even to most journalists and scholars, this portion of what is commonly called the "ethnic press" remained virtually invisible for generation after generation.

"That so many Negro newspapers were coming and going for 120 years on the mass of land between the Atlantic and Pacific Oceans, Mexico and Canada is itself remarkable," note journalists Gene Roberts and Hank Klibanoff in a recent account of the press and the southern Civil Rights movement. "More extraordinary is that white people did not know about it."[5]

The white population's ignorance of this new press did not diminish its profound impact on the individual communities it served, nor did it erase the moral challenge those pioneering newspapers posed to the white press. Despite very distinct origins in different regions of the country, the papers of each group displayed a remarkable common purpose. Not that all of those editors spoke with a unified voice on major issues: there was a substantial diversity of outlooks between them, even racial or ethnic bias exhibited at times from the editors of one group toward another. The *Phoenix*, for example, carried several articles filled with racist stereotypes about blacks. Likewise, several prominent nineteenth-century Hispanic editors firmly supported slavery, such as José Agustín Quintero, editor of *El Ranchero*, a San Antonio newspaper of the 1850s.

Conflicts that reflected class, race and political allegiances frequently developed between editors within the same ethnic group, as evinced by the polemics between Frederick Douglass and Martin Delaney in the 1840s over the best way to abolish slavery, the bitter debates over Cuban independence in the 1850s between white Cuban Cirilo Villaverde, editor of New York's *La Verdad*, and Afro-Cuban Carlos de Collins, editor of that city's *El Mulato*, or between Robert Abbott of the *Chicago Defender* and Robert Vann of the *Pittsburgh Courier* over the *Amos 'n' Andy* controversy in the 1930s, or the dueling views of borderland Mexican editors over the Mexican Revolution in the early 1900s.

Despite such differences, early editors of color generally shared common views, faced common obstacles, and challenged a reigning newspaper narrative that was deeply imbued with Anglo white bias. In the process, they promoted reasoned debate over sensationalism and hyperbole in news coverage, they opposed a centralized and commercially driven news media system, and they persistently pleaded for the news media to adopt a more responsible social role in relation to the public. They were also more skeptical of America's territorial expansion and more critical of our nation's imperial rise than the dominant white press. In January 1848, for example, Frederick Douglass wrote a scathing denunciation in his *North Star* of the "disgraceful, cruel and iniquitous war" with Mexico.[6]

The Early Spanish Press in America

Traditional histories of the US press have long claimed that German immigrants were responsible for the bulk of the nation's foreign-language newspapers before the Civil War, but virtually all of those accounts have failed to note that at least eighty Spanish-language papers were started before 1860 in what is now the United States.

That such a robust Hispanic press even existed can be attributed to several factors: a long print and newspaper tradition in Latin America that was distinct from that of the Anglo-Saxon press; the geographic proximity of Mexico, Cuba and Puerto Rico, the main countries from which early Latino journalists migrated; and the reality that a large portion of the settler population of the American west and southwest was Spanish-speaking before those areas were annexed into the nation.

We often forget that the first printing press in the New World was introduced into Mexico, not the British colonies. In 1534, less than two decades after Cortés and his band of conquistadores vanquished the Aztec empire, a Spaniard named Esteban Martín founded a printing business in Mexico City. No copies of Martín's work survive, but those produced by the second printer in Mexico are well-known. Juan Pablos, an Italian type composer who worked for Juan Cromberger, the German owner of a major publishing house in the Spanish city of Seville, migrated to Mexico City five years after Martín. It was from the Cromberger enterprise that the first known American news sheet, or *hoja volante*, was produced in 1542. Titled *Relacion del Espantable Terremoto*, it gave an account of the destruction of the City of Guatemala on September 10th and 11th, 1541 by an earthquake and storm.[7]

That news sheet pre-dated many produced in Europe and was issued some eighty years before the first English news-sheet or *coranto* appeared. A second pioneering center of New World publishing was Lima. At least thirteen *hojas volantes* produced there between 1623 and 1640 are said to be preserved in the National Library of Paris. By comparison, printing did not even begin in the English colonies until Harvard University installed a press in 1638.[8]

In 1693, only a few years after Benjamin Harris launched his *Publick Occurrences* in Boston, the first news periodical in Latin America, *Mercurio Volante*, was founded by Carlos de Sigüenza y Góngora, a scientist at the University of Mexico, while *La Gaceta de Mexico*, the first newspaper to be regularly printed in Spain's New World empire, began operation on January 1, 1722, just eighteen years after Campbell's *Boston News-Letter*.

The modern United States thus became the meeting ground for two distinct printing and newspaper traditions. The main one, of course, came from England. It took root in Boston with Benjamin Harris and John Campbell, branched out through the Thirteen Colonies, and spread westward as white settlements expanded. The second and less well-known tradition originated in Spain, took root in Mexico City with Juan Pablos and Carlos de Sigüenza y Góngora, spreading northward with the early Spanish and Mexican settlers into Florida, Louisiana, Texas, New Mexico and California. This second tradition, as we will see next, soon spawned a new dissident Latino press within the US.

5

Priests, Mobs, and Know-Nothings: The Early Spanish-Language Press

Afterwards, two Mexicans were found hanging from a tree, and near there another with two bullets in the head. On the road from Tejon another company had encountered two poor peddlers (always Mexicans) who were arrested and hanged as suspects.

El Clamor Público, Los Angeles, March 21st, 1857

In September 1808, John Mowry, the federalist editor of the *Louisiana Gazette* in New Orleans, began publishing a new Spanish-English semi-weekly news-paper for that city. Mowry's intent was to stir Louisiana's Spanish inhabitants to oppose the recent occupation of their homeland by Napoleon's army, and his publication, *El Misisipí*. was the nation's first Spanish-language periodical, appearing regularly until 1810.[1]

Only two editions of the paper are known to have survived. The lead article in the October 10, 1808 issue featured a blistering attack on the arrival of an additional 70,000 French troops in Spain, on the crowning of Napoleon's brother Joseph as the new Spanish king, and on the traitor-ous collaboration of a Spanish archbishop with the occupiers. Signed by "a correspondent," it praised those Spaniards who were resisting the "French yoke" and confidently predicted that the armies of the Spanish patri-ots would "increase and improve in a far greater degree than those of the enemy."[2]

New Orleans thus emerged as the birthplace of the Spanish-language press in the United States. In the decades that followed, that press grew at a breathtaking pace, with scores of new publications sprouting in New York, South Texas, New Mexico, and California, many of them remarkably diverse in content and rich in literary quality.

Foremost among those early Hispanic editors was a group of Cuban exiles that spearheaded in the 1850s an extraordinary Hispanic literary ren-aissance on US soil. But you would not know from general chronicles of the American media that a vibrant Spanish-language press existed during the nineteenth century.[3] More than eighty Spanish-language papers were launched in the United States before the Civil War—an astonishing number given the small Spanish-speaking population of the country at the time. Another twenty-five were published in either Matamoros or Brownsville, near the mouth of the Rio Grande. Since those papers provided news coverage on both sides of the Lower Rio Grande, and since they counted many Mexican inhabitants of the contested borderlands of South Texas among their subscribers, it is our view that they were essentially part of the Hispanic press tradition in this country. If so, that would place the number of pre–Civil War Hispanic papers at more than one hundred, and it would make Spanish newspapers second in number among the foreign-language press only to the 199 publications established by German immigrants before 1860.[4]

When it came to the Spanish press, however, our libraries reinforced the nation's white racial narrative by failing to preserve Hispanic newspapers. "Of an estimated 165 Spanish-language newspapers believed to have existed in borderland Texas (including Matamoros) from the time of the Texas Revolution to the ousting of Mexican President Diaz, approximately thirty-five have any sort of surviving record, either in microfilm or original copies," notes historian Edward Lee Walraven.[5]

In recent years a new generation of scholars has begun to unearth the amazing work of those nineteenth-century Latino editors. Those scholars have called for a new perspective on the evolution of the US news media, an outlook that is transnational, multilingual, and interconnected. The Spanish-language press, they argue, can no longer be pigeonholed as just another in a string of marginal "foreign-language" immigrant media. Rather, it should be regarded as a parallel and integral component of the US media.

New Orleans, Cradle of the US Spanish-language Press

New Orleans emerged in the early 1800s as a popular destination for both refugees fleeing the region's independence wars and rebels conspiring to launch them. With its disorderly mix of nationalities and languages, and its large number of *gens libres de couleur* (free people of color) and black slaves, it was unique in North America for its racial amalgamation. "No city perhaps on the globe presents a greater contrast of national manners, language, and complexion," noted an astonished visitor in 1816. This extraordinary intermingling produced in journalism and the arts what one modern scholar has called "hybrid cultural spaces and alternative aesthetic possibilities."[6]

El Misisipí was the first Spanish-language newspaper, but it was not the first Hispanic-owned paper. Rather, Mowry and Johnson pioneered a trend that is still prevalent in US journalism today: foreign-language newspapers owned and operated by Anglo-Americans. The distinction of being the first Hispanic-owned newspaper belongs more properly to *El Mensagero*

Luisianés, which started as a semi-weekly in September 1809 and listed Joaquín de Lisa and Joseph Antonio Boniquet as publishers. Like *El Misisipí*, its news coverage focused on the Spanish population's war against Napoleon's occupation. *El Mensagero*, however, was not a defender of the Anglo-American newcomers to Spain's American colonies. Its edition of October 13, 1810 contained a sharp condemnation of a group of Anglo settlers who had taken advantage of the Napoleonic wars in Europe to seize control of a section of West Florida claimed by Spain. *El Mensagero's* denunciation of the revolt appears to have been one of the earliest examples of domestic press criticism of American expansionism.[7]

Altogether, more than twenty-five Spanish-language publications appeared in New Orleans before the Civil War, turning the city into the seat of a remarkably vibrant and extensive Spanish-language press. Among the most enterprising was *El Telégrafo*, launched in November of 1825 by Francois Delaup and Manuel Ariza. Delaup had been a printer in the French colony of Saint-Domingue who fled to Cuba after the successful Haitian revolution. He subsequently joined a second exodus of some 5,800 French refugees and their slaves who left Cuba for New Orleans in 1809, probably as a result of the hostilities created by the French invasion of Spain.

A similar influx of wealthy refugees from Mexico reached New Orleans in the late 1820s, after General Santa Anna's troops defeated the Spanish army's campaign to reconquer its former colony. The subsequent arrival of hundreds of pro-Spanish refugees in the city gave rise to dueling papers: *El Español* (1829) denounced the new Mexican government and defended Spain and the new arrivals, while *La Abeja,* the Spanish supplement of the bilingual *L'Abeille de la Nouvelle Orléans* (another paper started by Delaup), excoriated the refugees as "enemies of the liberty of the Americas ... men vomited onto this soil by absolute kings and hypocrites."[8]

A Rebel Priest and El Habanero

Rev. Felix Varela was a professor at Havana's prestigious San Carlos Seminary and a newly elected representative to the Spanish Cortes when he introduced a daring proposal to that legislative body in 1821, calling for the abolition of slavery in Cuba. Before it came up for a vote, King Ferdinand VII reclaimed absolute power from the Cortes and requested help from France to crush pro-democracy advocates. The French army eventually captured Cádiz, seat of the Cortes, whereupon Ferdinand ordered the arrest of the priest-politician and all other opposition deputies who had sided with the resistance. From that point on, no dissident press was allowed to operate in Spain or in its two remaining colonies in the New World, Cuba and Puerto Rico. Unable to return home, the young priest fled with two other fellow Cuban deputies, first to Gibraltar and then to England, where they boarded the *Draper* bound for the United States. A royal decree in May 1824 then ordered Varela's execution.

Shortly after the three arrived in New York, a group of fellow Cuban exiles, several of them former students of Varela at San Carlos, asked him to head a newly formed committee in the United States to advocate for the island's independence. To advance the group's efforts, Varela moved to Philadelphia and started producing a 5-by-8-inch periodical he called *El Habanero*. It became only the fifth Spanish-language publication in the country after *El Misispí,* and the first outside the South.[9] Varela called it a "political, scientific and literary" journal, and wrote most of the articles himself. He filled each edition with long polemics against Spanish colonialism and short updates on the independence struggle, interspersed with patriotic poetry and scientific treatises, such as: "The Effect of Magnetism on Titanium," "The Propagation of Sound," and "The Temperature of the Sea at Various Depths." His supporters would then smuggle copies of *El Habanero* into Cuba.

In 1825 Varela returned to New York to assume the post of pastor of Christ Church on Ann Street, that city's third Catholic parish. He continued to publish *El Habanero*, however, and the uproar the first issues sparked among Cuba's elite became so great that in March of 1825 Spanish officials dispatched an assassin to the United States to kill him. For reasons that have never been clear, the killer returned without accomplishing his assignment. In the third issue of *El Habanero*, Varela scoffed at the plot against him: "Do you believe you can destroy the truth by killing he who speaks it? ... I do not know the war of assassins, nor have I waged any battle but that of reason ... I have done nothing more than seek that men know each other and their situation ..."[10]

El Habanero ceased publication after only seven issues. In 1828, Varela and fellow Cuban exile José Antonio Saco launched a second pro-independence newspaper, *El Mensajero Semanal*. Like its predecessor, *El Mensajero* was short-lived, closing for good in 1831. By then, Varela had immersed himself in the mounting problems of his impoverished Irish and German congregation. In 1825 he launched the *Truth Teller,* a weekly bilingual Catholic newspaper aimed at Irish youth, and in the years that followed he established dozens of schools, social service organizations, day-care centers, and an orphanage, and he helped to found the New York Catholic Temperance Association.[11]

Appointed co-vicar general of the New York Archdiocese in 1829, Varela somehow managed to write for or directly launch a remarkable number of religious newspapers, journals and ecclesiastical treatises. Those publications cemented his reputation as the major intellectual leader of the American Catholic church in the nineteenth century.[12] Still revered today in Cuba as the greatest thinker of his era, Varela never returned to his homeland, which was still under Spain's iron grip when he died in 1853 in St. Augustine, Florida.[13]

Bridging Cultures in Time of War: La Patria

On October 1st, 1847, in the midst of the Mexican-American War, *La Patria* ("The Motherland"), the first Spanish-language daily in the United States, began publication in New Orleans. It rapidly became the most quoted and most controversial of the early *periodicos*. At the time, New Orleans boasted a highly competitive and respected group of English-language papers, and was the main source of news for the rest of the country about Latin America.

The daily *La Patria* was itself a successor to *El Hablador* ("The Talker" or "The Tattler"), a weekly that began in 1845, and it later underwent yet another name change to *La Unión*.[14] All three publications were owned and edited by Eusebio Juan Gómez and Victoriano Alemán. While little is known about the personal lives of either man (the 1850 census reported only that Gómez was thirty years old and born in Louisiana), they pioneered a unique, transnational vision of journalism in the New World—one that continues to infuse the work of many modern-day Latino editors and writers, even though few have ever heard of its principal founders or of the newspaper that first practiced it.[15]

Gómez and Alemán subtitled their paper the "organo de la población española de los Estados Unidos" ("organ of the Spanish population of the United States"). Its masthead featured a man seated before an inkwell, surrounded by the flags of the United States, Spain and Mexico. To achieve their cross-border vision, they established their own network of agents and correspondents in Mexico, Cuba, Trinidad, and in several towns across Texas and the American South.[16] They then augmented dispatches from those correspondents with news distilled from scores of Latin American papers that arrived each week through the postal system at *La Patria*'s offices at 68–70 Exchange Alley. They even translated into English key articles from those papers. As a result, *La Patria*'s reports were frequently reproduced in US newspapers during the Mexican War. One review of eight major papers for that period—including the Baltimore *Sun*, the Charleston *Courier*, the Boston *Daily Mail*, the *New York Tribune*, and the Philadelphia *Public Ledger*—found 134 citations and translations of *La Patria* articles.[17]

While *La Patria*'s staple was political and commercial news, it also devoted considerable space to poetry and fiction. Gómez and Alemán sought to showcase the beauty and value of Spanish and of Latin American culture, to convince "Anglo-Americans that Spanish speakers were as lettered, diverse, and intelligible as they—if not more so," notes literary scholar Kirsten Silva Gruesz. For a short period in 1848 they even attempted to launch an English-language section.[18]

Gómez and Alemán rarely shied away from criticizing the pompous prose often employed by the city's English-language papers. In October 1848, for example, *La Patria* lampooned its competitors as journalists who pass in society as sensible men, and who believe that they have great judgment because they edit a newspaper in English—which, seen properly, is the simplest thing in the world when it's done the ordinary or customary way in the United States, which consists of cutting up pieces from here and there and filling entire columns this way. Naturally, some men who don't know how to do anything else besides edit a paper with scissors and starch start talking nonsense like crazy men as soon as they have to leave their little sphere and take up a pen to deal with a serious matter, or they fire more shots than words ...[19]

While *La Patria*'s articles and editorials generally challenged derogatory views of Spanish culture and condemned filibuster activities on Latin American soil, its editors also published items on occasion that displayed strong sentiments against Spanish colonialism. Take, for example, this anonymously written poem, also titled *La Patria*, which appeared in 1846:

> What does it matter, dumb slave
> that you fall asleep, carefree,
> to the sound of the chains
> of your barbarous oppression? ...
> What does it matter that today you cry out
> as long as you know, beloved country,
> that someday a day will dawn
> with celestial brilliance?
> Then, although the tyrant
> should thunder in anger and ire,
> the American world will become
> lord of the Old World.[20]

Gómez and Alemán supplemented their paper's revenues by running a bookstore and lending library, offering Spanish lessons to the public, and producing for a time a humor magazine called *La Risa* ("Laughter"). In the highly competitive world of the New Orleans penny press, they were masters at self-promotion. On July 4, 1847, for example, they printed *La Patria* on red paper with gold ink, and whenever major news broke they frequently issued "extra" editions.[21] The *Daily Delta*, which was not always on good terms with Gómez and Alemán, nonetheless acknowledged that their paper was "conducted by a society of able and intelligent writers."[22]

La Patria soon garnered a respectable daily circulation of more than 800, placing it among the city's top five publications. But once the Mexican War broke out, the paper engendered substantial public resentment for publishing dispatches that often contradicted rosy accounts by US officials of the progress of the fighting. The city's major English-language papers, the

Picayune, the *Delta,* the *Crescent,* the *Commercial Times,* and the *Bulletin,* were all such cheerleaders of the conflict that they came to be known throughout the country as the "War Press" of New Orleans.[23]

"We cannot look on with indifference, as the people of the United States, robbing themselves of their sincerity and their healthy principles, adopt doctrines so contrary to their founding, " *La Patria* proclaimed in a June 1846 editorial, "The war with Mexico ... is an unjust war and dangerous to the North American Union."[24]

In 1847, *La Patria* was condemned by newspapers around the country after it published an article that detailed the war plans of the Polk administration. "The foreign editor who made public the revelations should be arrested for aiding and comforting the enemy," declared the Philadelphia *Public Ledger.* "[S]ome of these articles were very anti-American in their tenor, and derogatory to the United States and their citizens," wrote William L. Hodge, editor of the New Orleans *Commercial Bulletin.* Critics of Eusebio Gómez alleged he had illegally obtained secret military documents, though most of the material he used came from public records.[25]

As the war dragged on, *La Patria's* relations with the city's Anglo inhabitants grew increasingly tense. Its editors publicly complained that their postal deliveries of exchange newspapers were being stolen and offered a $100 reward for information on those responsible.[26] Alemán received so many physical threats that he began carrying a sword cane for his protection. In 1848, he was severely beaten by a competing editor following a street-corner political argument. His assailant was none other than William Walker, the fiery proponent of US expansionism who only a few weeks before had replaced Walt Whitman on the staff of the *Crescent.* Walker would later become infamous for his filibuster escapades in Central America, foremost of which was the bizarre and short-lived dictatorship he established in Nicaragua.[27]

Despite the enmity they faced, Gómez and Alemán often praised the liberties enjoyed by the American people, they celebrated the Fourth of July, and, like all Southern editors, they supported slavery. Their paper ridiculed the failed monarchy established by Iturbide after Mexican independence, it disdained the regime of military strongman Santa Anna, and it often lampooned Mexico's perennial political instability.[28] In July 1848, shortly after Mexico was forced to cede its northern territories to the US in the Treaty of Guadalupe-Hidalgo, *La Patria* published a satirical poem about a famous actress in Spain who was regretting her decision to move to Mexico to work:

> Isabel, what good
> can you expect from a building
> that finds itself with no roof?
> So much (and when you board

for that distant shore,
you'll hear heartfelt sobs)
goes from those discordant states
to the *United States!*[29]

The Sacking and Looting of La Unión

Once the Mexican War ended, Gómez and Alemán attracted even greater hostility from white Southerners by opposing several filibuster expeditions aimed at liberating Cuba from Spain. The annexation of Cuba gripped the American public's imagination during the late 1840s and early 1850s. All of our early presidents assumed that, once Spanish rule ended, the island would come under US control.[30] Since slavery was so central to the Cuban economy—36 percent of the island's 900,000 inhabitants were held in bondage—many in this country feared an independence movement could explode into a Haiti-style uprising.[31] Southern planters, on the other hand, regarded Cuban annexation as the best way to expand slavery in the Union. They avidly sided with Manifest Destiny advocates among Northern Democrats to press for its annexation, and most did not care whether their goal was accomplished by peaceful or violent means. Several expansionist governors and members of Congress started providing their own financial backing to filibuster efforts aimed at wresting the island from Spain by force.[32]

A central figure in most of those conspiracies was the notorious separatist general, Narciso López. Born into a wealthy merchant family in Caracas in present-day Venezuela, López had fought in Spain's colonial army for many years. By the late 1840s, however, he became disgruntled with his treatment by the governor of Cuba and joined the Club de la Habana, a secret anti-Spanish organization that advocated the island's annexation to the United States. Its leaders were some of the richest creole planters and merchants on the island. By then, annexation had gained a wide following among Democratic Party leaders in the North and Southern politicians. Many of those annexationists regarded López as the pivotal leader on the island who could lead the effort.

After the Spanish authorities foiled an incipient revolt of López followers in 1848, the general fled to the United States and sought money and volunteers for an armed invasion. The federal government disrupted his first attempt in 1849. His second effort, an invasion of the city of Cárdenas in 1850 with 600 men, almost all of them American, ended in failure, and López returned to the US, where he began organizing another excursion from New Orleans.[33]

As the general hastily organized his next effort, *La Patria*'s editors Gómez and Alemán were changing the name of their newspaper to *La Unión*. They released the first edition under its new masthead on January 3rd, 1851. The reconstituted paper, a tri-weekly, was to be "a spokesman for the neglected and often maligned Spanish-speaking person in a hostile environment." The two editors, who had always regarded López as an instrument of US domination, also declared their paper would oppose "the imperialistic designs of Great Britain and the United States."[34]

On August 3rd, 1851, the new López-led escapade, some 400 men, most of them North Americans, reached Cuba after setting sail from New Orleans. Spanish troops once again routed the invaders, but this time López and his men did not escape. On August 13, a patrol of some fifty Americans led by Colonel William L. Crittenden was captured. All were tried by a military court the next day and summarily shot by a firing squad in Havana. López was captured two weeks later with more than 160 of his followers. Island authorities promptly executed him and shipped his men off to Spanish prisons.

The swiftness and ferocity of the Spanish repression sparked widespread outrage in the United States, with most newspapers labeling it a "massacre" and printing gruesome details of how crowds in Havana had supposedly cheered the executions of the American captives, then mutilated the bodies.[35] Front-page headlines in the New Orleans papers blared: "Massacre of 51 Patriots!" "Fifty-one Americans Captured and Butchered in Cold Blood," and "The Cuban Massacre."[36] Lost in all the sensational accounts was the obvious fact that the López expedition had violated US neutrality laws. What made the incident even more embarrassing for the federal government was the leading role played by Crittenden, who happened to be a West Point graduate, a decorated Mexican war hero, and the nephew of US Attorney General John Crittenden.

The public furor stoked by the New Orleans papers grew so intense that angry crowds of Anglo residents quickly formed in the streets of that city demanding revenge for the dead Americans. On August 21, only days after Crittenden's execution, a mob invaded the offices of La Unión. The attackers demolished the newspaper's printing equipment, physically assaulted co-editor Victoriano Alemán in front of his wife and children, and then rampaged through the city's French Quarter, sacking the Spanish consulate and wrecking numerous Hispanic businesses.[37] By the time peace was restored, La Unión had been silenced for good.

The Filibusteros and the Desterrados

A new generation of Latin American journalists emerged in the US during the 1850s. Their papers sparked the first Latino literary renaissance on US soil, and several of the editors even landed work writing for English-language newspapers. Cuban poet Miguel Teurbe Tolón, for instance, edited a Latin America section of the New York Herald in the 1850s. In addition to his articles and poetry, Tolón translated Tom Paine's *Common Sense* and directed two Spanish-language newspapers, *El Papagayo* and *El Cometa*.[38] His fellow exile poet José Agustín Quintero launched San Antonio's first Hispanic-owned paper in 1855, and eventually became a respected editor at the New Orleans *Daily Picayune*. Dominican essayist Alejandro Angulo Guridi, who arrived in the US in the 1840s and quickly became an American citizen, worked for a time as a correspondent for the New York *Herald* and the *Daily News*.[39] Cirilo Villaverde, author of the first great Cuban novel, translated Longfellow and Tennyson and wrote articles for John O'Sullivan's *United States Magazine and Democratic Review*.

All of the Cuban editors were followers of Narciso López, and all were based at some point in New Orleans, the center of the general's filibustering activities. Most also came from wealthy families that directly benefited from Cuban slavery. As members of Cuba's white elite, their yearning to throw off Spanish rule was always tempered by their fear of an uprising by Cuba's black masses, which helps to explain why most preferred annexation to the US over outright independence.[40]

Once the Spanish authorities had executed López in 1851, the general's exiled followers sought to keep his movement alive through their own writings and through financing new filibuster schemes. They penned scores of patriotic poems that frequently appeared in Spanish-language periodicals here, and they eventually collected those poems in several books that were published in New York. Tolón's *Leyendas Cubanas* ("Cuban Legends") and Pedro Santacilia's *El Arpa del Proscripto* ("The Banished Man's Lyre"), for example, both appeared in 1856, while *El Laúd del Desterrado* ("The Exile's Lute") was published in 1858. The latter was the first anthology of exile literature to be produced in the United States. It included poems by Tolón, Quintero, Santacilia, Pedro Ángel Castellón, Leopoldo Turla, and Juan Clemente Zenea. One historian has estimated that half the poems in *El Laúd del Desterrado* were originally published in US Spanish-language papers.[41]

These Cuban exile writers found their stay in the United States both liberating and filled with torment. Their efforts to overthrow Spanish rule repeatedly ended in failure, and though they sought to emulate American ideals, they were often frustrated by how little regard most Anglo-Americans displayed for Cuba's condition or even for Spanish culture. Despite this, the exile writers managed to produce a remarkable body of poems, news accounts and even works of fiction, some of which rank among the best Cuban literature of the nineteenth century.

Cirilo Villaverde, John O'Sullivan and La Verdad

Perhaps the best-known exile journalist of the mid nineteenth century was Cirilo Villaverde, who arrived in New York in 1849 and spent the next fifty years in the United States, editing several Spanish-language newspapers.[42] Born in the Cuban province of Pinar del Río in 1812, Villaverde was already a popular writer of short fiction in his homeland when he met General López and enlisted in the separatist cause. He was among the group of López disciples that Spanish authorities arrested in the aborted uprising of 1848. Convicted of treason and sentenced to life in prison, Villaverde spent six months in a Havana cell before pulling off a daring escape with the help of a guard. He then boarded a ship to Florida and made his way to New York.

Reunited with López in the United States, Villaverde abandoned fiction-writing and immersed himself in revolutionary work, serving for several years as the general's secretary and chief assistant. Soon after his arrival in New York, he met John O'Sullivan, the Democratic Party leader and apostle of Manifest Destiny. O'Sullivan was already intimately involved in Cuba conspiracies through his brother-in-law Cristóbal Madan, a Cuban planter and ship owner. Madan had helped to found the Club de La Habana and presided as well over a parallel New York–based group of rich creoles known as the Cuban Council, which also advocated Cuba's annexation.[43] Madan joined with O'Sullivan and Moses Y. Beach, editor of the *New York Sun*, to create a bilingual newspaper aimed at fostering support for Cuban annexation.

That newspaper, *La Verdad*, was financed by the Cuban Council and printed on the presses of Beach's *Sun*. Its first issue appeared on January 9, 1848, and the paper lasted in different formats until 1860. Unlike the *Sun*, it contained virtually no local New York news or advertisements. Each issue featured several polemics about Cuban annexation along with letters from anonymous correspondents in Cuba—all aimed at stirring up the island's inhabitants against Spanish rule. "The annexation of Cuba is the most important question of the day with us," proclaimed an early issue. "It is the complement of the great system which is to reign in America from Cape Horn to the Arctic Sea."[44]

The editor and principal writer of *La Verdad* during its early years was Jane McManus. The daughter of a US congressman and a fervent advocate of Manifest Destiny, McManus wrote under the pseudonym of Cora Montgomery and led a storybook career as a journalist, land speculator and secret diplomat. She was the first woman to report from behind enemy lines during the Mexican War, was rumored to have had romantic ties at different periods in her life with former US vice-president Aaron Burr and former Texas president Mirabeau B. Lamar, and was on friendly terms with many of the leading politicians and journalists of her era, including Horace Greeley, James Polk, and James Buchanan. In 1849, McManus married William Cazneau, who, like her, was a wealthy Texas landowner and a proponent of US annexation of Latin American lands.[45] As editor of *La Verdad*, McManus made sure not only to smuggle the paper into Cuba, she also distributed it to each member of Congress, thus assuring its outsized influence in Washington and among the American opinion-makers when it came to Cuba policy. Among the exiles who worked with her to edit the paper were poets Miguel T. Tolón and essayist Gasper Betancourt Cisneros.[46] Even though they favored annexation to the US, the Cubans who grouped around *La Verdad* frequently disagreed on the best way to end Spanish rule, on how much autonomy they imagined Cuba would enjoy as a state of the union, and on the role North Americans should play in their struggle.[47]

During his early years in New York, Villaverde wrote occasional items for *La Verdad* and also collaborated with O'Sullivan on two articles about Cuba for the latter's *United States Magazine and Democratic Review*. One of those articles, titled "General Lopez, the Cuban Patriot," appeared in Febraury 1850. It offered a glowing account of the rebel general's exploits on the battlefields of Latin America and Spain. "[H]is democratic principles have naturally generated a habitual sympathy with the poor and oppressed," Villaverde said of López, conveniently glossing over his early career in Spain's colonial army and his stint as a Spanish provincial governor in Cuba. The general had "undertaken the noble mission of emancipating Cuba from the yoke and abomination of Spanish tyranny, with a view of her entrance into our union," Villaverde noted.[48]

La Verdad's stance eventually encountered stiff opposition from other exile editors. Most prominent of those was José Antonio Saco, the disciple of Félix Varela and former co-editor with him of *El Mensajero Semanal*. Like Varela, Saco was an ardent foe of slavery and advocated total independence for Cuba. From Europe, where he had gone to live, Saco penned a series of bitter polemics against *La Verdad* and its editors. Many of his articles appeared in *La Crónica*, a competing New York paper that routinely criticized annexation efforts while glorifying Spain. Saco condemned the US acquisition of Florida and Louisiana, the "infamous" seizure of Texas, and the war with Mexico. He labeled the various filibuster efforts by Americans in the Caribbean as "the criminal ambition of a runaway democracy," and he chalked up the US public's widespread support for the acquisition of Cuba to "a desire for expansion and the interests of slavery." Annexation, he predicted, would force an end to Cuba's "nationality, and even the last vestige of its language." Despite his nationalist rhetoric, Saco's anti-colonial perspective was deeply flawed, however, by his preference to maintain Spanish rule over his homeland if that meant keeping it free from US domination.[49]

"We have not been able to comprehend what nationality it is of which Saco speaks," Betancourt and Cisneros responded, "whether it is the one belonging to government, or the one appertaining to nature or race. The first Cuba does not possess, unless the condition of *enslaved colony* of Spain is the glorious nationality worthy of being inscribed on armorial bearings …" Later, Villaverde produced a string of furious rebuttals to Saco in *La*

Verdad, labeling the elder writer a hypocrite and "a man completely lost for Cuba."[50]

Villaverde took over as editor of *La Verdad* for a few months in early 1852, and it was at that point that his own views on Cuban liberty began to change. He started to condemn any further US-backed conspiracies to invade and annex the country, advocating instead an armed uprising from within Cuba itself to achieve full independence. The change brought him into conflict with the rich New York City creoles who financed the paper, and they soon forced him to resign. He then moved to New Orleans, where in 1853, together with fellow exile Manuel Antonio Mariño, he launched a new bilingual newspaper, *El Independiente*, to counter *La Verdad* and other pro-annexation sheets. Among those other sheets were Miguel T. Tolón's *El Cubano* and *El Filibustero*, which first appeared in April of the same year.

Race and Class Conflicts Within Cuba's Exile Press

The proliferation of competing Cuban newspapers in the mid 1850s reflected a sharpening divide in the exile community over class and race, over American hegemony, and over the nature of Cuban liberation. In 1854, a young Afro-Cuban exile named Carlos de Collins launched *El Mulato*, while poet Francisco Aguero Estrada began publishing *El Pueblo* in 1855. Both newspapers sharply attacked *La Verdad* and the filibuster conspiracies promoted by wealthy creoles. *El Pueblo* and *El Mulato* were even more radical in their views than Villaverde's *Independiente*. Cuba's liberation movement, De Collins declared in the pages of *El Mulato*, could only succeed by making the abolition of slavery an integral part of its program. Annexation to the US, he feared, would doom Cuba's black population to perpetual servitude. He openly accused *La Verdad* of being an organ for Cuba's upper classes. "We feel repugnance upon seeing that one of the organs of the revolution is in the hands of royalists, a satellite of despotism," he wrote.[51]

De Collins' fellow populist editor Aguero Estrada went even further. He urged the incorporation of the island's black population into the revolutionary movement. "One of the capital errors of those who have so far directed our revolution has been to attempt to exclude a large class of the Cuban people," *El Pueblo* argued in 1855.[52] His paper even challenged alleged corruption and financial mismanagement by the head of the Cuban Council of New York. It called for new revolutionary leaders "who do not aspire to monopolize glory and are not avid about riches." Aguero Estrada especially questioned an aborted filibuster plot the Council had arranged after the death of López, this time with former Mississippi Governor John Quitman as commander. After raising hundreds of thousands of dollars, Quitman had suddenly abandoned the plan in 1855 without accounting for any of the money raised.

The Civil War brought to an abrupt end the era of Cuban filibustering. Several followers of Narciso López sided with the Confederacy and even enlisted to fight in the rebel army. But the Northern victory extinguished all desire in the US for annexing Cuba. After the war, some Cuban exile writers returned home or moved to Mexico, while others, like Villaverde and Quintero, chose to make their permanent home in this country. Villaverde returned to his first love, fiction-writing. In 1882 he completed his final version of *Cecilia Valdés*, the tragic story of an illicit affair between a Cuban mulatto woman and her white lover, an earlier edition of which he had penned in 1839. Published in a series of newspaper installments here in the US, the book has long been considered the first great novel in Cuban literature. Quintero, as we shall soon see, became an integral part of Southern journalism.

Thus did the amazing renaissance of Cuban literature on US soil come to a close. In their poetry and political polemics, through their fiction and furious conspiracies, this small band of exile editors managed to forge a parallel Spanish-language literary movement in mid-nineteenth-century America. It was a movement that battled over the relation of art to politics and war, that confronted Anglo-American biases against Latin America, that challenged accepted notions of freedom and empire, and that fought internally over questions of race and class. Its writers conducted their debates through newspapers articles, fiction and poetry; they crafted their work on the streets of New York, in the alleys of New Orleans and the barrios San Antonio, from colonial Havana all the way to Paris and Madrid, in a transnational literary upsurge that remained virtually invisible to the English-language press and to the American public.

The Forgotten Press of Matamoros and the Mexican Borderlands

In 1825, the year Félix Varela commenced his work as a parish priest in New York City, a Connecticut merchant named Francis Stillman landed with a cargo ship of hay and oats at the Mexican port of Matamoros, near the mouth of the Rio Grande. Impressed by the demand for his goods, Stillman dispatched his son Charles, future founder of First National City Bank, to set up a branch of the family business. Don Carlos, as the Mexicans respectfully called him, quickly became the biggest merchant and landowner in the region. Some 300 foreigners, most of them North American businessmen, moved to the Matamoros area by 1832, transforming the once-sleepy town into the key shipping port for Northern Mexico.[53]

As Matamoros grew into a commercial crossroads, newspapers began sprouting in the city, with at least twenty sheets published there prior to 1848. One of the earliest was *El Mercurio del Puerto de Matamoros*, founded in 1834 by George Fisher, an immigrant from Serbia and a naturalized Mexican citizen. Fisher's experiment in Spanish-language journalism didn't last very long; he was expelled from the country after he threw his paper's support behind the liberal Mexican federalists who were battling the regime of President Santa Anna, and his paper then passed into the hands of Mexican editors. Apart from Fisher's brief venture, all the early Matamoros newspapers were Mexican-owned and were aimed at Spanish-speaking readers on both sides of the Rio Grande. Technically, they formed part of Mexico's newspaper legacy, though we believe they warrant some consideration as components of the early US Hispanic press, since it was not until the Treaty of Guadalupe-Hidalgo in 1848 annexed all land north of the Rio Grande into the US that Matamoros suddenly became a "border city." Only at that point did that town's early papers become a "foreign" press.[54]

The early decades of Mexico's independence were marked by bitter and often violent rivalries between federalists and centralists. Those political battles, as one might expect, dominated the news in the Matamoros papers. By the late 1830s, however, some of the city's editors began to criticize aggression against Mexico from the north. When federalist leader General José Antonio Canales, for example, joined forces with a group of Texans and crossed into Mexico to declare his own Republic of the Rio Grande, *El Ancla* of Matamoros condemned the rebellion. It labeled the Texans "bandits" and asked why any Mexicans should be "so obsessed or so stupid as to serve in any army under the orders of Canales ... delivering their own possessions, their own wives, their own sons into the hands of a foreign enemy."[55]

Reports that Anglo settlers were abusing Mexican residents also became more frequent. In 1839, Vicente de la Parra's *La Brisa* accused Texans of stealing cattle and horses and engaging in smuggling. The Texans, the paper observed, were out "to enrich themselves with the spoilation of our properties. Our lands, our livestock, our equipment and all we possess will undoubtedly capture their greediness."[56] In 1844, the editors of *El Justo Medio* likewise condemned the proposed annexation of Texas as motivated by American greed. In his *Aguila del Norte* just before the outbreak of the Mexican War, editor Martin Salazar labeled the United States "a suspicious nation, avid for lands to the extreme of obtaining what it desires with calls false and traitorous."[57]

So influential was the Matamoros press in the Rio Grande Valley that, once the war erupted and US troops occupied the city, one of the army's first acts was to shut down the only five newspapers still in operation. The war itself caused a sharp decline in the city's fortunes. While its population at the start of the occupation had hovered around 15,000, by the time the fighting ended half of Matamoros's residents had fled.

"A new period was about to begin for the Spanish-reading public" of the Rio Grande Valley, notes historian Edward Lee Walraven, as "newspapers produced by Anglos" and "presenting an Anglo perspective" became the norm.[58] Several of those papers were based not in Matamoros but in Brownsville, the small army post on the US side of the Rio Grande. Samuel Bangs, a former editor of the Corpus Christi *Gazette* and of a half-dozen other newspapers in Galveston and Houston, moved into the Valley in 1846 and began to publish the English-language *Reveille* in Brownsville. Bangs also created a Spanish-language section that he called *La Diana de Matamoros*. That same year, Isaac Fleeson, a former Bangs associate, launched the *Republic of the Rio Grande* in Matamoros. Edwin Scarborough purchased the paper two years later, renamed it *American Flag*, and relocated it to Brownsville. Scarborough also published a Spanish-language version named *Bandera Americana*. The two versions often presented starkly different perspectives on the news. On May 15, 1852, for example, Scarborough's Spanish edition reported on a new Mexican ambassador to the United States, a volcano in Hawaii, and events in Europe. The same day, his English version featured prominently a story headlined: "MORE DEPREDATIONS. Five men killed by a gang of motley Indians and Mexicans." Bangs later started a second Spanish paper, *El Liberal*, but that paper was forced to close and Bangs was temporarily jailed after he published several articles critical of army activities.[59]

San Antonio and the Transformation of the Latino Press

With the end of the Mexican War, the center of Spanish-language journalism shifted to San Antonio, Santa Fe, and Los Angeles. Until that point, Hispanic editors in New Orleans, New York, and Matamoros had used their papers primarily to influence political events in their homelands, and only secondarily to help fellow Hispanics acclimate to life in the United States. But, beginning in the 1850s, editors in the west and southwest began to forge a "native" Spanish-language press.[60]

This new press arose during a period of bitter and often violent conflict, as the established *Mexicano* settlers found themselves suddenly dispossessed of their land by more recent arrivals from back east, and the English-speaking courts they established.

Of the sixteen newspapers started in San Antonio between 1848 and 1860, virtually all were English-language publications—even though Anglos numbered only about a third of the town's 10,500 residents, the rest being Mexicans (4,000) and German immigrants (3,000). San Antonio's first foreign-language paper, in fact, was the German-language *Zeitung*. Founded in 1853 by Adolph Douai, an immigrant teacher and social reformer, it quickly turned into a liberal voice for the area's German farmers.

The presence of so many German immigrants in Texas no doubt helped fuel local support in the mid 1850s for the fiercely anti-immigrant and anti-Catholic American Party, commonly known as the Know-Nothings. In

1854, Know-Nothing members captured a majority of the San Antonio city council, and logged impressive victories in Austin and Galveston as well.[61]

The Know-Nothings' most influential organ in Texas was the *Bastrop Advertiser*. Published only eighty miles from San Antonio, it counted many of that city's residents as subscribers. It was not only hostile to Irish and German immigrants, it also vehemently opposed any extension of political rights to the original Mexican settlers of Texas. "There is hardly a good feature in the Mexican character," one *Advertiser* article proclaimed. "Do you desire this race, in which no one is superior to your Negro in morals or education, to have a right to vote?"[62]

San Antonio's first Spanish-language newspaper, *El Bejareño*, came into existence in 1855, though it was not Hispanic-owned. The paper's founders were Xavier Blanchard DeBray, a Frenchman and former diplomat under Napoleon III, and an Englishman named Alfred A. Lewis. Their paper sought to marshal support from the town's Mexican community for the Democrats against the Know-Nothings. It aimed to instill Anglo values in the town's Spanish-speaking readers. The Rio Grande "separates, on this continent … progress and ignorance, the future and the past," proclaimed *El Bajereño's* inaugural issue. Unfortunately, the paper also promoted territorial expansion and Manifest Destiny—views that most *Mexicanos* saw as threats to their very existence.[63]

When *El Bejareño* and *Zeitung* challenged the *Bastrop Advertiser* and the Know-Nothings, they tended to do so in muted tones, rarely questioning the second-class status of *Mexicanos*. *El Bejareño* instead urged the Mexican community to improve its image and to instruct its youth in a way that would eliminate "the false idea that the Mejico-Tejano does not have the moral requisites for a member of a free state."[64]

A second and more assertive Spanish-language paper—the first to be Hispanic-owned—appeared in San Antonio in 1856. It was called *El Ranchero* ("The Rancher"), and it immediately redefined the boundaries of press dissent in Texas by championing the interests of the *Mexicano* community and by launching defiant editorial condemnations of the Know-Nothing movement.

Surprisingly, the new paper's founding editor, José Agustín Quintero, was neither a *Mexicano* nor a long-time resident of Texas. Born in Cuba in 1829, he was the son of a wealthy island tobacco planter and an upper-class English mother whose parents sent him to the United States at a young age to study at Harvard. A handsome and charismatic young man, Quintero soon became a favorite in Boston's literary circles, cultivating friendships with some of the country's most influential intellectuals and writers, among them Emerson and Longfellow. After completing his studies and returning to Cuba, he joined the budding Narciso López movement against Spanish rule, and collaborated with fellow writer Cirilo Villaverde on various reformist publications in Havana. Like Villaverde, he was jailed by the Spanish authorities, convicted of sedition, and condemned to death, but he managed to escape from prison and wound up in New Orleans, where he reconnected with his mentor Villaverde and another Cuban exile, Manuel Antonio Marino, and assisted them in publishing *El Independiente*.[65]

While in New Orleans, Quintero struck up friendships with two prominent Southerners—Mirabeau Lamar, the former president of the Texas Republic, and Mississippi Congressman John A. Quitman. The latter was a former Mexican war hero and twice governor of Mississippi who repeatedly hatched filibuster plots aimed at annexing Cuba. In 1851, Quitman successfully fought federal charges of neutrality law violations for aiding the López expedition.

Quintero's other friend, Lamar, was a firm advocate of close relations with Mexico and Latin America, and as Texas president from 1838 to 1841, had opposed the Lone Star Republic's annexation to the US. He was also an amateur historian, and appears to have been so impressed by Quintero that he hired him as an assistant. In 1855, the two men returned to Lamar's estate in Richmond, Texas, where Quintero was put to work translating and organizing Spanish documents from the former president's personal papers. During his stay at the ranch, Quintero traveled the countryside and met many *Tejano* landowners who were fighting to save their properties from the machinations of new Anglo settlers. He also served for a time as clerk for the Texas House of Representatives, reviewing and translating numerous Spanish land titles. As he grew more familiar with land records, he began to sympathize deeply with the *Tejano* population. At the same time, he became increasingly impatient with *El Bejareño*'s moderate opposition to the Know-Nothings, with its defense of what he called "particular individuals rather than principles."[66]

Quintero soon decided to launch *El Ranchero* with the help of Mexican-American businessman Narciso Leal. Their paper wasted no time in publicly attacking the xenophobic *Advertiser*. "We want the rights and privileges of free citizens because [Know-Nothings] are priests of corrupt forces," Quintero declared in his first editorial. He even translated his commentaries into English so the town's Anglo population could read them. His outspokenness prompted so many threats on Quintero's life that his name disappeared from the paper's masthead, even as he continued to contribute articles to the paper.

Despite challenging the anti-Mexican bias of the Know-Nothings, Quintero held white-supremacist views himself, as did most of the white Cuban exile editors and disciples of Narciso López. So did Quintero's Mexican-American partner and successor as editor of *El Ranchero*, Narciso Leal. Once the Civil War began, both men enlisted in the Texas Quitman Guards and fought for the Confederacy. In September 1861, Quintero personally met

Jefferson Davis in Virginia and was appointed by him a secret agent for the Confederate states in Mexico, serving in that capacity throughout the war. After the Union victory Quintero moved to New Orleans, where he landed a job as an editor for the city's main newspaper, the *Daily Picayune*. He was still working at that paper when he died in 1885. "In New Orleans no man was more widely known or more generally beloved," noted his obituary in the *Picayune*. He thus became one of only a handful of early-nineteenth-century Hispanic journalists to make his mark in both the English-language and Spanish-language press.[67]

Cultural Conflicts in New Mexico

New Mexico and California were backwater northern provinces of Mexico in the 1830s, their inhabitants scattered in remote mission towns and ranches and totally isolated from the latest news and culture. That slowly began to change in 1834, when Antonio Barriero, a Mexican government official in Santa Fe and two prominent *Nuevomexicanos*, Rev. Antonio José Martínez and Ramón Abrey, arranged to purchase the city's first press.

Martínez, an admirer of Mexico's founding father Miguel Hidalgo, started New Mexico's first school in his home in Taos. Abreu immediately used the new press to publish the territory's first newspaper, *El Crepúsculo de la Libertad* ("The Dawn of Liberty"). In 1835 the three partners moved the press from Santa Fe to Taos, where Martínez used it to publish the territory's first book, a Spanish primer. He also took on the role of publisher of *El Crepúsculo* and continued to issue the paper until 1837. A second publication, *La Verdad*, appeared in Santa Fe in 1845 using the same Martínez press. But just as in Matamoros, *Nuevomexicano* publishers were silenced once war broke out between the US and Mexico, when US troops marched into Santa Fe in August 1846. General Stephen Kearny promptly commandeered the Martínez press, using it to print his declaration of military rule and subsequent pronouncements to the territory's inhabitants.[68]

The military occupation provoked a deep estrangement between *Nuevomexicanos* and the territory's new American rulers, and it aborted for many years the development of Hispanic-owned newspapers. In the decades that followed, Anglo settlers launched their own newspapers in Santa Fe, Taos, Las Vegas, and Albuquerque.[69] But unlike California, which had a small Mexican population before annexation, New Mexico boasted more than 50,000 Spanish-speaking inhabitants. Anglo publishers and editors quickly realized they would need to print their papers either totally or partially in Spanish if they hoped to succeed, and that meant employing *Nuevomexicanos*, though they appear to have kept the number of such jobs to a minimum. Despite the predominance of Spanish articles in the territory's early papers, only about ten of some eighty journalists who worked at them were

Spanish-Americans, with most *Nuevomexicanos* employed as translators or printers.[70]

Still, *Nuevomexicanos* "shaped much of the scope and nature of early Anglo-American periodical activity," says historian A. Gabriel Meléndez, because they remained the territory's majority throughout the century.[71]

Francisco Ramírez and the California Editors

Little is known about California's early Hispanic press. One study lists at least forty-six Spanish-language California newspapers during the nineteenth century, mostly in San Francisco and Los Angeles, though seven of those were actually bilingual editions of English-language sheets. Another bibliographic compilation claims more than seventy existed, while a third posits a far bigger and more questionable number of 132 by the turn of the twentieth century.

Everyone agrees, however, that Anglo editors of the bilingual sheets soon recognized the financial reward they could reap by publishing the laws and decrees of the new American government and by running advertisements to reach the Spanish-speaking residents. The *Californian*, for example—the first newspaper published in the state—was bilingual. It was launched on August 15, 1846, in Monterrey by two Americans with close ties to the US troops who occupied the town. The second bilingual paper, *La Estrella*, began publication in 1851 as a translation of the Los Angeles *Star*.[72]

This early press helped reinforce Anglo control over the Mexicans of the west and southwest. As journalism historian Felix Gutiérrez notes:

> The conquering group establishes media for the conquered group, but then controls the media by restricting employment opportunities, establishing a dual labor market, controlling the context of the news, and delivering even that news a week later to members of the conquered group. A more concise description of the neo or internal colonial control of the press could not be more clear.[73]

The first genuine Hispanic-owned newspaper in California was San Francisco's *La Cronica* ("Chronicle"). It was launched by J. Joffre and J. T. Lafuente in 1854, and began as a twice-weekly bilingual sheet—three pages in Spanish and one in Italian. The Italian section was dropped within a few months, and the paper then continued publishing entirely in Spanish.[74]

Early Hispanic editors attempted to give voice to the landed class of *Californios* whose status and wealth were threatened by the new miners and settlers flooding into the state. No editor performed that role more valiantly or for a longer period of time than Francisco Ramírez, the giant of nineteenth-century Californian Hispanic journalism. Ramírez was only seventeen when he decided in 1855 to start his own newspaper, following a short stint as a compositor on the Spanish edition of the *Los Angeles Star*. He called his paper *El Clamor Público* ("Public Clamor"). Ramírez was pro-business, pro-Californian statehood, a strong advocate of Mexicans learning the English language, and an early recruit to the Republican Party; he thus garnered enthusiastic support at first from the Anglo settlers, even securing a small subsidy for his newspaper from the city of Los Angeles.

But he eventually grew disillusioned with the new settlers. In one August 1855 editorial, he wrote:

> Since 1849, there has existed an animosity between Mexicans and Americans, so foreign to a magnanimous and free people to such an extent that these have wished with all their heart that all of the Mexicans had just one neck so that it could be cut off all at once. They [Mexicans] have suffered many injustices, and they have especially been mistreated and abused with impunity in the mines. If a Mexican has the misfortune to place a suit in a court of this state, he is sure to lose it.[75]

In 1852, the state's Board of Land Commissioners started to verify the old Spanish and Mexican land grants. By then, many of the original California landowners were losing their titles during costly legal battles that were conducted under newly adopted property laws. Ramírez and other Hispanic editors were the only ones who dared expose the rampant abuses against those *Californios*. On April 26, 1856, *El Clamor Público* reprinted a stirring speech before the state legislature by *Californio* leader Pablo de la Guerra:

> I have seen old men of sixty and seventy years of age weeping like children because they have been cast out of their ancestral homes. They have been humiliated and insulted. They have been refused the privilege of taking water from their own wells. They have been refused the privilege of cutting their own firewood. And yet those individuals who have committed these abuses have come here looking for protection, and surprisingly the Senate sympathizes with them. You Senators do not listen to the complaints of the Spanish citizens. You do not sufficiently appreciate their land titles and the just right to their possessions.[76]

Perhaps the biggest affront to the cultural pride of *Californio* editors was the way white newspapers advocated the militant rhetoric of Manifest Destiny. As one historian noted, "between 1856 and 1859 one can hardly scan a California newspaper without seeing a slur on Mexico's honor, a plan or a rumor of a filibuster, or advocacy of colonization somewhere in the south."[77] The Spanish-language press, on the other hand, frequently condemned conspiracies against Latin American lands. William Walker, the San

Francisco journalist and filibuster hero, for example, was a frequent target of *El Clamor Público*.

To Ramírez, a "lynchocracy" was operating against Mexicans in the state. In 1857, he translated and published a letter that had first appeared in a French-language paper in San Francisco. The letter warned that vigilantes near the town of San Gabriel were terrorizing Mexicans and hanging some on the mere suspicion of theft:

> [T]he two unfortunates were hanged—despite the protests of their coun-trymen and their families. Once hanged from the tree, the ropes broke and the hapless ones were finished being murdered by shots and knife thrusts. The cutter of heads was fatigued, or his knife did not now cut! Perhaps you will believe that this very cruel person was an Indian from the mountains, one of those barbarians who lives far from all civilization in the Sierra Madre. Wrong. That barbarian, the mutilator of cadavers, was the Justice of the Peace of San Gabriel! ... He is a citizen of the United States, an American of pure blood ...[78]

The San Gabriel attack was no isolated incident, as the article made clear: "Afterwards, two Mexicans were found hanging from a tree, and near there another with two bullets in the head. On the road from Tejon another company had encountered two poor peddlers (always Mexicans) who were arrested and hanged as suspects."[79]

Recording crimes against Mexicans was just one of the unique services *El Clamor Público* provided its readers. Like many Spanish-language papers of the nineteenth century, it also fostered the spread of literature and high culture and the preservation of the Spanish language. One of his earliest issues, for example, contained a front-page article on the French symbolist poet Gérard de Nerval, and the paper routinely published "Poesías Escogi-das," a section that reprinted poetry from Cuba, Puerto Rico, or other parts of the Spanish-speaking world—even verses by unknown local scribes.[80]

While he often championed the rights of all *Californios*, Ramírez none-theless remained a loyal member of and spokesman for the community's wealthiest members. On at least one occasion he sided with his fellow *ricos* against more oppressed *Mexicanos*. In 1857, for example, *El Clamor Público* strongly backed a joint posse of affluent Mexicans and Anglo settlers that hunted down and captured Juan Flores and Campo Daniel, two "bandits" who were leading what was in effect a revolt of poor Mexicans against Anglo rule.[81]

The many abuses against Mexicans that he witnessed so embittered Ramírez that he began urging his readers to flee California. In 1859, he shuttered his newspaper and moved to Mexico, where he continued his journalism career as editor of *La Estrella de Occidente* ("The Western Star").

But his self-imposed exile did not last very long. He had returned to California by 1862, editing several other papers over the next few decades, practicing law, and even vying unsuccessfully for a seat in the state legislature on the Republican ticket. Unfortunately, his illustrious career was suddenly derailed in 1881 when Los Angeles authorities charged him with fraud. He promptly fled for a second time to Mexico, and appears to have lived out the rest of his life in Baja California.[82]

We have provided here only a cursory sketch of the vibrant and diverse Hispanic press that existed in the United States prior to the Civil War. The best of these Cuban- and Mexican-born editors displayed uncommon perseverance as they sought to chronicle the stories, the hopes and dreams, the verse and literature of our nation's early Latino population. They promoted American ideals of liberty and freedom of the press while defending their otherwise powerless communities against racial and linguistic hostility from white settlers. As the United States annexed greater swaths of western territory, Spanish-speaking editors were among the few to challenge the Manifest Destiny drumbeat from the country's most powerful publications. In many ways, their achievements are comparable to those of the patriot printers of the Revolutionary War era, or of their better-known contemporaries in the black press such as Frederick Douglass and Martin Delaney.

The Indian War of Words

It is up to the true poet to use his pen, his chisel, or his pencil ... to give us pictures of our noble selves.

John Rollin Ridge, Cherokee writer and
founding editor of the *Sacramento Bee*

With the founding in 1828 of the *Cherokee Phoenix* (*Tsa-la-ge-Tsi-hi-sa-ni-hi*), the world's first Indian newspaper, Native Americans began to fashion a radically different, more comprehensive image of their reality than could be found in the white press. During the decades that followed, a handful of Native journalists would distinguish themselves by heading commercial newspapers aimed largely at white readers, among them the Sacramento *Bee* and the *San Diego Union*.

To appreciate fully the enormous leaps Native Americans made in mass communication during the nineteenth century, it is necessary to review the tragic state of Indian–white relations up to the age of Jackson.

Civilized Nations and the Broken Treaties

From early colonial days, the Creeks, Chickasaws, Choctaws, Seminoles, and Cherokee had inhabited a large buffer territory in the South between the Spanish colony in Florida, the Anglo settlers of Tennessee, Georgia, and North Carolina, and the French along the Mississippi. Known by whites as the Five Civilized Tribes because they readily adopted European dress, tools, and farming methods, and because many became Christianized, the Indians of the South numbered around 125,000 by the early 1800s.[1]

After the Revolutionary War, US leaders sought peace with the various tribes on the frontier, paying special attention to the Cherokee, who had been fierce allies of England during the war. In a series of pacts that began with the Hopewell Treaty in 1785, the federal government recognized the sovereignty of the Cherokee nation in portions of what today are North Carolina, Georgia, Alabama and Tennessee, and it guaranteed that Cherokee land would be off-limits to American settlers.[2]

But new white settlers, their thirst for land almost unquenchable, simply ignored the treaties and continued to squat on Indian land. The incursions led to repeated incidents of violence and retribution from both sides. Each time new fighting erupted over a treaty violation, Congress retroactively recognized the illegal white settlements, offered the Cherokee leaders cash for the expropriated land, and then negotiated a new treaty, which again promised the Indians sovereignty over their own territory.[3] Once the Louisiana Purchase had placed vast new territory west of the Missis- sippi under US control, Southern whites quickly secured the backing of President Jefferson for the eventual removal of the Cherokee from their homeland, and in 1804 Congress authorized the president to grant land in the Louisiana territory to the Indians in exchange for their current hold- ings. Jefferson left office before that policy could be implemented, and his successors James Madison and James Monroe both espoused the same long- range goal but refused to move forward unless the Indians voluntarily agreed to move.[4]

Negotiations over a new treaty were interrupted by the War of 1812. During that conflict, Major Ridge, principal chief of the Cherokee, recruited 500 of his warriors to fight alongside Andrew Jackson's Tennessee militia against a radical faction of Creek Indians, the Red Sticks, who had allied with the British.[5]

Jackson's Cherokee allies in that victory were led by a trio of mixed-race Christian chiefs: Major Ridge and Charles Hicks, both successful planters and slave-owners, and Lt. "Little John" Ross, a short, stocky Scottish-descended merchant who claimed one-eighth Cherokee blood and who had been edu- cated in eastern American schools. All three men would play pivotal roles in the destiny of their tribe during the decades that followed. Another brave who fought at Horseshoe Bend that day would become the most famous Cherokee of all, and would lay the basis for the first Indian mass media. His English name was George Gist (or Guest). His father was a Virginia colonel who deserted George's Cherokee mother when he was just a boy. After the Creek War, Gist landed work as a silversmith and became widely admired among his fellow Indians for his skill at drawing animals and human faces. Tribe members called him by his Indian name: Sequoyah.

Old Hickory's Indian Treaties and Land Deals

Jackson emerged as a national hero following his defeat of the Red Sticks and his victory over the British at New Orleans the following year. Once the War of 1812 ended, white settlers on the southern and western fron- tier increased the pressure on Congress to solve the "Indian problem," with Jackson becoming the country's most prominent spokesman for Indian removal.

Following his victory over the Red Sticks, for example, Jackson forced the Creeks, including his White Sticks allies, to sign the Treaty of Fort Jackson on August 9, 1814. In that agreement the Creeks ceded to the United States 23 million acres—half of all the land they possessed—as reparations for the hostilities. It amounted to roughly three-fifths of the current state of Alabama and one-fifth of Georgia. In the words of Jackson's best-known biographer, Old Hickory "converted the Creek civil war into an enormous land grab and ensured the ultimate destruction of the entire Creek Nation." He also secured a piece of land for himself as a "gift" from the Creek leaders.[6] From then on, Jackson repeatedly bribed, bullied and lied to tribal leaders, while steadily increasing at their expense the size of his land holdings and those of his relatives and friends. He appointed John Coffee, his nephew by marriage and a veteran of the battle of Horseshoe Bend, as surveyor of the lands in Alabama that the Creeks had ceded to the federal government. Coffee later organized a land speculation company based in Tennessee and Philadelphia and arranged for its investors, including Jackson, to buy large parcels at below-market prices.

Jackson and Coffee arranged a series of additional land cession treaties with the Cherokees, Choctaws and Chickasaws. Through those agreements, Old Hickory managed to amass for the federal government an estimated 50 million acres of new lands by 1820.[7] Included in those acquisitions were some 13 million acres he pressured the Choctaws to relinquish in the heart of the fertile Mississippi delta region in exchange for land in southern Oklahoma and southwestern Arkansas. White settlers in Mississippi had long been eager to move out the Choctaws. In January of 1820, the *Mississippi State Gazette* demanded the tribe's removal from lands "which they hold to the great detriment of the state." Jackson, the paper declared, was the unanimous choice of the state's leaders as a treaty commissioner to negotiate the land swap. He soon won the appointment, and the result was the Treaty of Doak's Stand, signed on October 18, 1820. Mississippi leaders were so grateful to Jackson that they named their capital after him. As for Old Hickory, he ended up with a 2,700-acre plantation on former Choctaw land.[8]

Despite the many white settler incursions on their land, the Cherokee prospered in the decades after the War of 1812. Missionary churches spread across Cherokee territory; tribal leaders built their own capital, New Echota, and established their own courts and legislature; they adopted their own Constitution, and they built their own schools to teach their children English. A report to the War Department in 1825 by Thomas L. McKenney, head of the Office of Indian Affairs, praised their remarkable progress:

> The Natives carry on considerable trade with the adjoining States; some of them export cotton in boats down the Tennessee to the Mississippi and down that river to New Orleans ... There are many public roads in

the nation, and houses of entertainment kept by natives. Numerous and flourishing villages are seen in every section of the country. Cotton and woolen cloths are manufactured ... Industry and commercial enterprise are extending themselves in every part. Nearly all the merchants in the nation are native Cherokees.

McKenney noted, in addition, a surprising trend that seemed to shatter the stereotype of the "skulking Indian enemy" propagated for so long by the country's commercial press. A large number of whites, he wrote, were living peaceably as part of Indian society, where they "enjoy all the immunities and privileges of the Cherokee people, except that they are not eligible to public offices."[9] A census conducted that year by Indian leaders tallied 147 white men and 73 white women living in tribal territory, most of them spouses of Indians, along with 13,563 Cherokees and 1,277 slaves. Cherokee society, in other words, was becoming multi-racial.[10]

Indian Images in the Commercial and Religious Press

By the 1820s and early 1830s, few Americans along the eastern seaboard could even claim much direct contact with Native Americans, most of whom had been pushed far from the major population centers. The only mention of them in the commercial press came largely from accounts that originated in Southern and eastern publications and reached the eastern press through postal newspaper exchanges. Those accounts invariably reinforced historic stereotypes of both the Noble Indian and the Ruthless Savage. In 1835, for example, a Georgia newspaper said of Indians: "Their [sic] are no greater thieves in existence than Indian dogs; not even excepting the old squaws ... With the last, it is a matter of habit, and practice; but with the former it is instinct."[11] A satiric 1837 poem in a Tennessee weekly blamed devilish Indians for spreading the habit of smoking:

> Tobacco is an Indian,
> It was the d[evi]l sowed the seed;
> It drains your pockets—scents your clothes,
> And makes a chimney of your nose.[12]

As with African slaves, the most sympathetic portrayals of Indians tended to be stories of those who sided with whites. In the midst of the Semi-nole Wars, for instance, the Washington *Telegraph* published the story of a seventeen-year-old Seminole girl who showed her "singular development of noble feeling and humanity" by interceding among her tribesmen to prevent their execution of a captured white soldier.[13]

There was one wing of early American newspapers, however, that provided a far different portrayal of Native peoples than the commercial sheets. Evangelical and religious publications began increasingly to depict Indians as the victims of white conquest. Throughout the 1820s and 1830s, papers like the Presbyterian *New York Observer*, the *Missionary Herald*, the *Religious Intelligencer*, and the Congregational *Boston Recorder* urged a more benevolent policy toward Indians and sought to expand missionary work among the various tribes.[14] They condemned forcible seizures of Indian land by the southern states, and even published on occasion the words of Indians themselves. In 1824, for instance, after the Cherokee were forced to cede yet another piece of land, a story in the *Boston Recorder* quoted an elderly Indian as saying, "White people kill my people and no notice is taken." The *Religious Intelligencer* even decried the false portrayals of them in the press: "White men make inroads into the Indian territory, destroy their game, and steal their furs. If the natives, indignant at such outrages, make any resistance, we immediately find articles in newspapers, headed with '*Indian Barbarities, Murders,* etc. etc.!!'"[15]

The Birth of the Cherokee Phoenix

In 1821 the young Indian silversmith who had fought with Jackson at Horseshoe Bend finally achieved his decades-long obsession. Sequoyah had dreamed since before the War of 1812 of devising a written version of the Cherokee language so his people could communicate with each other the same way white people did. He spent years crafting individual symbols for some 2,000 Cherokee words, but eventually abandoned that strategy in favor of creating one sign for each syllable. He finally completed his eighty-six-character syllabary in 1821, but his fellow tribesmen in Arkansas, thinking him crazy, refused his entreaties to study it. Undaunted, Sequoyah embarked on a relentless campaign among tribal leaders until they finally agreed to a test of the alphabet's power among a group of young men. The test proved so successful that the Cherokee Council endorsed it, and before long tribal members were using tree bark and even the walls of their houses to memorize the letters, with virtually all Cherokees, the young as well as the old, learning to read and write the new language by 1828. An astonished contemporary of Sequoyah who observed this grassroots literacy movement in action, wrote: "That the mass of people, without schools or books, should by mutual assistance, without extraneous impulse or aid, acquire the art of reading, and that in a character wholly original is, I believe, a phenomenon unexampled in modern times."[16]

White missionaries initially rejected Sequoyah's alphabet, until they realized its potential for spreading the gospel.

One of those missionaries was Rev. Samuel Worcester, a tall, slender linguist who would soon play a pivotal role in the creation of the Indian press.

Born in Vermont and educated at Andover Theological Seminary, Worcester had begun his ministry with the Cherokee in Georgia in 1819, and he
soon befriended a brilliant young schoolteacher named Buck Watie, who
was the secretary of the tribal council and also nephew of Cherokee chief
Major Ridge.[17] Watie had been among a small group of Cherokee youths
who were sent in 1818 to study at a new college the American Board of
Missions had established in Cornwall, Connecticut. On his way to the
school, Watie spent a night at the New Jersey home of Dr. Elias Boudinot, a member of the mission's board and a longtime member of Congress.
Boudinot took such an immediate liking to the Indian youth that he offered
to finance his education, whereupon the grateful Buck Watie decided on the
spot to change his own name to Elias Boudinot.

Once the Indian youths arrived at the Cornwall school, however, both
Boudinot and the handsome John Ridge, son of Major Ridge, made the
unpardonable mistake of falling in love with white women. Ridge shocked
local town residents by marrying Sara Northrop, who had nursed him
through an illness, while Boudinot soon after wed Harriet Gold, daughter of
Cornwall's Colonel Benjamin Gold. The two interracial weddings sparked
such a fury in Connecticut that funding for the school dried up, and it was
forced to close its doors.[18]

In 1826 John Ross, who would later become the Cherokee's principal
chief, convinced his fellow chiefs to launch a tribal newspaper. Ross believed
that such a publication would be "an important vehicle in the diffusion of
general knowledge" and a "powerful auxiliary in asserting and supporting
our political rights." While it was to be an official tribal organ, Ross envisioned the paper as having a degree of independence.[19]

He chose Boudinot, who was only twenty-seven at the time, as its editor,
and Samuel Worcester immediately volunteered to organize a speaking tour
of northeast churches to raise money for the project. The first edition of the
paper appeared on February 21st, 1828. Printed in both English and Cherokee, it included spelling and grammar lessons for the new language, as well as
copies of Cherokee laws and tribal reports. In the spirit of Varela's *El Habanero* and of *Freedom's Journal*, Boudinot's opening editorial promised reasoned
and balanced reporting: "We shall reserve to ourselves the liberty of rejecting
such communications as tend to evil, and such as are too intemperate and
too personal. But the columns of this paper shall always be open to free and
temperate discussions of matters of politics, religion, & c."

The final words in that first commentary were an eloquent call for an end
to the 140-year-old anti-Indian racial narrative in American newspapers:

> We now commit our feeble efforts to the good will and indulgence of the
> public, praying that God will attend them with his blessings, and hoping
> for that happy period when all the Indian tribes of America shall rise,

Phoenix-like, from their ashes, and when terms like "Indian depredations," "war whoops," "scalping knife," and the like shall become obsolete and forever buried "under deep ground."[20]

Each issue of the weekly *Phoenix* faithfully chronicled Cherokee efforts to prevent incursions on their land by Georgia's white settlers. Worcester, who served as Boudinot's main assistant, shared much of the writing duties with him. Only a few copies were printed in the paper's early days; so few that they were initially apportioned one per village, but soon subscription requests came pouring in from throughout the United States and from as far away as Europe, from people eager to read the first newspaper created by Indians. The *Phoenix* was born at a critical time for the Cherokee. Gold was discovered on tribal land in northeast Georgia the following year. The influx of white prospectors soon despoiled the area's rivers and streams, and their competing claims led to rampant trafficking in fraudulent land titles. In December 1829 the Georgia legislature passed a raft of new laws aimed at forcing the Cherokee from their land. Indians were barred from testifying in any trial involving white men, and any testimony on their part henceforth required corroboration by at least two white witnesses. The legislature even outlawed meetings of the Cherokee council except for the purposes of ceding land.[21]

Boudinot exposed and criticized each new assault on Indian rights in the pages of the *Phoenix*. After Georgia passed its anti-Indian laws, he reported a campaign of harassment and physical attacks against members of his own staff. At one point after he exposed the local postmaster's sale of liquor to Indians, the post office cut off delivery of the newspaper's supplies and exchange papers. "This new era has not only wrested from us our rights and privileges as a people," Boudinot responded, "it has closed the channel through which we could formerly obtain our news. By this means the resources of the *Phoenix* are cut off."[22]

Similarly, Elijah Hicks, who later replaced Boudinot as the paper's editor, noted in 1833 that he had spotted a sign in the Nashville post office ordering the curtailment of all newspaper exchanges with the *Cherokee Phoenix*.[23] It thus appears that the postal system was used intermittently to cripple the ability of the *Phoenix* to reach its readers—much as occurred with abolitionist newspapers mailed to the South.

Some copies of the paper nonetheless reached editors in other sections of the country, and occasional Boudinot articles were then reprinted in both the evangelical press and a few influential commercial newspapers in the North, among them *Niles' Weekly Register* in Washington, DC.

Unfortunately, the *Phoenix* also displayed racist views toward blacks. The tribe's constitution, published periodically in the paper, declared that no Negro or mulatto could vote or hold office, it outlawed intermarriage between black slaves and Indians, and it denied slaves in Cherokee territory the right to own horses, cattle, or hogs. On occasion, Boudinot would publish anecdotes in black dialect that viciously satirized blacks, much as white newspaper editors were then accustomed to doing. One *Phoenix* article, titled "Negro Fun," ridiculed a fictitious "brudder Sam" and "brudder Mingo," both attempting to discuss "Gin'ral Washington's defeat of Cornwallis."[24]

At the same time, the *Phoenix* was one of the few Southern newspapers that permitted debate on the merits of slavery. On several occasions, Boudinot published articles opposed to African bondage, and he sometimes sought to portray blacks in a positive light. When more than 77,000 slaves were sold in Rio de Janeiro in 1826 and 1827, Boudinot pointed out that Africans were being "placed in a situation as debasing to the human mind and infinitely worse as regards physical suffering than the ordinary condition of the brute creation." And in an article reprinted from the *Raleigh Register*, the *Phoenix* recounted the story of "an extraordinary young slave" who wrote poetry and had made a name for himself among students at the University of North Carolina.[25]

Jackson and Indian Removal

Andrew Jackson's electoral victory over President John Quincy Adams in 1828 immediately thrust the issue of Indian removal into the national spotlight. In his first address to Congress, in December 1829, Old Hickory called for a massive resettlement effort, and he suddenly announced he would no longer defend the Five Civilized Tribes against land expropriations by state governments in the South.[26]

The pro-Jackson press had rallied voter support for him among Northern workers, but Jackson's solid sweep of the South had rested largely on his promise to complete the removal of the Indian tribes. So important was the issue to that region that, even before he was sworn in, state governments in Georgia, Alabama and Mississippi quickly passed new laws declaring their sovereignty over Indian territory.[27]

The financial importance of Indian removal to the Southern oligarchy is not often understood. As historian Anthony Wallace has noted, by the mid 1830s half of all the cotton consumed by the world's estimated 450 million people was coming from the American South, and the demand for manufactured cotton goods was skyrocketing. Since a single acre of land was capable of producing 200 pounds of cotton, a 500-acre plantation could generate a yearly profit as high as $6,000—a huge sum for that time. Removing the Five Tribes from the approximately 100 million acres they still possessed was essential for white cotton growers to expand slavery and the plantation system. Jackson, the Democrat and populist, willingly served as the political instrument of that expansion. Moreover, the sale of those lands was itself a main source of federal income, since by 1835 half of all federal revenue was coming from the sale of government land.[28]

Jackson repeatedly sought to portray removal as a humane policy—one that benefited Native Americans. Only by emigrating beyond the Mississippi, he argued, could the Indians survive as a race. It was a view espoused by one of the nation's most prominent experts on Indian language and culture, Lewis Cass, who Jackson appointed Secretary of War in 1831. Cass produced a series of highly influential articles in the *North American Review* elaborating in great detail the intellectual justification for what was, in effect, a campaign of ethnic cleansing. In 1827, for example, Cass blasted any belief "in that system of legal metaphysics, which would give to a few naked and wandering savages, a perpetual title to an immense continent." [29]

In a subsequent piece in the magazine, in 1830, Cass said of Indians:

> Existing for two centuries in contact with a civilized people, they have resisted, and successfully too, every effort to ameliorate their situation, or to introduce among them the most common arts of life ... And in the whole circle of their existence, it would be difficult to point to a single advantage which they have derived from their acquaintance with the Europeans ... There must be an inherent difficulty, arising from the institutions, character, and condition of the Indians themselves.[30]

Such arguments found cruder expression in the commercial press, especially in those papers that backed Jackson. In 1837, for instance, when the *New York Sun* printed a first-person account by a western trapper about his kind treatment by Indians in the Black Hills, the paper's editor added: "Trust to their honesty and they will steal the hair off your head."[31]

Despite the rationales offered by Cass and Jackson, bitter resistance erupted in Congress and around the country against the president's Indian Removal Bill. In town hall meetings, in petition drives, and in scores of resolutions by municipal governments throughout the North, a sizeable portion of the American public condemned the plan. Much of that opposition was organized by the ecclesiastical press and the new women's movements, with feminists such as Catherine Beecher and Angelina Grimké, and writer and poet Lydia Sigourney, all spearheading defense of the Indians.[32]

On March 28, 1830, after months of intense debate and a close vote in Congress, Jackson officially signed into law the Indian Removal Act. It authorized the president to relocate all Indian tribes west of the Mississippi, where they would receive new land "in perpetuity." Jackson promptly withdrew from Georgia all federal troops that had been protecting the Indians from local settlers. State officials then began to survey all Cherokee land, divide it into allotments, and award it to white settlers in a lottery.

Phoenix *Editors Attacked, Jailed and Censored*

But the *Cherokee Phoenix* soon became a major obstacle to Indian removal. Boudinot's many articles in defense of Indian rights kept finding their way into newspapers in the North, where they helped to stir up public opposition to the tactics of the Georgians. So effective was the paper's editorial campaign that local settlers escalated their efforts to silence it. "Boudinot was occasionally ordered to come forth from the *Phoenix* office and answer for his editorials before armed Georgia troops and civilians, but the fear they hoped to instill in him did not change his views or his writings," notes historian John Ehle.[33]

In 1831, the state legislature passed a new law requiring all non-Indians living in Cherokee territory to be licensed and to swear allegiance to Georgia laws. Tribal leaders immediately declared the law invalid on Indian land, since existing treaties with the federal government recognized the Cherokee as a sovereign nation. Boudinot's assistant on the *Phoenix*, Rev. Samuel Worcester, and several other white missionaries refused to comply with the new law and were promptly arrested by the Georgia Guard. Their jailing prompted an outcry in the Northern press. "Is it honest then to seize on, and take by force, a piece of property that pleases our fancy, but does not exactly belong to us?" asked the New York *American.*

Jackson and his Democratic majority in Congress ignored the growing Indian rights movement in the North, and the Supreme Court seemed at first to back him up. In a July 1831 decision by the court, *Cherokee Nation v. Georgia*, Chief Justice John Marshall concluded the Cherokee were not a foreign nation but a "domestic, dependent nation," one "in a state of pupilage" to the United States. The Court thus sanctioned federal power over Indian tribes.

But the question of state power over those tribes was another matter— and that issue soon came to a head in the case of jailed editor Worcester, who had decided to appeal his four-year sentence, handed down by Georgia authorities. In a separate decision issued in 1832, the Supreme Court handed a stunning victory to the cause of Native American rights. In that case, *Worcester v. Georgia*, Justice Marshall ruled that, though the Cherokee were not a sovereign nation, they were still "a distinct community occupying its own territory ... in which the laws of Georgia can have no force, and which the citizens of Georgia have no right to enter, but with the assent of the Cherokees themselves, or in conformity with treaties, and with the acts of Congress."[34] Jackson was furious at the new ruling, and defiantly insisted on supporting the Georgians. "John Marshall has made his decision," Jackson is reputed to have said, "now let him enforce it." Taking their cue from the president, Georgia officials simply ignored the Court and refused to release Worcester from jail. As for Jackson, he declined to dispatch federal troops to implement Marshall's ruling.[35]

Jackson then moved quickly to convince the Cherokee leaders, many of whom he had known personally for years, to consent to their own removal through a new treaty. The Civilized Tribes had so far done everything white society had demanded of them. They had established thriving farms and towns, they had adopted the Christian religion and the white man's customs and dress, and they had created laws, courts and a bicameral legislature in the American style. But the Georgians, backed by the federal government, were now demanding the Indians abandon everything they had built.

Cherokee tribal leaders dispatched John Ridge to Washington as their chief negotiator. Under pressure from Indian friends in Congress and the American Board of Missions, Ridge eventually agreed to back the new pact that Jackson sought. When word of Ridge's concession reached Chief John Ross, he rejected it as "one of the most consummate acts of treachery."[36] Fierce divisions promptly arose among Cherokee leaders over the new pact. Ross and the majority of the Cherokee population opposed it, while a small group, including many of the tribe's more educated and affluent leaders, reluctantly decided they could no longer resist so many white settlers overrunning their land. John Ridge, his father Major Ridge, and *Phoenix* editor Elias Boudinot emerged as chief spokesmen for what came to be known as the Treaty faction.

Ross ordered Boudinot not to publish any reports in the *Phoenix* about the raging debate inside the Cherokee Council. Rather than submit to such censorship, the young editor chose to resign. Boudinot penned his final words as editor in the August 11, 1832 issue of the paper: "I could not consent to be the conductor of this paper without having the privilege and the right of discussing those important matters … I should think it my duty to tell them the whole truth. I cannot tell them that we shall be reinstated in our rights when I have no such hope."[37]

The Indian Press after Boudinot

Ross appointed his son-in-law Elijah Hicks to replace Boudinot, and the new editor continued the paper's campaign against Indian removal, though the vigor and quality of the writing declined after Boudinot's departure.

In 1835, twenty members of the Ridge-Boudinot faction signed the New Echota Treaty with the Jackson administration, and agreed to move to the newly designated Indian Territory in present-day Oklahoma. That same year, Ross and the Cherokee Council decided to move the *Phoenix* to a more secure location on Cherokee land in Tennessee. Tragically, the Georgia Guard intercepted the wagon train that was carrying the newspaper's equipment, seized the press at gunpoint, and dumped its lead type into a well, and so ended the extraordinary saga of the world's first Indian newspaper.[38]

Despite the efforts of the Ridge-Boudinot faction, most members of the
Cherokee nation remained loyal to Chief Ross. They refused to recognize
the New Echota Treaty and continued to peacefully resist removal from their
land for several more years. In the winter of 1838, Jackson's successor, Martin
Van Buren, ordered federal troops under General Winfield Scott to forcibly
march Ross and more than 18,000 of his tribesmen to the federal land set
aside for them in the west. The infamous Trail of Tears, as the march was
called, claimed the lives of at least 4,000—some estimates put it as high as
8,000—who perished in army stockades or along the route of the march.[39]

It didn't take long for Ross's followers to exact a grisly price on the
leaders of the Treaty Party for their betrayal. On June 28, 1839, a group of
Indians accosted Boudinot outside his farmhouse in Park Hill, Indian Territory, and stabbed him to death. The same day, another band ambushed and
killed his uncle Major Ridge near the Arkansas border, while a third group
burst into the home of his cousin John Ridge and hacked him to death in
front of his wife and children.[40]

Once the survivors of the Trail of Tears were firmly established in their
new land, Chief Ross and the Cherokee Council voted to launch a new
tribal newspaper. They chose as its editor William P. Ross, the chief's nephew
and a Princeton graduate. The first issue of the *Cherokee Advocate* rolled off
the presses on September 26, 1844. A six-column bilingual weekly that also
used Sequoyah's alphabet, it would become the longest-running and most
influential Indian newspaper of the nineteenth century, publishing with only
a few brief interruptions until 1906.

The *Advocate*, however, was not the first newspaper directed at Indians in
the new territory. In 1839, *Siwinowe Esibwi*, or the *Shawnee Sun*, a monthly
printed completely in the Shawnee-Sioux language, began operation at
the Baptist mission press in the region, while in August 1844 the *Cherokee Messenger*, another Baptist mission newspaper, was launched in Westville,
Oklahoma, and appeared intermittently until 1858. The *Shawnee Sun*, *Cherokee Advocate*, and *Cherokee Messenger* were followed by the *Cherokee Rose
Bud* (1848), the first magazine produced by Indian women; the Choctaw
Telegraph (1849), and its successor, the *Intelligenser* (1850), the latter two being
bilingual weeklies that were printed in Doaksville, Oklahoma, capital of the
Choctaw nation; and the *Chickasaw Choctaw Herald* (1858), which appeared
solely in English in Tishomingo, capital of the Chickasaw Nation. Most
of the new publications were run not by Native Americans, but by white
missionaries or businessmen eager to reach Indian readers.

Both white-owned and Native-owned publications in the territory supported the plantation slave system that had become essential to the economy
of the Five Civilized Nations. As a result, after the outbreak of the Civil War,
many Indians in the territory joined the Confederate army, and all newspapers in Indian country were forced to suspend publication.[41]

Native American Editors of Anglo Newspapers

Indian Territory was not the only place Native American writers left an impressive journalism legacy during the nineteenth century. A handful of Cherokee writers played important but unheralded roles on mainstream white newspapers.

When fellow Indians assassinated Treaty faction leader John Ridge in 1839, one of the witnesses to the murder had been his twelve-year-old son Yellow Bird. The boy's white mother later sent him to the Great Barrington School in Massachusetts, and after he completed his education, Yellow Bird, also known as John Rollin Ridge, pursued a career in law and opened his own practice in Fayetteville, Arkansas. Ten years after his father's death, Ridge got into dispute with a fellow Indian he thought to be one of his father's assassins. He killed the man and fled the state to escape prosecution.

He eventually made his way to California, where he began a new career as a writer and journalist. In 1854, he published *The Life and Adventures of Joaquín Murieta*, a fictionalized account of the notorious California bandit. Ridge depicted Murieta as a folk hero who had turned to crime only after white miners hanged his brother and raped his sister. His book is generally considered the first novel written by a Native American.

Ridge, who was working at the time as the deputy clerk of Yuba County, then tried to launch a California newspaper to defend Indian rights. "I want to write the history of the Cherokee Nation as it should be written and not as white men will write it and as they will tell the tale, to screen and justify themselves," he wrote in a letter to his cousin Stand Watie, the brother of Elias Boudinot. Unable to raise the necessary funds for the paper, Ridge took a job instead as a writer for the *California American*.

Violence against Indians was then rampant in the state. In 1852, for example, the *Daily Alta California* reprinted an account from Weaversville, Trinity County, of "a fearful act of retributive slaughter recently committed in that district. A rancheria of 148 Indians, including women and children, was attacked, and nearly the whole number destroyed." An article the following year in the San Francisco *Union* noted: "The Indians have committed so many depredations in the North, of late, that the people are enraged against them, and are ready to knife them, shoot them, or inoculate them with smallpox—all of which have been done."

Two 1859 articles in northern California papers reported separate instances of brutal killings of individual Indians. "An old Indian and his squaw were engaged in the harmless occupation of gathering clover on the land of a Mr. Grigsby," noted the first article in the Marysville *Democrat*,

> when a man named Frank Harrington set Grigsby's dogs upon them (which, by the way, are three very ferocious ones), and before they were taken off of them, they tore and mangled the body of the squaw in such

a manner that she died shortly after. It is said the dogs tore her breasts off her. The Digger man escaped without any serious injury, although bitten severely.

The second item in the Shasta *Courier* reported:

> A few days ago, the Indian boy who set fire to the house of Col. Stevenson was taken from the custody of Sheriff Dunn, by a number of citizens, and hanged. The Sheriff had taken him to the Court House and left him in a room adjoining the Courtroom, and while absent for a few moments, the boy was taken by the mob. This is really horrible, and reflects no credit to the parties concerned.

The paper's criticism, however, was hardly inspired by sympathy for Indians. "The boy deserved hanging, if he was capable of appreciating the magnitude of his crime," the paper's editor went on to say, insisting only that the youth should have been "hung in a legal manner."[42]

In 1856, General James Allen, a leader of the state's Know-Nothing Party, launched the *California American*, the paper where Ridge began his journalism career. The Know-Nothings captured many of the state's top political posts later that year, including the governorship, whereupon the *American*, as the party's chief organ, won a lucrative contract as official state printer. By then, Ridge was both editor and part-owner. But the period of Know-Nothing rule was a disaster for California, as vigilante violence between political factions engulfed the state. Even though Ridge publicly rejected his party's handling of the violence, the popularity of the Know-Nothings plummeted, and so did the influence of his newspaper. To clean up its tarnished image, Ridge organized a group of Sacramento businessmen to buy the paper from Allen and replace it with a new publication. They called it the *Daily Bee*, and it began operation on February 3rd, 1857, with Ridge promising his readers to maintain it free of political partisanship.[43]

During the six months he served as the *Bee*'s editor, Ridge filled the paper with deftly written editorials and with his own poetry. And while it was a general circulation sheet aimed at white settlers, Ridge nonetheless featured many articles in the paper about the plight of California's Native population. "The speech of the North American warrior or chief in council is full of metaphor and the essence of poetry," Ridge wrote. "It is up to the true poet to use his pen, his chisel, or his pencil ... to give us pictures of our noble selves."[44]

The *Bee* often defended the Digger Indians, a California tribe that was then facing extinction. Ridge, however, regarded the tribe's members as inferior to his fellow Cherokee, calling them a "poor, miserable, cowardly race" that "permit themselves to be slaughtered like sheep in a shambles."

He even acknowledged hiring one of the tribe's leaders as a household servant.

Perhaps more amazingly, given the tragic course of Cherokee-white relations, Ridge was a firm proponent of Manifest Destiny. "In the march of events," he once wrote, "those races which have an affinity will be brought together; the others will be improved while they last, and afterwards become extinct. But the time is rapidly approaching when the world will be inhabited by a few leading races ..." His paper praised American filibuster movements in Mexico and Central America, especially the escapades of the notorious William Walker in Guatemala, and when it came to land conflicts between the original *Californio* land-grant holders and the white settlers, Ridge and the *Bee*, unlike Francisco Ramírez and *El Clamor Público* and other Hispanic publications, sided with "settlerism," labeling the *Californios* an "aristocratic few who would rob and oppress" those who merely wished to work the land.[45]

In July 1857, James McClatchy, a young Irish-born reporter at the *Bee* who had worked previously for Horace Greeley's *Tribune*, purchased the newspaper from Ridge and his partners. The paper would go on to become the flagship property of the McClatchy Company, one of the nation's biggest newspaper chains, yet few journalism accounts, even the company's official history, acknowledge that Cherokee journalist John Rollin Ridge was its founding editor. As for Ridge, he continued to play a prominent role in California journalism for another ten years, first at the *California Express*, where he became a leading voice for anti-abolitionist Democrats, then as the editor of the San Francisco *Evening Journal*, where his frequent articles condemning President Lincoln and the Emancipation Proclamation made him increasingly unpopular.[46]

Ridge's remarkable but brief journalism career (he died in 1867 at the age of forty) reveals a fascinating but deeply flawed figure. A proud Cherokee and fervent defender of Indian rights, he nonetheless championed the complete assimilation of Indians into white society, and revealed bigoted views toward less developed Indians such as the Diggers. As a celebrated author, he extolled Mexican rebellion against white settlers in his novel *Joaquín Murieta*, yet he later became an avid supporter of Anglo seizure of Mexican lands. Similar contradictions can be found in other nineteenth-century Cherokee journalists, all of them of mixed race, who functioned in a social and psychological limbo—as intermediaries between white society and the masses of their own people.

No group more clearly symbolized that identity crisis than the members of the Ridge-Watie (Boudinot) family. Elias Cornelius Boudinot, son of the founding editor of the *Cherokee Phoenix*, became co-owner and editor in 1859 of the Fayetteville *Arkansian*, a newspaper on the border of Cherokee land. He then served, from 1860 to 1861, as editor of the *Arkansas True*

Democrat. At both newspapers, Boudinot was a staunch supporter of slavery, once claiming:

> All of the abettors of Abolition from the Chief down should be publicly warned that although the South is the natural protector of the Cherokee, Creeks, and Choctaws, yet the South will sweep from its frontier every one who is so base bold, or insidious, as to raise thereon the Black Flag of Abolition.[47]

When war broke out between North and South, Boudinot enlisted in Stand Watie's Confederate Indian Brigade, where he rose to the rank of Lieutenant Colonel.

Another Cherokee who made his mark in the white press was Edward "Ned" Bushyhead. After learning the printing trade in the offices of the *Cherokee Messenger* in 1844, Bushyhead moved to California and became one of the founders of the *San Diego Union* in 1868. His partners were Colonel William Gatewood and a young printer named J. N. Briseño, with Bushyhead serving as the paper's principal owner until his retirement in 1873.

The Native American press before the Civil War thus followed a dramatically different trajectory from the African-American or Latino press. As we have noted, the mere existence of an Indian press during that era was itself an astonishing accomplishment. But only Boudinot's paper in Georgia, and later the *Cherokee Advocate* and *Cherokee Rosebud* in Oklahoma, were actually owned and operated by Indians. Meanwhile, a handful of gifted Indian journalists such as John Rollin Ridge, Elias Cornelius Boudinot, and Edward Bushyhead achieved startling breakthroughs by editing commercial newspapers that were directed mainly to a white readership. Two of those publications, the *Sacramento Bee* and *San Diego Union*, are today considered among California's most important newspapers. So while African-American and Latino journalists pioneered a more authentic "national" press under their own control, Native Americans achieved greater success when it came to integrating, and even running, mainstream "white" newspapers.

To Plead Our Own Cause: The Early Black Press

Our vices and our degradation are ever arrayed against us, but our virtues are passed by unnoticed.

Freedom's Journal, March 16, 1827

Mexico seems a doomed victim to Anglo Saxon cupidity and love of dominion.

Frederick Douglass's *North Star*, January 21, 1848

Freedom's Journal, the first black-owned newspaper in America, marked the beginning of a new opposition press for the nation. That press not only expanded the boundaries of acceptable news and opinion on slavery, it also spawned an independent communications network among black freedmen that led to the historic Black Convention movement.[1]

The founding editors of *Freedom's Journal*, Samuel Cornish and John Russwurm, never made the abolition of slavery their paper's main cause. For two black men to do so in 1827, even in a Northern state such as New York, would have risked courting fierce retribution from whites. Instead they saw their primary job as chronicling the progress of the 500,000 free blacks living in the North, where even whites who opposed slavery still backed separation of the races and believed in the inferiority of blacks.

The words of *Freedom's Journal*'s first issue have amazing resonance even today:

From the press and the pulpit we have suffered much by being incorrectly represented. Men whom we equally love and admire have not hesitated to represent us disadvantageously, without becoming personally acquainted with the true state of things, nor discerning between virtue and vice among us. The virtuous part of our people feel themselves sorely aggrieved under the existing state of things—they are not appreciated.[2]

Determined to challenge all manner of racial stereotype, Cornish and Russwurm devoted much attention to chronicling the school programs, intellectual accomplishments and lifestyle of the emerging Northern black middle class.[3] At the same time, they evinced an intense pride in their African roots and an unwavering commitment to their enslaved brethren:

> Useful knowledge of every kind, and everything that relates to Africa, shall find a ready admission into our columns; and as that vast continent becomes daily more known, we trust that many things will come to light, proving that the natives of it are neither so ignorant nor stupid as they have generally been supposed to be. And while these important subjects shall occupy the columns of the FREEDOM'S JOURNAL, we would not be unmindful of our brethren who are still in the iron fetters of bondage. They are our kindred by all the times of nature; and though but little can be effected by us, still let our sympathies be poured forth, and our prayers in their behalf, ascend to Him who is able to succor them.[4]

On more than one occasion, Cornish and Russwurm publicly challenged racial bigotry in other New York City papers. On July 4, 1827, for example, the remaining slaves of New York State were about to be emancipated. The city's black leaders planned a large parade and celebration for the historic day. The week before emancipation, Cornish and Russwurm reprinted a disturbing item from the *Morning Chronicle*. The article predicted the freed slaves would bring a "manifest increase" in the city's "criminal calendar, pauper list and *dandy* register," and it condemned this "Jubilee nonsense" from a black population that "our citizens already find to be almost intolerable from their numbers and public habits."

In their response, Cornish and Russwurm noted the "disposition in the inferior class of our editors, and newspaper writers, to indulge in low, mean, and vulgar abuse" of black people. "The tendency of such little-minded efforts, is to excite hostile feelings, between the lower classes of the white population, and the people of colour," the *Journal* warned, and could lead "to consequences disgraceful to our city." While acknowledging "bad" behavior among some blacks, the *Journal*'s editors reminded the *Chronicle* that the freed slaves "are an injured people and we think it beneath the character of a public Editor, to add insult to injury."[5]

In its May 11, 1827 issue, *Freedom's Journal* singled out an article on slavery in the *New-York Evening Post*. Written by the *Post*'s venerable editor William Coleman, the article claimed the condition of blacks on Southern plantations, despite some "occasional exceptions," was "one of contentment, of gaiety and happiness," and it described the master-slave relationship as "one of mutual attachment." Slaves in the West Indies, Coleman noted, were likewise "better off when they had a good master and mistress to provide for them." Cornish and Russwurm immediately scorned those conclusions:

Where Mr. C. obtained his information we cannot conceive. The idea that a mind, the least enlightened, should be more contented and happy in a state in which it was not allowed to act from its own volition, but must be the tool of a superior human agent, is too gross to be calculated in this enlightened age of the world.[6]

They also challenged the anti-black diatribes that frequently appeared in Mordecai Noah's *New York Enquirer*. In one article titled "Negroes," Noah lamented the emancipation of New York's last slaves, declaring: "The free negroes of this city are a nuisance incomparably greater than a million slaves."

Cornish and Russwurm reminded Noah that, as an influential Jewish leader, he should be even more aware of the dangers of bigotry. "Major Noah's efforts to increase the prejudice of the lower orders of society against our brethren, is exceedingly unkind," they wrote. "The mob want no leader. Blackguards among whites are sufficiently ready to insult decent people of colour. The Major ought to have gained experience from the situation of his brethren in other countries and learned to be more cautious."[7]

The number of subscribers to *Freedom's Journal* was never very large; some estimates place it around 800 per week. But its reach was still significant, given that the largest-circulation daily newspaper, James Watson Webb's *Courier and Enquirer*, had only 4,500 subscribers. The mere existence of the *Journal* "redefined the rest of the New York City media as a white press, expressing the opinions of their white constituents, and publishing in the interests of white people," concludes historian Craig Steven Wilder.[8] Cornish and Russwurm's success may have even inspired the city's nascent movement of white mechanics and workingmen to start their own press, since the first workers' paper appeared in the city only four years after the launch of *Freedom's Journal*.

The *Journal's* impact on the black population outside New York, moreover, was far greater than its circulation numbers might indicate. A letter that appeared in William Lloyd Garrison's *Liberator* in 1831 hints at the paper's extensive underground reach. Written by a man who had traveled a few years earlier through a Southern slave state, the letter noted:

I chanced one morning, very early, to look through the curtains of my chamber window, which opened upon a back yard. I saw a mulatto with a newspaper in his hand, surrounded by a score of colored men, who were listening, open mouthed, to a very inflammatory article the yellow man was reading ... I afterwards learned that the paper was published in New York, and addressed to blacks.[9]

Freedom's Journal provided the first public forum for blacks to debate among themselves strategies for their own liberation. Chief among those debates was how freedmen should regard the influential American Colonization Society. The paper's May 18, 1827 issue, for instance, contained a stinging rebuke to a speech by Henry Clay at the American Colonization Society's annual meeting in Washington. Identifying himself only as "A Man of Colour," the writer insisted that the Society's growth "cannot be viewed in any other light, then a desire to get effectually rid of the free people." Both Southern slaveholders and Northern philanthropists "who have at all times espoused the cause of the oppressed" were united around the Society's plan, he warned, and were ignoring widespread black opposition to it. "At a meeting lately held in Philadelphia of the most respectable people of colour, consisting of nearly three thousand persons, to take this subject into consideration, there was not one who was in favor of leaving this country; but they were opposed to colonization in any *foreign* country whatever."[10]

While the *Journal* initially editorialized against the ACS, it later published some articles supportive of its goals. Cornish and Russwurm quickly adopted opposing views on the issue, and some historians have suggested those differences led to the severing of their partnership and to the resignation of Cornish as co-editor just six months after they launched the paper.[11] Others discount that as the reason for their split. They point out that Russwurm continued to editorialize against the ACS after Cornish resigned, though the paper's criticism of colonization became less frequent and less emphatic.[12]

Russwurm continued to publish *Freedom's Journal* until March of 1829. By then he had turned bitterly pessimistic about the future for blacks in America, and he shocked New York's freedmen by suddenly announcing he had adopted the Colonization Society's goals of emigration to Africa. "In the bosom of the most enlightened government, we are ignorant and degraded," he declared in his last issue, on March 28. "Under the most republican government, we are denied all the rights and privileges of citizens, and what is worse, we see no probability that we as a community will ever make it our earnest endeavor to rise from our ignorance and degradation."[13]

Shortly after he closed the paper, Russwurm abandoned New York and moved to Liberia. There he became editor of the *Liberia Herald* and later served as superintendent of that country's public schools.[14]

Samuel Cornish and The Rights of All

After Russwurm's departure, Cornish moved to fill the void by launching a new publication, *The Rights of All*. In the first issue of the new paper he expressed surprise at his former partner's conversion. Returning to Africa might help a few free blacks that emigrated, Cornish acknowledged, but, "[a]s it respects three million that are now in the United States ... we think [colonization] in no wise calculated, to meet their wants or ameliorate their condition."[15]

Unfortunately, *The Rights of All* survived for only a few months, and once it closed its doors no other black publication appeared for another eight years. In January 1837, Philip Bell and a group of the city's black abolitionists began to publish the *Weekly Advocate*. They immediately enlisted as its new editor Cornish, who in the intervening years had turned even more hostile toward any colonization schemes. "It matters not to us what features it may assume whether it present itself in the garb of philanthropy, or assumes the mild and benign countenance of Christianity, or comes with the selfish aspect of Politics," he wrote in the new paper. "[W]e will believe, assert and maintain (So help us God!) that we are opposed to the exclusive emigration and colonization of the People of Color of these United States."[16]

Another New York clergyman, Charles Bennett Ray, joined Cornish and Bell in their new publishing venture. Ray hailed originally from Massachusetts, had attended Wesleyan University, and had worked as a boat-maker in New York before being ordained in 1837. The three men changed the paper's name to the *Colored American* and pledged in its inaugural issue to disseminate the "well-known sentiments" of blacks "on the subjects of Abolition and Colonization—the enactment of equal laws, and a full and free investiture of their rights as men and citizens."[17]

The *Colored American* continued to publish until 1841, and during that time it became an uncompromising advocate for the citizenship rights of black New Yorkers. When city officials denied licenses to black carters and porters, for instance, the *Colored American* took up their cause. "Any colored citizen, who with a respectful petition and recommendation in his hand, applies for a license as a carman or porter, is entitled to them," the paper told its readers, "and the authority which withholds them, alike violates the laws of the land, of humanity, and of God."[18] The paper sharply criticized the lack of standards in the mainstream press. One article in 1840 labeled James Gordon Bennett's *Herald* so abysmal as "to vitiate all correct tastes, corrupt all the social and moral habits, and morally degrade human beings."[19] Cornish blasted fellow white editors for their growing obsession with newspaper revenues. "How corrupt the journals of our country and the world," he wrote in 1837. "How much self-interest is apparent on the face of most of our newspapers! A greater disposition to court public favor, to proselytize public sentiment, and to procure gold and silver patronage, cannot be found among any class of the community, than among editors."[20]

The Second Generation

By the 1840s, a new and more outspoken generation of black editors and publishers began to emerge in the North. The first generation—Russwurm,

Cornish, and Bell—had all been prominent members of the country's small black middle class. Born free men, each had managed to secure an excellent education. They had utilized their newspapers to appeal to white society in a civil and respectful—some would say an almost submissive—manner. But they dared not directly champion the abolition of the slave system. That submissive tone changed dramatically with the second generation of editors, a group that included Frederick Douglass, Henry Highland Garnet, Martin Delany and David Ruggles. Several of these men were one-time slaves, and largely self-educated, and they harbored no illusions about the hostility they faced from white America.

The papers they founded clamored boldly for full emancipation, and they consciously used their list of subscribers to create a national network of black freedom advocates. Just as Benjamin Edes and Samuel Adams had once used the rebel colonial sheets to agitate for independence from England, black editors sought to organize and give voice to a two-pronged freedom struggle: against slavery in the South and for full citizenship in the North.

By 1833, white abolitionists William Lloyd Garrison and Arthur Tappan had founded the radical American Anti-Slavery Society (see Chapter 3). As the new group stepped up its opposition to the American Colonization Society, the ranks of the abolitionist movement swelled and cooperation began to blossom between white and black anti-slavery editors. White abolitionists even started to subscribe to black newspapers, and in the case of Douglass's *North Star* they at times outnumbered its black subscribers by as much as five-to-one.[21]

Perhaps the most audacious of all the black editors of the period was David Ruggles, the founder of the *Mirror of Liberty*. Born in Norwich, Connecticut, in 1810 to lower-middle-class parents, Ruggles actually bridged the two generations, though he was spiritually closer to the second. He moved to New York at the age of seventeen, and found work initially as a seaman, before opening a grocery store that he gradually turned into the country's first black-owned print shop and bookstore. An early convert to the temperance movement, Ruggles sponsored advertisements in *Freedom's Journal* warning fellow blacks about the dangers of alcohol. By 1833 he had joined the anti-slavery movement and become an agent and correspondent for the *Emancipator*, an abolitionist weekly. He also wrote for Samuel Cornish's *Colored American*.

But Ruggles was more than a man of letters. He risked his life repeatedly to protect fugitive slaves from the many white bounty hunters in the city—men who would routinely kidnap blacks, then quietly arrange, with the connivance of local officials, to ship their shackled captives back South. The victims were often children or local residents who had been legally born free citizens in the North. As an organizer and treasurer of the New York City Vigilance Committee, Ruggles offered food, sanctuary, and legal assistance to escaped slaves and openly confronted the kidnappers of black youths, all of which earned him the enmity of the city's most influential slavery advocates. He was jailed several times in such street-corner confrontations, and a mob once burned down his print shop. Nonetheless, he persevered, and on two occasions he even secured the arrest of white ship captains under federal anti-slave-shipping laws.[22] Both the *Colored American* and Ruggles's own *Mirror of Liberty* publicized numerous examples of such abductions. "A colored man, named Rufus Kinsman, is now confined in the Calaboose in New Orleans as a fugitive slave," the *Colored American* reported in 1841. "He affirms he is a free man, is a native of New Haven, Conn., has sailed as a seaman from Hartford and NY."[23]

One of the fugitive slaves Ruggles protected was Frederick Douglass, who arrived in New York in 1838 after fleeing from Baltimore. "I had been in New York but a few days, when Mr. Ruggles sought me out, and very kindly took me to his boarding house at the corner of Church and Lespenard St. [also the offices for the *Mirror of Liberty*]," Douglass revealed in his autobiography. "Mr. Ruggles was then ... attending as well to a number of other fugitive slaves, devising ways and means for their successful escape; and, though watched and hemmed in on almost every side, he seemed to be more than a match for his enemies."[24]

By 1837 the Vigilance Committee proudly reported that its members had protected 335 blacks from being sent back into captivity. Despite that extraordinary success, Ruggles fell into financial ruin and disgrace only a few years later. The cause of his downfall was an article he wrote in 1839 for the *Colored American*, in which he accused a black hotel owner of assisting white slave-catchers. The man sued the paper for libel and won a $600 judgment. It was a financial calamity for Cornish and his cash-strapped newspaper. The elder editor had always been uncomfortable with the younger man's militant activities. Cornish now turned against Ruggles, condemned him in the pages of the *Colored American*, and sought to ostracize him from the city's anti-slavery movement. Ruggles, who was already suffering from chronic health problems and going blind, felt deeply betrayed. He abandoned the city and moved to Massachusetts, where he died in 1849—at the tender age of thirty-nine.[25]

By the time of Ruggles's death, Douglass had moved to Rochester, founded his own newspaper, the *North Star* (1847), and emerged as a national spokesman for the abolitionist movement. He had also become a close friend and disciple of William Lloyd Garrison. The latter's paper, the *Liberator*, was in many ways a "black" newspaper; or at least our nation's first racially integrated paper. For one thing, Garrison expressly aimed it at the country's black inhabitants, even addressing them in its pages as "my countrymen." Not surprisingly, the majority of subscribers in its early years were African-American. Garrison was also the first white editor to publish prominent black writers of his era, including Douglass, poet Phyllis Wheatley, and abolitionist agitator Maria W. Stewart.[26] Garrison seldom missed an opportunity to laud black progress. As his finest biographer, Henry Mayer, has noted,

> The columns of The Liberator hailed the accomplishments of black students in the schools the editor regularly visited, and the newspaper faithfully reported the musicales, oratorical contests, and self-improvement lecture courses in Boston's black community. The Liberator, too, could be counted on to promote and publish the proceedings of the growing number of black political conventions ...[27]

The Black Convention Movement

The series of black conventions that occurred before the Civil War were historic gatherings where black leaders openly debated the most effective methods and tactics to achieve their freedom in America. Black editors publicized those gatherings in their papers, they participated actively in the debates among the delegates, and they reprinted the key speeches and resolutions.

Both Samuel Cornish and Philip A. Bell, who would later work together on the *Colored American*, for example, were among the forty delegates to the first National Negro Convention in Philadelphia in 1830.[28] At least four black editors were among the seventy delegates who attended the contentious August 1843 convention in Buffalo, New York. Douglass represented Massachusetts at that gathering, though he had not yet launched the first of what would be six different newspapers he would be associated with. Also attending that convention were Charles B. Ray, former editor and publisher of New York's *Colored American*, Henry Highland Garnet, co-editor of the *National Watchman* (1842–1847) in Troy, New York, and J. H. Townsend, who would later found and co-edit the *Mirror of the Times* (1856), California's first black newspaper.

The 1843 convention was dominated by a now legendary dispute between Douglass, the meeting's vice-president, and Garnet, chair of the assembly's business committee. Their dispute centered on the appropriate strategy blacks should pursue to end slavery. Like his mentor Garrison, Douglass espoused racial assimilation. He favored moral and religious appeals to the white majority and deeply believed in the country's Democratic ideals. Garnet, on the other hand, favored open rebellion—the approach first espoused in *David Walker's Appeal* fourteen years earlier. In a speech to the delegates, Garnet urged an immediate uprising:

> You had far better all die—immediately—than live slaves and entail your wretchedness upon your posterity. If you would be free in this generation,

here is your only hope. However much you and all of us may desire it, there is not much hope of redemption without the shedding of blood. If you must bleed, let it all come at once—rather die freemen, than live to be slaves.[29]

His words electrified the convention, brought many delegates to tears, and swayed most of those present against the less confrontational approach of Douglass. Garnet's passionate oratory no doubt drew fuel from the enormous suffering he had endured throughout his life. Tall and handsome, the proud grandson of a Mandingo warrior prince, he had been just nine years old when his father led their family of eleven in a daring escape from slavery in Maryland in 1824. The family eventually settled in New York City's Five Points section. One day in 1829, Garnet returned home from a stint working as a cook and steward on a ship only to learn that, during his absence, slave-catchers had surrounded his parents' home, captured his sister, destroyed their belongings, and scattered the rest of the family into hiding. The following year, while working on a farm in Long Island, he suffered a severe knee injury that reduced him to walking on crutches for the rest of his life. By then he had begun to study for the ministry.

In 1835, Garnet and Alexander Crummell, son of New York black leader Boston Crummell, enrolled in an interracial school in New Hampshire that had been founded by abolitionists. A mob of local townspeople attacked the school, set it on fire, and began shooting into the students' living quarters. Garnet bravely discharged his own gun at the attackers in self-defense. He and Crummell somehow escaped, fled back to New York State, and eventually completed their education at the Oneida Institute in Whitesboro. Garnet was still hobbled by his knee injury, however, and doctors were forced to amputate his leg in December 1840. He was appointed first pastor of the Liberty Street Presbyterian Church in Troy two years later. There, together with fellow abolitionist William H. Allen, he founded the *National Watchman*. Unfortunately, no copies of their newspaper or of more than a dozen other ante-bellum black newspapers have been preserved.

Given the repeated violence and misfortune that marked his life, Garnet's fiery call for a black uprising at the Buffalo convention is understandable. But his speech brought determined opposition from Douglass. "There was too much physical force, both in the address and the remarks of the speaker," Douglass said afterward, perhaps also seeing in the charismatic Garnet a threat to his own leadership.[30] Militant rhetoric was not the only thing that distinguished Garnet from Douglass. Garrison and Douglass rejected the ballot box and called instead for a moral awakening of white society as the only way to end slavery—a stance Douglass would later renounce. Garnet believed that free blacks should abandon the United States, though not as part of any movement allied to the American Colonization Society.

Like another black nationalist editor, Martin R. Delany, who founded and edited the *Mystery* in Pittsburgh (1842), and who worked for a time on Douglass's *North Star*, Garnet came to believe that any other country would be more hospitable to free blacks than the United States. He developed his own plan for blacks to immigrate to Jamaica—a proposal strongly opposed by Douglass—and he even founded the African Civilization Society in 1859 to promote his goal. After the Civil War, Garnet put his beliefs into practice; he abandoned the United States for Liberia, where he died in 1881.[31]

Those early black editors and the national convention movement they helped initiate shaped the seminal differences in outlook and strategy that still exist today in African-American society—between assimilation and separation, between moral reform and militant rebellion, between arousing the masses of oppressed blacks to achieve full equality or depending on the talent and economic progress of a rising middle class to lift the entire population into full citizenship. Even as those editors debated their differences in print, they waged difficult personal battles to keep their publications afloat financially. Given the hostility they faced from white society, the paucity of advertising their papers attracted, the difficulty their subscribers had in paying on time, and the small percentage of blacks who were even literate, their publications had predictably short life-spans, and few achieved financial success. As a result, black editors and publishers were invariably forced to resort to full-time work as ministers, merchants, doctors, educators, or abolitionist lecturers, while they toiled in their spare time to produce their papers.

Douglass, Mary Ann Shadd Cary and the Rights of Women

Douglass, who would eventually edit six different newspapers, towered over all his colleagues in both the power of his writing and the influence of his publications. In early 1848, John O'Sullivan, editor of the *Democratic Review*, became so incensed at his growing fame that he published a particularly vicious attack on the "black vagabond Douglass, who spent his time in England propagating his filthy lies against the United States, which were greedily swallowed by English hypocrites and fools." When O'Sullivan learned that a ship's captain had allowed Douglass to socialize on deck with whites during a return voyage from England, the *Review* called for the captain to be thrown overboard the next time he docked in New York harbor. Douglass reprinted the article in full, then reprimanded the *Review* and several other anti-black New York newspapers:

> Had the New York Express, Sun, or Herald, used the language above, we
> should not have taken any notice of it; their pro-slavery malice being

widely known and well understood; and being also understood to belong to the bloodhound class of American newspapers, whose business it is to hunt negroes for their Southern masters. From such as these we might well expect such things, but not from the Democratic Review. This periodical has for some time been regarded as a decent and respectable print; and it is therefore somewhat surprising to find it dealing in coarse and vulgar abuse, and coolly counseling the citizens of New York to Lynch Capt. Judkins.[32]

The ethical and political challenge Douglass and other black editors posed to our nation's established commercial press went far beyond the issues of slavery and racial discrimination. Like Garrison and other leading abolitionists, Douglass was far ahead of his time as an outspoken champion of women's rights. He attended the July 1848 Seneca Falls convention that launched the modern feminist movement and signed its declaration. An article in the *North Star* the following January headlined "Girls Hold Up Your Heads" urged the need for women to achieve the "complete development" of their intellectual powers, and it lampooned men who viewed women as a "mere satellite, a plaything, an ornament—anything, in short, but a being possessing equal rights."[33]

Douglass backed up his rhetoric by providing space in his newspapers for several black women writers, among them Mary Ann Shadd Cary, the educator, feminist and abolitionist who would become the first African-American woman to edit a newspaper in North America. A light-skinned mulatto, Shadd had been born into a prosperous free black family in Delaware. She ran several schools for black children throughout the North, and later taught the children of fugitive slaves in Canada. [34]

Shadd's biggest impact, however, came through the combative ideas she expressed in her writings. Her first article in the *North Star*, in 1849, delivered a stinging rebuke against a "corrupt clergy among us" who were "inculcating ignorance as a duty, superstition as true religion." Such clergymen, she said, urged their congregations to "pay no attention to your perishing bodies … but get your souls converted … Thus any effort to a change of conditions of our people is replied to, and a shrinking, priest-rid people, are prevented from seeing clearly." Shadd penned those words in direct response to an article by Rev. Henry Highland Garnet, which Douglass had published a few weeks earlier. She went on to ridicule the rest of the established black leadership: "We have been holding conventions for years—have been assembling together and whining over our difficulties and afflictions, passing resolutions on resolutions," she noted, yet "we have made but little progress" and "have put forth few practical efforts to an end. We should do more, and talk less." She even took a subtle swipe at Douglass by criticizing leaders who claimed "[t]he elective franchise would not profit you."[35]

Shadd remained deeply skeptical throughout her life that any real support for black liberation would come from outside the black community. She favored instead a strategy of self-reliance by free blacks on their own abilities, while at the same time she defended the rights of women within the broader emancipation movement. Her pessimism eventually turned her into an advocate of emigration. After Congress passed the Fugitive Slave Law, she left the country for Canada, where she founded a weekly newspaper, the *Provincial Freeman*, in Windsor on March 24, 1853, and convinced veteran journalist Samuel Ringgold Ward to become the paper's editor.[36] In a measure of her stature, Frederick Douglass himself praised Shadd's "unconquerable zeal and commendable ability," noting, in 1855, "We do not know her equal among the colored ladies of the United States."[37]

Douglass and the Mexican War

Douglass mounted eloquent challenges to another accepted view of his contemporary white editors—Manifest Destiny. He condemned the US war against Mexico as an act of aggression, and boldly asserted the conflict was fueled by racial prejudice toward the Mexican people. It was not an easy stance to take, even for a white editor. It is in times of war, after all, that freedom of the press confronts its greatest test. Editors who dare to oppose our nation's wars have faced not only the fury of the public and of advertisers, but official condemnation, censorship, suspension of postal privileges.

Not surprisingly, most American newspapers backed President Polk's call for war with Mexico, though some Whig papers did so reluctantly. The New York penny papers, along with the New Orleans dailies, took the lead in coverage of the conflict.[38]

A few months into the war, the *New Orleans Tropic* blasted Polk for the "national disgrace" of considering peace talks before the American military had totally conquered Mexico. "We hope that Mr. Polk will not *sue for peace under any circumstances*," warned an editorial. "Let our Government dictate one in the city of Mexico, to that weak and imbecile Government—we want no compromise ..."[39]

Not all US papers, of course, favored the war. A handful of abolitionist and religious publications generally condemned it as a naked grab for more territory, one aimed at expanding Southern slavery. They criticized opposition Whigs in Congress who kept voting more funds to pay for the fighting. In the early days of the conflict, the editor of one of those anti-war publications, the *Cincinnati Weekly Herald and Philanthropist*, directly chastised his colleagues for their cowardice:

There are those editors who in their hearts abhor the Mexican war, and could scarcely be forced to march upon Mexico themselves, but are loud in their exhortations to others to enlist in defense of their country. Why are they not honest? Why have they not the courage to rise above the pitiful denunciations of treason, and proclaim their true sentiments?[40]

Douglass, meanwhile, published several front-page anti-war articles and speeches by its major critics in his *North Star*, and penned his own scathing criticisms of the conflict's origins and progress. On January 21st, 1848, he pilloried all the major political parties, the national press, and "our slave-holding president," saying:

> The taste of human blood and smell of powder seem to have extinguished the senses, seared the conscience, and subverted the reason of the people … "Fire and sword" are now the choice of our young republic. The loss of thousands of her own men, and the slaughter of tens of thousands of the sons and daughters of Mexico, have rather given edge than dullness to our appetite for fiery conflict and plunder.

Douglass rebuked the country's religious leaders for being "silent as the grave," adding:

> [T]heir silence is the greatest sanction of the crime. They have seen the blood of the innocent poured out like water, and are dumb; they have seen the truth trampled in the dust—right sought by pursuing the wrong—and have not raised a whisper against it; they float down with the multitude in the filthy current of crime, and are hand in hand with the guilty.[41]

Two months later, a front-page article in the *North Star* depicted horrific scenes of civilian carnage and lamented the lack of public outcry. Its apocalyptic words seem today an eerie precursor of anti-war sentiment that would unfold generations later during similar US military adventures in the Philippines, Vietnam and Iraq:

> We have seen for eighteen months, the work of mutilation, crime and death go on, each advancing step sunk deeper in human gore. By every mail has come some new deed of violence.—Cities have been attacked, and the cry of helpless women and children has risen, amid the shrieks and agony of death and dishonor. The living have gone forth, and dead corpses encased in lead have returned. Thousands of widows and orphans have sent up to the heavens their pitiful wail …
> And yet all is quiet as under the most perfect despotism. There is no united appeal, which would make the rulers tremble; no thronging voices of petition, no indignant rebuke, no prayer, "Lord, how long?"[42]

To Douglass the cause of the war was obvious, no matter what political leaders in Washington claimed: "[T]his, from the first, has been a war of conquest. No conditions of peace have been offered except coupled with the demand of surrender of Territory ..."[43]

As the most influential black editor of the nineteenth century, Douglass made opposition to empire an acceptable view among black journalists. After him, the black press would prove far more willing to question America's foreign wars than any other section of the national press.

"The Chinese Must Go!"

[T]he Brannan Street butchers set their dogs on a Chinaman who was quietly passing with a basket of clothes on his head; and while the dogs mutilated his flesh, a butcher increased the hilarity of the occasion by knocking some of the Chinaman's teeth down his throat with half a brick. This incident sticks in my memory with a more malevolent tenacity, perhaps, on account of the fact that I was in the employ of a San Francisco journal at the time, and was not allowed to publish it because it might offend some of the peculiar element that subscribed for the paper.

Mark Twain, 1875

Thousands of impoverished immigrants from southern China were among the flood of prospectors from around the world who sought instant wealth in California during the Gold Rush of 1849. Over the next few decades, the Chinese turned San Francisco into a booming metropolis of 100,000 people and formed an essential part of the labor force of the Far West. During construction of the transcontinental railroad's western spur, for instance, some 15,000 of the 17,000 laborers hired by the Central Pacific Company were Chinese; once the railroad was completed, many of those laborers turned to agriculture, so that by 1886 nine out of ten farm workers in the state were Chinese.[1]

After a brief initial period in which the press portrayed them with benign curiosity, California newspapers and a few influential sheets back east took to denigrating and demonizing the Chinese as a threat to the American way of life. They were "a worse class to have among us than the negro," said one 1853 editorial in the *San Francisco Daily Alta Californian*. "They are idolatrous in their religion—in their disposition cunning and deceitful, and in their habits libidinous and offensive ... They do not mix with our people and it is undesirable that they should ..."[2]

The first Chinese-language newspapers to appear in the US, *Golden Hills News* (1854) and the *Oriental* (1855), were published by American missionaries and merchants who wanted both to spread the gospel and to market goods to the bourgeoning population of Chinese consumers. Those early

sheets helped the new arrivals adjust to life in America, and they provided
Anglo society with a more dispassionate picture of the immigrants through
uplifting accounts of the community that were translated into English.

Independent Chinese journalism in America did not take hold until 1856,
with the publication of the *Chinese Daily News* in Sacramento—the first
Chinese-language paper in the world. By the end of the nineteenth century,
more than twenty-five Chinese papers had appeared in eight US cities. A
surge of Chinese, Japanese, and Korean publications in both the US and
Hawaii followed during the early twentieth century. Unfortunately, virtually
none of our early journalism historians read Chinese, and American libraries preserved few copies of those early papers. A more accurate portrayal of
the Chinese press in America only began to emerge in the 1970s, when a
handful of scholars such as Karl Lo and Him Mark Lai published the initial
results of their research into personal records of early Chinese immigrants.

Until the Civil War, anti-Chinese stereotypes appeared mostly in the
newspapers of the Far West, but xenophobia toward the new immigrants
soon seeped into the wider culture to such an extent that it prompted Congress to pass the Chinese Exclusion Act of 1885—the first racially based
immigration policy in US history.

Opium, Gold and Early Chinese Immigration

On the eve of the Gold Rush, a mere fifty-four Chinese nationals resided in
San Francisco, but the number jumped to 789 the following year, and by 1852
there were 25,000 residing in the Golden State.[3] A handful of American and
British shippers had established ties with China as early as the 1820s, largely
through their illicit trafficking in opium. Narcotics soon represented two-
thirds of all British imports there, while virtually every American trading
house was shipping opium into China by 1840.[4]

The Chinese government's opposition to the trade led to the first Opium
War (1839–42). British warships occupied Shanghai and Hong Kong and
imposed the Treaty of Nanking, which forced China to cede control over
Hong Kong and effectively legalized the opium trade. Over the next 150
years—until its reversion to Chinese sovereignty in 1997—Hong Kong
served as the principal colonial outpost for the British Empire in Asia. In the
aftermath of the war, economic and social devastation spread across southern
China, with opium imports doubling and drug addiction spiraling.

In Canton, the city that had served for centuries as the only Chinese port
through which foreigners could legally conduct commerce, tens of thousands of dockworkers lost their jobs. Many of them fled abroad in search
of work, thus giving rise to the infamous coolie trade. By 1844 the British
were shipping Chinese coolies to their American colony of Guiana. A few
years later, Spain started using them on its plantations in Cuba and Peru.

American merchants shared in the wealth by transporting most of the contract workers to the New World. US merchant ships, for example, carried up to 6,000 Chinese laborers annually to Havana between 1847 and 1862.[5]

Changing Press Images of the Chinese

Initial press accounts of California's Chinese extolled them as model immigrants. "The quietness and order, cheerfulness and temperance which is observable in their habits is noticed by everyone," claimed one 1849 article in *Little's Living Age* about a group of Chinese construction workers. The following year, the *California Courier* praised the "China Boys" after they marched in spotless holiday attire in a local procession and received a bundle of religious pamphlets that city leaders imported for them from Canton. "We have never seen a finer-looking body of men collected together in San Francisco," the *Courier* reported. "In fact, this portion of our population is a pattern for sobriety, order and obedience to laws, not only to other foreign residents, but to Americans themselves."[6] As late as 1852, one San Francisco paper praised the "large number of celestials" in the city, noting, "the China Boys will yet vote at the same polls, study at the same schools and bow at the same altar as our own countrymen."[7]

But the frantic competition for gold soon transformed the Chinese into social outcasts. At first, the biggest conflicts in the gold fields were between Anglos and some 13,000 Mexican and Latin American migrant prospectors. Many of the latter were experienced miners, and they enjoyed greater success in the hunt for gold than the novice arrivals from back east.

In April 1850 the state legislature passed the Foreign Miners Tax. The law initially required all non-citizens to pay $20 each month for the right to mine, but Mexican, French, and German immigrants balked at paying the exorbitant fee. White vigilante groups then began expelling the tax resisters from the mining camps at gunpoint, and they usually targeted the Mexicans and Pacific Islanders for the harshest treatment. A wave of violence ensued, which prompted the state to lower the tax to $3 or $4 a month. But the damage was done.[8] A raft of new racially inspired laws were adopted with the aim of ensuring that white miners would dominate the gold fields. One ordinance stipulated that "no black or mulatto person, or Indian, shall be allowed to give evidence in favor of, or against a white man." Another banned all marriages between whites and Negroes or mulattos. Meanwhile, the new state constitution excluded blacks from citizenship by restricting the right to vote to "white male citizens."[9]

People v. Hall *and Racial Identity*

By 1852, white miners were once again complaining of foreign workers—
this time it was the Chinese. Influential papers like the *Daily Alta Californian*
began claiming that the Chinese were not white, and therefore should
be classed with blacks and mulattos as ineligible for any basic rights. An
investigation by the State Assembly concluded that the well-being of white
American workers was threatened by the "vast numbers of the Asiatic races
... and many others dissimilar from ourselves in customs, language and
education."[10]

Debate over the racial identity of the Chinese intensified after a white
man named George W. Hall killed a miner named Ling Sing in Nevada
County. A court convicted Hall of murder in October 1853 and sentenced
him to hang. But since the jury's verdict rested on the testimony of one Caucasian and three Chinese witnesses, Hall's lawyer appealed and claimed that
all statements from the Chinese witnesses should be invalidated by virtue
of California's 1850 criminal statute prohibiting testimony against whites by
blacks, Indians and mulattos.

The question of whether the Chinese were white thus fell squarely before
the California Supreme Court. Chief Justice Hugh C. Murray issued the
court's majority opinion in *People v. Hall* the following year, ruling that the
Chinese were non-white and that the testimony of the three Chinese witnesses was therefore inadmissible. The Chinese, Murray concluded, were "a
race of people whom nature has marked as inferior" and were "incapable of
progress or intellectual development beyond a certain point ... differing in
language, opinions, color and physical conformation; between whom and
ourselves nature has placed an impassable difference."[11]

The Hall decision further emboldened white miners; vigilantes soon
began terrorizing the Chinese in their own camps and ordering them to
leave the fields altogether. As Iris Chang has documented, in 1856 whites in
Mariposa County gave the Chinese ten days to evacuate or "be subjected to
thirty-nine lashes, and moved by force of arms," and in El Dorado County,
white miners burned Chinese tents and mining equipment.[12]

So deeply did Sinophobia pervade Californian culture that even Native
Americans and *Californios* took to persecuting the new arrivals. One
Sacramento newspaper reported in 1853 that

> a party of six "digger" Indians came down from the mountains a few days
> since and ... met an equal number of Chinamen. The chief advanced and
> demanded their poll-tax. This they obstinately refused to pay. The chief
> then demanded of them to show their receipts. They refused to do this
> also. The Indian then shot one of them, whereupon they capitulated and
> paid over $18. The "diggers" then returned, evidently well satisfied.[13]

Likewise, the following article appeared in a San Francisco newspaper in 1860:

> A party of Indians entered a China cabin with thieving intent, and indignant at not finding any money, proceeded to chop the Celestial occupants up in a cruel manner. One of them has died since. Instances are related where Diggers have taken the cue from the Sheriff, and compelled Chinamen to pay [the miners'] license ...[14]

Joaquín Murieta, the Mexican bandit immortalized by John Rollin Ridge in his novel, repeatedly attacked Chinese miners in their camps, tortured them to reveal where their gold dust was hidden, tied their pigtails together, and on occasion slit their throats.[15]

It did not take long for anti-Chinese stories to appear in papers far removed from the gold fields. In 1854, Bayard Taylor, the famed correspondent for the New York *Tribune*, described the Chinese in one dispatch as "uncivilized, unclean and filthy beyond all conception ... Pagan in religion, they know not the virtues of honesty, integrity or good faith." A Hong Kong correspondent for *Harper's Weekly* described Chinese coolies in 1858 as "half-horse, [and] half stevedore," and described "Celestial ladies" as having the "baboon-like faces of Hong-Kong women."[16]

Mark Twain and the Chinese

One of the few journalists in California to depict the Chinese sympathetically was Mark Twain, who worked at several state newspapers during the 1860s and 1870s. But even Twain was known on occasion to lend his acid pen to racial stereotypes. In one article, he described his visit to the city jail to view nineteen Chinese girls who authorities had detained after their arrival on a ship from Hong Kong. The girls, Twain learned, had been kidnapped in China to be sold into slavery in America. "Some of them are almost good-looking, and none of them are pitted with small pox," Twain wrote. "We would suggest, just here that the room where these unfortunates are confined is rather too close for good health, and besides, the more fresh air that blows on a Chinaman, the better he smells."[17]

But Twain also produced some richly detailed accounts of Chinese life, as in this report on the opening of a new Chinese temple in the city:

> The house and its embellishments cost about eighty thousand dollars ... and will be well worth visiting ... There was one room half full of priests, all fine, dignified, intelligent looking men like Ah Wae, and all dressed in long blue silk robes, and blue and red topped skull caps with broad brims turned up all round like wash-basins ... and those who are fond of that

sort of thing would do well to stand ready to accept the forthcoming public invitation.[18]

In "John Chinamen in New York," a sketch he wrote years later about a New York tea merchant, Twain wrote:

> Is it not a shame that we, who prate so much about civilization and human-ity, are content to degrade a fellow-being to such an office as this ... In my heart I pitied the friendless Mongol. I wondered what was passing behind his sad face, and what distant scene his vacant eye was dreaming of. Were his thoughts with his heart, ten thousand miles away, beyond the billowy wastes of the Pacific? Among the ricefields and the plumy palms of China? Under the shadows of remembered mountain peaks, or in groves of bloomy shrubs and strange forest trees unknown to climes like ours?[19]

C.O. Cummings was another California journalist who stood out for his occasional sympathetic reports on the Chinese. As editor of the *Watsonville Pajornian*, Cummings even showcased the writings of a Chinese immigrant. In 1871, he published Chung Sun's account of his first harrowing months in the US, including an incident where the newcomer was beaten and robbed in Los Angeles. "The ill treatment of [my] own countrymen may perhaps be excused on the grounds of race, color, language and religion," Chung said in his first letter, "but such prejudice can only prevail among the ignorant." In a second letter he called the United States "a jumble of confusion and a labyrinth of contradictions."[20]

White Labor Leads the Attack

By the 1870s, white hostility toward the Chinese had reached fever pitch, much of it fueled by newspaper stereotypes. Western workers had watched with increasing dismay during the previous decade as corporations like the Central Pacific railroad dispatched agents to China to recruit thousands of laborers to build the transcontinental railroad. They were furious that the railroad barons then used those Chinese, who were usually willing to work longer hours for less pay than their white counterparts, as pawns with which to resist demands for better salaries and working conditions from their American employees.[21]

Massive rallies of San Francisco's unemployed became commonplace, and out of those gatherings arose Dennis Kearney, leader of California's Work-ingmen's Party. An Irish immigrant and former railroad employee with a knack for fiery speeches, Kearney steered workers' rage not only against the railroads and land barons, but also against the Chinese. Every Kearney speech ended with the war cry: "The Chinese must go!"

During the Great Railroad Strike of 1877, San Francisco's labor leaders called for a massive support rally on July 23rd for strikers back east. More than 7,000 showed up near City Hall. As the rally ended, a section of the protesters broke off and descended on Chinatown, destroying fifteen Chinese laundries and shooting several Chinese bystanders. Over the next two days, four people were killed and fourteen wounded in the worst rioting in the city's history.[22] "Nothing can be said in defense of such violence," the *Bulletin* warned the following day. "It is the beginning of anarchy and the destruction of all lawful government."[23]

But while they railed against the lawlessness, the local papers shared the disdain of the workers for the Chinese and urged their eviction from town. The *Bulletin*, for instance, published a statement by the "Committee of Safety," a vigilante group of prominent city leaders that formed to help police restore order:

> In common with all the inhabitants of the State we are embarrassed by what is properly called the Chinese question, and are most desirous to see its early solution in a manner satisfactory to our whole people ... But however desirable it may appear that this disturbing element should finally be withdrawn and removed from our midst, we are unanimous in the conviction that violence will not hasten its proper adjustment, and may produce incalculable injury to all.[24]

Subsequent *Bulletin* articles alerted readers about a meeting of the anti-Chinese Workingmen's Association in San José, which urged "systematic organizing" as the "the best method of opposing the Chinese evil." The platform of the Sacramento Republican Party, the paper noted, called for a new treaty with China because "the interests of labor in California suffer so deeply from the great and constantly increasing number of Chinese."[25]

Most major newspapers and public figures in the country soon began to demand restrictions on further Chinese immigration.[26] Chinese exclusion became a "panacea for a complex web of problems," notes historian Andrew Gyory, "with politicians striving to turn a regional, cross-class issue into a national working-class demand."[27] The five most important Irish newspapers in New York all espoused anti-Chinese views. "We want white people to enrich the country, not Mongolians to degrade and disgrace it," wrote the editor of the *Irish Citizen*, thus replicating the same kind of intolerance Irish immigrants had themselves encountered a generation earlier.[28]

But it was in the mining areas of the Far West that such views found the most receptivity. "Mongolian hordes" were preventing women in Helena from "making a living," claimed an 1866 report in the *Radiator*. "We are being ruined by Chinese thieving," began an 1879 article in Wyoming's *Cheyenne Daily Leader*. In Southern Wyoming, Legh Freeman, editor of the *Frontier Index*, openly called his newspaper anti-black, anti-Indian and anti-Chinese. "The RACES and SEXES in their respective spheres as God Almighty created them," was the motto of his editorial page.[29]

One 1878 article in the *San Francisco Chronicle* described "how the Mongolian octopus developed and fastened its tentacles upon the city," while a study of newspaper articles in Astoria, Oregon, found such denigrating statements as: "It is just as natural for a Chinaman to steal as it is for a sponge to absorb water," and "Every Chinaman is a faucet inserted into the land, draining a stream of gold, small or large, into the land of his birth."[30]

Such sentiments were not unique to the western press. In 1870, columnist John Swinton wrote in the New York *Tribune*: "Can we afford to permit the transfusion into the national veins of the blood more debased than any we have known? Can we afford to offer the opportunity for this sort of mongrelism?"[31]

The Democratic Party, which had been dramatically weakened as the party of slavery, consciously sought after the Civil War to build support among western workers by attacking Chinese immigrants. This manufactured public outcry culminated in the Chinese Exclusion Act of 1882, which effectively banned new immigration from China for ten years. The new law marked a dramatic shift in US immigration history, by introducing race-based restrictions on who could enter the country.[32] Congress would repeatedly extend the Exclusion Act in the decades that followed. But instead of mollifying opponents of the Chinese, the new law only inspired a movement to expel those immigrants already in the country. It was called the "Driving Out" movement, and was marked by horrific mob violence, with several Chinese communities in the west subjected "to a level of violence that approached genocide," according to Iris Chang.[33]

In November 1885, for example, angry whites raided Chinatown in Tacoma, Washington, dragged 600 Chinese from their homes, and herded them onto train cars in a driving rain, where they were transported to Portland. Two of the immigrants died in the process. The incidents in Tacoma and several other cities came on the heels of an even more tragic outbreak in the mining community of Rock Springs, Wyoming. On September 2nd of that year, a white mob furious at increased competition for jobs from local Chinese surrounded the large Chinatown neighborhood there, ordered its residents to leave within an hour, then began setting fire to their shacks and shooting down the fleeing victims. When the smoke cleared, twenty-eight Chinese lay dead, fifteen had been wounded, dozens were missing, and some 100 houses had been destroyed. It was the worst incident of anti-Chinese violence in our nation's history.[34]

The Early Chinese Press

A handful of Chinese-language newspapers provided the only consistent counterpoint to reigning Sinophobia in nineteenth-century America. That press was born on April 22nd, 1854, when the merchant firm of Howard & Hudson began publication of *Kin Shan Jit San Luk* ("The Golden Hills News"), a weekly, four-page lithographed sheet whose articles were handwritten by Chinese brush.[35]

William D. M. Howard, the firm's principal owner and one of California's earliest Anglo pioneers, arrived in the territory in 1839 and established himself as a merchant in Yerba Buena, the village that later became San Francisco. During the Gold Rush years, Howard made a fortune supplying prefabricated houses for the thousands of new arrivals and built the city's Central Wharf. He also became a prominent philanthropist, was active in civic work among local Chinese residents, and established a post office for the new immigrants.[36]

One of the earliest editions of *Golden Hills News* noted that Rev. William Speer, a former missionary in China, had recently established a Chinese chapel at the Stockton Street Presbyterian Church, and that both the chapel and the newspaper were "intended to relieve the pressure of religious ignorance, settle and explain our laws, assist the Chinese to provide their wants and soften, dignify and improve their general character." *Golden Hills News* appears to have lasted only a few months, however, and very few copies have been preserved.[37]

The second newspaper, *Tung-ngai san-luk* ("The Oriental"), was launched by Rev. Speer himself on January 4, 1855. It was published three times a week, was more religious in tone, and featured a weekly column in English where its owner penned items to enlighten the Anglo community about Chinese affairs. In the inaugural edition, Speer promised the paper would be a "vehicle of religious and general knowledge, of late news, or whatever may tend to draw the Chinese into the tide of our nation's advancement."[38] He named as his associate editor Lai Sai, a former student at the Morrison Education Society School in Hong Kong and the first Chinese elder in San Francisco's Presbyterian Church. Lai Sai (also known as Lee Kan) was largely responsible for the Chinese content of the *Oriental*.[39] The pages of the *Oriental* provide an invaluable record of events in the Chinese community. In February 1855, for instance, the paper printed the reply by San Francisco's Chinese merchants to Governor Bugler's anti-Chinese message to the legislature. The following year it printed the first directory of Chinese businesses in the city.[40]

Unfortunately, *Golden Hills News* and the *Oriental* both perpetuated a white racial narrative. Like the earliest newspapers in China that arose around the same time, they were started and managed by American businessmen and missionaries who considered the Chinese an inferior group, and who—in their own benign but thoroughly paternalistic manner—saw their role as spreading Christianity and Western ideals among a heathen population.

In December 1856, around the time the *Oriental* ceased publication, Ze Too Yune, a Chinese businessman in Sacramento (he was also known as Hung Tai), launched the *Daily News*. Priced at 25¢ a week, its circulation was only around 200, yet it holds the distinction of being the first Chinese-owned daily published anywhere in the world, since it was launched more than a year before mainland China's first daily, *Chung ngoi san po* (1858). The Sacramento *Daily News*, like its predecessors in San Francisco, survived less than two years. Its frequency of publication dropped first to tri-weekly, then weekly, then to irregular intervals, before it finally shut down. Nearly twenty years would pass before another Chinese newspaper was started in the US. In 1874, two American businessmen founded the *San Francisco China News*, a mercantile newspaper, while *T'ang fan kung pao* was launched by Chock Wong and J. Hoffman. The latter newspaper would last into the twentieth century under a variety of owners and names.[41]

Wong Chin Foo Demands Respect

The most celebrated immigrant Chinese editor of the nineteenth century was undoubtedly Wong Chin Foo, who founded the *Chinese-American*, a bilingual weekly, in New York City in 1883. By the time he turned to publishing, Wong was already a much sought-after public lecturer and a frequent contributor to English-language newspapers and magazines with his poems, sketches, and articles on Chinese culture and Buddhism. Having arrived in San Francisco in 1869 under the sponsorship of an American lady philanthropist who had met him in China, Wong quickly won a name for himself in the press for defending the rights of Chinese workers and for advocating an end to the use of opium in his own community.[42]

A slender man, smaller in stature than the average Chinese, with an angular face and large sparkling eyes, Wong cut a flamboyant figure in New York's literary society with his exquisite dark velvet jackets and petticoats, a black silk skull cap over his lustrous queue, and ornate shoes with thick one-inch soles. His razor-sharp humor, astonishing eloquence in English, and pointed challenges to stereotypes of Chinese life, endeared him to the large American crowds that turned out to hear him throughout the country. During one lecture at New York's Steinway Hall before a packed audience of more than 600, Wong provoked raucous laughter when he quipped: "I never knew that puppies were good to eat until I was told by American people."[43]

In an August 1883 article in the *New York Times*, he ridiculed the commonly accepted belief that Chinese ate rats and cats, even offering a $500 reward if anyone could prove otherwise. But his foray into newspaper publishing fizzled quickly. When he tried to expose gambling and opium smoking in New York, some Chinese toughs invaded his office and beat up his staff," notes journalist Arthur Bonner in a delightful portrait of Wong, while a major Chinese gambler promptly slapped the new editor with a libel suit.[44]

The colorful Wong nonetheless remained a favorite of the city's Anglo press. In 1883, Denis Kearney, the chief spokesman for the anti-Chinese movement in America, visited New York. The city's Central Labor Union denied Kearney's request to address its members, whereupon he rented Cooper Hall on Astor Place to speak. Wong then publicly challenged Kearney to a duel to the death. "I give him his choice of chopsticks, Irish potatoes, or Krupp guns," he told one reporter. Kearney refused, and derided the challenge from a "representative of Asia's almond-eyed lepers."[45]

Despite the failure of the *Chinese-American*, and of a second paper he ran briefly in Chicago, Wong continued producing humorous and often provocative poems and articles for *Pucks* magazine and other publications. In one 1887 piece for the *North American Review*, titled "Why I am a Heathen," he wrote: "Love your neighbor as yourself is the great divine law which Christians and heathen alike hold but which Christians ignore. That is what keeps me the heathen that I am."[46]

He also kept up his zealous advocacy of the rights of his fellow immigrants, and was actually one of the first Chinese to coin the term Chinese-American. In 1892, Wong became a founding member of the Chinese Civil Rights League. The following year he testified for the League in Congress in opposition to further extension of the Chinese Exclusion Act, and in the decades that followed he repeatedly campaigned for extending the right to vote to Chinese-Americans.

Such are the outlines of the early Chinese-language press. Small in number and circulation, and largely controlled at first by American merchants and missionaries, it was for generations the least known of all the news media produced by people of color in this country. Robert E. Park's 1922 classic, *The Immigrant Press and Its Control*, for example, contained exhaustive tables on foreign-language publications in the US, but Park erroneously claimed the first two Chinese-language newspapers had appeared as late as 1885; Alfred McClung Lee's 1937 book, *The Daily Newspaper in America*, gave 1880 as the first year for a Chinese newspaper and listed only four publications before the turn of the century; Frank Luther Mott's highly regarded *American Journalism*, first published in 1962, mistakenly identified the earliest newspaper as San Francisco's *Wah Kee*, and gave its period of publication as 1875–79. All three histories, in other words, were off by more than twenty years in dating the start of the Chinese press.[47]

Even today, information on Asian-American journalism is distressingly inadequate. Much investigation remains to be done, not just to sketch a comprehensive picture of the Chinese press and its pioneering practitioners, but to unearth the contributions of Korean, Japanese, Filipino, Vietnamese, and most recently Southwest Asian journalists to the rich and increasingly diverse history of the American news media.

III

The Age of News Networks

Wiring the News

The news furnished to every leading citizen and almost every other daily paper comes from one source, and its preparation, wherever it is collected, is under the direct supervision of the agent of the seven associated papers in New York. It is inevitable that the views, opinions, and interests of those seven papers should be expressed through this channel, especially by the full or short reports upon topics they favor or oppose and by the bias of the writer's mind.

US Senate Report 624, 1875

The advent of the telegraph dramatically transformed America's system of mass communication. It altered the pace and pattern of news dissemination, sparked the consolidation of a national market for goods, and brought "the speed of electronic communication within reach of the potential empire builder."[1] It fostered, as well, a change in the actual content and style of news reporting, so that racial stereotyping and the white racial narrative became systemic and widespread in American journalism.

Until that point our media had evolved into a decentralized network of hundreds of local newspapers. While most of those papers were filled with partisan political views, they at least operated independently of each other, and collectively they managed to produce a rich and relatively diverse civic discourse. Thanks to low entry costs and generous postal subsidies, scores of journalists of color were able during the early nineteenth century to reach the public.

But the telegraph soon spawned an entirely new model for diffusing knowledge: one that was far more centralized and commercially driven. Individual publishers increasingly depended on standardized news dispatches transmitted over privately owned wires, instead of a government-owned postal network, and their operating costs escalated sharply. Within decades of the building of the first telegraph lines, the nation witnessed the rise of its first industrial monopoly, the Western Union Co., and of its first communications cartel, an alliance between Western Union and the Associated Press. That cartel proved so abusive in its pricing policies and stranglehold over the information flow that a popular movement soon arose to national-ize Western Union, and while the movement ultimately failed, it marked the first sustained citizen effort at structural reform of the mass media. Its defeat allowed the Western Union-AP cartel free reign in shaping public opinion on an industrial and nationwide scale.

The Associated Press had been formed in the late 1840s as a newsgather-ing cooperative by a handful of powerful publishers in New York City, and thanks to its relationship with Western Union it rapidly emerged as the main gatekeeper to the nation's supply of information. But the new technology's instant speed and its monopoly pricing structure demanded shorter and simpler news items, action over reflection, screaming headlines over nuanced analysis. The stories most likely to meet those requirements were those that triggered common stereotypes in the mind of the average reader, that rein-forced pre-existing biases instead of challenging them.

Because of that, AP's dispatches were often filled with blatantly racist distortions, and its member papers then replicated those accounts across the nation, fueling public anxiety against one racial minority after another. A disturbing number of publishers actually instigated horrific acts of racial violence—from the New York Draft Riot of 1863, to Indian massacres in the Far West, to Klan terror and the epidemic of lynching during the Jim Crow era, to armed assaults on black communities in Vicksburg, Mississippi (1874), and Wilmington, North Carolina (1898).

African-Americans and Indians were the main victims of those press campaigns, but so were Mexicans and Chinese. More than a few courageous black and Mexican journalists tried to use their own newspapers to expose injustices by white settlers, only to be met with physical attack or arrest by local authorities; a few even had their papers burned down. Thus, the cen-tralization of news delivery in late-nineteenth-century America represented a huge setback for the portrayal of race relations.

A Wondrous New Network

In 1843, the federal government appropriated $30,000 to pay inventor Samuel Morse for construction of the country's first telegraph, a forty-mile line between Washington, DC, and Baltimore. Congress and the White House were both controlled at the time by the Whigs, who strongly favored government financing of internal improvements.[2]

On May 1st, 1844, the new line, which extended then only to Annapo-lis, transmitted its first message to the nation's capital: the news that the Whig convention in Baltimore had nominated Henry Clay as its candidate for president. At first, the Morse line was operated by the Post Office. The inventor, fearing private control of the new technology, quickly offered to sell his patents to the government for $100,000. A debate ensued in the press over the merits of federal ownership. "Government must be impelled to take hold of it" and make it part of the postal service, urged Bennett's *New York Herald*, while Jeremiah Hughes, publisher of the influential *Niles' National Register*, predicted that private ownership could ensure "communities would be better served and their interests better taken care of."[3]

Whig presidential candidate Clay, on the other hand, sided with Morse. "Such an engine should be exclusively under control of the government," Clay urged. But since Democrats had long resisted federal sponsorship of internal improvements, when James Polk defeated Clay for the presidency in 1844 and the Democratic Party swept control of Congress, any hope of a government purchase of the Morse telegraph died.[4]

Public debate dragged on for most of the century over whether the federal government should intervene to control this new form of mass communication. A string of federal postmasters and national leaders, including President Grant, repeatedly urged such a course. But industrial and financial executives were determined to make it serve, first and foremost, their own needs. "Distant markets beckoned firms the moment the telegraph enabled businessmen to 'speak to' a correspondent or banker or supplier in Boston or New York and 'get a response *in the same hour*,'" noted one economic historian. Given the breakneck speed and cutthroat nature of the era's financial speculation, investors and dealmakers came to depend on the telegraph for providing them with access to the best intelligence hours or even minutes ahead of their competition.[5]

As soon as Congress rejected his offer to sell the government his patents, Morse embarked on the creation of his own Magnetic Telegraph Company. The Morse group decided to franchise its patent rights to private regional consortiums that would actually build and operate separate trunk lines. It secured the investment of many leading newspaper executives, and even recruited one of them—Amos Kendall, the former postmaster general under President Jackson—as president of the new company. Given his years of postal system expertise, his political and administrative skills, his previous stints as a newspaper editor, and his training as a lawyer, Kendall seemed the perfect choice to oversee the new nationwide communications network.[6] But his ambitious plan to fashion an interlocking group of companies controlled through the Morse patents quickly foundered. Between 1848 and 1852, scores of new firms raced to build their own competing systems. Repeated court battles ensued over patent infringement claims. Meanwhile, state legislatures took to granting the new companies local charters and rights of way over public lands at no charge. Those state charters created a glut of telegraph lines, and the glut led to a period of frenzied competition, poor service, low profits and high rates of failure among the start-up companies.[7]

The Western Union Monopoly

By the early 1860s, one telegraph firm, Western Union, had managed to gobble up most of its troubled competitors at fire-sale prices. Rochester businessman Hiram Sibley headed the firm during those years. The key to Sibley's phenomenal success was a strategic alliance he fashioned with the railroad industry; he negotiated exclusive deals with the biggest lines to run Western Union's telegraph wires along their existing rights of way. In exchange, Western Union offered the railroads preferential access and discounted rates for telegrams, thus allowing them to better track and manage their trains. By 1866 Western Union had absorbed its biggest remaining competitors, American Telegraph and United States Telegraph, to become the nation's first industrial monopoly.[8]

That same year, Congress codified its own power to take over the system with the Telegraph Act of 1866, but it never actually moved to exercise that power. Its decision to keep the telegraph in private hands was virtually unique in the world, with only Canada following suit after 1868. All European and Asian governments opted instead for public systems; even Britian, which started with a private one in the 1840s, abolished it and merged all domestic telegraph services into its existing Post Office by 1870. European systems featured low rates that made the telegraph accessible to their masses of citizens. Message costs charged by American companies, on the other hand, were so high that only commercial firms and the wealthiest citizens could afford them. One Congressional study found that Western Union's rates per mile were more than twice those in Europe. Within Britain, the government telegraph charged only a third of what Western Union charged its domestic customers. By 1890, company president Norvin Green testified before a Congressional committee that 46 percent of all messages the company transmitted were "purely speculative—stockjobbing, wheat deals in futures, cotton deals in futures, pool room, etc.," while "34 percent is legitimate trade." The "press business" (newspaper and wire service dispatches) comprised 12 percent of the company business, Green testified, "while a mere 8 percent was 'social' messages," i.e., telegrams between ordinary Americans.[9]

Western Union's monopoly, in short, brought back class stratification to our nation's system of mass communication. The penny papers of the Jacksonian era, together with the federal government's low newspaper postal rates, had begun to narrow the information gap between the masses of Americans and the country's elite. The telegraph reversed that trend, with business executives and wealthy individuals gaining access to the most important news and information of the day far ahead of ordinary Americans.

AP and Western Union Join Forces

As early as 1827, a group of New York City editors began creating informal associations or alliances to pool their newsgathering efforts. The rise of the telegraph in the mid 1840s, combined with the public demand for the latest news from the war with Mexico, eventually led to the creation of the New York Associated Press.[10]

Around the same time, a group of newspapers in upstate New York had united to transmit news from Albany via telegraph to their cities. They called their group the New York State Associated Press. AP's own official history, however, traces its origins to a pony express created that same year by New York City publisher Moses Y. Beach and his *Sun* to speed delivery from the South of news from the Mexican War. At the time, there was no direct telegraph service from New Orleans. Beach competed at first with some of the city's papers, but eventually joined forces with them to share costs.[11]

The year 1851 brought the official creation of the New York Associated Press, with the *Tribune* and the *Times* joining the group.

But the high telegram rates charged by the Morse companies (New England telegraph, for example, charged 50¢ for each ten words) soon led to growing protest from AP members. To keep costs down, AP began distilling the hundreds of daily reports it received from its member papers into one streamlined dispatch that it would then telegraph each night to papers around the country. Despite those efforts, telegraph expenses continued to devour more and more of every newspaper's budget. In 1865 alone, the New York *Tribune* paid $22,045 for "news by wire," more than half of what it spent on salaries for all its correspondents.[12]

To avoid the wrath of the publishers, Western Union began offering preferential rates to the members of AP, and at times refused to carry any other wire service. The company's rates for AP members dropped as low as six cents for twenty words, one Senate investigation found—half of what it charged non-AP papers. In return for those preferential rates, AP's leaders agreed, in the words of the association's chief agent D. H. Craig, "to ruin a paper that buys news from any competing telegraph line" and to refrain from criticizing the industry's giant. Thus was born one of the most powerful information cartels in US history.[13]

AP was already perfecting its own monopolistic practices. Member papers in any city or state could exercise veto power over new AP franchises within their circulation area. Any editor who publicly criticized the association could be ejected from membership. Such internal controls, when combined with the Western Union arrangement, made the holding of an AP franchise a crucial factor in the ability of any newspaper to survive.[14]

The power of this new communications cartel was astounding. By 1882, more than 80 percent of all the news that appeared in small-town mid-western newspapers originated from AP dispatches. In the words of an 1875 US Senate commission that investigated the Western Union-AP cartel:

> The news furnished to every leading citizen and almost every other daily paper comes from one source, and its preparation, wherever it is collected, is under the direct supervision of the agent of the seven associated papers in New York. It is inevitable that the views, opinions, and interests of those seven papers should be expressed through this channel, especially by the full or short reports upon topics they favor or oppose and by the bias of the writer's mind.[15]

One of the strongest critics of the Western Union-AP cartel was Gardiner G. Hubbard, a longtime director of the Bell Telephone Company and a proponent of a public telegraph. "The man who rules the Associated Press has an instrument for shaping the opinions of the millions," Hubbard warned in testimony to Congress. "Here is a power greater than any ever wielded by the French Directory, because in an era when public opinion is omnipotent, it can give, withhold, or color the information which shapes that opinion."[16]

So intense was the public antagonism to Western Union that more than seventy bills were introduced in Congress before 1900 calling for a government takeover. During that time, eighteen committees of the House or Senate issued reports on the issue, sixteen of them in favor of public ownership, but Western Union was able to prevent any action, thanks in good part to the unflinching editorial support it enjoyed from the members of the Associated Press and to the backing of the country's commercial elite.[17]

The Telegraph's Impact on Racial Coverage

Reliance on wire service dispatchers transformed the very content and style of news articles, especially at small town papers, which constituted back then—as they do today—the vast majority of US papers. The change did not result from conscious choices; rather it was a response by editors to the changing costs of news dissemination, to a new system where telegraph prices were pegged to the number of words a customer transmitted. "We want only the *material facts* in regard to any matter or event," wrote AP manager Daniel H. Craig in 1854 to his agents, "in the fewest words possible compatible with a clear understanding of the correspondent's meaning." Craig trained his correspondents to report only actions and avoid commentary.

In the absence of context, AP wire reports became fertile ground for the worst racial stereotypes. "The extensive use of the telegraph meant that news bulletins from the frontier—most involving violence or the threat of violence—became a common way of representing western Indians," notes journalism historian John Coward. "The headlines over these dispatches usually told a one-dimensional tale: 'Indian Troubles,' 'Indian Treachery,' 'Indian Murderers,' and the like."[18] As Richard Schwarzlose notes, "Craig could offer a politically inoffensive news report to newspapers occupying a wide political spectrum; the newspapers, in turn, could editorially make of this objective report whatever their political leanings dictated."[19]

The Sand Creek Massacre and the Rocky Mountain News

A clear example of how AP stories influenced national perceptions of race occurred in 1864, following a brutal army massacre of nearly 200 peaceful Cheyenne and Arapaho at Sand Creek, Colorado. At the time, William Newton Byers, the editor of the daily *Rocky Mountain News*, the chief AP paper in the Colorado territory, was one of the principal proponents of Colorado statehood and a fierce advocate of Indian removal. For months, Byers had published articles predicting an imminent Indian war. Following the Sand Creek incident, wire stories out of Denver, all based on coverage in Byers's paper, lauded it as a great military victory and praised the soldiers for subduing marauding savages, with the *Rocky Mountain News* extolling "the needed whipping of the 'red skins.'" But eyewitness accounts began to filter out several weeks later with a far different story. The army had slaughtered the Indians, many of them women and children, in an unprovoked attack, the witnesses claimed—and when a few eastern newspapers printed those allegations, Byers jumped to condemn the "humanitarian" eastern papers as anti-western.[20]

AP editors in New York relied on a vast network of local member papers and correspondents to wire them raw stories each day from which the central headquarters then filtered and edited those deemed newsworthy for the daily dispatch. A coterie of correspondents for the biggest eastern newspapers and magazines at times supplemented those wire stories with more extensive reports filed from the western frontier. Many of those correspondents, one press historian noted more than half a century ago, "spread before their readers the kind of highly-colored accounts of Indian raids and 'massacres' that the most sensational yellow journal of a later period would have envied."[21]

Local newspaper editors such as Byers were generally considered the "authority" on events in their area, and they typically sought to present even the most horrific examples of racial violence by their white neighbors in the best light possible, even if it meant distorting or burying key facts.

"Righteous Retribution" at Camp Grant, Arizona

On the morning of April 30th, 1871, a band of Anglo and Mexican settlers from Tucson, joined by their Papago Indian allies, surrounded and attacked an encampment of Arivaipa Apaches near the US Third Cavalry's base at Camp Grant in the Arizona Territory. The vigilantes were determined to avenge several fatal attacks on white settlers during the previous weeks by an unknown band of Apaches. They proceeded to slaughter more than one hundred Indians who were asleep in their tents, virtually all of them women and children. The assailants also abducted twenty-eight Apache children, who were later distributed to some of Tucson's most prominent citizens as slaves. Among the leaders of the attack were William S. Oury, later elected a Tucson alderman, Sidney R. DeLong, who within weeks became the city's first elected mayor, and rancher Jesus Maria Elias, one of Tucson's most prominent Mexican-Americans.[22]

The grisly massacre was especially noteworthy for the role played by the territory's three English-language papers—John Wasson's Arizona *Citizen* and P. W. Dooner's Weekly *Arizonan*, both published in Tucson, and John H. Marion's *Arizona Miner*, printed in Prescott. As with the *Rocky Mountain News* and the Sand Creek massacre, the three Arizona papers openly sought to stir up violence against the Apaches beforehand, even accusing local US soldiers of supplying arms to the Indians. The territory's white settlers were furious that federal troops were adhering to President Grant's instructions to seek a peaceful solution to Indian-settler conflicts by relocating the Indians in protected camps. The three papers, while differing in their views on Mexicans, all agreed that only "dead Indians should be called 'good Indians.'" The *Weekly Arizonian*, for example, urged settlers in January to "receive them [the Apaches] when they apply for peace, and have them grouped together and slaughtered as though they were as many nests of rattlesnakes."[23]

After the massacre, the response of the territorial papers ranged from jubilant to defiantly supportive. "To say this instance shows a spirit of barbarism in our people, would be a gross slander," declared a May 6th editorial in the *Citizen*. "While the killing is a matter for regret, the necessity for it is still more to be deplored."[24] The *Arizona Miner* more than 200 miles away in Prescott did not even report the story until May 27th. When it did so, under the headline "125 Indians Killed, Righteous Retribution," it proclaimed: "we applaud and glorify the deed, and rejoice in the establishment of the reservation in Arivipa [*sic*] Canyon, where 125 good Pinals shall rest without hunger or thirst till resurrection."[25] The *Citizen's* publisher later admitted in print that he had been informed beforehand of the attackers' plan to butcher the Apaches but chose not to prevent it by informing the local army commander.[26]

No telegraph line existed in Tucson at the time, so it took almost two weeks before news of the killings reached the rest of the nation. The San

Diego *Union*, the first paper to receive an overland report from the *Citizen*, wired it to San Francisco on May 11th, and from there it immediately reached New York AP via Western Union's transcontinental wire.

"The dispatch was a masterly whitewash of the attack," historian William Blankenburg concluded in his study of press coverage of the Camp Grant massacre. Once again, AP transmitted word for word a grossly distorted version of events.[27] That account appeared the following day on the front page of the *New York Times*: "The suffering and exasperated people have commenced the work of retaliation on the Indians," it reported. "Early on the morning of the 30th they dashed into the Indian camp, killing eighty-five savages and taking twenty-eight Indians prisoner." Nowhere did the dispatch mention that those killed had been virtually all women and children, or that all the "prisoners" were also children.[28] Not until a month later, when President Grant personally labeled the incident "pure murder" and a handful of northeast publications reported his remarks, did a different narrative begin to emerge. Nearly three months after the massacre, the *New York Times* published the contents of a letter from Lt. Royal Whitman, the army commander in charge of the Apaches at Camp Grant. Whitman reported that the Indians had been peaceful, that almost all the victims had been women and children, and that the territorial press had been "puerile" in its reports.[29]

The ensuing furor over Camp Grant prompted federal indictments of one hundred of the assailants, including Tucson's Mayor Sidney DeLong. After a one-week trial, during which Arizona newspapers repeatedly condemned the federal prosecutors for daring to file the charges, and during which lawyers for the vigilantes produced testimony about a string of unrelated Indian attacks on whites, a Tucson jury took a mere nineteen minutes to acquit all the defendants.[30]

While Blankenburg condemns the Arizona papers for their "venom" and their "reinforcement of anti-Indian sentiment," he concludes they "can't fairly be called murderers," since the massacre "would have occurred even without a supporting press." Given the state of Indian-settler enmity at the time, he calls it "wishful thinking" to expect those Arizona editors to have gone against their neighbors.[31]

But the Arizona newspapers were guilty of more than simply spreading racist "sentiment." Though their editors did not participate in the massacre, they incited and legitimized anti-Indian violence, and they played a key role afterward in creating the public climate in which jurors acquitted the killers and kidnappers. Camp Grant, after all, was not the first time American journalists confronted the moral choice of challenging a bias deeply held by the majority. Ben Franklin's revelations about Pennsylvania's Indian massacre in the 1750s, William Lloyd Garrison and Frederick Douglass's ringing exposés of the evils of slavery, and the editorials by Francisco Ramirez in

El Clamor Público, provided clear example of courageous editors daring to report inconvenient facts, even when faced with a public outcry. One kind of journalism deserves emulation, the other condemnation.

In Search of Mexican Border Bandits

In 1890, Jonathan Gilmer Speed, a correspondent touring the borderlands for *Harper's Weekly*, wrote of the local Mexican residents, "though they have been American citizens for more than forty years, [they] are almost as much an alien race as the Chinese, and have shown no disposition to amalgamate with the other Americans."[32]

A recurrent theme of borderland Anglo newspapers was the hunt for Mexican-American bandits. But those papers rarely delved into what drove much of the so-called banditry—the pivotal battle over land. Newly arrived Anglo settlers were determined to use any means they could to wrest the land from the original Mexican titleholders and to stamp out all resistance from the various Indian tribes. Lawlessness and violence thus dominated press accounts of the borderlands for decades. For more than fifteen years, for example, local newspapers feverishly chronicled the relentless efforts by the Texas Rangers and the US army to capture Juan Cortina and his band, which waged its own guerrilla war in stubborn effort to defend the land titles of Mexicans by force of arms.[33]

Violence and repeated lynching of Mexicans along the border continued deep into the twentieth century. On November 11th, 1922, for example, a Mexican named Elías Zarate was lynched after being arrested for getting into a fistfight with a white man. A week later, a *New York Times* editorial remarked, "the killing of Mexicans without provocation is so common as to pass almost unnoticed."[34]

The border troubles led to several Congressional investigations, with the official record of those probes usually providing more accurate information about the causes of the unrest than what appeared in the southwestern press.[35]

By 1880, the US Public Land Commission, which had been appointed by Congress the previous year to investigate the resolution of land claims by original residents of the former Mexican territories, reached an astounding conclusion. Over a nearly thirty-year period, more than 1,000 claims had been filed with the federal government, but Congress had only acted on seventy-one. The federal government, in short, had failed to abide by a provision of the Treaty of Guadalupe-Hidalgo that guaranteed all Mexicans who became US citizens that their property rights would be recognized.[36]

Spanish-language papers, on the other hand, saw land disputes as the crux of the enmity between Mexicans and Anglos. In 1891, for instance, Justo Cárdenas, editor of *El Correo de Laredo*, warned his readers that a new law under consideration in the Texas legislature threatened to cripple the ability of Mexicans to own land.[37]

By then, the border towns of Laredo and El Paso had grown dramatically in size, thanks to new railroad lines connecting them to the outside world, and had surpassed Brownsville and San Antonio as the centers of Spanish-language journalism. The first Laredo newspaper, *El Horizonte*, appeared in 1879, two years before James Saunders Penn started publishing the English-language *Laredo Times*. A total of eleven Spanish-language papers were launched in the city during the 1890s. During a smallpox outbreak in 1899, clashes erupted between white law enforcement authorities and the Latino community over the quarantine order aimed at Mexican laborers. Cárdenas, the most influential of the city's Latino editors, criticized in his paper the heavy-handed enforcement of the edict by the Texas Rangers. The *Laredo Daily Times* accused him of causing a panic, and the Rangers tossed him and twenty other Mexicans into jail.[38]

Catarino Garza—Journalist and Revolutionary

Many Spanish-language publications began in the late 1880s to sympathize with a growing movement to overthrow Mexican President Porfirio Díaz.[39] The Díaz regime had left Mexico's peasantry in ruins. The nation's most fertile soil, along with most railroads and mines, was now owned by American and British firms.

At the center of the anti-Díaz movement was a fiery journalist named Catarino "Cato" Garza, who wrote for a time for *El Libre Pensador* ("The Free Thinker") in Eagle Pass, Texas. After Garza penned several articles criticizing the Texas Rangers, however, a group of white Texans destroyed the paper's press, prosecuted him for criminal libel, and jailed him for thirty days. He then moved to Corpus Christi and began publishing *El Comercio Mexicano*. There, he once again enraged white settlers by accusing Texas Ranger John Sebree of unjustly killing a Mexican in Rio Grande City. The Rangers promptly arrested Garza again on charges of criminal libel and took him to Rio Grande City. There, Sebree shot and wounded him in a confrontation on September 21st. Hundreds of the Mexican editor's armed *Tejano* followers responded by occupying the town with guns. They attempted to apprehend Sebree, but he managed to find refuge at a local army base. The sensational incident came to be known as the Rio Grande City Riot of 1888.[40]

Garza moved quickly from being just a gadfly editor to a full-fledged revolutionary. In 1891 he led an armed band of more than 1,000 men into Mexico in an effort to topple the Díaz government, dashing back and forth across the border in gun battles with both the Mexican and US armies. Garza's War, as it was called, galvanized press attention on both sides of the border, much of it inaccurate and contradictory.[41] The reports could not even agree on his physical size and appearance, whether he was an ordinary bandit or a revolutionary, whether his army was real or a myth, or how much public support he enjoyed. "Journalists liberally wove fact with fiction, cutting and pasting from rumors and reports to construct engaging and suspense-filled narratives," says historian Elliot Young.[42] The coverage served primarily to perpetuate an image of the Southwest border in the American mind as a place of lawlessness and savagery.

Eventually driven out of the borderlands by the US army and the Texas Rangers, Garza fled to Central America, where he wandered from one Latin American revolution to another and was finally killed in 1895, while leading a guerilla assault on a prison in present-day Panama.

The Garza War left only one thing clear: the Spanish-language press in the southwest was now opposed to President Díaz and his US-backed program of industrialization. Latino editors in this country were deeply divided over Garza's armed tactics, but most openly sympathized with his goals. Those editors so influenced anti-Díaz perceptions by Mexicans on both sides of the border that the Garza revolt is today recognized as the precursor of the tumultuous Mexican Revolution that erupted in 1910.

The New York Draft Riots and the Civil War

In July 1863, only weeks after the disastrous defeat of the Union army at Gettysburg, thousands of working-class whites in New York City erupted in the worst rioting the country had ever seen. The violence began as a protest against a new federal law that allowed wealthy Americans to avoid military conscription by paying substitutes to serve in their place. It rapidly turned into a four-day orgy of assaults by Irish workers against black residents, one that devastated the city and claimed more than 100 lives. Anti-black fervor in those years was primarily stoked by newspapers aligned with the Copperhead wing of the city's Democratic Party, which was headed by Fernando Wood, the city's three-time former mayor. Wood, who also represented New York for a time in Congress, had successfully opposed efforts in the 1850s to extend voting rights to free blacks. Wood's brother Benjamin was the notoriously bigoted editor of the Daily News, and himself served for a period in the House of Representatives. Another Wood brother, Henry, was a partner in the Christy Minstrel Company, one of the most popular blackface troupes in the country.[43]

Before the Civil War, such performances by minstrel companies were wildly popular among working-class whites in the North, and afterward they grew even more prevalent in the South. Wherever they were performed, the shows, featuring grossly stereotyped figures such as "Sambo," "Tambo and Bones," "Jim Crow," and "Zip Coon," served to rationalize and trivialize white oppression of blacks.[44]

In 1860, the *Daily News* warned its readers that if Lincoln and the Republicans won the election, "we shall find negroes among us thicker than blackberries swarming everywhere." For a short time after the start of the war, the postmaster general suspended postal delivery of the paper because of its pro-Confederacy stance. But once the 1863 draft riot began, several other influential city dailies joined the *News* in stoking the violence. The mobs "were encouraged in their racial bestiality by ... the *Herald*, the *World*, and the *News*, which tagged the riot as a 'popular insurrection,'" notes one historian. Republican sheets like Greeley's *Tribune* and Henry Raymond's *New York Times*, however, roundly condemned the violence. They called on soldiers and police to crush the riots, whereupon they became targets of the mobs.[45]

Thomas Morris Chester's Civil War Chronicles

As war dragged on between North and South, New York City's Republican editors began to conclude that the battlefield dispatches they were receiving from the Associated Press were distorted, especially when it came to the role of black soldiers in the fighting. Greeley biographer Lurton Ingersoll described one *Tribune* staff meeting where a managing editor exclaimed:

> Now, this Associated Press dispatch is evidently a Rebel lie—two hundred armed negroes attack fifty unarmed whites, and two whites are wounded and fifty negroes killed—what perfect nonsense! Reid, you write an article on this business ... [L]ook up the other cases in which the Associated Press dispatches are toned by the rebels.[46]

Few editors, however, made any consistent effort to ensure accurate accounts of the war's racial aspect. Of all the major papers, only the *Philadelphia Press* is known to have employed an African-American correspondent during the conflict. That correspondent, Thomas Morris Chester, was the first black writer for a big-city American daily. Chester's mother Jane Marie had been born a slave in Virginia but had escaped to Harrisburg, Pennsylvania. His father George was Harrisburg's only agent for Garrison's *Liberator*, and owned a restaurant that served as a hub for the town's abolitionist movement. Their son Thomas was born in 1834, and studied at Allegheny College before becoming an agent of the American Colonization Society. In his late twenties he moved to Liberia, where he worked at first as a teacher and then as a journalist, founding and editing the *Star of Liberia* in the late 1850s. But Chester soon came into conflict with Liberian officials over his editorial policies, so he decided in 1859 to return to the United States. He landed a job as a Liberia recruiter for the ACS, but the outbreak of the war and Lincoln's emancipation decree forced a reversal in his thinking. Chester renounced his long-held view that free blacks should return to Africa, and began instead to recruit black volunteers for the Union army, even pressing publicly for the appointment of black officers.[47]

In August 1864, John Russell Young, editor of the *Philadelphia Press*, offered Chester a job as a war correspondent covering black Union troops. For the next eight months he provided almost daily dispatches from the front, documenting the role those black soldiers played in the conflict. His dispatches provided unusual glimpses into black life, as shown by this article on an escaped slave who reached union lines:

> Justenia Gerard, a quadroon of rather prepossessing appearance, sooner than marry in Richmond, where the laws refused to recognize the sacred-ness of the compact, fled with her betrothed to our lines, where they arrived after having concealed themselves many days, traveled many nights, and waded through cold streams of water up to their necks. A short time before leaving rebeldom, she, with a number of other ... colored people, was arrested and confined in prison for three days for attending the wedding of a friend in the country, and only escaped the disgrace of stripes at the public whipping post through the earnest aid of counsel, pleading that they were assembled upon a white man's plantation.[48]

Chester was one of the first Northern correspondents to reach the Con-federate capital of Richmond with black soldiers from the 5th Massachusetts Cavalry and the XXV Army Corps. In the following dispatch—one difficult to imagine any white journalist of his era writing—he describes the jubila-tion of Richmond's black population when President Lincoln visited the captured rebel capital a few days later:

> Everyone declares that Richmond never before presented such a spec-tacle of jubilee. It must be confessed that those who participated in this informal reception were mainly Negroes. There were many whites in the crowd, but they were lost in the great concourse of American citizens of African descent. Those who lived in the finest houses either stood motion-less upon their steps or merely peeped through the window-blinds, with a very few exceptions.[49]

During Reconstruction, Chester won an appointment as a general in the Louisiana state militia and served for a time as a superintendent of public schools, at least until Democrats returned to power in the state in 1877. He never returned to journalism, however, working instead as federal govern-ment appointee, lawyer and businessman until his death in Harrisburg in 1892.

The White Press Imagines Reconstruction

The end of the war signaled a marked change in the way northern newspapers portrayed the freedmen of the South. Even stalwart anti-slavery newspapers such as the *New York Tribune* began to depict every aspect of Reconstruction in the most negative and distorted fashion. Correspondents sent South by Northern newspapers and magazines sent back alarming accounts about the role of "carpetbaggers." They described this unprecedented experiment in self-government by millions of freedmen as a colossal failure. The *Tribune's* James Shepherd Pike, for example, portrayed a South Carolina state legislature ruled by "colored men whose types it would be hard to find outside the Congo; whose costume, visages, attitudes, and expression, only befit the forecastle of a buccaneer." Similar reports came from Charles Nordhoff of the *Herald* and H. V. Redfield of the *Cincinnati Commercial*. "It is no more trouble to buy their votes than to buy spring chickens in the Cincinnati market," Redfield wrote of Southern black legislators.[50]

Press historian Mark Wahlgren Summers has documented repeated examples of vicious stereotyping of black politicians and voters by Reconstruction-era reporters. The *Chicago Tribune*, for example, labeled as a "reign of terror" efforts by federal marshals to protect black voters in North Carolina. The paper described the Ku Klux Klan as a mere response to the "diabolical teachings to the blacks ... which lit up the skies ... with midnight conflagrations, and made every Southern mother press her babe closer to her bosom."[51]

Of all the Northern correspondents, no one perpetuated the white racial narrative more than Zebulon L. White, the Washington bureau chief for the *New York Tribune*, then the country's most respected commercial newspaper. In a series of reports from the South in 1874, White repeatedly portrayed blacks as inferior, falsely characterized Reconstruction efforts, and openly sided with the region's Democratic planters to pave the way for the return of white rule.

"White's reports were worse than misleading," according to Summers. Among the things they told *New York Tribune* readers were

> that at the end of the war, freed slaves refused to work and, as a result, died of starvation by the thousands; that whites were generally kind to blacks, whereas blacks were "insolent" and "provoking in conduct"; that cotton planting failed to pay simply because blacks stole one-fourth of the crop and every pig or chicken they could lay hands on; that the Alabama legislature of 1868 was almost entirely composed of "illiterate blacks or white thieves and murderers" ... that freedom had led to the moral and physical degeneration of the Negro race ...[52]

The daily dispatches from the South by the Associated Press were equally odious. AP headquarters in New York relied on southern papers to supply raw copy from the region, and all of them were partial to Democratic opponents of Reconstruction. "From Republicans came the complaint that telegraph operators did their best to quash or color dispatches sent out," Summers notes. "The head of the local [New Orleans] White League instructed the manager of Western Union to submit all dispatches referring to racial disturbances in Louisiana to him in advance; and while a revolutionary Democratic government held the city, it inspected every telegram going out."[53]

Once those dispatches reached New York, the filtering of stories by editors at AP headquarters compounded the problem. "'Every insignificant offence committed by a negro has been exaggerated into an outrage, if not developed into a bloody and brutal riot,' complained the New York *Graphic* in 1875, 'while the telegraph seldom reports the shooting of negroes by whites, even though a score are massacred at a time.'"[54]

Summers concludes that biased coverage was inevitable "given the racial assumptions that correspondents shared with virtually all their white contemporaries."[55] We do not share his view. After all, the dispatches of Thomas Morris Chester, and the articles by black editors such as Douglass, Delany, and Shadd Cary, provided far different and invaluable news accounts. But by excluding black writers from their staffs, Northern commercial newspapers guaranteed that a white-washed narrative of Reconstruction would prevail.

Meanwhile, in the South, the black papers that did exist after the Civil War "found their task well nigh impossible," according to Summers. In Alabama, at least a dozen survived for a year or more. As late as 1880, two were publishing in Huntsville, one in Marion, and one in Montgomery. But they remained almost invisible to white society. News about the South in black papers was "ignored entirely" by the Associated Press, those papers were excluded from AP membership, and few copies were even preserved by local libraries.[56]

So while Reconstruction succeeded for a time in bringing blacks into Southern politics, it failed utterly to offer African-Americans a voice in the country's major media. That failure virtually guaranteed that the press would provide the public with a fundamentally false picture of that pivotal era in our nation's history. Would perception of Reconstruction have been much different if a strong biracial press had existed? To Summers, the answer

is necessarily conjectural, but from those surviving issues of black journals like the Arkansas Freeman or the Washington National New Era, one can surmise a few things. First, the terrorism and violence that was used against Southern Republicans would have received greater coverage; the freedmen would have appeared as less comic figures, less passive followers of white leaders, and the issues on which Southern politics turned might have shown a smaller emphasis on taxes, railroads, levees, and development, and more on the transformation of social custom, religion and educational practice.[57]

Newspapers and Lynching

Nothing reflected the terror and violence of the Jim Crow era more than the epidemic of lynching that swept the United States in the decades after Reconstruction. Between 1889 and 1918 more than 3,200 people were lynched. Over that thirty-year period, an average of two people a week were killed, and 78 percent of them were black, though, as we will see in the next chapter, a significant number were Mexican. Newspaper editors were obsessed with covering this most brutal of American rituals. Even those that strongly condemned the practice, such as the *New York Times*, often provided the most minute and gory details of the atrocities mobs perpetrated against their victims, and sometimes sought to rationalize the violence. In an 1893 editorial where it condemned the killing by a mob of a black man accused of rape, the *Times* remarked: "it is true that the crime for which lynch law is even more frequently invoked than for murder is one to which the Southern negroes are peculiarly prone."[58]

What explains this press fascination with lynching? In Perloff's view, each news report of such mob action "could be guaranteed to contain information that would arouse prurient interest, engage racist citizens, and uphold a social order that was dependent on the systematic oppression of Blacks by Whites."[59]

A few Northern newspapers displayed remarkable consistency in condemning the practice. The *Chicago Tribune*, for example, waged a relentless editorial campaign that helped turn public opinion against lynching by the 1940s. Despite that change, Congress resisted pleas from the NAACP and other humanitarian organizations to pass a federal anti-lynching law.

As for Southern editors and publishers, few dared to condemn the practice. At the height of the Jim Crow era, the South's big city dailies cheered mob killings of blacks. The *Atlanta Constitution*, for example, offered a $500 reward in 1899 for the capture of Sam Holt, a black man who was a suspect in the rape of a white woman and the murder of her husband. Holt was eventually caught and hanged by a mob.

Bill Arp, a longtime columnist for the *Constitution*, former Confederate soldier, and the South's most widely syndicated commentator, wrote in 1902: "I repeat what I have said before; let the good work go on. Lynch 'em! Hang 'em! Shoot 'em! Burn 'em!" Arp (his real name was Charles Henry Smith) mixed unrepentant racism with homespun country humor that endeared him to thousands of loyal readers. One example of that macabre humor was his reaction in another 1902 column to a letter from a North Carolina friend asking his opinion of Charles Carroll's *The Negro a Beast*. The Carroll book, then a bestseller among poor whites in the South, quoted biblical scripture to prove that people of the "red, yellow and brown races" were not human. In his column, Arp responded: "He asks, 'Do you believe the nigger is a beast?' I answered at the bottom of his letter, 'Which nigger?'"[60]

Rural Southern publishers often saw lynching as a tool to keep the large black populations in their counties submissive to white rule. One of the few in-depth studies of lynching and the Southern press concluded that those papers often used "sympathetic language" when depicting white mobs and provided "moral, if not legal, justification" for the mob actions. The small-town editor who openly called for lynching—and there are numerous examples of those who did—knew the impact his words could have on readers. "What's the use of forever apologizing for doing something [lynching] that is necessary and proper," proclaimed a 1903 editorial in Georgia's *Crawfordville Advocate-Democrat*. Unlike the big city dailies, small-town publications were typically weeklies that operated on a bare-bones budget. Their editors worked long hours and usually served as the paper's only full-time writer and reporter—even as its ad salesman. Still, the enterprise was usually profitable and its owner enjoyed a coveted status of key opinion-maker, his words carrying enormous power.[61]

The Statesboro Mob of 1904

On the morning of July 29th, 1904, Henry Hodges, a prosperous white Georgia farmer, his wife Claudia, and three of their children were all brutally murdered and burned to death on their isolated farm six miles west of the town of Statesboro. The aftermath of the Hodges tragedy revealed the classic interplay between Southern newspapers and white lynch mobs. In the days after the murders, fifteen black men were rounded up and arrested by a posse under the direction of Bulloch County Sheriff John Kendrick. Two of those men, Paul Reed and Will Cato, were quickly charged with the murders.[62]

The gruesome nature of the acts attracted widespread press attention throughout the country. "The wholesale butchery ... of the Hodges family near Statesboro by dehumanized brutes adds another to the long list of horrors perpetrated in this state since the emancipation of the African slaves in 1865," said an editorial in the *Macon Telegraph*. The *Statesboro News* warned that local farmers were "living in constant danger" because "human vampires live in their midst, only awaiting the opportunity to blot out their lives." The *Atlanta News* labeled the Negroes of South Georgia "a lot of irresponsible and half-savage vagabonds, apparently hopeless to the redeeming efforts of civilization" and a "continual menace and threat to the peace and safety of the people."[63]

Nearly two weeks before the trial of Cato and Reed was to begin, an editorial in the *Statesboro News* proclaimed the town's residents "anxious to know that these murderers are hanged high and hanged until they kick out their bloody and criminal existence between heaven and earth."[64]

Georgia papers proclaimed no doubt about the guilt of the accused men. For months after the killings the Statesboro paper, along with several others, reported wild rumors that gangs of blacks had secretly formed "Before Day Clubs" to slaughter whites in their beds. The *Statesboro News* even claimed that one of the accused killers, Reed, had confessed to membership in the secret club and had admitted he and Cato were planning to kill more whites. Such news accounts created widespread fear, even though they were never verified.

An estimated 5,000 people from all over the state converged on the States-boro courthouse for the trials of the two men, which took place separately on August 15th and 16th, 1904. Both Reed and Cato took the stand and professed their innocence. The chief prosecution witness at both trials was Reed's frightened wife Harriet, who had claimed after police arrested her that her husband and Cato were the murderers. She changed the specifics of her story several times, but still her testimony sealed the men's fate. By noon of the second day, jurors had declared both men guilty. Superior Court Judge Alexander Daley immediately sentenced them to hang on September 9th.

Prior to the trials, a group of town leaders and KKK members had openly hatched plans to lynch the men. Georgia Governor Joseph Terrell, having learned of the plans, dispatched a squad of state troopers from Savannah to assist the local sheriff in protecting the prisoners.

Despite those precautions, as soon as Judge Daley pronounced sentence several hundred people in the street rushed into the courtroom and dragged Cato and Reed out with nooses around their necks, without any action by the troopers. Once outside of town, the mob chained Cato and Reed to the stump of a tree, poured kerosene over them and burned them to death. The vigilantes, their faces uncovered, encouraged reporters and photographers to record their grisly vengeance.

A front-page story in the *Atlanta Constitution* the next day described the scene in detail:

> As the flames touched Reed's naked oil-soaked skin, he twisted his head around in an endeavor to choke himself and avoid the fearful torture. [Cato's] heavy hair was almost the first thing the flames fastened on and screaming with agony, while the hemp rope became a collar of fire around his neck, a thrill of horror ran through the frames of the more timid ... As soon as it was seen that the men were dead, the crowd commenced dispersing. A large number remained behind, however, pilling more fuel on, until both bodies were burned all except the trunks.[65]

At least one newspaper had been notified beforehand of the planned lynching, but had done nothing to alert authorities. "When the information was
given to the *Savannah Morning News* correspondent," the paper reported the
day after the lynching, "he was made to understand in no uncertain manner
that a divulgence of any of these plans would provoke trouble."

Even more chilling than the mob violence and the complicity of some
journalists was the terror that befell the black population of the entire state.
"A week after the Statesboro incident," Smith notes, "there was a lynching
in Cedartown, Georgia, where a reported eight thousand whites 'pulverized'
the body of a black man with bullets who had been accused of 'outraging'
a white girl." By the end of August a half-dozen other black men had been
lynched in Georgia. The violence became so widespread that many blacks
fled the county.[66]

Ethnic Cleansing in Vicksburg, Mississippi

In December of 1874, newspapers in New York and other northern cities
were filled with alarming reports that hundreds of armed black men had
attacked the white residents of Vicksburg, Mississippi. Twenty-five blacks and
one white had been killed in the gun battle that ensued, and "the negroes in
the country [are] burning dwellings and ginhouses." The violence erupted,
the wire stories claimed, when a black mob tried to force reinstatement of
Peter Crosby, the county's black sheriff. Crosby and several black office-
holders had reportedly been pressured to resign a few days earlier by an
association of taxpaying "citizens," who accused them of corruption. The
Associated Press dispatch blamed state Republican leaders, especially "car-
petbagger" Governor Adelbert Ames, for inciting "the invasion of this city
by negroes." Other reports claimed that the black crowd had opened fire
first and that black leaders had talked of the need to "slaughter the white
women and children."[67]

A subsequent Congressional investigation of the Vicksburg uprising
depicted a far different story. The taxpayer association, it turned out, was
actually called the White League. Federal investigators learned that a local
election that summer had been marred by an openly racist campaign among
whites to oust all blacks from political office. Armed bands of white citizens
had formed before election day to intimidate blacks into staying home, and
as a result Republicans were swept out of office. The fraudulent Democratic
victory then emboldened white leaders to remove the few remaining black
county officials, including Crosby, even though their terms were not set
to expire for another year. In early December, 500 whites marched to the
courthouse and forced Crosby at gunpoint to sign a resignation later. The
sheriff appealed to Governor Ames, who pledged his support. Ames urged
Crosby to take his case to court first, while suggesting the sheriff organize a

citizen's posse. A few days later a flyer appeared, signed by Crosby, calling on county residents for help in restoring him to office.

Blacks in the county immediately began arming themselves, at which point Governor Ames had a change of heart and tried to convince Crosby to retract his call. But by then it was too late. More than a hundred blacks had begun to march on the town. Vicksburg Mayor Horace H. Miller intercepted the march on the outskirts of town, and he appeared to have convinced its leaders to turn back, when the first shots suddenly rang out. Witnesses later differed on which side fired first, but there was no disputing that blacks suffered the greatest casualties. In the days that followed, white bands crossed into Vicksburg from Louisiana and joined members of the White League in a systematic slaughter throughout the county. As many as 300 blacks were reportedly killed, many with their throats slashed and ears cut off.[68]

Once again, the early wire stories had gotten the facts wildly wrong. Once again, newspapers all over the country disseminated those erroneous reports to millions of Americans. "Northern newspapers never seemed to learn," Summers notes. "Each scare was accepted as credulously as if it were the first to appear." The Chicago *Tribune* was one of the few white-owned papers to question the obvious pattern, noting: "If anyone is punished, it is a negro; if anyone is driven from home, it is a negro. If anyone is killed, it is a negro; and if anyone is to blame, of course it is a negro."[69]

Josephus Daniels and the Armed Revolt in Wilmington, North Carolina

On November 10th, 1898, three months after the end the Spanish-American War, 2,000 white residents of North Carolina, including many of the state's political and economic elite, converged on the city of Wilmington, surrounded the local black newspaper, the *Daily Record*, and burned it to the ground. Over the next few hours the rioting mob terrorized the town's black majority in a series of gun battles in which as many as sixty blacks were killed. The mob's leaders promptly removed the elected mayor and city alderman, fired all black city workers, ordered other black leaders to leave town, and installed the chief of their insurrection, former Confederate Army Colonel Alfred Louis Waddell, as the city's new mayor.[70]

The Wilmington incident marked the first successful armed overthrow of a local government in US history. In a 600-page report that was published in 2006, the Wilmington Race Riot Commission, an official body established by the state of North Carolina to investigate the violence, concluded that none of those who killed black residents that day and seized control of city government were ever arrested or brought to justice. The federal government likewise never intervened. It would take 108 years for the state even to acknowledge the crimes committed that day. The Commission's report vividly described the Wilmington Coup as one of the darkest chapters in the reign of terror suffered by American blacks after Reconstruction.

Equally astonishing is the report's documentation of how some of North Carolina's biggest white-owned newspapers directly fomented and assisted the armed coup. A principal conspirator identified by the commission was Josephus Daniels, one of the era's most famous Southern editors. A Democratic Party statesman and follower of William Jennings Bryan, Daniels was publisher and editor of the Raleigh *News and Observer* from the 1890s until his death in 1948.

The troubles in Wilmington began in early 1898, when two North Carolina white-supremacist groups, the Red Shirts and the "White Government Union" clubs, began a campaign to drive all blacks from elected office. At the time, blacks comprised a majority of Wilmington's 19,000 residents, and an alliance of black Republicans and white populists was running the city's government. The program of the Fusionists, as they were called, centered on economic justice, public education and equal voting rights for all. But white planters and the local business elite were determined to divide and destroy this interracial movement.[71]

In his autobiography, Daniels would later acknowledge the deliberate campaign he and other white leaders devised to intimidate black voters prior to statewide elections that year: "At some places in the black districts, guns were fired and the white supremacy people surrounded the polls in great numbers ... in places where the Negro vote was large, the impression prevailed among the Negroes that it was not safe for them to make any show of resistance."[72]

The vote on November 8th was marked by considerable ballot-stuffing on the part of whites, according to the Race Commission report. Daniels proudly described how he used his newspaper to whip up the anger of whites against black voters:

> Day and night we worked, for I rarely went home until two or three o'clock in the morning, getting the news and writing the editorials and conferring with Democratic leaders. Never a day passed that two or three or four county chairmen did not come to Raleigh to secure speakers, report, or give suggestions. We would meet at Democratic headquarters or they would come to my office, and every one of them had a story of something they thought would tell against the Fusionists.[73]

Many of the state's white-owned newspapers joined in the anti-black crusade, with Daniels proudly calling his own *News and Observer* "the militant voice of White Supremacy."[74] As part of that crusade, he published a series of articles that depicted "unbridled lawlessness and rule of incompetent officials," a "worthless police force," and "incidents of housebreaking and robbery in broad daylight," all of which, according to the *News and Observer*, had occurred in Wilmington "under Negro domination."[75]

Throughout the summer, the paper also published numerous articles blasting Alex Manley, the publisher of Wilmington's only black newspaper, the *Record*. Manley's most flagrant transgression had been to print an article that questioned whether some instances of alleged rape of white women by black men had actually been consensual sexual unions. Daniels declared that article an outrage against all Southern white women.

After Democratic candidates captured two-thirds of the legislative seats in the November 8th election, victorious white supremacists targeted Wilmington for immediate regime change, even though the town's leaders were not scheduled to run for re-election for another year. On November 9th, a committee of white supremacists demanded that Manley's paper be closed. The following day, a mob gathered at the paper's office. Daniels provided this eyewitness account of what happened that day:

> The white supremacy people determined to expel Manley from the city, and to set fire to his building and burn it as a lasting evidence that no vestige of the Negro who had defamed white women of the State should be left. His building was gutted and burned but Manley escaped ...[I]t was an armed revolution of white men of Wilmington to teach what they believed was a needed lesson, that no such defamer as Manley should live in the city and no such paper should be published.[76]

After the burning of Manley's paper the violence spread and massacres of blacks began, until all black leaders had been driven from town. Daniels then presided at a huge celebration in Raleigh, at which a "motion was made to thank the *News and Observer* for its leadership in the fight."[77]

Josephus Daniels was not simply some crazed white-supremacist editor. He went on to become a chief strategist for the presidential campaigns of Woodrow Wilson, and served as Wilson's secretary of the navy during World War I. During that time Daniels, along with other top Wilson appointees, segregated all federal departments in Washington, establishing separate black and white toilets and cafeterias and reversing a trend of racial integration that had prevailed among government employees in the nation's capital.[78] Secretary Daniels was a friend and mentor to the young Franklin D. Roosevelt, who was then an assistant naval secretary. When the federal government placed all radio broadcasting under the control of the navy during World War I, Daniels exercised significant influence over government policy toward the new medium, though Congress ultimately rejected his plan for radio to be brought under permanent government control. Decades later, after FDR was elected president, he named Daniels his ambassador to Mexico.

We are thus left with a picture of this influential American publisher who was also the leader of a racist and murderous insurrection. Even more amazing, Daniels went on to enjoy a stellar career as a respected historian and top federal appointee under two of our most revered presidents. Yet his leadership role in the Wilmington massacre, one of the most shameful events in the history of the American press, has somehow been turned into a minor footnote of his otherwise "distinguished" career—when it is mentioned at all. Consider, for example, how Daniels is portrayed in *The Press and America: An Interpretive History of the Mass Media*. This widely acclaimed textbook, one of the few that goes beyond passing references to the non-white press in the US, describes Daniels as a crusading, populist editor who campaigned for state-funded public schools and editorialized against the monopolists of the Southern Railway and the Duke family's North Carolina tobacco trust. No reference is made to his leadership role in the Wilmington Coup and massacre.

Such is the power of the white racial narrative in American news.

In fairness to the Daniels family legacy, we note the positive role later played by his son Jonathan Daniels, who took over the reins of the *News and Observer* after his father's death. After serving as a special assistant to Franklin D. Roosevelt in the White House, the young Daniels became one of a handful of Southern editors during the 1950s—the group included Mark Ethridge of the Louisville *Courier-Journal*, Ralph McGill of the Atlanta *Constitution*, and Hodding Carter Jr., of the *Delta Democrat-Times* in Greenville, Mississippi—that gradually broke with the pro–Jim Crow policies of the region's elite and supported the Civil Rights movement.[79]

Even in the darkest days of the Josephus Daniels era, however, a courageous group of journalists of color emerged to challenge the white racial narrative, to defend the best principles of a free press. We turn now to some of those unsung editors and writers of the Progressive Era.

The Progressive Era and the Colored Press

The Negro of this country is a freeman and yet a slave. Talk about fighting and freeing poor Cuba, and of Spain's brutality; of Cuba's murdered thousands, and starving reconcentrados. Is America Any Better Than Spain?
Cleveland Gazette, 1898

We are foot soldiers of the community, guarding its rights …
La Voz del Pueblo, Santa Fe, New Mexico, 1889

In January 1880, a young Cuban writer with a lustrous mustache and dark, receding hair settled in New York City after wandering for nearly a decade as a political exile in Europe and Latin America. Twenty-seven-year-old José Martí quickly landed work as a correspondent for several of Latin America's top newspapers and as an occasional contributor to the New York *Sun*. He would spend the next fifteen years in that city, producing a remarkable body of literature and newspaper articles on life in the United States.

Martí's marvelous dispatches should long ago have accorded him a special place among America's nineteenth-century newsmen, but because he wrote in Spanish he remains largely unknown in the very country where he practiced his finest journalism. Writing, however, was not Martí's greatest gift; he was also the spiritual voice and organizational genius of the Cuban fight for independence, and is known today as one of the great revolutionaries of Latin American history.

In 1889, a young African-American schoolteacher named Ida B. Wells began editing a tiny publication in Memphis, Tennessee. Her paper, the *Free Speech and Headlight*, sought to chronicle the disparate treatment the town's black residents were receiving from the white community.

Soon after Wells took the reins of the paper, a shocking incident occurred that would alter her life. Three black male friends of hers, all business partners in the People's Grocery store in town, were thrown in jail following an altercation at the store that resulted in the wounding of several white men. Wells later discovered that her friends—Thomas Moss, Calvin McDowell, and Will Stewart—had fired in self-defense to repel an attack by white competitors who were trying to drive them out of business. But initial accounts of the incident in the local white newspapers erroneously claimed that "negro desperados" had assaulted the white men without cause. Soon after, a mob broke into the Memphis jail, dragged Moss, McDowell and Stewart from their cells, and shot them to death. Wells was so outraged by the killings and by the failure of authorities to prosecute the murderers that she dedicated herself from then on to exposing America's epidemic of lynching and race hatred.[1]

Martí and Wells exemplified an aggressive new style of advocacy journalism that blossomed in the non-white press of the late nineteenth and early twentieth century, a period of breakneck industrial expansion, of a widening gap between rich and poor, and of the rise of an American colonial empire. In the media, this was the heyday of Western Union and the Associated Press, of the first great newspaper chains, of the centralization of news dissemination, and of the birth of a worldwide news cartel.

In response, a band of courageous scribes began chronicling the social calamity wrought by corporate monopolies and political corruption, and their startling exposés soon captivated the public. Known as the "muckrakers," the group included Upton Sinclair, who shocked the nation with his descriptions of conditions in the meatpacking industry; Lincoln Steffens, who turned the spotlight on municipal corruption; Ida Tarbell, who exposed the ruthless rise of the Standard Oil monopoly; and Ray Stannard Baker, who depicted the oppressive conditions of the Jim Crow South. Their searing investigative pieces did not appear for the most part in daily newspapers, but in a raft of popular middle-class magazines like *McClure's*, *Cosmopolitan*, *Collier's*, and *Everybody*. The new form of advocacy journalism they championed left an indelible imprint on the turbulent period that came to be known as the Progressive Era.

But, as we will see in this chapter, journalists of color were battling for justice long before the muckrakers became household names. We sketch below how Martí and Wells pioneered social justice journalism, and we outline the contributions of other little-known journalists of color who followed in their footsteps, among them T. Thomas Fortune of the *New York Age* and Jesse C. Duke of the Montgomery *Herald* in Alabama, Enrique Salazar of New Mexico's *Voz del Pueblo* and *El Independiente*, and Ng Poon Chew of San Francisco's *Chung Sai Yat Po* ("China West Daily"). All saw themselves as sentinels and guardians for their communities, assisting their readers in standing up to and negotiating with the broader society.

This "colored" press of the late nineteenth and early twentieth century has at times been erroneously lumped together with the hundreds of foreign-language newspapers that flourished around the same time among European immigrants. But while the immigrant press successfully helped new arrivals assimilate to their new nation, racial segregation in the US never permitted such an option for blacks, Native Americans, Asians and the largely mixed-race Mexicans and Latin Americas. Non-white minorities were quickly relegated to a rigid second-class status, and as a result colored editors turned into persistent opponents of racial bigotry directed against their own com-munities—though not always of bigotry in general. Excluded from the halls of "mainstream" journalism, these editors were forced to launch their own press organizations, such as the Alabama Colored Press Association (1887), the Afro-American Press Association (1890), and New Mexico's Hispanic American Press Association (1891). They thus constituted a separate but vibrant wing of the country's muckraking press, though one that remained largely invisible to white society.

Martí's Forgotten US Chronicles

A handful of exile journalists and political figures from the Spanish-speaking Caribbean made New York their second home during the late nineteenth century, but none compared to Martí in the quality of writing, the depth of insight, or the literary legacy they left behind.[2]

Martí's canvas was the New World itself. In 1885, for example, he attended the historic Mohonk Indian conference in upstate New York. There, he heard Sen. Henry Dawes of Massachusetts defend his plan to end all com-munal ownership of Indian lands. Congress would approve the senator's proposal, better known as the Dawes Act, two years later. In a dispatch he wrote about the conference, Martí penned a stirring condemnation of US treatment of Native Americans:

> He [the Indian] is forced by onerous treaties to give up his land; he is cut off from the place where he was born, which is like cutting the roots off a tree, and he thereby loses the greatest object of life; he is forced, under the pretext of making a farmer of him, to buy animals to work a patch of land that does not belong to him; he is compelled, under the pretext of schooling him, to study in a foreign language, the hated language of his masters, textbooks that give him some vague notion of literature and the sciences, whose usefulness is never explained and whose application he never understands. He is imprisoned in a confined space, where he mills around among his corralled companions, their only horizon the hucksters who sell shiny geegaws [sic], weapons, and alcohol for the money that, in accordance with the treaties, the government distributes on the reserva-tion each year.[3]

Two months earlier, Martí had written in Argentina's *La Nación* about the "barbaric killings of Chinamen," in Rock Springs, Wyoming. In 1892, he produced a chilling account of the brutal lynching of a black man named Ed Coy in Texarkana, Texas, for allegedly insulting a white woman:

> And the bound black man comes along at a trot—"out of town, in the open countryside where everyone can get a good view"—and behind him, as he trots along, the five thousand souls come running. He reached the only tree. One compassionate man wanted to climb it with a rope, asking that at least they hang him, but his compassion was diminished by the mouth of a rifle. Coy was trussed against the tree trunk with iron hoops. They threw buckets of petroleum over his head until his clothing was drenched ... And when Mrs. Jewell [the alleged rape victim], in a triangular scarf and hat, came out from among the crowd, on the arms of two relatives, the crowd burst into a round of cheers: "Hurrah for Mrs. Jewell!" The ladies waved their handkerchiefs, the men waved their hats. Mrs. Jewell reached the tree, lit the match, twice touched the lit match to the jacket of the black man, who did not speak, and the black man went up in flames in the presence of five thousand souls.[4]

Whether his subject was a professional boxing match or the death of Karl Marx or simply a day at Coney Island, Martí brought a poet's touch and an artist's eye to each event, as in this closing paragraph of his account of the May 1883 opening of the Brooklyn Bridge:

> Thus they have built it and thus it stands, the monumental structure, less beautiful than grand, like a ponderous arm of the human mind. No longer are deep trenches dug around embattled fortresses; now cities embrace one another with arms of steel. No longer do sentry posts manned by soldiers guard populations; now there are booths with employees ... who collect the penny of peace from the laborers that go past. Better to bring cities together than to cleave human chests.[5]

During his fifteen years in the US, Martí did far more than report the news. He also founded the Cuban Revolutionary Party in 1892, was elected its first leader, and founded its newspaper *Patria*. He finally returned to Cuba in 1895 to join his fellow revolutionaries in their guerrilla war against the Spanish army. By then, he had spent almost as much time in the United States as he had in his own homeland. Shortly after landing in Cuba, he was killed in a battle with Spanish troops. He was only forty-two at the time of his death.[6]

Enrique Salazar and the Hispanic American Press Association

By the late nineteenth and early twentieth century, the southwest had surpassed New York, New Orleans and California as the center of the Hispanic press in the United States. At least 190 Spanish-language newspapers were launched between 1880 and 1935 in the former Mexican territories of the southwest.[7]

New Mexico proved the most fertile ground for the new Hispanic journalism. This was to be expected, since the territory boasted the largest Mexican population of the areas annexed by the US. Anglo settlers launched virtually all of the initial New Mexico publications (except for a couple mentioned in Chapter 5)—even the territory's bilingual sheets. But that began to change after the arrival of the railroad in 1879, for *Nuevomexicano* intellectuals found it easier to buy and import their own printing presses. As a result, some thirty-five Spanish language and eleven bilingual newspapers were in operation in the territory by the 1890s.[8]

So many Spanish-language weeklies appeared that Latino editors met in Las Vegas, New Mexico, in December 1891 to found La Prensa Asociada Hispano-Americana (the Hispanic American Press Association), the first known organization of Latino journalists in the nation. At that meeting, Victor Ochoa, editor of *El Hispano-Americano* in Las Vegas, was elected the group's president, and Carlos Padilla, then editor of *El Mosquito* in the town of Mora, its vice-president. The outlook of the New Mexico *periodistas* (journalists) was radically different from that of the typical foreign-language immigrant press in the US. They were not foreigners or immigrants, after all; they wrote for a community that had been long established, and Spanish was the native tongue of the majority of the territory's inhabitants. They were determined to preserve that language and their *Mexicano* culture, and they saw the mission of their newspapers as reaching "consensus on the measures and means best suited and needed for the progress and betterment of the community [the association] represents."[9] They regarded their work as journalists, in other words, as a way to defend the *Nuevomexicano* way of life. They sought, in addition, to facilitate news exchanges among their publications and to pressure railroad, telegraph and postal officials "to provide association members and the communities they represented with improved service."[10]

A pivotal figure in the association was Enrique Salazar, editor of *La Voz del Pueblo* ("The People's Voice"). Born in 1858, Salazar was a graduate of St. Michael's College, a preparatory school founded by the Christian Brothers that would become the training ground for many of the territory's Hispanic leaders. He learned the printing trade and journalism as an employee of the English-language *Santa Fe New Mexican*, and worked at papers in Taos and Chihuahua before returning to Santa Fe in 1889 as co-publisher of *La Voz del*

Pueblo with fellow journalist Nestor Montoya. They moved the paper to the town of Las Vegas in 1890, and quickly won a following with their stinging criticism of Thomas Catron, political boss of the territory's Santa Fe Ring. "[I]t is diminution for our people to be governed by upstarts and strangers when we have among us good and competent men to fill all positions from the first to the last of them," Salazar declared in an early editorial.[11]

He was equally critical of fellow *Nuevomexicanos* who accepted such treatment or who assisted the white minority's control. "We have become so fond of the role of seconding plans that benefit outsiders that we have forgotten that our innate autonomy should be the guiding start of our proceedings," he wrote in another of his newspapers. And if those outsiders "throw us aside" and "despise us continually for our servility and subjugation," he said, "who should we blame if not ourselves?" After New Mexico gained statehood in 1912, Salazar's one-time partner Montoya won election to the US Congress in 1920.[12]

Trouble in San Miguel County

Las Vegas, a booming town in San Miguel County in the east-central part of the territory, soon became the cauldron for land conflict between new Anglo settlers and poorer *Nuevomexicano* residents. The Spanish tradition of family land tenure and common grazing areas collided head-on with the American practice of treating land as a commodity—one whose parcels could be individually bought and sold. As Anglo settlers purchased more land, they laid claim to large swaths of the old communal areas and began to fence in their claims. "Legislators collaborated to pass laws that would virtually strip *los pobres* [the poor] of their interest in their grants," notes historian Robert Rosenbaum. "Men conspired with the surveyor general of the territory and with land registrars, even on the floors of Congress, to gain title to as many acres as they could."

Mexicanos, however, still outnumbered whites in the county by five to one, with many of San Miguel's leading families tracing their land grants as far back as the 1790s.[13] Territorial judges initially backed *Mexicano* farmers in the dispute, but Anglo settlers simply chose to ignore the courts and continued to fence in their claims. In April 1889, nightriders began tearing down the fences of two white landowners and their Mexican allies. The secret group called itself Las Gorras Blancas (The White Caps), for the white hoods they wore to disguise themselves on their raids. Several of the group's leaders, authorities later learned, were *Mexicano* members of the Knights of Labor, the anti-capitalist fraternal order that reached its apogee during the 1880s.

A grand jury indicted more than two-dozen people for the attacks. That November, more than sixty armed members of the White Caps rode into

Las Vegas and surrounded the local courthouse in a show of force.[14] With the territory careening toward civil war, editors Salazar and Montoya decided to move their newspaper from Santa Fe to the scene of the conflict. In their final Santa Fe edition, Salazar told his readers:

> We are foot soldiers of the community, guarding its rights; for this reason, believing the battle nears, we wish to place our batteries where they are most effective and where they will cause the most damage to our enemies. This is, after all, the reason for our move to the city of Las Vegas.[15]

Sabotage of white farms, railroads and timber companies by the White Caps continued off-and-on for the next two years. The group enjoyed so much support from *Mexicano* residents that authorities found it hard to prosecute its members, and efforts to expand Anglo land-holdings in San Miguel ground to a halt. Salazar's newspaper never explicitly endorsed the vigilante group's actions, but it steadily condemned the land policies of the region's Anglo-American settlers.

Supporters of the White Caps decided to challenge the grip of the Santa Fe Ring on territorial politics through a more peaceful approach, by launching a third political party to challenge the Democrats and Republicans. The party they formed, El Partido del Pueblo Unido ("The United Peoples' Party"), vowed to oppose monopolies, the railroads, and land thieves. The *Las Vegas Daily Optic*, the town's leading Republican paper, ridiculed its chances, but the new group proceeded to shock the territorial establishment in 1890 by capturing more than 60 percent of the vote in San Miguel County. Salazar's paper, with its regular editorials defending the rights of *nuevomexicanos*, was a major factor in the party's success. The main issue in the nation, *La Voz* warned readers, was "the millionaire against the middle-class, the rancher and the worker."[16] The party's success was short-lived, however. By 1894 it had collapsed from internal divisions. That year, Salazar sold *La Voz del Pueblo* and launched another newspaper, *El Independiente*, vowing this time to steer the paper clear of partisan politics. The new weekly became the state's most successfully Hispanic paper, with Salazar editing it for the next thirty-four years.[17]

Carlos Padilla *and* Revista Illustrada

Another key founder of the Prensa Asociada Hispano-Americana in 1891 was Carlos Padilla, the foremost proponent of a *Nuevomexicano* literary tradition in the United States. Born in 1865, Padilla got his start in newspapers at the Santa Fe *New Mexican*, where he worked as a compositor for ten years before he decided to spend time traveling around the US. In 1890 he was appointed private secretary to New Mexico's territorial delegate to the

House of Representatives, a job that required him to live in Washington, DC, while Congress was in session. He began publishing his own paper, *El Mosquito*, while in Washington, traveling back home to work on the paper during Congressional breaks. In later years, he worked in the US Government Printing Office and as a translator for the State Department.

In 1907 Padilla moved to El Paso, Texas, and launched *Revista Ilustrada*, a literary magazine that would soon blossom into the nation's premiere venue for Spanish-language poetry, fiction, essays, graphics, and historical studies. "Its inclusiveness," notes historian A. Gabriel Meléndez, "reduced the tendency to view *Nuevomexicano* issues and concerns as unrelated or disconnected to realities in other areas of the Southwest, and made patent a cultural affinity to the El Paso border area, to Mexico, and to other part of the Hispanic world."[18]

The pages of *Revista Ilustrada* offered unmistakable evidence that a robust Hispanic American culture and literary tradition had taken root on US soil. We must emphasize that Padillla, Salazar, and their fellow Spanish-language editors were in no way foreigners or immigrants. They were as "native" to the southwest as anyone who practiced the craft of journalism in the region. The mere existence of their papers established the Hispanic press as an integral part of American journalism.

Ida B. Wells

When she took over as editor of the Memphis *Free Speech* in 1889, Ida B. Wells had already made something of a name for herself challenging racial bigotry. Born into slavery in Holly Springs, Mississippi, on July 16, 1862, she was the oldest of seven children of James and Elizabeth Wells. Her father, a tireless advocate for the state's freedmen and a Republican Party leader, instilled in his oldest daughter a passion for education and for social justice. His training no doubt influenced her response in 1884 to a conductor on the Chesapeake and Ohio Railroad train who directed her to sit in an all-black car. She refused do so, whereupon the conductor threw her off the train. She then filed a civil rights suit against the railroad. A lower court initially upheld her claim, but the Tennessee Supreme Court overturned that decision in 1887. Two years later, Wells joined a group of investors to publish the weekly Memphis *Free Speech*. She took over editing of the paper while also teaching at a Memphis school for black children.

On May 21, 1892, two months after the mob killing of her three friends, Wells issued an editorial that stunned the city:

> Eight negroes lynched since last issue of the "Free Speech," one at Little Rock, Ark., last Saturday morning where the citizens broke (?) into the penitentiary and got their man; three near Anniston, Ala., one near New

Orleans, and three at Clarksville, Ga., the last three for killing a white man, and five on the same old racket—the new alarm about raping white women ...

Nobody in this section of the country believes the old threadbare lie that Negro men rape white women. If Southern white men are not careful, they will over-reach themselves and public sentiment will have a reaction; a conclusion will then be reached which will be very damaging to the moral reputation of their women.[19]

Many alleged incidents of African-American men raping white women, she suggested, were actually cases of consensual sex. Lynching, in her view, was Southern white society's way of punishing and preventing interracial unions and keeping black men subservient. A more explosive claim could not be leveled at Southern society. The *Commercial Appeal*, the city's main white newspaper, immediately issued a furious response and a barely veiled threat: "There are some things that the Southern white man will not tolerate, and the obscene intimations of the foregoing have brought the writer to the very outmost limit of public patience. We hope we have said enough."

The same day, the white-owned *Evening Scimitar* issued an even stronger warning: if Negroes failed to squash such further comments in the press, whites would "tie the wretch who utters these calumnies to a stake at the intersection of Main and Madison Sts., brand him in the forehead with a hot iron and perform upon him a surgical operation with a pair of tailor's shears."[20]

Shortly afterward, a mob destroyed the offices of the *Free Speech*, forced its business manager to leave town, and threatened to kill Wells, who was away in New York on vacation when the attack occurred. Within days she discovered that creditors had taken possession of her newspaper. The frenzied reaction only convinced Wells that she had exposed a key source of the lynching epidemic.

She then moved to Chicago and launched a systematic investigation of the hated practice around the country. T. Thomas Fortune, editor of New York's main black newspapers, immediately offered to print her stories in his *New York Age*. Over the next few years, Wells documented in a riveting series of newspaper articles—and also in a powerful book, *Southern Horrors*—the hidden facts behind America's wave of lynchings. "Over a thousand black men, women and children have been thus sacrificed the past ten years," she declared. "Three human beings were burned alive in civilized America during the first six months of this year [1893]. Over one hundred have been lynched in this half year. They were hanged, then cut, shot and burned." Nearly a third of those killed, she reported, had been charged with sexual abuse of white women. More were lynched for rape than for murder, and some for such minor offenses as quarreling with white men or making threats.[21]

And while black men were lynched for the mere allegation of having raped a white woman, Wells found numerous examples of white men who had been convicted of sexually assaulting black girls, yet went unpunished. One of the cases she investigated was that of Ed Coy, the man whose lynching in Texarkana, Texas, José Martí had witnessed and chronicled. More than a year after Coy's grisly death, Wells revealed that the woman he was accused of assaulting was "generally known to have been criminally intimate with Coy for more than a year" and had been "compelled by threats ... to make the charge against the victim."[22]

Wells was also a civil rights leader and fervent feminist. Along with W. E. B. DuBois and William Monroe Trotter, editor of the Boston *Guardian*, she was one of the founders of the Niagara Movement in 1905, and of the NAACP in 1913. In 1898 she was part of a delegation of black leaders who met with President McKinley to demand prosecution of the South Carolina mob members who had shocked blacks across the country by murdering Fraser Baker, a local black postmaster whose appointment whites had opposed. A friend of both Susan B. Anthony and Jane Addams, in 1913 Wells also founded the first black women's suffrage club, and marched in Washington, DC, that year in support of women's right to vote.

T. Thomas Fortune and the New York Age

The most famous black editor of the late nineteenth century was T. Thomas Fortune. Born in 1856 in Jackson County, Florida, Fortune was descended from a mixed family of blacks, Seminoles and Irish immigrants. His father, Emmanuel Fortune, was a prosperous farmer who had dared to rebuff at gunpoint several attacks by the local Ku Klux Klan on the family farm. Emmanuel Fortune then fled with his wife and children to nearby Duval County, and settled in the city of Jacksonville. There he won election five times to the post of city marshal on the Republican Party ticket.

As a boy, Thomas Fortune worked in the office of the Marianna *Courier*, and once his family moved to Jacksonville he landed a job as a compositor at the *Daily Union*. At the age of eighteen, he went to work for the local post office and was appointed to deliver mail between Jacksonville and Chattahoochee, but he left the postal job in 1876 to study at Howard University. He subsequently moved to New York City and found a job as a compositor on the *Weekly Witness*. His first day on the job, the paper's white typesetters were so enraged, they walked out on strike rather than work beside him. But the owner, a devout Christian, refused to bow to his employees' action, and they eventually returned to their jobs.[23]

By 1880, Fortune embarked on his career as newspaper editor. He joined with two other black New Yorkers to launch *Rumor*, a weekly newspaper for the African-American community that became an instant success.

They changed the paper's name in 1881 to the *Globe*, but after a falling out among the partners Fortune struck out on his own. He founded the *Freeman* in 1884, and then changed its name to the *New York Age* in 1887. He called the new paper the "Afro-American Journal of News and Opinion," thus becoming one of the first writers to use the term "Afro-American."

Fortune routinely highlighted incidents of abuse against blacks that the white press was ignoring. In 1886, for instance, the *Freeman* reported on the lynching of Robert Smith, a black laborer in St. Bernard Parish, Louisiana. Smith had been arrested for fatally shooting a plantation overseer who had broken into his home one night with two other men to beat him. The following day, the *Freeman* reported that a mob had dragged Smith out of jail and lynched him in broad daylight:

> Smith is the seventh colored man mobbed in the South last week as follows: Kentucky mobs one and shoots one. Georgia one, Louisiana one, Mississippi one and Virginia one. There are from six to eight colored men or women murdered by white men in the Southern States weekly … The white press doesn't publish half the crimes committed upon colored people by their white brothers. Premise they are ashamed to put them on record.[24]

Fortune also devoted considerable space in his paper to news about the conditions and concerns of black workers. He repeatedly urged blacks to find common cause with white laborers, and he often counseled them against being used as strikebreakers, as in this article on May Day 1886:

> The hour is at hand when the wage workers of all races are organizing for the purpose of forcing a more reasonable distribution of the products of labor … The black man who arrays himself on the side of capital as against labor would be like a black man before the war taking sides with the pro-slavery as against the anti-slavery advocates.[25]

The following year, Fortune left his elder brother Emanuel, Jr., in charge of the *Age* and went to work as writer for the New York *Sun*. He spent four years there, but in 1891 decided to resume the reins of the *Age*.[26] By then, black newspapers were blossoming around the country. Historians of the black press differ on how many existed at the beginning of the 1880s (estimates range from thirty-one to sixty-six), but it seems clear there were more than 150 by 1890. Some believe that as many as 1,184 black papers were launched between 1865 and 1900—an astonishing figure considering that the illiteracy rate among blacks was about 70 percent at the time. So many new papers appeared that in 1890 a group of black editors convened in

Indianapolis to found their own National Afro-American Press Association, and they promptly elected Fortune as their chairman.[27]

In January of that same year many of the country's black leaders held a national convention in Chicago to devise common strategies to confront segregation and racial violence. Delegates to that gathering voted to found a new Afro-American League, an idea that Fortune had been espousing for years—and they elected the New York editor as the new League's chairman. The League's militant program called for an end to lynching, voting rights for blacks, an end to segregation in public transportation, and equal funding for black and white schools. Despite the great fanfare that accompanied its creation, however, the new organization floundered from internal divisions, and folded after only a few years.[28]

Most of the black newspapers that arose in the 1880s and 1890s disappeared just as quickly. Those that did survive usually suffered from tiny circulation and anemic revenues. Many could not have remained in existence were it not for the financial help they received from the Republican Party—subsidies which the party then expected those newspapers to repay by mobilizing black voters behind its candidates. Even some of the biggest papers, like Fortune's *Age*, received Republican National Committee subsidies from time to time. The black leader who wielded the most say on those Republican subsidies was Booker T. Washington. Washington's critics, among them W. E. B. DuBois, claimed "he subsidized the Negro press in order to promote his own views and his claims to race leadership," notes historian Emma Thornburgh. Washington always denied the charges, but substantial evidence has since emerged to the contrary. In the early 1900s, for instance, Washington gave repeated cash infusions to the *Age* and directly purchased or exercised control over more than 40 percent of the shares in the newspaper.[29]

In return for that aid, Fortune and his fellow editors frequently printed the institute's news releases and advertisements. Washington never openly criticized lynching or the South's Jim Crow system, but at least he refrained from pressuring Fortune to adopt his policies of racial accommodation. The *Age* thus remained firm in its militant stance against lynching and its support of the need for black workers to organize themselves into unions. In 1907, the year Washington gained financial control of the paper, Fortune suffered a nervous breakdown and relinquished control.[30]

Jesse C. Duke and the Montgomery Herald

In April of 1886, Jesse C. Duke, a young black postal worker in Montgomery, Alabama, was fired from his post for being an "offensive partisan." Duke was a prominent leader of the state's black Republicans at the time, and a trustee of Selma University, a school founded and financed by black Baptists. A month after losing his job, Duke published the first issue of the weekly

Montgomery *Herald*, one of twenty-nine black papers that appeared across Alabama during the 1880s.

With the slogan "Equal and Exact Justice to All Men" emblazoned on his paper's masthead, Duke quickly distinguished himself with his bold new style of crusading journalism.[31] His *Herald* editorialized repeatedly for better schools for the black community, and called on the legislature to outlaw separate black and white cars on the railroads. Duke also blasted the servile attitudes among his own people, once urging his readers to show some "race pride ... and manhood," and stop "crawling on your belly to lick white men's boots."[32] Even more radical than Duke was C. M. Brown, editor of the Montgomery *Weekly News*. In 1884, Brown sparked a huge controversy when he suggested in an editorial on lynching that blacks "take two or three white devils along ... and stop being shot up and killed ... like dogs."[33]

Duke soon garnered an enviable following, largely because of his extensive ties to both the Republican Party and the state's Baptist hierarchy. Less than a year after starting the *Herald*, he organized a convention of black editors and was elected the first president of the new organization they founded, the Alabama Colored Press Association. Not long after the association's founding, a white mob lynched a Montgomery boy who had been accused of raping a white girl, and dragged the boy's body by rope through the town's black neighborhood. Duke, who personally witnessed the incident, responded with a stinging rebuke of the town's white community:

> Every day or so we read of the lynching of some negro for the outraging of some white woman ... There was a time when such a thing was unheard of. There is a secret to this thing, and we greatly suspect it is the growing appreciation of the white Juliet for the colored Romeo, as he becomes more intelligent and refined.[34]

Duke's comments, reprinted within days in the local white press, infuriated town leaders. More than seventy-five white citizens immediately met to discuss how to deal with his "outrageous and indecent" remarks. The vigilantes ordered him to leave town immediately and dispatched men to the train station and to black neighborhoods to find him. And while Duke sent word to the group offering a written apology for his "hastily composed" editorial, his offer was refused and he was forced to flee. In the days that followed, newspapers throughout Alabama and the South denounced the "scoundrel" Duke and thanked the "noble white men" of Montgomery for their actions. The Columbian *Shelby Sentinel* called Duke "a menace to that which the Southern white men regards as a priceless jewel, the unsullied reputation of the women of the South." The Chattanooga *Times* suggested it would have been better to hang "the filthy beast and thus make sure he would not live to spread his devilish opinions ... such a monster deserves no mercy at the hands of civilized men of any race."[35]

The mob response to Duke's editorial, together with the widespread condemnation he received in the Southern press, sent a clear message: black editors were only free to publish if they remained subservient to white power. After leaving Montgomery, Duke relocated to Pine Bluff, Arkansas, and began practicing a more sedate form of journalism. He edited four different newspapers between 1889 and 1898 before enlisting at the age of forty-five as a second lieutenant in a black regiment during the Spanish-American War. After the war he returned to Pine Bluff, where he edited the *Weekly Herald* from 1901 to 1908.

Ng Poon Chew and the New Asian-American Press

At least twenty-six Chinese-language newspapers had appeared in the United States during the second half of the nineteenth century, but it was not until a young clergyman named Ng Poon Chew launched a daily in 1900, San Francisco's *Chung Sai Yat Po* ("China West"), that the Chinese press in America came of age. No other Chinese-American editor left so indelible a mark on his community as did Ng. Raised in his homeland to become a Buddhist monk, he converted to Christianity after migrating to California as a youth. He soon entered the Presbyterian ministry, became fluent in English, joined the Masons, and emerged as a fervent proponent among his fellow immigrants of Republicanism, American progress, and cultural assimilation.

Chinese communities were then isolated enclaves within the broader society. As Peter Kwong has documented, "By 1910, the Chinese completely disappeared from the labor market. They were forced to retreat to self-employment in laundry and restaurant trades or to do domestic work for white patrons."[36] Ng Poon Chew was determined to end that isolation. He sought to enlighten white Americans about the Chinese community by lecturing extensively across the country, and, in a sign of his commitment to assimilation, was one of the first Chinese to voluntarily cut off his queue.

Ng's most powerful podium, however, was the press. After starting a tabloid weekly in Los Angeles called *Wa Mi San Po*, he decided to move the paper to San Francisco and changed its name to *Chung Sai Yat Po*. Launched on February 16, 1900, it was the second Chinese-owned daily in the US, after the short-lived Sacramento *Chinese Daily News* nearly a half-century earlier.[37]

San Francisco's newspaper world was dominated at the time by the sensationalism of Hearst's *Examiner*. Ng eschewed that style and refrained from publishing reckless stereotypes. "It is peculiar, but nevertheless true," he told a reporter in 1909, that in San Francisco the yellow man gets out the white paper and the white man gets out the yellow paper. We run a conservative paper in every way. It is cleanly edited and our whole aim is to educate and elevate the Chinese people; to make them better citizens and better people.[38]

At the paper's offices on Sacramento St., Ng put together a remarkable staff of young Chinese, many of them educated at American universities and well versed in American culture, and they quickly turned his paper into an indispensable item for every Chinese immigrant. By 1905, *Chung Sai Yat Po* boasted a circulation of 4,000. "[One could] scarcely enter a Chinese home in California without seeing a copy," noted one writer for the Oakland *Tribune* in 1922.[39]

Ng assured his countrymen the latest information on American laws and regulations, on political and civic activities that directly affected the immigrant community, and on the importation of Chinese goods and food staples. He constantly urged his readers in front-page editorials to celebrate the way of life of their adopted country. Public education of Chinese children, he told them, was the best way to end the community's exclusion and isolation from US society.[40]

After the destruction of Chinatown in the San Francisco earthquake of 1906, several of the city's English-language newspapers proposed permanent relocation of the Chinese from downtown, but Ng strenuously opposed those proposals; he instead encouraged his readers to seek full claim payments from local insurance companies and urged them to move back to Chinatown and rebuild.

"The city government or the administration have no power to force the Chinese to live in a place they designate," he said in one editorial. "According to the US Constitution, Americans and foreigners in the United states are both protected by its provisions to choose where they want to live ... we Chinese can simply ignore [local officials]."[41]

Even though Chinese immigrants could not become citizens, Ng's paper repeatedly urged them to get involved in pressuring American politicians to prevent racial discrimination, claiming in a 1911 editorial: "We have been cruelly and meanly treated by Americans. The United States can betray humanity as such, because our people have no political awareness, no concept of how a government works, and we have contributed to our situation by giving up many of our rights."[42]

It is difficult to imagine the physical obstacles Ng faced in simply putting out a Chinese-language paper during the era of lead typesetting. English-language printers only had to worry about twenty-six letters when putting together the words for their newspapers. Chinese compositors, on the other hand, worked from a type font that held 11,000 pieces of lead to express the separate Chinese characters most commonly used in writing. "To set up the limited type required for a small four-page daily paper, the constant labors of eight or nine skilled Chinamen are required for twelve or thirteen hours," noted one shocked American writer who visited Ng's composing room in 1902.[43]

Chung Sai Yat Po continued to publish until 1951, making it one of the longest-running and most influential Chinese papers in American history. Throughout most of that time, Ng persevered against intense competition, as other publications garnering significant followings in San Francisco's Chinese community. The staffs of those competing papers included several writers who would later become major figures in the political history of modern China.

The most famous was Sun Yat-Sen, the first president of the Chinese Republic, who worked on two Chinese-language papers in what is now the United States, and directed the creation of a third. Born in 1866 in Guangdong Province to a peasant family, Sun moved to Hawaii when he was thirteen years old. During a long return visit to China in 1883, he was radicalized by the extreme poverty and backwardness he witnessed there.

He eventually moved back to Hawaii, and in 1894, along with several fellow Chinese exiles founded the Revive China Society, the forerunner of the Chinese Nationalist Party or Kuomintang. Sun went back to China the following year to organize a revolt against the emperor, but when the plot failed, he was forced to leave again. Returning to Honolulu, he took over *Lug Kee Bao* ("The Hawaiian Chinese News"), and made it an organ of the Revive China Society, publishing several of his own articles.[44]

Sun left Hawaii for San Francisco in 1896, and became an American citizen after the United States annexed the Hawaiian Islands two years later. During his stay in San Francisco, he worked on the staff of the city's *Chinese Free Press*, an early competitor to Ng's *Chung Sai Yat Po*. Founded by Chinese Masons in 1902, the *Free Press* quickly attracted other young radicals and reformers to its staff, with much of its news coverage geared to events in China. In 1909, supporters of Sun founded *Young China*, the paper that would become the main organ of the Chinese Nationalist Party in the US.

Another formidable competitor of *Chung Sai Yat Po* was the *Chinese World*. Followers of K'ang Yu-wei, the exiled political leader of China's Reform Movement, founded the paper in 1898 as a weekly opposed to the imperial government. Three years later, they turned the *World* into a daily, with a circulation second only to *Chung Sai Yat Po*. From that point on, most Chinese newspapers in America became organs of one or another political faction or secret society in China. Among those early newspapers, only *Chung Sai Yat Po* maintained its editorial independence.[45]

The Early Japanese and Korean Press

The first Japanese-language newspaper in the US, *Shinonome* ("Dawn"), began publication in 1886 in San Francisco. Fewer than 25,000 Japanese lived in the US at the time. A handful of other Japanese papers appeared over the next few years, including a daily called *Soko Shimbun* ("San Francisco News") in 1892. By the 1920s, more than 130,000 Japanese had settled in Hawaii and at least ten Japanese newspapers sprang up to service the immigrants; other papers appeared in Los Angeles, Seattle, Salt Lake City and Denver.[46]

The first Korean-language paper, *Konglip Sinbo*, appeared on November 22nd, 1905, in San Francisco. A competing paper, *Taedong Kongbo* ("Great Unity News") began publication two years later. Both were soon absorbed by a third publication, which was founded on February 10, 1909, by one of San Francisco's earliest Korean mutual aid societies. That publication, *Shinhan Minbo* ("New Korea"), emerged as the most influential and long-lasting newspaper in the Korean immigrant community of the United States, and is still being published today as a monthly in Los Angeles.[47]

The Age of Empire

Following the mysterious explosion aboard the USS *Maine* in Havana harbor, "the building of [imperialist] frenzy and newspaper circulation [went] hand in hand," media historian Erik Barnouw once noted. Hearst, Pulitzer and E. W. Scripps, having cobbled together the first giant newspaper chains, then spearheaded the efforts of American editors to win public support for an overseas colonial empire.[48]

Even as newspaper barons celebrated American might, the Associated Press was extending its own news empire. In 1893, AP quietly joined a little-known European communications cartel, which included Britain's Reuters, France's Havas and Germany's Wolff news agencies. The cartel had begun as early as 1869 to divide among its members the responsibility for disseminating news dispatches for Asia, Africa and the western hemisphere. Once AP joined the group, Reuters and the other agencies agreed to stay out of the United States. AP agreed, in turn, to exclusively supply the European members with news from the US and Latin America.[49]

The wire services thus carved up the world's information flow in the same way the European colonial powers carved up the world's resources and peoples. As press historian Anthony Long has noted:

> It is no accident, then, that the same nations which controlled physical transportation around the globe and which thereby maintained contact with their centres of trade and their colonies, also constructed the first

news networks to sell information to the world's newspapers. The traders and overseas administrators, like the explorers before them, were in themselves the basic sources of knowledge of the world and it was their view which was implicit in imperial society's creation of the political realities of the globe.[50]

Journalists of Color Challenge the Empire

Non-white journalists generally regarded the holding of a colonial empire as contrary to American democratic traditions. Most black newspapers in 1899 and 1900 were "anti-annexationist," according to one study of the era's minority press. Since US military interventions were invariably directed against non-white populations, black editors believed the federal government "could not deal justly with dark-skinned peoples, as evidenced by its do-nothing record at home."[51]

Moreover, the war erupted at the worst possible time for the country's black population. The Supreme Court's *Plessy v. Ferguson* decision two years earlier had officially sanctioned the spread of Jim Crow segregation. That ruling was followed in 1898 by two shocking incidents of mob terror, which the federal government refused to prosecute despite widespread appeals for action from the black community.

The first occurred on the night of February 21, less than a week after the explosion of the USS *Maine*. Fraser Baker, a black postal worker, and his infant son were murdered by a white mob in Lake City, South Carolina. President McKinley's decision to appoint Baker as local postmaster had enraged South Carolina politicians and the state's white citizens. "The placing of a Negro in an official position over white men of the South is a criminal outrage of the most flagrant type," warned one state newspaper. When Baker refused to resign, an armed mob in Lake City attacked and burned his home, which also doubled as a temporary post office. Baker, his wife, and his four children tried to escape the flames, but were met by gunfire. The volley of bullets wounded father and son. They then fled back into the house and were burned to death. His wife and other children managed to survive, but all suffered serious injuries.[52]

The second incident occurred in November, when North Carolina editor Josephus Daniels and other white Democratic leaders staged their bloody riot and armed overthrow of Wilmington's city council (see Chapter 9). Neither crime had a "federal aspect," McKinley claimed in his annual message to Congress.[53] Black papers wasted no time in blasting the president's response. "In the midst of the great war excitement let it not be forgotten that the South Carolina murderers of Postmaster Baker are yet unpunished," warned the black-owned Kansas City *American Citizen*. "There should be peace at home as abroad," it added. "To take in Cuba is but a beginning to swallow up all the West Indies. Do we actually need them for the safety of our republic?"[54]

One after another, black newspapers questioned the Cuba invasion, the mistreatment of black volunteers for the army, and the refusal of many states to allow black officers to command black troops. In May, after Congress declared war, the black-owned Cleveland *Gazette* published a stinging condemnation of the government's claims to be seeking Cuba's liberation:

Talk about fighting and freeing poor Cuba, and of Spain's brutality; of Cuba's murdered thousands, and starving reconcentradoes [sic]. Is America Any Better Than Spain? Has she not subjects in her very midst who are murdered daily without a trial of judge or jury? Has she not subjects in her borders whose children are half-fed and half-clothed because their father's skin is black and cannot labor side by side in her factories, etc. etc. with the white man?[55]

Following Spain's surrender, black editors stepped up their questioning, especially after President McKinley rejected the declaration of Filipino independence by that country's rebel leader General Emilio Aguinaldo and US troops became mired in a war against Filipino guerrillas.

The Coffeyville *American* reflected the sentiment of the black press:

The conduct of men in the future can only be determined by observing their conduct in the past … [I]t would be deplorable to have the inhabitants of the Philippine Islands treated as the Indians have been treated or the people of Cuba or Puerto Rico ruled as the Negroes of the South have been ruled.[56]

Some, like the Salt Lake City *Broad Ax*, were even more vehement in denouncing the Filipino occupation:

This war is simply being waged to satisfy the robbers, murderers, and unscrupulous monopolists who are ever crying for more blood! This country is not invested with any valid title to those islands; and her troops should not be permitted to trample upon the rights and liberties of the Filipinos.[57]

A number of mainstream white newspapers, such as Pulitzer's *New York World*, also editorialized against the occupation of the Philippines, but the strident opposition from the black press was unprecedented. Its editors repeatedly linked their own community's fight for racial equality to the desire for national freedom among non-white peoples in other parts of the world.

Latino newspapers likewise questioned the fervor for empire, though not always with the consistency of the black press. Some Latino editors who had long backed the liberation of Spain's remaining New World colonies welcomed the Spanish-American War as a way to achieve Cuban independence. Others saw the conflict as a naked US attempt to replace Spain's domination. A few weeks before the sinking of the battleship Maine in Havana harbor, for example, Pablo Cruz, the influential editor of the San Antonio *El Regidor*, wrote:

> Spain has nothing more left than a piece of American land and another portion of Puerto Rico, and who knows if tomorrow those will not be hers? ... Cuba is lost for Spain because of the just castigation of its impiety, the lack of humanity and religious beliefs, and of the horrible crimes always carried out in the name of Spain in America.[58]

But even *El Regidor* refused after the Maine explosion to accuse Spain of culpability. Two days after the tragedy, Cruz published a sober and balanced account, quoting Spanish claims that the explosion was an accident, and detailing the assistance Spain had provided to the US investigation. But once war was declared and US troops were on their way to Cuba, *El Regidor* and other key Texas papers, such as the influential *La Crónica* in Laredo, actively backed the war, and blasted in their editorials those newspapers in Mexico that were condemning the US effort.[59]

The Muckrakers and Race

The rise of business-friendly and chain-dominated American news did not go unchallenged for long. As so often happens in a society, a powerful trend soon spawns its own opposition. This time, however, that opposition did not come from the daily press. By the turn of the century, urban newspapers had grown so large and the power of the big chains so great that prospective new entrants to the field faced almost insurmountable challenges. The cost of printing presses had soared, and so had the influence of advertisers. While ads accounted for 44 percent of newspaper and magazine revenue in 1879, that figure rose to 55 percent by 1899, then to 60 percent over the next ten years.[60]

Advertisers naturally preferred the newspaper that offered the biggest audience and the lowest cost per reader. They tended to ignore smaller publications with narrow followings, and directed their money instead at those papers that could appeal to all political views. As a result, the number of newspapers plunged and competition in many cities waned. The second decade of the twentieth century marked the highpoint for US dailies (around 2,400) and for weeklies (around 16,000).[61]

The failures of the commercial press to address the country's mounting social problems soon gave rise to a new form of journalism—muckraking. Its chief practitioners were a handful of dogged investigative reporters who wrote mostly for radical middle-class magazines such as *McClure's*, *American Magazine*, and *Everybody's Magazine*. Lincoln Steffens, Upton Sinclair, Jacob Riis, Ida Tarbell, and Ray Stannard Baker emerged as national heroes for their chronicles of abusive social conditions, for their exposés of political and corporate wrongdoing, and for their radical critiques of class bias and corruption in the commercial media.

The publishers of those marvelous exposés, however, routinely ignored similar work by journalists of color. Ida Wells' explosive accounts of Southern lynching, for example, pre-dated Ray Stannard Baker's celebrated 1908 series in *American Magazine* by more than fifteen years. Articles by William Monroe Trotter in his Boston *Guardian* newspaper in the early 1900s, exposing Booker T. Washington's efforts to buy control of the black press, appeared several years before *The Brass Check*, Sinclair's classic 1919 indictment of corruption in the media. Likewise, Martí produced his brilliant dispatches on the ethnic cleansing of Native Americans in 1885, only four years after Helen Hunt Jackson published *A Century of Dishonor*, her riveting and immensely popular indictment of federal Indian policy. But unlike the white muckrakers, who soon became household names, Wells, Trotter, Martí, and the colored muckrakers remained virtually invisible outside their own communities.

The dissident tradition in American journalism thus evolved along parallel but segregated tracks—one white, one non-white. Once before, in the 1830s, the editors of white working-class newspapers had failed to bridge their differences with non-white journalists over slavery and western territorial conquest. The same dynamic repeated itself at the beginning of the twentieth century, and both journalism and the American public's understanding of race suffered as a result.

Muckraking in the white press largely disappeared by the 1920s, as the magazines that pioneered it went out of business or were scooped up by big commercial publishers. By then, the Progressive movement had achieved laudable social and political reforms—the nation's first consumer and environmental laws, the creation of social programs for the urban poor, the anti-trust legislation of the Roosevelt era—and it had touched off a storm of public criticism against the powerful barons of the press.[62]

But the progressives and muckrakers fell short in two key areas: they failed to build public support for closing the growing divide between workers and capitalists in America, and they did almost nothing to confront the spread of racial segregation. As Michael McGerr notes in his brilliant study of the Progressive Era: "True to their mission to create a safe society for themselves and their children, the progressives turned to segregation

as a way to halt dangerous social conflicts that could not otherwise be   •
stopped."[63]

The middle-class reformers of the era supported segregation not "out
of anger, hatred and a desire to unify whites," McGerr asserts, "but they
certainly expressed plenty of condescension and indifference, as well as
compassion" toward racial minorities. Most were not willing to derail their
effort to transform American society with a bitter battle over segregation.
Some of the most prominent muckrakers, like Sinclair, even had a tendency
to sprinkle their articles with racist references to blacks.[64]

Nonetheless, the muckrakers did provide relentless criticism of press corruption and complicity with the Captains of Industry. "Journalism is one
of the devices whereby industrial autocracy keeps its control over political
democracy," Sinclair declared in *The Brass Check*. "[I]t is the day-to-day,
between-elections propaganda, whereby the minds of the people are kept
in a state of acquiescence, so that when the crisis of an election comes, they
go to the polls and cast their ballots for either one of the two candidates of
their exploiters."[65]

Such attacks became so popular that they soon prodded the media industry to reform the worst excesses of its news-reporting methods. Between
1900 and 1915, several major universities created journalism schools to train
a new generation of reporters, while in 1922 executives of the country's
major newspapers founded the American Society of Newspaper Editors,
which soon adopted the newspaper industry's first code of ethics.[66]

The industry's decision to temporarily police its most corrupt practices,
together with the failure of white muckrakers to unite with their non-white
colleagues into a single, united media reform movement, effectively cur-
tailed any hope for structural change in the nation's mass media at the dawn
of the twentieth century. The celebrated Progressive Era ended with further
consolidation of giant news chains, further dominance of advertising over
news, and further consolidation of the white racial narrative. But even as that
era came to a close, yet another advance in technology touched off a seismic
upheaval in the media and opened new opportunities for a more democratic
system of news. That technology was wireless telegraphy.

IV

The Age of Broadcasting

Words with Wings

> Since the dawn of history, each new medium has tended to undermine an old monopoly, shift the definitions of goodness and greatness, and alter the climate of men's lives.
>
> Erik Barnouw, *A Tower in Babel*

On October 4, 1899, Guglielmo Marconi amazed the American public with his marvelous "black box" for sending messages through thin air. Shortly after launching Marconi Wireless Telegraph Company Ltd. in England, the young inventor traveled to the United States to showcase the instrument by providing "real-time" reports on that year's America's Cup race.

Under the sponsorship of James Gordon Bennett of the New York *Herald*, Marconi stationed himself on the deck of a steamer off the coast of New York, where he could follow the progress of the contending yachts. He used Morse code to transmit periodic updates on the race to two receiving stations in Manhattan, one of which was located at the *Herald*'s office on 34th Street. Bennett's employees then posted those reports on bulletin boards outside the newspaper, and from there the news was relayed to thousands of yachting fans lining the shores. America had discovered wireless telegraphy —the new medium that would evolve by the 1920s into modern radio.

The saga of that medium's early years has been amply chronicled by others, but radio's enormous impact on American race relations has received far less attention. In the pages that follow we summarize the pivotal federal policies that shaped radio's evolution into a largely commercial system dominated by a handful of national networks, we chronicle the handful of little-known minority radio pioneers who took to the airwaves in the early 1900s, and we reveal how the federal agencies Congress formed to regulate the airwaves in the public interest ended up condoning or ignoring racial bigotry in radio programming, thus helping to solidify further the white racial narrative in the US mass media.[1]

Even more than the Post Office and the telegraph, wireless communication compressed time and space as never before. It offered millions of Americans instant access to news, information and the performing arts. The public was "stirred at the prospect of telegraphing through air and wood and stone without so much as a copper wire to carry the message," proclaimed the *New York Times*. "We are learning to launch our winged words." As those winged words evolved from rudimentary point-to-point communications to full-fledged radio broadcasting, and then into huge national networks, they bound the public more tightly together in a new shared experience. Radio, after all, could reach everyone within range of an inexpensive transmitter, and it soon became the most ubiquitous mass medium in history. Millions of people listening to the same shows on the same day, often at the same hour, emerged with a new sense of their common identity—both as citizens and as consumers.[2]

Wireless telegraphy, moreover, proved invaluable for the US military, which had just emerged from the Spanish-American War with the pressing need to administer a new colonial empire. It gave naval commanders stationed in far-flung outposts like Puerto Rico, Cuba, the Philippines, and later the Panama Canal, the ability to communicate quickly with each other and with political leaders in Washington.

As the enormous potential of this new medium both to democratize knowledge and to influence public thought became apparent, considerable controversy arose during the 1920s and 1930s over what role, if any, the government should play in its development and regulation. Such constitutive debates, however, were confined largely to elite groups with a direct stake in the outcome—the executives of a few major electrical corporations; newspaper publishers eager to protect their dominant position in news dissemination; the burgeoning and mostly middle-class amateur radio movement; educational reformers with ambitious plans of turning the medium into a vehicle for cultural enrichment; and top bureaucrats at the US navy, the Post Office, and the Commerce Department, all of whom were vying to stake out bureaucratic control of radio for their separate departments.

The policies that emerged were eventually codified in the Federal Radio Acts of 1912 and 1927 and the Federal Communications Act of 1934. Key among them were: the airwaves are public property; the military's needs for communication must take precedence over civilian needs; the government can license and regulate use of the electromagnetic spectrum to private companies, but those companies must operate in a manner that serves the "public interest, convenience or necessity"; government regulation should seek to ensure economic competition and a diversity of viewpoints for the public; and local broadcasters must address the particular needs of their local communities.[3]

Our leaders fashioned, in effect, a market-based media system with moderate government regulation—a far different model from the publicly funded systems that developed in Britain, Canada and other industrial nations. In exchange for a government license to privately mine what was essentially a limited public resource—the electromagnetic spectrum—broadcasting companies agreed to serve certain information needs of the listening public. Much of the political history of American broadcasting since then has involved a series of battles between broadcasters, the government, and citizen groups over the definition of "public interest." As occurred in previous eras with the Post Office, the telegraph, and the telephone, those communications battles often hinged on a fundamental question: whether federal policy would promote a centralized or decentralized media system, and to what degree the government should intervene to preserve the existence of one or the other model. Citizen groups and political leaders of small, rural states usually favored laws to protect their locally based media from extinction, while politicians and businesses from large industrial states typically urged a system that privileged a handful of large national companies that could take advantage of economies of scale.

But each new model Congress adopted rarely survived for very long. The reason for that was simple: technological innovation is itself a revolutionary force. The emergence of new communications media, or even new methods for transmitting the old mediums (smart phones and personal digital assistants vs. desktop computers, for example), inevitably leads to upheaval in the existing order. In the case of wireless telegraphy, once thousands of amateur operators took to the airwaves in the early decades of the twentieth century and began to transmit their own "news" and entertainment, the amateur radio movement emerged as a threat to the centralized gatekeeper function that the big newspaper chains and Associated Press monopoly had wielded over information for decades.

Innovative technologies also create unexpected opportunities for new entrants, so it should not be surprising that people of color managed to establish a little-known beachhead as amateur radio operators, as on-air performers, and as providers of wireless content. But, beginning with the Radio Act of 1927, the government knocked scores of amateur and college radio stations off the air, turning the most powerful frequencies over to a handful of centralized commercial radio networks such as NBC, CBS and Mutual Broadcasting. That reorganization, with its heavy emphasis on advertiser-sponsored radio, betrayed the early hopes of educators who envisioned the new medium would act as a force for democratizing human knowledge, and for breaking down cultural barriers between peoples. Among the amateurs knocked off the air were dozens of people of color who had gravitated to wireless before World War I. As a result, racial minorities were virtually shut off from commercial radio licenses for decades. Until now, radio historians have believed that the first Hispanic and African-American commercial stations began in the mid-1940s. But our research has uncovered at least one Hispanic American who obtained a commercial license as far back as 1922. That year, Mexican-American John Rodriguez, owner of the Alamo

Electric Company in San Antonio, launched the second commercial station in that city and the first minority-owned station in the country, WCAR.

Other than Rodriguez, however, radio broadcasting in the United States remained white-owned throughout the 1920s and 1930s, even as newspapers published by people of color surged in number, circulation and influence. Some non-white entertainers did manage to perform on the air, and an occasional news show would touch on the condition of blacks or other racial minorities, but radio programs in those early decades invariably disseminated a "white" view of the world, and when they did portray non-whites, it was often through demeaning stereotypes.

Media historian Robert McChesney has painstakingly chronicled the heroic but unsuccessful campaign that educational reformers waged between 1927 and 1934 to carve out federal protections for non-commercial broadcasting. But even as the educational reformers pursued their goal, a separate and even more popular effort to reform federal broadcast policy was underway among people of color—the massive protest by African-Americans to force the popular *Amos 'n' Andy* off the air, the first of many attempts by African-Americans and Latinos to challenge the racial bigotry of broadcasters.

Despite those early citizen movements, both the Federal Radio Commission and its successor the Federal Communications Commission permitted—we would even argue, abetted—the evolution of a system that was racially exclusionary in ownership, in its hiring practices, and in its news and entertainment content. Not until the government opened radio up to a rash of new entrants in the late 1940s and early 1950s did people of color enjoy the first real benefit from the new medium.

Wireless Communications and Great Power Rivalry

The US government first began to pay attention to wireless communication during the Spanish-American War. Despite his stunning victory against the Spanish armada in the Philippines, Admiral George Dewey found himself unable to communicate from his ships at sea to army commanders on the ground, and he had even more difficulty reaching his superiors in Washington.

That lesson was reinforced during the Russo-Japanese War of 1904, when Japan's effective use of wireless communications gave its army a decided advantage over Russian forces. Soon after Japan's victory, President Teddy Roosevelt created the Interdepartmental Board of Wireless Telegraphy to coordinate and accelerate US efforts to develop this new medium. The board called for the creation of a coastal network of navy-operated wireless stations, and it urged that no private company be allowed to erect a station where its signal might interfere with military operations. The military use of wireless, in other words, was to have priority over any commercial use, with the navy in charge. At the same time the board proposed that all private stations should henceforth be licensed and supervised by the federal Department of Commerce and Labor.[4]

By 1899 Marconi was supplying the British and Italian navies with point-to-point wireless equipment. That year he established the Marconi Wireless Telegraph Company of America and started to solicit contracts from the US navy. He proposed to sell and erect the actual transmission equipment, whether aboard ships or on shore, then to supply his own operators to send and receive the messages. But company policy prohibited clients who leased Marconi equipment from communicating with firms that used competing instruments. Marconi, in other words, wanted total control of communications through the ether. It was a revolutionary concept, since no one had ever sought to lay claim to the air over any sovereign country.

The Marconi business model, as one might expect, soon sparked controversy among the major imperial powers. In 1902, the German government protested British dominance over the new industry and called for an international conference to discuss wireless communications. The US navy, which was understandably worried about the emergence of a second international communications monopoly since Britain already dominated the world's ocean cable lines, rejected the Marconi model and took the lead instead in funding wireless research in the US by its competitors.[5]

Enter Amateur Radio

Military and commercial leaders in the US soon confronted a new and unexpected group with ambitious plans for the ether: amateur radio operators. By 1905 an eighteen-year-old immigrant from Luxembourg named Hugo Gernsback had set up a company to sell radio sets to hobbyists. Gernsback's complete system included a bare-bones transmitter and receiver, and it became so popular that thousands of young people, most of them white middle-class males, began taking to the airwaves. One hundred and fifty amateur stations were operating by the end of 1905, and by 1910 600 radio clubs had been formed, with *Electrical World* reporting that an astonishing 800 amateur stations were up and running in the Chicago area alone. Hugo Gernsback then began to organize his fellow amateurs into the new Wireless Association of America.[6]

The navy was at first hostile to the amateur radio community, and sought legislation to curtail its growth. It accused ham operators of hampering rescue efforts by clogging frequencies and transmitting prank orders to naval ships, even though in several documented incidents amateurs were the first to hear and relay distress signals not picked up by navy or commercial operators.[7]

The Titanic *Tragedy Changes Wireless History*

The defining event in the early history of wireless was the sinking of the *Titanic* during its maiden voyage on April 15, 1912. The calamity not only shocked the public, it prompted Congress to adopt strict federal control and licensing over the infant wireless industry.

A US Senate Commerce Committee investigation of the disaster later concluded that the 1,500 passengers who perished that night, several of them prominent members of America's richest families, might have been saved if several vessels cruising near *Titanic* had responded immediately to the ocean liner's distress signals. The ships nearest to *Titanic* did not immediately learn of its troubles because they did not have wireless operators on duty round-the-clock.

Initial press reports of the catastrophe accused amateur operators of concocting messages that the *Titanic* had been saved. The Senate investigation found no evidence that anyone deliberately spread false information, but it did criticize amateurs for creating confusion during the rescue by refusing to vacate the airwaves. Moreover, the committee concluded that the 800 survivors would have perished as well if not for the SOS signals that were heard by the wireless operator of another ship, the *Carpathia*, which was fifty-eight miles away from the site of the accident.[8]

The Senate investigation established for the whole world the critical importance of wireless telegraphy. The true heroes of the *Titanic* calamity, the press concluded, were Marconi and his wireless company. One company employee in particular, a twenty-one-year-old Russian immigrant named David Sarnoff, achieved instant fame for his handling of the incident. After arriving at work on April 14 at a Marconi station on the roof of Wanamaker's department store in New York City, Sarnoff had heard the first faint coded message relaying news from the *Carpathia* of the loss of the Titanic and the search for survivors. He stayed on the air non-stop over several days receiving and decoding the intermittent messages from rescue ships and passing on the names of survivors to anxious reporters and government leaders.[9] Marconi rewarded his young employee with a promotion. But Sarnoff turned out to be a relentless self-promoter who took to embellishing even further his role in the *Titanic* affair. Still, the enormous press attention showered on him ignited Sarnoff's rise. He would go on to found the National Broadcasting Company and would emerge as one of the most influential executives in twentieth-century radio and television.[10]

The Federal Radio Act of 1912 was a direct response by Congress to the public outcry that followed the *Titanic* disaster. The new law required that all radio operators be licensed by the Department of Commerce and Labor; it divided up the electromagnetic spectrum for use by commercial ships, government and amateurs; it gave priority to distress communications and

mandated stiff fines for any "malicious interference" or irresponsible transmissions; and it gave the president the power to take control of the airwaves
during wartime.[11]

The act also sought to reduce the number of amateur operators by rel-
egating them to what was then the least desired short-wave portion of the
spectrum—200 meters or below. That restriction, however, did not diminish the ranks of amateur operators or the problem of interference. Many
simply chose to transmit without a license, since the Commerce Department lacked effective power to enforce its new regulations.[12] By 1914, the
number of radio clubs had climbed to an astonishing 10,000—and that
year Hiram Percy Maxim formed the American Radio Relay League, a
grass-roots effort that allowed ham operators to develop their own national
network for passing on vital information on natural disasters. In 1917 alone
(the year of the US entry into World War I), the government issued more
than 13,000 amateur radio licenses.

One of the most innovative of the early stations was 9XM at the University of Wisconsin. Teachers in the physics department there had started as
early as 1909 to experiment with point-to-point communication, then with
broadcast services. By 1917 Professor Earle M. Levy was sending out weather
reports in Morse code to hundreds of farmers on the outskirts of Madison,
and that year he and his students completed construction of a "wireless
telephone" transmitter. Another early innovator was Charles "Doc" Herrold
of San Jose, California, who founded his own college of engineering in
1909 and began experimenting with voice transmissions from a station he
erected atop a bank in San Jose. Despite having no formal training, Herrold
quickly attracted dozens of students from the growing amateur community in the Santa Clara Valley. Herrold's weekly show continued without fail
for years, even though the quality of its voice transmission was spotty. San
Francisco schoolteachers often brought their students to tour the station,
and it received widespread attention at the 1915 Panama Pacific Exposition
in San Francisco.[13]

The entry of the US into World War I in April 1917 brought a temporary
halt to the amateur craze. The federal government immediately shut down
all amateur stations and took over operation of commercial ones. It also
required wireless companies to mass-produce a variety of communications
equipment for the war effort. To facilitate cooperation by those companies, the government placed a moratorium on all patent disputes, it allowed
radio manufacturers to use "any patented invention necessary" to meet
US military needs, and it placed most radio experimentation under direct
supervision of the navy.[14] As would later happen with the early development
of the Internet, the military needs of the US government thus subsidized
and accelerated research into a new communications medium. In the words
of radio historian Eric Barnouw, radio "was a development financed by

government, coordinated largely by the navy ... With few restrictions as to funds, it became the inspirer and guiding patron of diverse assembly lines and research laboratories ..."[15]

African-Americans and the Wireless Era

Only a few non-whites were featured on amateur radio before World War I, most of them musicians. In November of 1914, for example, white amateur Victor H. Laughter transmitted a Memphis concert by W. C. Handy, the "Father of the Blues." The first wireless transmission of a sporting event was of the legendary 1910 boxing match between Jack Johnson, the first black heavyweight champion, and his white challenger Jack Jeffries (see Chapter 12).[16]

Black radio operators were deeply involved in the early amateur radio movement, but you could only know that by reading the pages of the black press. In 1910, for example, the *Chicago Defender* published an account of Robert Gillespie, a black high school student and member of the Wireless Club of America who had astonished visitors to the Electric Show at the Chicago Coliseum with the radio he had erected in his own home electric shop. Gillespie had "the distinction of being one of only three colored wire-less operators in America," the *Defender* noted.[17] Four years later, the *Defender* reported that a "near riot" had occurred when Harry T. Daily, a black man who had acquired radio skills while serving in the navy, reported to work at his new job as a wireless operator for the Red Star line, but was then sum-marily dismissed because of the angry protest of white radio operators.[18]

By 1915, the Woodlawn Radio Association, a black radio club in Chicago, was holding regular meetings.[19] In Baltimore, another black amateur operator, Roland Carrington, started to recruit youths from his community in 1916 to experiment with the new medium. The city's weekly *Afro-American* reported in March of that year that Boy Scout Troop 2 was "taking up wireless and semaphore signal codes."[20] Nearly a year later, Carrington offered in a letter to the paper to assist local black Boy Scouts in setting up their own station:

> [I]f there were enough of our boys and Boy Scouts interested in wireless they could erect a wireless station at the park and I am most sure that arrangements could be made to have another station erected either at the Afro-American Building or at the YMCA. But as yet, we have not enough boys interested to do so. Let us try and get together and form a good and up-to-date Radio Club in our city. I will be more than pleased to help.[21]

Carrington's plans were interrupted a month later when the navy shut down all radio stations because of the war. On May 5 he promised the readers of the *Afro-American* he would resume radio work after the ban was lifted:

I am still interested in wireless work but I am not receiving any wireless messages now because the government has ordered all aerials taken down. All wireless instruments are now sealed in a box by the United States Radio Inspector. Don't get discouraged at this restriction but let us hope that we may get on the job soon when the present troubles are over and the ban lifted. Great times will follow.[22]

The war itself created a huge need in the army for radio operators. With prominent black editors loudly condemning racial segregation in the military, the government responded by authorizing all-black signal battalions and training their recruits in wireless. Emmett J. Scott, an assistant secretary of the War Department and one of the military's highest-ranking black officials, spearheaded training of the all-black 325th Signal Battalion in Richmond, Virginia.[23] In 1917, at the federal government's request, Howard University began to offer courses in radio engineering—the first black college to do so.[24]

The Great War and Mass Propaganda

World War I was the first armed conflict to prove the strategic value of mass propaganda for military success. The federal government systematically utilized the news media, both the wireless and newspapers, to win tens of millions of people around the world to the allied cause.[25] As part of that effort, President Wilson appointed George Creel, a muckraking journalist and former editor of the *Rocky Mountain News*, to run the Committee on Public Information and manage public opinion. At the same time, Congress moved to suppress press and citizen opposition to the war at home by passing the Espionage Act of 1917. The new law barred false statements that interfered with the war effort or any statement that encouraged "insubordination, disloyalty, mutiny" or refusal to serve in the military. It also empowered the postmaster general to deny mailing privileges to any publication he thought violated any provisions of the Act. In October 1917, Congress passed the Trading With the Enemy Act, authorizing the Post Office to censor foreign-language publications. Finally, in May 1918 came the Sedition Act, which barred any "disloyal, profane, scurrilous or abusive language" about the government, the military, or the flag. More than 2,200 Americans were prosecuted under the new laws, and nearly half of them were convicted. The government canceled the mailing privileges for some forty-four newspapers during the first year of the Espionage Act, and it permitted another thirty to use the mails only after their publishers agreed to produce no more stories about the war. Among those denied access to the mails were the *American Socialist, Appeal to Reason*, the *Milwaukee Leader*, and the magazine *The Masses*. Victor Berger, the Austrian-born editor of the *Leader*—the first socialist to be elected to the US Congress—was convicted of conspiracy to violate the Espionage Act and sentenced to twenty years in prison. Eugene V. Debbs was sentenced to ten years in prison for speaking out against military recruitment, while fellow socialist Rose Pastor Stokes was slapped with a ten-year sentence for writing a letter to the editor of a Kansas City newspaper that proclaimed: "I am for the people and the government is for the profiteers."[26]

More significant than direct government censorship, however, was the massive propaganda machine created by Creel, enlisting hundreds of newspapers and thousands of journalists around the world, the entire Allied wireless industry, and scores of naval transmitting stations.[27] Creel convinced publishers to accept a voluntary code of self-censorship for troop and ship movements, and recruited major advertisers and the infant film industry to help "sell" the war effort to the American people. The United States was no different in this regard than the other major belligerents. In a classic study of the immigrant press written a few years after the war, sociologist Robert E. Park noted the key role of the press, especially foreign-language and ethnic newspapers, in the propaganda effort. Belligerent governments tried not only to win over their own migrant nationals living inside the states of their enemies—they sought to stir the racial and ethnic minorities of those states against their governments. While modern science had "multiplied the engines of destruction," Park noted, advances in mass communication, along with the growth of international labor migration, had transformed modern warfare into an "internal or internecine struggle" as well. "Under these circumstances, propaganda, in the sense of an insidious exploitation of the sources of dissension and unrest, may as completely change the character of wars as they were once changed by the invention of gunpowder."[28]

Creel's efforts were not simply confined to foreign countries. He also sought to ferret out and neutralize propaganda efforts by Germany and its allies here at home, spearheading a huge surveillance operation against pacifists, socialists, and war critics in the immigrant and African-American press. The German government likewise poured significant resources into controlling its image in the press of other countries. Before the war, for example, the German officials purchased the New York *Daily Mail* for $750,000, and even sought for a time to buy the New York *Sun* and the *Washington Post*. They secretly kept a number of American correspondents on payroll, and bankrolled or sought to control several foreign-language papers in the US. One of those newspapers was New York City's *Staats-Zeitung*, the country's main German-language newspaper. Founded in 1834, the paper had been purchased in 1896 by German-American Herman Ridder. Under Ridder it had become the most influential foreign-language paper in the country, with its circulation of 60,000 surpassing even that of the *New York Times*. But it also became the unofficial organ of the German government in this country.

After Ridder died in 1915, leaving the paper heavily in debt, Germany tried to save it from bankruptcy by secretly providing Ridder's sons with $15,000 in aid.[29] *Staats-Zeitung* survived its financial troubles only by agreeing to reject further German help and to line up behind the US war effort. After the war, Ridder's descendants used the newspaper to launch what eventually became one of the most influential newspaper chains of the late twentieth century, Knight-Ridder. The chain lasted until 2006, when the McClatchy Company purchased it.

Creel's effort to counter the influence of *Staats-Zeitung* was one small part of a worldwide strategy he fashioned to win what he called the "verdict of mankind." In that immense clash, Creel later wrote, "America put her chief dependence on radio, finally reaching a peak of operation that used the air lanes of the whole world, reaching every country on the globe with the American message." Packages of news and information prepared by the CPI staff, as Creel's operation became known, were wired each day from a station in Tuckerton, New Jersey, to a network of wireless stations around the globe. Virtually every country in Asia, Latin America and Europe had a government-owned wireless station by then. Once Creel's daily dispatch arrived, his agents in each country would immediately translate it into the local language for insertion into that country's newspapers for publication. And so it was that millions of people worldwide were exposed to America's view of the war in their local newspaper each morning.[30]

Josephus Daniels and the Navy's Creation of the Radio Trust

To harness radio effectively for the war effort, Creel worked closely with Secretary of the Navy Josephus Daniels, whom Wilson had appointed an ex-officio member of the Committee on Public Information. Daniels was the same former newspaper publisher who less than two decades earlier had played such a pivotal role in North Carolina's white-supremacy movement and the Wilmington race riot (see Chapter 9). Despite their distinguished careers as journalists, Creel and Daniels showed no reluctance to squash news stories which they felt undermined the nation's war effort. In his cabinet diaries, Daniels mentioned numerous wartime meetings with Creel on the subject. In one entry, Daniels describes how navy officials convinced the Associated Press bureau chief in Washington to kill a story about US ships torpedoed by submarines en route to France.[31]

A longtime populist and follower of William Jennings Bryan, Daniels had advocated federal ownership of wireless even before the war. Once America entered the fighting, he spearheaded the navy's building of its own system of wireless transmitters and supervised the takeover of two powerful stations the Germans had erected on the east coast. He even quietly arranged for the navy to purchase control of the Marconi shore-to-ship network, as well as a competing network run by Federal Telegraph on the west coast. Through those efforts, Daniels and his deputies fashioned the navy's wartime monopoly over radio. But in his eagerness to perpetuate the monopoly after the war, Daniels ran afoul of Congress and key members of America's business community, who favored a return to a privately owned radio system. When Congress discovered Daniels' unauthorized actions, its members launched an investigation and demanded that the navy return the Marconi stations to the company. Several lawmakers even threatened to impeach Daniels. But he and his subordinates refused to back down. "Monopoly of wireless must be in hands of one government or one corporation," Daniels said. "Interference makes anything else weaken or destroy the value of wireless."[32]

As with the debate over telegraph ownership in 1846, a change of political power in Washington significantly altered the course of federal media policy. Republicans gained control of Congress in the 1918 elections, and their victory dashed Daniels' hopes for a government monopoly over the new medium. Daniels and his aides, fearful of a possible British hegemony over radio communications, then quickly moved to derail a proposed Marconi technology partnership with the General Electric Company. In April 1919, Commander Stanford Hooper from the navy's bureau of engineering, and Rear Admiral W. H. G. Bullard, the director of naval communications, met with General Electric chairman Owen Young to press him for an alternate radio strategy. The navy's position was simple: any postwar wireless system in the United States had to be controlled by Americans. Bullard assured Young of government backing for the creation of a new company that would ensure that goal.[33]

Young and navy officials then mapped out their strategy. They agreed that key participants in the American wireless industry would all hold shares in the new entity and make their patents available to each other. Foreigners such as Marconi would be limited to a minority stake, and the navy itself would have a seat on the board of directors. Since the navy was still in control of Marconi's US facilities, it wielded enormous power. Simply put, it was an offer Marconi could not refuse. The new Radio Corporation of America officially came into existence on October 17, 1919. Marconi's US subsidiary promptly transferred all of its assets to the new RCA; General Electric's Owen Young became chairman, and Admiral Bullard assumed a post on the board of directors as the navy's official representative. So while Daniels had failed in his plan to nationalize radio, his fallback plan—control of wireless by a single company closely tied to the navy—had won the day. Amazingly, this pivotal moment in early broadcast history went largely unreported to the American public.[34]

Over the next two years, Young recruited as major shareholders of RCA the American Telephone and Telegraph Company, along with its Western Electric subsidiary, the Westinghouse Corp., and the United Fruit Co., which operated its own radio network throughout Latin America. And so it was that the navy engineered the creation of the American Radio Trust, better known as RCA. All the members of the new trust agreed to share their patents and divide up their areas of interest "so that the world of electronic communication, as the conferees viewed it in the early months of 1920, might be developed co-operatively rather than in competition."[35] The group of companies that comprised RCA would go on to dominate commercial broadcasting for much of the twentieth century in much the same way as Western Union had dominated the telegraph in the late nineteenth century.

Even today, the early political history of broadcasting is unknown to most Americans. Modern media executives who call for an end to government regulation, for a private media system where competition reigns, rarely acknowledge that the handful of networks that dominated radio and television broadcasting throughout the twentieth century were born through direct government sponsorship and enjoyed huge wartime federal subsidies for their early research.

The Birth of Radio Broadcasting

The members of the new Radio Trust originally expected to use wireless only for point-to-point commercial and government communications in Morse code. But a few visionary employees at those companies soon began to imagine potential consumer applications for the new technology— transmission of the human voice itself to individual homes, each equipped with its own inexpensive receiver. One of those visionaries was David Sarnoff. As a mid-level manager at American Marconi, Sarnoff had moved over to RCA when his old company was absorbed into the new entity. He soon proposed to his superiors that the company start manufacturing radio receivers for the public—boxes that could receive different frequencies and offer listeners an array of lectures and music. Sarnoff called his idea the "Radio Music Box." RCA officials were slow to respond, and by the time they did others had already begun transmitting live events. Sarnoff would later claim he had been the first to develop the idea of broadcasting.[36]

But as we have seen, amateur operators like Charles Herrold and Earle Levy were conducting serious experiments with transmitting music, news and educational programs long before Sarnoff. Levy and his colleagues at the University of Wisconsin had even managed to escape the federal wireless ban during World War I, when the navy granted him a waiver to continue his experiments. As soon as the war ended, Levy's 9XM resumed public broadcasts of weather reports and road conditions in both Morse code and voice, and it even began to transmit music. Between 1921 and 1925, some 176 colleges and universities received operating licenses from the federal government.

One of the earliest radio enthusiasts among newspaper publishers was William E. Scripps, owner of the *Detroit News*. Scripps purchased some radio equipment for his son in 1920, installed the equipment in a file room at the *News*, and began to experiment with an amateur station, using the call letters 8MK. Scripps ordered a teenage office boy at the paper with a good singing voice to begin crooning each night into an Edison gramophone horn that was connected to a telephone mouthpiece and the transmitter; he then told the boy to keep asking periodically if any radio operator out there could hear him. Scripps even tried to attract listeners by publishing announcements of the station's programs in his paper. On August 31 of that year, the *Detroit News* radiophone transmitted the results of a local Democratic primary election, with the paper praising its experiment as a "gigantic step" in "the history of man's conquest of the elements."

All over the country amateurs were engaged in similar efforts at radio broadcasting, with most relying on music as their staple product. The transmission of live news soon became a huge draw for both operators and listeners. On Election Day 1920, the *Detroit News* station, now renamed WWJ, transmitted the results of the Harding-Cox presidential race. WWJ actually shared the honor of that first national election broadcast with Pittsburgh's KDKA, but the latter managed to generate so much press attention for its effort that WWJ has long been relegated to the footnotes of radio histories. The following year KDKA initiated regular news reports from the offices of the Pittsburgh *Post*. Meanwhile, WJC in Norfolk, Nebraska launched a daily news show, and by the late 1920s WOMT in Manitowoc, Wisconsin, was producing news "every hour on the hour." In 1922 the *Brooklyn Eagle* initiated New York's first news and commentary show on AT&T's WEAF station, featuring the paper's star reporter H.V. Kaltenborn. With his melodious, patrician voice, incisive social commentaries, and unwavering opposition to corporate and government abuse, Kaltenborn would soon become one the best known and most respected journalists in America.[37]

More than any other early radio broadcast, KDKA's transmission of the 1920 presidential election signaled the start of the commercial revolution in radio. The station's founder was Westinghouse employee Frank Conrad. The company promptly secured its own radio license on November 2nd, 1920, and KDKA became the nation's first commercial radio station to go on the air. Operating from a makeshift tent atop the roof of the Westinghouse building, Conrad used his inaugural broadcast to provide listeners with the presidential returns, just as Scripps was doing with his amateur station in Detroit. The mad rush of voices to the airwaves was on. By the end of the decade this astonishing new medium would transform America's system of mass communication.[38]

The success of KDKA shifted the economic model for wireless from the selling of transmission equipment and services for point-to-point communication to the selling of radio sets to American consumers. Radio ceased to be merely a medium for individual amateurs to entertain and inform each other; it became instead a commercial tool for building an audience, then selling that audience consumer products. More than 3 million sets were sold from 1922 to 1925, as the percentage of homes that owned a radio skyrocketed from 0.2 percent to 10 percent, mostly among white, middle-class or wealthy families.[39] So few blacks or other people of color owned radios in those early days that broadcasters paid virtually no attention to those communities, except in some of the big cities, and even then the programs were geared to a white audience. In 1923, for instance, RCA's first station, WJZ, aired a half-hour show every Tuesday called "Negro Dialect Stories."[40]

The government licensed only twenty-eight commercial stations in 1921, but the following year the number zoomed to 500. "In twelve months radio phoning has become the most popular amusement in America," the *New York Times* noted in March 1922. "In every neighborhood people are stringing wires to catch the ether wave currents." Secretary of Commerce Herbert Hoover called the new radio fever "one of the most astounding things that [has] come under my observation of American life."[41]

By then individual members of the Radio Trust were rushing to start their own stations. On October 5, 1921, Sarnoff launched WJZ in Newark, NJ. Its first broadcast was a play-by-play account of the World Series from the Polo Grounds. A few months later engineers at AT&T proposed the creation of a network of thirty-eight stations linked by the company's long-distance telephone lines. In the summer of 1922, AT&T initiated what was to become one of New York City's most important stations, WEAF. In those wild and confusing early years of broadcasting, when no one was quite sure how the medium would develop or pay for itself, AT&T settled on a plan to link stations into national and regional networks, then to charge those stations and programmers for its services rather than create its own original content.[42]

The barons of the newspaper industry and the wire services, meanwhile, had been caught flat-footed by the new technology. In the wake of the *Detroit News* experiment, publishers who had voiced initial hostility to the new medium now began entering the field purely as a defensive measure— to guard against any threat to their gatekeeper role as disseminators of news and information. More than 100 papers had launched their own stations by 1922, most of them in the 25–50 watt range. Colonel Robert McCormick of the *Chicago Tribune*, for example, began in December 1921 to supply news and market reports to that city's first radio station, Westinghouse Electric's KYW. Radio sets were not yet available in stores, but amateurs were rushing to buy individual components and then assemble their own, so that by 1922 more than 20,000 sets were in Chicago homes. Soon, whole sets came on the market with names like Grebe, Aeriola and Radiola, and stores could barely keep them in stock.[43] When a 1924 *Tribune* survey revealed that more than 100,000 receiving sets were operating in the Chicago area, McCormick rushed to lease the bulk of time on a Zenith-owned station, rechristening the station WGN (World's Greatest Newspaper). The new *Tribune* station's opening-night program, on March 29, 1924, consisted largely of broadcasts of band concerts from Chicago's Drake Hotel, interspersed with news bulletins from the paper's staff and an "Agricultural Program" produced by the American Farm Bureau.[44] The following year, WGN pulled off a brilliant move by broadcasting the final days of a trial in Dayton, Tennessee, that had begun to attract considerable attention—the Scopes "Monkey Trial." It cost the station more than $1,000 a day to transmit the dramatic courtroom showdown between legendary defense attorney Clarence Darrow and the fiery but aging William Jennings Bryan for the prosecution, but the broadcast drew a huge audience and further awakened the public to the awesome power of live radio.[45]

A few papers soon began printing daily radio logs and program listings to increase their own circulation and as a way of developing ties with local stations. Department stores, electrical companies, and automobile dealerships all joined the stampede for radio licenses in an effort to boost sales for their primary product. Even churches, schools and local governments sought licenses to better reach their members or constituents.[46]

Herbert Hoover and the Federal Radio Act of 1927

The radio craze sweeping the country soon forced the federal government to devise a long-term policy toward the new medium. No leader played a more decisive role in fashioning that policy than Herbert Hoover. As secretary of commerce under two presidents from 1921 to 1929, Hoover had inherited the responsibility for licensing radio operators and assigning station frequencies—a power delegated to the Commerce Department by the Radio Act of 1912.

A successful businessman and mining engineer, Hoover was a firm believer in the key role of science and technology in modern society and a fervent champion of corporate standardization of mass production to advance prosperity. He was also an advocate of "associationalism"—the theory that leaders of industry and citizen groups could come together to informally solve disputes and regulate themselves.[47]

His department was just one of three federal agencies that became locked in a bureaucratic battle over control of radio after World War I. The Commerce Department, as the agency most closely allied with American business, favored keeping radio in private hands, much like the early telegraph, and because of that the major radio companies regarded Hoover as their "protector and champion."[48]

The Radio Trust also relied on the support of another powerful interest group—newspaper publishers. For the most part, publishers began advocating a privately owned radio system after World War I. As Susan Douglas points out, "while in 1919, the navy enjoyed titular power over America's radio networks, it was no match for the communications corporations," which had cultivated for years a "bias against government control of public utilities."[49] The navy hierarchy may have fathered the Radio Corporation of America in 1919, but it was powerless to control the growing chaos on the airwaves from thousands of amateurs experimenting with radio broadcasting. Ever since 1912, virtually anyone had been granted a license merely by applying to the secretary of commerce. As the number of stations mushroomed, congestion and interference between radio signals became constant and intolerable. Everyone realized only federal intervention could resolve the problem.

Hoover convened four national radio conferences during the early 1920s to address all issues affecting the radio industry, particularly the question of interference. He skillfully used those gatherings to maneuver between competing interests of the military, private business, and the amateurs, and thus cemented his role as the government's principal broker on radio policy. Despite his public claims that he was balancing the interests of all stakeholders, Hoover routinely assigned amateurs and low-power stations the least desirable frequencies.[50]

The fourth radio conference, in 1925, recommended a moratorium on new licenses to curtail rampant interference. Hoover promptly imposed that moratorium, and when a station run by Zenith Radio Corp. switched its transmission to another frequency without asking for Commerce approval, Hoover went to court to stop the station. A year later, an Illinois federal judge dealt a severe blow to the radio moratorium. In *U.S. v. Zenith Radio,* the court ruled that under the Federal Radio Act the Commerce Department did not have the legal right to assign frequencies or to deny a license to any applicant.[51]

Following Hoover's defeat in the Zenith case, more than 200 new stations rushed to get on the air; scores of others simply jumped to whatever broadcast frequency they preferred. The resulting free-for-all produced so much signal interference that virtual anarchy reigned for months. Even before that new stampede of stations, radio in the US had mushroomed to include 15,111 amateur stations, 1,902 ship stations, 553 land stations for maritime use, and 536 broadcasting stations.[52] Ordinary Americans were furious at the chaos on the airwaves, though some historians have seen a positive aspect to the upheaval. "The undisciplined and unregulated voice" of so many amateurs, notes Mark Goodman, "interfered with corporate goals of delivering programming and advertising on a dependable schedule to a mass audience."[53]

The mad rush to the airwaves prompted angry public cries for federal intervention, and Congress responded by hurriedly passing the Radio Act of 1927. The new law established the basic rules of the American broadcasting system that are still in operation today. It made clear for the first time that the federal government had the authority to regulate the nation's airwaves, and it revoked all existing licenses and created a five-member Federal Radio Commission to divide up the spectrum, issue all licenses, assign frequencies, and otherwise supervise broadcasters. Due to the finite number of frequencies available, the law also limited the number of radio license holders, and it required that all radio stations, as a condition of possessing a license, serve the "public interest, convenience or necessity."

The Federal Government Favors the Networks

The FRC's subsequent reallocation of frequencies gave larger radio companies and networks unparalleled control over the fledgling radio industry while reducing the number of independent voices. The agency immediately removed 150 of the 732 broadcast stations then on the air, including many educational stations, and it forced others onto less desirable frequencies.[54] Until then considerable variety had existed on the air, with educational institutions and colleges holding a large share of the licenses, and with few stations in the habit of selling airtime. Even the labor movement had won a license—WCFL in Chicago in 1926; and in New York one station, WEVD, was closely associated with the Socialist Party.

To justify its new allocation of licenses, the Commission claimed network and commercial stations served the public interest requirement of the law because they had better operating and engineering standards, and could therefore produce better-quality radio signals. Larger stations, the FRC argued, provided greater diversity of viewpoint to listeners than smaller, nonprofit stations that aired programs only to niche groups.[55] In fact, the new national networks had only just been formed. RCA created the National Broadcasting Company in 1926 and immediately launched two chains of affiliates, the NBC Red and Blue networks. Businessmen George A. Coats and Arthur Judson formed the United Independent Broadcasters in January 1927, using Philadelphia station WCAU as their base of operations. The following year Columbia Records purchased United and rechristened it the Columbia Phonographic Broadcasting System.[56]

It soon became apparent that the FRC was setting aside the most desirable, clear channel licenses—those with the highest power and the longest reach—to benefit the commercial broadcasters, while banishing others to regional and low-power frequencies. The agency ordered the University of Arkansas's KFMQ, for example, to share time with a commercial station—one-fourth of the time for the university, and three-fourths for the commercial station. It allotted Nebraska Wesleyan's WCAJ one-seventh of the time on the same frequency with WOW, a commercial station in Omaha. Many church-owned stations were simply bought out, sometimes with the purchaser agreeing to continue broadcasting the church's Sunday services.[57] In 1927 there were fifty network-affiliated stations; by 1931, NBC alone had sixty-one affiliates in *each* of its Red and Blue networks, while the CBS boasted seventy-nine station affiliates.[58]

The emergence of the networks, with their ability to sell lucrative advertising to national sponsors, placed enormous financial pressures on independent stations. It also began to restrict the relative freedom of station owners from both government and advertiser interference in their programming. Some of those dangers had become apparent as early as 1924. That year, William Harkness, the manager of AT&T's WEAF, removed H.V. Kaltenborn from the air. Kaltenborn had made the mistake during a news show of criticizing Secretary of State Charles Evan Hughes for refusing to extend diplomatic recognition to the Soviet Union. Aides to Hughes lodged furious complaints directly to AT&T's representative in Washington, and since the company, according to one executive, had a policy of "constant and complete cooperation" with government agencies that had anything to do with communications, Harkness immediately sacked Kaltenborn.[59]

As network programs with corporate sponsorships mushroomed, the need for local talent to perform live for individual stations diminished. "The word came to many—orchestra leaders, lady organists, pianists, singers, monologists, speakers—that they would not be needed," Barnouw has noted.[60] And it did not take long for the networks to switch from direct corporate underwriting of whole programs to selling blocks of airtime to hawk products directly. In 1930, NBC president Merlyn Aylesworth told a US Senate committee: "I am opposed to direct advertising on the air." Two years later, a newspaper study of one day's broadcasting—2,365 hours on 208 stations across the country—found 12,546 interruptions for advertising. Radio stations were devoting more time to sales pitches than to news, education, lectures and religion combined, the study noted.[61]

The Davis Amendment and Local Control

The Commission's obvious bias in favor of members of the Radio Trust sparked immediate opposition from members of Congress in the Southern and western states. They argued that the Radio Act of 1927, which had divided the country into five geographic regions of roughly the same population, required equitable distribution of licenses, but the agency was giving favored treatment to stations in only one region, the northeast. Since the Act also required Congress to reauthorize the agency the following year, the dissatisfied representatives threatened in 1928 to hold up that renewal. US

Rep. E. L. Davis (D-Tenn.) noted during the reauthorization debate that the Commission had granted the northeast "nearly twice as much increased power as all the other four zones combined, or putting it differently, the city of New York ... was granted 15,000 more watts than was granted all the other forty-seven States in the Union." Davis pushed through an amendment requiring equitable distribution of radio licenses, station power, and time on the air for all states and regions. His effort echoed the nineteenth-century battles in Congress over second-class postal rates, in which congressmen from small states had championed special postal discounts for their local newspapers so they would not be overwhelmed by bigger east-coast publications. While Davis never questioned the increasingly commercial nature of American radio, his proposal did at least mandate a more decentralized, and thus more democratic, character to the system. President Hoover signed into law the Davis Amendment on March 28, 1928. Its provisions quickly forced the FRC to increase the number of radio stations based in the South.[62] As the agency did so, the influence over radio programming by that region's industrial and agricultural elite also increased.

The Radio Commission's first year of operation was an especially turbulent period. Two of its five founding members, Admiral W. G. H. Bullard and John F. Dillon, died within months of their appointment, while a third, Henry A. Bellows, quickly resigned. The new agency was forced to depend on Commerce Secretary Hoover's staff from the department's Bureau of Standards to develop many of its earliest technical and licensing decisions.[63] Hoover thus wielded immense influence over those decisions.

Licensing a Klan Station

Southern businessmen who launched radio stations in the 1920s and 1930s were invariably segregationists. Most were convinced that Jim Crow would last forever, and they were determined to prevent any views that challenged those beliefs from reaching their audiences. Southern affiliates of the big national networks routinely objected to or removed from their local stations network shows that presented any other outlook on white-black relations.

The FRC exacerbated this problem by refusing to consider avowed racists as ineligible to hold licenses. In 1927, for example, the Commission granted a radio license to the Independent Publishing Company, a Washington, D.C. firm that published a weekly newspaper openly associated with the Ku Klux Klan.[64] James S. Vance, one of the two owners of Independent Publishing, was an influential Washington journalist and member of the National Press Club. He had begun his career in the press as the business manager of a Scottish Rite publication in 1910, and later worked on the staff of the *Analyst*, a financial paper published by the *New York Times*.[65] Vance and George Fleming, his partner at Independent

Publishing, were both Masons when they joined together in 1921 to launch their newspaper, the *Fellowship Forum*. They called it "The World's Greatest Fraternal Newspaper," and claimed its mission was to disseminate "religious and patriotic doctrines."[66]

The *Forum* became an integral part of the resurgence of the KKK among white Americans in the 1920s. Klan leaders hired public relations experts Mary Elizabeth Tyler and Edward Young Clarke to refashion their organization's public image into one that depicted Klansmen as devoted to "Pure Americanism." Membership skyrocketed from just a few thousand at the beginning of the decade to some 5 million, while subscriptions to the *Fellowship Forum* zoomed from a mere 1,000 in 1921 to more than a million by 1927.[67] By then the paper boasted a staff of 125, and its editors could claim:

> In every portion of the Nation God-fearing and liberty loving citizens look upon The Fellowship Forum as the National Voice of Protestant and Fraternal Americanism and have come to know that they can safely depend upon its utterances as the statement of truth unembellished by mundane influences ... by either political and sectional doctrines.[68]

Franklin D. Roosevelt would later estimate that the *Forum* spent between $2 million and $5 million on the paper's publication.[69]

In 1927 the *Fellowship Forum* decided to apply to the new Radio Commission for permission to begin broadcasting in the Washington, DC, area. The details of its little-known effort can be found in Department of Commerce records at the National Archives. In July of that year Vance purchased a failing radio station owned by the Twelfth Assembly District Republican Club of Brooklyn and applied to the FCC for permission to move the station to a Virginia property that had once been part of George Washington's Mt. Vernon estate. The goal of his station, Vance claimed, was "to pierce the ether frequently with talks on pure patriotism by some outstanding American" and to provide a venue for patriotic and fraternal organizations.[70]

But the *Forum* was then considered so disreputable that an acting supervisor of radio for the Commerce Department questioned whether granting Vance a license would serve the public interest requirements of the Radio Act. Amazingly, the supervisor was concerned, as the following note shows, only with the *Forum*'s anti-Catholic bigotry, not with its racism:

> There is enclosed herewith application for radio station construction permit submitted by the Independent Publishing Company, Washington, D.C.
>
> Confidential inquires concerning this publishing company indicate that the above concern is connected with the Ku Klux Klan and that it is their policy to denounce in their publication, the Catholic Church.

It would seem on the strength of the above that it is safe to assume that this applicant, should a broadcast station be erected and licensed, would carry on religious propaganda to the extent that it would be questionable whether such a station would be in the interest of public convenience, interest and necessity.[71]

Despite the obvious concerns of its staff, the FRC approved the *Fellowship Forum*'s license. Vance quickly secured more than $65,000 to build the station. It no doubt helped that his newspaper—and presumably the new station—*could* be counted on to assist Hoover in his upcoming campaign for president in 1928. Hoover knew by then that New York's Governor Al Smith, a Catholic, was the leading contender for the Democratic nomination. He also knew that, in order to capture the White House, he would need to weaken Smith's support in the solidly Democratic South.

In August 1927, the FCC approved the license transfer to Vance and the *Fellowship Forum*. The station's call letters were changed to WTFF (for The Fellowship Forum).[72] Shortly after securing the license, Vance petitioned the Commission for an enormous increase in the station's power. Before the year was out, the FRC had granted WTFF a jump in power to from 50 to 10,000 watts, making it one of the most powerful stations in the South.[73]

Once the presidential campaign began, the *Forum* launched a stream of attacks against Smith. One issue of the paper showed a cartoon of a supposed Smith "cabinet meeting." It included the pope and a dozen fat priests all drinking liquor around a table, and depicted Smith as their obsequious waiter. The crusade against Smith was aided immeasurably by the fact that Vance now controlled both a national newspaper and a radio station that could blanket the South.

The *Forum*'s attacks were so relentless that even some Republicans were aghast. Emily Marx, the Republican candidate for state assembly in Manhattan's Ninth District, for example, condemned Vance in a letter and demanded he stop sending her copies of his newspaper.[74]

At one point in the campaign, Smith publicly accused Hoover of links to the KKK and *Fellowship Forum*. While the Republican National Committee denounced Smith's allegation in an October 1928 press release, it also sought to distance itself from the *Fellowship Forum*. Hoover, meanwhile, never denounced the Klan tactics or the attacks of Vance's newspaper and radio station against his opponent. After Hoover's victory, *Time* described the enormous influence of Vance's organization on the outcome:

The Fellowship Forum, a national weekly newspaper devoted to the fraternal interpretation of the world's current events, achieved more fame than it ever had before and, in percentage, it won more circulation and showed a greater increase in gross revenue than any other US publication.

From the publisher's standpoint, it won the campaign. "Fraternal" means that the Fellowship Forum is the organ of the Ku Klux Klan and all those who believe that the Pope and Al Smith want to hang 100% Protestant-American babies from the trees on the White House lawn. The Fellowship Forum boasts that its "million readers are a unit against Al Smith because he is wet and they are ardent prohibitionists, but were he is dry, most of them would oppose him on religious grounds."[75]

Soon after the 1928 election, the *Forum* changed the station's call letters from WTFF to WJSV, for the initials of its principal founder James S. Vance, and it became the main CBS affiliate in the nation's capital, with CBS assuming responsibility for most of its programming. As the Depression deepened, and as public discontent over Hoover's economic policies grew, Vance and the *Fellowship Forum* fell on hard times. In 1932, George Barr Baker, a member of Hoover's political inner circle and a frequent intermediary for him with the press, asked the White House for some financial assistance for Vance.[76] Baker sent Hoover's secretary, Walter H. Newton, a copy of "a plea advanced by Jas. S. Vance for funds to carry on the work of the *Fellowship Forum*."[77]

If any help came, it appears to have been insufficient, for Vance sold the station completely to CBS. The network then moved its transmitter to Alexandria, Virginia, in October 1932. By the late 1940s the old Vance station—its call letters now changed to WTOP—was purchased by the *Washington Post*, and it eventually adopted an all-news and talk format. Currently owned by the Hubbard Radio company, WTOP has in recent years been the most popular station in the nation's capital, yet its role in the KKK propaganda efforts that helped catapult Herbert Hoover into the White House in 1928 remains unknown to most of its listeners.[78]

The Federal Radio Commission saw no contradiction in those early years between the public interest requirements of the Radio Act and issuing a license to a white-supremacist group like the *Fellowship Forum*.

The agency's unflagging favoritism toward big commercial networks, as we will see in Chapter 13, led to the curtailing of many innovative, independent experiments in radio programming by racial minorities that had flowered during the early days of radio; it made it almost impossible for African-Americans, Hispanics and Native Americans actually to own radio stations until after World War II; and it sparked the first great national movement against racial bias in American broadcasting—the black community's campaign in the 1930s against the *Amos 'n' Andy* show.

But while radio had begun to drastically alter the dissemination of news and entertainment, the main battleground in the media when it came to race—at least during the first half of twentieth century—remained the world of newspapers. Americans, after all, still relied primarily on print publications to make sense of their world. They depended on local newspapers, for instance, to explain to them the vast conflagration sweeping Europe, the rash of race riots that erupted around the same time at home, and the outbreak of revolution and civil war in neighboring Mexico—all of which suddenly posed frightening threats to the tranquility and prosperity of American society.

Trouble in the Streets

The newspaper reports of what is happening in Washington have most frequently indicated that the causes of the outbreaks were attacks by colored
soldiers on white women. Though this is a serious and sinister charge to
repeat day after day in dispatches that go to the entire nation, the fact is
there have been no supporting details, no particulars of knowledge or
information such as any court of law or any intelligent person requires
before arriving at an opinion or conviction.

Carl Sandburg on the Race Riots of 1919

On July 4th, 1910, America's first black heavyweight boxing champion, Jack
Johnson, defended his title against big Jim Jeffries, a former champ who
had come out of retirement vowing to regain the title for the white race.
Their bout was the biggest news story of its day and the first major sports
event to be reported live to the public via wireless telegraphy.[1] Held before
12,000 screaming spectators in Reno, Nevada, it climaxed with Johnson's
stunning knockout of Jeffries in the fifteenth round. Within moments of the
dramatic finale, white mobs launched spontaneous attacks against blacks in
cities throughout the country, thus providing the first glimmer of the new
medium's awesome potential to affect public opinion.

But newspapers still reigned as the main source of information, and
most publications continued to generate bigoted and inflammatory news
about racial minorities, especially in times of crisis. During World War I, for
example, an epidemic of race riots gripped the nation. The troubles began
in East St. Louis and Houston in 1917, and then spread during the Red
Summer of 1919 to Chicago, Washington, DC, Omaha, Elaine, Arkansas, and
other locales. Several resulted in staggering property destruction, unprecedented loss of life, and massive black flight. In virtually every one of the
conflicts, influential white newspapers in the affected towns stirred racial
hostility before and during the violence by falsely magnifying black crimi-
nality and minimizing abuses by whites.

Black- and Hispanic-owned newspapers, on the other hand, tended
to be more accurate in reporting the actual events, and frequently

questioned the response of law-enforcement agencies. Government leaders responded by targeting the most outspoken minority editors for surveillance and censorship. A handful ended up in jail for alleged violations of espionage and sedition laws; others were detained on spurious local charges. Black and Latino journalists thus joined the anti-war and socialist publishers of their era as the main victims of government repression against the dissident press.

"Do Not Point Your Nose Too High"

By the time he stepped into the ring against Jim Jeffries, Jack Johnson was already the most photographed and controversial man in America—a flesh-and-blood symbol of the country's raw racial divisions. The brash bruiser from Galveston, Texas, had captured the heavyweight championship in 1908, shattering long-held beliefs that black boxers were inferior to whites.

Like the legendary Muhammad Ali, who would capture the heavyweight title a half-century later, Johnson was larger than life. In the ring he toyed with his opponents, boasted of his prowess, and loved to predict to the press the exact round he would emerge victorious; outside of it, he sported outlandish clothes, flaunted a life of luxury cars and endless revelry and—most unforgivable of all to white America—dared to publicly date and marry a string of white women. So hated was he by the white press that sportswriters routinely referred to him as "dinge," "coon," and "nigger."[2]

The press openly depicted the Johnson-Jeffries fight as a racial battle; many papers even dubbed Jeffries the "Great White Hope." "If the black man wins, thousands and thousands of his ignorant brothers will misinterpret his victory as justifying claims to much more than mere physical equality with their white neighbors," predicted the New York Times a few months before the fight.[3] The Omaha Daily News questioned whether Jeffries could "beat down the wonderful black and restore to the Caucasians the crown of elemental greatness as measured by strength of brow, power of heart and lung, and withal, that cunning and keenness that denotes mental as well as physical superiority."[4]

Although the bout took place in Reno before an all-white crowd, Americans of all races were able for the first time to follow a sports event as it was happening, thanks to amateur wireless operators who relayed minute-by-minute updates. More than 30,000 people, for example, camped outside the New York Times building on the day of the fight to receive updates from an outdoor bulletin board the paper set up. When the champ began to wear Jeffries down with his withering blows and finally knocked him out, blacks were jubilant and whites were enraged.[5]

"Do not point your nose too high," the Los Angeles Times warned African-Americans afterward. "Do not swell your chest too much. Do not boast too loudly ... Remember you have done nothing at all. You are just the same member of society you were last week ... No man will think a bit higher of you because your complexion is the same as that of the victor at Reno."[6]

In Wheeling, West Virginia, a white mob angry at the defeat of Jeffries pulled an African-American man from his car and lynched him. In Houston, a black man aboard a streetcar had his throat slit for cheering for Johnson. In Uvalda, Georgia, whites fired upon African-Americans at a construction site, killing three. In New Orleans, "George Johnson, a half-demented negro, was set upon and beaten by a crowd in Newspaper Row while returns were coming in on the Johnson-Jeffries fight," reported one newspaper. Estimates of the number of victims of post-fight violence, most of them black, ranged from eleven to twenty-six dead, with hundreds more injured. Several states immediately banned film footage of the fight in local theaters for fear it would lead to further bloodshed.[7]

The Black Press and the Great Migration

A few years after the Johnson-Jeffries fight, the US entered World War I. The conflict cut off the nation's traditional supply of immigrant labor from Europe and forced industries in the North to start recruiting black workers from the South. More than half a million African-Americans joined the Great Northern Migration of 1915 to 1920. Many of them filled jobs in the steel, rubber and aluminum industries. In Pittsburgh, for example, Carnegie Steel employed only 1,500 blacks in 1916; within two years that number had more than doubled to 4,000.

Those migrants ended up in already overcrowded and substandard slums in Pittsburgh's Hill District, in the South Side of Chicago, in the South End of East St. Louis, or in Harlem. "Blacks were living in every conceivable place—attics, cellars, storerooms, even abandoned boxcars," notes one historian. Even as the Northern black migration mushroomed, D. W. Griffith's *Birth of Nation* burst on the scene, captivating the public with its frightening depiction of black men lusting after white women and its portrayal of the Ku Klux Klan as heroic defenders of white honor. Released in 1915, the film played to sold-out theaters across the country. It quickly led to angry pickets by black leaders, random attacks on blacks, and more than a few racial brawls.[8]

To expand the size of the military for the war effort, the government was forced also to step up its recruitment of black soldiers, and it found support for that policy both in the black press and in some of the biggest white Northern newspapers. "This is no time to discuss race problems, our duty now is to fight and continue the fight until this war is won," proclaimed the Chicago *Tribune* in May 1918, "then we will adjust the problems that remain in the life of the colored man." Black editors echoed that view, and encouraged their readers to enlist. "In loyalty to this country, the Negro people of the United States yield to none," declared the *New York Age* in March 1917. The paper proudly pointed out that in many areas of the South military reg-istration of the Negroes exceeded that of the whites, noting as an example Mississippi, where "74,579 colored registered against 64,334 whites."[9]

The sight of so many blacks in uniform and carrying guns unnerved many whites, especially those who lived in Southern towns next to military bases. Meanwhile in the North, officials hastened to devise laws and regula-tions to confine the new migrant black workers to all-black neighborhoods. Racial discrimination in public schools, hospitals, public accommodations, and the judicial system became pervasive and entrenched. As a result, black leaders became restive, and black newspapers ever more indignant. Some took to condemning the most flagrant examples of Jim Crow—lynching and segregation in the military. Wilsonian democracy, they reminded the nation, must be practiced at home, not just abroad.

Some black editors were so perturbed at the federal government's failure to act against KKK terror that they began urging blacks to abandon the South en masse. The most enthusiastic proponent of this strategy was Robert Abbott, owner of the *Chicago Defender*. Each week, Abbott's paper featured stories about groups of Southern blacks filling up railroad cars and heading North in what the *Defender* labeled the "Flight Out of Egypt." The paper even declared May 15th, 1917 the launch date for the "Great Northern Drive."[10]

The exodus campaign in the black press was not completely altruistic. Its editors knew that, as black people shifted from farm labor and domestic servitude in the South to industrial work in the North, the migrants would need to learn all they could about their newly adopted cities: where to find jobs, where to rent living quarters, where to shop. They would naturally turn to the pages of the black press and to the sermons of black ministers for guidance.

With their repeated campaigns for equal treatment for newly arrived blacks in public services, the *Defender* and Robert Vann's *Pittsburgh Courier* emerged as champions of the new black working class. The *Defender* became the most popular black newspaper in the country during World War I, boast-ing an unprecedented circulation of more than 200,000, with two-thirds of those copies sold across the South.[11]

The Great War and the East St. Louis Riot

Only months after the US entered World War I, a frightening wave of racial violence rocked the country. The troubles began in East St. Louis in the spring and summer of 1917. The second of those disturbances culminated in one of the worst massacres of blacks in US history.

Located on the banks of the Mississippi in southern Illinois, East St. Louis had a population of 75,000 at the time. The town was dotted with huge, foul-smelling slaughterhouses, and was home to the sprawling American Aluminum Company, a critical component of the new US aviation industry. The town was also notorious throughout the Midwest as a center for vice, gambling and political corruption, with scores of prostitutes operating in the open in a notorious red-light district next to City Hall and police head-quarters. Many of its 12,000 black residents were farm workers who had only recently fled poverty and Jim Crow terror in the South. They lived in a segregated black section of town known as the South End.[12]

As industry expanded in East St. Louis, factory managers began con-fronting demands from their white workers for higher wages and for union recognition. In July 1916, 4,000 workers at the Swift, Armour and Morris meatpacking plants walked off the job in an effort to secure a union contract. Plant owners immediately brought in 1,500 new black workers as replace-ments. By the end of the year, more than 2,500 blacks had found jobs in the packing plants, usually in the lowest-rung and most dangerous jobs, and they soon comprised 40 percent of the entire meatpacking work force. Many of the Polish and Lithuanian immigrants who had joined the unions suddenly found themselves unemployed, prompting the Central Trades Council to denounce the influx of black strike-breakers.[13] Racial tensions in the plants rapidly spilled over to the rest of the city.

The main paper in town was the *East St. Louis Daily Journal*. Closely tied to the Democratic Party and the city's labor leaders, it was an evening paper widely known for its sensational reporting and for its open hostility to the new black workers. Editor and publisher James Kirk considered himself a reformer, but like so many populist politicians of his era he regarded non-whites as generally unfit to govern themselves, whether at home or in the country's newly acquired colonial possessions of Puerto Rico and the Philippines.[14]

During late 1916 and early 1917, the *Journal* printed a string of front-page stories alleging a crime wave by blacks against whites. "[S]ome of the black crime reported so luridly in the *Journal* did not turn out be black crime at all," notes Harper Barnes, a longtime editor of the *St. Louis Post-Dispatch* and author of one of the best accounts of the 1917 riots. In October 1916, Kirk's *Journal* openly declared that "black colonizers" were responsible for the spike in crime. "Negroes come to East St. Louis, are not known, shoot or rob someone, and get out before we know who they are," the paper claimed. In May 1917, a story headlined "Race Riot" gave an account of a street brawl between black and white gangs. A few days later, the paper played up a report that leaders of the city's Central Trades Union were planning to confront the mayor and the city council to complain about all the new blacks into the city.

The day of the city council meeting, May 28th, the *Journal* printed an ominous front-page headline: "POLICE WATCH MANY THREATEN-ING NEGROES." That same evening, word spread that a black holdup man had shot a white man in the downtown area. Bands of angry white residents quickly gathered on the streets of downtown, randomly attacking black pedestrians and setting fire to black homes and businesses. Peace was only restored when several hundred members of the Illinois National Guard occupied the town the following day. No one was killed in the May distur-bance, but two blacks were shot and several were badly beaten.

"The trouble arose over the large influx here of penal and shiftless negroes from the south …" Kirk's *Daily Journal* declared in a front-page editorial that clearly aimed to excuse the rioters. "Amongst them are many lawless and violent characters who have resorted to assaults upon white people." According to the paper, the incident was not "really a race one" since the city's whites harbored no animosity against the "older, law abiding and long resident portion of our negro population."[15]

The only black-owned newspaper in the area, the weekly *St. Louis Argus*, depicted things far differently. "UNION LEADERS START RACE RIOT," it proclaimed in a June 1 front-page story, attributing the surge in anti-black feeling in East St. Louis to whites who were angry at being "displaced by Negroes."

The *Daily Journal* was the main paper in town, but across the river in St. Louis, five dailies were locked in feverish competition. They included the *St. Louis Post-Dispatch*, the flagship of the Pulitzer chain, known for its liberal views on race and its frequent crusades against local corruption; the *Globe-Democrat*, a morning paper associated with the Republican Party; and the *St. Louis Republic*, another pro-Democratic paper with openly racist views. All the St. Louis papers operated bureaus in East St. Louis, and each sought to build its circulation there.[16]

Early on the morning of July 2nd, 1917, a second racial incident mush-roomed out of control. Weeks of sensational articles in the *Daily Journal* after the first May 28th event had created a tinderbox, with wild rumors circulating throughout the town that both blacks and whites were plan-ning violence during the upcoming July 4th celebrations. One June 15th article in the *Daily Journal* had called for another "race riot" to put an end to the supposed crime wave by blacks.[17] On the evening of July 1, bands of white men began attacking black pedestrians. At least one carload of whites in a Model T Ford sped through the city's black community shooting into homes. Hoping to prevent a repeat of the terrifying May 28th assaults, black residents gathered on the streets with rifles and shotguns.

Around midnight, white detectives Samuel Coppedge and Frank Wodley were dispatched to investigate reports of armed black patrols. They drove to Tenth and Bond Avenue in the heart of the South End in an unmarked

Model T Ford. Accompanying them were a handful of uniformed cops and two newsmen, Roy Albertson, an eighteen-year-old cub reporter for the *St. Louis Republic*, and the veteran Robert Boylan of the *Globe-Democrat*. As their car arrived at the corner, the crowd of blacks unleashed a volley of bullets, fatally shooting Coppedge and Wodley. The two reporters and other cops survived unscathed and managed to flee back to police headquarters. When they arrived, police officials decided to wait until daylight before mobilizing the town's tiny force to restore order.

The front-page headline and story in the *St. Louis Republic* the next morning made it appear that blacks had erupted in a deliberate and open revolt. "POLICEMAN KILLED, 5 SHOT IN EAST ST. LOUIS RIOT. NEGROES, CALLED OUT BY RINGING OF CHURCH BELL, FIRE WHEN POLICE APPEAR. OUTBREAK FOLLOWS BEATING OF WATCHMAN BY BLACK SATURDAY NIGHT." Young Albertson's eyewitness story claimed that the detectives had identified themselves before the mob shot them down in cold blood. It mentioned nothing about car-loads of whites that had shot into black homes prior to the confrontation at Tenth and Bond. The prominence the story gave to the ringing church bell made it seem that the murder of the cops was part of a broader insurrection by black leaders.[18]

Once again, the black-owned *St. Louis Argus* reported a far different set of "facts." In its July 6th issue, the paper disclosed interviews with several black witnesses to the police shooting. No words had been spoken before the bullets began to fly at Tenth and Bond that night, the witnesses claimed. The dead cops, the witnesses said, had never identified themselves. Instead, they had been tragically "mistaken for rioters" by black residents, who opened fire as their car approached the intersection. The unmarked Model T police car, it turned out, was eerily similar to the car that had transported the drunken white thugs who had shot up the neighborhood earlier that night.[19]

But the only "eyewitness" accounts city residents read on the morning of July 2nd were those of the *Republic* and the *Globe-Democrat*. The latter reported that police had poured into the black community after the shooting but could not contain the violence—another fabrication meant to portray the police in a more positive light. By that afternoon, thousands of angry whites began sweeping into black neighborhoods in a rampage of arson and gunfire that would last for several days.

The lead article in the next day's neighboring *Belleville News-Democrat*, a white-owned paper that provided generally accurate coverage of the incident, revealed the extent of the carnage:

> Negroes were lynched, shot to death, clubbed to death, incinerated in their flaming homes and drowned in Cahokia Creek. Men, women and children participated in the rioting ...

The frightfulness of the entire spectacle—a spectacle which will never be forgotten by those who witnessed it—was augmented tenfold by the death cries of the negroes as they were either shot down in their tracks or suspended with ropes from telephone and telegraph poles.[20]

One of the most chilling accounts came from Carlos Hurd, a star reporter for the *Post-Dispatch*. Hurd had already covered some of the era's biggest stories, but nothing had prepared him for the savage slaughter he witnessed. "I have heard stories of the latter-day crimes of the Turks in Armenia, and I have learned to loathe the German army for its barbarity in Belgium," he wrote. "But I do not believe that Moslem fanaticism or Prussian frightfulness could perpetrate murders of more deliberate brutality than those which I saw committed, in daylight, by citizens of the State of Abraham Lincoln."[21]

The official death toll in the July riot, according to an investigation conducted afterward by the House of Representatives, was thirty-nine blacks and nine whites, but some estimates place the number of fatalities as high as a hundred. Several hundred blacks were injured. More than 300 buildings were destroyed by fire, and more than 7,000 African-Americans were forced to flee the city during the violence.[22]

The carnage so outraged the country's black population that thousands staged a silent march down Fifth Avenue in New York City a few weeks later—the first public protest for civil rights in the country's history. Membership in the NAACP, which had hovered around 9,200 in 1917, skyrocketed to 44,000 the following year, and both the National Urban League and Marcus Garvey's Negro Improvement Association often pointed to East St. Louis as they recruited thousands of new members. [23]

Mutiny in Houston

A few weeks after East St. Louis, another racial disturbance broke out. This time, however, it was violence by blacks that stunned the nation, when more than a hundred soldiers in a black company of the Illinois National Guard mutinied on August 23rd at Camp Logan, a military base outside of Houston, Texas. The soldiers then marched on the city's downtown, fired on white residents, and fought pitched gun battles with police. Fifteen whites, four of them policemen, died in the rampage that day, as did four of the attackers. More than a dozen people were wounded. White America's worst nightmare had been realized—black soldiers had killed white civilians. The government response was swift and merciless. Over the next few months the army tried and convicted 110 members of I Company in what became the largest court-martial in US history. Nineteen of the soldiers were hanged and more than sixty received life sentences in federal prison.[24]

But missing from most news coverage of the shocking incident was any dispassionate explanation of the specific events that had triggered the mutiny, or of the tense racial climate in Houston during the preceding months. Like East St. Louis, Houston was a city synonymous with corruption, where gambling and prostitution flourished in open view of top officials. The city's police force was notorious for protecting the heads of vice operations while running roughshod over the city's black population. Throughout the early part of 1917, black residents were repeatedly shot by police or falsely accused of crimes they had had no hand in, according to one study of the mutiny.[25]

By the time they arrived at Camp Logan in late July, the black soldiers from Illinois were already in an uproar over the tragedy in East St. Louis. They had followed those events closely in the *Chicago Defender* and other papers, and had even set up a fund among themselves to help the victims of that riot. They were also fuming at reports that fellow white national guardsmen deployed to East St. Louis had joined in attacks on blacks. They became further enraged when they realized that Houston police had decided to employ an iron hand with any black soldier found outside Camp Logan. During late August "blacks were routinely assaulted on the streets by private citizens and by police," notes journalist and historian Harper Barnes.[26]

Houston's longtime black residents were more accustomed to the constant harassment and racial slights of Southern white society, but the young black soldiers from up North refused to accept such indignities. And since they were armed, each refusal became a potentially violent confrontation. On the morning of August 23rd, Corporal Charles Baltimore, a black MP, went into town and sought to intercede with local police over their arrest of a black soldier. The soldier, Baltimore learned, had challenged the police for their treatment of a black woman he knew in Houston's Fourth Ward. But when Baltimore questioned cops about the incident, they assaulted and arrested him as well. Word of what happened to Baltimore soon reached the Illinois guardsmen on the base, and the angry soldiers decided to teach the whites of Houston a lesson. They grabbed their weapons and marched on the town.

Government Intimidation of the Black Press

The events in East St. Louis and Houston unnerved the nation. Many leaders in Washington quickly concluded that the black press was undermining the war effort with its constant calls for an end to racial discrimination. George Creel's Committee on Public Information saw foreign provocateurs at work. German agents "had thousands of propagandists among the Negroes, exciting them with stories of impossible atrocities committed against the colored people," one of the Committee's circulars said.

Creel and the Justice Department started paying special attention to dissent by black newspapers against the war or the government. Most of that dissent was directed not at the war itself, but at rampant segregation in the ranks of the military and at home. Robert S. Abbott's *Chicago Defender* and Robert Vann's *Pittsburgh Courier*, for example, were reporting extensively on the growing anger and frequent complaints from black units stationed in the South about their mistreatment by local white civilian leaders.

In an attempt to quiet such criticism, the War Department and Creel's CIP convened a conference of forty-one black leaders in Washington in June 1918, most of them newspaper editors. While Creel's tone at the meeting was conciliatory, and he appealed for their help in marshaling black support for the war, behind the scenes the government launched "a massive investigation of black papers," notes historian Patrick Washburn, and it pressured those it considered "most objectionable" in a crackdown that "involved little subtlety." [27]

When the black-owned *San Antonio Inquirer* editorialized against the executions of the mutinous Houston soldiers, the Justice Department promptly indicted its editor G. W. Bouldin for violating the Espionage Act. Bouldin had been traveling outside of San Antonio when the article appeared in his paper—but a jury found him guilty nonetheless, and he was quickly sentenced to two years in prison. Bouldin was one of three black editors jailed during the war. The other two were A. Philip Randolph and Chandler Owens, publishers of the socialist monthly the *Messenger*. Both were arrested on August 4th, 1918 in Cleveland and held for several days for disseminating an editorial and making speeches that ridiculed government claims of pro-German sentiment among blacks. The actual reason for black discontent, Randolph and Owen had dared to claim, was "peonage, disfranchisement, Jim-Crowism, segregation ..." [28]

Meanwhile, military and civilian agencies repeatedly investigated Robert Abbott's Chicago *Defender* for its war coverage. Typical of the items that aroused their concerns was a *Defender* cartoon that depicted white American soldiers shooting fellow black soldiers in the back during battles with German troops. In May 1918, a black army officer named Major W. H. Loving visited Abbott and warned him he would be "held strictly responsible and accountable for any article appearing in his paper ... that would give rise to any apprehension on the part of the government." A few days later, a worried Abbott wrote to Loving and proclaimed his patriotism. Abbott assured Loving that he had "more than once advised my staff writers to refrain from expressing their views on problems that would precipitate national strife ..." [29]

The Post Office and the Immigrant Press

The federal government also used the Espionage and Sedition Act and the Trading with the Enemy Act to intimidate and censor dissident foreign-language publications. Among those targeted were several Spanish-language papers whose editors had been radicalized by the Mexican revolution of 1910. In his study of the immigrant press, Robert Park minimized the impact of that suppression campaign. Yes, some newspaper offices were raided by the Justice Department, he acknowledged, but the number actually denied service by the Post Office was "very small, probably not more than ten."[30]

Park's assessment, however, ignores the chilling impact such restrictive laws had on all foreign-language editors. The Trading with the Enemy Act of 1917, for instance, required publishers of all non-English newspapers to file a translation with the government of all articles about the war—unless authorities specifically granted a waiver. Since immigrant papers usually operated on a shoestring budget, the time and cost required to meet the new requirement undoubtedly discouraged many editors from writing about the war, and it certainly dissuaded them from any criticism of the US effort. Moreover, all foreign-language newspapers had to register a copy of each edition with the Post Office, where an army of foreign-language readers then perused them for questionable items. Editors knew that violating the Espionage Act could lead to denial of their postal privileges, or even arrest. Among the Spanish-language papers the federal government targeted was *Voluntad* ("Will Power"), a New York sheet whose postal privileges were revoked in 1916, and New York's *Cultura Obrera* ("Workers' Culture").[31]

The Government Campaign Against Ricardo Flores Magón

Perhaps the most flagrant persecution of Hispanic journalists before and after World War I was the effort the government waged against anarchist editor Ricardo Flores Magón and his two brothers Jesús and Enrique. Ricardo Flores Magón was born in 1873 to a poor Indian mother and *mestizo* father in the southern state of Oaxaca. As a university student, he was attracted to the theories of Russian anarchist Peter Kropotkin, and became a fierce opponent of Mexican dictator Porfirio Díaz. He founded a newspaper in Mexico City that he called *Regeneración* ("Regeneration"), and became a leading voice for the newly founded anti-Díaz Liberal Reformist Association. The Díaz government closed the newspaper in 1903 and briefly jailed Ricardo, whereupon Mexico's Supreme Court banned him from either printing a paper or writing for other publications. The three brothers fled to the United States, where they resumed publishing *Regeneración* in San Antonio, Texas, in 1904, and developed a network of followers to smuggle copies of each issue into Mexico.[32]

A fiery speaker with thick, curly black hair and a handle-bar mustache, Ricardo and his brothers attracted such a devoted following among Mexican political dissidents that the Díaz government decided to silence them. It offered a reward of $20,000 for their capture and sent its own agents to the

US to pursue them. Thugs twice forced their way into the San Antonio house where Flores Magón was living, and assaulted him. He and his brothers evaded capture by moving to St. Louis. In that city, they restarted their paper and also founded the Partido Liberal Mexicano ("Mexican Liberal Party"), an organization that would later play a significant role in the Mexican Revolution. The brothers hoped to base the new party in Mexico's emerging urban working class, but the US government was equally determined to prevent the spread of a radical, anti-Díaz movement on US soil.

In 1905, Flores Magón was arrested and threatened with extradition to Mexico to face charges of criminal libel. He posted bond and came out of jail, only to discover that the Post Office had suspended mailing privileges for *Regeneración*. Convinced that certain death awaited him back home, Flores Magón fled to Canada, moving constantly from place to place in an effort to evade Díaz's agents. In 1906, he returned secretly to the US and lived as a fugitive in Los Angeles. But with federal agents circulating his picture on wanted posters and offering a $25,000 reward, he could not evade capture for long. In both 1907 and 1911, he and several of his followers were jailed and charged with violating federal neutrality laws. Convicted in two controversial trials, Flores Magón served separate prison stints of three years and eighteen months. He was jailed again in 1917 after he published an article condemning Texas Rangers for the killing of Mexican-Americans. The unrelenting persecution garnered Flores Magón an even bigger following among both Mexican immigrants and radical labor groups like the Wobblies.

Spanish-language newspapers along the US-Mexican border reported regularly on the exploits of the brothers and their Partido Liberal. The party's followers, known as *Magonistas*, played a major role once the revolution against Díaz began, eventually "liberating" several towns in Morelos and other Mexican states in early 1911. By then the circulation of *Regeneración* is said to have reached nearly 30,000 per week, most of it in the peasant villages of Mexico. Emiliano Zapata, one of the Revolution's most enduring figures, even adopted as his battle cry the slogan, "Land and Liberty," which Flores Magón and the Liberal Party had first espoused.[33]

In March 1918, only months after the Russian Revolution, Flores Magón issued his own anarchist manifesto in *Regeneracíon*. US authorities immediately charged him with violating the new Espionage Act. Convicted in yet another federal trial, he was sentenced to twenty years in Leavenworth prison. This time, however, his health deteriorated rapidly, and he died in prison only four years later.[34]

Laredo's La Cronica *and Jovita Idar*

Even as the Flores Magón brothers were defying US and Mexican authorities, a young Mexican-American editor named Jovita Idar was inscribing her own trail of dissent across South Texas and Northern Mexico. Born in the border town of Laredo in 1885, Idar was one of eight children of Nicasio and Jovita Idar. Her father was a former railroad worker from Brownsville who had traveled throughout Mexico and Texas as a union organizer. By the time the family settled down for good in Laredo in the 1890s, the town boasted several Spanish-language newspapers, including *El Coreo de Laredo* ("The Laredo Mail") and *El Democrata Fronterizo* ("The Frontier Democrat"), both weeklies published by the outspoken Justo Cárdenas (see Chapter 5). Whites were such a tiny minority of the town's population then that even the daily *Laredo Times* contained some Spanish-language articles and advertisements. Nicasio Idar soon became one of Laredo's leading figures. He opened a small print shop, served for a time as assistant city marshal and justice of the peace, founded a Masonic journal called *La Revista*, and was an organizer of the Mexican fraternal organization known as *La Orden Caballeros de Honor*.

In 1895 he launched his own weekly newspaper, *La Crónica*, and enlisted the help of his sons Clemente and Eduardo. His only daughter Jovita initially tried her hand at teaching in Laredo public schools, but she grew quickly disillusioned over the horrendous conditions in the ramshackle, segregated schools *Tejano* students were forced to attend, so she quit teaching and went to work with her family on *La Crónica*. Jovita and Clemente edited the paper under their father's direction, while their brother Eduardo traveled throughout the lower Rio Grande Valley as a roving correspondent. Among the frequent contributors the Idars recruited to the paper was poet Sara Estela Ramírez. The most popular female writer in South Texas, Ramírez was also a close friend of Ricardo Flores Magón. She would later join the Mexican Liberal Party and edit two radical papers of her own in Laredo in the early years of the century, *La Corregidora* ("The Corrector") and *Aurora* ("Dawn").

La Crónica, however, was no radical, gadfly sheet. It rapidly established itself as the best Hispanic paper along the border. In well-documented stories and passionate editorials, most of them written by Jovita or her brother Clemente, the paper repeatedly exposed not only segregation in the public schools, but the unjust seizures of *Tejano* land, and lynchings of Texas Mexicans. It also urged its *Mexicano* readers to preserve their culture and Spanish language by establishing their own private schools.[35]

Tejano editors who devoted space to such controversial matters often incurred the enmity of local white settlers. In 1908, for example, Everardo Torres, editor of *El Aldeano*, a small newspaper in the nearby town of Uribeño, in Zapata County, published an article criticizing some Anglo county officials. Torres was promptly jailed on fabricated charges.[36]

In June 1910, *La Crónica* condemned the decision of the school board in the West Texas town of San Angelo to admit only white children to a new school that had just opened its doors. According to the paper, the board had assigned all *Tejano/Mexicano* children to the town's older, run-down school, a decision that had prompted 300 Latino parents to organize a boycott of classes. *La Cronica* praised the boycott as a "dignified ... protest."[37] A few weeks later, the paper condemned the pervasive segregation in Texas public schools, warning: "[I]t is in the interest of this country to give education to the youth of whichever race, to remove men from the obscure hole of ignorance ... The law concedes to the inhabitants of Texas equal rights and identical privileges. Then, in what is based this odious distinction?"[38]

Later that year, a young Mexican named Antonio Rodriguez was accused of killing an Anglo-American woman on a ranch near Rocksprings, Texas. A crowd of whites immediately surrounded the jailhouse, pulled Rodriguez from his cell, tied him to a tree, and burned him to death. In a front-page story titled "Barbarism," *La Crónica* blasted both the mob and the sheriff's deputies for failing to prevent the jail break-in. "The crowd cheered when the flames engulfed his contorted body," Jovita Idar wrote of the incident. "They did not even turn away at the smell of his burning flesh and I wondered if they even knew his name."[39]

On June 19th, 1911, barely seven months after the Rocksprings incident, fourteen-year-old Antonio Gómez stabbed to death a German-American who had tried to eject him from a store in Thorndale, Texas. After the youth was arrested, a mob of whites seized him from the authorities and beat him to death. His killers then tied the teenager's body to the back of a buggy and dragged it through the streets of town. *La Crónica* urged the government to act against the lynch mob, and it bitterly predicted the boy's killers would "be freed on bail and after public opinion has subsided with the appearance of a trial," for "until now we know of no [Anglo] American who has been punished for the lynching of a Mexican."[40]

Such anti-Mexican terror was more common in the southwest than is generally known. Between 1848 and 1928, Anglo mobs lynched at least 597 Mexicans, most of them in the annexed Mexican territories, according to one study. The rate of lynching for the tiny Mexican-American population during the first thirty years of that period was an appalling 473 per 100,000—far higher than the 52.8 per 100,000 rate among African-Americans in Mississippi, the state with the worst lynching problem. And from 1880 to 1930, the lynching rate for Mexicans was 27.4 per 100,000, not far behind the 37.1 rate for African-Americans.[41]

The complicity of local authorities in such vigilante violence—or at least their condoning of it—provoked mounting discontent among the region's Mexican-American majority. After the killing of Gómez, the Idar family took the lead in convening an unprecedented meeting of *Mexicano* leaders to address the issues of lynching, school segregation, illegal land expropriations, and the condition of Mexican women. Publisher Nicasio Idar's fraternal group La Orden de Caballeros spearheaded the historic gathering, El Primer

Congreso Mexicanista de Texas ("First Mexican Congress of Texas"), which took place from 14th to 22nd September, 1911, in Laredo, while *La Crónica* and other Spanish-language papers gave extensive coverage to the event.

Not surprisingly, the state's English-language press barely mentioned it. A *Houston Post* report during the gathering did acknowledge that because of the "Alamo" mentality, "[Mexicans] have felt the vengefulness of violated law to a harsher and more exacting degree than even the negroes ..." [42] "We have all known before the *Post* told us ... that thousands of verdicts in Texas courts are against the Mexicano, inspired by vengeful blood that accompanies the cry, 'Remember the Alamo,'" a writer for *La Crónica* pointedly responded. [43]

The *Laredo Times* and the *San Antonio Express* each published small articles on the gathering, but both papers "deliberately or otherwise ... misrepresented the tone and content of the meeting," according to historian José Limón. The *Express*, for example, claimed the group's "principal work will be the enlightenment and elevation of the Mexican element in the State of Texas, with a view of making them more desirable and better citizens and a credit to the Texas cities in which they make their homes." When another delegate, J. M. Mora, gave a speech during the Congress about the need for *Mexicano* workers to unite against abuses by their employers, the *Laredo Times* described Mora as urging Mexicans to "better their social positions by their own individual efforts." [44]

The entire Idar family participated actively in the Congress. Family patriarch Nicasio opened the gathering and was elected vice-president of the new *Gran Liga Mexicanista de Beneficencia y Protección* ("Grand Mexican League for Mutual Benefit and Protection"). The following month Jovita and other Laredo women launched *La Liga Feminista Mexicana* ("Mexican Feminist League"), which met for a time in the offices of *La Crónica*, and its members elected twenty-six-year-old Jovita as their first president. The group immediately embarked on a campaign to provide food, clothing, and free schools for poor Mexican children in the state, with *La Crónica* providing frequent coverage of its activities.

Jovita Idar's attention, however, was increasingly drawn to the titanic conflict unfolding across the river in Mexico after the fall of dictator Porfirio Díaz. She began writing articles in *La Crónica* favorable to rebel general Pancho Villa. When a major battle erupted between rebel and government forces in Nuevo Laredo in March 1913, she crossed into Mexico to treat wounded fighters as part of a group of Laredo women recruited by her friend Leonor Villegas de Magnón, one of Laredo's wealthiest residents. Idar traveled for several months throughout Mexico with a new medical group founded by Villegas de Magnón called La Cruz Blanca ("White Cross"), nursing wounded soldiers from both sides of the conflict. [45]

By the time she returned to Laredo, Idar had been converted to the revolutionary cause. She took a job as editor of a radical newspaper, *El Progreso*, where she published an editorial in 1914 that criticized President Wilson's decision to dispatch American troops to the border. A company of Texas Rangers responded by riding into Laredo, surrounding the paper's officers, and ordering it shut down. Idar greeted them at the door as a large crowd of *Tejanos* gathered on the street outside, and refused to step aside, instead lecturing the stunned lawmen on the US Constitution and her First Amendment rights. Several tense moments ensued before the Rangers finally rode off. By doing so, they sealed the legend of Idar that endures to this day in *Mexicano* folklore. Her victory, however, was largely symbolic, since the Rangers returned that same night and wrecked the press.[46]

Shortly after the incident, Idar's father died and she returned to *La Crónica* to operate the paper with her brothers. She remained there until she married in 1917 and moved to San Antonio. Once settled in San Antonio, she founded a free kindergarten, edited *El Heraldo Christiano*, a publication of the Methodist Church, and became a respected leader of that city's Democratic Party. She remained in San Antonio until her death in 1946.

Red Summer and the Chicago Race Riot of 1919

It was called the Red Summer of 1919. Over the span of several months, race riots erupted in twenty-six cities and towns, the worst occurring in Elaine, Arkansas, where as many as 800 people died. But there were major outbreaks as well in Washington, DC; Omaha, Nebraska; Charleston, South Carolina; Long View, Texas; and Knoxville, Tennessee. This time, however, the victims were not confined to one side. After fighting to defend democracy in Europe, many of the black veterans who returned home from the war were less disposed to accept racial abuse than prior generations.

The disturbance that garnered the most press attention was in Chicago, where thirty-eight people died and more than 500 were injured during several days of street battles between blacks and whites. Once again, white newspapers were part of the problem. Early press reports disseminated wild rumors that often only inflamed white anger, frequently mischaracterized the numbers of victims among blacks and whites, and failed to explain accurately what had sparked the troubles.

"Two colored men are reported to have been killed and approximately fifty whites and negroes injured, a number probably fatally, in race riots that broke out at south side beaches yesterday," said the lead story in the Chicago *Tribune* the day after trouble began. The account went on to say:

> The rioting spread through the black belt and by midnight had thrown the entire south side into a state of turmoil.

Among the known wounded are four policemen of the Cottage Grove avenue station, two from west side stations, one fireman of Engine Company No. 9, and three women ...

One Negro was knocked off a raft at the Twenty-ninth street beach after he had been stoned by whites. He drowned because whites are said to have frustrated attempts of colored bathers to rescue him. The body was recovered, but could not be identified.

What the *Tribune* story failed to note was that the Negro "knocked off a raft" was a seventeen-year-old boy named Eugene Williams who had been attacked and drowned after he had mistakenly drifted past the imaginary line that confined blacks to a particular section of the segregated beach.[47]

According to an investigation conducted months later by the Chicago Race Commission, blacks at the beach became furious when a policeman refused to arrest a white youth named George Stauber, who witnesses claimed had thrown the rock that led to the teenager's death. "At this crucial moment [the policeman] instead arrested a Negro on a white man's complaint," the Commission reported, prompting angry blacks to attack the police. "These two facts, the drowning and the refusal of the policeman to arrest Stauber, together marked the beginning of the riot."[48] The weekly *Chicago Defender*, the city's major black-owned newspaper, produced a far more accurate account in its first issue a few days later. The lead paragraph of the *Defender*'s story noted that the "refusal of Policeman Daniel Callahan (white) ... to arrest George Stauber (white) ... after the latter had knocked Eugene Williams ... from a raft ... fanned into action one of the worst race riots in the history of Illinois."[49]

The *Defender* also chronicled the brutal acts committed by black rioters. It reported that, after Williams's death, "the whole South Side was in an uproar," with crowds of blacks invading streetcars and pulling "every white face ... from the cars" and attacking them. But the paper's stories left no doubt that the bulk of the victims of the violence were black—something the white newspapers failed to do. The Chicago Commission noted that white newspapers erroneously reported more whites injured and killed than blacks, as when the *Chicago Tribune* reported on July 29th that thirteen whites and seven coloreds had been killed, when "the true figures were nearly the opposite."[50]

The *Defender* was not only more accurate than the *Tribune* in its general assessment of the tragedy—it provided more vivid details that captured the bone-chilling savagery of some rioters:

In all parts of the city, white mobs dragged from surface cars black passengers wholly ignorant of any trouble, and set upon them. An unidentified young woman and a 3 months old baby were found dead on the street at the intersection of 47th street and Wentworth Avenue. She had attempted to board a car there when the mob seized her, beat her, slashed her body into ribbons and beat the baby's brains out against a telegraph pole. Not satisfied with this, one rioter severed her breasts, and a white youngster bore it aloft on a pole, triumphantly, while the crowd hooted gleefully. All the time this was happening, several policemen were in the crowd, but did not make any attempt to make rescue until too late.[51]

According to the Commission, of the thirty-eight people who were killed in Chicago, twenty-three were black and fifteen white; of the 520 people injured, 342 were Negro and 178 were white; yet blacks comprised an astounding two-thirds of the 229 people arrested and accused of crimes. "The fact that twice as many Negroes appeared as defendants and twice as many Negroes as whites were injured, leads to the conclusion that whites were not apprehended as readily as Negroes," the Commission concluded.

In the months after the violence, the *Defender* repeatedly accused the authorities of biased prosecutions of those arrested. A front-page article on September 6th reported that 10,000 blacks had gathered in a public meeting and petitioned the Illinois attorney general to take the riot-related cases out of the hands of the local state's attorney because of the "prejudicial manner in which the present investigation is being conducted." The article claimed that "through the jugglery of the state's attorney's office 52 Colored men have been indicted and only 17 whites."[52]

That same edition of the paper carried several numbing accounts of the epidemic of racial violence sweeping across the country. "Races Clash at Knoxville" was the screaming headline of one article; it provided details of a major riot that had just occurred in Tennessee. In that incident a white mob had tried to storm the local jail to lynch Maurice Hayes, a black man accused of killing a white woman. Groups of blacks and whites immediately broke into hardware stores to secure guns, and a pitched battle ensued in town. National Guard troops dispatched to the scene had set up machine guns in the black community and had begun firing into homes after some blacks greeted them with bullets, the paper said. Alongside the Knoxville report was the biggest story of the day: "Mob Burns Churches: Whites Apply Torches to Lodge Halls and Temples of Worship: Celebrate With Lynching." The church story, datelined Eastman, Georgia, told of a mob killing on August 28th of Eli Cooper, an elderly black farmer. According to the story, Cooper had urged blacks in the area to arm themselves to protect against growing violence from whites. Soon after, a band of intruders had dragged him from his house, riddled his body with 500 shots, taken his remains to a nearby church, and set the building ablaze.

Poet Carl Sandburg's own report on the Chicago riot and other racial incidents that year quoted a scathing critique that Chicago's deputy super-intendent of police gave of white press coverage:

The newspapers' reports of what is happening in Washington have most frequently indicated that that the causes of the outbreaks were attacks by colored soldiers on white women. Though this is a serious and sinister charge to repeat day after day in dispatches that go to the entire nation, the fact is there have been no supporting details, no particulars of knowledge or information such as any court of law or any intelligent person requires before arriving at an opinion or conviction.[53]

The Omaha Bee *and the Lynching of Will Brown*

The failures of the *Chicago Tribune* paled in comparison to the scandalous reports produced by Nebraska's highly regarded *Omaha Bee* when racial troubles erupted in that city a few months later. The *Bee* was then the most influential Republican newspaper west of the Mississippi. Its long-time publisher Edward Rosewater had served on the Republican National Committee and had twice run unsuccessfully for the US Senate.

On the night of September 25th, 1919, a young white woman named Agnes Loeback was attacked and raped at gunpoint in Omaha by a black man as she was walking home with her disabled boyfriend. Police quickly arrested a forty-one-year-old packinghouse worker named Will Brown, and within a few hours both the victim and her boyfriend identified him as the assailant. The next morning, Omaha residents awakened to a screaming front-page headline in the *Bee*: "Black Beast First Stick-up Couple." The accompanying report began with the words: "The most daring attack on a white woman ever perpetrated in Omaha occurred one block south of Bancroft street near Scenic avenue in Gibson last night."

Omaha in the early twentieth century was a turbulent city, infamous for bitter rivalries between corrupt political machines. The most powerful of those machines was controlled by Tom Dennison, the boss of an illegal gambling ring in town. An alliance between Rosewater and Dennison had long ensured that the latter would receive sympathetic news coverage in the *Bee*. But when a reform-minded Democrat named Edward P. Smith captured the mayoralty in 1918, the new mayor immediately vowed to eradicate corruption in Omaha. In response, Rosewater launched a string of sensational stories in the *Bee* about more than twenty violent assaults in the city. Virtually all of the stories were about white women attacked by black men, and they usually featured lurid details of each incident. Rosewater's aim was to convince the public that under Smith's leadership the police department was permitting a "carnival of crime," and was incapable of protecting law-abiding citizens.

By the time police locked Brown up for the rape of Agnes Loeback, the *Bee* had whipped the city's white community into a fury. Within hours of the arrest, a throng of more than 5,000 people converged outside the town courthouse. Police tried at first to keep the crowd at bay, but shots rang out and two people fell fatally wounded in the hail of bullets from both sides. Mayor Smith rushed to the scene and courageously tried to reason with the mob leaders. Several of them grabbed the mayor, knocked him down, and lynched him from a nearby lamppost. Luckily, police rushed in to rescue him within moments.

The jailed defendant Brown was not so fortunate. Still proclaiming his innocence, he was pulled from the jail around 11 p.m., beaten unconscious, stripped of his clothes, and hanged from another lamp pole. His attackers then riddled his body with bullets, set it ablaze, and dragged its charred remains in jubilation through Omaha's downtown streets. The army was called in to restore order, and though more than one hundred rioters were later arrested and a grand jury convened, no one was ever prosecuted for the violence.

Omaha Police Commissioner Dean Ringer later claimed a direct cause of the riot had been "the crystallization of the mob spirit ... by vicious, unprincipled and false newspaper criticism of the police department." Rosewater and his *Bee* deserved considerable responsibility for creating the riot conditions that led to Brown's death. The city's other major white newspaper, the *Omaha World-Herald*, on the other hand, distinguished itself by refusing to engage in biased reporting. Two days after the violence, *World-Herald* editor Harvey E. Newbranch, wrote:

> Omaha has had an experience in lawlessness. We have seen, as in a nightmare, its awful possibilities. We have learned how frail is the barrier which divides civilization from the primal jungle—and we have seen clearly what that barrier is. It is the law! May the lesson sink deep.[54]

The *World-Herald's* restrained coverage and its powerful editorials against the lynching of Will Brown provided such a stark contrast to the racial arson practiced by Rosewater and the *Bee* that the paper was accorded a Pulitzer Prize the following year. Its actions showed that white journalists were perfectly capable of challenging racial bigotry even when faced by a mob of their fellow citizens. Still, the disturbing fact remains that Rosewater's *Bee*, a respected newspaper in a major mid-western city, made it acceptable for thousands of otherwise sane residents of Omaha to attack their own police officers and mayor, and then kill and mutilate a black man who no jury had yet found guilty of a crime.

The first two decades of the twentieth century witnessed the maturing of two starkly divergent trends in the American press. On the one hand were the established white-owned newspapers, which continued for the most part to perpetuate the white racial narrative. On the other hand, African-American and Latino newspapers mushroomed in circulation and influence within their own communities, operating in a parallel world where they challenged the reigning narrative but remained mostly invisible to white America. The Great Migration, the Mexican Revolution, and World War I created tens of thousands of new readers for the bourgeoning non-white press, and the editors of that press became increasingly critical of segregationist policies. The federal government responded with efforts to intimidate or silence the most vocal of those papers. By the end of the war, however, the new medium of wireless telegraphy had been transformed into radio—and, once again, journalists of color would fight to be heard.

Other Voices: Amos 'n' Andy, the "Sunshine Lady" and Los Madrugadores

By portraying blacks as one-dimensional buffoons, Radio provided white listeners with a convenient rationale for the plight of African Americans...

> William Barlow, *Voice Over: The Making of Black Radio*

> It's Pedro J. González
> who we're going to sing about.
> He was a radio announcer
> who became quite popular ...
>> "The Ballad of Pedro J. González"

Early radio introduced an astonishing diversity in the content of programs and a highly decentralized form of mass communications, and thus posed a direct challenge to a central racial narrative. Many station owners were desperate to fill time slots with live musical performances, and as a result African-American musicians started popping up on the airwaves in unprecedented numbers: more than 800 stations featured black artists on their shows between 1920 and 1930. Millions of white Americans were thus exposed for the first time to the sounds of Duke Ellington, Louis Armstrong, and Fletcher Henderson, and the enormous popularity of "race music" on the radio paved the way for the cultural renaissance we now call the Jazz Age.[1]

Several of the biggest jazz bands of that era also featured musical stars from Cuba and Puerto Rico who had settled in New York after World War I. As early as 1921, one of the best-known Latino bandleaders of the era, Vincent Lopez, began drawing large audiences for radio broadcasts of his weekly performances from the city's Pennsylvania Grill. Lopez's orchestra offered an elaborate mix of musical forms, as suggested by this 1930 review in the *Amsterdam News*: "The evolution of the blues, from the tribal chants of the Congo to their present highly polished symphonic arrangements, was featured last night by Vincent Lopez and an especially augmented orchestra of fifty-six musicians in the Pure Oil concert."[2]

But non-white radio pioneers did more than just perform on air. Several took to brokering time on major stations, where they produced a rich variety of shows aimed at their own communities, often with segments devoted to news and public interest. A handful even tried without much success to launch independent commercial stations. The most powerful radio owners and newspaper publishers, however, quickly stymied such independent efforts. Once they consolidated their control over the industry in the early 1930s, network executives began supplanting eclectic local shows with homogenized national programming aimed at the ideal white audience. "Network radio's penchant for lily-white melodramas and blackface comedy," says black radio historian William Barlow, "had the overall effect of seriously limiting the range of African American characters heard on the airways."[3] Meanwhile, "white musicians began to attain huge followings on radio," notes Susan Douglas, by "appropriating and diluting black jazz ... and selling it as 'the real thing' to whites."[4]

Racial bias in radio soon sparked new forms of resistance from minority communities. In 1931 a massive public campaign arose among African-Americans against *Amos 'n' Andy*, the era's most popular radio show. Out west, the government's persecution and jailing of Pedro J. González, a Los Angeles radio performer and immigrant advocate, aroused widespread furor in the Mexican-American community. But perhaps the most bizarre example occurred along the US-Mexico border, with a handful of powerful outlaw "Border Blaster" stations. Owned by maverick Anglo businessmen, these stations managed to circumvent the major networks' stranglehold on national content. In the process, they created the first major Latino presence on US radio, making it possible for scores of Mexican performers and radio technicians to secure valuable experience in broadcasting.

Early Black Radio

From the inception of wireless telegraphy dozens of African-Americans showed a keen interest in the new technology. That interest continued once radio took off after World War I. Miles Hardy founded the Pioneer Radio Club in New York City in December 1921 and Roland Carrington founded the Banneker Radio Club in Baltimore in 1922.[5] In one of several columns he penned for the *Afro-American* on the subject, Carrington wrote:

> We are offering an invitation to all radio fans, novice or expert. The fellows with crystal sets are as welcome as the ones with audions to join the club. We are in the game to help in every way possible anyone who desires our assistance. Operating on a non-commercial basis, there is much in the club to be gained.

partnered with the *Chicago Defender* and *Pittsburgh Courier* to produce several programs, including the first newscast for African-Americans in the midwest, and he even financed a mobile unit to go out to the community to report breaking news. In 1946 he started *Listen Chicago*, the first roundtable show geared to the black community. No other African-American radio operation of the era could compare to Cooper's, prompting *Ebony* magazine to label him the "Dean of African-American Disc Jockeys."[12]

The National Urban League and Radio

In 1928, soon after the creation of the Federal Radio Commission, the National Urban League concluded that radio could be used as a tool to further interracial understanding. By appearing on programs such as *Wings Over Jordan* during the late 1930s, the NUL sought to spread a new national image of black self-improvement.[13] The League's conciliatory and gradualist approach to ending segregation, along with its emphasis on education and respectable action by blacks, reflected the philosophy of Booker T. Washington, the country's most influential black businessman, and because of that, shows that included NUL figures were even aired by many Southern radio stations. In the words of radio historian Brain Ward, *Wings Over Jordan* "raised few alarms among whites and provided a model for much black-oriented public affairs and political broadcasting for the next two decades."[14]

Even as they broadcast the NUL's productions, however, the networks clung to discriminatory practices in their own operations. It was not until 1935, for instance, that an NBC vice-president reluctantly ordered that the word "nigger" be eliminated from songs aired on the network "wherever possible." Even then, the network acted not because such derogatory words were objectionable but because, as one executive put it, they "always bring complaining letters from Negro listeners."[15]

Breaking the Newspaper Color Line: Maria Coles Lawton and Lester Walton

The newspaper industry's abysmal record on racial integration improved only slightly during the first half of the twentieth century. As we have previously noted, Thomas Morris Chester of the *Philadelphia Press* and T. Thomas Fortune of the New York *Sun* were among only a handful of black journalists employed at major American dailies during the 1900s (see Chapter 7). The only known black editor of a white newspaper during the century was Henry O. Flipper, who spent a few months in 1889 as editor of Arizona's *Nogales Sunday Herald.*[16]

One of the first African-American women to break the color line in the twentieth century was Maria Coles Perkins Lawton, who worked as a reporter at the daily *Brooklyn Standard Union* between 1907 and 1927, and who wrote her stories under the byline M. C. Lawton. The wife of a prominent Presbyterian minister, Lawton would go on to become an influential civil rights advocate, a founder of social service programs for blacks in Brooklyn, and a chief organizer of the National Association of Colored Women's Clubs. She distinguished herself by spearheading the successful campaign by the Brooklyn chapter of NAACP to get papers in the borough to stop using the derogatory term "darkies" in their articles.[17]

While Lawton was at the *Standard Union*, another young black writer, Lester A. Walton, was making his mark in both the African-American and white press. A native of Missouri, Walton began his newspaper career with the *St. Louis Star* in 1902, becoming the first black reporter for a daily in that town, and years later also wrote for the *Globe-Democrat*. In 1906 he moved to New York City, and within two years was named the theatrical director of the city's most prestigious black newspaper, the *New York Age*.

On April 25th, 1913, Walton, who by then had married the publisher's daughter and become the *Age*'s managing editor, sent a letter to the editors of the Associated Press. It was a stirring and thoughtfully crafted plea for a simple change in AP's writing style, one that the black press had been demanding for decades. He asked AP to capitalize the word "Negro." Small as the request was, it rocked the staid and imperious group of New York press barons, for it challenged a style that had been used for centuries. "In the daily press," Walton noted,

> you frequently read an article that is written something like this: 'Every race was represented at the conference held in Carnegie Lyceum Tuesday evening. The Indian, Chinese, Japanese, Italian and negro were much in evidence.' What a rank injustice to the Negro to use the lower case 'n' in this instance![18]

Most Negroes were not black, Lawton insisted, for "in the grouping of my race you can put the black, brown, mulatto, near mulatto, and near white under one head—Negroes," so that "using the term 'Negro' as an adjective, meaning black, is misleading." In defense of his argument, Walton used a phrase that in all likelihood inspired a legendary phrase in Martin Luther King Jr.'s "I Have a Dream" speech half a century later: "It is not that the members of our race are ashamed of being black, far from it," Walton wrote, "for the color of one's skin does not determine character or intelligence. In many cases our darkest Negroes are the most representative. However, we do think that it is wrong to classify millions of people as black who are not, thus creating an improper impression." After Walton's plea, AP changed its style, though it would take until the 1950s for most newspapers to follow suit.[19]

The AP controversy won Walton considerable attention from the city's white editors, especially from those at the liberal New York *World*. Immigrant publisher Joseph Pulitzer had purchased the *World* in 1877 and turned the paper into the main voice in the city for immigrants, and for the downtrodden. By the 1920s, the *World* also became the first white newspaper to champion the concerns of blacks. Herbert Bayard Swope, the paper's executive editor, commissioned Walton, a former classmate and co-worker of his in St. Louis, to write a series of articles in 1922 on the migration of Southern blacks to the city. Swope was so impressed by the quality of the series that he hired Walton as a special correspondent and assigned him to produce a Sunday column about black life in New York. Swope also lured Heywood Broun, a popular sports writer and drama critic, away from the *New York Tribune*. Broun launched a new syndicated column, "It Seems to Me," where he often crusaded against racial discrimination, social injustice, and press censorship. Meanwhile, the *World's* reporters turned out stinging investigations of Ku Klux Klan violence and exposed the slave-labor conditions of black farm workers in Florida, garnering the Pulitzer Prize for the paper in both 1922 and 1924.

The hiring of Walton and Broun caused the *World's* circulation in Harlem to skyrocket, and it drew praise from all the major black weeklies in the country. The paper's competitors, on the other hand, sought to undermine that success by urging advertisers to drop their business with the *World* and accusing it of bias toward blacks.[20] This remarkable period of enlightened news coverage came to a sudden end when Swope resigned from the *World* in 1928 and Broun left for the *Herald-Tribune*. The Pulitzer paper folded three years later, a victim of the Depression. "No stouter, no firmer friend to freedom and justice ever labored against the brutality of American race prejudice than the *New York World*," the *Chicago Defender* noted in appreciation.[21]

As for Walton, he followed Broun to the *Herald-Tribune* as a feature writer, but resigned within a short time after that paper refused to give him a byline on his articles, and returned instead to the *New York Age* as an associate editor. An active member of the Democratic Party, Walton served as publicist for the national party's Colored Division for many years. President Franklin Roosevelt named him special US envoy to Liberia in 1939, and New York's Mayor Robert Wagner subsequently appointed him to the New York City Commission on Human Rights.

George Schulyer's Scorching Satire

As influential as Walton was, he never became as towering or controversial a figure among black journalists as George Schuyler, the satirical columnist and editorial writer for Robert L. Vann's *Pittsburgh Courier* for more than thirty years. A close friend of H. L. Mencken and frequent contributor to a variety of white publications, including the *American Mercury*, the *Nation*, and the *New York Evening Post*, Schuyler was the most famous black writer in the country at the pinnacle of his career, yet many black journalists and intellectuals reviled and shunned him because of his extreme right-wing views.

Born in 1895 in Providence, Rhode Island, and raised in Syracuse, Schuyler enlisted in the army when he was only seventeen, and quickly reached the rank of First Lieutenant before a racial incident derailed his promising military career. While he was stationed in Hawaii, a Greek immigrant who was supposed to shine Schuyler's shoes refused to do so. Schuyler became so angry at the racial slight that he went AWOL. When he returned to his unit he was court-martialed and sentenced to five years in prison. He served nine months before being released and discharged from the military. He then moved to New York, where he found work as a handyman and became immersed in the study of literature. He was also drawn to the socialist movement, and took his first stab at journalism on the staff of A. Phillip Randolph's *The Messenger*.

Schuyler's love affair with the radical movement, however, died as quickly as it had flared up. He soon turned into a fierce critic of the American left, and once he joined the staff of the *Courier* he emerged as the most outspoken black conservative of his era. During the 1950s, he championed Senator Joseph A. McCarthy's anti-communist campaign and even authored a controversial 1968 article, "The Reds and I," for *American Opinion*, the John Birch Society magazine. These words from a 1939 Schuyler article in the *American Mercury* evince both his razor-sharp sharp wit and his bitter enmity toward the left:

> Naturally the communists regarded Negroes as sure-fire converts, and have proselyted them these twenty years. They have tried every bait, device, dodge, and argument to win black adherents. Holding interracial dances, defending Negroes afoul of the law, bulldozing landlords, inundating Negroes with "literature," staging countless demonstrations and marches, endorsing Father Divine, nominating black nobodies for office, and courting Negro leaders.[22]

The Poston Brothers and the Garvey Movement

While Lawton, Walton and Schuyler each played pivotal roles in piercing the color line in twentieth-century journalism, no black writer accomplished more in this regard than Kentucky-born Ted Poston.

Born on July 4th, 1906, in the small town of Hopkinsville, near the border with Tennessee, Poston was the youngest of seven children born to Ephraim

Poston and Mollie Cox. Both parents were educators and prominent members of the town's small black community, and the Poston household was famous throughout Hopkinsville for its well-stocked library and for the many black newspapers to which the couple regularly subscribed.[23]

In 1918, two of Ted's older brothers, Ulysses Simpson and Robert Lincoln Poston, were inducted into the US army and quickly promoted to sergeants. But, while stationed at a military base near Louisville, they grew outraged at the brutal treatment meted out to their fellow black soldiers by their white superiors. The brothers spoke up in protest, only to find themselves summarily demoted. Their dispute with the army attracted extensive coverage in the pages of the *Negro World*, the influential weekly newspaper of Marcus Garvey's United Negro Improvement Association.[24] At its apogee, the *Negro World* boasted a worldwide circulation of more than 50,000. Black seamen routinely smuggled copies of it into Europe's African colonies to circumvent a ban on the paper by colonial authorities. Here in the United States, prominent African-American writers and intellectuals like Zora Neale Hurston, Arturo Schomburg and T. Thomas Fortune were among its regular contributors.

After their discharge from the army, Robert and Ulysses Poston decided to launch their own newspaper. They called it the *Hopkinsville Contender*, and their younger brother Ted, only fourteen at the time, became the paper's copyboy. The *Contender's* editorials against segregation aroused the fury of the town's white residents. Robert and Ulysses moved the paper's operations to Detriot in 1920, and changed its name to the *Detroit Contender*.

Soon after the brothers arrived in Detriot, Marcus Garvey, the charismatic former printer from Jamaica, visited the city and spoke to a large crowd at Utopia Hall. Garvey's movement was already attracting tens of thousands of followers around the world, yet Detroit's white newspapers completely ignored his visit. The Poston brothers were so inspired by his militant Pan-African message that they closed their paper and followed Garvey back to Harlem. Robert rose rapidly up the ranks, becoming the group's assistant secretary-general, while Ulysses was elected to administer its various business enterprises. His chief assistant in those enterprises was J. Raymond Jones, who would later become the first African-American leader of New York's Tammany Hall.

The editor of the *Negro World* when the Poston brothers arrived in the city was Hubert Harrison. A teacher, orator, labor organizer and writer from St. Croix, Harrison was then the most influential black socialist in America. Garvey's organization and newspaper were actually inspired by the previous work Harrison had done during World War I, when he founded the all-black Liberty League and the *Voice* newspaper. Harrison's tenure as managing editor of the *Negro World* in 1920 led to a huge increase in the paper's circulation. The following year, Harrison suddenly resigned from the paper and broke with Garvey. The reason for their split, Harrison said, was his refusal to keep quiet about fraudulent claims that Garvey was making to his followers.[25]

With Garvey's movement mushrooming in membership, UNIA decided in 1922 to launch the *Negro Times*, a daily version of the *Negro World*. Garvey named Ulysses Poston as the paper's managing editor. Poston worked under the direction of T. Thomas Fortune, the great former chief of the *New York Age*, who was then sixty-six and nearing the end of his career. The *Negro Times* collapsed after only twenty-six issues, however, following a series of crippling crises within UNIA. First, Ulysses resigned in a falling-out with Garvey; then an unknown assassin shot to death the association's provisional president Rev. James W. H. Eason in 1923; then Garvey himself was convicted of mail fraud and sentenced to prison in connection to his bankrupt Black Star shipping line. The following year, Robert Poston died of pneumonia while returning from a UNIA trip to Africa.[26]

While the Poston brothers were assuming key roles in the Garvey movement, their youngest brother Ted was studying journalism at Tennessee Agricultural and Industrial College. To pay for his studies, Poston found part-time work on the railroads as a Pullman porter. The railroad job exposed him once again to black newspapers from around the country, including the *Chicago Defender*, *Pittsburgh Courier*, and Baltimore *Afro-American*, all of which black railway employees frequently disseminated along their routes. It also introduced him to the American labor movement and led to his joining the Brotherhood of Sleeping Car Porters, the union for black railroad workers that A. Phillip Randolph had organized.

Ted Poston Helps Launch the Newspaper Guild and Covers the Scottsboro Trial

In 1928, Ted Poston graduated from college, followed his older brothers Ulysses and Robert to New York City, and settled in Harlem, then the center of an astonishing cultural renaissance.

While he waited for his chance to break into journalism, Poston worked intermittently as both a railroad porter and a waiter at the Cotton Club. His brother Ulysses, who by then was one of Harlem's biggest politicians, hired Ted for a while to do composition work on the *Contender*, the old family paper that he still published as a political sheet. Poston got his first real newspaper job in 1931, when the *Pittsburgh Courier* agreed to publish a gossipy column of his called "Harlem Shadows." The *Courier* paid him nothing for his work, but his tongue-in-cheek style and the sharp-edged poems he composed to kick off each column soon attracted a following. In April, for instance, he began one column with "Our Gift, O Magi":

We're quite reluctant in confessing
(Admittedly, it is so depressing)
That our sole gift is acquiescing
To their cruel savagery of heart ...
We lent our ears while Negro mystics
Urged us to be idealistic—
Even while pale mobs, sadistic,
Tore our poor black souls apart ...[27]

Four months after Poston started "Harlem Shadows," the *Amsterdam News* lured him away from the *Courier*. He began writing light and humorous pieces, but he soon switched to producing a riveting series of articles which catalogued gruesome details of lynching incidents around the country. In one 1935 article, he described the "swinging and mutilated bodies" of blacks lynched outside an Indiana county courthouse, and the "bloodthirsty white women who drove their sharp heels into the eye sockets of the victims."[28]

The *Amsterdam News* assigned Poston in 1933 to cover the retrial of the Scottsboro boys—nine black youths accused of raping two white women. No black reporter was accredited to cover the proceedings in Decatur, Alabama, so Poston had to sit upstairs in the Negro section, disguised as a local country boy, while he surreptitiously took notes. Years later he recounted how fellow white reporters secretly helped him get his stories out to New York. "There were so many decent white guys working on papers who were willing to do the right thing, but knew that their papers would never print what they knew I could print, and they wanted the truth to get out," Poston recalled. "I just happened to be lucky enough to be the conduit."[29]

In October of that same year, Poston and his best friend at the *Amsterdam News*, Henry Lee Moon, responded to a public call from the city's most revered newspaperman, Heywood Broun, to found a union for newspaper writers. They learned of the effort in an article in the Communist Party's *Daily Worker*, and attended the first meeting of the new group, the Newspaper Guild, in Broun's apartment. They then recruited every member of the editorial staff at the *Amsterdam News* to join them. Over the next few months they dragged those new recruits to picket lines at both the *Brooklyn Eagle* and *Newark Star-Ledger* to win union recognition.

Before long, Poston and Moon found themselves locked in a bitter fight with Sadie Warren Davis, their publisher. Davis, who ruled the paper with an iron fist, canceled all vacations for the staff in 1935, and she threatened to fire any employee who was a Guild member, thus provoking her staff to walk out. Poston and Moon turned that strike into a *cause célèbre* for the entire city. Broun and other big-name newsmen from downtown showed up regularly on the picket lines, as did many of Harlem's influential figures, such as Rev. Adam Clayton Powell of Abyssinian Baptist Church and writer Zora Neale

Hurston. As the walkout dragged on, however, Davis was eventually forced to declare bankruptcy. In December of that year, she sold the paper at a fire-sale price to two Harlem doctors.[30]

The new owners immediately fired the key strike leaders, including Poston. But Poston did not stay out of journalism for long. In 1936, Walter Lister, city editor at the *New York Post*, gave him a chance to break into the white press. The owner of the *Post* at the time was J. David Stern, a liberal businessman who had signed the first labor contract with the Newspaper Guild. Lister offered to pay Poston 30¢ per inch of copy if the young writer could come up with an exclusive front-page story. Poston met the challenge immediately. On his way home on the subway that day, he witnessed an incident in which a white man jumped a subway turnstile and was then attacked by a group of blacks. Poston assisted a transit policeman in saving the white man from the mob; he then feverishly penned a stirring first-person account that appeared the next day in the *Post*.[31]

From that point on he established himself as an essential member of the *Post* staff. In a period when no other New York paper employed a black reporter, he managed to keep a full-time job, says his biographer Kathleen Hauke, because he "crafted his stories to fit the stereotype of the amusing, cunning, Hambone-like Negro." Poston often chronicled, for instance, "the antics of the famous Harlem character Father Divine, the preacher who renamed his followers (e.g., Faithful Mary), required celibacy of everyone but himself, and took the paychecks of his flock in exchange for providing food and living accommodations."[32]

But he also had a keen eye for detail, an uncanny sense of the importance of humor in a newspaper, and a determination to expose racial abuse wherever he found it. In 1955, for instance, he traveled to Montgomery, Alabama, to cover the bus boycott organized by Martin Luther King, Jr. Poston cultivated close ties with all the important figures in New York's black community, many of whom often provided him with invaluable news tips ahead of any other reporter. One of his Harlem neighbors was civil rights attorney and future Supreme Court Justice Thurgood Marshall. Except for a few years when he left the paper to head the Negro News Desk at the Office of War Information during World War II, Poston remained at the *Post* until his retirement in 1972. By then, he had spent more than thirty years on the paper and was no longer the only black reporter in the white press.

Native Americans and Early Radio

The first Native American broadcaster, Ora Eddleman Reed, came from a family of Cherokee print journalists. Her father, David Eddleman, was a successful white rancher and a former mayor of Denton, Texas, while her mother, Mary Daugherty, was of Cherokee descent and had grown up in Arkansas.

The Eddlemans became part owners of the *Muskogee Morning Times* in February 1897, with David, Mary and her cousin Charles Daugherty all among the group of shareholders that controlled the paper. One of the Eddleman's daughters, Myrta, served as business manager. Another daughter, Ora, who was only a teenager at the time, worked as a reporter and proofreader while attending Henry Kendall College, forerunner of the University of Tulsa. When Mary Eddleman's partners sold out because of financial problems, she ended up the paper's principal owner. Despite being a journalism neophyte, she turned the paper's finances around, and even arranged to contract with the Associated Press to receive wire copy. The *Morning Times* thus became the first Indian-owned paper to boast an AP membership.

In 1898, Mary's daughter Myrta decided to expand the family's interest beyond newspapers by launching *Twin Territories*, a monthly Indian literary magazine. She promptly hired her sister Ora as the magazine's editor and chief writer. A petite, 100-pound woman who was fiercely proud of her Cherokee heritage, Ora used the new magazine to showcase the finest Indian authors of her era and to dispel stereotypes about Native Americans. She also began writing fiction under the pseudonym of Mignon Schreiber, and became one of the founders (and the only female member) in 1896 of the Indian Territory Press Association. She resigned from *Twin Territories* in 1904, after marrying Charles Reed, a correspondent for the Associated Press from Kansas City, and the magazine folded a few months afterward.

Twenty years later, Ora Eddleman Reed embarked on an entirely new career in radio. She and her husband were living in Casper, Wyoming, when a friend of theirs launched that state's first radio station, KDFN, in 1924. Ora offered to host a "talk-type" show to draw listeners and advertisers to the station. She started with a half-hour skit that she filled with commentaries on how to achieve contentment in everyday life. Calling herself the "Sunshine Lady," she answered calls and letters from listeners "with [a] homespun, optimistic doctrine of happiness," notes one historian. The show became wildly successful, and it remained on the air until 1932, when Ora and her husband moved to Tulsa.[33]

Given that Native Americans had relied for centuries on oral tradition to preserve their history and heritage, radio proved to be a natural medium for them to use. During the late 1930s, John Collier, the commissioner of Indian affairs, used federal money to finance radio stations for Native villages in Alaska. As part of that effort he launched a new show on January 1st, 1937, focused on educating the public about Native American history and news. It eventually aired on 170 stations across the country.[34]

Latino Radio Brokering and the Border

The first Latinos in radio followed a path very similar to Hispanic news-paper editors of the early nineteenth century. The geographical proximity of Mexico, Cuba, and Puerto Rico meant that Latino media professionals, whether in print or broadcasting, were able to draw repeatedly on the inde-pendent traditions of the media industries in their home countries, whether for professional training, technological experimentation, or temporary employment. Radio did not explode in popularity in Mexico as quickly as it did in the US because few people in the country owned receivers during the early 1920s, but that began to change by the end of the decade. By then, Mexican audiences were receiving Spanish-language programs from both the US and Latin American countries, and the country's fledgling indus-try emerged as the incubator for a new transnational "Hispanic" broadcast culture—since radio waves are impervious to national boundaries.

As early as the 1920s, Latino brokers began purchasing airtime on southwestern stations to produce Spanish-language programming for the country's small but growing Mexican population. To pay for their slots, the brokers would sell sponsorships to companies doing business with Latinos. These early brokers were mostly Mexican nationals who had attended US schools and who had returned home for a time to work in their country's fledgling radio industry. In Mexico, they did not confront the kind of racial discrimination in hiring that was prevalent in the early US radio industry, so they were able to hone their skills rapidly.

Constantino de Tárnava, Jr., for example, attended high school in Austin from 1913 to 1917, then studied engineering at Notre Dame. While in Austin, he began experimenting with wireless. "During my summer vacation from college in 1921, I set up experimental station 24-A in Monterrey," he noted years later. "Late in 1923, I changed the station status from amateur to com-mercial, the call letters shifting from 24-A to CYO. Later CYO became XEH, today one of Mexico's oldest radio stations."[35]

In 1913, Ignacio E. Lozano, a Mexican immigrant who had fled his country during the Mexican revolution, founded a newspaper in San Antonio that was aimed at his fellow immigrants. *La Prensa* soon became the most widely circulated Spanish-language paper in the United States, and by 1928 Lozano was using its popularity to delve into radio. He began by purchasing airtime on San Antonio's local station, KONO.[36] When the demand for subscrip-tions to *La Prensa* from Latinos in California skyrocketed, he launched a sister newspaper in Los Angeles in 1926, *La Opinión*. The latter paper, still operated today by the Lozano family, is one of the oldest Hispanic newspa-pers in the country.[37]

Similarly, Rodolfo Hoyos, another early radio pioneer, purchased airtime on a Los Angeles station to produce programming for the city's Spanish-language community. Hoyos's was largely a one-man operation. He not only produced his show, which consisted of live music, poetry, drama, and discussion, he also sold advertising and made the collection rounds.[38]

Pedro J. González and Los Madrugadores

The most influential of the early Latino radio pioneers was undoubtedly Pedro J. González, the Los Angeles announcer, singer, and guitar player whose velvet voice, trademark ten-gallon hat, and on-air defense of Mexican immigrants made him a legend throughout the southwest. Born and raised in Mexico, González was only a fifteen-year-old telegraph clerk working in a tiny village in the state of Chihuahua in 1910, when revolutionary leader General Francisco "Pancho" Villa caught him secretly sending information to government officials about the rebel army. Villa immediately conscripted the youth at gunpoint into the rebel forces as a telegraph operator. Over the next few years, González crossed the border several times with Villa's army, even taking part in its infamous raid in March of 1916 on the town of Columbus, New Mexico. Wounded by US soldiers one day as he crossed back into Mexico, González was recuperating from his wounds when he was suddenly jailed by Villa's aides, who accused him of siding with Pascual Orozco, a former rebel general turned counter-revolutionary.

Villista loyalists were preparing to execute him when a young schoolteacher saved his life. The teacher led her pupils to surround him and dissuaded the soldiers from carrying out the sentence. In 1923, González and his wife, Maria Barajas, drove to Los Angeles, where he landed a job as a longshoreman. But the one-time revolutionary turned dockworker also had a gift for writing songs and possessed a hypnotic voice, and those skills helped him find part-time work doing Spanish-language radio commercials for radio station KMPC in 1929. The following year he recorded his first song, and it turned him into an overnight Spanish-language star. He then teamed up with two guitar-playing brothers, Jesús and Victor Sanchez, and they secured their own show on KEWL in Burbank. The group they formed called itself *Los Madrugadores* ("the Early Risers"), after the 4 to 6 a.m. slot they chose for their show. At those hours, they could reach the thousands of Mexican laborers who rose before dawn each day to work in the fields and factories of southern California.[39]

The love ballads and *corridos* González performed on the air made him a household name among the Latinos, but it was the prose he uttered between those songs that turned him into a public hero, for he was the first radio announcer to chronicle the condition of Hispanic immigrants and to publicly condemn abuses against them. This was in the midst of the Great Depression. The Hearst newspapers and other influential publications like the *Chicago Tribune* and the *Saturday Evening Post* began to stoke anti-Mexican sentiment, urging a government crackdown on illegal immigration.[40]

In response, President Hoover's Secretary of Labor William N. Doak launched the biggest immigrant roundup and deportation campaign in US history. Without offering much evidence, Doak claimed that more than 400,000 illegal Mexican immigrants were residing in the country. During the first year of the Hoover administration, more than 17,000 Mexicans were detained and deported from the Lower Rio Grande Valley of Texas alone. The White House was not motivated merely by public sentiment. Hoover had encountered stiff opposition to his economic policies from the country's trade union movement, so he specifically directed Doak to use the massive deportations to "create a diversion to counteract organized labor's hostile attitude."

Agents from the newly created Border Patrol of the Immigration and Naturalization Service conducted indiscriminate sweeps throughout the country from 1930 to 1932. They raided factories and farms, they surrounded and locked down whole Mexican neighborhoods, they searched houses without warrants and demanded identification from every resident, and they detained people in public parks, on buses and trains. Those they arrested were often held incommunicado until they agreed to be "voluntarily" deported. The federal government's own Wickersham Commission, which investigated the deportation campaign, later condemned the dragnets. "The apprehension and examination of supposed aliens are often characterized by methods [which are] unconstitutional, tyrannic and oppressive," the Commission concluded. Estimates of the number of Mexicans forced to leave the country in the early years of the 1930s vary wildly, from a low of a few hundred thousand to as many 2 million, though it seems certain that at least 1 million were repatriated.[41]

As the dragnet spread, radio announcer Pedro González was the lone voice on the airwaves alerting his fellow Mexicans to impending raids. "They say that this government campaign is to secure jobs for North American citizens," González told his listeners in one broadcast. "It's a trick. It isn't true. It's really nothing more than a racist attack against all Mexicans. We are neither illegals nor undesirables."[42]

González was especially critical of Los Angeles District Attorney Buron Fitts for his anti-Mexican bias. In 1934, Los Angeles police suddenly arrested González and charged him with raping a sixteen-year-old girl. The city's Mexican residents regarded the arrest as a government plot to silence their most effective spokesman. He refused a plea bargain, was found guilty, and was sentenced to one to fifty years in San Quentin Prison. Even in prison, however, he continued to speak out. He organized the first major protest in San Quentin's history: a hunger strike by 10,000 inmates against intolerable prison conditions—an action that led to major reforms in the state's penal system.

Meanwhile, Dora Versus, the girl González had been convicted of raping, recanted her story and admitted that the authorities had pressured her to accuse him falsely. The convicted man's wife then spearheaded a grassroots campaign to win her husband's freedom. Her effort garnered unprecedented support on both sides of the border, "The Ballad of Pedro J. Lopez" became one of the era's most popular *corridos*, and two Mexican presidents eventually called for his release. González was finally freed in 1940. As soon as he was released, the government deported him to Mexico. On his trip to the border, thousands gathered at Union Station in Los Angeles to express their support and wish him goodbye. He then settled in Tijuana, where he continued his broadcasting career. He died in Lodi, California in 1995 at the age of ninety-nine. Over the years, his remarkable story has been immortalized in a *corrido*, a PBS documentary, and a feature film, yet few histories of the US media mention the pioneering role he played in public-interest broadcasting among Latinos, or the government conspiracy to silence him.[43]

Latino Radio Ownership in the 1920s

Latino involvement in early broadcasting went beyond brokering and the production of individual programs to include actual ownership and operation of radio stations. Until now, all accounts of Hispanics in broadcasting have claimed that the first Hispanic to hold a commercial radio license in the United States was Raoul Cortez, who founded KCOR in San Antonio in 1945. But Hispanic involvement in radio began much earlier, during the medium's infant years. John C. Rodriguez, president of the Alamo Radio and Electric Company in San Antonio, was granted a commercial radio license by the federal government on May 9th, 1922, according to records found in the National Achives. Rodriguez's WCAR made its debut that same year as the second commercial station in that city, and while little is known about his personal story or the kind of programming his station produced, he appears to have been involved with radio even before World War I. A 1916 Department of Commerce Radio Service Bulletin lists Rodriguez as receiving a license to operate amateur station 5ZR that year in San Antonio. He went on to run WCAR under the name Southern Radio Corporation of Texas until 1926, at which point the station was sold to the Lone Star Broadcasting Company. The new owners then changed the station's call letters to KTSA, the name by which it continues to operate today with an all-news and talk format.[44]

The year before Rodriguez launched WCAR, a burly, silver-tongued Mexican shoe-salesman named Emilio Azcárraga Viduarreta began his own experiment with radio below the border, in Mexico City. Born in the northern industrial city of Monterrey in 1893, Azcárraga was the son of a low-level government worker. His parents enrolled him at St. Edward's University in Austin, Texas, where he became a star on the university's 1912 football team—but he dropped out of school before graduation and decided to set out across Mexico's vast countryside as an itinerant shoe-salesman. Within a few years, Don Emilio, as he came to be known, had acquired the rights to sell several fashionable brands of American shoes, and had established a prosperous enterprise. His sales touch proved so magical that he quickly took on a raft of products, peddling everything from automobiles made by Henry Ford to record players manufactured by the Victor Talking Machine Company.

In 1921, Azcárraga and his four brothers decided to start a small radio station in Mexico City. They abandoned the project after three years—Don Emilio would later claim that they launched it strictly "for fun"—but the experience they gained proved priceless. In 1929, NBC bought the Victor Talking Machine Co., and Don Emilio, as Victor's Mexican agent, began selling radios as well. One day a customer complained to Azcárraga that he could only hear "gringo music" on the radios that Don Emilio was peddling. Azcárraga suddenly glimpsed a whole new market beckoning. He dispatched his brother Raúl to New York to receive technical training in broadcasting from NBC, and on March 19th, 1930, the Azcárragas launched a new station in Monterrey, XET. It proved so successful that nine months later they started XEW, a 5,000-watt station in Mexico City. Don Emilio called it "La Voz de la America Latina desde Mexico" ("The Voice of Latin America from Mexico"). Such was the origin of a broadcast firm that would evolve into the most powerful and storied media empire in all of Latin America: Televisa.[45]

Border Blasters Open Opportunities for Latinos

When the Azcárragas started XEW there were just thirty private and ten government-owned educational radio stations operating in Mexico. All of these stations faced a huge obstacle to further growth: the imperialistic communications policy of their neighbors to the north. Mexico's radio pioneers quickly discovered that US and Canadian stations had already snatched up all the available frequencies on the electromagnetic spectrum, and had divided those frequencies between themselves in 1924. Even worse, the bigger 50,000-watt American stations were creating havoc with Mexico's domestic signals.[46]

The Mexican government sought repeatedly to reach agreement with US and Canadian officials on an equitable reallocation of frequencies, but its efforts were repeatedly rebuffed. Its response was to license a group of high-powered radio stations along its northern border. The new stations, dubbed

Border Blasters, would have a dramatic impact on North American radio for several decades. While their transmitters were technically located in Mexico, the new stations were owned mostly by US citizens, many of them medical quacks, salesmen and psychics who actually operated from studios on the US side of the border, and who then connected those studios to transmitters on the Mexico side. The Border Blaster transmitters were so powerful that their signals blanketed huge sections of the US, causing constant interference with American and even Canadian stations. Perhaps the most famous figure the Border Blasters produced was Wolfman Jack, the late-night madcap disc jockey for XERF who was heard all over America in the early 1960s.

The first of the mega-stations was XER. It began operating on October 21st, 1931 from Villa Acuña, Mexico, just across the Rio Grande from Del Rio, Texas. While it billed itself as the "Sunshine Station Between Nations," XER's owner and operator, Dr. John R. Brinkley, was notorious throughout the US for his wild claims of restoring the virility of impotent men by implanting goat glands in them. Brinkley had originally promoted his exotic cure on KFKB in Milford, Kansas, for which he obtained a radio license in 1923. Within six years, KFKB was the most popular station in the country and Brinkley had become a multi-millionaire. He succeeded despite a relentless campaign against him by the American Medical Association, which accused him of quackery. The influential Kansas City *Star*, owner of a competing radio station, soon joined the anti-Brinkley bandwagon as well. So did many of the state's key politicians, who became spooked after Brinkley ran for governor as an independent populist and nearly pulled off a stunning upset. His enemies eventually banded together in 1930 and convinced the Federal Radio Commission to revoke Brinkley's radio license. The good doctor responded with a brilliant countermove: he relocated his operation to Del Rio, Texas, secured a radio license from the Mexican government, and built a 75,000-watt transmitter on the other side of the border, making his station more powerful than any in the US.

Brinkley was followed by a host of other American businessmen peddling medicinal miracles, psychic advice and the like on Border Blasters all along the Mexican border. Among them was Norman Baker, the political populist and cancer-curer who had his Iowa radio license revoked by the FRC only to pop up again as the owner of XENT in Nuevo Laredo, Mexico. Baker's station went on the air in late 1933. It included two 300-foot towers and an astounding 150,000-watt transmitter. So powerful was its signal that when local residents tuned into the station, their radios boomed with explosive, ear-splitting sounds.

The advent of the Border Blasters, however, also provided an enormous boost in radio opportunities for Hispanics—a byproduct their founders had never intended. The maverick American broadcasters, after all, had to curry favor with both Mexican government officials and the largely Mexican-

American business elite on the US side of the border. In addition, the Mexican government required the station owners to offer at least 25 percent national content in their programming.[47] Some Mexican businessmen even became part-owners of the new stations. Carlos M. Bres, a Mexican entrepreneur and former mayor of Piedras Negras, for instance, was one of the founding owners of XEDN in 1932. With its staggering 100,000-watt signal and its largely English format, XEPN could be heard over much of the United States.[48]

Given their borderland location, their outlaw status, the reach of their signals, and their comparatively large budgets, the Border Blasters emerged as the first white-owned radio stations to substantially integrate Mexican technicians and performers into their staffs and Hispanic shows into their programs. A typical evening broadcast on Baker's XENT, for example, included not only shows such as *Tune Corral* and *Memory Lane*, but also the *Mexican String Orchestra* and the *Cuban Orchestra*, and the station always signed off at dawn with the music of the Mexican Típica Orchestra. At XER, J. R. Brinkley employed as his chief engineer Isaías Gallo, a former inspector of radio and telegraph for the Mexican government; in addition, the station featured the music of both the Studio Mexican Orchestra and the Sabinas Orchestra, along with performances by soprano Rosa Domínguez, who station managers dubbed "Mexico's Nightingale." Meanwhile, XEPN, where C. M. Bres was part-owner, was among the first to produce Spanish-language programming for a US audience.[49]

Amos 'n' Andy

On August 29th, 1929, a few months before the stock market crash, the NBC Blue Network launched *Amos 'n' Andy*, a new comedy series. Before long, more than 40 million people—half the national radio audience at the time—were tuning in to NBC each night from 7 to 7.15 p.m. to chuckle at the latest exploits of the two bumbling owners of the "Fresh Air Taxicab Company of America, Incorpulated," their sleazy sidekick Kingfish, and all the other members of the "Mystic Knights by the Sea" fraternal group. In the words of one radio historian, it became a "national addiction, as hotel lobbies, movie theaters, and shops piped the show ... so as not to lose customers. Telephones remained still, toilets weren't used, taxis sat unhailed while the show was on."[50]

The program's lead performers, Freeman Gosden and Charles Correll, both white vaudeville actors and veterans of blackface minstrel shows on Chicago radio, became the highest-paid and most celebrated performers of their era. Using an exaggerated "Negro dialect" that they sprinkled with endless malapropisms, Gosden and Correll evoked for their listeners the slapstick images and sounds that ostensibly captured the foibles, fears, and frustrations of black urban life in the midst of the Great Depression.

Blackface minstrelsy had been a feature of American popular theater since the early 1800s, but *Amos 'n' Andy* spawned a resurgence of the demeaning genre. Those who rushed to imitate the show's success inevitably depicted three main racial stereotypes of blacks: Coons, Toms and Mammies. Most programs rejected African-Americans as leading actors for not sounding black enough, and those that did employ them attempted to coach them on how to speak with a "proper" black dialect.[51]

Gosden and Correll were brilliant comedians, and their show no doubt brought considerable cheer to a nation faced with the calamity of the Great Depression. Because of that, many radio accounts have tended to discount the show's damaging effect on American racial attitudes. Some have preferred to focus instead on the more benign image of the two loveable bumpkins as reflecting the quest of ordinary people to make sense of an increasingly strife-ridden world.

In *The Early Days of Radio Broadcasting*, for example, George H. Douglas notes:

> *Amos 'n' Andy* seems to have appealed to all kinds and classes of people, rich and poor, simple and educated. Most black listeners seem to have been every bit as amused by the show as the whites. This was probably partly due to the fact that all of the central characters were human, likeable and sympathetically rendered. If the writers were using them for evoking laughter, they were making fun with them, not of them.[52]

In her spellbinding study of American radio, *Listening In*, historian Susan Douglass acknowledges that *Amos 'n' Andy* played on stereotypes about the "incompetence, duplicity, and shiftlessness of black men," yet she asserts that the show's "power" came from the way "white men put into the mouths of blacks their sense of helplessness in a world where all too many men suddenly felt superfluous, stymied, throttled."[53]

Gosden and Correll, however, did much more than simply portray universal human foibles. As black radio historian William Barlow has noted, the show's theme song, "The Perfect Song," from D. W. Griffith's classic white-supremacist film *Birth of a Nation*, signaled each night to educated black listeners the overriding message of its creators—black inferiority.[54]

Those black leaders who recognized the message for what it was refused to dismiss the show as innocuous comedy, and a huge public outcry and bitter debate ensued among black Americans over how to respond to *Amos 'n' Andy*. The result of that debate was a pioneering movement for media reform and against racism in broadcasting.

That movement began in 1931, when Robert Vann, the *Courier's* publisher, issued a public call to take *Amos 'n' Andy* off the air. Vann declared in an editorial:

> No people in the world would stand for the exploitation but Negroes. No people would sit idly by and allow themselves to be so portrayed but Negroes. Certainly, the white people exploiting us would not dare exploit any other race of people on earth. They could not get away with it.[55]

Vann urged a massive petition campaign by African-Americans to the Federal Radio Commission to complain of the show's negative depiction of the black community. The result was an unprecedented flood of letters expressing outrage against the show. "I am neither Amos nor Andy and would not like to be called either of the two," said J. Alexander McNeill of Fayetteville, NC. "I consider this program harmful to the American Negro." "Whites like this program better than any other because it shows the Negro just as they like to see him," wrote Arthur Tucker of Canton, Ohio. "This program should be stopped, if possible."[56]

Norman E. Jones, secretary for the NAACP Memphis branch, described the show's dreadful impact on white residents of his town:

> Recently when Dr. J. E. Walker, president of the Universal Life Insurance Company of this city appeared before the investigating committee of State Affairs in Nashville, a daily paper of Memphis carrying the story used the phrase that "Dr. Walker answering all questions in a calm and intelligent manner, was no Amos and Andy type of Negro." With the insinuation that he was rather an exception to the type that these radio entertainers portray in general.[57]

Publisher Vann pronounced the survey responses proof that action was needed: "From almost every corner of the United States come letters telling us that the Negro is the only one who would sit idly by while his whole past is ridiculed and his future darkened by two high powered salesman whose love of money makes Negroes of white men ..."[58]

Vann proceeded to feature a thermometer on the paper's front page to track the number of petition-signers calling for the show's cancellation. By July, the thermometer had reached his original goal of 100,000; by August, it had surpassed 300,000; and by October, it had reached 675,000 letters of protest against *Amos 'n' Andy*.[59] The paper then called for 5,000 ministers to take part in a national day of protest against the program. Vann set the date of the protest for October 25th, and he urged all participating ministers to preach their sermons that day on the subject of self-respect.[60]

While Vann did not reach his final goal of 1 million signatures, the 740,000 he did collect represented an extraordinary achievement. Since the nation's total black population at the time was only 9.7 million, the *Courier* petitions thus represented more than 7 percent of the entire community, and a far higher percentage of its adults.

"The fight to silence the insidious propaganda broadcast by *Amos n'Andy* is the greatest movement toward the uplift of the race that has ever been attempted," Vann boasted.[61] While his claim was certainly exaggerated, the *Amos 'n' Andy* campaign nonetheless deserves recognition as perhaps the first black-led nationwide movement to challenge racial bigotry in America's mass media.

Its success was even more remarkable when you take into account the vehement opposition Vann faced from several of his fellow black publishers. The *Chicago Defender's* Robert S. Abbott, for example, was not only a fan of the show, he was a personal friend of Gosden and Correll. In the midst of Vann's campaign, Abbott publicly invited the duo to a picnic sponsored by the *Defender* at a local city park. The *Courier* responded with a hilarious cartoon that depicted Amos and Andy changing the name of the *Chicago Defender* to "*Chicago Surrender.*"

But Abbott was not alone. In Jacksonville, Fla., the black-owned *Florida Sentinel* rebuked Vann's efforts.[62] New York's *Amsterdam News* also defended the show, saying:

> It cannot be denied that there are imperfections in Amos 'n' Andy's depictions of Negro life ... But these errors are inaccurate rather than objectionable. Amos and Andy have presented the Negro in a more favorable light than much of the literature written by Negro authors ...
>
> Wholly apart from the fun they have brought to millions, Amos and Andy have done more to lessen race prejudice than anything else in contemporary literature.[63]

Vann shot back with a scathing condemnation of his fellow publisher:

> [W]e must have all sorts to make a backward group. We must tolerate the vacillating editor, the fawning apologists, the guffaws and asinine writers until the light of intelligence penetrates even every dense quarter of Harlem. Harlem has given us many things—some of value and then some of—well shall we include an "Editor Andy"?[64]

The debate over *Amos 'n' Andy* reflected a major divide among black journalists over how to respond to the dissemination of racist ideas on a nationwide scale—a problem made more immediate by the new radio technology. In many ways, it was a continuation of the disputes between Frederick Douglass and Henry Highland Garnet nearly a century earlier, and of W. E. B. DuBois and Booker T. Washington in the early 1900s, for they

sharpened for black intellectuals and journalists differences in their strategies for tackling slavery or Jim Crow. The simple fact that Vann managed
to garner nearly a million supporters for his campaign, however, suggests
that the masses of conscious blacks repudiated the *Amos 'n' Andy* stereotypes
and identified more with the *Courier's* strategy of direct confrontation.

As for the federal government, it completely ignored the massive outcry
against the show. In early 1932, the Federal Radio Commission dismissed
the petitioners' call for a hearing. Vann's prediction that Washington would
not ignore the will of the African-American community turned out to be
exceedingly naïve.

Hoover and Radio Politics

By refusing to respond to black protests against *Amos 'n' Andy*, the infant
Federal Radio Commission helped to preserve the white racial narrative in
broadcasting. In much the same way, the FRC exhibited arrogance toward
our Mexican neighbors by refusing to negotiate an equitable allocation of
radio frequencies between the two countries. Both responses were a sharp
contrast to how the agency handled the appeals of many white American
publishers and radio station owners in those early years. President Hoover's
direct involvement in many of these appeals can be found in his presidential
papers.

In November of 1930, for example, newspaper publisher Frank Gannett
wrote to George Akerson, Hoover's assistant, to request the White House's
help in preventing a New York radio station from falling into the hands of a
rival Hearst newspaper.

Gannett, who owned the *Knickerbocker Press* and *Evening News*, made
clear in his letter that he was seeking the station only as a maneuver against
Hearst, though his correspondence with FRC Chairman Charles McKinley
Saltzman spoke only of the public good that would be served by granting
his request. Gannett claimed he wanted to move WOKO, a Poughkeepsie
station in which his company had a stake, to Albany so that the Gannett
papers there could provide a higher quality of news broadcasts for the Albany
community.[65]

Likewise, a 1931 letter to Walter Newton, Hoover's assistant, from Republican National Committee member George Vits sought the White House's
help in securing a radio license for the Call Publishing Company of Racine,
Wisconsin, which Vits called "one of our very good supporters in the state."
The company, which owned the *Racine Times-Call*, belonged to Wisconsin Senator Walter Goodland, who was also the paper's editor. Vits attached
to his letter a note from Senator Goodland explaining the real political
purpose behind his efforts to secure a 100-watt station. "Conservatives in
Wisconsin are very weak in active radio support," Goodland wrote. "If we

get the license we are going to see that it gets actively into the next campaign. I do not know much about the business personally, but it is said that it is difficult to get a license and a lot of backing is required."[66]

Julius Liebman, the vice-president and editor of the *Milwaukee Sentinel*, traveled to Washington, DC, in early June 1931 for a meeting in the White House with Hoover assistant Walter Newton to discuss increasing the power of the newspaper's radio station from 250 to 500 watts, which required a waiver from the FRC. That summer Liebman stressed to the White House the importance to the Republican cause of increasing the station's power:

> ...we felt it would be to the advantage of others, besides ourselves, to have this station in a position to be heard in a wider area than is now possible. Our Democratic competitor in Milwaukee, as I told you, has 1,000 watts and can be heard throughout the State while our station can be heard only in the immediate vicinity of Milwaukee.

So while politically connected publishers and the major radio networks consolidated their power over broadcasting during the 1930s, people of color saw their presence in the new medium sharply diminished. African-Americans and Latinos fought back against racial stereotypes through mass movements such as the campaign against *Amos 'n' Andy*, through the movement to free Pedro J. González, and through support for the outlaw Border Blaster stations. But President Hoover and the Federal Radio Commission ignored calls for greater racial diversity, and instead actively assisted the networks and publishers in strengthening their domination. Only the outbreak of a new world war and yet another wave of race riots in the big cities would finally convince our government leaders and major media companies that it was time to dramatically alter the white racial narrative.

14

Uniting the Home Front

The Negro press is far more than a mere expression of the Negro protest.
By expressing the protest, the press also magnifies it, acting like a huge
sounding board.

Gunnar Myrdal, *An American Dilemma*

Americans fell in love with radio between the Great Depression and the end
of World War II. They were awed by its magical ability to penetrate their
homes and stir their deepest emotions, by its wondrous capacity to convey
live musical performances and crucial events from far-off places at any hour
of the day or night. But the new medium quickly began to replicate many of
the same racial stereotypes that had long characterized white-owned newspapers and magazines.

The structure of the nation's broadcasting system, moreover, did not
permit people of color to offer some alternative or competing portrayal of
American life in the same way they had done with the printed word: they
now needed a federal license to start their own station, or they were forced to
rely on appeals to government regulators or on community pressure against
license-holders to provide more balanced and inclusive programming.

Luckily for the reformers, the Communications Act placed broadcasters
under government regulation and required them also to serve the public
interest. The regulatory structure established by the 1934 law survived for
more than seven decades, despite continuous advances in mass communications technology, fierce contention among media owners, periodic upsurges
of citizen discontent with the broadcast system, and frequent battles in
Congress over whether to expand or diminish the government's power. As
the years passed, the FCC and the federal courts gradually defined the nebu-
lous concept of the "public interest" to encompass three main policy goals:
promoting competition in the broadcast marketplace, requiring local stations to serve the needs of their local community, and ensuring a diversity of
viewpoints on the public airways. Commonly referred to as "localism, diversity, and competition," these goals are still considered the bedrock principles
of federal communications policy.

At first, however, the FCC made no effort to preserve the relative diversity of voices that radio had evinced in the 1920s. The agency even refused to guarantee a place for the noncommercial and educational stations that had been a feature of the medium's early years. Instead, it allowed the handful of commercial broadcast networks to consolidate enormous control over hundreds of local stations. Those networks promptly transformed radio into a huge commercial and entertainment platform, one whose main goal was to deliver the biggest audience possible to the corporate advertisers who bankrolled its content.

The programs the networks produced during the 1930s tended to steer clear of contentious social issues or dissenting viewpoints that might anger those advertisers. They often even avoided transmitting any real news. By 1940, for example, the four national radio networks (NBC Red, NBC Blue, CBS and the Mutual Broadcasting System) "provided listeners with 59 daytime hours of sponsored programs weekly," according to an FCC analysis of programming, with fifty-five of those hours devoted to soap operas.[1] Invariably, the networks sought to attract a white audience. Part of this was no doubt driven by the huge racial disparities in ownership of radio sets. The proportion of American households that owned radios spiraled from 65 percent in 1934 to 81 percent in 1940, but ownership by African-Americans and Hispanics lagged far behind.[2] In North Carolina, for example, only 1 percent of blacks owned a radio in 1930, and while the rate had climbed to 33 percent by 1940, it was still dramatically lower than for whites. Ownership statistics, on the other hand, did not fully capture the popularity of radio among non-whites, since many listened to programs in public venues such as taverns, clubs and barbershops.[3]

The outbreak of World War II, however, promoted new government efforts to diversify radio content. In 1943, another wave of racial violence engulfed the country and the federal government sought to ease racial tensions by encouraging the radio networks to showcase the positive contributions of black people to American life. Unfortunately, the change in programming was never extended to another racial minority: Japanese Americans. Most newspaper and radio coverage during the war served only to reinforce long-held anti-Asian biases and to justify our government's wartime internment policies toward the Japanese.

The Early Fight Against Network Dominance

The Radio Act of 1927 had always been regarded as a temporary measure. The law required annual reauthorization by Congress, and it offered no assurance to radio license-holders that a privately run system would remain in place in the future. Great Britain, for instance, had already opted for a government-sponsored model, the British Broadcasting Corporation. In the

US, annual reauthorization debates meant broadcasters faced the constant worry that their programs would provoke the ire of individual members of Congress. At the same time, a small but persistent group of educators, amateur radio enthusiasts, labor unions, and citizen groups had continued to lobby Washington lawmakers for a more direct government role in radio. The reformers especially sought guarantees that a portion of spectrum space would be devoted to educational and non-commercial broadcasting.

In the end, the federal government opted for a system run solely by private business, much as it had with the nineteenth-century telegraph.[4] It did so even though numerous surveys made it clear that Americans were already fed up with rampant commercialism on the airwaves. "Radio broadcasting is threatened with a revolt of the listeners," *Business Week* warned in 1932. "Newspaper editors report more and more letters of protest against irritating sales ballyhoo."[5]

On May 15th, 1934, the Senate approved by a simple voice vote the most important media legislation since the creation of the Post Office—the Communications Act. Before doing so, the senators first defeated by a vote of forty-two to thirty-five a last-minute proposal by the Catholic Church to reserve 25 percent of all radio channels for non-profit broadcasters. But while Congress ignored major concerns of the public-interest groups, it did at least uphold the basic principle that the electromagnetic spectrum was a national resource, and it agreed to preserve the original language of the Radio Act stating that broadcasters must operate in furtherance of "the public interest, convenience, or necessity."

Ironically, the most liberal chief executive in the country's history, Franklin D. Roosevelt, ended up approving a law that gave the giant radio networks the near-total control they had been seeking. In signing the Communications Act, Roosevelt was attempting to ensure his political survival. His close friend, mentor, and former boss, Navy Secretary Josephus Daniels, had repeatedly urged him to hold out for government control of radio, but Roosevelt had been in office then for only thirteen months, and he was locked in a fierce battle with the nation's newspaper publishers. Most of those publishers had opposed his election, and during the early days of his administration they used their newspapers to vilify his New Deal policies. The radio owners, on the other hand, offered Roosevelt a free platform to speak directly to the public.

The previous winter had been one of deepening despair for millions of Americans, with bank failures spreading and unemployment spiraling out of control. To calm the population, Roosevelt and his aides spoke on radio some 150 times during the first ten months of his administration, and he soon institutionalized his legendary fireside chats. He thus outflanked the newspaper publishers and guaranteed himself a way of mobilizing public support for his New Deal reforms. The logic of Roosevelt's political compromise with the networks was perhaps unassailable, but its long-term legacy—a privately run, centralized broadcast system infused with hyper-commercialism —remains with the American people to this day.[6]

What made FDR's approval of the Communications Act even more disastrous for people of color were the subsequent appointments he made to the FCC. Of twelve Democrats named to the agency during his presidency, nine came from segregationist Southern states, including its first chairman Eugene Sykes (1934–35), a former Mississippi state Supreme Court justice and a holdover from the previous Radio Commission.[7] Two successors to Sykes were Charles McNinch of North Carolina (1937–39), and James Lawrence Fly of Texas (1939–44). Southern domination of the Commission during its early years ensured that the agency did virtually nothing to address racial diversity in broadcast ownership.

During McNinch's tenure, Congress and the agency did begin to voice some unease over the extraordinary concentration of radio ownership that was occurring. By 1938, for instance, 46 percent of the 700 broadcast stations operating in the country had fallen under the ownership or control of the major networks, while more than 200 were owned by newspaper interests.[8]

Once Fly became chairman, the agency released a report on chain broadcasting that confirmed what most Americans already knew: the networks were exerting too much control over their affiliates. The FCC then ordered reforms that allowed local stations to air shows from other networks and that permitted them to determine their own ad rates.[9] It also concluded that NBC's ownership of the Red and Blue networks constituted an unjustifiable monopoly and ordered the company to divest itself of one of them. NBC executives fiercely opposed the order. The Supreme Court finally upheld the FCC action in 1943, forcing NBC to relinquish its Blue Network, which became the American Broadcasting Company.[10]

The Racial Narrative Between World Wars

Despite radio's growing popularity, most literate adults in the 1930s still relied on daily papers for the bulk of their news and information. The country boasted 2,000 daily newspapers at the beginning of the decade, and those papers had a circulation that surpassed 40 million. One of every three inhabitants, in other words, purchased a paper each day. But the Great Depression coincided with a sharp decline in newspaper circulation, stirring further fear among publishers of competition from radio.[11]

Those newspapers, however, were still firmly wedded to the white racial narrative. In 1932, for example, researcher Noel Gist published a study of sixty days of news coverage in seventeen metropolitan newspapers. He found that 46 percent of all space devoted to blacks contained "anti-social" news, with about a third of it devoted to theft or violent crimes. In several papers, more than half of all news about blacks was "anti-social." The worst offenders were the *New Orleans Times-Picayune* (67.2 percent), the *Atlanta Constitution* (58.8 percent), the *Washington Star* (59.3 percent), and the *Indianapolis News* (52.2 percent).[12]

Another study of racial coverage in twenty-eight Texas newspapers found that 78 percent of items about blacks in the state's urban publications and 62 percent in rural ones were anti-social, "most of it involving attacks on women, liquor charges, thefts, robberies, and murders." Considerably more space was given "to items that might substantiate the beliefs among Southern white people that Negroes are superstitious, simple, ignorant, childish, clown-like, sincere believers in the power of a rabbit's foot, voodoo and fortune tellers of the most absurd type," researcher Ira B. Bryant noted.[13]

To Bryant's surprise, however, there were substantial disparities in the sheer volume of racial bias, even among newspapers in the same area of the state. The Houston *Chronicle*, for example, devoted more than 86 percent of its news space about blacks to anti-social items, while the nearby Galveston *News* devoted 58 percent, despite crime rates among blacks in both cities being similar. Galveston contained only one-fifth the number of professional blacks that Houston did, yet its paper depicted ten times more professional blacks in its news pages than did the *Chronicle*. The main variable Bryant found between the cities was that Galveston's black residents could vote in local elections, while those in Houston could not. He thus reached the startling conclusion that the relative political power of African-Americans in a community affected how well white newspapers depicted them. The same pattern existed throughout the state. Overall, the "five papers, taken from the cities where Negroes are not permitted to vote in the city elections, are more likely to make use of opprobrious references than [eleven] newspapers published in cities where the Negro participates in local elections," Bryant noted.[14]

Such systemic press bias was not confined to the South. A 1937 study of four Philadelphia newspapers found "an absolute decrease" in space devoted to Negro news between 1908 and 1932, even though the city's black population during that time increased from 7 to 11 percent. The proportion of articles devoted to crime news was astonishingly higher for blacks than for whites—only 10 percent of total news space in the four papers. But the "percentage of Negro crime news in all Negro news space [ran] from 27.7 percent in the *Public Ledger* in 1918 to 79.9 percent in the Philadelphia *Record* in 1923!" White readers, the researcher concluded, had been presented "an unreal picture of Negro life from their newspapers."[15]

The Birth of Broadcast Journalism

World War II marked the dawn of broadcast journalism. As the war spread, the amount of radio time devoted to news skyrocketed, with news specials or news reports comprising nearly 20 percent of all network programming by 1944. "From broadcasters such as Eric Sevareid in Paris, William L. Shirer in Berlin, Edward R. Murrow, Robert Trout, and Charles Collingwood in London, listeners in the United States heard bombs and bullets tear apart European civilization," is how one radio historian describes the advent of the new journalism. Those daily dispatches established the critical importance news broadcasting would henceforth play in shaping mass opinion in wartime.[16]

During the war, several notorious attempts by corporate chiefs and politicians to silence radio reporters came to light. In 1939, for instance, General Mills withdrew its sponsorship of H.V. Kaltenborg's news broadcasts on CBS after Catholic listeners complained of his criticism of the Church's role in the Spanish Civil War. In 1943, following complaints from the Johns-Manville Company, a major CBS advertiser, that newsman Cecil Brown's commentaries were too friendly to the Soviet Union, network executives sought to reduce his editorial comments. Brown's subsequent resignation triggered a national debate over censorship. "If radio becomes guilty of making its commentators take sides—or pull their punches—in order to curry favor with advertisers, it will have much to account for," warned an editorial in *Time*.[17] That point was brought home again in 1949, when William L. Shirer resigned from CBS after the network lost its sponsor for his popular prime-time show. Shirer blamed the show's cancellation on the growing corporate hostility to liberal views on the air. Altogether, some two-dozen left-of-center commentators were dropped from the four radio networks in the years immediately after the war, according to one report in the *New Republic*.[18]

The Press and the 1941 Civil Rights March on Washington

Black newspapers soared in popularity before and during the war. In 1932, about 150 black papers had an estimated combined circulation of 600,000. By 1940, with the country's black population at 13 million, circulation of black weeklies had grown to 1.2 million; it then zoomed by 1945 to 1.8 million. Black weeklies typically were held longer and passed around more frequently than their white counterparts, so that one researcher has estimated some 3.5 to 6 million blacks read the papers each week—about 25 to 50 percent of the entire black population. Just five papers, the Chicago *Defender*, the *Pittsburgh Courier*, the New York *Amsterdam News*, the Baltimore *Afro-American*, and the *Norfolk Journal and Guide*, claimed the bulk of the paid circulation of about 740,000. Known collectively as the Big Five, these papers exercised far more influence over the views of blacks nationwide than their competitors in the white press did among the general public.[19]

The *Pittsburgh Courier*, for instance, played a pivotal role under its legendary editor and publisher Robert Vann in convincing black voters to abandon their historic ties to the Republican Party in 1932 and vote for Franklin Roosevelt. Eight years later, both the *Courier* and the Baltimore *Afro-American* switched their support to Republican Wendell Wilkie in his effort to unseat Roosevelt. They did so, despite strenuous pressure from Roosevelt's "black cabinet" to keep them in the Democratic camp, because Wilkie and the Republicans were promising to enact a federal anti-lynching law, voting rights for blacks, and an end to discrimination in the military—all issues that FDR had shelved during his first eight years in office in order to shore up his support among Southern white Democrats. Not surprisingly, the paper's militant stance generated its biggest circulation gain ever, and it soon emerged as a national paper, with separate editions and offices in several cities. After Vann's death in 1940, his successor, Ira Lewis, and other black leaders and editors, concluded the time had come to press the Roosevelt administration to end racial exclusion in the defense industry. In early 1941, A. Philip Randolph, the president of the Brotherhood of Sleeping Car Porters and the country's best-known black labor leader, made a public call for thousands of blacks to march on Washington, DC, to demand an immediate end to segregation in both the military and the defense industry.

The white press initially ignored Randolph's announcement, and even mainstream black organizations like the Urban League and the NAACP gave it a lukewarm reception. But extensive coverage in black newspapers prompted huge support for the protest in black communities across the country. "Labor Leader Says Group to Parade in Washington for National Defense Jobs," was the headline in a January 31 article in the black-owned Kansas City *Call*. "Power is the active principle ... of the masses united for a definite purpose," the article quoted Randolph as saying. "Call Colored Americans to Washington, DC for Jobs and Equal Participation in National Defense, July 1," proclaimed the Boston *Guardian*. "Let the Negro Masses Speak," blared a headline in the *Amsterdam News*. 'Negro Won't Get Jobs as Before," predicted the Atlanta *Daily World*.[20]

As the July 1 date of the protest neared, Roosevelt tried everything he could to stop it. He even agreed to meet with Randolph and other march organizers like William White, head of the NAACP, and Mary McLeod Bethune, of the National Youth Administration. The president warned that the protest could "create serious trouble," but he refused to issue a presidential order ending discrimination in the military. He then enlisted the help of several white figures who were well-regarded in the black community to convince Randolph to cancel the event.

Less than a month before the scheduled event, a barrage of sensational articles in Washington's white press depicted an epidemic of street crimes and sexual assaults on women in the city. On June 18th alone, the *Washington Post* published three articles with ominous headlines like: "Super-Police Squad Hunts Sex Slayer of DC Girls," "Murder Leads Mrs. Roosevelt to Warn Girls," and "Legislators Seek Investigation of Police, FBI Intervention." Three days later, more *Post* articles fueled the atmosphere of crime and crisis with headlines such as: "DC Crime Wave Rolls On, with Six Felonies in One Day," and "Randolph Asks Military Police Help for DC." Since blacks allegedly committed most of the street crimes, the coverage was undoubtedly meant to deepen fears among Washington's white residents about a black march.[21]

And the *Post* was not alone in propagating such hysteria. "The troubles in Washington reflected a nationwide sense of racial instability that stemmed from the [war] preparedness effort," notes Daniel Kryder in his study of racial relations during the war. As African-American migration to the cities increased, press reports about "crime waves" in those cities became more frequent. Likewise, as more young black men from the North enlisted in the army and were dispatched to Southern military bases, black soldiers "assumed a new prominence" in reports about racial conflicts. This was especially true in the black press. In 1941, for instance, seventeen of the nineteen incidents of racial violence that appeared in black newspapers involved black soldiers. The black-owned Nashville *Globe and Independent*, for instance, reported on April 25th that an army investigation had failed to find the killers of a black soldier who had been found lynched in the woods at Fort Benning, Georgia. An April 20th brawl between white and black soldiers at Fort Jackson, South Carolina, prompted a story in the Atlanta *Daily World*, headlined, "Race Soldiers, White CCC Boys Clash in SC." And the April 5th shooting death of a black private at Fort Benning by an MP prompted a story in the Baltimore *Afro-American* headlined, "Unruly Soldier Killed by MP at Ft. Benning." All of this coverage translated into even greater support for Randolph's march.[22]

When the president learned that the projected size of Randolph's civil rights march had grown to more than 100,000, he was furious. But despite the pressure from Roosevelt and Washington's white press to call off the march, Randolph and White refused to do so. They stood fast to their demand that the president first issue an order desegregating the army and the war industry. Articles in the black press, meanwhile, firmly supported Randolph and conveyed a starkly different image of the plans for the march. "Roosevelt Won't Address Marchers to Washington," the *Amsterdam News* reported on June 28th. "Race Leaders Stand Pat on Job Demands," was the headline in the Chicago *Defender* that same day.[23]

Faced with the possibility of the largest mass protest in US history, and by a potential eruption of violence between Washington's largely white police force and Randolph's black marchers, Roosevelt chose to compromise. Only days before the start of the march, and over the objections of his military chiefs, the president issued Executive Order 8802, which prohibited racial discrimination in federal government employment or by defense contractors, and he established a temporary Fair Employment Practices Commission. Roosevelt refused to budge on Randolph's other demand, the desegregation of the armed forces, but his major concessions convinced Randolph, White, and Bethune to call off the march. Two of the president's first appointees to that seven-member commission turned out to be influential newsmen: publisher Mark Ethridge became chairman of the Commission, and RCA chief David Sarnoff became one of its unsalaried members.[24]

Roosevelt's executive order was the first major reform of federal policy toward African-Americans since Reconstruction. It came about because of an unusual convergence of factors: growing racial unrest across the country, and a fearless and skilled group of civil rights leaders. But the role of the black press should not be underestimated. By daring to expose the racial injustices that were occurring inside the US military, by giving consistent voice to the plans and statements of Randolph and the other organizers of the civil rights movement, black newspapers were a huge factor in marshaling pressure on the White House to act.

Radio Unites the Home Front

The war itself led to a surge in positive portrayals of black Americans on radio, as national leaders sought to reduce black-white tensions at home. In a repeat of World War I communications policy, the government rushed to create a massive radio propaganda apparatus through the Office of War Information, the Armed Forces Radio Service, and the Office of Censorship. Former CBS commentator Elmer Davis, the director of the OWI, negotiated a voluntary agreement with NBC, CBS and Mutual to assist the war effort by adopting control over their own content. The networks thus avoided a repeat of the federal takeover of radio that had occurred during World War I, and the government avoided the need for direct censorship of broadcasts, though some network news commentators, such as Walter Winchell and Drew Pearson, routinely offered their scripts to the Office of Censorship for clearance.[25]

As part of the new policy, "various federal agencies were directed to develop radio shows that addressed the race issue in a progressive manner and showcased African-Americans in a positive light," according to radio historian William Barlow. Government officials secretly worried that African-Americans might succumb to propaganda from the Axis powers, and those fears were not entirely misplaced. Prior to the war, W. E. B. DuBois and other black leaders had openly expressed admiration for Japan's rise, and many followers of Marcus Garvey and the Nation of Islam's Elijah Muhammed later chose to go to prison rather than fight against Japan. A 1942 survey by the OWI revealed that an astonishing 50 percent of black residents of New York City believed their lives would be better off or the same under Japanese rule.[26]

Public affairs programs until then had rarely addressed race relations or featured African-American guests, but that began to change during the war. NBC's *America's Town Hall Meeting on the Air* and CBS's *People's Platform* highlighted African-American support for the war, with the latter even airing an episode where the guests were all black.[27] Among the first programs to emerge from the new propaganda initiative was *Freedom's People*, an eight-part NBC series that dramatized the contributions of African-Americans to science, sports, education, the arts and the military. Produced by the Federal Radio Education Committee of the US Office of Education, the series featured in its cast many of the country's most renowned black figures, including A. Philip Randolph, Paul Robeson, Jesse Owens, George Washington Carver, Count Basie, and Cab Calloway. Some seventy Southern affiliates of NBC agreed, for instance, to broadcast the network's first installment of *Freedom's People*.[28] In early 1942 the War Department's public relations office also asked the networks to make changes in their entertainment lineup, as well as in news programs. Soap opera producers Frank and Ann Hummert immediately responded by inserting positive black characters in two popular series—*Our Gal Sunday* and *The Romance of Helen Trent*. Meanwhile, CBS aired shows such as *They Call Me Joe* and *The Negro at War*, which profiled the contributions of people of color in the military.[29] Another program that drew enormous praise was the National Urban League's *Salute to Freedom* show, which was broadcast in 1944 by NBC and narrated by popular actor Frederick March.[30]

The Double V Campaign and Threats of Press Suppression

While African-Americans welcomed the radio networks' newfound sensitivity, it did nothing to ease the sting of day-to-day racial discrimination. Once the war began, black leaders rushed to challenge Jim Crow in two institutions where it had become most glaring and indefensible—among the troops and among military contractors. On February 7, 1942, the *Pittsburgh Courier* launched its legendary "Double V Campaign," in which it called for victory against both Nazism abroad and segregation at home.[31] Once it began, the paper's crusade spread rapidly in black neighborhoods across the country—so rapidly that White House officials hastily convened a meeting in Washington on March 20th with some fifty black leaders to address the discontent. Editors from the *Courier*, the *Afro-American*, the *Michigan*

Chronicle, the NAACP's *Crisis* magazine, and the Associated Negro Press were among those invited to the gathering. Archibald MacLeish, director of the federal Office of Facts and Figures, requested their help in toning down any public criticism of the federal government from the black community until after the war. MacLeish thus repeated the same strategy toward the black community that George Creel had employed during World War I. But the leaders would not be mollified. They advised MacLeish that black morale for the war would improve only if the federal government stepped up its efforts at racial integration, and they refused to dampen their criticism unless the Roosevelt administration adopted such reforms.[32]

Faced with the near-unanimous rejection of his appeal, MacLeish and his aides opted for a more aggressive policy. They urged Attorney General Francis Biddle to warn black newspapers that the federal government would be monitoring their activities. "The Negro press is flagrantly abusing the privilege [of Freedom] of the press every day," one MacLeish aide wrote in an internal memo a few weeks after the meeting. "Much of the present unrest among the Negro population is due to the inflammatory and extremist tenor of the Negro papers ... As long as the Negro Press is permitted to continue its present practices with impunity, we can expect very little improvement in morale of the Negro population."[33]

Before long, a handful of prominent white journalists began to parrot the same allegations in print. One of the first to step forward was Virginius Dabney, the legendary liberal editor of the Richmond *Times-Dispatch*. In an April 1942 editorial titled "The Negroes and the War," Dabney pointed with alarm to the growing number of "race riots" near Southern army bases. The "prevailing assumption," Dabney wrote, was that the "bloody encounters" were being instigated by black newspapers. Two days after his comments appeared, syndicated columnist Westbrook Pegler also lashed out at the black press, comparing the *Pittsburgh Courier* and *Chicago Defender*'s "inflammatory bias in the treatment of news" to subversive efforts by the Communist Party press.[34]

Black editors, however, were simply voicing the profound resentment among their readers against racial segregation, and against the white press for refusing even to debate the matter publicly. A sign of that resentment came in the spring of 1942, with the Office of War Information survey of how black men in Harlem viewed the war. The results were shocking. Only 11 percent of those surveyed believed conditions would improve for African-Americans if the US won the war.[35]

If anything, the black press was actually understating the problem. It was less skeptical about the government's war effort and about the prospects of ending Jim Crow than the bulk of its readers. The *Courier*, for instance, repeatedly displayed a greater commitment to racial diversity in its pages than any white publication of its era. At various times the paper counted among its stable of regular columnists an Indian, a Chinese, and two white journalists. Other black papers such as the *Age*, the *Defender*, the California *Eagle*, and the Savannah *Tribune* also featured white columnists.[36] Unfortunately, the views of black people were of such marginal concern during the war that most Americans did not even know the black press existed. Gunnar Myrdal described this astounding media divide in his classic study of US race relations, *An American Dilemma*:

> Through all the Negro press there flows an undercurrent of feeling that the race considers itself a part of America and yet has no voice in the American newspaper. Members of this group want to learn about each other, they want the stories of their success, conflicts, and issues told, and they want to express themselves to the public.[37]

Top officials in the Roosevelt administration so resented wartime criticism from black papers that they launched extensive investigations of several publications through the Office of War Information, the army's Military Intelligence Division, the Justice Department, the FBI, and the Post Office. The most determined in this regard were J. Edgar Hoover's FBI and the Post Office. Top officials at both agencies repeatedly urged that sedition charges be lodged against several black editors, and at one point Roosevelt himself mulled the possibility, but Attorney General Biddle repeatedly beat back any pressure to initiate such prosecutions, and thanks to his efforts, black newspapers escaped any overt suppression during the war.

The Black Press and Racial Strife in the Military

In 1942, the army's Intelligence Division urged camp commanders to "reduce and control the publication of inflammatory and vituperative articles in the colored press."[38] At the time, some three-quarters of the training facilities for black troops were located in the South. African-Americans assigned to those camps often faced rancorous abuse from local citizens and law enforcement, even from camp commanders and military police. The camps and the towns around them became racial cauldrons, with confrontations flaring up whenever local or military police arrested a black soldier for some alleged infraction. More than 200 such racial incidents occurred between 1942 and 1945, some two-thirds of them in the South.[39]

The peak period for racial disturbances came during the bloody summer of 1943, with major clashes at Camp Stewart, Georgia; March Field, California; Fort Bliss, Texas; and Camp Breckinridge, Kentucky. Once again, black newspapers were the only publications that consistently exposed the racial insults, inferior living conditions, and physical abuse the black soldiers faced. In May, for instance, Harlem's *People's Voice*, a radical tabloid edited then by Adam Clayton Powell, Jr., the future congressman, warned in a front-page story headlined "Georgia HELL-HOLE," about "unspeakable conditions at Camp Stewart down in Georgia, where Jimcrow is riding high, wide and handsome." A week later, the *Voice's* more conservative competitor, the *Amsterdam News*, printed a letter from a member of New York's all-black 369th infantry unit. Headlined "Cold Cuts for the 369th Unit," it complained about the lack of proper food for black troops.[40] Black soldiers at Camp Stewart had complained repeatedly to their superiors and to the NAACP that MPs harassed them and the black women from nearby Savannah that soldiers would visit. On June 9th, word spread that two black soldiers had been assaulted and a black female companion of theirs killed by MPs. That night, several angry soldiers ambushed convoys of white MPs, killing one and wounding four.[41]

In the aftermath of the Camp Stewart incident the black press once again sought to expose the roots of the violence. "Guns and Clubs Used to Enforce Mass Jim Crow," was the headline in the June 12th edition of the Baltimore *Afro-American*. The article reported that Savannah police had been routinely stopping black soldiers and their female companions and demanding health cards from women to prove they did not have venereal disease. "Alleged Attack on Negro Woman Causes Clash at Camp Stewart," was the headline of a June 17th article in the black-owned *Savannah Tribune*.[42]

During that same summer of 1943, major race riots erupted in New York, Los Angeles, Philadelphia, Mobile, and Beaumont, Texas. The worst outbreak was in Detroit. Mobs of blacks and whites clashed repeatedly over a three-day period in June, with the city's white police force joining in attacking black citizens. More than thirty-four people were killed, most of them African-American; some 600 were injured and nearly 2,000 arrested. The fighting ended only after President Roosevelt sent federal troops to occupy the city. So widespread were the disturbances that summer that the army's chief of staff sent a memo in July to top generals warning that racial unrest had become an "immediately serious problem."[43]

The Sleepy Lagoon Hysteria and the Zoot Suit Riot

Only days before troubles erupted in Detroit and at Camp Stewart, the infamous Zoot Suit riot engulfed Los Angeles. Between June 3 and 13, thousands of white sailors and marines rampaged through the city's Mexican community. They especially targeted *Pachucos*—young Mexicans they suspected of being gang members because of the trademark Zoot Suits they wore. The sailors grabbed scores of Mexicans, ripped off their clothes, and beat many severely, but they also attacked other non-whites. Local police, according to several reports, stood by or joined in the attacks, then arrested the victims instead of the perpetrators. Miraculously, no one was killed, but the violence sparked a pattern of similar attacks on Zoot Suiters that summer in a half-dozen other US cities.

The Los Angeles troubles had been building for more than a year. They followed publication of a series of articles by the city's major newspapers about a supposed wave of assaults on women and incidents of gang violence.

On the morning of August 2nd the body of a young man named José Díaz was found on a dirt road in East Los Angeles, near a gravel pit that local Mexican youths often used as a swimming hole. The dead man's head had been fractured, his face was badly bruised, and he had been stabbed several times. Witnesses told police that Díaz had left a gang fight which had broken out at a neighborhood party. The press immediately labeled it the "Sleepy Lagoon Case," after the name of the local swimming hole, and a spate of sensational accounts depicted a sordid story that was supposedly emblematic of violent *barrio* life.

On the nights of August 10th and 11th, police sheriffs and California highway patrolmen encircled and blockaded several Mexican neighborhoods throughout Los Angeles County. They pulled residents from their cars and homes and arrested more than 600 youths, most of whom had done nothing wrong. They eventually charged twenty-five—all alleged members of the 38th Street Gang—with the killing of Díaz. The Sleepy Lagoon proceedings became the biggest mass trial for murder in US history. Despite the absence of any concrete evidence or witnesses tying the accused youths to the homicide, seventeen of the defendants were convicted in early 1943 on various counts ranging from assault to second-degree murder.[44]

The hysteria among white residents over the Sleepy Lagoon case was unprecedented for the southwest—though it was eerily similar to the climate surrounding the trial of the Scottsboro Boys in the passions it aroused. Two days after Díaz's death, for example, William Randolph Hearst's *Los Angeles Evening Herald and Express* called in an editorial for an immediate police crusade against gangs. "Youthful Gang Evil: Vigorous Action Imperative in View of Seriousness of Situation," was the editorial's headline. During the latter half of 1942, other *Evening Herald* articles were headlined: "Brutal Attack on Woman" (August 8th); "3 New Attacks on Women" (September 28th); "2 Women Beaten, Robbed," (October 28th); "Victim of Gang Holdup" and "Robbery: Zoot Suit Boy Held in Woman Slugging" (November 6th).[45]

A local tabloid magazine named *Sensation* published a series of stories purporting to provide an inside look at the horrors of gang life. One article, headlined "Smashing California's Baby Gangsters," described Pachucos as "reckless madbrained young wolves." Written by the chief of the criminal division of the Los Angeles sheriff's office, the article praised the sheriff for organizing a special anti-gang squad and moving swiftly to "stop the wolf-packs before they committed further murders." The term "wolf-packs," notes

Eduardo Obregón Pagán, a historian of the Sleepy Lagoon case, "was a well-understood reference to the tactics of the feared Unterseebooten of Nazi Germany that silently stalked Allied ships and sunk them in coordinated surprise attacks." By linking domestic Latino youth gangs in the public consciousness to German U-2 submarines, *Sensation* further demonized them as a threat to the nation and as deserving of no mercy.[46]

In more recent times, the term "wolf pack" was resurrected in the New York press in 1989 after five black and Hispanic youths were charged with the vicious beating and rape of a young female investment banker in Manhattan's Central Park. The incident, which came to be known as the Central Park Jogger attack, provoked hysteria and rage among local white residents that was similar to that of the Scottsboro Boys and Sleepy Lagoon cases. Press accounts, all leaked by New York City detectives, alleged that the youths had laughed and joked about the attack when they were questioned. Those reports created such a furor that billionaire real estate developer Donald Trump sponsored full-page ads in all the major papers, calling the young men "animals" and urging the reinstitution of the death penalty in the state. Much as in the Scottsboro and Sleepy Lagoon cases, the convictions against the New York youths were suddenly overturned thirteen years later, after DNA evidence linked another man—a career criminal and sex offender—to the crime, and that man, Matias Reyes, later admitted his involvement.[47]

Just as with the Trump ads during the Central Park Jogger case, the *Los Angeles Times* printed many angry letters from readers during the Sleepy Lagoon affair, including one that asked: "[W]hen are the Sheriff and the Chief of Police going to issue instructions to their men to go out and give the same rough treatment to these hoodlums that [they] give their victims?"[48]

Hostility toward Mexicans was so engrained in the public's mind in 1943 that one of the prosecution experts who testified in the grand jury against the youths, Lieutenant Edward Duran Ayres of the LA County Sheriff's Department, told the jurors they needed to understand the "biological" nature of Mexican Indians to grasp the seriousness of the "Mexican problem" in the US. "The Indian from Alaska to Patagonia ... shows many of the Oriental characteristics, especially in his utter disregard to human life," Ayres testified.[49]

Many Latinos in Los Angles believed from the start that the young men had been railroaded. Several prominent city leaders soon spearheaded a massive movement to demand justice for the Sleepy Lagoon defendants. Among the organizations that carried on that fight were the Sleepy Lagoon Defense Committee (SLDC), co-chaired by longtime California progressive Carey McWilliams, and the Citizens' Committee in Defense of Mexican American Youth (CCDMAY), an outgrowth of the International Defense League.

Not until months after the arrests did the public learn that most of the accused youths had held down ordinary working-class jobs and were not violent thugs at all. Several of those convicted spent more than two years in jail, until an appeals court in October 1944 unanimously overturned all the convictions for insufficient evidence. By then, the propaganda machine of the Axis powers had repeatedly attempted to use the Sleepy Lagoon case to subvert support for the war in Latin America and among Hispanics in the US.[50]

While the Sleepy Lagoon defendants sat in jail, the Zoot Suit riot erupted. Once again, local press helped create a hostile racial climate. According to one study of that city's papers conducted more than a decade later, press coverage of Mexicans grew increasingly negative in the weeks before the rampage. Once the riot began, several newspapers, including the *Los Angeles Times*, the *Daily News*, and Hearst's *Herald-Express* condoned the attacks and egged on the servicemen with claims that Mexicans were planning to attack them. "44 Zooters Jailed in Attacks on Sailors," read the main headline in the *Daily News* on June 7th; it was followed the next day by: "Zoot Suit Chiefs Girding for War on Navy." An editorial in the *Herald-Express* suggested the riots would "rid the community of ... those zoot-suited miscreants." The smaller Eagle Rock *Advertiser* lamented that "servicemen were called off before they were able to complete the job. Most of the citizens of the city have been delighted with what has been going on."[51]

A June 7th front-page headline in the *Times* stated, "Zoot Suiters Learned Lesson in Fight With Servicemen." The paper's lead article evinced obvious delight at the actions of the sailors:

> These gamin dandies, the zoot suiters, having learned a great moral lesson from servicemen, mostly sailors, who took over their instruction three days ago, are staying home nights.
>   With the exception of 61 youths booked in County Jail on misdemeanor charges, wearers of the garish costume that has become a hallmark of juvenile delinquency are apparently "unfrocked."[52]

In the midst of the bedlam, the local papers made one outlandish and distorted claim after another about Mexican youths. On June 9th, for instance, the *Los Angeles Times* printed a sneering photo of a twenty-two-year-old Mexican-American woman holding up her fist. "Brass Knuckles Found on Woman 'Zoot Suiter,'" the paper's headline declared. Only by closely reading the story did one learn that the young woman was not a gang member at all. She was merely carrying brass knuckles, she said, to protect herself from Zoot Suiters who frequently gathered near her home.[53]

The following day the *Herald Examiner* featured a story about an anthropologist who claimed nine Mexican-American girls had confessed to being

part of a plot to seduce and murder sailors. Like the alleged murder conspiracies against whites in Statesboro, Georgia, in 1904, no evidence of such
plots was ever uncovered, nor was anyone charged with participating in
such a plot. The unfounded press accounts, however, made an already tense
situation even worse.[54]

The only papers to depict a different reality were Al Waxman's Jewish
Eastside Journal and *La Opinión*, Ignacio Lozano's Spanish-language daily.
"Belvedere Fears Another 'Invasion' of the Sailors,'" was the banner headline
across the top of the June 6th issue of the Spanish-language *La Opinión*,
followed by the subhead: "Alarm in the Mexican neighborhood, Sailors
Announce They Will Return to Continue War Against Gangs." Waxman's
newspaper, meanwhile, published a riveting eyewitness account of Mexican
men and women being beaten by sailors and police.[55]

Radio Responds to the Riots

Faced with mushrooming racial violence throughout the country, the federal
government and the network chiefs consciously sought to use radio as an
instrument to promote social harmony. CBS, for instance, aired *An Open
Letter on Race Hatred* in 1943 as a direct response to the bloodshed. Produced
by respected radio dramatist William Robson and personally reviewed by
CBS chief William Paley, it was the most powerful condemnation of racism
the new medium had yet produced. The show's startling opening words
signaled to listeners that this was no ordinary broadcast:

Dear Fellow Americans: What you are about to hear may anger you …
We ask you to spend thirty minutes with us, facing quietly and without
passion or prejudice, a danger which threatens all of us. A danger so great
that if it is not met and conquered now, even though we win this war, we
shall be defeated in victory; and the peace which follows will be for us a
horror of chaos, lawlessness, and bloodshed. This danger is race hatred.

The provocative script went on to compare attacks on blacks in Detroit to
fascist "gangs of German youth armed with beer bottles and lead pipes." It
warned that two-thirds of America's allies in the war "do not have white
skins." Those non-white allies, the narrator declared, had "long and hurtful
memories of the white man's superior attitude in his dealings with them"
and "[r]ace riots in Detroit, Los Angeles, and Beaumont, Texas, do not reas-
sure them … Such an attitude within our borders is as serious a threat to
freedom as is the attack from without … It is essential that we eliminate it
at home as well as abroad."[56]

Wartime racial violence, in other words, had so shaken the nation that
CBS, with the clear backing of the federal government, was forced to

tacitly acknowledged the "Double V" campaign started by black newspaper publishers. So powerful was the impact of the *Open Letter* documentary that the show won the prestigious Peabody Award that year, and Henry Luce's *Time* magazine called it "one of the most elegant programs in radio history."[57]

The final years of the war witnessed a string of similar public affairs radio shows that depicted a more humane image of African-Americans. They included NBC's *The Army Hour*, a weekly series spotlighting the exploits of black soldiers, and *Too Long, America*, a show on racial discrimination in the workplace narrated by movie star Edward G. Robinson.[58]

Japanese Internment and the Media

On February 19th, 1942, President Franklin Roosevelt signed Executive Order 9066, authorizing the US military to exclude any resident of the country from certain designated military zones for national security purposes. Government officials proceeded to round up some 120,000 Japanese nationals, more than two-thirds of them US citizens, and forcibly relocate them to military camps for the duration of the war. Japanese internment was to become one of the most shameful government actions in the nation's history. Critics saw it as a gross violation of democratic principles and due process rights, especially since US participation in the war was aimed at defeating Axis aggression and the Nazi ideology of racial supremacy. More than forty years later, Congress finally apologized for the internment policy and awarded $20,000 in compensation to each surviving victim.

Press historians, however, have paid scant attention to how biased press coverage fueled public hysteria against the Japanese. Following the attack on Pearl Harbor on December 7th, 1941, many of the country's most influential newspapers backed the internment of first-generation Japanese immigrants (*Issei*), as well as second- and third-generation Japanese who were already US citizens. The *Los Angeles Times*, *San Francisco Chronicle*, and *New York Times* were among the many papers that published stories questioning the loyalty of ethnic Japanese. Some stories even claimed local Japanese were helping their homeland government prepare an attack on the west coast.[59]

Several California papers launched a crusade in support of Lieutenant General John L. DeWitt, the Western Defense commander who claimed that a Japanese fifth column existed on the west coast. DeWitt openly framed his allegations in racial terms, stating:

> A Jap's a Jap, and that's all there is to it. I am speaking now of the native-born Japanese ... In the war in which we are now engaged racial affinities are not severed by migration ... The Japanese race is the enemy race and while many second and third generation Japanese born on the United

States soil, possessed of United States citizenship, have become "Americanized," the racial strains are undiluted.[60]

The day after Pearl Harbor, the *Los Angeles Times* reported that some Japanese could very well be upstanding good citizens, but "what the rest may be we do not know, nor can we take a chance in the light of yesterday's demonstration that treachery and double-dealing are major Japanese weapons." Later, the *Times* called for the removal of the Japanese, declaring, "A viper is nonetheless a viper wherever the egg is hatched—so a Japanese American, born of Japanese parents, grows up to be a Japanese, not an American."[61]

Scripps-Howard columnist Westbrook Peglar advocated executing a hundred detained Japanese for every American killed in the war, suspending habeas corpus for all Japanese, and placing them under government surveillance.[62] While a few papers initially defended the Japanese minority, even those papers changed their tone after government officials warned of possible spies among the immigrants. California Attorney General Earl Warren, for example, testified to Congress that the nation was being "lulled into a false sense of security" when it came to Japanese at home. "Our day of reckoning is bound to come," warned Warren, who would later become chief justice of the Supreme Court.[63] On December 13th, the *New York Times* reported that US and Mexican government sources were concerned about unidentified aircraft flying near a secret airbase in the Southern California desert, where a large population of Japanese was "rumoured" to reside.[64]

At the same time the federal government began subsidizing radio portrayals of the Japanese as subhuman. In the *Treasury Star Parade,* a federally sponsored series aimed at promoting the sale of war bonds, one episode, titled "A Lesson in Japanese," described the Japanese as monkeys and reptiles and still "savage beast[s]." Another depicted a scene of an American soldier dismembering the genitals of a Japanese soldier.[65]

Little wonder that public feeling against the Japanese was far greater than against German nationals. A survey by the US Office of Facts and Figures in April 1942, for example, found three times as many Americans backed war with Japan as with Germany. In a separate survey by the Office of War Information, respondents commonly described Japanese as "sly," "cruel" and "treacherous," while they described Germans as "warlike," "cruel" and "hardworking."[66] Admittedly, some of this was due to the simple fact that Japan, not Germany, had launched a direct surprise attack on US territory; still, the ferocious cruelty Americans countenanced toward the Japanese during the war was bewildering. In a Pulitzer Prize–winning study of the Pacific conflict, historian John Dower called it a "bloody racist war." It was "virtually inconceivable," Dower noted, "that teeth, ears, and skulls could have been collected from German or Italian war dead and publicized in Anglo-

American countries without provoking an uproar, and in this we have yet another inkling of the racial dimensions of the war."[67]

Once the war ended, so did efforts by radio broadcasters to improve the image of African-Americans. The few post-war shows the networks did launch soon encountered stiff resistance from Southern broadcasters, and this time the network chiefs quickly capitulated. Southern stations, for example, refused to broadcast a 1946 CBS show honoring the national Negro newspaper, which included Frank Sinatra and Ella Fitzgerald. The network also encountered hostility for airing a program called *Night Life*, which featured a racially mixed cast broadcasting live from Harlem. When the Mutual Broadcasting System aired a four-part series dramatizing President Truman's Commission on Civil Rights, Southern politicians demanded and received equal time to rebut the show's accusations. NBC canceled the Nat King Cole show in 1946 after only three months because so many Southern stations refused to carry it. A few years later, Cole experienced a similar fate with the cancellation of his TV show.[68]

15

The Color Line and the Public Interest:
The Post-War Period

> Tonight the Negro plantation worker in the Delta knows from his radio
> and television what happened in the world. He knows what black people
> are doing and he knows what white people are doing. He can see on the
> 6 o'clock news screen the 3 o'clock bite by a police dog ... He knows
> about the new free nations in Africa and knows that a Congo native can
> be a locomotive engineer but in Jackson he cannot even drive a garbage
> truck.
>
>   James Meredith, speaking on WLBT-TV in Mississippi in May 1963,
>   three weeks before his assassination

Jackson, Mississippi, the capital of our nation's poorest state, is a long way
from the New York City skyscrapers that house the titans of our national
broadcast networks, yet it was in Jackson that a pivotal battle unfolded during
the 1950s and 1960s to dismantle the color line in the American media.

The turmoil over the color line resumed shortly after World War II, as
African-American veterans returned home from the battlefield brimming
with a new sense of their rights as citizens, and some began to challenge
how the media portrayed black people. Their efforts gained unexpected
impetus from a series of post-war reform efforts that suddenly jolted the
nation's major media executives, and by technological advances that further
revolutionized mass communications.

The advent of television, for example, spurred unintended changes in
how radio addressed racial minorities. As broadcast network executives
shifted their attention and resources to television in the 1950s, many experts
initially predicted that TV would be the doom of radio. But just the opposite occurred: the number of AM stations mushroomed from 948 to 2,824
between 1946 and 1954. What did change was the two-decade-old centralized network model for producing radio shows. Station owners forced to
compete against television for new ad revenues decided to create new programs geared to their own local listeners, or even to smaller niche audiences

within those communities.[1] A significant number even switched to black-appeal programming in order to tap the burgeoning and still largely ignored black consumer market.

As a result, scores of non-white communities across the country were suddenly introduced to a new and powerful type of public figure—the local black DJ. Those DJs emerged as an important new force in the Civil Rights movement, joining black ministers and black newspapers, the other established voices of the nation's African-American masses. By the mid 1960s, Civil Rights leaders adopted an unprecedented strategy: they filed direct challenges to the licenses of a handful of white-owned radio and television stations in the South. The most important of those challenges was to be the fourteen-year campaign against racial discrimination in Mississippi television, which culminated in 1969 with a federal court revoking the license of a white-owned station in Jackson, WLBT. The court's decision was a seminal moment for proponents of media reform and for people of color seeking an end to racial bias. That victory might never have been possible, however, were it not for the moral outrage and the relentless pressure that black journalists and black veterans stirred up against another bastion of racism in American society—professional baseball.

Jackie Robinson and the Crusade of the Black Press to Integrate Baseball

No national institution felt the post-war pressure to end segregation more sharply than major league baseball. In August 1945, Brooklyn Dodgers General Manager Branch Rickey was contemplating a move that would end up transforming American sports. He was preparing to break the color line in baseball. Rickey held his first meeting with Jackie Robinson, a young World War II veteran and former star black athlete at UCLA, who was then playing baseball for the Kansas City Monarchs in the American Negro League.

As early as the 1930s, a few isolated columnists in the white press had begun to question segregation in baseball—among them Heywood Broun, Westbrook Pegler of the *Chicago Tribune*, and Jimmy Powers of the New York *Daily News*.[2] Blacks were then allowed to compete alongside whites in only a few sports, but they were completely excluded from the country's most cherished game, professional baseball.

The journalist who spearheaded that effort was Sam Lacy, one of the best-known black sports columnists of his day. In a career that spanned more than seventy years, Lacy worked at various times for the Washington *Tribune*, the Chicago *Defender*, and the Baltimore *Afro-American*. Born in 1903 in Mystic, Connecticut, to a black father and a full-blooded Native American mother, Lacy sold peanuts as a youngster in the Jim Crow section of Griffith Stadium in Washington, DC. He later enrolled at Howard University, and began writing full-time at the black-owned Washington *Tribune* after graduation.

Lacy sparked a national controversy with his reporting in 1937, when he revealed that a Syracuse University football star named Wilmeth Sidat-Singh was not of East Indian descent, as school authorities had been claiming, but had actually been born in the District of Columbia to African-American parents. The all-white University of Maryland team, which was about to play a game with Syracuse, threatened to pull out of the contest after Lacy's article appeared. Syracuse responded by removing its star player from its squad. The team lost the game, and Syracuse incurred condemnation throughout the North for its appeasement of segregation.

Following the Sidat-Singh affair, Lacy questioned why major league owners kept excluding the greatest players of the Negro leagues. In 1938 he published an extensive interview in the *Afro-American* with Clark Griffith, owner of the Washington Senators. "Both the commissioner [of baseball] and I know that colored baseball is deserving of some recognition in the organized game," Griffith told Lacy. "However, I am not sure that the time has arrived yet … A lone Negro in the game will face rotten, caustic comments. He will be made the target of cruel, filthy epithets."[3]

By then, the *Pittsburgh Courier* had started its own campaign to integrate baseball.[4] The paper's effort gained steam after a young Detroit native named Wendell K. Smith joined the staff in 1938 and began writing a column titled "Smitty's Sports Spurts." From his first pronouncement on the issue, Smith minced few words. He blasted both the owners and his fellow blacks who accepted the status quo:

> Why we continue to flock to major league ball parks, spending our hard earned dough, screaming and hollering, stamping our feet and clapping our hands, begging and pleading for some white batter to knock some white pitcher's ears off … is a question that probably will never be answered satisfactorily … Major league baseball does not want us. It never has … We keep on crawling, begging, and pleading for recognition just the same.[5]

Smith was especially critical of Griffith for the latter's insistence that blacks should remain in the Negro leagues. He was furious that Griffith employed Latin ballplayers but refused to hire blacks. "Griffith is one of those league owners," Smith wrote,

> who prefers to go outside the borders of these United States and bring in players, rather than hire American citizens of color. He has so many foreigners on his team it is necessary to have an interpreter, and if you ever hear this conglomeration of personalities talking to each other in the airport, you'd swear you were sojourning in Madrid, Lisbon, or Havana.[6]

Lacy and Smith were the most prominent voices in the black press calling for an end to the color line in sports, but they were hardly alone. As far back as 1936, Roy Wilkins had written a scathing article in the *Amsterdam News* about the treatment of black athletes. The occasion was a trip by the all-white University of North Carolina football team to play an integrated team from a Northern school:

> There were no boos and in my section of the stand I heard none of the familiar cries of "Kill the Negro!" So far, the University of North Carolina is still standing and none of the young men representing it on the gridiron appears to be any the worse off for having spent an afternoon competing against a Negro player …[7]

For the most part, the white press ignored the pleas of the country's black sports columnists. That was until a scrappy white sports columnist named Lester "Red" Rodney launched an even more militant campaign to integrate baseball. Between 1936 and 1958, Rodney edited the sports section of the *Daily Worker*, the main organ of Communist Party, single-handedly transforming its once lifeless pages into a venue for chronicling the achievements of baseball players in the Negro leagues. He convinced the party's Young Communist League to leaflet New York's major ballparks, and spearheaded a petition campaign among baseball fans that eventually logged more than a million signatures in favor of integration.[8]

In response to the growing crusade, Commissioner Kenesaw Mountain Landis agreed to allow Paul Robeson, one of the country's best-known black figures, and several members of the Black Newspaper Publishers' Association, to make a personal appeal to the owners during their December 1943 meeting in Cleveland.

Landis, a crusty and bigoted former federal judge, was determined to keep blacks out of baseball. While on the bench, he once sentenced heavyweight champion Jack Johnson to a year in prison for violating the Mann Act—thus forcing him out of boxing. "There is no rule, nor to my knowledge, has there ever been, formal or informal, or any understanding, written or unwritten, subterranean or sub anything, against the hiring of Negroes in the major leagues," Landis said. Robeson, John Sengstacke of the *Defender*, Ira Lewis of the *Courier-Journal*, and Howard Murphy, business manager of the Baltimore *Afro-American*, each attended the meeting and appealed for baseball to change its practice.[9]

Lacy, who left the *Defender* for the *Afro-American*, was surprised when the owners agreed to set up an integration committee. Even more astonishing, they named Lacy, along with Dodgers executive Branch Rickey and the New York Yankees' Larry MacPhail, to the new committee. MacPhail sought to derail the effort by refusing to attend any of the committee meetings, but Rickey persevered and decided the Dodgers would take the lead by themselves. As luck would have it, Happy Chandler replaced Landis in 1945 as baseball commissioner, and was more open to ending segregation.

Before he could sign Robinson, however, Rickey wanted to gauge how he would handle the inevitable hostility that would come from major league fans. The young baseball phenomenon had already gone through a trial by fire as a second lieutenant at Fort Hood, Texas. After boarding a bus on the base in July 1944, he was arrested by MPs for refusing the directive of a white bus driver to sit in the back and brought before a court martial for drunkenness and disorderly conduct. Robinson reached out to the NAACP, which turned his case into a public crusade. Eventually cleared of all charges, Robinson was given an honorable discharge at the end of 1944 and went on to play baseball with the Monarchs.

During the first meeting, Rickey was so impressed by Robinson that he immediately assigned him to the Dodgers' Montreal farm team for the 1946 season. Black writers like Lacy and Smith chronicled every step of Robinson's amazing journey. Promoted to the Dodgers the following year, he became an instant star and was voted baseball's Most Valuable Player in 1949. Only three years later, WNBC-TV in New York hired Robinson, who was then still playing baseball, as its director of community relations, thus making him the first black executive at a broadcast network.

Cracks in the System

The same year that Rickey held his initial meeting with Robinson, the Supreme Court issued a ruling that would establish a key precedent for the modern American media. The case, known as *Associated Press v. United States*, was touched off in 1941 when the *Chicago Sun*, a daily recently founded by retailer Marshall Field to compete with the *Chicago Tribune*, sought and was denied membership in the Associated Press cooperative. Without access to the AP wire, the *Sun* was at a severe disadvantage against the *Tribune*. Ever since the advent of the AP-Western Union alliance, the member papers wielded unparalleled control over news dissemination through their power to deny a franchise to competitors and their ability to charge higher prices to non-members. The *Sun's* editors decided to challenge that power by filing an anti-trust complaint with the Justice Department. The department's investigation concluded that AP's exclusionary rules did indeed violate the Sherman Anti-Trust Act.

The legal battle between the federal government and AP dragged on for years. It eventually ended up in the Supreme Court, which soundly rejected AP's claim. The court ruled that the organization's by-laws created an illegal monopoly over news distribution. The First Amendment "rests on the assumption that the widest possible dissemination of information from diverse and antagonistic sources is essential to the welfare of the public," wrote Justice Hugo Black in the majority opinion. By monopolizing the flow of news and information, AP, the "chief single source of news for the American press," was stifling the access of the American people to other sources of news. "Freedom to publish means freedom for all and not for some," Black added. "Freedom of the press from governmental interference under the First Amendment does not sanction repression of that freedom by private interests."[10]

In a separate, concurring opinion, Justice Felix Frankfurter noted that the news media were markedly different from any ordinary businesses. "The business of the press, and therefore the business of the Associated Press, is the promotion of truth regarding public matters," Frankfurter wrote. "Truth and understanding are not wares like peanuts or potatoes," he added, for the press served "the most vital of all general interests: the dissemination of news from as many different sources, and with as many different facets and colors as is possible."[11]

In the decades since that ruling, Congress and the FCC have repeatedly referred to the AP decision as a pivotal principle of federal communications policy, one that requires the government to preserve diversity of voices—and therefore of ownership—on the airwaves. At the same time, white media reform groups often refer to the 1945 case as the legal underpinning of their efforts to oppose excessive control of the news media by a small number of private companies.

The year before the *Associated Press* decision, Henry Luce, founder of the *Time-Life* Company, created a blue-ribbon panel of leading American intellectuals to examine the role of a free press in the post-war democratic world. Public dissatisfaction with the unbridled power of the press was then on the rise, and many groups in American society were calling for some kind of action against the major media companies. Luce was leery of those who sought to clamp down on news organizations. He regarded any such attempts as a direct threat to democracy. The greatest peril, in his view, originated elsewhere: from advertisers seeking to eliminate controversial news and opinion, and from politicians intent on muzzling press criticism of their policies. The group Luce created, known as the Commission on the Freedom of the Press, or the Hutchins Commission, included philosopher Reinhold Niebuhr, historian Arthur Schlesinger, and poet Archibald MacLeish, the former head of the Office of Facts and Figures. Its final report, released in 1947, called on the press to adopt new ethical standards, and it promulgated several hallmarks of responsible journalism. The last and perhaps most important hallmark was the Commission's call for journalists to "project a representative picture of the constituent groups in the society."

Unfortunately, broadcasters and publishers ignored the recommendations and doggedly resisted any serious efforts at racial integration of their staffs.

As late as 1964—nearly twenty years after the Hutchins Commission—the Newspaper Guild of America could identify only forty-five blacks among more than 50,000 employees at the country's daily newspapers.[12] The Hutchins Commission's biggest impact was felt in higher education, where journalism schools began inculcating certain minimal standards of fair and objective reporting among a new generation of students.[13]

In 1946, the FCC spelled out for the first time public service guidelines for broadcasters, known as the Blue Book. The report noted numerous instances in which station owners had received licenses after promising to establish educational or public-service programs, but had then failed to do so. Many of those broadcasters had turned instead to network-generated entertainment programs and had saturated their airtime with advertising. Between 1937 and 1944, industry revenues more than doubled, from $114 million to $275 million—and income on that revenue nearly quadrupled, from $22 million to $90 million.[14]

The Blue Book called on station licensees to provide more local and public-service programming, and it reminded them of the requirement for them to "serve significant minorities among our population." It thus anticipated similar conclusions to those that would be reached by the Hutchins Commission the following year.[15]

The FCC also formally adopted new rules on editorializing in 1949. Those rules, which came to be known as the Fairness Doctrine, mandated station licensees to broadcast opposing viewpoints on controversial issues of public importance in a fair and balanced manner. In adopting the new rules, the agency specifically referred to the Supreme Court's 1945 Associated Press ruling.[16]

Taken as whole, these post-war developments reflected a tacit acknowledgement by key segments of the country's ruling circles that broadcasters and newspaper chains had achieved a troubling influence over public opinion. Those networks and chains, in the view of many, posed a growing threat to the free flow of diverse views needed in a robust democracy. This was especially true when news accounts pertained to racial or ethnic minorities.

The Rise of Black-Appeal Radio

The rise of television in the 1950s, and then of FM radio in the 1960s, led to the first significant change in broadcasting's practice of racial exclusion. The most popular network stars and national advertisers migrated increasingly to commercial TV, with the networks virtually abandoning radio. The proportion of stations affiliated to the major networks plummeted between 1947 and 1955, from 97 percent to only 30 percent.[17] Local radio owners were left scrambling to find new sources of advertising dollars. The flipside of that scramble, however, was the sudden independence those owners gained from those same networks that had once supplied them with so many hours of programming. Television thus inadvertently ushered in a new era, wherein radio stations experimented with locally produced shows.[18]

In their search for untapped markets, an increasing number of white owners changed the format of their stations to serve communities of color. For most, the decision was purely economic. African-American purchasing power had grown to $15 billion by 1953 and advertisers were suddenly intent on reaching black consumers. The first station to switch to a black-appeal format was WDIA in Memphis, in 1948. Its owners opted to implement the change gradually, so as not to attract much attention, and at first they did not even inform their sponsors.

Radio owners in Chicago, New York, and other Northern cities showed far less reticence. In 1949, Harry and Morris Novik, two liberal white businessmen, purchased WLIB from *New York Post* publisher Dorothy Schiff. They promptly moved the station to Harlem, switched it to an all-black format, and launched *The Walter White Show*, hosted by the NAACP's executive secretary. The following year, three more independent stations moved their studios to Harlem—WWRL, WNEW and WMCA—and began producing more than twenty hours per week of black-oriented programming. By 1955, twenty-eight stations had adopted black formats, most of them in Southern markets, and more than 260 others were providing specific programming for black listeners. Those numbers mushroomed to more than one hundred black-formatted stations by 1965.[19]

The sudden increase in black-appeal radio stations produced another major, though largely unintended, consequence: the popularity of rhythm and blues and rock and roll among America's white teenagers. Several radio historians have pointed to the pervasiveness of black music during the 1950s as the first cultural sign that the Jim Crow system was doomed. Rhythm and blues was impervious to "whites only" signs, and quickly became the signature music for a new generation of "cross-over" white DJs. The 1950s witnessed the remarkable rise of celebrities such as "Daddy-O" Dewey Phillips in Memphis, Alan "Moon Dog" Freed in Cleveland, and the legendary Robert "Wolfman Jack" Smith, who boomed his outlandish late-night rock-and-roll show to legions of young listeners across the country from a Border Blaster station on the other side of the Mexican border.

Crossover DJs pioneered a new racial ventriloquism, imitating the slang and mannerisms of urban black America. While they harkened in some way to the "black minstrelsy" performers of prior eras, the new radio announcers were markedly different, for they did not aim to ridicule or denigrate blacks or to reinforce white superiority.[20]

Raoul Cortéz and Jesse Blayton Pioneer Minority Ownership

More than two decades after John Rodriguez received his license for WCAR in San Antonio, the next two commercial stations owned by people of color went on the air. Raoul Cortéz launched KCOR in San Antonio in 1946, and Jesse Blayton began operating WERD in Atlanta in 1949. A San Antonio businessman and veteran of the Spanish-speaking media, Cortéz secured his license in 1945. It was the first the FCC had ever issued to a Hispanic (Rodriguez had received his in 1922 from the old Commerce Department—before the FCC or its predecessor, the Federal Radio Commission, had even been formed).

Born in Veracruz in 1905, Cortéz moved to the US with his parents during the Mexican Revolution.[21] The family settled in San Antonio, where Cortéz began buying airtime on Anglo-owned stations and producing Spanish-language broadcasts during the 1930s. While working as a salesman for the Pearl Brewing Company, Cortéz launched a show called *La Cervecería Perla* on station KMXT.[22] He established a local theater to showcase films from Mexico, and he was leasing two hours of airtime daily to advertise these films. Cortéz agreed to manage the radio slot and book artists both to perform at the theater and have their performances broadcast.[23]

Cortéz was also a reporter for Ignacio Lozano's *La Prensa*, even as he continued to produce Spanish-language variety shows on that city's KMAC station in his spare time. The radio brokering became so lucrative that Cortéz decided to apply for his own FCC license. He promised in his application to increase support for the war among the city's Spanish-speaking majority, but by the time the station went on the air on February 15th, 1946, the war was over.[24]

KCOR (its call letters were based on Cortéz's last name) quickly became a hit throughout Texas. Its owner recruited Mexican actor Lalo Astol and musician and DJ Mateo Camargo to host a theater program, *La Hora de Teatro Nacional*. Latin American and *Tejano* music and a weekly political talk show, *Frente Al Pueblo*, the first major forum on radio for Spanish-speaking Americans to discuss contemporary issues, also aired on the station.[25]

A few years after launching KCOR, Cortéz created the "Sombrero" network, a chain of Spanish-language stations that banded together to share resources. Then, in 1955, he won FCC approval for the first UHF television channel in the country, KCOR-TV Channel 41. He thus became the nation's first Hispanic television station broadcaster[26]—an extraordinary feat at the time given the anti-Mexican bias and rigid racial segregation that prevailed in Texas. Cortéz owed much of his success to the close ties he cultivated in the Tejano community. Besides his radio work, he was national president of the League of United Latin American Citizens from 1948 to

1950, head of San Antonio's Hispanic Chamber of Commerce, and a leader of the Pan American Progressive Association. He was such a prominent civic leader and broadcaster that he secured meetings with both President Harry Truman and Mexican President Miguel Aleman to advocate for improvements in the Bracero Program for Mexican migrant workers.

Meanwhile, in Atlanta, Jesse B. Blayton was overcoming similar barriers.[27] Born in Fallis, Oklahoma, in 1897, Blayton graduated from the University of Chicago in 1922, then moved to Georgia, where he became the state's first black certified public accountant and a part-time college teacher. In the great ideological debate of the early twentieth century between W. E. B. DuBois and Booker T. Washington over the best strategy for black emancipation, Blayton was a devout disciple of Washington's philosophy that individual self-improvement and economic advancement were essential for the survival and progress of the black community. But Blayton was, above all, a savvy investor obsessed with accumulating capital. In pursuit of that vision, he would eventually gain control of a significant share of Atlanta's black businesses.

A frugal and unpretentious man, Blayton often cut a rumpled figure among Atlanta's refined black elite.[28] He knew something about radio, having spent time as an occasional teacher and patron of the Midway Radio and Television School, preparing African-American students for careers in electronic media; so when a white Atlanta businessman and major stockholder in the Radio Atlanta consortium offered in 1949 to sell him a money-losing station that no white businessman in town was willing to take over, Blayton jumped at the chance. Unable to find investors, he gambled his entire personal fortune on the $50,0000 purchase price for the 1,000-watt station, WERD, and inherited its all-white workforce.

Shortly after assuming control, Blayton was forced to move the station's offices out of downtown Atlanta because his landlord objected to African-Americans coming in and out of his building. He set up new offices at the Prince Hall Masonic Lodge building on Auburn Ave., in the center of the city's black middle-class neighborhood. He immediately changed the station to a black-appeal musical format, with a heavy emphasis on rhythm and blues, while retaining several of the station's veteran white employees. Along with his son, Jesse, Jr., whom he appointed station manager, Blayton began slowly introducing new black voices on the air. Several of the newcomers would become legendary figures in Atlanta radio history—among them Jack "Jockey Jack" Gibson, who doubled as both disc jockey and program director.[29]

As the first truly integrated station in the country, WERD offered a starkly distinctive perspective on racial matters. In 1950, for example, Blayton hired the head of the state's NAACP chapter, William Boyd, who was then a professor at Atlanta University, to produce news digest about the black community three times a week. The following year, the station rocketed to first place in the city's radio market. WERD's meteoric rise coincided with the flowering of Atlanta as the center of the nation's Civil Rights movement. The Southern Christian Leadership Conference (SCLC), the Student Non-Violent Coordinating Committee (SNCC) and the Southern Regional Council (SRC) all had their headquarters there. SCLC's main office, in fact, was located one floor below WERD in the same Auburn Ave. building. Relations between the station and SCLC became so close that program director and DJ Gibson later recalled:

> If Dr. King wanted to make an announcement, he'd take a broomstick and hit on the ceiling ... [I]f I was on the air, I'd say—"[W]e interrupt this program for another message from the president of the SCLC, Martin Luther King Jr. And now here is Dr. King!" But while I was saying it, I'd let a microphone out the window, and it would come down to him, and he'd pull the microphone in from his window, and he'd make his announcement.[30]

Blayton himself never joined SCLC, SNCC or the NAACP. Nor did he publicly support their confrontational challenges to the Jim Crow system. He preferred instead to be associated with the more conservative National Urban League. He even refused to provide the NAACP with airtime for its national radio show unless it paid the regular sponsorship rates. This was in keeping with his goal of turning his station into a big tent for the black community, one where all contending viewpoints could be heard but none would be favored. In the early 1960s, for example, on Sunday mornings the station carried *Muhammed Speaks*, the regular show of the Nation of Islam that was produced from XERF, a Border Blaster station in Mexico.[31]

Despite the successful trailblazing efforts of Cortéz and Blayton, the FCC granted only a handful of broadcast licenses to non-white applicants during the late 1940s and 1950s. One of these went to Andrew "Skip" Carter, an army veteran who attended the RCA School of Electronics and New York University after the war. Carter launched KPRS-AM, a 500-watt daytime operation, in Kansas City, Missouri, in 1950. The station was the first black-owned outlet to begin broadcasting west of the Mississippi.[32] That same year, KLVL in Pasadena, Texas, near Houston, received its FCC license. Felix Hessbrook Morales, the owner of KLVL, pioneered the use of Spanish-language radio dramas (*radionovelas*) and his station featured several community interest shows like *Yo necesito trabajo* ("I Need a Job"), and *Que Dios se lo pague* ("May God Reward You"). In the latter show, Angie Morales, the owner's wife, served as the host, soliciting contributions for needy families in the community.[33]

The rise of black radio was hardly a smooth one. Several owners of those stations received anonymous death threats, and their offices became targets of racial violence. In Birmingham, Alabama, for instance, three stations— WJLD, WEDR, and WBCO—had turned to black-appeal formats by the mid 1950s. Half of Birmingham's black population owned their own homes by then, and white broadcasters saw a goldmine in black programming. As one WBCO sales pitch boasted, "It's a proven fact that the best way to sell the Birmingham area's quarter million Negroes is with ALL-NEGRO radio."[34] But WEDR's transmitter was attacked by the KKK in 1949, and again in 1958. Peggy Mitchell, the host of a daily show on the station during the late 1950s, was repeatedly threatened because of her friendship with Martin Luther King, Jr. At one point her car was run off the road, and on another occasion thugs shot up her house. Rev. Erskine Fausch, the host of a morning gospel show on Birmingham's WENN, was also hounded by the KKK, and was threatened many times on the air. In the early 1960s, the Klan cut down the station's tower.[35] And such terror was not confined to the South. In 1968 and 1969, vandals twice toppled the transmitting tower for WUFO, a black-appeal station in Buffalo, New York.[36]

Racism and Federal Broadcasting Policy

It would take until 1978 for the FCC to adopt its first official policy to promote minority ownership of broadcast stations. At the time, people of color comprised less than 1 percent of all station-owners. In all the decades prior to adoption of that policy, the agency had repeatedly ignored or failed to respond to complaints against broadcasters who denigrated blacks on the air or denied them employment. In 1947, for example, the NAACP lodged a protest with the agency that WFOR, a station in Hattiesburg, Mississippi, was refusing to air any network programs that concerned race and Civil Rights. The agency did nothing. In 1955, the agency granted a construction permit for a new station to Shreveport Television Co. even though one of the company's owners, Don George, operated segregated movie theaters. The FCC concluded that George was only abiding by the Jim Crow laws of Louisiana.[37]

In 1970, the agency renewed the licenses of the Alabama Educational Television Commission, which operated several public television stations around the state, despite numerous complaints that AETC would routinely refuse to broadcast black-oriented programs distributed nationally to all public television stations, and replace them with its own shows. The conflict over AETC's programming and hiring policies dragged on for a decade, and while the agency confirmed the allegations in 1975, it eventually allowed all nine stations in the Alabama network to retain their licenses.[38]

The FCC was also aware that radical hate groups like the Ku Klux Klan had managed to secure control of some citizen radio licenses—and perhaps other types of commission licenses—to spread their hate propaganda. The agency's archives reveal, for example, that on March 3, 1969, Henry Geller, its general counsel, wrote FBI director J. Edgar Hoover to ask for an update on such owners who held commission licenses:

> From time to time you have furnished the Commission with reports containing names of persons who are suspected of being members of either the Klu Klux Klan or minutemen organization. Those persons were reported to have used radio equipment in their organizational activities, and in some instances were said to be Commission licensees. In order to complete and update our information, the Commission would appreciate your furnishing the names, addresses, and birth dates of any additional persons whom you believe should be brought to our attention.[39]

Geller wrote similar letters in 1969 to J. Walter Yeagley, assistant attorney general for the International Security Division, to the US Commission on Civil Rights, and to Francis J. McNamara, director of the House Committee on Un-American Activities.

There is no record that the FCC initiated any efforts to investigate the use of FCC licenses by such hate groups. There is ample evidence on the other hand that the agency ignored complaints from black leaders of discriminatory actions by Southern white stations. In December 1952, for instance, H. Calvin Young, the white owner of WSOK, a station in Nashville, Tennessee, that had recently adopted a black-oriented format, suddenly fired Ed Cook, a popular black announcer.[40]

In 1963, the agency did threaten to revoke the construction permit of a radio station in Broward County, Florida, but this was after the station's white owners announced their intention to adopt an all-black format to serve the area's African-American community! The agency directed the station to alter those plans and provide programming for the entire community—that is, to the *white* community. Sadly, it did not require the same of Southern stations located in areas with large black populations.

A similar double standard developed in the awarding of FM licenses to colleges and universities during the 1950s. Southern black colleges had promoted radio education among their students long before the advent of FM broadcasting. Howard University, as we noted earlier, launched its first course in radio engineering during World War I, and more than twenty black colleges offered classes in various aspects of radio by the early 1940s.[41]

Despite those pioneering efforts, when the FCC began assigning FM licenses to educational institutions in the 1950s, all the permits it issued went to segregated white schools. The University of North Carolina's WUNC-FM, for example, received its license in 1952, three years before the college admitted its first black undergraduate; KUT-FM at the University of Texas was granted its license in 1958, only two years after the first black student was admitted. The University of Alabama's only student-operated station began as an AM commercial station, BRN (Bama Radio Network) in the 1940s. Alabama did not admit its first black student until 1963, following Governor George Wallace's infamous bid to oppose integration.

FM radio had been in operation for twenty years before the FCC granted the first non-commercial radio license to a black college. It went to Durham's WAFR, an FM station sponsored by North Carolina Central University, which went on the air in 1971. Not only did white colleges get licenses far sooner than black colleges—the power level granted to their stations was significantly higher than for black college stations.[42] The agency's de facto exclusion of black colleges in license allocations greatly delayed the racial integration of American broadcasting. These were, after all, licenses for *educational* stations. If there was one arena where federal policy could have spurred public-interest programming and ensured a diversity of views, this was it. Yet the federal government's allocation of college radio licenses during the 1950s and 1960s denied an entire generation of black students the kind of educational radio opportunities that white college students routinely enjoyed. Quite simply, the FCC handed America's white youth a ten-to-twenty-year training advantage over black youth for careers in broadcasting—in what was arguably the most influential industry of modern society.

Radio's Black DJs and the Civil Rights Movement

The 1950s signaled the coming of age of a new cultural and political voice for black America—the black radio DJ. "Numerous African American DJs gained stature as political activists and race leaders in their respective communities; they marched on picket lines, spoke at protest rallies, helped raise money for the cause, and served as officers in local civil rights organizations," notes William Barlow.[43]

One of the most influential of those DJs was Georgie Woods, the "Guy With the Goods." Born in Burnett, Georgia, in 1927, Woods became a towering presence and an idol of the Philadelphia black community on stations such as WHAT and WDAS. His father had been a preacher and outspoken defender of Civil Rights, so much so that in 1936, when Woods was just a boy, the family fled north after the KKK burned a cross outside their home. They eventually settled in Harlem, and Woods joined the navy during World War II, then enrolled in broadcasting school on the GI Bill. His first job was as a DJ on New York's WWRL.[44] Founded in 1926 by a young ham radio operator named William Reuman, WWRL had long provided news and entertainment not only for African-Americans but for dozens of immigrant communities in their own languages.[45] Woods didn't last long at the station; he was fired after only a few months for playing a song that promoted alcohol.

He got a second chance in 1953, when Philadelphia's WHAT hired him to host the station's morning wake-up show. There he joined other rising DJs like Jocko Henderson and Larry Dixon. He landed an afternoon show, *The Snap Club*, which he renamed the *House of Jive* when he moved it to WDAS. To supplement the tiny income radio gave him, Woods began promoting black concerts and dances. Before long he was the main black music promoter in the city, even rivaling his legendary contemporary Dick Clark. By the early 1960s, however, Woods was turning increasingly political. He joined the NAACP and started to promote what he called "Freedom Shows" at the Uptown Theater in the heart of North Philadelphia, where he worked closely with fiery Civil Rights lawyer Cecil B. Moore and used his radio shows to mobilize thousands of blacks to demand jobs at city construction sites. "I'd go on the air and tell people where I was going to be demonstrating, and a mob of people would show up and I had a microphone and I was directing people," Woods recalled later.

In 1963, Woods invited Martin Luther King, Jr., to Philadelphia. Two years later, he joined King in his historic desegregation march in Selma, Alabama, and was among the protestors who were beaten by state police on the Pettus Bridge that day.

Like Woods, other black DJs played militant roles as organizers of the movement. They included figures like Louise Fletcher of WSOK in Nashville; Hot Rod Hulberth of WITH in Baltimore; Mary Mason of WHAT in Philadelphia; Hal Jackson and Jocko Henderson of WLIB in New York City; Larry Dean Faulkner and Martha Jean "the Queen" Steinberg of WHBC in Detroit; and Purvis Spann, Herb Kent, and Wesley South of WVON in Chicago.

It is almost impossible to overstate the important of these black DJs to the freedom struggles. "You have to understand that we were the voice that the people listened to," Gibson once explained, "and if you gave us a message to say, 'There will be a meeting tonight of the SCLC at the First Baptist Church' ... we would go ahead and elaborate all around it and do our own thing.'"[46]

The Southern Media and the Battle Over Integration

Soon after World War II, two brothers who had served in the conflict, Charles and Medgar Evers, returned home to Mississippi. Like so many African-American veterans, they would no longer quietly accept the oppressive conditions of Jim Crow. Charles landed a job as one of the state's first black DJs at a radio station in Philadelphia, Mississippi, where he quickly began using the airwaves to urge his listeners to pay their poll taxes and vote. Outraged white listeners complained to the station, and Evers was forced to resign after a few months on the job.[47] Meanwhile, his brother Medgar, who had become a leader in Mississippi's NAACP Youth Council, tried to enroll in the University of Mississippi law school in 1954, only to be rebuffed by school authorities.

By then, the Supreme Court's *Brown v. Board of Education* decision had stirred widespread hope among Southern blacks and an equal amount of anger among whites. Key newspapers and television stations in the region repeatedly condemned the federal courts. "Mississippi will not obey the decision," wrote Frederick Sullens, editor of the *Jackson Daily News*. "If any effort is made to send Negroes to school with white children, there will be bloodshed. The stains of the bloodshed will be on the Supreme Court steps."[48]

Immediately following the Brown decision, Robert B. Patterson, a plantation manager and former paratroop major during the war, convened a meeting in a private home in the Mississippi Delta's Sunflower County.[49] The fourteen white men who attended Patterson's meeting, all middle-class pillars of their community, founded the first White Citizens' Council. Blacks comprised 68 percent of the population of the county at the time, but only 0.03 percent of them were registered voters. By 1955 there were more than 160 Citizens' Councils throughout the South; the group had even created its own regular fifteen-minute program, *Citizens' Council Forum*, to distribute to TV and radio stations in the region, and an estimated 300 stations were said to broadcast the show. As part of its campaign to maintain segregation, the Mississippi Sovereignty Commission helped finance the television and radio programs of the White Citizens' Councils.[50]

In Jackson, the Hederman family—one of the South's most powerful media families, emerged as a major supporter of the Citizens' Councils. The Hedermans owned both the Jackson *Daily News* and *Clarion-Ledger*, and they controlled WJTV, the first TV station in Mississippi, as well as a radio station. In addition, they owned considerable real estate and sat on the boards of banks and the local power company. Both Hederman newspapers joined that effort, often spiking stories on integration that were deemed too controversial by the Sovereignty Commission.[51]

The year 1955 was especially perilous for Civil Rights leaders in Mississippi. On the night of May 7th, Rev. George Washington Lee, one of the few blacks since Reconstruction to register to vote in Humphreys County, was driving through the small delta town of Belzoni, a place so infamous for its lynching of blacks that it was nicknamed Bloody Belzoni, when a fatal shotgun blast from a passing motorist blew off most of his face. The Jackson *Clarion-Ledger*, in an article headlined "Negro Leader Dies in Odd Accident," dutifully reported the sheriff's conclusion that there had been no foul play involved.

The same fate befell Lamar Smith, a black farmer and World War II veteran, a few months later. Smith had been urging fellow black residents to register to vote in statewide elections by absentee ballot. One Saturday afternoon, as he was walking in broad daylight on the lawn of the Lincoln County court-house in the town of Brookhaven, he was surrounded by a group of white men and shot to death. The story on the murder in the combined Sunday edition of the *Clarion-Ledger and Daily News* was headlined, "Links Shoot-ing of Negro with Vote Irregularities." Without bothering to interview any friends or associates of the dead man, the reporter quoted law-enforcement officials as saying Smith had been "linked to voting irregularities." Even though the murder occurred in front of numerous bystanders, a grand jury heard from no witnesses who could identify the assailants, and no one was ever prosecuted.[52]

Given the First Amendment's protection for the press, blacks leaders could do nothing about the systemic bias exhibited by Mississippi newspa-pers. But local broadcasters were another matter. In 1955, the local NAACP wrote the FCC to lodge complaints about racially discriminatory pro-gramming by Jackson television station WLBT Channel 3, the local NBC affiliate, and against radio station WJDX, both owned by the Lamar Life Insurance Company. The civil rights organization urged the commission to consider revoking the stations' licenses. Fred Beard, the station manager of WLBT, also happened to be a board member of the Jackson White Citi-zens' Council. Beard boasted in a newspaper article that he had knocked off the air a network program featuring NAACP lawyer Thurgood Mar-shall and replaced it with a "Sorry, Cable Trouble" sign. In September 1957, after President Eisenhower appeared on an NBC broadcast to discuss the school integration crisis in Little Rock, Arkansas, WLBT aired a Citizens' Council ad urging, "Don't let this happen in Mississippi."[53] During the Little Rock integration battle the station featured a panel of segregationist leaders, but it denied Medgar Evers' request to be included on the panel. Evers promptly filed a complaint with the FCC, demanding "equal time." The agency responded that its equal-time provisions only covered candidates for political office, not controversial issues.[54]

Despite all the examples provided by the NACCP, the commission renewed WLBT's license in 1959, calling the incidents "isolated" and "honest" mistakes. Meanwhile, the Hederman-owned Jackson *Daily News* said of Dr. A. H. McCoy, state president of the NAACP, "the fanatical mouthings of McCoy have reached the limit. If not suppressed by his own race, he will become the white man's problem."

Mississippi Television and the Birth of Media Reform

As the NAACP's campaign against WLBT was unfolding in Missis-sippi during 1956 and 1957, Rev. Martin Luther King, Jr., who was then leading the Montgomery bus boycott in Alabama, began holding occasional meetings with leaders of the Northern-based Congregational Christian Board of Home Missions. In those meetings, King and fellow SCLC leader Rev. Andrew Young repeatedly complained about the biased and derogatory news coverage by radio and television stations in the South.

Around the same time, the director of the church's Office of Communication, Rev. Everett C. Parker, undertook a fact-finding trip throughout the South to observe first-hand how the region's stations were portraying African-Americans.[55] That trip convinced Parker, who had been involved with broadcasting since his high school days in the 1930s, that Southern broadcasters who promoted segregationist views had to be challenged. Following his return, he convened meetings with leaders of the National Council of Churches, the United Methodist Church, the Presbyterian Church, and the United Church of Christ. The church groups jointly petitioned the National Association of Broadcasters to urge all local stations to adhere to the FCC's Fairness Doctrine, and to present more diverse views on the air, to "bring about change, if possible, in an orderly [and] friendly way," as Parker later recalled.

Former Florida governor Le Roy Collins was the NAB's president at the time. A moderate Democrat and a respected member of the small group of "New South" leaders who opposed the worst excesses of Jim Crow, Collins enthusiastically backed Parker's proposal and presented it to the NAB board of directors, only to encounter their unanimous rejection of it.[56]

In early 1962, Robert L. T. Smith, a black Methodist minister and grocery store owner in Jackson, Mississippi, decided to run for Congress against segregationist John Bell Williams. As the first African-American to run for federal office in the state since Reconstruction, Smith repeatedly tried to buy air time for his campaign commercials on WLBT and on WJDX, but executives at both stations repeatedly refused his requests. He then filed a formal complaint with the FCC, and when the agency declined to take action, he appealed to sympathetic journalists, labor leaders and politicians around the country for help. Burke Marshall, the head of the civil rights division at the Justice Department, interceded on Smith's behalf, as did former first lady Eleanor Roosevelt, who personally called FCC chairman Newtown Minow to complain. In response to the pressure, the FCC directed WLBT station manager Fred Beard to run a Smith commercial. The day Smith taped the commercial at WLBT, "station manager Fred Beard walked him out of the station to the edge of the Pearl River (which ran in front of the WLBT property), put his arm around him and said, in Smith's words, that 'my home and my place of business would likely be blown up and my body would likely be found floating in the Pearl River.'"[57]

Later that same year, the US Supreme Court sided with the NAACP Legal Defense and Educational Fund in a long-running lawsuit against the University of Mississippi for refusing to allow James Meredith to register as a student. Justice Hugo Black ordered that Meredith be immediately enrolled in classes for the fall term that was about to start. The court's order touched off one of the most violent conflicts over federal power since the Civil War. Ten days after the decision, Mississippi Governor Ross Barnett, backed by the state legislature, personally blocked Meredith's admission to the Ole Miss campus at Oxford. "There is no case in history where the Caucasian race has survived social integration," Barnett declared. Mississippi, he vowed, would not "drink from the cup of genocide."[58]

With network television chronicling each step of the unfolding crisis on the evening news, Americans watched in awe as the governor defied the Supreme Court, the Kennedy White House, and federal marshals by repeatedly blocking Meredith's efforts to register. Mississippi newspapers and broadcast stations played a pivotal role in exacerbating the crisis. "The media played up all the negatives that could possibly happen," Myrlie Evers, Medgar's widow, recalled in an interview years later. "THOUSANDS SAID READY TO FIGHT FOR MISSISSIPPI," blared a headline in the Jackson *Daily News*. The paper exhorted its readers to learn the words to a new protest song, "Never, No Never." The lyrics praised the governor's stand with the couplet: "Ross's standing like Gibraltar / He shall Never Falter;" and it defiantly proclaimed, "to hell with Bobby K." Meanwhile, WSUH, an Oxford station owned by the Colonel Rebel Radio Company, and WRBC in Jackson, repeatedly played "Dixie" as a protest against the presence of the federal agents.

"The television was terrible. It was so slanted, so biased," recalled Gordon Henderson, a political science professor during the crisis at nearby Millsaps College, "[I]t was unbelievable how much they stirred things up." While most media outlets in the state expressed similar abhorrence to integrating Ole Miss, there were some notable exceptions. The *Delta Democrat-Times*, for example, ran editorials by Hodding Carter III warning that opposition to the federal courts was useless.[59]

Events turned more ominous on September 26th, when former Major General Edwin A. Walker, a hero of the Korean War and leader of the John Birch Society, issued a passionate call over KWKH, a 50,000-watt station in Shreveport, Louisiana, for Southerners to join him at Oxford to stop Meredith's registration. Walker had been in command of the federal troops sent to Little Rock by President Eisenhower in 1957 to enforce integration of that city's Central High School. The experience had turned him into a bitter enemy of the federal government and the national media, and he came to believe that both were deeply infiltrated by communists. "It is time to move," Walker declared in his KWKH interview, "if the President of the United States commits or uses any troops, federal or state, in Mississippi." The next day, September 27th, armed groups of white supremacists began congregating in Oxford. Meredith himself would later recall that "[t]he radio stations ceased all regular programming and were devoting full time to reporting the preparations for the coming battle." [60]

The showdown erupted just two nights later. Attorney General Robert Kennedy dispatched border agents, deputy federal marshals, and Justice Department lawyers to escort Meredith secretly to a dormitory on the Oxford campus. Within an hour of Meredith's arrival an angry crowd of several thousand students and militant segregationists had gathered in front of the university's Lyceum. The mob started to attack the federal agents, and it quickly turned from bricks and bottles to Molotov cocktails and guns. The agents, under orders from Attorney General Kennedy not to discharge their own weapons, sought without luck to disperse the crowd with tear gas. Fighting raged through the night and did not end until federal troops occupied the town under orders from President Kennedy. By then, two bystanders were dead and 160 marshals had been injured, twenty-eight of them wounded by gunfire. Meredith did manage to register for classes, but thousands of soldiers and marines continued to occupy Oxford until his graduation in 1964.

The Murder of Medgar Evers

The FCC later cited eight Mississippi stations for violating the Fairness Doctrine in their coverage of the Oxford events. The agency declined, however, to order strong sanctions against any of them. [61] The following year it notified all broadcasters that the Fairness Doctrine applied to any coverage of integration, and it directed stations to present the viewpoints of African-Americans on the issue. [62]

Medgar Evers promptly put the agency's new directive to the test by petitioning for local Jackson stations to provide him with equal time to counter segregationist views expressed by Mayor Allen Thompson on their airwaves. WLBT agreed to his request, and on May 20th, 1963, Evers made a stirring seventeen-minute appeal for an end to segregation. In that appeal he especially noted the role the news media were playing in advancing civil rights—whether consciously or not:

> Tonight the Negro plantation worker in the Delta knows from his radio and television what happened in the world. He knows what black people are doing and he knows what white people are doing. He can see on the 6 o'clock news screen the 3 o'clock bite by a police dog. He knows that Willie Mays, a Birmingham Negro, is the highest paid baseball player in the nation. He knows the Leontyne Price, a native of Laurel, Mississippi, is a star of the Metropolitan Opera in New York. He knows about the new free nations in Africa and knows that a Congo native can be a locomotive engineer but in Jackson he cannot even drive a garbage truck.

He sees a city where Negro residents are refused admittance to the City auditorium and the Coliseum; his children refused a ticket to a good movie in a downtown theater; his wife and children refused service at a lunch counter in a downtown store where they trade ...[63]

The speech stunned white citizens in the state. Many called the station to protest. It also made Evers a target. "[B]efore this moment, Medgar Evers had just been a name in the newspapers," notes journalist Mary Anne Vollers. "Very few white people could even recognize him. The televised reply put Medgar too out front." Less than a month later, on June 12th, 1963, Evers was assassinated in the driveway of his home.[64]

The Ole Miss riot and the assassination of Evers further convinced the United Church of Christ and Rev. Everett Parker that it was time to make an example of Mississippi broadcasters by challenging their licenses before the FCC. In March 1964, Parker recruited twenty-eight volunteers, all of them white, to secretly monitor and log a week's worth of programming by WJTV and WLBT in Jackson. Parker chose the two stations because their continued abuse of the local black community was so flagrant. Blacks comprised 45 percent of the population of the signal area of the two stations, yet no blacks were employed at the stations except as janitors. The monitors found that, while two-thirds of all program time on WLBT consisted of entertainment, no blacks appeared on the air except on a few network-originated shows, and even the Sunday programs devoted to religious services featured no black churches.

Parker felt he now had enough ammunition to challenge the license renewals of the stations for failing to serve the public interest and abide by the Fairness Doctrine. But most legal experts he consulted saw no chance of success. Never before had the FCC considered a license challenge unless it had come from a businesses with a "substantial" interest in the agency's decision, and that had always been interpreted to mean an economic interest by a party seeking to obtain the license for itself or to prevent electromagnetic interference. Since Parker was not applying for the license, he would never be granted the standing to challenge its current holder, the experts told him. But Parker was convinced he could catch the station owners in direct lies to the FCC about the content of their programming. He was sure he could set new precedents in communications law when it came to defining the "public interest."

Before he could petition the agency, Parker needed to recruit some local citizens of Jackson as complainants. Medgar's brother Charles refused. He recommended instead that Parker approach Aaron Henry, the president of the state's NAACP and a leader of the historic challenge to Mississippi's delegation to the 1964 Democratic Party convention. Henry agreed, and so did Robert L. T. Smith, the man who only two years before had battled Fred

Beard and WLBT over that station's refusal to run his campaign commercials in his race for Congress.

When the petition arrived in Washington, FCC staffers were unsure at first how to handle it. The Commission decided to send the chief of its office of complaints and compliance, Bill Ray, down to Mississippi to investigate the claim. Ray's report, never released publicly, "confirmed all the allegations and then some," according to historian Robert Horowitz. Yet, even if agency staff recommended revocation of the licenses, the full FCC ruled on May 20th, 1965, by four votes to two, to dismiss the United Church of Christ petition. In doing so, the commissioners did not rule on the merits of the charges, rather they denied the procedural "standing" of the petitioners. But, in a clear sign that WLBT had violated public interest requirements, they also announced a form of probation for WLBT—a one-year renewal.[65]

Parker and the petitioners promptly appealed the agency's decision to the federal courts. The following year a three-judge panel of the District of Columbia Court of Appeals stunned the broadcasting world with its unanimous decision against the FCC. In its historic ruling, the Court said:

> The Communications Act of 1934 did not create new private rights. The purpose of the Act was to protect the public interest in communications ... Congress gave the right to appeal to persons "aggrieved or whose interest are adversely affected" by Commission action ... But these private litigants have standing only as representatives of the public interest. [emphasis in original].[66]

The opinion was even more remarkable because its author was a conservative Republican, Warren Burger, who would later be named chief justice of the Supreme Court. "Legitimate listener representatives," Burger wrote, could serve as instruments to protect the public interest. More importantly, he expressed clear displeasure with how little attention had been paid until then to the public interest. "After nearly five decades of operation," Burger went on to say, "the broadcast industry does not seem to have grasped the simple fact that a broadcast license is a public trust subject to termination for breach of duty."[67]

The Court ordered the FCC to hold a public hearing on WLBT's application for a license renewal before reaching a final decision. The agency reluctantly conducted that hearing, but it continued to ignore the overwhelming documentation of racial bias that Parker and his allies had presented against WLBT, and in 1968 it voted once again to grant the station a three-year license. Parker responded with a second appeal to the federal courts, and the following year the same three-judge appeals panel once again ruled against the agency. This time, however, the Court concluded that the FCC's "administrative conduct in this record is beyond repair." It ordered a new comparative licensing hearing, one where other applicants, including WLBT, could compete for the license on an equal basis. It was the first time a federal court had revoked a station's license for failing to meet the public interest. During the comparative hearing process that followed, a consortium of groups that included African-Americans obtained the new license and Aaron Henry, one of the original petitioners, emerged as chairman of the new station.[68]

The WLBT case thus became a pivotal victory for civil rights and public accountability in the US media, as historic for the broadcasting industry as *Brown v. Board of Education* was for public education, for it established the right of citizens to sue before the FCC over a station's failure to fulfill the public-interest requirements of its license, and it had even broader ramifications for the power of citizen challenges to administrative law decisions in all federal agencies.[69] By combining two social movements that until then had operated separately—the movement of African-Americans for racial equality and the movement of progressive white Americans to make our media system more accountable to ordinary citizens—the struggle in Mississipi over revoking WLBT's license marked a new era in mass communications and public policy.

Fierce Rebellion, Furious Reaction: 1963–2003

If what the white American reads in the newspapers or sees on TV conditions his expectation of what is ordinary and normal in the larger society,
he will neither understand nor accept the black American. By failing to
portray the Negro as a matter of routine and in the context of the total
society, the news media have, we believe, contributed to the black–white
schism in the country.

Kerner Commission, 1968

Network news cameras were rolling that spring of 1963 when Sheriff "Bull"
Connor's deputies turned their fire hoses and dogs on black youths who had
organized sit-ins for integration in Birmingham, Alabama. They were rolling
on "Bloody Sunday," March 7, 1965, when police on horseback mauled
hundreds of marchers peacefully crossing Selma's Edmund Pettus Bridge to
demand their voting rights.[1]

Those searing images on the evening news stunned the nation. Along
with riveting eyewitness reports by young correspondents like Dan Rather
and John Chancellor, they stirred up enormous public sympathy for the
Civil Rights movement and played a pivotal role in convincing the federal
government to outlaw racial segregation.

It was the Golden Age of television news.

But despite that brief interlude of courageous network coverage, most
local news organizations during the Civil Rights era continued to disseminate racial stereotypes and biased reporting on the country's growing
non-white communities.

This chapter chronicles the vast citizen movement that forced many of
the nation's all-white newsrooms to open their doors to people of color
during the late 1960s and 1970s, and outlines the subsequent emergence of
our modern media system.

While it is common knowledge today that the Civil Rights movement
and the urban rebellions of the 1960s prompted landmark federal legislation
to outlaw segregation in education, voting, and public accommodations,
few Americans are aware that those upheavals also cracked the longstanding

color line in the mass media. As the first big wave of minority journalists began to enter mainstream newsrooms, they sparked dramatic changes in the actual content of the news and entertainment Americans received.

Such momentous change did not come easily. Many broadcasters and publishers only agreed to integrate their institutions after African-American and Latino groups launched angry protests and boycotts against them or challenged their broadcast licenses. Between 1971 and 1973, more than 340 such license challenges were filed in virtually every major city in America. At least forty-nine advocacy organizations were founded across the country to reform communications policy in the brief period between 1967 and 1975.[2]

It was the most widespread movement for media reform in US history. Spearheaded by little-known local and national activists such as William Wright, Emma Bowen, and Domingo Nick Reyes, it garnered scant attention from the mainstream press, yet its startling success prompted the nation's broadcasters to launch a concerted campaign to rewrite federal regulations so as to reduce the accountability of their stations to the public.

That counter-attack from the broadcasters gained considerable force in 1980 with the election of Ronald Reagan as president. And once the Republican Party gained a majority in both houses of Congress in the mid 1990s, federal lawmakers moved to abolish the only FCC program that had managed to achieve a substantial increase in minority ownership of radio and television stations. Meanwhile, an increasingly conservative federal judiciary began to shift decidedly against such affirmative action efforts.

By then, however, it was too late to resurrect the old order, for media companies had already admitted into their newsrooms several thousand Hispanic, Asian- and African-American journalists. Those new hires were shunned at first, and ridiculed by white colleagues who regarded them as unqualified and inferior. They responded by forming their own professional organizations of African-American, Asian, Hispanic and Native American journalists, all of which prodded the industry to further integrate, and they became watchdogs against racial bias in news coverage. The most daring members of the new groups even filed historic racial discrimination lawsuits against major media companies such as the *New York Times*, the *Washington Post* and the *Daily News*.

Meanwhile, two separate developments, one in federal media policy and the other in communications technology, were beginning to further roil the nation's system of news dissemination. In 1967, Congress created the Corporation for Public Broadcasting as a new non-commercial alternative to the existing market-driven media system. The Public Broadcasting Act specifically charged the new CPB with fostering programs that addressed "the needs of unserved and underserved audiences, particularly children and minorities." Shortly afterward, cable television began reaching the big cities.

The proliferation of new cable companies and their dramatic expansion of channel capacity offered hope at first for a new era of expanded democracy and racial diversity in both programming and media ownership.

Neither public broadcasting nor cable, however, fulfilled the dreams of their early proponents. As the former matured, it evolved into a news and entertainment venue geared largely to the upper-classes throughout the country, though it did on occasion provide more nuanced and comprehensive portrayals of racial minorities than the commercial system. Cable was marked during its early years by the mushrooming of hundreds of small companies, a surprising number of which were initially minority-owned, but as cable franchises grew increasingly lucrative in subsequent years, a wave of mergers began to sweep the industry. In a replay of the telegraph mergers of the 1860s (see Chapter 9), the bigger providers swallowed the smaller ones until only a handful of giant companies were left.

Consolidation in cable mirrored similar trends in traditional media. The 1980s and 1990s became the era of huge and unwieldy media conglomerates. Synergy and convergence were the new buzzwords, with firms racing to place newspapers, TV and radio stations, book-publishing subsidiaries, cable networks, even film studios, under one corporate umbrella. The biggest conglomerates then launched a relentless lobbying effort in Congress to further deregulate mass communication. They accomplished much of their goal with the passage of the Telecommunications Act of 1996, the most sweeping change to our media and telecommunications system since the creation of the FCC. The new law unleashed an even bigger wave of ownership consolidation in the final years of the twentieth century.

Even as media moguls were savoring their achievement in Congress, however, a new and unexpected citizen movement burst on the scene in 2002. Its members began clamoring for an end to media consolidation and for greater accountability on the part of giant news organizations to their local communities; the movement eventually convinced Congress and the federal courts to overturn Bush administration attempts to further consolidate ownership of the nation's media companies. Forty years after the historic popular revolt that broke the color line in the American media, a new generation of activists thus achieved an equally stunning victory. Those two revolts are the bookends to this tumultuous era of media history we will now explore.

The Kerner Commission and the Press

In 1967, more than eighty people died in outbreaks of racial violence in Detroit, Newark, and other US cities. Over the next two years, at least 1,100 racial disturbances occurred in every region of the country. Such riots became so pervasive for a time that national leaders grew justifiably fearful of a race war breaking out. President Lyndon Johnson created the National Advisory Commission on Civil Disorders, better known as the Kerner Commission, to investigate and report on the causes of the violence.[3]

The Commission's groundbreaking report, issued in the spring of 1968, reached the startling conclusion that, despite the abolition of slavery a century earlier, and despite the inroads made against the Jim Crow system after the Supreme Court's *Brown* decision, the nation was "moving toward two societies, one black, and one white—separate and unequal." The report particularly faulted the press for exacerbating the racial divide. "Far too often, the press acts and talks about Negroes as if Negroes do not read the newspapers or watch television, give birth, marry, die, and go to PTA meetings," the report stated. African-Americans, it warned, harbored a deep mistrust and "contempt" of the news media; they regarded journalists as instruments of the "white power structure," too often simply publishing information they received from authorities during racial troubles without even speaking with members of the affected communities. A primary reason for the failures of the media in this area, the Commission concluded, was the absence of black journalists in mainstream newsrooms. Press executives had been "shockingly backward in seeking out, hiring, training and promoting Negroes," with only 5 percent of all newsroom employees and just 1 percent of editors and supervisors being black, most of them working for black-owned companies. The report urged a concerted effort by the entire industry to hire and promote non-whites in all areas of news organizations, and it called for the creation of a new "Institute of Urban Communications" to train young blacks for jobs in journalism.[4]

Other federal actions also influenced changes in news industry practices. Following the passage of the 1964 Civil Rights Act, for instance, the Justice Department created the Community Relations Service and gave it the specific mission of acting as a "peacemaker" in racial and ethnic disputes. Several of the original leaders of CRS came out of the media industry. As a result, CRS adopted an unusual role for a government agency: its staff began organizing and training minority activists to pressure media companies for reform. To direct that organizing, CRS hired Ben Holman, one of the country's most respected black journalists. Holman had been the first black reporter at the *Chicago Daily News* in 1952, before going on to work as a correspondent at both CBS and NBC network news.[5]

The efforts of CRS received a major boost in 1969, when the FCC adopted Equal Employment Opportunity regulations, the first official federal communications policy to target racial inequality specifically. The new rules did not simply ban racial discrimination in hiring, they required broadcasters to maintain a workforce that reflected the communities they were serving.[6]

The News Industry Responds to Kerner

In the aftermath of the Kerner report, several top media executives con-cluded that racial integration of their industry could no longer be postponed. The speed with which the industry tackled the problem, however, varied greatly among its various sectors. The American Society of News Editors, for instance, had many Southern members during that period who were staunch segregationists. Harry M. Ayers of the *Anniston Star* reflected the views of that segregationist wing. In 1956, Ayers had gotten into a heated exchange during an ASNE convention panel integration. "[M]any Negroes are dirty, are unreliable, are liars," Ayers said.

> I asked the county health office just before I left home—I had gotten the figures from the State Health Department—and he said that of all the vene-real cases he treats in Calhoun Country, 90 percent of them are Negroes ... We do not want to subject our children to that sort of thing.[7]

ASNE did not even admit its first black member until 1965, when John N. Sengstacke, editor and publisher of the *Chicago Daily Defender,* joined the organization. Five years later, as protests by blacks activists against media companies were at their height, Senstacke became ASNE's first black board member.[8]

The editors' group formed a "Diversity Committee" in 1972, which con-ducted the association's first ever survey of newsroom employees. What it found was shocking: African-Americans comprised just 1 percent of per-sonnel at the nation's daily newspapers—235 out of 23,111.[9] Nonetheless, it took ASNE until 1978—a decade after the Kerner Report—finally to adopt an integration policy. That year, its leaders established an ambitious goal: to have the racial composition of the nation's newsrooms reflect the general US population by the year 2000. An annual newsroom survey launched to gauge the progress of member newspapers revealed that, in 1978, minority journalists comprised just 4 percent of newspaper staffs. While that certainly represented a significant increase from the group's initial 1972 headcount, it still lagged woefully behind the 17 percent minority population of the country, with hundreds of papers reporting no people of color in their newsrooms.[10]

ASNE's slow response to the Kerner recommendations stood in marked contrast to the lightning-fast actions of Fred Friendly, one of the legendary figures of American broadcast journalism. Friendly had resigned from CBS in 1966 after the network chose to run a scheduled episode of *I Love Lucy* instead of televising US Senate hearings into the conduct of the Vietnam War. He then moved to the Ford Foundation, where he directed funding for media programs. In 1968 he secured a Ford grant for a summer program to train minority journalists at Columbia University, and directed the program himself. The new initiative would go on to graduate more than 200 journalists of color over the next seven years, placing them in jobs throughout the industry. The program relocated to the University of California at Berkeley in 1975, this time with new funding from the Gannett Foundation. There, it became the flagship project of the Institute for Journalism Education—a new organization that had been established by a pioneering group of journalists. The group's founders included Robert C. Maynard, then a reporter at the *Washington Post*; Dorothy Gilliam, a columnist at the same paper; fellow *Post* reporter Roy Aarons, who would later found the National Lesbian and Gay Journalists Associaiton; Earl Caldwell of the *New York Times*; and Frank Sotomayor of the *Los Angeles Times*.

Meanwhile, the Radio-Television News Directors Association conducted its first newsroom employment survey for the broadcast industry in 1972. It revealed a much bigger proportion of racial minorities in television newsrooms—13 percent—than in newspapers; but it also found that 40 percent of all stations employed no minorities at all. Even those dismal numbers understated the problem because none of the major network news organizations participated in the survey.[11]

The ten years following the Kerner Report thus produced significant changes in racial attitudes among major media executives. Most began publicly espousing the integration of their newsrooms, though in reality they were slow to reform hiring practices, invariably claiming that there was an insufficient pool of qualified journalists of color.

Challenge Their License: The Birth of a Grassroots Movement

As industry leaders conducted their studies and cautiously mulled their responses to Kerner, a grassroots movement for media reform began sweeping the country. Groups of blacks and Latinos, inspired by the victory in Mississippi against WLBT, suddenly marched into media company offices in scores of cities, demanded an end to biased news coverage, and threatened to challenge the license renewals of individual broadcasters.

In 1969, a coalition of African-American groups contested the license of KTAL-TV in Texarkana, Texas. They complained to the FCC that, even though blacks comprised 25 percent of the city, the station routinely covered only issues that affected whites. The station owners opted to negotiate. They agreed to hire at least two full-time African-American reporters for their news staff, to include both black and white participants whenever they aired controversial programming, and to meet regularly with the community to discuss the station's programming policies.[12]

That same year, fifteen black residents of Washington, DC, contested the license of WMAL-TV, an ABC affiliate owned by Evening Star Newspapers. They pointed out that their city's population was 70 percent black, yet the station employed virtually no African-Americans, and they labeled its coverage of the black community "derogatory and insulting." A key figure in that challenge was William Wright, a slender thirty-eight-year-old African-American and former dental technician who was then directing Unity House, a community-organizing project sponsored by the Unitarian church.[13]

"Most folks will see something on TV that makes them mad and they'll call up 25 friends to tell them about it but they won't call the station," Wright said at the time. "They don't know that complaints of this sort must be reported to the FCC by the station, and that all the letters of complaint that they might write setting forth their views can be used as ammunition on their behalf when a station's license renewal time comes up."[14]

Wright went on to found Black Efforts for Soul in Television (BEST), and quickly became the black community's leading voice against racial bias in news coverage. He sponsored workshops around the country to train community leaders in how to file a "Petition to Deny" against a station before the FCC, and he spearheaded pressure on the Nixon administration to name the first African-American to the FCC. Those efforts culminated in 1972, when Nixon named Benjamin Hooks, a lawyer and former television host for Memphis station WMC-TV, to the Commission. During his five-year tenure at the agency, Hooks went on to champion equal-opportunity reforms and pressed for greater minority ownership. He resigned his seat in 1977 to become head of the NAACP.[15]

Lonnie King and the Battle in Atlanta

In Atlanta, Lonnie King, president of the local NAACP chapter, decided in 1969 to take on his city's entire broadcast industry. A former civil rights compliance officer for the Department of Health, Education and Welfare, King tried at first to create a summer training program for high school students interested in broadcast careers. He then urged some local stations, asking them to hire some of his graduates.[16]

When the stations ignored him, King convinced several Atlanta Civil Rights leaders to form the Community Coalition on Broadcasting. The group immediately threatened to contest the renewal of twenty-eight radio and TV licenses in the Atlanta market, all of which were up for review in April 1970. Coalition members submitted the same demands to all stations: air new programming that addressed the black community's needs, provide scholarships for black youths, hire black employees, and spend money with black institutions. They also requested that any agreement be made a condition of a station's future license renewal.[17]

The stations uniformly rebuffed the coalition, whereupon King petitioned the FCC for more time for negotiations. The agency then startled the broadcasters by agreeing to the Coalition's request. It was the first time the Commission had ever granted a deadline waiver for those seeking to challenge a license renewal. "What kind of Republican politics is this?" wrote Rep. Fletcher Thompson (R-GA) to President Nixon's FCC Chairman Dean Burch. Thompson called on the Commission to reverse its "unprecedented federal backing" of "certain groups in the Atlanta area."[18]

The widespread support King enjoyed in Atlanta's black community, along with the FCC's tacit support of the effort, convinced nearly all of the city's broadcasters to reach a settlement. *Jet* magazine promptly declared the events in Atlanta a demonstration of "audacious black power," adding:

> Little David and Goliath fought a re-match in Atlanta. The issue: the giant Atlanta broadcasting industry's reasonability to black people and its failure to act responsibly ... And when the giant fell flat on his face before his adversaries, jittery broadcasters across the nation paused to listen to a few words from little David's sponsors.[19]

Following his victory, King was inundated with phone calls from black groups in other cities eager to take on their local broadcasters. The movement spread so rapidly that *Broadcasting* magazine, the main industry organ, began urging federal legislation to protect station owners from what it labelled "the tide of black revolution that has begun to beat against the television establishment."[20]

The citizen groups achieved further leverage in 1971, however, when the FCC adopted new "ascertainment" guidelines that required station owners to solicit information actively on the problems, needs, and interests of their audience, and to respond to them. That same year, two Washington-based citizen groups—William Wright's BEST and the Citizens Communication Center—challenged the licenses of nine TV stations owned by the Alabama Educational Television Commission (AETC). Even though blacks made up 30 percent of the state's population, they noted, the AETC had never employed a single African-American professional in its seventeen-year history, and it had no blacks on its programming board. In addition, it had refused to air any national black-oriented public television programs, such as the weekly *Black Journal*.[21]

At first, the FCC rejected the challenge, but after it received additional complaints in 1975, and after Ben Hooks became a Commission member, it changed course and revoked all the licenses. The decision was "a thunderbolt" heard round the country, Albert Kramer, the first head of the CCC noted decades later, since "no one ever thought that would happen to the public broadcasting community."[22]

The FCC subsequently reversed its Alabama decision a second time. It restored the licenses of six AETV stations when they faced no new charges of discrimination. It also renewed the licenses of three others in 1980, after the stations reached an agreement with local citizen groups to reform their hiring and programming practices.[23]

Emma Bowen Takes on the New York Media

Harlem community activist Emma Bowen was invited in 1970 to speak to a group of New York City's black reporters. The journalists, many of them the first non-whites to work in their newsrooms, complained to Bowen that their editors routinely dispatched them to dangerous riot situations in the black community but rarely sent white reporters to cover the same stories. A young widow and mother of three, Bowen had already earned a reputation for her willingness to tackle racial segregation by successfully campaigning in 1965 to get the US Senate to hire its first black page, Lawrence Bradford, Jr.

As a mental health professional, Bowen was convinced that the constant stream of negative press accounts about African-Americans was producing deep psychological damage to black youth. In 1971 she founded Black Citizens for a Fair Media, and initiated a series of meetings between the group and the major broadcast networks and New York area stations. She went on to negotiate voluntary agreements with several stations to increase minority hiring, develop community affairs programs, and improve minority content in programming, and challenged the licenses of those broadcasters who refused to reach a settlement.

All over the country, citizen groups won similar concessions. As a result, local broadcasters started airing public-interest shows that presented non-white communities in a more positive light, and hundreds of black and other minority journalists secured their first jobs in the industry.[24]

But the sprawling, loosely connected citizen movement was also fraught with weaknesses. Some of its leaders wielded the cudgel of community pressure largely to secure jobs and business opportunities for close friends or relatives. Some station executives promised change, but then reverted to their old practices once the community pressure dissipated. One of the movement's most influential pioneers, Albert Kramer of the CCC, later concluded that he and his fellow reformers had failed to achieve any lasting structural change in the industry. "No licenses got lifted, nobody got designated for a hearing," Kramer noted. "And the only one they had the courage to go after and only because they were dead in their tracks if they didn't was the educational authority in Alabama."[25]

Despite such setbacks, Kramer and his fellow activists in the black community waged a heroic and seminal struggle. After all, most reforms forced on a powerful elite by a popular movement tend to be fragile; all are susceptible to being whittled away or eventually dismantled by their opponents once the original movement's strength begins to wane, once conditions change.

But even when they are defeated, great reform movements leave an indelible imprint on the institutions they challenge. Moreover, they provide critical lessons for future generations of activists. Which is why the media reformers of the late 1960s and 1970s did more to transform the white racial narrative in American news than any other group in the nation's history.

Frito Bandito and the Chicano Movement

In 1967 the Frito-Lays Corporation launched a national ad campaign to promote its popular corn chips. The ads featured a cartoon character named Frito Bandito, a potbellied Mexican who wore a sombrero, sported a handle bar mustache, and robbed people of their chips at gunpoint.

Frito soon became so popular with white audiences that other companies started using the *bandido* figure to sell everything from cars to cigarettes and watches. One TV commercial featured the leader of a gang of Mexican *vaqueros* using a Bristol-Myers deodorant. "If it works for him, it'll work for you," the narrator advised.[26] A newspaper ad for Elgin even portrayed one of Mexico's revolutionary heroes as a watch thief, proclaiming:

> Emiliano Zapata, the Mexican Robin Hood and revolutionary, tacked up this notice in a western railroad station: Any engineer or conductor found not carrying an Elgin watch will be killed for concealing valuables ... It's a good thing Emiliano Zapata's gone. He'd be stealing Elgins as fast as we could make them.[27]

The ads sparked almost unanimous outrage among Mexican-American leaders, and became instant targets for a spate of militant Chicano newspapers that had arisen in the nation's *barrios*—publications such as *La Raza* in Los Angeles, *El Grito del Norte* in New Mexico, and *El Gallo* in Colorado.[28] "Seldom a day goes by in the United States without at least one young Mexican-American being called a Frito Bandito," Stanford University sociologist Thomas M. Martinez concluded in a study of the effect of the ads on Mexican-American youth.[29]

To combat such stereotypes, Chicano activists launched the National Mexican-American Anti-Defamation Committee (NMAADC) in Washington, DC, in 1968. They chose Domingo Nick Reyes, a one-time radio DJ and television producer, and a former staff member at the US Commission on Civil Rights, to head the group, and demanded that Frito-Lay stop running the Frito Bandido commercial.

When the company refused to do so, NMAADC and other Mexican-American groups launched a campaign against it. They also threatened in 1969 to file a Fairness Doctrine complaint with the FCC against any station that aired the commercial. Chicano groups in California successfully pressured Los Angeles station KNBC and San Francisco's KRON and KPIX to decline to air it. Finally, Reyes and his fellow activists threatened a defamation lawsuit against Frito-Lay in federal court in 1971. The relentless pressure finally convinced the company to cancel the commercial.[30]

While the Frito Bandito campaign targeted advertising and not actual news coverage, it represented a milestone for Latinos in media reform. For the first time, the country's small but growing Chicano community had successfully challenged the broadcast industry over its public service responsibilities. On the heels of that victory, NMAADC published a "Brown Paper" denouncing the overall portrayal of Latinos by the media and calling for Chicanos to control their own news and entertainment companies.[31]

Racial Conflicts in the Media Reform Movement

Chicano media reformers at first spurned any alliances with their counterparts in the black or white communities. Many were skeptical that BEST or the CCC would defend the particular needs of Latinos, while a few even exhibited racial bias toward blacks and whites. *Los Angeles Times* reporter and columnist Ruben Salazar condemned such views. In a 1970 column, he openly confronted simmering tensions between African-Americans and Chicanos:

> Blacks, scarred by the bitter and sometimes bloody struggle for equality, consider Mexican-Americans or Chicanos as Johnnies-come-lately who should follow black leadership until the Chicanos earn their spurs.
>
> Chicanos, not untouched by bigotry, and wary of the more sophisticated black leadership, insist on going on their own because as they put it, "our problems are different from those of the Negroes."
>
> Despite the loud mouthings of radicals, most blacks and Chicanos want the same thing: a fair chance to enter the mainstream of American society without abandoning their culture or uniqueness.[32]

Salazar's admonition failed to sway the most nationalistic Chicano leaders. They preferred instead to work on media reform with officials of the Community Relations Service. At the time, CRS was almost unique among federal agencies in employing several Hispanics in key positions. It also hosted several conferences of Latinos on media reform. At one gathering in 1970, in the Plaza Hotel in New York, Salazar played a pivotal role in launching the National Chicano Media Council, and was the keynote speaker. Several mainstream executives, including *Washington Post* publisher Katherine Graham, participated in the New York meeting and expressed support for the new organization.[33]

Shortly afterward, Time–Life Broadcasting announced it was selling five television stations to McGraw–Hill, and Chicano leaders immediately banded together to oppose the deal. FCC rules barred any company from owning more than two VHF stations in any of the fifty biggest markets, and the sale would leave McGraw–Hill over that limit in three of those markets—yet the Commission initially approved the deal. The coalition of Latinos filed a formal complaint against the transaction, claiming the stations slated for sale had not been adequately serving the large Hispanic and African-American audiences in their signal area. The coalition chose Domingo Reyes, the prime organizer of the Frito Lay campaign, to lead the new effort. By then, however, Reyes was becoming a divisive figure. He so alienated the members of the McGraw–Hill coalition with his inflammatory rhetoric and anti-Semitic remarks that they turned against him and sought legal guidance instead from the CCC, the United Church of Christ, and MALDEF.[34]

Despite its internal problems, the coalition garnered so much community support that McGraw–Hill eventually agreed to form community advisory boards at its stations, to hire more journalists of color, and to broadcast more content about African-Americans and Chicanos. Several similar efforts by Chicanos in the west and southwest prompted other station owners to follow suit.[35]

Taking on Public Television

Latino leaders turned their sights in early 1972 on the new public broadcasting system. Jesus Treviño, one of the few Chicano film producers employed at Los Angeles station KCET, issued a letter that year condemning the station's abysmal record on hiring Latinos and its lack of Latino-themed programming. Treviño organized about twenty Latino employees at KCET (mostly janitors, secretaries, and technicians), and they all threatened to quit en masse unless the station created a weekly Chicano show. KCET agreed to sponsor *Acción Chicano*, a low-budget talk show on southern California's Mexican-American population. Treviño used the new program both to address current events and to showcase documentaries by Chicano filmmakers.[36]

As the KCET conflict unfolded, a group of Puerto Rican community activists in New York, including Gilberto Gerena Valentín, Esperanza Martell, Diana Caballero, and Julio Rodríguez, formed the Puerto Rican Education and Action Media Council. They began working with filmmaker José García, whose efforts to launch a Latino public affairs show had been repeatedly rejected by the city's main PBS station, WNET. The activists then decided on an audacious approach. They secretly gained access to the WNET building by disguising themselves as volunteers for its pledge drive. During a live fundraising pitch, they seized the microphone, issued a statement of protest on the air, and announced a sit-in. Their action triggered the first ever shutdown of the station's signal. Police were summoned to arrest those inside, while several hundred supporters picketed outside the station with a banner that read: "20% Hispanic population, 0% programming." The disturbance prompted WNET to create a new Latino show called *Realidades*. Under the leadership of García and Humberto Cintrón, an East Harlem community activist who was named executive producer, that show became the most influential national Latino program in the history of the PBS system and a launching pad for many of the country's finest Latino documentary filmmakers.[37]

As their media victories mounted, Civil Rights groups began encountering resistance to their movement from the federal courts. In 1971, for example, a coalition of South Texas groups joined the American GI Forum and the League of United Latin American Citizens to challenge the license of WOAI, a San Antonio television station. They accused the station's management of violating both the FCC's Equal Employment Opportunity rules and its ascertainment requirements, which mandated that stations hold periodic community meetings to determine the needs of their listeners. But a federal court ruled years later that, even if the racial composition of a station's staff differed substantially from a station's listening audience, that was not sufficient to prove discrimination. Moreover, in a major setback to the citizen reform movement, the judge also ruled that a station's owners, not the public, had ultimate authority over programming decisions.[38]

Ruben Salazar's Uncommon Journey

The founders of the Chicano Media Council who met in New York City in early 1970 selected as their first chairman Ruben Salazar, the most influential Latino journalist of his era.

Born in Juárez, Mexico, on March 28, 1928, Salazar was just a baby when his parents, Luz and Salvador Salazar, crossed the Rio Grande and settled in El Paso. After graduation from high school and a stint in the army, he returned to El Paso, earned a bachelor's degree in journalism at Texas Western University in 1954, and landed a job on the *El Paso Herald-Post*. As that paper's first Latino reporter, he quickly displayed an uncommon talent for newsgathering. Within days of his arrival, he got himself locked up on a phony drink charge, then wrote a scathing exposé of conditions in the city jail. For another story, he posed as a drug addict and described how easy it was to buy heroin in the *barrio*.

Salazar soon moved to a bigger stage, joining the staff of the *Los Angeles Times* in 1959. He again found himself the first and only Latino in the newsroom, but he resisted being pigeonholed into simply covering the "taco beat." Before long, he was writing dispatches from the Dominican Republic during the 1965 US invasion of that country, and reporting from the battle-fields of Vietnam. When Mexican soldiers massacred protesting students just before the 1968 Olympic games, Salazar covered the tragedy as a member of the paper's Mexico City bureau. Soon after, *Times* editors called him back home to help chronicle the mounting social upheaval in the *barrios* of southern California. The paper had still not hired any other Latino reporters during his absence.

Salazar surprised everyone around him, however, by resigning from the *Times* and taking a job as news director at KMEX, then a little-known Los Angeles Spanish-language television station. From his first day at KMEX, Salazar instituted an aggressive style of advocacy journalism that was then unknown in Spanish-language television. "The press's obligation is to rock the boat," he declared at the time. His station produced a startling report on police brutality in the Latino community, one that incurred the enmity of police officials and city leaders. At the same time, Salazar continued to write a weekly op-ed column for the *Times*, where he gave unique expression to the problems of Mexican-Americans.[39]

During the founding conference of the Chicano Media Council in early 1970, for instance, the forty-two-year-old Salazar made a stirring plea for the nation's media executives to pay more attention to the gathering storm in the barrios:

> We ask you—almost beg you—to help us inform this nation about the tragic plight of 8 million invisible Chicanos whose lives often parallel those of black people. There is much bitterness in our Mexican-American community, gentlemen, an ever-increasing bitterness against school systems that psychologically mutilate the Chicano child, against certain police who habitually harass our brown brothers, against local and federal governments that apparently respond only to violence. Consequently, there are some Chicanos who have finally concluded that we must have a Watts-type riot to catch your attention—to force the establishment to pay heed.
>
> We prayerfully hope this won't happen ... We hope that reason will finally prevail, that you leaders of the national media will help us to push for the kinds of governmental reforms and changes in public attitudes that will help better the lot of the much-ignored Chicano. In all candor gentlemen, I can't say I'm entirely hopeful. It may be too late to forestall the violence of long-festering frustration, but I think we should try.[40]

His warning proved tragically prophetic. A few weeks later, on August 29, 1970, Salazar left his KMEX offices to cover an anti–Vietnam War protest by young Chicanos. The all-day event—organizers called it the National Chicano Moratorium—was scheduled for Laguna Park in east Los Angeles.

More than 25,000 participants from throughout the west converged on the park, making it the largest Latino street protest in the country's history at that time.

What began as a festive and peaceful demonstration of Latino pride soon escalated into a violent and bloody confrontation. Following a minor disturbance a block away from the main rally, police decided to end the main event. In doing so, they grabbed and arrested one of the key speakers, Corky Gonzales, head of Colorado's La Raza Unida Party, before he could even reach the podium. They then swept into the crowd with clubs and tear gas. Hundreds of angry youths resisted, and a riot ensued in which more than forty cops were injured and twenty-five police cars destroyed.

At one point Salazar and his camera crew sought refuge from the mayhem in a nearby bar, the Silver Dollar Café. Minutes after they entered, police surrounded the building—they would later claim they had received a report of a man entering the bar with a gun. Without warning to those inside, an LA County deputy sheriff fired a tear-gas canister through the open front door. The projectile tore into Salazar's head and killed him instantly. [41]

Two other people died in the riot that day, scores were injured, and hundreds arrested in what would become for US Latinos the equivalent of the Kent State massacre for white America, or Bloody Sunday in Selma for the Civil Rights movement. The sudden death of Salazar shocked the residents of Los Angeles and Latinos across the nation. Scores of Latino editors and reporters had faced abuse and even persecution for their work in the past, but none had ever been killed. Since that day, numerous Latino organizations have sought to preserve Salazar's legacy, creating awards and scholarship funds in his name, and even convincing the US Post Office to issue a commemorative stamp in his honor in 2008. Yet mainstream media associations and most textbooks on contemporary journalism rarely cite his extraordinary story or his personal contributions to freedom of the press in his adopted country.

Salazar's killing was also an enormous setback for Mexican-American efforts at national media reform. The Chicano Media Council he had been elected to lead slowly disintegrated a few months later. [42]

The Broadcasters Attempt to Stifle Competition

By the late 1960s the nation's broadcasters faced not only a powerful new citizen movement but also new competitive threats to their licenses. Ever since its creation by Congress in 1934, the FCC had been required to hold a comparative hearing whenever two applicants were vying for the same license, and to give preference to the applicant who would better serve the public interest. In practice, however, the agency never established fair criteria for how to choose between competing applications, and it had traditionally favored incumbent broadcasters. That all changed in 1965, when the FCC adopted new guidelines for comparative hearings. Thereafter, the agency announced, it would consider such factors as diversity of ownership, whether a license-holder was directly involved in a station's management, and what kind of program services the station offered its viewers or listeners.

The Commission relied on those new guidelines in 1969 to revoke the license of Boston's WHDH, a television station owned by the *Boston Herald-Traveler*, and to award it instead to a competing applicant, Boston Broadcasting Inc. In doing so, it specifically cited the concentration of ownership of Boston's mass media as one of the factors it had considered.[43] FCC commissioner Nicholas Johnson played a key role in the WHDH decision. Appointed to the FCC by President Lyndon Johnson in 1966, he had quickly emerged as the most outspoken and liberal commissioner in the agency's history. An Iowa law professor and former clerk to Supreme Court Justice Hugo Black, Johnson was a relentless critic of chain ownership and of what he described as television's "sick influence in our society." A few years into his term, he authored a path-breaking report that documented the growing trend of cross-ownership between daily newspapers and local television stations in many cities. The report found that daily newspapers controlled local stations in 250 cities in 1967, with the local paper having no competition from any other daily in 213 of those cities. Between them, newspapers and broadcast chains owned an astounding 81 percent of the nation's VHF television stations. Johnson incurred the lasting enmity of industry chiefs by authoring *How To Take Back Your TV Set*, a guide for local communities on how to make broadcasters more accountable.[44]

Station owners eventually raised such a furor in Congress over the FCC's comparative hearing guideless that the agency revised them in 1970. Henceforth, the Commission announced, it would approve an incumbent broadcaster for a license renewal application unless it first determined that the station had failed to serve the public interest. Black Efforts for Soul in Television and the Citizens Communications Center immediately challenged the new policy in federal court. They claimed it violated their First Amendment rights by preventing people of color from gaining access to the media. The courts subsequently sided with the citizen groups and nullified the FCC change—a decision that further infuriated the industry's chiefs.[45]

By the late 1970s, the combination of massive grassroots pressure and FCC policy changes produced significant advances in the hiring of minorities and in the racial content of news and entertainment at hundreds of stations. By then, however, a new technology had begun to challenge traditional television broadcasters for the public's attention—cable.

The Broken Promise of Cable Television

In 1948, John Walson, a lineman for Pennsylvania Power and Light, attached a wire to a TV set in his appliance store in Mahoey City, Pennsylvania. He then stretched the wire to an antenna he had set up on a nearby hill. The homemade invention provided crystal clear TV reception from Philadelphia stations located nearly 90 miles away. Visitors to Walson's store were so impressed by the TV's picture quality that they began pleading with him to connect their sets to his line. He decided to charge each household $2 a month and, to his amazement, he quickly garnered 727 subscribers. Thus was born one of the first commercial Community Antenna Television, or CATV.[46]

By 1955, there were 400 CATV systems in the United States, serving 150,000 subscribers, and some systems started adding more channels to provide their customers with movies. Hollywood film studios, fearing a backlash from theater owners and broadcast stations, balked at selling their content to the new cable operators. Television executives thus exhibited the same fear of the nascent cable industry that newspaper barons had shown toward early radio.[47]

The broadcasters correctly regarded the new technology as a threat to their dominance, so they pressured the FCC to shield them from competition. In 1966 the agency restricted cable operators from importing distant TV signals. It then adopted regulations in 1966 that prevented cable companies from developing their service in the 100 largest markets—where 87 percent of the country's population resided.[48]

By then, however, an unusual alliance of organizations had emerged to support cable's expansion into the cities. Civil Rights leaders, for instance, regarded cable with the mix of hope and naïveté that has marked public perception of every new technological advance in communications. As William Wright of BEST saw it:

> The potential of cable television is beyond imagination … With the increased number of channels possible with cable TV, we should make certain that some of those channels are set aside for us. It is fantastic what we would be able to do with them. We could begin to communicate with each other, something we desperately need to do. This is really our big chance and if we blow this one, we might as well forget it.[49]

"Cable represents the only avenue available for Hispanics to gain substantial control over a communications medium," proclaimed a 1977 article in *Agenda*, a publication of the National Council of La Raza. "[I]f Hispanics do not immediately begin to actively pursue cable franchises they will find themselves in the same situation as they are now with the broadcast industry:

desperately trying to pry a few jobs and programs from an Anglo-controlled medium."

Calling cable "the last communications frontier for the oppressed," the Urban Institute's Charles Tate likewise predicted that minority ownership of cable systems could bring enormous progress to ghetto neighborhoods. Tate's main worry was that most community leaders knew little about the political debate going on in Washington between cable operators, broadcasters, and the handful of media reform advocates.[50]

Civil Rights leaders weren't the only ones impressed by the new technology's potential. Military think tanks like the Rand Corporation and the MITRE Corp., concerned about the dangers of more urban rebellions, warned that the central problem confronting inner-city ghettos was political and social isolation caused by inadequate communication systems. Cable could be used to end that isolation, they argued, by providing social welfare services such as banking, shopping, adult education, medical consultations, and civic participation.[51]

In 1970 the Alfred P. Sloan Foundation's Commission on Cable Communications recommended that the government develop cable systems fostering community interaction and critical social services. Meanwhile, another study by the National Academy of Engineering concluded that communications technology, including cable, could enable cities to provide job training for non-white media professionals and create anti-crime surveillance for poor communities.[52]

At first, even the federal government seemed to agree. A communications policy task force created by President Johnson had already concluded in 1967 that cable had the potential to maintain peace and spur economic development in poor, urban areas through the creation of two-way municipal channels that aired programming produced by the public and provided job and educational training.[53]

Nonetheless, when the FCC finally lifted its restrictions on allowing cable operators to enter the top 100 markets in 1972, it largely ignored recommendations from Civil Rights and media reform groups. The agency instead permitted privately owned cable companies to establish virtual monopolies in each city through locally issued franchises, while requiring them to pay franchise fees for using the public rights of way. In a minor concession to the public interest groups, the agency required that at least three channels on each system be set aside for public access, municipal government, and educational purposes. These PEG (Public, Education and Government) channels, as they came be known, turned out to be the only portions of the cable television bands that actually served any broader public service function.[54]

Cable in the Cities: Minority Empowerment or Rent-a-Citizen Schemes?

By the time the cable companies came knocking on their doors, most big-city governments were facing shrinking tax bases. Because of that, few municipal leaders wanted to risk financing their own cable systems. Instead, they typically negotiated agreements with private firms to build out and operate a local monopoly franchise. After landing those franchises, the companies often cherry-picked the affluent, white neighborhoods for the earliest connection and delayed for years stringing their wires in the poorest neighborhoods. Most importantly, the companies rarely offered interactive, two-way cable service—the type of advance that held the greatest promise to spur greater civic participation.

Local politicians routinely used their leverage over cable operators during franchise negotiations to demand funding for projects that had nothing to do with video services. It was common for a cable company to subsidize the planting of trees or the construction of public libraries and firehouses. New York City Mayor John Lindsay called cable franchises "urban oil wells beneath our city streets."[55] John Malone, the head of cable giant TCI, initially refused to get his company involved in such shadowy deal-making. "We weren't going to build libraries, give away free fire engines and send the mayor's eighteen illegitimate kids to college," Malone once quipped.[56]

To help them secure a local franchise, cable companies often recruited local civic leaders by offering them a stake in their cable operations. Once the cable company prevailed, however, those leaders usually sold their interest and walked away with a financial windfall. A perfect example was the partnership Warner Communications and American Express formed to win a fifteen-year franchise in Pittsburgh in 1980. The venture gave the local Urban League, the United Negro College Fund, and other local African-American groups a 20 percent stake in the local cable company. The arrangement touched off a federal probe into possible bribery and influence-peddling, but Warner/Amex was never charged with any wrongdoing.[57]

Billionaire Warren Buffet called the "rent-a-citizen" scheme a "national scandal" after cable operators sought his help in securing a franchise in his hometown of Omaha.[58]

In Houston, five franchises were awarded in 1979 to companies that hired several people connected to the mayor. An unsuccessful bidder, Affiliated Capital Corp., challenged the award in court, and a federal jury later found the mayor and the cable operator had conspired to "limit competition." The court awarded $6.3 million in damages to Affiliated Capital Corp.[59]

Other than the much-publicized scandals involving minority front companies, the early years of cable were marked by limited progress in media ownership by African-Americans and Latinos. One of the first minority-owned cable systems in the country was Olympic Cable TV, which was

founded in 1971 in Port Orchard, Washington. The system had twelve
channels and served more than 4,000 subscribers. The first known Hispanic-
owned cable system, Tele-Vu, received a franchise in 1972 to operate in
Grants, New Mexico, and had more than 2,000 subscribers. Another
Hispanic-owned cable company, Mecure Telecommunications, was able to
secure five franchises in New Mexico as well.

In 1980, Connection Communication Corp., a minority-owned company,
won the franchise to serve Newark, New Jersey, while in Chicago, Continental Cablevision, the nation's eleventh-largest cable company, signed a
contract with Stellar Cable in 1982 to provide cable services to the city's far
south side. Stellar Cable was made up of prominent black business leaders,
including John H. Johnson, publisher of *Jet* and *Ebony*.[60]

Other black-owned franchises set up shop in the mid 1980s in
Metlakatla, Alaska; East Cleveland and Columbus, Ohio; Greensville,
Mississippi; Pompano Beach, Florida; Huntsville, Alabama; and Carrboro,
North Carolina. But few people of color held on to their systems for very
long. By the middle of the 1980s, blacks owned a mere sixteen systems
nationwide, and Hispanics just eleven, even as the overall number of franchises more than doubled between 1980 and 1990—from 4,225 to 9,575.[61]

Only the biggest minority-owned firms were able to survive. In 1979,
for example, the Mexico-based Azcárraga family, owners of Spanish International Communications Company and Spanish International Network,
launched the Galavisión cable channel. The new network, which focused
on movies, sporting events, and *telenovelas*, only solidified SIN's domination
of the US Hispanic market. Likewise, Robert Johnson, a native of Hickory,
Mississippi, launched Black Entertainment Television in 1980. He found a
willing partner in the legendary cable mogul John Malone, the head of
Tele-Communications Inc.

Malone and other cable operators had discussed for years the importance
of creating a channel that would increase the number of African-American
cable subscribers in the big cities. He ended up lending Johnson $320,000 to
launch the network, and purchased a 20 percent share of the company. TCI's
stake in BET marked the first time the company had made an investment
in a cable network. Johnson and BET subsequently came under intense
criticism from African-American leaders for the network's stereotypical programming and for its paucity of news and public affairs content. Nonetheless,
BET turned into a bonanza for Malone and Johnson—the first black-owned
and controlled company to trade on the New York Stock Exchange. When
Johnson sold the network to Viacom in 2000 for $3 billion, he became the
nation's first black billionaire.[62]

Meanwhile, two of the country's most prominent African-American
businessmen, Don Barden and Percy Sutton, also joined the cable gold rush.
Barden, a native of Detroit, initially bought a small stake in cable operations

in Lorain and Elyria, Ohio. In 1983 he won a fifteen-year contract from the city of Detroit. When the big cable companies began consolidating in 1994, Barden sold his Detroit franchise to Comcast and walked away with a profit of $115 million.[63]

Sutton expanded his Inner City Broadcasting by the 1980s beyond New York to include stations in Detroit, Los Angeles, and the San Francisco Bay area. He also acquired a 50 percent share of Sheridan Broadcasting, the second-largest black radio news network, with 108 radio affiliates. Sutton then decided to seek a slice of the cable franchises that New York City was about to award. He secured a $300 million loan to bid on serving all of Queens and used his political skills to land a franchise for a third of the borough, beating out major companies such as Westinghouse, Time Inc., and Warner Amex.[64]

Once Congress passed the 1984 Cable Act, effectively ending local and national restrictions on cable prices, industry revenues skyrocketed from $900 million in 1976 to almost $12 billion in 1987. The larger operators gobbled up the smaller ones, and by 1996 the top five companies had amassed control of 66 percent of the industry.[65]

The cable companies consolidated even further once Congress passed the 1996 Telecommunications Act. While the new law allowed telephone companies to begin competing against cable for video services, the telephone companies did not begin rolling out their fiber-optic video and data services until a decade later. Meanwhile, cable company mergers continued at an alarming pace. By 2004, the ten largest cable operators served nearly 60 million of the 72 million basic cable customers in the US. Comcast Corp. and Time Warner Cable today control nearly 40 percent of the market. Minority ownership of cable systems is almost non-existent.[66]

Minority Journalism Associations: The New Media Watchdogs

As we have seen, by the early 1970s the Civil Rights movement had succeeded in cracking open the nation's major newsrooms to a small number of minority journalists. Those journalists encountered both overt and subconscious hostility from their white colleagues, and most concluded that the best way to survive in the newsroom was by forming their own organizations for mutual support.

After the death of Ruben Salazar, for instance, a handful of young Mexican-American reporters in California banded together in 1972 to create the California Chicano News Media Association. Among CCNMA's founders were Frank Del Olmo, who began working at the *Los Angeles Times* the year Salazar was killed, Joe Ramirez of KNBC-TV, and Estela López of KABC-TV.

Three years later, forty-four black journalists met in Washington, DC, to launch the National Association of Black Journalists. Its founders included Les Payne of *Newsday*; DeWayne Wickham of the *Baltimore Sun*; Acel Moore of the *Philadelphia Inquirer*; Max Robinson, who would later become the first black anchor of a national evening news show with ABC; Vernon Jarrett of the *Chicago Tribune*; and Chuck Stone, a columnist at the *Philadelphia Daily News* and a former editor of both the *Chicago Defender* and the *New York Age*. The group elected Stone, a former Tuskegee Airman during World War II and former speechwriter for Harlem Congressman Adam Clayton, Jr., as NABJ's first president.

In October 1982, more than 200 Latino media workers met in San Diego at the first national Hispanic media conference. The gathering led to the formation of a national organizing committee that spearheaded the founding of the National Association of Hispanic Journalists in Washington, DC, in 1984. Among the new group's founding directors were Maria Elena Salinas, the veteran anchor of Univision's national news; Maggie Rivas Rodriguez, then a reporter with the Dallas *Morning News*; Guillermo Martínez Marquez, a former editorial board member of the *Miami Herald*; and Juan Manuel García Passalacqua, a longtime radio host and newspaper columnist. Gerald García, then the publisher of the *Tucson Citizen*, was elected the NAHJ's first president.[67]

In the late 1970s, *Los Angeles Times* reporter Bill Sing set about creating a national group to represent the interests of Asian-American journalists. Sing met KNBC anchor Tritia Toyota, who shared in his vision, and they joined with David Kishiyama and Nancy Yoshihara of the *Times*, television producer Frank Kwan, and Dwight Chuman, an editor at a local Japanese-American paper. The group, known as the Original Six, founded the Asian American Journalists Association in 1981.[68]

In 1983, thirty Native American journalists met at Pennsylvania State University to discuss the state of Native American media. They reconvened a year later at the Choctaw Nation in Okalahoma and created the Native American Press Association. The group changed its name to the Native American Journalists Association in 1990 to reflect its desire to include those working in the broadcast industry.[69]

In the decades that followed, these minority associations pried open the doors of many newsrooms for more young journalists of color. They continued to challenge stereotypical news coverage, and even convinced many news organizations to eliminate the use of racially insensitive terms; they championed the integration of university journalism schools and raised scholarship money for minority students; they conducted valuable content research on issues concerning race and the media. In short, they emerged as permanent watchdogs within the industry on issues of race and ethnicity.

But the minority journalists' groups played another vital role that has rarely been acknowledged. The annual conventions they sponsored became the only periodic venues for rank-and-file reporters and editors to dissect the impact of key industry trends and of government policies on the American media in general. By providing forums for both media executives and their employees to analyze the relationship of journalism to the public interest, the groups thus became a new voice of conscience for the entire profession.

Unfortunately, that voice was not always an independent one. For the first few decades of their existence, minority journalism associations depended largely on the big media chains and media-related foundations to finance their operations, either through outright grants or through individual companies underwriting the travel and registration fees of employees who attended the annual conventions. The Gannett Foundation, under the leadership of its longtime chief Gerald Sass, for example, provided more than $4 million in grants to the groups.

The biggest chains even openly encouraged their top-ranking minority employees to run for leadership posts within those associations. The more money that media companies gave them, the harder it became for the leaders of those associations to publicly question the policies of the big companies.[70] Perhaps even more troubling, by the 1990s all minority journalism organizations had begun accepting large donations from major non-journalism corporations and US government agencies. Executives at those companies increasingly regarded those contributions as providing them with valuable access to this rising group of opinion-makers.

As the years passed, generational conflicts also emerged between the original founders of the minority associations and their younger members. The old-timers had always understood the debt they owed to the civil rights movement for forcing open the doors of the mainstream media. The newer members, having no direct experience with that movement, tended to believe their success was due solely to their own individual skill and effort, and they thus adopted a more technocratic and less confrontational approach to achieving progress in the industry.

The number of journalists of color grew modestly in the newspaper industry during the 1970s and the 1980s, while it increased rapidly at local TV stations. The reason for this, as noted earlier, was the regulatory power over broadcasters held by the FCC. As a result, journalists of color achieved national recognition and prominence on television far more quickly than in newspapers. Max Robinson became the first African-American network anchor when he joined ABC News in 1978. Ed Bradley was a CBS and White House correspondent before becoming a Sunday night fixture on 60 Minutes. Charlayne Hunter-Gault, who was one of two students to break the color line at the University of Georgia, joined the MacNeil/Lehrer News Hour on PBS in 1978, becoming the first black female to anchor a national newscast. Bernard Shaw worked as a correspondent for CBS News in 1971 and the Miami bureau chief for ABC news, before becoming an anchor at

CNN in 1980. Geraldo Rivera became the first Hispanic correspondent on a national news show, ABC's *Good Morning America*, and the first to be named broadcaster of the year, in 1972, by the New York State Associated Press Broadcasters' Association. And Connie Chung served as the first Asian-American to anchor a network evening news show, first with *NBC Nightly News* from 1983 to 1989, and then as co-anchor of the *CBS Evening News* from 1993 to 1995.[71]

Black Journalists Confront the Media Industry

Despite significant efforts by some media companies during the 1970s to dismantle the long-established color line, editors and managers at newspapers remained almost all white. The critical behind-the-scenes decisions those editors made—about what stories to cover and how to frame them—profoundly shaped how ordinary Americans perceived people of color during this period of intense racial turbulence. A report by the US Commission on Civil Rights, for instance, found that only nine out of 230 network news stories it examined in 1974–75 focused on racial minorities. Of the eighty-five field correspondents who appeared in 131 stories, only three were women of color (two African-American and one Asian), and only two were black men.[72]

It did not take long for those first minority reporters to take an even bolder step. In 1972, seven black journalists at the *Washington Post* filed an EEOC complaint against their employer for racial discrimination in hiring and promotion. One of the group's most determined leaders, Leon Dash, had joined the *Post*'s metropolitan staff in 1968, soon after his graduation from Howard University. Dash had been deeply influenced by the assassination of Martin Luther King, Jr., that year, and by the urban rebellions that erupted immediately afterward. Ironically, the *Post* was then considered one of the most liberal papers in the country on racial matters. Its management prided itself on having the highest percentage of minority reporters—9.3 percent—of any major US daily. But with African-Americans comprising 71 percent of the Washington, DC, population, the paper's record was still glaringly inadequate. Dash and several other black reporters—they came to be known as the Metro 7—pressed the *Post*'s management to set a goal of 35 percent black employment.[73]

A subsequent EEOC investigation upheld the group's initial complaint. The decision enraged the *Post*'s management, though the company did begin to hire and promote more black journalists, and sought to burnish its image in the black community. The Metro 7 eventually decided they could not afford the financial cost of a protracted legal fight against the *Post*'s powerful battery of lawyers, so they "embraced their partial victory and moved on," says journalism historian Pamela Newkirk.[74]

By then, black employees at the *New York Times* had filed their own racial discrimination class-action. Among the reporters joining the suit was Earl Caldwell, who had gained national attention in the late 1960s by refusing to turn over to a California grand jury and to the US Justice Department his notes on his interviews with members of the radical Black Panther Party. Caldwell's stance had led to a Supreme Court decision on the case, and had sparked the passage by New York State of a reporters' shield law. The *Times* reporters also reached a negotiated settlement in 1979, in which the paper adopted a new affirmative-action hiring policy but admitted no past discrimination.[75]

In 1978, women and African-American journalists at the Associated Press filed a discrimination complaint. At the time, AP did not employ a single black or female bureau chief, editor, or executive. In the same fashion as their fellow reporters at the *Post* and the *Times*, however, AP's employees quietly settled their complaint in the early 1980s.[76]

Major news organizations thus quickly established a pattern of response to racial discrimination complaints from their own minority reporters: deny all charges, stall in court in hopes of exhausting the plaintiffs financially, then quietly reach a settlement.

The Historic Daily News Battle

That pattern was broken in 1987 at the most storied tabloid of the twentieth century—the *Daily News*. Founded in 1919 by Joseph Medill Patterson, grandson of the legendary *Chicago Tribune* publisher, the *Daily News* boasted a circulation of more than 2.5 million during its 1950s glory days. By the 1970s, that circulation had begun to plummet. As the city's working class became increasingly black and Puerto Rican in composition, so did the dwindling though still substantial readership of the *News*. The paper's reporting staff, on the other hand, was stuck in a time-warp. It remained overwhelmingly Italian and Irish, and politically conservative, with only a token handful of African-Americans and Hispanics—most of them assigned to cover non-white communities.

In 1980, a group of veteran black journalists at the paper filed a little-noticed racial discrimination complaint with the New York City Human Rights Commission. The group's main leader, David Hardy, had worked as a sports writer for the *Plainfield Courier* in New Jersey before joining the *Daily News* in 1967. A tall man with the lumbering build of a football lineman, an easy smile, and piercing eyes, Hardy had been so deeply affected by his experience covering the 1967 Plainfield race riot, during which he witnessed an angry mob of blacks beat to death a white policeman for shooting a young black man, that he later testified before the Kerner Commission about unchecked violence in the black community and about the negative role of the press.[77]

In 1969, he left the *News* for a job at the *Washington Post*, and he was still working at the latter paper when the Metro 7 filed their dramatic lawsuit in 1972. That same year he returned to the *Daily News* for a second stint, and soon discovered that black reporters at that paper were equally frustrated by their treatment from white editors and reporters. Hardy and his colleagues formed a black caucus to press the management for some reforms. Twelve caucus members filed their initial complaint with the city's Human Rights Commission in 1980, and eventually sued the paper in federal court in 1982. The EEOC followed with a class-action suit against the paper, as well on behalf of all black employees.[78]

The case of *Hardy et al. v. The Daily News* went to trial five years later. By then, only four of the original complainants were still involved. The others had all reached individual settlements with the company. Publisher James Hoge decided to risk a courtroom battle with the remaining four instead of agreeing to a quiet settlement. A graduate of Exeter Academy and Yale University, Hoge had cut an elegant figure in New York's high society since taking over as president and publisher of the *News* in 1984. While he possessed the charm and looks of a Hollywood star and a wide-ranging intellect, Hoge often seemed out of touch with the rough-and-tumble world of the city's working-class and non-white communities.

Even among black employees at the *News*, however, support for a lawsuit was not unanimous. An early member of the black caucus who broke with his colleagues was Bob Herbert. The company had responded to the lawsuit with a series of promotions for Herbert, making him the paper's first black investigative reporter, then, in 1985, its first black city editor, and later a columnist and member of the editorial board. Lawyers for the *News* repeatedly pointed to Herbert's promotion as proof that the company was willing to promote qualified minority journalists. During the 1990s Herbert left the paper to become a columnist at the *New York Times*, and for the next two decades was the most prominent a liberal voice on that paper's opinion pages.

Neither the National Association of Black Journalists nor the *Amsterdam News*, the city's main black newspaper, spoke out on behalf of Hardy and the other plaintiffs. NABJ's refusal to take a stand was especially perplexing, since the organization's stated mission had always been to promote the hiring and promotion of black journalists. Other major black organizations like the NAACP and the Urban League also declined to support the lawsuit.[79]

The trial itself was a fierce and bitterly contested affair—the first public examination of both race relations and ethics inside an American media company—with every twist and turn of the testimony closely monitored by industry executives across the country. Hardy and the three remaining plaintiffs—features editor Joan Shepard, copy-editor Causewell Vaughn and assistant news editor Steven Duncan—came under scathing personal attacks from Tribune lawyers, who portrayed them from the start as malcontents, unproductive employees, mediocre writers, and even as unethical.[80]

In fact, the four plaintiffs were all veteran journalists who had worked at a variety of media companies. Vaughn, forty-four, had started his career as a copy boy at the *New York Post*, worked as a stringer at the *Buffalo Evening News*, then been a copy-editor at the *New York Times*, before landing a job at the *Daily News* in 1973. Duncan, sixty-three, had begun his career in the 1950s in the black press—first at the St. Louis *Argus*, then the *Baltimore Afro-American*, where he had covered the Emmett Till trial and the Civil Rights movement. Sheppard, forty-five, had joined the *Daily News* after working at *Women's Wear Daily* and as a consumer affairs reporter at WINS Radio.[81]

Perhaps the most damaging evidence presented by their lawyer, Daniel Alterman, was an EEOC study that had uncovered "substantial" disparities at the *News* between black and white staff members in pay, work assignments, and promotions. White reporters, the agency found, were promoted to the title of special reporter within fifty-nine months, compared to 113 months for African-Americans. They also received an average of $118 a year in bonuses compared to $50 for black reporters from 1979 to 1981. The agency could not find a single instance where the salary of a black or Hispanic staff member equaled or surpassed that of white colleagues. Out of forty-seven people promoted into *Daily News* management from 1979 to 1981, the agency found that not a single person had been African-American.[82]

On April 15, 1987, the jury declared *Daily News* management culpable in twelve of twenty-three discrimination allegations, whereupon the paper agreed to pay plaintiffs $3.1 million. For the first time in US history, a major news organization had been convicted in a federal court of racial discrimination.[83]

The *Daily News* trial, much like the WLBT federal court decision nearly twenty years earlier, was a seminal moment for racial reform in the US media. But you would not guess that from the scant attention the case has received in studies of the media industry since then. Many media firms subsequently stepped up the racial integration of their newsrooms. In the five years before 1987, for instance, the percentage of minority employees at the nation's newspapers had increased by only 1 percent (from 5.5 to 6.5 percent); in the five years after the *Daily News* trial, it jumped from 6.5 to 9.4—almost a 3 percent gain.[84] While there is no way to prove a direct cause-and-effect relationship, there is little doubt that news organizations became more conscious of their treatment of black and other minority employees following the *Daily News* verdict.

The Long Battle Over Minority Ownership

Opening up entry-level jobs for minority journalists at major newspapers was just one step toward ending centuries of racial bias in the media. A bigger and more difficult step remained: shattering the color barrier at the highest levels of the industry—among editors, publishers, station managers, and owners.

By 1971, only ten of the nation's 7,500 radio stations were owned by people of color. The industry's racial track record was so abysmal that the National Association of Broadcasters finally adopted a goal in 1973 of doubling the number of black-owned stations over the next three years—one that it failed to meet.[85]

Many Americans questioned then—and still do today—whether increasing minority ownership of news media is a necessary or even legitimate goal for our society. The skeptics have little knowledge of the unique role the minority press played during the nineteenth and early twentieth centuries in challenging racial stereotypes and bigoted reporting. The expansion of minority ownership, in our view, is even more important for transforming news content than is simply hiring more minority journalists into white-owned companies. A series of studies commissioned by the FCC in the late 1990s seems to bear this out. Those studies found a clear connection between minority ownership and the diversity of a station's programming content. One study found that 73 percent of minority-owned stations showed live broadcasts of community events, compared to only 55 percent of white-owned radio stations. Minority stations were also more likely to broadcast programs about issues of concern to senior citizens (60 percent) than white-owned stations (30 percent), and they were more likely to produce shows geared to women (81 percent) than white stations (57 percent). In addition, 66 percent of minority owners reported that they played a direct role in their radio station, compared to only 31 percent of white owners. Finally, as one might expect, minority-owned stations were also far more likely to hire non-white staff and on-air talent than white-owned stations.[86]

The most successful black broadcast owner in the late 1960s was legendary rhythm and blues singer James Brown. He purchased WRDW in Augusta, Georgia, in 1967, then acquired two additional stations to create the first black-owned radio chain. But the handful of other black owners soon grew frustrated by the lack of opportunities to expand. Skip Carter of KPRS in Kansas City, along with Pierre Sutton, vice-president of New York's Inner City Broadcasting, spearheaded the creation of the National Association of Black Owned Broadcasters in 1976.[87]

The first black-owned television station did not sign on until 1975, in Detroit, two years after the FCC awarded a UHF license to a Detroit black fraternal group, the International Free and Accepted Modern Masons, Inc.

Dr. Willie Banks, the group's founder, set out to make the station, WGPR-TV, responsive to the news and informational needs of the city's black community. He initially hired twelve reporters, but had to lay off half of them within a month because of insufficient revenue. The station remained black-controlled until it was sold to CBS in 1995.[88]

As bad as the situation was in radio and television in those early years, it was even worse in newspapers. A handful of Spanish-language and black-owned dailies existed in the 1970s, but they were read almost exclusively within their own communities and were virtually unknown to white America. Not until 1979 did an African-American become the editor of a mainstream US daily. That year Robert Maynard took the helm of the Gannett-owned *Oakland Tribune*. Two years later, Gannett named Gerald Garcia publisher of the *Tucson Citizen*, making him the first Hispanic publisher of a major English-language daily. In 1983, Maynard purchased the *Tribune* from Gannett for $23 million and became the first African-American to own a major US newspaper.[89]

But for most minority journalists seeking to own their own company, access to capital remained the key obstacle to success. Banks were simply unwilling to lend large sums of money even to the most highly successful people of color. That discrimination was best symbolized by Percy Sutton's forays into the media business. A successful lawyer who had once represented Malcolm X, Sutton was for decades one of Harlem's most prominent figures. He won election to the New York State Assembly in 1965, and subsequently served as the first African-American borough president of Manhattan. Despite those accomplishments, when Sutton sought to purchase Harlem-based WLIB-AM in 1972 from its longtime owner, Harry Novick, more than seventy financial institutions rejected his loan request before he finally obtained the $2.5 million he needed. A few months later, Sutton also purchased WLIB-FM for $600,000. The station soon grew into the largest black-owned business in Harlem, and it did so by offering more public-service programming than any black-oriented station in the country.[90]

Sutton and other black media executives were so convinced that racial bias in lending was the chief roadblock to minority ownership that they appealed to the Congressional Black Caucus to pressure the FCC and the Carter administration on the issue. Just forty of the nation's 8,500 radio stations, they noted, were minority-owned—less than half of 1 percent of the total.

Carter's FCC responded with several new policies. In 1978 the agency amended a little-known tax certificate program that had been in existence for decades and turned it into a vehicle for expanding minority ownership. Under the original program, the federal government had allowed NBC to defer paying capital gains taxes after the Supreme Court's 1943 anti-trust ruling had forced the company to spin off its Blue network, and thus given birth to ABC. In subsequent years, the FCC had awarded more than 170 tax certificates under the program.[91]

The agency altered the tax certificate regulation in 1978 to allow any broadcaster who sold his license to a person of color to likewise defer capital gains taxes. It also approved a new "distress-sale" policy that permitted a broadcaster faced with revocation of a license to sell his station to a person of color at 75 percent of its market value. Finally, the agency agreed to award extra credit to a minority broadcast applicant during a comparative hearing.[92] The three new FCC policies led to an immediate spurt in minority broadcast ownership. The agency issued 364 tax certificates between 1978 and 1995—290 for radio, forty-three for TV, and thirty-one for cable stations—and total minority radio ownership jumped dramatically from 1 to 3 percent.[93]

The first person to take advantage of the distress-sale policy was a thirty-three-year-old African-American woman from Omaha, Nebraska, who had been managing the Howard University station and had been nurtured by journalist Tony Brown, the founder and first dean of Howard's school of communications. Her name was Cathy Hughes, and she succeeded in purchasing ailing station WOL-AM in Washington, DC, in 1980. Like Sutton, Hughes would later recall that she was turned down thirty-two times for a loan before securing the $1.5 million she needed—from a Latina loan officer. Today, Hughes is CEO of the largest and most influential radio company in the black community, the fifty-four-station Radio One network.[94]

One of the few bright spots for racial diversity in non-commercial broadcasting toward the end of the twentieth century was Pacifica Radio. Lewis Hill, a pacifist and conscientious objector during World War II, joined with other writers and artists in 1949 to launch KPFA-FM in Berkeley, California, pioneering the concept of listener-sponsored radio. Hill then created the non-profit Pacifica Foundation to support the effort. Over the next two decades, the Foundation's network grew to include stations in Los Angeles, Houston, Washington, DC, and New York, and it became the main anti-war and left-oriented radio operation in the country. It was also the most multiracial in terms of both its staffing and programming—so multiracial that the Houston station was bombed off the air twice during its first year of operation by the Ku Klux Klan.

Over the past decade, three of the network's five stations, WPFW in Washington, WBAI in New York, and KPFK in Los Angeles, have been classified by the FCC as minority-owned, since more than 50 percent of station management and staff at those stations are non-white.[95]

The Rise of Spanish-Language Television

It is one of great ironies of US broadcasting history that a foreign-owned company has produced the best example of diversified news coverage in our domestic media system. During the early 1950s, Mexico's most powerful broadcast mogul, Emilio Azcárraga Vidaurreta (see Chapter 13), attempted to expand his television empire by establishing a presence north of the border. Azcárraga teamed with a US businessman in San Diego to launch that city's second television station, XETV, in 1953. With a transmitter located in Tijuana and a license from the Mexican government, the station broadcast in both English and Spanish, and sought to reach a southern California audience.[96]

Azcárraga then tried to sell Spanish-language programming from his Telesistema Mexicano company (later named Televisa) to US networks. Unable to find any buyers, he decided to create his own Spanish International Communications Corporation to buy TV stations in US cities with large Latino populations. He started in San Antonio in 1961, purchasing the station originally owned by Raoul Cortéz and rechristening it KWEX. He then bought KMEX in Los Angeles (1962), New York's WXTV (1968), and Miami's WLTV (1971). He also founded a second company in 1961, the Spanish International Network (SIN), as a US distribution arm for his Mexico-produced shows. Azcárraga directed the operations of both SICC and SIN until his death in 1972, at which point his son Emilio Azcárraga Milmo assumed the reins.[97]

The Azcárragas' control of SICC was a breach of federal communications law, which prohibits foreigners from owning more than 20 percent of a domestic broadcast station. But since foreign ownership of programming is not prohibited, the family managed to cloak its control of SICC for many years by claiming majority control only of SIN. Rene Anselmo, the president of SICC and SIN, was a US citizen, as were other majority investors in SICC, but he was also a close friend of Azcárraga, and he functioned, in practice, as an agent of the Mexican mogul. By 1979, SIN was distributing sixty-four hours of programming a week to SICC stations and affiliates, and Televisa's programming accounted for fifty of those hours. Most of the shows were *telenovelas* (Spanish soap operas) and variety productions.[98]

Because of SICC's convoluted and hidden corporate structure, Mexico's Televisa thus ended up spearheading the development of Spanish-language TV in the United States. One journalism historian who studied the process has labeled it a form of "reverse neo-colonialism." "It's a Latin American network taking what Yankees have done to them by doing it to Latinos in the United States," claims University of Southern California Professor Félix Gutiérrez.[99]

Thanks to the historic exclusion of Latinos from US broadcasting, however, the Azcárraga stations became an invaluable resource for the nation's growing Spanish-speaking population. Their local newscasts covered many news events in the Latino community that the Anglo media routinely ignored, thus helping millions of Latin American immigrants assimilate to and maneuver within US society.[100] SIN, and later Univisión, provided a stream of daily coverage of major events in Latin America, keeping the newcomers informed about and connected to their homelands. Finally, the Azcárraga companies began to foster a new "Hispanic" consciousness among the disparate Latino ethnic groups within the United States. They not only popularized a new standard Spanish diction among their reporters—they also forged and branded a new "Hispanic market," and then functioned as the prime advertising conduit for corporate America to penetrate and exploit that market.

By the mid-to-late 1970s, the FCC was coming under increasing pressure to stop ignoring foreign control of SICC. In 1980, the Spanish Radio Broadcasters Association challenged the licenses held by SICC and accused it of violating US foreign-ownership restrictions. "The FCC is allowing a monster to be created that will ultimately stifle the development of TV programming by Hispanic Americans," Ed Gomez, the group's president, said at the time.[101]

In 1986, an FCC investigation finally concluded that SICC was indeed foreign-owned. The agency then refused to renew the network's thirteen broadcast licenses. Several bidders immediately stepped forward to purchase the valuable licenses, among them a domestic Latino-owned company named TVL. But the FCC allowed SICC to sell its stations to Hallmark Cards for $301 million. As part of the sale agreement, Televisa's SIN remained the main source of programming for the new Hallmark station group.[102]

One critic of the agency's approval of Hallmark was Henry Rivera, a former Albuquerque Democratic Party lawyer and the first Latino appointed to the FCC. A member of the Commission from 1981 to 1985, Rivera suggested instead that the stations be put up for a distress sale, which would have guaranteed their acquisition by minority broadcasters in the US. Hallmark promptly changed the name of its newly acquired network to Univisión, and in 1988 went on to purchase the network's programming arm, SIN, for an additional $274 million.[103]

Hallmark held on to its new network for only five years. During that brief period, Univisión depended less on programming from Televisa and began producing more than 40 percent of its content in the US. But the network struggled financially, and failed to produce the return its investors had expected. So in 1992 Hallmark sold it for $550 million to Hollywood producer and Republican Party financier A. Jerrold Perenchio. The deal marked the return of Azcárraga's Televisa, but this time the Mexican conglomerate teamed up with Venevisión, the powerful media group owned by the Cisneros family of Venezuela, as joint minority shareholders. Not surprisingly, Televisa and Venevisión emerged as suppliers of 94 percent of Univisión's programming by the mid 1990s.[104]

By then, a second Spanish-language network had become firmly established in the US. That network, Telemundo, originated in Puerto Rico, where a local media entrepreneur, Angel Ramos, launched *Telemundo Canal 2*, the island's first chain of stations, in 1952. Unable to break Univisión's monopoly over programming from Mexico, the smaller Telemundo network tried instead to produce more Spanish-language shows in the US, supplementing those shows with content imported from Brazil, Colombia and other Latin American countries. But the new network could not break the 70 percent stranglehold on advertising dollars that Univisión has always enjoyed in the US market. As a result, Telemundo passed through a succession of owners, until General Electric's NBC-Universal subsidiary purchased it in 2002. When they sought FCC approval of the purchase, NBC executives promised to expand Telemundo's news operations to serve the public interest more effectively. Despite those promises, the new owners gradually eviscerated or discontinued much of the reporting staffs and local news programming at the member stations.[105]

Over the past fifty years, Spanish-language television has become a major factor in propelling the diversification of content in American news. By the turn of the century, local Spanish-language evening news programs in several US cities were drawing more viewers than their English-language competitors. Their popularity was indicative not only of "the desire of Latinos to access programming that is relevant to their experiences," one analyst has noted, but of "the need of corporations to reach an audience segment of the US population that has been relatively untapped."[106]

The potential for that new trend to affect national discourse became most evident in the spring of 2006, when scores of Spanish-language radio and television stations across the country provided sympathetic coverage, and even helped to fuel the spread of the most massive series of public protests in American history. Those protests by several million Latinos over immigration rights, and against the Sensenbrenner Bill—a proposal in Congress that would have made it a felony crime for any immigrant to be in the US illegally or for anyone to assist or aid a person they knew to be an undocumented immigrant—took both the country's political class and most of the English-language media completely by surprise.

Toasters and Television: Mark Fowler and the Industry Fight Back

Former California governor Ronald Reagan entered the White House in 1981 promising a new era of freedom from government regulation. The Reagan appointee who most eagerly implemented that new direction in the mass media was Mark Fowler. A lawyer and former radio DJ, Fowler had worked as a communications counsel to Reagan presidential campaigns in 1976 and 1980, and became the new president's first FCC chairman.

Under his direction, the agency rescinded regulations that required broadcasters to operate a station for a minimum of three years before selling it. It increased from seven to twelve the cap on the number of AM and FM radio stations a company could own, and it increased caps on ownership of TV stations, so long as those stations did not reach more than 25 percent of the national viewing audience. Fowler transformed the licensing process into a mere formality by eliminating the need for broadcasters to fill out detailed program logs, by ending ascertainment requirements, and by allowing stations to apply for renewals by postcard application. He also ended any aggressive enforcement of equal employment regulations and eliminated a broadcaster's obligation to air a certain percentage of public-service programming.[107]

Fowler was so dismissive of the agency's public-interest mission that he once quipped, "TV is nothing more than a toaster with pictures," and boasted to a Washington reporter that he kept a Mao cap with a red star on his shelf, to be used as a dunce cap for the staffer who offered "the most regulatory idea of the week."[108]

His revamping of FCC rules sparked a buying spree in the industry. It was during Fowler's tenure that Capital Cities Communications gobbled up ABC, that General Electric Company acquired NBC, and that Rupert Murdoch purchased Metromedia Broadcasting, thus paving the way for the Australian-born magnate to launch his Fox Television empire. Such mega deals, of course, required enormous sums of money. "Broadcasters are now [so] heavily burdened by debt," the New York Times noted in the midst of the spree, that they had made "the profit imperative all the more powerful."[109]

Civil Rights and media reform leaders did not realize at first the profound reversal that Fowler's policies represented. "What we thought was structural changes turned out to be temporary," Nolan Bowie, a former head of the CCC, said. "We did not realize [the 1970s] was sort of the golden age of reform." Consumer advocate Ralph Nader would later accuse Fowler of inflicting more damage on democracy than any of Reagan's top one hundred officials. And Nader was hardly alone in his assessment. After Fowler stepped down as FCC chairman in 1987, the Washington Post's television critic Tom Shales declared: "We are as well rid of him as the indignant villagers were well rid of Dr. Frankenstein. Fowler was one for the books: a mad scientist who kept trying to burn down his own laboratory."

Industry executives, on the other hand, celebrated Fowler's tenure. "If Rip Van Winkle went to sleep in 1981 and awakened now, the difference in the communications landscape would be unrecognizable," NAB President Eddie Fritts said. "[Fowler] was so far ahead of us that all we could do was to monitor the changes coming at us."[110]

One reform that Fowler repeatedly sought to dismantle was FCC policy aimed at expanding minority ownership, but he was thwarted by Congress. He had a "philosophical aversion to the notion of affirmative action," said former FCC Commissioner Henry Rivera, who often bumped heads with Fowler.[111]

After Fowler had left the agency, a federal court case challenged the Commission's use of race as a factor in both comparative hearings and distress sales. But the case, *Metro Broadcasting v. FCC*, then moved to the Supreme Court, which upheld the commission's policies by a five-to-four vote in 1990.[112] "The diversity of views and information on the airwaves serves important First Amendment values," the High Court's majority opinion said. "The benefits of such diversity are not limited to the members of minority groups who gain access to the broadcasting industry by virtue of the ownership policies; rather, the benefits redound to all members of the viewing and listening audience."[113]

The *Metro* decision salvaged the agency's rules for promoting minority ownership, but only temporarily. Once the Republican Party took control of both the House of Representatives and the Senate in 1995, Congress moved to eliminate those FCC programs. Republicans killed the tax-certificate program altogether by attaching an amendment to an unrelated bill extending health insurance deductions to freelance workers. President Clinton, still reeling from the Republican Congressional victory, agreed to sign the law. Thus was eliminated the most effective government program ever devised to promote minority ownership of the media.

Then, in 1998, the US Court of Appeals for the District of Columbia declared the Commission's EEO rules unconstitutional. Following the ruling, the Commission eliminated a requirement for broadcasters to submit annual reports to the agency on their progress in hiring blacks, Latinos, Asian Americans and Native Americans.[114] Four years later, the FCC replaced its EEO rules with a race-neutral policy that required broadcasters only to publicize job openings widely.[115]

The Telecommunications Act and the Rise of Mega Media

The 1996 Telecommunications Act was the culmination of a furious two-decade campaign by media company executives to dismantle government regulation of their industry. It weakened FCC policies aimed at serving the public interest and crippled the ability of non-white communities to challenge and transform the white racial narrative in news. It removed, for example, national caps on the number of radio stations any broadcaster could own. Until then, a single company was limited to no more than forty radio stations. It also extended the limit on the cumulative reach of TV stations owned by one company from 25 percent of the national viewing audience to 35 percent, and it stretched the term for TV and radio licenses from five and seven years, respectively, to eight.[116]

The Telecommunications Act paved the way for the biggest media mergers in history. CBS purchased Infinity Broadcasting for $4.7 billion, only to be purchased by Viacom in 1999 for $50 billion. Rupert Murdoch's News Corp. purchased twenty TV stations, turning his Fox Television into the largest network in the country. The Tribune Company absorbed Times Mirror for $6 billion, while Time Warner spent $160 billion in a disastrous purchase of America Online.[117]

The new law's impact was most severe in the radio industry. In 1996, the top fifty radio companies owned about 800 stations; two years later, ten companies owned 1,300 stations. Just one firm, Texas-based Clear Channel, went from owning forty stations to owning 1,200. In the first decade after the enactment of the new law, the number of radio owners declined by 39 percent.[118]

The media buying frenzy drove the price of individual stations to unprecedented levels, it severely taxed the ability of small owners to compete for ad revenues against the new conglomerates, and it virtually closed off the chance for people of color to enter the industry. "When you approve legislation that allows the big fish to gobble up the little fish—and all African-Americans are in the little fish pond—you run the risk of having no black ownership by the turn of the century," Radio One founder Cathy Hughes, the country's largest black broadcaster, said at the time. "Some of these major white corporations are making offers to small black companies and small white companies that they can't refuse ... What the federal government has done is opened up the floodgates that will literally drown black ownership."[119]

Shortly after the new law was enacted, President Clinton appointed William Kennard as the first African-American chairman of the FCC. Ironically, it was during Kennard's tenure that broadcast ownership by racial minorities started to decline. Hughes and a few black owners sought to survive by buying up other black stations. She took her Radio One company public in 1999, and then partnered with cable giant Comcast in 2003 to launch the cable network TV One.[120] Even the big Spanish-language networks became takeover targets in the post–Telecommunications Act era. In 2002, NBC purchased Telemundo for $2 billion, while a private equity firm acquired Univisión in 2007 for $12 billion.

Only three years after the passage of the Telecommunications Act, an FCC study concluded that "the barriers of entry have been raised so high that, left standing, they appear virtually insurmountable." The report's conclusion forced Kennard to acknowledge that "the pace of consolidation was probably more dramatic than anyone predicted."[121]

A New Peoples' Movement for Media Reform

In December 2000, President-elect George W. Bush named Michael Powell, son of soon-to-be Secretary of State General Colin Powell, as chair of the FCC. Much like Fowler during the Reagan era, Powell had complete disdain for the "public interest" requirements of communications law. In a speech to the American Bar Association in 1998—after he had been named to the Commission but before his elevation to the chairmanship—Powell had declared:

> The night after I was sworn in, I waited for a visit from the angel of the public interest. I waited all night, but she did not come. And, in fact, five months into the job, I still have had no divine awakening and no one has issued me my public-interest crystal ball.[122]

Powell quickly proposed the most drastic relaxation of ownership rules in the nation's history. His plan would have permitted a single company in the larger markets to own eight radio stations, three TV stations, a local daily newspaper, and the local cable operating system in larger markets.[123]

With most experts predicting that the new rules would win easy approval, some of the biggest media companies, including NBC and Viacom, pressed for even greater deregulation. Powell, meanwhile, dismissed public concerns about media consolidation as overblown. He pointed to the explosion of the Internet and to the hundreds of channels available on cable as proof that the free market was already providing huge diversity in programming to the American people.

But Powell and the industry chiefs drastically underestimated the public response to deregulation. The idea of giving huge media companies even more control over the airwaves appalled not only the country's traditional liberal and progressive sectors, but many conservatives as well. Small-state Republican senators such as Ted Stevens of Alaska, Trent Lott of Mississippi, and Olympia Snowe of Maine, for example, were leery of the enormous power that major media companies—most of them headquartered in New York—wielded over their own constituents and over their own political futures. They thus echoed the same concerns that rural legislators in nineteenth-century America had expressed when they championed the use of postal subsidies as a way to protect the viability of their own local newspapers (see Chapter 2), or that Tennessee's populist Senator E. L. Davis had advocated in 1928 against the radio networks with his Davis Amendment to the Federal Radio Act (see Chapter 11).

Meanwhile, Christian fundamentalists were furious at the big media companies for their unbridled dissemination of sex and violence on TV. The Parents Television Council, for example, conducted a survey of approximately one hundred network–owned-and-operated TV stations in the country in 2003, and found that only one station had ever refused to air a program due to indecency.[124]

The initial public outcry against Powell's proposals emboldened the two Democratic commissioners on the five-member FCC—Michael Copps and Jonathan Adelstein. Both called for the FCC to hold public hearings around the country to solicit the views of the American people. Powell ignored their request, and eventually held just one hearing in Virginia.

Copps and Adelstein then opted for an unusual strategy: they presided over a dozen or so unofficial town hall hearings across the country. Those hearings, sponsored by local citizen groups, drew huge and enthusiastic audiences despite a virtual blackout of news coverage of them by the major commercial media companies.[125] Citizen groups as diverse as Common Cause, the Parents Television Council, the Leadership Conference on Civil Rights, the Family Research Council, the Media Access Project, and Code Pink all called on Powell to stop media deregulation. Several minority journalism groups, led by the National Association of Hispanic Journalists, also challenged the new rules. Nearly 3 million people contacted either the FCC or Congress on the issue, and the sentiment was overwhelmingly against further consolidation. Even the National Rifle Association—a longtime foe of the major national media companies—joined in, delivering more than 300,000 postcards from its members in opposition to further media consolidation.[126]

Despite the public outcry, the Commission voted on June 2nd, 2003, to implement Powell's plan and lift the ownership rules. The final three-to-two vote was strictly along party lines. After the FCC vote, the Prometheus Radio Project, a non-profit, low-power radio group in Philadelphia, challenged the new rules in federal court. A year later, the US Third Circuit Court of Appeals in Philadelphia jolted the media industry by ruling in favor of Prometheus and overturning the new rules. The FCC, the court concluded, had failed to justify how the changes served the public interest. Furthermore, the panel admonished the agency for failing to address the issue of minority ownership. As with the Supreme Court's *Associated Press* decision in 1945 and its *Metro v. FCC* ruling in 1990, and the DC Circuit Court's WLBT decision in 1969, the federal courts had once again upheld the principle that the government has a key role in ensuring that the American people hear a diversity of voices in their news media.[127]

Powell resigned shortly after his plan was defeated. His successor, Kevin Martin, then pursued partial deregulation instead of the wholesale effort championed by his predecessor. One of the last major acts of the Martin-led FCC in the waning days of the Bush administration was to eliminate the ban on newspapers owning broadcast stations in the largest markets, and to weaken those restrictions in smaller markets. That change opened the door to mergers of newspapers and broadcast stations, making it easier for big-city papers, most of which function as monopolies, to buy up the few minority-owned stations still left.[128] But in 2011, the Third Circuit Court once again rebuked the FCC and vacated the rule.

The second half of the twentieth century witnessed a fierce democratic rebellion by people of color against racial discrimination in the mass media. That rebellion achieved a partial desegregation of the nation's newsrooms and led to significant increases in minority ownership of media companies, especially in broadcasting. For a time, it succeeded in dramatically changing the white racial narrative that had long existed in American news. The movement's success, however, provoked a furious reaction during the 1980s and 1990s from the media owners, who pressured Congress and the federal courts to dismantle many of the previous reforms. Those efforts culminated with the Telecommunications Act of 1996. The new law sparked a surge of mega media conglomerates, but it also ignited a new citizen movement for diversity, democracy, and increased accountability in our news institutions. The new media reform movement achieved a startling victory in 2004 when it defeated industry efforts to dismantle federal regulations over broadcast ownership. No one, however, had fully anticipated how profoundly a new technological advance would disrupt our media system once again. That advance was the Internet.

V

The Age of the Internet

Controlling the Means of Transmission: Old Media's Fall and New Media's Rise

When the interests of the nation in an informed citizenry and the demands of the shareholders for ever-increasing profits are at odds, which take priority?

Jay Harris, former publisher of the *San Jose Mercury News*

It was three o'clock one Saturday morning in March 2001, and Jay Harris, a newsman at the pinnacle of his career, was tossing in bed as he pondered quitting the job he loved. Only seven years earlier, at the age of forty-six, Harris had capped a meteoric rise up the corporate ladder of the Knight Ridder newspaper chain to become chairman and publisher of the *San Jose Mercury News*. In the process, he had also become one of the country's most prominent African-American media executives. The staff at the *Mercury News,* already one of the most racially diverse papers in the country, welcomed his arrival, even though his pinstripe suits, button-down shirts, bright suspenders, and hard-nosed style seemed to evoke a Wall Street trader more than a rumpled reporter.

Despite his corporate image, Harris was deeply committed to the social role of the media in society. Having come of age during the turbulent 1960s, he was especially determined to eliminate vestiges of racist coverage by the industry. As an instructor at the Medill School of Journalism in 1978, he had designed the American Society of Newspaper Editors' first newsroom census to track the hiring of minority journalists. Shortly after being appointed executive editor of the *Philadelphia Daily News* in 1985, Harris had convened a private reception at his home with members of the paper's Third World caucus. He personally thanked the caucus members for pressing the paper's management to improve its coverage and hiring of minorities, and he urged them not to let up.[1] Within a few years of his arrival at the *Mercury*, the paper produced an explosive and controversial series by its top investigative reporter, Gary Webb, chronicling how the CIA-backed Nicaraguan Contras had partially financed their guerrilla war by selling crack-cocaine in

America's inner cities, and had thus helped to fuel the 1980s drug epidemic that devastated many black communities.

But Harris had become increasingly dismayed by 2001 at a spreading malady within his own industry—profit mania. That year, Knight Ridder's corporate headquarters ordered him to ramp up profits beyond the enviable 22 to 29 percent levels the *Mercury* had averaged over the past decade. Harris knew the only way to meet such demands from the top was to slash newsroom staffs—to eviscerate his paper's ability to produce good journalism. On March 19, 2001, a few days after that sleepless night, he announced his resignation from the *Mercury*. He then shocked many in the industry by publicly condemning Knight Ridder's continuing cuts. "When the interests of the nation in an informed citizenry and the demands of shareholders for ever-increasing profits are at odds, which takes priority?" he asked in a startling speech a few weeks later at the annual gathering of the American Society of Newspaper Editors. His words were met with enthusiasm from his fellow editors. Finally, one of their own had dared to give voice to their worst fears in such a public forum.[2]

Harris was virtually alone among major media executives back then in peering over the precipice and pointing to the calamitous fall that awaited the industry.[3] Daily newspapers, after all, had been declining in readership for decades, but newspaper chiefs had ignored the trend. They sought instead to build monopolies in their individual markets and gear their publications toward more affluent readers. They went on buying and selling sprees, turning traditional family-owned newspapers into publicly traded corporations and erecting national chains fueled by debt. Many even folded their news operations into huge entertainment conglomerates, then sought to cash in on a new wave of prosperity wrought by sheer size. In the few short years between 1994 and 2000, there were 719 transactions that involved the sale of a daily newspaper—this in a country with less than 1,500 dailies. Some papers changed hands three and four times during that period.[4] But none of this frenetic trading displayed any real comprehension of the gathering media revolution represented by the Internet.

Shortly after Harris's resignation, Chris Rabb, a former White House aide under Bill Clinton, launched Afro-Netizen, one of the first successful Internet blogs by an African-American. Rabb happened to be the great-great-grandson of John H. Murphy, the founder of the Baltimore *Afro-American* newspaper, and he was a member of the newspaper company's board of directors. But he, too, grew frustrated during the late 1990s as he watched the venerable black newspaper refusing to embrace the technological revolution in media. At one point, he started collecting news items he considered important and emailing them to friends, and was shocked when his email list grew almost overnight to more than 10,000 people. He then transformed the list into a blog, Afro-Netizen, and by its second year of operation it became so popular that his was one of only forty blogs credentialed to cover the Democratic Party's national convention in Boston.

A few years later, two African-American social activists, James Rucker, a software engineer who had worked for a time with MoveOn.org, and Van Jones, a San Francisco environmental attorney, launched a new web-based advocacy organization for the black community. Rucker and Jones, angry at the federal government's failure to aid the victims of Hurricane Katrina in New Orleans, called their site ColorOfChange.org. It quickly filled a gaping void by providing a national voice to challenge racial injustices that commercial newspapers and more established white-owned websites were simply ignoring. When law enforcement in Jena, Louisiana, for example, filed attempted murder charges against six African-American high school students in 2006, ColorOfChange spearheaded a national campaign to challenge the prosecutions as a modern-day racial lynching. The black students were charged with severely beating a white student following a series of racial conflicts at a local high school, among which had been an attempt to intimidate black students by the hanging of a noose in the school courtyard. Rucker's website quickly turned Jena into a national cause. It raised more than $275,000 to pay for the students' legal fees, gathered more than 320,000 signatures to a letter calling on the state's governor to drop the charges, and helped mobilize thousands of people to march in Jena in support of the students, in a campaign that galvanized the attention of the major television networks.[5]

The Harris resignation, along with the emergence of Afro-Netizen, ColorOfChange and other online organizations, symbolizes the two principal trends for the American news media in the early twenty-first century. The first is the startling decline of Old Media (newspapers, television, and radio) and the parallel collapse of the advertiser-financed model of journalism that has held sway for more than 150 years. The second is the emergence of thousands of citizen journalists on the Internet—a movement that harks back to the early days of newspapers and ham radio. Both trends, moreover, have occurred just as the nation's white population is on the verge of turning into a minority.

We explore in this final chapter the ramifications of these trends on the delivery and content of news to local communities and people of color. Has the digital revolution ignited a parallel social revolution in which every citizen can now become a publisher, as some claim? Or is cyberspace already evolving, like the telegraph, radio, and cable before it, into just another way for entrenched power groups to exercise greater vigilance and more sophisticated control over the mass of their populations? Will the new medium finally achieve racial diversity in the flow of information, circumventing and undermining the power of the media conglomerates that arose in the late twentieth century? Or are we heading toward a de facto apartheid system in the US, where a white minority controls the production of news in both the old and new media? To answer these questions adequately, we will need to delve in part into an esoteric area: federal telecommunications policy.

Washington lawmakers have adopted a series of decisions since the 1960s that made possible the most powerful communications medium in history—the Internet. There was no one seminal moment in that process. Rather, government policy evolved through a long-running series of debates and decisions in Congress, at the FCC, and in the courts. Those debates were reminiscent of the numerous nineteenth-century battles in Congress that produced our early postal system (see Chapter 2). As with the postal system, the telegraph, and the radio, the government played a key role in subsidizing the research and development of the Internet. The American people, in other words, made substantial investments through our taxes in the information superhighway. In a reflection of that investment, government policy initially fostered a highly decentralized and open architecture for that highway; it sought, in other words, a democratic and autonomous Internet. But now that the medium has matured and offers enormous commercial potential, huge battles keep erupting over the character and degree of federal regulation, and over how open the new medium should remain.

The citizen media reform movement that rebuffed the FCC's deregulation of Old Media less than a decade ago (see Chapter 16) has increasingly turned its attention to cyberspace. The movement's key leaders argue that the Internet's original non-discriminatory and open architecture must be preserved if the nation wants to maintain a robust, diverse and democratic press, if we are to achieve the widest possible dissemination of knowledge, as its founders believed was essential to preserving democracy. Key business groups and their allies in government think otherwise. Their aim is to centralize the new system, as was done with the other technologies like the telegraph and radio, to ensure private control of the "pipes" and navigation tools through which all content on the Internet must travel.

Meanwhile, the dominant center of the US media has shifted noticeably during the past few years from the traditional companies that create content (newspapers, book publishers, broadcasters, and movie producers) to those that control the networks or online operating systems (telecom and cable companies, and smart phone makers like Apple). Cablevision's purchase of *Newsday* and Comcast's acquisition of NBC/Universal/Telemundo are just two recent manifestations of that shift.

The pivotal mass communications issue facing the American people today is whether to permit a few private companies to gain effective control of the means of transmission over the Internet. The opposing camps on this issue are best exemplified today in the most important Washington policy debate that the average American has never heard of—the battle over "net neutrality." Quite simply, "net neutrality" means that Internet service providers (ISPs) should be prohibited from blocking, discriminating against, or degrading access to the content and applications a consumer chooses online. At first glance, this may seem like an arcane debate among computer geeks, yet it has rapidly become the main dividing line between advocates of a decentralized and democratic media system and those seeking greater centralization and control. We examine in this chapter not only this key battle over net neutrality, but a handful of related issues that will determine how local communities and the country's non-white populations receive their news in the future.

The Collapse of Old Media in the Twenty-First Century

For more than 200 years, newspapers were the main source of news to the US public. Even as successive waves of technology transformed our media system, and even though more people received their news from radio and television by the middle of the twentieth century, newspapers remained the primary source of information for the entire nation. This was especially true when it came to local events. The reason for this was simple: on any given day, the average metropolitan daily newspaper boasted more full-time reporters than all other media outlets in a city combined. That paper could assign full-time staff members to specific beats, such as public schools, City Hall, police, labor, environment, health, the state capital, investigative teams, high school sports—even one reporter for each professional sports teams in town, and so on. Those reporters accumulated so much in-depth knowledge about their beats and produced such a wealth of information in their articles that radio and TV stations, unable to duplicate their research, usually resorted to bare-bones recitations of what had first appeared in the daily papers.

Radio and TV, in other words, offered snapshots of news to a broader audience, but daily papers, even as they declined in circulation, remained the fountainhead of our country's news and information system. Along with magazines, they were also the main providers of in-depth stories about societal trends.

In 1940, when the US population barely surpassed 140 million, there were 1,900 daily papers being published in the country. Today, only about 1,400 dailies remain, even though the population has more than doubled in the intervening years. While total newspaper circulation did not begin falling until 1990, it was largely because the surviving papers managed to establish monopolies in their towns, and thus sell more copies to their growing populations. Still, the overall market penetration of printed dailies—the percentage of Americans who regularly read newspapers—has been plummeting steadily since 1950, from about 380 copies sold per 100,000 Americans to about 150 today, according to a recent study by Robert McChesney.[6]

When Jay Harris walked away from the *San Jose Mercury News* in 2001, the newspaper industry was still basking in extraordinary profits. Average operating margins had soared from 14.8 percent in 1990 to an astonishing 21.5 percent by 2000. That year, *Fortune* listed the publishing and printing industry as having the eleventh-highest profit rate out of forty-eight major industries. "The old line in the newspaper industry is that a bad year was earning a 21 percent profit margin," one newspaper analyst has noted.[7]

How was this possible, given the extraordinary erosion of its readership? *Columbia Journalism Review* ascribed the publishers' "long winning streak" to the combination of a strong economy and the monopoly status of most dailies. Being a monopoly allowed the average metropolitan paper to tailor its shrinking circulation to the most affluent readers in its community. It could then charge higher rates to its advertisers, who provided the overwhelming share of the paper's revenues. Another way to maintain such astronomical profit levels was through massive reductions of labor costs. In 2008, the McClatchy chain registered a 21 percent profit margin while cutting one-third of its workforce; the Gannett chain boasted an 18 percent profit while eliminating 3,000 jobs.

As with all goldmines, the good fortune eventually ran out—but too many publishers, blindly assuming it would last forever, neglected to build up cash reserves to withstand inevitable economic downturns. Instead, many took on more debt in a mad rush to swallow up smaller competitors. When the nation's subprime mortgage crisis that began in 2006 exploded in the following years into a Great Recession, newspaper ad revenues went into free-fall. Circulation declined nationwide by nearly 5 percent during a six-month period in 2008, with big-city dailies the hardest hit. The *Chicago Tribune*'s circulation fell by 7.7 percent; the *Boston Globe*'s by 10.1 percent; the *Philadelphia Inquirer*'s by 11 percent. The following year, things got even worse. Circulation plummeted another 10.6 percent nationwide from that of the previous six months. The *San Francisco Chronicle* lost an astounding 25.8 percent of its readers, the Newark *Star-Ledger* and *Dallas Morning News* 22 percent each.[8] Since 2000, newspaper circulation has shriveled by an astounding 25.6 percent.[9]

The big chains suddenly found themselves with mountains of debt and evaporating profit margins. From 2005 to 2010, several of the most powerful chains disappeared or collapsed into bankruptcy.[10] Papers that managed to survive did so by slashing news staffs even further—among them the *New York Times*, *Washington Post*, and *Boston Globe*—or by closing some of their properties. The E. W. Scripps Company, for instance, closed both the 150-year-old *Rocky Mountain News* and the eighty-six-year-old *Albuquerque Tribune*. The Gannett Company shuttered the 139-year-old *Tucson Citizen*. No one knows for sure how many reporting jobs have been lost. According to ASNE, daily newspapers have cut 25 percent of their full-time newsroom workforce since 2001—about 15,000 reporters and editors—leaving an estimated 41,000 still working at dailies in 2010, the lowest level since the mid 1970s. But the ASNE Census covers less than 70 percent of the country's 1,400 dailies, and does not bother to count layoffs or buyouts at more than 6,000 weekly newspapers in the country. In just the past few years, for example, the once-iconic *Village Voice*, now owned by a chain operator of alternative weeklies, dismissed such legendary writers as Nat Hentoff, James Ridgeway, and Wayne Barrett. The Project for Excellence in Journalism recently reported that 11,000 journalists lost their jobs just in 2008 and 2009. Others place the losses far higher—as many as 12,000 during 2008 and 24,000 in 2009.[11]

Wall Street and the American Newspaper

How did the newspaper industry go from record profits at the beginning of this century to doom and gloom less than ten years later? According to the most popular current narrative, the Internet is the primary culprit. Commercial websites like Craigslist and Monster.com drained away newspaper ad revenues, while aggregators like Google and Yahoo profited unfairly from using as their own content the news they appropriated from the free websites of daily papers. While some of this is no doubt true, we believe Old Media's crisis was largely a result of self-inflicted wounds. Quite simply, the industry steadily capitulated to an insatiable demand from Wall Street investors for maximum short-term profit.

The average American does not realize that our nation's biggest papers only became publicly traded companies in the 1960s. Until then most dailies were typically owned or controlled by an individual or a family—even the few that were grouped into chains. Since most papers enjoyed a monopoly in their city, they could secure considerable power and wealth for their owners, and those who ran them never had to worry about pleasing an army of absentee shareholders. But gradually the patriarchs of the big publishing families died off, and their descendants began searching for ways to avoid paying higher estate taxes. Wall Street was more than ready to help. Take the Gannett Company, the country's biggest newspaper chain, as an example. Its founder, Frank Gannett, started with one tiny publication in 1906 in Elmira, New York, and over the next few decades he cobbled together a chain of lucrative small-town papers that was headquartered in Rochester. In 1967, ten years after Gannett's death, his successors as heads of the company, Paul Miller and Al Neuharth, issued company stock on Wall Street and began buying up a slew of papers. From 1960 to 1980, a total of fifty-seven publishers sold out to Gannett.[12]

Soon other companies started to emulate Neuharth's model. From 1969 to 1973, ten newspaper companies became publicly traded companies, including the *New York Times*, *Washington Post* and *Times-Mirror*, and by 1977 two-thirds of all papers had become part of a newspaper corporation.[13]

The full effect of this new business model did not become immediately apparent, since many of the original families at first retained nominal control. "In the early stages of this transition we knew the first generation of people who began building the public newspaper companies and laying the foundation for today's concentration of ownership," notes Frank Blethen, the publisher and owner of the *Seattle Times*. "They were experienced newspaper operators, often with news backgrounds. For the most part, they had respect for quality, local journalism, and our public-service stewardship."[14]

Their successors, however, were a different breed. They increasingly insisted that financial performance was paramount, at the expense of journalistic mission. The goal of winning more readers by providing more or better news—a notion that had always been more of an ideal than a reality—was now increasingly abandoned. "In bad times, chain owners convince themselves that less news, less space, fewer journalists, less money spent on reporting is still enough," former *Washington Post* editor Len Downie noted in the midst of the crisis, adding:

> By instinct, no editor is likely to agree, but instinct can be modified. If the editor's personal compensation is closely tied to the paper's overall profitability, he or she can develop a new appreciation for meeting the corporation's financial goals. And editors of chain papers rarely have the autonomy to resist pressures from corporate headquarters. Like it or not, editors generally make the cuts demanded of them.[15]

Meanwhile, radio and television broadcasters who had long enjoyed profit levels even more astounding than newspaper publishers began pursuing similar staff cuts. The number of full-time journalists working in commercial radio and television newsrooms has been sharply reduced in recent years, though cable television has spawned more "news" networks, such as CNN, Fox News, ESPN, MSNBC, Headline News, Bloomberg News, and CNBC. An estimated 1,600 local television newsroom jobs were lost in 2008 and 2009, with many companies increasingly relying on part-time correspondents to provide their content. McChesney has estimated that the workforce in broadcast radio and television news dropped from about 0.15 per 100,000 population in 1982 to 0.09 in 2008.[16]

The Decline of Racial Integration in Newsrooms

One of the little-noted victims of Old Media's collapse has been racial integration in the newsroom. While the country's Hispanic and non-white

Table 17.1 % Minority Population in the US and on Daily Newspaper Staffs*

	In US	In US daily newspaper employment
1980	20.2	4.89
1990	24.8	7.86
2000	29.3	11.85
2010	35	13.26

*Includes black, Asian, Native American, and Hispanic populations. *Sources*: US Census Bureau, "United States—Race and Hispanic Origin 1790–1990" and "Overview of Race and Hispanic Origin 2000," both available at www.census.gov.

population has continued to skyrocket, surpassing 35 percent of the US population in 2010, only 13 percent of professional employees at daily newspapers are Hispanic or from racial minorities. In 2009, the number of those from minorities in daily newspapers shrank to just 5,500—800 fewer than the previous year, and the lowest since 1993.[17]

If you compare the increase in the country's minority population over the past few decades to that of daily newspapers, it becomes apparent that the rate of racial integration in US newsrooms has slowed steadily, especially between 2000 and 2010 (see Table 17.1).

The rate of increase in the overall minority population has been about 20 percent each decade since 1980. Minority employment in newsrooms, on the other hand, jumped by 60 percent in the 1980s, by 50 percent in the 1990s, but by only 12 percent since 2000.

Even highly successful efforts at racial diversity have been stymied by Old Media's economic crisis. In 2003 and 2004, for instance, the National Association of Hispanic Journalists, Latino community leaders in Denver, and the local *Rocky Mountain News*, an E. W. Scripps newspaper, launched an innovative partnership called the Parity Project to hire more Latino journalists and to improve coverage of Hispanics in Denver. In a few short years the paper more than doubled the number of Latinos on its staff, and won plaudits from Denver's Hispanic leaders for the changes in its coverage. Top Scripps executives like Mike Phillips, the head of the chain's news division, and John Temple, the editor and publisher of the *Rocky Mountain News*, devoted considerable time and energy to eradicating racial bias in reporting. Temple even hired the *Rocky*'s first Native American reporter—an act of enormous symbolic importance given that paper's notorious anti-Indian prejudice and its horrific role in the Sand Creek Massacre of 1864 (see Chapter 9).

The Parity Project's success sparked similar efforts between NAHJ and other media companies in more than two-dozen cities. But when Scripps' corporate headquarters closed the 150-year-old *Rocky* in 2009, the company not only ceded Denver's newspaper market to the monopoly control of the *Denver Post*, it also abruptly cancelled the gains the Parity Project had achieved in that city. By then, Phillips, the chain's forceful advocate for racial diversity, had retired, while Temple subsequently left the chain.[18]

The stagnating pace of racial integration in newsrooms has had a direct effect on how people of color are portrayed in the media. In 2009, the Pew Research Center for the People and the Press and the Project for Excellence in Journalism studied the content of news reports from fifty-five major US news outlets over a six-month period. What they discovered was astounding. Even though African-Americans, Latinos, and Asians made up an estimated 32 percent of the US population, only 7.5 percent of more than 34,000 news reports made a "substantial reference" to one or another of the three minority groups. Hispanics, for example, were mentioned in just 2.9 percent of the reports, though they made up 15.8 percent of the population, with more than half of the "Hispanic" reports centered on two storylines: the nomination and confirmation battle over Supreme Court Justice Sonia Sotomayor (39 percent) and the Mexican drug war (13 percent).[19]

A separate and even bigger Pew Research Center study, in 2010, found that media coverage of minorities was even more abysmal during the first full year of Barack Obama's presidency. Only 3.4 percent of more than 67,000 national news reports that Pew reviewed between February 2009 and February 2010 gave "significant" mention to African-Americans (1.9 percent), Asian-Americans (0.2 percent) or Hispanics (1.3 percent). Three storylines represented more than 40 percent of all the stories that significantly mentioned African-Americans: the arrest of Harvard professor Henry Louis Gates (19.4 percent), the Obama presidency (17.6 percent), and the death of Michael Jackson (5.7 percent).[20]

In contrast, very little attention has been devoted in the media to examining major stories that would provide a more nuanced view of the lives of people of color in the US: the disproportionate impact, for instance, that the home mortgage crisis has had on the family assets of African-Americans and Hispanics, or the sharply rising number of Latinos serving in the US armed forces.

At the same time, it must be recognized that many media companies are today more sensitive to the industry's historic role in perpetuating racial bias. Several major newspapers have issued formal public apologies for their coverage. The *Tallahassee Democrat* apologized in May 2006 for not covering the city's bus boycott following the arrest of Rosa Parks in Montgomery, Alabama, in 1955. "Leaders in that journey toward equality should have been able to expect support in ending segregation from the local daily newspaper, the *Tallahassee Democrat*," the paper wrote. "They could not."

The *Charlotte Observer* and the Raleigh *News & Observer* apologized in November 2006 for their role in the 1898 riots in Wilmington, North

Carolina (see Chapter 10), that resulted in the death of more than sixty black residents and the first overthrow of a local government in our nation's history.

That same year, the Waco *Tribune-Herald* in Texas apologized for the role of its predecessor paper in the lynching of Jesse Washington, a seventeen-year-old African-American who was arrested and accused of killing his employer's wife in 1916.[21] "We recognize that such violence is part of this city's legacy," the paper stated. "We are sorry any time the rule of passion rises above the rule of law. We regret the role that journalists of that era may have played in either inciting passions or failing to deplore the mob violence."[22]

The Takeover of Spanish-Language Media

For a short while during the last decade, the big fad at many newspaper firms was creating new Spanish-language publications. The Tribune Company launched *Hoy* newspapers in New York, Chicago and Los Angeles in 2004; Belo and Knight Ridder launched competing papers in the Dallas–Fort Worth area, *Al Dia* and *La Estrella*, that same year. New York's *Daily News* created *El Daily News*, while scores of other English-language dailies launched weekly Spanish-language supplements.

Unfortunately, all of these efforts were hampered from the start by flawed strategies. Even though they initially led to modest increases in the hiring of Latino reporters, the new publications were typically launched with skeletal editorial budgets, their reporters and editors relegated to lower salaries and benefits than their counterparts on the paper's English-language side. The Spanish-language publications thus became second-class enclaves within their newsrooms.

Advertising departments were usually the prime advocates for the new papers, and since company executives expected them to turn a quick profit, they often urged those in charge of editorial content to fill their pages with celebrity and lifestyle coverage, and discouraged them from tackling controversial issues. They became geared more toward exploiting the Latino "market" than informing Latino readers. Some papers even out-sourced the writing of their Spanish-language news content to low-wage firms across the border in Mexico.

In 2005, for instance, the *San Jose Mercury News* closed its nine-year-old Spanish-language weekly, *Nuevo Mundo*. The paper's parent company, Knight Ridder, then replaced *Nuevo Mundo* with a new Spanish-language weekly, *Fronteras de la Noticia*, that used a novel outsourcing strategy. A year-old publication that was then appearing in fourteen US markets, *Fronteras* offered mostly non-local news and features, with only two pages of local copy set aside for each of its cities. But even that scant local news was made up of English-language articles from the *Mercury* that had been "out-

sourced for translation to a company in Mexico," with the layout then sent
back digitally to California, noted industry watchdog *Columbia Journalism
Review*.[23]

As you might expect, such cheaply produced papers failed to stir much
reader loyalty. Their founders then summarily folded them, thus quickly
extinguishing the "Spanish paper craze." But by then the damage was done.
The sudden influx of Anglo capital transformed the Spanish-language newspaper industry almost overnight. What had been until then a loose network
of Latino family-owned businesses, each with deep ties to its local community, quickly became a market dominated by outside Anglo owners.

None of the surviving Spanish-language dailies in the United States
today are owned or controlled by Latinos. Even the most prestigious, such
as *El Diario/La Prensa* and *La Opinión*, are run by non-Hispanic investors
and executives. ImpreMedia, which acquired *La Opinión* and New York's
Hoy from the Tribune Company, and purchased *El Diario* separately, has
emerged as the largest publisher of Spanish-language dailies in the country,
with the Lozano family, former owners of *La Opinión*, holding a minority
share. Founded by Canadian entrepreneur John Paton in 2003, ImpreMedia
is a joint venture of three private equity firms—ACON Investments, Clarity
Partners, and Halyard Capital—with the specific aim of "consolidating the
Spanish-language newspaper sector."[24]

The Seeds of the Internet

At the turn of the new century, Old Media companies enjoyed such unparalleled profits that many owners could not feel the ground shifting under
them. Their reliance on local newspaper monopolies and on big-city television oligopolies, along with their enormous dependence on advertising
as their main source of revenue, left even the biggest firms unprepared to
cope with the digital revolution—most especially the expansion of broadband Internet usage by millions of Americans. The federal government, of
course, played an essential role in the development of the Internet, as it had
done with so many other breakthroughs in communications, including the
original postal system. Those who advocate a cyberspace run entirely by the
private market prefer not to dwell on those formative years, but we would
do well to review the initial visions of those Internet pioneers.

In 1958, following the Soviet Union's launch of *Sputnik*, President
Eisenhower created the Advanced Research Projects Agency (ARPA),
designed to reduce what was perceived to be a Russian technological advantage over the United States. The frenzied atmosphere of the Cold War soon
gave way not only to an arms race and a space race, but to a computer technology race as well. ARPA was housed within the Defense Department (its
name later changing to DARPA).

The first generation of computer scientists at places like MIT, UCLA, and Stanford received ARPA funding to conduct independent research aimed at developing networks of computer networks.[25] One of those early researchers, Paul Baran of the Rand Institute, concluded that AT&T's long-distance lines, which supplied both the civilian and military communications infrastructure, were too centralized and were incapable of transferring large amounts of information rapidly. The company's executives, Baran recalled years later, had long denied vulnerabilities within their network. "Their claims of invincibility were based upon distortions of fact, concealed weaknesses, and statements phrased in the common public relations style of the 1950s and '60s," Baran later noted.[26]

In a 1964 study, *On Distributed Communications*, Baran proposed a network of unmanned nodes that would all act as routers transferring information to other nodes in a "redundant" fashion, so as to overcome the disabling of any particular node. He also developed a more flexible means for computers to communicate with each other by breaking down data into digitized information packets, or electronic postcards. These packets would travel along different transmission paths on the network and be reassembled when they reached their final destination—a process called packet switching.[27]

The Defense Department asked AT&T executives to build the new distributed network using packet-switching technology, but they refused to do so. Ma Bell, as the company came to be known, had no interest in creating an open, autonomous system that might undermine the grand communication monopoly it had controlled for decades.[28]

The Rise of Ma Bell

To understand how a single company managed to acquire such colossal power—so much that the federal government finally decided in 1980s to dismantle it—we must briefly retrace the birth and evolution of the Bell system.

Thanks to the patents Alexander Graham Bell held, the Bell Company established a monopoly in the late nineteenth century over the licensing of telephone service in major US cities. It also acquired its own manufacturing arm, Western Electric, as the exclusive producer of telephone equipment for the new system. Bell then founded AT&T in 1884 to provide long-distance lines to connect cities in the northeast and midwest, thus offering the public a new and more convenient alternative to the expensive telegram service of Western Union (see Chapter 9). However, once Bell's original patents expired, in 1894, hundreds of new companies and citizen telephone cooperatives sprang up, creating a highly competitive and diverse communications marketplace. More than 1,000 such independents had been created by 1902, with telephone service registering a phenomenal 30 percent average

annual growth from 1895 to 1907. Three million phones were in service by
1904, and that number had mushroomed to 7.6 million by 1911. By then,
the United States boasted 67 percent of all telephones in the world. More
importantly, 60 percent of US cities with populations above 5,000 had competing telephone exchanges in 1904. And this extraordinary revolution in
mass communications was not limited to the cities. At least 30 percent of
American farms had telephone service by 1912—almost equal to the overall
35 percent rate among all US households.[29]

Still, the new technology had one terrible flaw: all those competing
phones were not interconnected. A person on one company's system could
not talk with someone in the same town using another system. AT&T's
answer was to eliminate all competition by buying the smaller companies
or denying them access to its long-distance lines. That strategy, coming as
it did at the tail-end of the antitrust era, provoked a flurry of lawsuits from
competitors. Several states, fed up with Ma Bell's arrogance, began passing
their own laws to regulate telephone service. Congress even considered for
a time nationalizing all long-distance lines.

Ma Bell started to alter its strategy after financier J. P. Morgan won control
of the company in 1907 and installed Theodore Vail, a former Bell officer, as
the new chief executive. Morgan and Vail embarked on a sophisticated effort
to form alliances with those firms willing to join the AT&T network. Vail
proposed to the federal government a vision of AT&T as a natural monopoly or regulated public utility—one that could ensure telephone access for
all. Ma Bell's desire for a single, centralized and closed model of communications was best summed up in Vail's favorite phrase: "One system, one policy,
universal service."

But after AT&T purchased a small Oregon telephone company in 1912,
the US attorney in Portland filed an antitrust lawsuit. The Justice Department then warned that AT&T's control of Western Union, which it had
purchased in 1909, was in possible violation of the Sherman Anti-Trust Act.
Unlike J. P. Morgan, Vail was keenly attuned to the public mood, and was
open to compromise; so after Morgan's death, in March 1913, he negotiated
a deal with the Justice Department. Under the arrangement, known as the
Kingsbury Commitment, AT&T agreed to sell off Western Union, to cease
for nearly ten years all efforts to buy up any more independents, and to allow
competitors to connect to the company's long-distance lines.

Vail's model thus prevailed. In exchange for achieving low-cost universal
service, lawmakers created a regulated monopoly in phone service, with the
federal government setting rates that guaranteed AT&T comfortable profits.
The AT&T network effectively became the backbone of the nation's telephone system, with the Bell Company eventually also re-establishing its
dominant position in local phone service in the major cities. For the next
seventy years, AT&T wielded unprecedented influence over the nation's

communications system. During the early years of radio, for instance, AT&T's lines made possible the development of national radio networks (see Chapter 11). By the 1970s, Ma Bell had become the largest corporation in the world.

Throughout that period, however, the company faced numerous challenges to its dominance, both from government regulators and from new technologies. Several technological advances in particular would have a big impact on the company's future and on the development of the Internet.

Out on the Range: AT&T's War Against the Carterfone

In the early 1950s, Thomas Carter, a crusty Texas cattle-rancher, wanted to solve a nagging problem: how to communicate with the outside world while managing his herd on the range. Carter kept tinkering around until he developed an acoustic coupling device that enabled him to connect a telephone handset to a radio transceiver. With his contraption, which he called the "Carterfone," he could make and receive phone calls while out on horseback. It worked so well that he decided to produce it for commercial use. Within a few years he had sold 3,500 Carterfones, mostly to oil-field workers in Texas. "We just showed up at oil company shows and started selling," he later recalled. "I just didn't believe anyone I wasn't harming had the right to tell me I couldn't be in business."[30]

"Anyone" was AT&T, which immediately objected.[31]

An obscure prohibition against "foreign" attachments to the phone network had previously been inserted into FCC policy at AT&T's request. But Carter was not about to back down. He decided to take on "Ma Bell" single-handedly by suing it in federal court and claiming a violation of the Sherman Anti-Trust Act. Company executives dragged him through more than ten years of legal battles, eventually forcing him to sell his ranch and home just to pay his legal fees. But in 1968, just as the case was about to go to trial, the FCC reversed its position and backed Carter by lifting its ban on "foreign devices." The agency's majority opinion was written by Commissioner Nicholas Johnson, the young one-time Iowa farmer and university professor who by then had already made a name for himself as the most liberal commissioner in the agency's history (see Chapter 16). Johnson's Carterfone decision sparked a new era in the manufacture of home telecommunications devices, among them the fax and answering machine, and it ultimately led to the development of the telephone modem and other peripherals that, when connected to phone lines, would become crucial to the development of the Internet.[32]

Telephones and Computers: The FCC's Computer Inquiries

Between 1966 and 1986, the FCC fashioned a triad of regulations that laid the basis for the Internet revolution. The agency gave this effort the deceptively prosaic name of Computer Inquiries, but the process signaled an intense and far-reaching effort by the federal government to grapple with what would become one of the fundamental policy questions of modern communications: how to address the convergence of the nation's old communications infrastructure of phone lines with the computer revolution.

AT&T's long-distance lines had been reliably providing Americans with instantaneous voice communication for nearly a century. Throughout that time Ma Bell had remained a government-regulated monopoly, its powerful executives repeatedly stifling innovation and doggedly defending the company's centralized network. But now computer scientists were developing powerful mainframe computers that could communicate over telephone lines with each other and with humans stationed at rudimentary endpoint terminals. This merging of phone lines and computer networks, the scientists predicted, was about to unleash a new era of innovative services, an explosion of knowledge and information for the general public, a huge expansion of commerce, and greater efficiencies in management. What exactly did this mean for the old information order? Computer networks, after all, were still dependent on the existing AT&T lines to transmit their information. The Communications Act of 1934 authorized the government to regulate common carriers of interstate phone and telegraph messages, but what did that mean for data services that traveled over the same phone lines?

Such questions formed the heart of the Computer Inquiries, the first stage of which lasted from 1966 to 1971 and was known as "Computer I." The agency decided to continue regulating the backbone of the nation's communications infrastructure: long-distance phone lines involved in what it called "pure communication." At the same time, it opted to promote innovation and economic growth by leaving to market competition all "data processing," which it defined as computer terminals receiving and changing the information they received through a phone line from a network.[33]

Ma Bell was free to use its computers to route "pure communication"— i.e. any voice and message communication that flowed unchanged through its network; but if it wanted to sell data-processing services it would need to create a separate subsidiary, with separate finances, separate workforces, and separate equipment, and it would have to pay the same rates to use its phone lines as other data-processing companies. So while the FCC chose not to regulate the emerging computer networks, it nonetheless played a pivotal role in their development by fostering an open, competitive and non-discriminatory system.[34]

A new stage in the computer revolution soon forced the FCC to review its decision. In 1969, scientists at UCLA and Stanford Research Institute working with the Defense Department's Advanced Research Projects Administration (DARPA) established the first two nodes of a new network of networks. By the end of the year, the University of California, Santa Barbara, and the University of Utah were connected to the network. They called it ARPANET and they gave its first public demonstration in 1972. Several other universities and defense contractors soon established links to ARPANET, though access was limited to computer scientists and other technical users at those institutions.

Meanwhile microcomputers started to come of age. By the late 1970s personal machines like the Apple I, TRS-80, and Commodore PET were becoming affordable to the middle class, and thousands of people began using dial-up modems to exchange emails and transmit documents. Suddenly, notes computer historian Robert Cannon, "there was intelligence at both ends of the line [not just with giant mainframes], and distributed computing had been born."[35]

The FCC now had to decide how to classify these different sets of computers that were using the same government-regulated phone lines. Thus arose "Computer II," which lasted from 1976 to 1980 and ended with the agency reinforcing and refining the policy it had adopted in "Computer I." The nation's communications infrastructure would continue to remain a neutral or open platform, and it would still be divided into two main parts, one regulated by government and the other unregulated. But the definition of the two parts of the system now changed. Henceforth, there would be regulated "basic services," which would include both the physical lines and some computer services that involved transmitting information, and there would be a separate and unregulated layer superimposed over it, to be known as "enhanced services." That second layer eventually encompassed a wide range of new competitive networking tools, including email, voice mail, newsgroups, the World Wide Web, fax store-and-forward, and audio text information services.[36]

Those who provided "enhanced services" had to be structurally separate from those who provided "basic services," the FCC ruled. It also prohibited common carriers—the phone companies—from bundling and selling their own equipment as part of their basic service. Such equipment included a variety of machines the public could use to connect to the phone lines: telephones, modems, fax machines, and other peripherals, all generally labeled Customer Premises Equipment (or CPE). The FCC thus ensured that neither local phone monopolies nor AT&T would create a bottleneck in the system by becoming sole suppliers of the hardware used to connect to it. The new policy unleashed a new industry of independent manufacturers of phone equipment, and led to a surge in innovative products.[37]

Shortly after "Computer II," the Justice Department ended its long-running antitrust case against Ma Bell by forcing the breakup of the Bell system. As part of the settlement, the government allowed AT&T to keep its long-distance lines, but forced the company to divest its local phone system in 1984 and divide it into several independent regional Bell companies, each of which became a dominant telephone service provider in its own geographical area. A federal judge subsequently overturned a key aspect of the FCC's rule that prevented the regional Bell companies from offering data as well as voice services.

In the aftermath of the AT&T breakup, the FCC was forced to redraw its rules once again in "Computer III," a process that did not conclude until 1986. This time the agency allowed the new regional phone companies to enter the data-service market, but it insisted that they had to fashion their phone systems so that any data-service competitor could use the phone lines on the same terms and conditions the phone company offered to its own data-service provider. The policy sparked a boom in public and commercial use of the Internet. The first commercial Internet service provider (ISP) was established in 1989, the World Wide Web began operation in 1991, and both Congress and the White House went online in the early 1990s. By 1998, 7,000 independent ISPs were operating in North America, and a vibrant, competitive market was in place.[38]

The Move to Privatize the Internet's Backbone

While the FCC grappled with how to preserve an open and competitive system for transmitting computer information over the phone lines, the White House and Congress attempted to solve a parallel problem: Who would build and operate the physical backbone of the nation's twenty-first-century "information superhighway" over which that data would travel? Fiber-optic lines, coaxial cable lines, and even wireless technology, which depended on the public airwaves, all offered potentially greater capacity and speed for transmitting voice, text, and even video than did the old thin copper AT&T wires that had long been the mainstay of the nation's telephone system.

By the early 1980s, ARPANET had grown to a network of about 200 mainframe computer networks, most of them located at major universities. The network, however, was still largely funded by the Defense Department, and was highly limited in access. At the same time, the National Science Foundation had begun subsidizing regional computer networks at universities. In the mid 1980s, the NSF contracted with several private companies to build six new supercomputer centers to serve as a high-speed backbone that connected the old ARPANET to various federal agencies, thus establishing the basic architecture of what we now know as the Internet. NSFNET became operational in 1987, and that year it officially replaced ARPANET. It quickly exploded in size. From just 200 networks and 1,000 hosts in 1985, it mushroomed to 11,000 networks and 2 million hosts by 1992. But while it provided access to a much larger number of people, NSFNET remained a largely government-funded project, one that was specifically limited to research and educational uses.[39]

Several of the key developers of ARPANET and NSFNET, joined by powerful leaders in both major political parties, began advocating that the government turn over to the private sector not only the transmitting of data, but the very backbone of the Internet itself. In 1989, a report by President George H. W. Bush's Office of Science and Technology urged "the deployment of the [third stage of the Internet that] will include a specific, structured process resulting in transition of the network from a government operation to a commercial service."[40] Shortly afterward, Congress passed the High Performance Computing Act of 1991. Al Gore, the Democratic senator from Tennessee and future presidential candidate, was the primary sponsor of that bill. It authorized more than $3.2 billion in federal funds over the next five years for the creation of an Internet that would be "designed, developed, and operated in a manner which ... will encourage the establishment of privately operated high-speed commercial networks."

Thus both Democrats and Republicans in Congress had joined together by the early 1990s to hand two decades of public investment in the Internet's backbone over to the private sector. The government's dramatic change in policy, however, still left in place some key federal regulations over the commercial companies that rapidly assumed control of the backbone.[41]

After the Telecom Act: The Fight to Control the Means of Transmission

We have already described how the Telecommunications Act of 1996 touched off a new stampede for consolidation in the broadcast media (see Chapter 16). But when it came to the Internet, the Act initially appeared to foster a more democratic system. It incorporated, for instance, the principles of competition and non-discrimination in telecommunications services, and it maintained the separation between those services and "information services" that the FCC had first established with its Computer Inquiries.[42]

The new law did not succeed, however, in preserving that separation during the rapid migration of Internet customers from dial-up modems to broadband. While in 2000 only 2 percent of US households had broadband access, seven years later that figure had soared to an astounding 60 percent. Once they realized the enormous potential of this new market, the major cable and telecom companies initiated a fierce lobbying campaign to prevent the competition and non-discrimination rules from applying to broadband. In 2002 they successfully pressured President Bush's first FCC chairman,

Michael Powell, to declare cable Internet service an information service rather than a telecommunication service, thus deregulating the broadband industry, freeing major providers from any legal obligation to allow competitors to use their lines to offer broadband services.[43]

Shortly afterward, a small Internet service provider in southern California named Brand X challenged that FCC decision in federal court. The company's president, Jim Pickrell, was a UCLA graduate who had launched the firm out of his Santa Monica home in 1994 to provide low-cost broadband Internet service. At first, Brand X relied primarily on dial-up DSL lines it leased from the phone companies, but when Pickrell sought also to rent local cable lines, he was rebuffed. His suit argued that because the cable company had a monopoly franchise to use local public streets for its coaxial lines, it was actually a common carrier providing telecommunications service and should thus be subject to the Communication Act's non-discrimination provision.[44]

In 2005 the Supreme Court rejected Pickrell's argument and backed both the FCC and Bush Justice Department. In a six-to-three decision authored by Justice Clarence Thomas, the Court ruled that the FCC had the jurisdictional authority to redefine broadband from a "telecommunications service" to an "information service," which allowed carriers to operate closed broadband networks. The Brand X ruling dealt a major setback to those who argued that the Internet's infrastructure must remain open and non-discriminatory. Soon afterward, the FCC told telephone companies they no longer had to allow competitors to use their DSL lines to offer broadband services. DSL would also be regulated as an "information" instead of a "telecommunication" service.[45]

The effect of both the Supreme Court and FCC decisions on the Internet service market was unmistakable. It wiped away thousands of independent ISPs that could not make the transition from dial-up to the broadband market and eliminated any incentive for giant companies like AT&T, Comcast, Verizon, and Time Warner to make their service more affordable. Today, cable and telephone companies control 97 percent of the residential broadband market, with AT&T and Comcast alone accounting for 42 percent of all customers. Meanwhile, our nation's broadband penetration and affordability has fallen shamefully behind many industrialized countries even though this was the birthplace of the Internet. In 2000, the US ranked fifth in broadband penetration worldwide, but by 2008 it had plummeted to twenty-second.[46]

The elimination of a competitive market in ISPs soon emboldened the emerging oligopoly of broadband providers to charge even higher prices to those using their lines, and also to control the public's access to content and applications. Telecom and cable executives have repeatedly proclaimed their intention to create a tiered and unequal Internet system, with those wanting their data to travel at faster speed being charged higher rates. As Ed Whitcare, the former CEO of AT&T, said in 2005:

> What they [Internet upstarts like Google] would like to do is to use my pipes free ... But I ain't going to let them do that because we have spent this capital and we have to have a return on it. So there's going to have to be some mechanism for these people who use these pipes to pay for the portion they're using. Why should they be allowed to use my pipes?[47]

But no one uses AT&T's pipes for free. Everyone, including online companies, pays for the bandwidth they use. Instead, the phone and cable companies want to control the public's ability to access content online in a way that protects their legacy businesses from competition. The carriers are concerned, for example, that customers could become less willing to keep paying high cable rates for TV services if they're able to watch more video online. In addition, the cable and telecom providers want to control the speed of delivery of video to customers, and to direct where Internet users go. As far back as 1998, for instance, AT&T devised plans to steer customers toward merchants that partnered with its @Home media.

Another way major broadband providers want to further monetize Internet access while limiting competition is to roll out tiered pricing for broadband usage. In 2008, for instance, Time Warner Cable began tiered pricing in Beaumont, Texas, then expanded it to San Antonio and Rochester, New York, the following year. The plan offered rates of $15 a month for a 1 gigabyte (GB) service, and from $22.95 to $54.90 per month for 5 to 40 GB, while charging $2 for every GB per month above that. Since a gigabyte equals about three hours of online video, frequent users of popular technologies such as AppleTV, Netflix, Xbox Live, and PlayStation 3 could thus find themselves facing huge overage charges.

"Watch one high-def episode of *Lost* online, and you're over the limit," said S. Derek Turner, the research director for Free Press. "By putting the cost of Internet video at such a premium, Time Warner is obviously trying to ensure that consumers continue to subscribe to the company's cable television service."[48] After public interest advocates protested and convinced New York's powerful US Senator Chuck Schumer and other politicians to condemn the plan, Time Warner pulled back, saying that it would instead explore other ways of regulating customer usage.[49]

Transforming the Digital Divide

Civil Rights leaders and some Internet experts have warned for several decades that the nation's persistent class and racial inequities were being replicated in cyberspace. But not everyone initially saw this "digital divide" as a major concern. President George W. Bush's first FCC chairman, Michael Powell, lampooned the concept shortly after assuming his post in 2001:

> I think the term ["digital divide"] sometimes is dangerous in the sense that it suggests that the minute a new and innovative technology is introduced in the market, there is a divide unless it is equitably distributed among every part of society, and that is just an unreal understanding of an American capitalist system ... I think there's a Mercedes Benz divide, I'd like one, but I can't afford it ... I'm not meaning to be completely flip about this—I think it's an important social issue—it shouldn't be used to justify the notion of, essentially, the socialization of deployment of infrastructure.[50]

Despite Powell's view, the digital divide has already had enormous consequences. Much as young African-Americans and Hispanics were denied opportunities to train in radio and television as those mediums initially developed, a similar pattern occurred in the early decades of the Internet. No one today, for instance, denies the importance of broadband access. But while the Obama administration made a commitment to expanding broadband services to underserved rural areas, the paramount issue when it comes to the digital divide is the huge number of households in the urban areas who are not yet *subscribing* to broadband. An estimated 96 percent of all households in the US have access to broadband, but just 69 percent of white households actually subscribe. That figure falls to 59 percent for African-Americans and 49 percent for Latinos. Meanwhile, broadband is deployed in only 10 percent of tribal lands. For too many families, the cost of broadband service is prohibitive. More than 93 percent of households earning over $75,000 have broadband, while only 52 percent of those earning less than $50,000 do, and only 40 percent of those earning under $20,000 do. Some simply lack digital literacy, while others do not yet understand the critical importance of being connected to a high-speed Internet service.[51]

The 2009 Federal Recovery Act called on the FCC to create a National Broadband Plan to ensure all households had affordable broadband access. But the nearly 400-page plan, released in March 2010, has been criticized by the public interest community for failing to take on the broadband industry on the issue of enhancing competition.[52]

Harvard University's Berkman Center for Internet and Society examined for the FCC the broadband Internet policy of countries around the world. It found that countries with robust broadband competition like Japan and South Korea had "open access rules" that forced carriers to allow competitors to use their networks to offer services. In those countries, broadband cost less, was faster, and was more widely deployed. The study also found the United States, which deregulated the broadband industry during the George W. Bush administration, was only "a middle-of-the-pack performer."[53]

The FCC ignored the Berkman Center report in its National Broadband Plan. Instead, FCC Chairman Julius Genachowski placed a great deal of hope in the idea that the emerging wireless industry would spur competition.[54]

The Obama Presidency and the Future of Net Neutrality

Few people imagined that cyberspace would quickly replicate the same racial disparities in ownership and employment of news professionals that existed during the heyday of newspapers, radio, and television. The election of Barack Obama seemed at first to herald significant progress in this regard. The Obama campaign, after all, was the first national political movement to harness the Internet to achieve victory. In doing so, it repeatedly bypassed the mainstream media and spoke directly to the public.[55]

"Through the Internet, people became excited about our campaign and they started to organize and meet and set up campaign activities and events and rallies," Obama noted a year after his election. "And it really ended up creating the kind of bottom-up movement that allowed us to do very well."[56] In effect, his campaign echoed a strategy previously employed by other populist Democrats at key junctures in US history. In 1828, as we have seen, Andrew Jackson adroitly used the rise of mass-circulation newspapers to catapult himself to victory (see Chapter 3). Nearly a hundred years later, Franklin D. Roosevelt made masterful use of radio to overcome the hammerlock the Republican Party held with newspaper publishers (see Chapter 14). John F. Kennedy subsequently utilized the power of television to spread his message against a more seasoned but less telegenic Richard Nixon in the presidential debates of 1960. Obama followed in their tracks, using a new medium to circumvent established power centers.

Perhaps because of those experiences, Obama pledged unflinching support throughout his campaign for the principle of net neutrality, and reiterated that position repeatedly after entering the White House. When Obama's FCC chairman, Julius Genachowski, announced in October 2009 a new rule-making procedure for the Internet, he made clear the administration's intention to codify the principle of net neutrality into law. Genachowski's initial proposal would have been, in effect, an extension of prior FCC efforts to safeguard non-discrimination in data services—a principle that goes back to the Computer Inquiries.

The cable and telecom companies responded with a fierce campaign to derail net neutrality regulations. Companies like AT&T, Comcast and industry trade groups employed more than 500 lobbyists and spent close to $75 million during the first nine months of 2009. Before we analyze the impact of that lobbying effort, we must first summarize some of the progress people of color had already achieved under a relatively open Internet.[57]

The Browning of the Internet

Thousands of African-Americans, Latinos, Asians, and Native Americans are using the Internet today to spotlight events and problems in their communities that the dominant commercial media continue to ignore. Many have become netroots citizen journalists and activists in the grand tradition of dissident reporting pioneered by John Russwurm, Ida B. Wells, Francisco Martinez, Jovita Idar, and Ng Poon Chew, and of the great political radio DJs like Pedro González and Georgie Woods. Bloggers like Marisa Trevino, founder of LatinaLista, and Pam Spaulding, publisher of the award-winning Pam's House Blend, have effectively used their blogs to provide a voice to people of color and the lesbian and gay community. Unfortunately, even the most successful have so far received scant attention from the mainstream media, and they have garnered little support from philanthropic foundations and private venture funds.[58]

We have already mentioned how James Rucker and ColorOfChange.org had an immediate nationwide impact with its campaign to defend the Jena Six. Rucker subsequently unnerved the black political establishment in 2007 by calling on the Congressional Black Caucus to ditch plans to sponsor a Democratic presidential debate on Rupert Murdoch's Fox News Channel. Citing the cable network's history of insensitive coverage of race, Rucker's group appealed to leading presidential contenders John Edwards, Hillary Clinton, and Barack Obama to withdraw from the scheduled debate. When the candidates agreed to do so, they embarrassed the Black Caucus, which had refused to pull its sponsorship, and forced Fox to cancel the event.[59]

ColorOfChange.org soon grew to more than 600,000 members. In 2009, the group targeted Fox News host Glenn Beck for calling President Obama a racist. It launched a campaign to get advertisers to pull their ads from Beck's show. By the end of the year, close to 300,000 people had signed a petition against Beck, and more than eighty companies had agreed to cancel their ads. Beck's popularity among die-hard conservatives eventually declined during the Obama years as the right-wing attacked campaigns made popular by MoveOn.org and ColorOfChange and other direct grassroots organizing efforts that sought to hold the media accountable.

Rucker went on to sponsor a Latino-focused counterpart, Presente. org, to reignite the energy of the historic 2006 immigration marches that saw millions of Latinos protesting for immigration reform in more than a hundred US cities. Salvadoran-American activist Roberto Lovato was one of the leaders of Presente.org when the organization launched Basta Dobbs, a web-based campaign to pressure CNN to fire Lou Dobbs for the anti-immigrant hysteria he had stirred up on his program for years. Other national Latino Civil Rights groups initiated a parallel boycott campaign against the Dobbs show. A widely watched video that BastaDobbs created on YouTube accused CNN of hypocrisy for producing the documentary "Latino in America" while still employing Dobbs. In November 2009, Dobbs suddenly resigned, and Presente.org immediately proclaimed it a victory for their movement.[60]

Another startling success of the brown blogger movement was the 2007 campaign against the Public Broadcasting System and one of the nation's most acclaimed documentary filmmakers, Ken Burns. In the spring of that year, Burns was preparing to air a much-publicized fourteen-hour series for PBS on the history of World War II. He and PBS suddenly confronted a grassroots opposition movement organized by Maggie Rivas Rodriguez, a journalism professor and former reporter for the *Dallas Morning News*. Rivas had for years headed up an oral history project at the University of Texas at Austin on Latino veterans of World War II. When she discovered that the Burns documentary would showcase the experiences of forty US veterans of that war but had failed to include a single Latino who served in the conflict, Rivas became deeply concerned. Her concern turned to anger when she contacted Burns and his production company and they refused her request to discuss the matter with her, and after she learned that PBS planned to launch the series during National Hispanic Heritage month.

Rivas responded by organizing the Defend the Honor campaign, a coalition of Latino veterans and community leaders. Relying largely on Internet postings and a string of community meetings and resolutions by Latino veterans' organizations, the group demanded that Burns re-edit the final version of his film to reflect contributions of as many as 500,000 Hispanic veterans to the war effort. PBS officials and Burns acknowledged their oversight but claimed it had been unintentional. They refused to violate what they called the "artistic integrity" of the film by making any changes under outside pressure. The public uproar and media attention over the controversy grew so intense, however, that both the network and Burns eventually agreed to add interviews with Latino soldiers—but only as part of a bizarre prelude to the film's opening episode. PBS then sought to placate widespread discontent in the Hispanic community by rushing into production several Latino-themed projects that had languished at the network for years.

Perhaps the most influential Latino political blogger in the country is someone not widely known for his Hispanic heritage. Markos Moulitsas Zúniga was born in Chicago in 1971 to a Salvadoran mother, and spent part of his childhood in El Salvador during that country's civil war. His family later moved back to the States, where Moulitsas served for a time in the army and then enrolled at Northern Illinois University. An anti-Mexican article he read in the *Northern Star*, his college paper, prompted him to write a rebuttal. He then joined the paper's staff, and eventually became its editor. Soon after he founded the Hispanic-Latino News Service, a website featuring stories about the country's growing Hispanic population.

In 2002, Moulitsas launched a new website as a way to vent his frustration over Republican victories in the mid-term elections. He called it Daily Kos, and it quickly became a must-read blog for many liberal Democrats, much as the Drudge Report is a premiere online destination for conservative Republicans. Joe Trippi, campaign manager for presidential candidate Howard Dean, subsequently hired Moulitsas as a technology adviser for the Dean campaign. Moulitsas continued to produce his blog while working for the Dean campaign, though he disclosed the political tie to his readers. In 2006 he coauthored *Crashing the Gate: Netroots, Grassroots and the Rise of People-Powered Politics*, in which he outlined his vision for how technology can empower a new citizen movement. That same year he started the annual conference known as Netroots Nation. With more than 2,000 participants, the conference now attracts participation from major national political figures.[61]

The websites represented at the Netroots conference, however, have come under increasing fire from bloggers of color for their lack of diversity in staffing and content. Much like the labor press of the 1830s and the muckrakers of the early twentieth century, the new Internet progressive press appears to have replicated some of the patterns of exclusion and neglect that characterized the old legacy media system.

In 2007, ASNE began counting newspaper employees who worked for its paper's online operations in its annual newsrooms census. It found that people of color accounted for 16 percent of online news employees. The group's 2010 survey found that journalists of color made up close to 20 percent of the 1,333 online workforce in 2009. That same year, ASNE also asked twenty-eight online news organizations to take part for the first time in its annual diversity survey, but only seven online news organizations agreed to do so. Among the largest online news organizations that did not respond were Yahoo!, the Huffington Post, Talking Points Memo, and the Daily Beast.[62]

Many journalists of color are deeply troubled by the severe lack of diversity at influential online news sites, but so far they have been unsure about the best way to make these new media ventures fulfill their responsibility to integrate their operations. Veteran journalist Richard Prince, who covers diversity in the media industry for the Maynard Institute for Journalism Education, commented:

> Having made my way in journalism at a time when news media either saw the need for affirmative action or were made to see it by community pressure, lawsuits or cases before the EEOC, I have no problem believing that the world of online journalism may have to feel the same heat in order to make progress.[63]

Cable Television's Public Access Channels and Media Diversity

When Congress passed the 1984 Cable Act, one of the law's key provisions authorized local franchising authorities to require that cable operators set aside channels for public, educational, or governmental ("PEG") use. Since the cable companies were using public streets for their wires, they had to provide a public benefit as well. They also had to finance PEG studios and the production costs of those channels, usually through a monthly public access fee per subscriber.[64]

Public-access channels came to represent a major attempt to democratize the media. For nearly three decades they have allowed ordinary citizens and local communities to produce their own programming without having to worry about attracting advertisers. PEGs became the equivalent of the Public Broadcasting System for over-the-air radio and television—except that their funding came from cable revenues instead of from the government. Originally there was much talk of their potential to utilize interactive technology to foster greater citizen involvement. A local government or community meeting, for example, could be viewed by residents sitting at home, and one day in the future those residents would also be able to send in questions and comments over their cable systems.

In practice, many local public-access channels became platforms for an eclectic and at times bizarre world of low-budget shows, often depending more on the perseverance of their producers in landing and keeping a time slot than on the quality of the program or its popularity with the public. Nonetheless, PEGs evolved into an important training ground in media for many young people, and provided a way for hundreds of thousands of ordinary Americans to have their voices heard. At its best, public-access TV offered unique forums for airing controversial issues, it brought light to the concerns of minority groups, and it sponsored important debates on local political elections that the commercial media routinely ignored. In some cases, as with the airing of alternative national news shows like *Democracy Now!* and Laura Flanders' *Grit TV*, and documentaries on international issues by Free Speech TV, public-access channels have kept alive the long tradition of dissident voices in the US news media. In 1999, for instance, Pacifica's *Democracy Now!* provided two hours of live coverage each morning on the massive public protests that paralyzed the city of Seattle, Washington, during a ministerial meeting of the World Trade Organization. By contrast, all the major commercial news organizations in the US were caught unprepared for the enormous turnout, the thousands of arrests, and the collapse of the world conference.

Despite such cases, the major cable companies have sought in recent years to grab back the valuable space that public-access channels occupy on their systems in order to use it for their own commercial purposes. The cable companies have resisted expanding the number of PEG channels even as the overall capacity of their systems has soared. When Time Warner began operating its cable franchise in Manhattan in 1983, for instance, PEG channels represented four of the original seventeen channels on the system—more than 20 percent. By 1993, Time Warner's Manhattan franchise had nine PEG channels out of a total of seventy-seven—less than 15 percent. Today, Time Warner in Manhattan boasts more than 500 channels, not including its hundreds of individual subscriber channels, yet the number of PEG channels on the system is less than ten—and only four of those are for public access.[65]

In other parts of the country, cable providers have sought to exile their few remaining PEGs to the least desirable channels on their systems. In today's digital world, channels function much like real estate, with location being paramount. The lower your number, the more valuable your channel, since viewers routinely surf with their remote from the lowest channel to the highest.

In Washington, Missouri, Charter Communications virtually disappeared its public-access channels, according to one recent article:

> Looking for your local town government meeting on Charter Cable? Missouri residents may have to send out a search party to find their local [PEG] channels, because Charter has moved them way, way up the dial for some of their subscribers. A Lewis & Clark–like expedition by Washington, Missouri councilman Guy Midkiff found his in the channel 900s range. [sic]

According to a blog post by the councilman,

> PEG programming has been given the heave-ho to stratospheric 900 plus channel … Apparently if your TV is more than 4 years old, you can't even get the PEG channels without a $5 per month additional fee and a converter box. What happened to them? Seems the state of Missouri took over the regulation of cable franchises back in 2007. What that meant was that local communities—like Washington—lost all leverage to demand cable hold up the longstanding bargain of making PEG programming available on the low channels. This was part of the original basic package of programming.[66]

Missouri is among some thirty states that have abolished the authority for local municipalities to negotiate franchise agreements with cable providers. In those states, franchise negotiations have been reserved for a statewide agency, thus weakening the ability of local communities to control what kind of service a cable company provides.

But perhaps the worst example of a cable company abusing public access is AT&T, which has been rapidly rolling out its U-verse video service in recent years. As a recent article in the *Chicago Tribune* noted,

> [P]ublic, educational and government programming [on U-verse] is consigned to a digital ghetto that makes public programming hard to use. Viewers must go to the dreaded Channel 99, and from there navigate toward the towns they want. While U-verse subscribers can digitally record up to four programs at once, they cannot digitally record from Channel 99. They can't even plan their viewing, because the digital guide available for all other U-verse channels is not available for public, educational, and government programming.[67]

Cable companies argue that, since the digital revolution now makes it possible for Americans to produce their own media over the Internet from a home computer, the original need that public access programming was meant to fill no longer exists. Public media advocates strongly dispute that claim. "Cable television viewership is still orders of magnitude higher than online, and the discrepancy is even higher in low-income communities," says Tony Shawcross, the director of Denver Open Media.[68]

Public access has also historically exhibited far greater racial and ethnic diversity in management and employment than have the commercial media. In most major cities, for instance, the boards of directors of public-access stations boast significant numbers of minorities and women.

The Failures of the Civil Rights Establishment in the Digital Era

We have already described how Civil Rights leaders spearheaded an unprecedented media reform movement during the 1970s that forced major media companies to dismantle pervasive practices of racial bias (see Chapter 16). They pressured the federal government for a more democratic and non-discriminatory media system, and secured better access to news and information for non-white communities. Unfortunately, many of our nation's leading Civil Rights organizations today are actively backing efforts by the largest telecom and cable companies to roll back those gains in communications policy.

The NAACP, League of United Latin American Citizens, and the Urban League—all of which used to rail against the injustices of the white media—can more often be found these days lobbying Congress and the FCC in support of more centralized control of our media system by major cable and phone companies. They routinely oppose the critical issue of net neutrality, and refuse to speak out against the dismantling of public-access channels by cable video providers.

This embrace of megamedia by established Civil Rights organizations represents the most startling and tragic setback in the modern history of the fight for social justice in the news industry.

But the transformation did not occur overnight. Companies like AT&T, Verizon, Comcast, and Time Warner have spent years cultivating close relationships with the main national Civil Rights organizations. They have hired scores of well-connected staffers of color to lobby these organizations, and have showered campaign contributions on key minority members of Congress. Most importantly, they have donated millions of dollars to support the work of the Civil Rights groups, bankrolling their annual conferences, financing scholarships for minority youth, even underwriting the general operations of several groups. AT&T's CEO, for example, chaired the NAACP's centennial campaign, the goal of which was to raise $5 million by 2010. LULAC, meanwhile, has received millions from AT&T to pay for the group's technology centers across the country. Comcast, Verizon and AT&T are all members of the National Council of La Raza's corporate advisory board.[69]

That financial support has no doubt played a role in convincing those groups to back the agenda of telecom and cable companies in Washington.[70] While major Civil Rights groups, for instance, have always been vocal opponents of Old Media consolidation because it stunted ownership opportunities for minorities, when it comes to the telecommunications industry they have backed some of the largest mergers in recent years, including the Verizon-MCI and AT&T–Bell South mergers of 2005/06. The AT&T–Bell South merger would "provide Hispanic consumers new educational opportunities through high speed broadband connections and better economic opportunities for Hispanic small businesses seeking to compete against larger better funded competitors," LULAC President Rosa Rosales claimed in a letter to the FCC.[71] The Urban League in Columbia, South Carolina, said it would be an "injustice" if the FCC didn't support the AT&T merger after the company pledged "to bring broadband service to every residential unit" in its service area.

Yet these mergers and others have actually ended up reducing the number of broadband competitors. They have also allowed cable companies to move toward tiered services. As we have already noted, the US has slipped from fifth among the world's nations in broadband penetration in 2000 to twenty-second by 2008.[72]

In 2007 Robb Topolski, an Internet expert, discovered that Comcast was violating the FCC's Internet Policy statement of 2005 by blocking him from using a file-sharing program to distribute legally his favorite barbershop quartet music. Topolski posted the results of a test he conducted online proving what the giant cable company was doing. The Associated Press then launched its own investigation and concluded that Topolski was right.

Comcast had prevented the news agency's reporters from using BitTorrent, a popular file-sharing program, to download a version of the King James Bible. The company eventually admitted that it interfered with certain applications, supposedly to relieve congestion on its network. It claimed, however, that it had not violated the FCC's Internet Policy statement, since that policy allowed for "reasonable network management." Public interest groups Free Press and Public Knowledge filed a complaint with the FCC that Comcast had violated the Commission's Internet Policy statement. The FCC agreed and ordered Comcast to end its discriminatory practices.[73]

Several national minority organizations immediately jumped to Comcast's defense, including the National Black Chamber of Commerce, the Labor Council for Latin American Advancement, the National Black Justice Coalition, the National Council of Women's Organizations, and the National Congress of Black Women.[74] "Given that about 70 percent of Latinos lack broadband service at home, the idea of some users taking P2P "sharing" to absurd levels and driving up the cost for all is galling," commented José Marquez, president of the Latinos in Information Science's and Technology Association. "These self-styled champions of 'equality' are actually defending the right of a minority of big users who clog the Internet for everyone else. That sounds like 'net inequality' to me."[75]

Backers of the cable and telecom providers thus echoed the claims of the companies that they can only increase broadband access in minority communities by requiring those who "hog bandwidth" to pay more for that privilege. No one denies that ISPs should have the right to manage their networks reasonably to eliminate occasional congestion, but the methods they use should be transparent and should be geared to preserving an open Internet. Unfortunately, in today's marketplace, with so little competition between broadband suppliers, the key players have little incentive to upgrade their networks continually. The nation's Internet backbone is fully capable of carrying almost limitless traffic, yet the ISPs who control the "last mile" connecting that backbone to the homes and personal devices of consumers can easily create artificial scarcity. They can then claim congestion and institute a pay-for-play system, where a wealthy company like Amazon or Disney can pay more to have its content uploaded faster than a small start-up firm; or they can favor some content, apportioning slower speeds to competitors like Hulu or Netflix than to their own movies. A perfect historical parallel can be found in the early decades of the telegraph, when Western Union used its monopoly position to offer priority telegraph services for those businesses willing to pay for them (see Chapter 9).

Moreover, many of today's major broadband providers have increasingly moved to deliver and market their own content on their pipes, much of it video. This dual role as both programmer and gatekeeper for transmission means the biggest Internet providers, Comcast and

Time Warner, are in direct competition for bandwidth use with small programmers.

Broadband service has already become more important to cable and telecom companies than their original legacy systems of video and phone service. In early 2010, Landel Hobbs, the CEO of Time Warner, admitted as much when he told an investors' conference in San Francisco that broadband had already replaced traditional video service as his company's anchor product. "Consumers like it so much that we have the ability to increase pricing around high-speed data," Hobbs said.

When FCC Chairman Genachowski moved to adopt net neutrality rules in 2009, the major cable and telecom companies fought back feverishly. "The 'net neutrality' rules as reported will jeopardize the very goals supported by the Obama administration that every American have access to high-speed Internet services no matter where they live or their economic circumstance," said AT&T's senior vice president, Jim Cicconi. A former deputy chief of staff to President George H. W. Bush and former special assistant to President Reagan, Ciconni warned: "That goal can't be met with rules that halt private investment in broadband infrastructure. And the jobs associated with that investment will be lost at a time when the country can least afford it."[76]

To the surprise of many in Washington, the companies won considerable backing within the Democratic Party to oppose Genachowski's efforts. A total of seventy-two House Democrats warned in a letter to the FCC that they were "suspicious" of the need for net neutrality rules. A third of the representatives signing the letter were from the Congressional Black and Hispanic Caucuses.[77]

In addition, many local and national Civil Rights groups, such as the NAACP, LULAC, and the National Urban League, filed comments reciting many of the industry's arguments: net neutrality would result in the loss of jobs and investment; the FCC should focus on implementing its National Broadband Plan to erase the digital divide rather than passing rules that might have the unintended consequence of widening it; and net neutrality was a solution in search of a problem.[78]

The result has been a growing public rift over net neutrality between the established Civil Rights groups on the one hand and minority journalists and progressive organizations of color on the other. The National Association of Hispanic Journalists, UNITY: Journalists of Color, the Center for Media Justice, the National Hispanic Media Coalition and ColorOfChange. org all supported net neutrality and opposed further centralization of power among both major media and telecom companies. So have many grassroots organizations in cities around the country. More than 60,000 members of ColorofChange.org signed the group's online petition urging the FCC to promote an open Internet. Meanwhile, James Rucker has blasted the established Civil Rights organizations' claim on several occasions that net neutrality would widen the digital divide.[79] "In other words, if Comcast—which already earns 80 percent profit margins on its broadband services—can increase its profits under a system without Net Neutrality, then they'll all of a sudden invest in our communities?" James Rucker wrote. "You don't have to be a historian or economist to know that this type of trickle-down economics never works and has always failed communities of color."[80] "It's ... time for a new generation of civil right leaders to be heard on this issue," said Malkia Cyril, the executive director of the Center for Media Justice. "We know that digital inclusion and closing the digital divide is only possible with affordable, accessible, and open high speed networks. True representation of people of color and the poor demands that the civil rights community fight for this as vigorously as we fight for equal access in our schools, services, and in the broader society."[81]

In December 2010, Genachowski and the Democratic majority on the FCC suddenly reversed course and sought to carve out a middle ground on net neutrality. They labeled the new rules an "Open Internet Order," but scores of critics from both the left and the right of the media policy spectrum blasted the final order. The rules would ban operators of fixed-line Internet services like Comcast and Time Warner from blocking access to sites and applications, but could still allow them to speed up or slow down web traffic, and would be far more lenient to wireless providers like AT&T and Verizon.

The order "leaves wireless users vulnerable to application blocking and discrimination," said a coalition of eighty media reform groups; it uses "unnecessarily broad definitions" and "would create a pay-for-play platform that would destroy today's level playing field." At the same time, Republicans in Congress vowed to defeat the new rules as unnecessary government intervention in the free market, and at least one giant telecom company, Verizon, immediately challenged the rules in federal court, thus ensuring that the fate of net neutrality will remain undecided for the foreseeable future.

The net neutrality debate is the latest manifestation of a fundamental divide that has always existed in America's media system: between those seeking centralized control over the content of news and how it gets transmitted, and those advocating local autonomy and decentralized transmission. In one camp can usually be found those who envision the role of the news media as providing the latest intelligence to an elite, molding the sentiment of the masses, and facilitating commercial exploitation. The other camp has generally been composed of those who favor the media providing Americans of all races and classes with the "widest possible dissemination of knowledge," who welcome the clash of dissident voices and who seek ways for information technology to strengthen democracy. Both camps have produced their share of heroes and villains, and throughout the history of our media system, key figures have at times shifted from one camp to the other. But the trajectories of individual protagonists should not obscure for us the fundamental choice Americans have repeatedly faced between a centralized and a decentralized system of news—or the pivotal role the latter model has played in preserving democracy.

Furthermore, our examination of America's media history provides abundant evidence that the white racial narrative has always been more virulent and exclusionary whenever our information system was most centralized and controlled from the top. Likewise, the nation's news has been more just and inclusive in those periods when its media system was more decentralized and autonomous. From the days of Benjamin Harris and the rebel printers, through the tribulations of José Martí and Ida B. Wells, to the bloggers of the Internet, the grand arc of the American press has been from news for the few and the powerful, to news for all the people.

Acknowledgements

This book had its genesis in a pamphlet Josreph Torres and I coauthored in August of 2004, titled "How Long Must We Wait? The Fight for Racial and Ethnic Equality in the US News Media." Joe was the deputy director at the National Association of Hispanic Journalists at the time, and I was completing a two-year term as the NAHJ's national president. That summer, more than 8,000 African-American, Latino, Asian and Native American journalists were meeting in Washington, DC, for the quadrennial convention of UNITY: Journalists of Color. As the largest gathering of professional journalists in American history, the event drew scores of the media industry's top executives, and since it was being held during a presidential election year, it also attracted major national figures such as President George W. Bush and his Democratic opponent John Kerry, who both spoke and submitted to grilling by the assembled reporters.

Joe and I hastily wrote our pamphlet in the weeks before the convention and we arranged to have a few thousand copies printed with the help of a private donor. By distributing it for free, we hoped to spark much-needed debate among our colleagues, not simply over the usual subject matter of these gatherings—the need for greater diversity in newsroom hiring and for improved coverage of racial minorities—but over the bigger picture that rarely gets discussed: the historic role of the press in spreading racial bias, and how our nation's news media system arrived at its current state.

One of the participants who read it was Jon Funabiki, who was then at the Ford Foundation. For years now, Funabiki has been one of the most influential figures among minority media professionals. He called us a few weeks later to let us know that, if we wanted to expand our pamphlet into a full-fledged book, Ford might be interested in underwriting our research.

Our thanks, therefore, go first to Jon, who urged us to dream big and offered us the resources to do so. Our gratitude, as well, to UNITY, whose board of directors kindly agreed in 2005 to be the sponsoring agent for the Ford grant. But our most enthusiastic champion throughout these seven years has been our editor Andy Hsiao. Even when we repeatedly missed our deadlines and the book's size kept spiraling, Andy never lost faith and never stopped encouraging us. His careful edits and many pointers for organizing the manuscript and smoothing out its weak spots were all invaluable.

We are indebted, as well, to several colleagues and friends, working journalists, media scholars, and media reform activists, who read portions of the manuscript and also provided us with feedback and comments. They include Ernie Sotomayor, Maggie Rivas, Félix Gutíerrez, Albor Ruiz, Federico Subervi, Dan Coughlin, Will Sutton, Jr., Craig Aaron, Andrew Jay Schwartzman, David Sandoval, Ivan Roman, Anna Lopez, Matt Wood, Coriell Wright, Onica Makwakwa. Ernie, in particular, spent so much time laboring over various drafts and provided us such detailed criticism and suggestions on improving the narrative that we have come to regard him as our second editor. The book was immeasurably improved by all of these individuals, though any errors remain ours alone.

Our thanks, also, to our employers, Free Press and the New York *Daily News,* for allowing us the time to complete this project. Our special appreciation to those outstanding figures in public interest journalism who have been such a huge inspiration to us, especially to Rev. Everett C. Parker, of the United Church of Christ, scholar and historian Robert McChesney, and Amy Goodman at *Democracy Now!*

We benefitted, as well, from the help of those unsung heroes of any historical study—the archivists at several libraries around the United States who were extremely generous with their time and with their advice. They include Christian Kelleher and Carmen Sacomani at the Benson Latin American Collection, University of Texas at Austin; Morgan Swan at the Beinicke Rare Book and Manuscript Library at Yale; Spencer Howard and Matt Schaefer at the Herbert Hoover Presidential Library in Ames, Iowa; Mary-Jo Miller of the Nebraska State Historical Society; Daniel Littlefield of Sequoyah National Research Center, University of Arkansas at Little Rock; Laura Schnitker, Chuck Howell, and Michael Henry at the Library of American Broadcasting, University of Maryland, College Park; as well as the staff of the Schomburg Center for Research in Black Culture of the New York Public Library and the staff of the National Archives in Washington, DC.

Our deepest gratitude as well to our researchers Bethsaida George-Rodriguez and Omar Rodriguez, who traveled relentlessly around the country to ferret out archival gems and illustrations from the personal papers of dozens of journalists of color and from scores of old newspapers.

Our agent, Frances Goldin, has always done more than simply represent her authors. For decades she has championed writing as another vehicle to serve the public good.

Finally our love and thanks to our wonderful partners, Sheala Durant and Niurka Alvarez, and to our daughters, Charis Torres and Gabriela González, for putting up with all those countless hours we spent away from home or locked in some office amidst piles of papers and books.

Notes

Introduction

1. Between 1985 and 2005, the believability of local TV news plunged from 85 percent to 62 percent; for newspapers it declined from 84 percent to 64 percent. All major networks experienced similar though less precipitous drops. See Pew Research Center for the People and the Press, "Public More Critical of the Press, But Goodwill Persists," June 26, 2005, available at peoplepress.org/reports/display.php3?ReportID=248.

2. Walter Lippman, *Public Opinion* (New York: Harcourt, Brace & Co., 1922): 81.

3. Ibid.: 83.

4. Anthony Smith, *The Geopolitics of Information: How Western Culture Dominates the World* (New York: Oxford University Press, 1980): 151.

5. Arthur M. Schlesinger, *Prelude to Independence: The Newspaper War on Britain 1764–1776* (New York: Alfred A. Knopf, 1958): 179, 285. Also, Sidney Kobre, *The Development of the Colonial Newspaper* (Peter Smith: Gloucester, Mass., 1960): 125–6.

6. Paul Starr, *The Creation of the Media: Political Origins of Modern Communications* (New York: Basic Books, 2004): 1–7.

7. David Paul Nord, *Communities of Journalism: A History of American Newspapers and Their Readers* (Urbana: University of Illinois Press, 2001): 81.

8. On a typical day in 1832, "the incoming mail at the Washington Post Office contained one tidy packet of letters and twenty-one enormous sacks of newspapers, each of which weighed between 150 and 200 pounds." See Richard John, *Spreading the News: The American Postal System from Franklin to Morse* (Cambridge: Harvard University Press, 1995): 39.

9. Dan Schiller, *Objectivity and the News: The Public and the Rise of Commercial Journalism* (Philadelphia: University of Pennsylvania Press, 1981): 15.

10. Ben Bagdikian, *The Media Monopoly*, first edition 1983 (Boston: Beacon Press, 2000): 3–26; Edward S. Herman and Noam Chomsky, *Manufacturing Consent: The Political Economy of the Mass Media* (New York: Pantheon Books, 1988): 1–35; James Fallows, *Breaking the News: How The Media Undermine American Democracy* (New York: Vintage Books, 1996): 47–73; Robert W. McChesney, *Rich Media, Poor Democracy: Communications Politics in Dubious Times* (New York: New Press, 1999): 16–29; Gene Roberts, Thomas Kunkel and Charles Layton, eds, *Leaving Readers Behind: The Age of Corporate Newspapering*

(Fayetteville: University of Arkansas Press, 2001): 109–56; Leonard Downie Jr and Robert G. Kaiser, *The News About the News: American Journalism in Peril* (New York: Alfred A. Knopf, 2002): 14–29.

11. Robert McChesney, *The Problem of the Media: US Communications Politics in the 21st Century* (New York: Monthly Review Press, 2004): 57–97; Bagdikian, *Media Monopoly*: 18–26.

12. S. Derek Turner and Mark Cooper, "Minority and Female TV Station Ownership in the United States: Current Status, Comparative Statistical Analysis and the Effects of FCC Policy and Media Consolidation," Free Press, 2006, available at www.stopbig-media.com/files/out_of_the_picture.pdf; S. Derek Turner "Off The Dial: Female and Minority Radio Station Ownership in the United States," Free Press, 2007, available at www.freepress.net/files/off_the_dial_summary.pdf.

13. David A. Copeland, *Colonial American Newspapers: Character and Content* (Newark: University of Delaware Press, 1977): 43; John Coward, *The Newspaper Indian: Native American Identity in the Press,* 1820–1890 (University of Illinois Press: Urbana, 1999): 13.

14. "Klan Radio Station Seeks 50,000 Watts," *New York Times*, October 9, 1927. For internal opposition by the Federal Radio Commission, see Department of Commerce, Navigation Service, April 19, 1927, "Records of the Federal Communications Commission Radio Division: Correspondence Relating to Applications for Broadcast licenses, 1928–1932."

15. John Tebbel, *The Media In America* (New York: Thomas Y. Crowell Company, 1974): 361–3.

16. Associated Press v. US, 326 US 1 (1945).

17. Andrew Buni, *Robert L. Vann of The Pittsburg Courier: Politics and Black Journalism* (Pittsburgh: University of Pittsburgh Press, 1974): xi.

18. In compiling those stories, we are indebted to the work of dozens of intrepid scholars of the ethnic press—people like Martin Dann, Frankie Hutton, Donna Halper, Jacqueline Bacon, William Barlow and Brian Ward for the black press; Karl Lo and H.M. Lai for the Asian-American press; John Coward and Mark Trajant for the Native American press; and A. Gabriel Meléndez, Nicolas Kanellos and Felix Gutiérrez for the Latino press.

19. *The Kerner Report: The 1968 Report of the National Advisory Commission on Civil Disorders* (New York: Pantheon Books, 1988): 389.

Chapter 1: "Barbarous Indians" and "Rebellious Negroes"

1. *Publick Ocurrences Both Forreign and Domestick*, September 25, 1690.

2. Frank Luther Mott, *American Journalism, A History:* 1690–1960 (New York: MacMillan, 1968): 9–11; also John Tebbel, *The Media in America* (New York: Thomas Y. Crowell Company, 1974): 12–15.

3. Smith, *Geopolitics of Information*: 34.

4. Elizabeth Eisenstein, *The Printing Revolution in Early Modern Europe* (Cambridge: CUP, 1983): 147.

5. Cited in Steven J. Shaw, "Colonial Newspaper Advertising: A Step Toward Freedom of the Press," *The Business Review* 33: 3 (Autumn 1959): 411.

6. Charles E. Clark, *The Public Prints: The Newspaper in Anglo-American Culture, 1665–1740* (New York: OUP, 1994): 79–81; Shaw, "Colonial Newspaper Advertising": 412–15.

7. William David Sloan and Julie Hedgepeth Williams, *The Early American Press, 1690–1783* (Westport: Greenwood Press, 1994): 5–9; also *Publick Occurrences*, September 25, 1690.

8. Copeland, *Colonial American Newspapers*: 42–5.

9. Ibid.: 44–61.

10. Ibid.: 47, 296.

11. Pete Steffens, "Franklin's Early Attack on Racism: An Essay Against a Massacre of Indians," *Journalism History* 5: 1 (Spring 1978): 8–10.

12. Ibid.: 10–11, 8.

13. Quoted in Clark, *Public Prints*: 93–4.

14. Copeland, *Colonial American Newspapers*: 127.

15. Ibid.: 147, 125.

16. Ibid.: 134.

17. Copeland, *Colonial American Newspapers*: 133; also Ira Berlin and Leslie M. Harris, eds, *Slavery in New York* (New York: W.W. Norton, 2005): 87.

18. Ibid.: 146.

19. Ibid.: 141–2.

20. Alfred McClung Lee, *The Daily Newspaper in America: The Evolution of a Social Instrument* (New York: MacMillan, 1937): 18; Sidney Kobre, *The Development of the Colonial Newspaper* (Gloucester: Peter Smith, 1960): 96–7; Clark, *The Public Prints*: 81–3.

21. Carol Sue Humphrey, *"This Popular Engine": New England Newspapers During the American Revolution, 1775–1789* (Newark: University of Delaware Press, 1992): 71.

22. Edwin G. Burrows and Mike Wallace, *Gotham: A History of New York City to 1898* (New York: OUP, 1999): 153–5; Mott, *American Journalism*: 30–5.

23. Cited in Mott, *American Journalism*: 36–7.

24. Lee, *The Daily Newspaper in America*: 32; Shaw, "Colonial Newspaper Advertising": 419.

25. Ibid.: 409.

26. Mott, *American Journalism*: 52.

27. David A. Copeland, "Fighting for a Continent: Newspaper Coverage of the English and French War for Control of North America, 1754–1760," *Early America Review* (Spring 1997), available at www.earlyamerica.com/review/spring97/newspapers.html.

28. Schlesinger, *Prelude to Independence*: 68.

29. Humphrey, *"This Popular Engine"*: 95.

30. Arthur M. Schlesinger, "The Colonial Newspapers and the Stamp Act," *New England Quarterly* 8: 1 (March 1935): 73.

31. Ibid.: 81.

32. Schlesinger, *Prelude to Independence*: 179.

33. Ibid.: 284.

34. Kobre, *Development of the Colonial Newspaper*: 122.

35. Eric Foner, *Tom Paine and Revolutionary America* (New York: OUP, 1977): 73, 89.

36. Humphrey, *"This Popular Engine"*: 125–7.

37. Ibid.: 137–8.

38. Garry Wills, ed., *The Federalist Papers by Alexander Hamilton, James Madison and John Jay* (New York: Bantam Books, 1982): viii–ix.

Chapter 2: In the Mail

1. Richard R. John, *Spreading the News: The American Postal System from Franklin to Morse* (Cambridge: Harvard University Press, 1995): 37.

2. Ibid.: 25; Richard B. Kielbowicz, *News in the Mail: The Press, Post Office, and Public Information, 1700–1860s* (New York: Greenwood Press, 1989): 1; Paul Starr, *The Creation of the Media: Political Origins of Modern Communication* (New York: Basic Books, 2004): 84–94.

3. Lee, *The Daily Newspaper in America*: 26–8.

4. John, *Spreading the News*: 29–30; Wayne E. Fuller, *The American Mail: Enlarger of the Common Life* (Chicago: University of Chicago Press, 1972): 109; Washington quoted in Dorothy Ganfield Fowler, *Unmailable: Congress and the Post Office* (Athens: University of Georgia Press, 1977): 10.

5. John, *Spreading the News*: 31–7.

6. There were 8,700 postmasters and only 6,300 soldiers in the army. See John, *Spreading the News*: 3.

7. Fuller, *American Mail*: 111–12.

8. Lee, *The Daily Newspaper in America*: 718; Ronald P. Formisano, *The Transformation of Political Culture: Massachusetts Parties, 1790s to 1840s* (New York: OUP, 1983): 16. Slightly different figures—106 papers in 1790, jumping to 1,258 by 1835—are cited in William A. Dill, *Growth of Newspapers in the United States* (Lawrence: Department of Journalism, University of Kansas, 1928): 11. There is general agreement, however, on a stunning increase of papers during this period. For British newspaper numbers, see Starr, *Creation of the Media*: 86.

9. Quoted in David J. Russo, "The Origins of Local News in the U.S. Country Press, 1840s–1870s," *Journalism Monographs* 65 (February 1980): 7.

10. Ibid.: 1.

11. Alexis de Tocqueville, *Democracy in America* (New York: Alfred A. Knopf, 1994 [1835]): 187–8.

12. Mott, *American Journalism*: 202 (footnote).

13. John, *Spreading the News*: 37; Richard B. Kielbowicz, "Origins of the Second-Class Mail Category and the Business of Policymaking, 1863–1879," *Journalism Monographs* 96 (April 1986): 4.

14. Ibid.: 84.

15. Wayne E. Fuller, "The South and the Rural Free Delivery of Mail," *Journal of Southern History* 25: 4 (November 1959): 511–19.

16. Robert V. Remini, *The Election of Andrew Jackson* (Philadelphia: J.B. Lippincott Company, 1963), gives a detailed account of the rise of the Jacksonian press; Sean Wilentz, *The Rise of American Democracy: Jefferson to Lincoln* (New York: W.W. Norton, 2005): 303.

17. Ronald P. Formisano, *Transformation of Political Culture*: 16.

18. De Tocqueville, *Democracy in America*: 188.

19. During the administration of John Quincy Adams from 1824 to 1828, 76 post offices received new postmasters, while during Jackson's first four years in office, 120 changed hands. See Formisano, *Transformation of Political Culture*: 248.

20. Ibid.: 325.

21. The town of Waltham, Massachusetts, for example, quickly changed from an agricultural to an industrial center, and as it did, the number of male taxpayers who owned no property jumped from 48 percent in 1822 to 62 percent by 1850. See Formisano, *Transformation of Political Culture*: 180.

22. Gerald J. Baldasty, "The Press and Politics in the Age of Jackson," *Journalism Monographs*, Association for Education in Journalism and Mass Communication, June 1984: 3; Wilentz, *Rise of American Democracy*: 309–10.

23. Alexander Keysar, *The Right to Vote: The Contested History of Democracy in the United States* (New York: Perseus Books, 2000): 40; Wilentz, *Rise of American Democracy*: 309.

24. For the British newspaper war, see Joel H. Wiener, *The War of the Unstamped: The Movement to Repeal the British Newspaper Tax, 1830–1836* (Ithaca: Cornell University Press, 1969); for Massachusetts labor unrest, see Formisano, *Transformation of Political Culture*: 227; for New York City wealth disparities, see Schiller, *Objectivity and the News*: 20.

25. Schiller, *Objectivity and News*, 45.

26. Sean Wilentz, *Rise of American Democracy*: 281–4; Eswin G. Burrows and Mike Wallace, *Gotham: A History of New York City to 1898* (New York: OUP, 1999): 511–20.

27. Burrows and Wallace, *Gotham*: 518–20.

28. Quoted in Fuller, *American Mail*: 90; see also Fowler, *Unmailable*: 17.

29. For several views on the Charleston mail-burning controversy, see Fuller, *American Mail*: 92–3; Wilentz, *Rise of American Democracy*: 410–12; Fowler, *Unmailable*: 26–31; Susan Wyly-Jones, "The 1835 Anti-Abolition Meetings in the South: A New Look at the Controversy Over the Abolition Postal Campaign," *Civil War History* 47: 4 (December 2001): 289–309.

Chapter 3: Inciting to Riot

1. *National Advocate*, August 3, 1821.

2. Burrows and Wallace, *Gotham*: 514.

3. *New York Enquirer*, November 21, 1826.

4. Anthony Gronowicz, *Race and Class Politics in New York Before the Civil War* (Boston: Northeastern University Press, 1998): 57.

5. Jacqueline Bacon, "The History of Freedom's Journal: A Study in Empowerment and Community," *Journal of African American History* 88: 1 (Winter, 2003): 2.

6. *Morning Courier and New-York Enquirer*, July 4, 1834.

7. Ibid., October 4, 1833.

8. Gronowicz, *Race and Class Politics in New York*: 61. Leonard L. Richards, *"Gentleman of Property and Standing": Anti-Abolition Mobs in Jacksonian America* (New York: OUP, 1970): 32.

9.   Richard A. Schwarzlose, *The Nation's Newsbrokers, Volume I: The Formative Years: from Pre-Telegraph to 1861* (Evanston: Northwestern University Press, 1989): 16.

10.   Henry Mayer, *All on Fire: William Lloyd Garrison and the Abolition of Slavery* (New York: W.W. Norton, 1998): 138.

11.   Burrows and Wallace, *Gotham*: 531–2, 551–2.

12.   *New York Courier and Enquirer*, October 2nd, 1833.

13.   Richards, *"Gentleman of Property and Standing"*: 27–30; Gronowicz, *Race and Class Politics in New York*: 61.

14.   *Morning Courier and New-York Enquirer*, October 4, 1833.

15.   Ibid., October 5, 1833.

16.   Richards, *"Gentlemen of Property and Standing"*: 114–15.

17.   Samuel Ringgold Ward edited the *Farmer and Northern Star* in Cortland, New York. He later continued the paper in Boston as the *Impartial Citizen* (1848), and was later a co-editor of the *Aliened American* (1852–56) in Cleveland, Ohio. In his 1853 autobiography, Ward said the riot of 1834 had been "gathered and sustained by the [city's] leading commercial and political men and journals."

18.   Richards, *"Gentlemen of Property and Standing"*: 113–18; Paul O. Weinbaum, *Mobs and Demagogues: The New York Response to Collective Violence in the Early Nineteenth Century* (Ann Arbor: University of Michigan Press, 1979): 21–35.

19.   *Morning Courier and New-York Enquirer*, July 8, 1834.

20.   *New York Sun*, July 9, 1834.

21.   Joanne Reitano, *The Restless City: A Short History of New York from Colonial Times to the Present* (New York: Routledge, 2006): 45–8.

22.   *Morning Courier and New-York Enquirer*, July 14, 1834.

23.   Richards, *"Gentlemen of Property and Standing"*: 69.

24.   Ibid.: 54.

25.   Mott, *American Journalism*: 203–4; Richards, *"Gentlemen of Property and Standing"*: 71–3.

26.   See David Paul Nord, "The Evangelical Origins of Mass Media In America, 1815-1835," *Journalism Monographs* 88 (May 1984); Mary Hershberger "Mobilizing Women, Anticipating Abolition: The Struggle Against Indian Removal in the 1830s," *Journal of American History* 86: 1 (June 1999): 18–19.

27.   Richards, *"Gentlemen of Property and Standing"*: 15–16.

28.   Ibid.: 86.

29.   Ibid.: 85–92.

30.   Mayer, *All On Fire*: 196–204.

31.   The press reports and details of the Cincinnati incidents are all from Richards, *"Gentlemen of Property and Standing"*: 92–100.

32.   Richards, *"Gentlemen of Property and Standing"*: 150–5.

33.   Gronowicz, *Race and Class Politics in New York*: 61.

34.   Mott, *American Journalism*: 216.

35.   Andie Tucher, *Froth and Scum: Truth, Beauty, Goodness and the Ax Murder in America's First Mass Medium* (Chapel Hill: University of North Carolina Press, 1994): 13–14.

36. New York *Sun*, September 2nd, 1833, cited in Mott, *American Journalism*, 223–4.

37. New York *Sun*, April 4, 1835, cited in James Stanford Bradshaw, "George H. Wisner and the New York *Sun*," *Journalism History* 6: 4 (Winter 1979/80): 118.

38. New York *Sun*, July 2nd, 1834.

39. Lee, *The Daily Newspaper in America*: 190; Mott, *American Journalism*: 220–7.

40. Philadelphia's first penny paper, the *Public Ledger*, was launched in 1836 by Arunah Shepherdson Abell and William M. Swain, both former printers at the *Sun*, and quickly became a spectacular success. Abell then moved south the following year to start the Baltimore *Sun*. See Alexander Saxton "Problems of Class and Race in the Origins of the Mass Circulation Press," *American Quarterly* 36: 2 (Summer 1984): 217; Mott, *American Journalism*: 228.

41. Ibid.: 226–7.

42. Tucher, *Froth and Scum*: 38; Saxton, "Problems of Class and Race": 215. While there have been several detailed studies of the Robinson-Jewett case, our analysis is based on Tucher's marvelous account and on Saxton's comparison of competing press reports.

43. Tucher, *Froth and Scum*: 38–9.

44. Mott, *American Journalism*: 218–20; John Tebbel, *The Media in America* (New York: Thomas Y. Crowell Co., 1974): 172–5.

45. Mott, *American Journalism*: 267–8.

46. Saxton, "Problems of Class and Race": 227. Mott, *American Journalism*: 268–9.

47. Saxton, "Problems of Class and Race": 212.

48. Tucher, *Froth and Scum*: 14.

49. Saxton, "Problems of Class and Race": 227.

50. New York *Sun*, July 8, 1834.

51. Cited in Saxton, "Problems of Class and Race": 232.

52. Interview with Day printed in New York *Sun*, September 2, 1933, quoted in Mott, *American Journalism*: 222–3.

53. Cited in Lauren Kessler, *The Dissident Press: Alternative Journalism in American History* (Beverly Hills: Sage Publications, 1984): 17.

54. Saxton, "Problems of Class and Race": 233.

55. Julia Ward Howe, "A Trip to Cuba," *Atlantic Monthly*, May 1859.

56. New York *Sun*, July 14, 1837, cited in Saxton, "Problems of Class and Race": 230; Tucher, *Froth and Scum*: 16.

57. Saxton, "Problems of Class and Race": 229–31.

58. Cited in Anders Stephanson, *Manifest Destiny: American Expansion and the Empire of Right* (New York: Hill & Wang, 1995): 42. See also Gronowicz, *Race and Class Politics in New York City*: 96–7.

59. Stephanson, *Manifest Destiny*: 44.

60. John M. Coward, *The Newspaper Indian: Native American Identity in the Press, 1820–90* (Urbana: University of Illinois Press, 1999): 57–8.

61. Ibid.: 78–9.

62. Ibid.: 92.

63. Ibid.: 2.

64. New York *Tribune*, September 29, 1854, cited in Andrew Gyory, *Race, Politics and the Chinese Exclusion Act* (Chapel Hill: University of North Carolina Press, 1998): 17.

65. Mott, *American Journalism*: 275.

66. Wilentz, *Rise of American Democracy*: 582–3.

67. Philip Ortego y Gasca and Arnoldo de Léon, eds, *The Tejano Yearbook: 1519–1798: A Selective Chronicle of the Hispanic Presence in Texas* (San Antonio: Caravel Press, 1978): 41.

68. Roy Sylvan Dunn, "The KGC in Texas, 1860–1861," *Southwestern Quarterly Review*, LXX: 4 (April 1967): 550.

69. Carey McWilliams, *North from Mexico: The Spanish-Speaking People of the United States* (New York: Praeger, 1990 [1968]): 124–5.

70. Cited in David Montejano, *Anglos and Mexicans in the Making of Texas, 1836–1986* (Austin: University of Texas Press, 1989): 28.

Chapter 4: A New Democratic Press

1. Despite Varela's amazing career, there is little written in English on his life. We are indebted for our account of his religious and literary career to: Roberto Esquenazi-Mayo, ed., *El Padre Varela: Pensador, Sacerdote, Patriota*, a collection of essays based on a 1988 Library of Congress symposium (Washington, DC: Georgetown University Press, 1990); Carlos Manuel de Céspeda Garcia-Menocal, "Pensamiento del Padre Félix Varela Acerca de La Esclavitud," *Revista Bimestre Cubana* 3: 6 (June 1997), Havana, Cuba.

2. Jacqueline Bacon, "The History of Freedom's Journal," *Journal of African American History* 88: 1 (Winter 2003): 2–5; Craig Steven Wilder, *In the Company of Black Men: The African Influence on African American Culture in New York City* (New York: New York University Press, 2001): 86, 147–9.

3. Elias Boudinot, "An Address to the Whites: Delivered in the First Presbyterian Church on the 26th of May, 1826," cited in James E. Murphy and Sharon Murphy, *Let My People Know: American Indian Journalism, 1828–1978* (Norman: University of Oklahoma Press, 1981): 24.

4. Ibid.: 23–5; Barbara F. Luebke, "Elias Boudinot, Indian Editor: Columns from the Cherokee Phoenix," *Journalism History* 6: 2 (Summer 1979): 1.

5. Gene Roberts and Hank Klibanoff, *The Race Beat: The Press, the Civil Rights Struggle, and the Awakening of a Nation* (New York: Alfred A. Knopf, 2006): 13.

6. *North Star*, January 21, 1848.

7. Carlos E. Castañeda, "The Beginning of Printing in America," *Hispanic American Historical Review* 20: 4 (November 1940): 671–5, provides an excellent summary of the early Mexican printers.

8. Al Hester, "Newspapers and Newspaper Prototypes in Spanish America, 1541–1750," *Journalism History* 6: 3 (Autumn 1979): 73–6. For Lima *hojas volantes*, see Ella Dunbar Temple, *La Gaceta de Lima del Siglo XVIII: Facsimiles de seis ejemplares raros de este periodico* (Lima: Biblioteca de la Sociedad Peruana de Historia, 1965): 5; Nicolás Kanellos and Helvetia Martell, Hispanic Periodicals in the United States, Origins to 1960 (Houston: Arte Público Press, 2000): 3.

Chapter 5: Priests, Mobs, and Know-Nothings

1. A copy of the October 12, 1808 issue of *El Misisipí* (vol. I, no. 10) is held by the Wisconsin Historical Society. The American Antiquarian Society has a photostat copy of the December 10, 1808 (vol. I., no. 27) issue, the original of which is in Seville, Spain, at the Archivo General de las Indias (Papeles de Cuba, Legajo 185). See Raymond R. MacCurdy, *A History and Bibliography of Spanish-Language Newspapers and Magazines in Louisiana 1808–1949* (Albuquerque: University of New Mexico Press, 1951): 8–9.

2. *El Misisipí*, October 12, 1808.

3. In his classic 1937 study, *The Daily Newspaper in America*, for example, Alfred McClung Lee erroneously claimed that only three Spanish-language newspapers were published in the US before 1860. He listed the earliest as appearing in 1839—some thirty years after *El Misisipí*. In his seminal texbook, *American Journalism*, first published in 1941, Frank Luther Mott took note of the various immigrant presses in the US, including French, German, Yiddish, Chinese, Serbian, Russian, and Hungarian newspapers, but did not mention a single Spanish-language newspaper. See Lee, *The Daily Newspaper*: 735; Mott, *American Journalism*: 121, 317, 493–4, 588–9, 623, 730–1.

4. Ibid.: 734.

5. Edward Lee Walraven, "Ambivalent Americans: Selected Spanish-Language Newspapers' Response to Anglo Domination in Texas, 1830–1910," doctoral thesis, (Texas A&M University, August 1999): 247. South Texas scholar Cipriano A. Cárdenas echoes Walraven's concern: "While many public libraries devotedly kept copies of English-language newspapers, such was not the case for Spanish-language periodicals," he concludes. "Consequently, virtually all records of Mexican-American life in Rio Grande Valley, as reflected in their publications, have been lost." See Cipriano A. Cárdenas, "Hispanic Journalism in Brownsville Texas," in Milo Kearney, Anthony Knopp, and Antonio Zavaleta, eds, *Studies in Matamoros and Cameron County History* (Brownsville: University of Texas at Brownsville, 1997): 227.

6. William Darby, *A Geographical Description of the State of Louisiana* (Philadelphia, 1816 [publisher unknown]): 186; Kirsten Silva Gruesz, *Ambassadors of Culture: The Transamerican Origins of Latino Writing* (Princeton: Princeton University Press, 2002): 109.

7. The best overview of the early New Orleans press is still MacCurdy's *A History and Bibliography*.

8. Ibid.: 12–14.

9. Besides *El Misisipí* and *El Mensagero Luisianés*, the early Spanish-language papers were *La Gaceta de Texas* (1813), *El Mexicano* (1813), and *El Telégrafo de las Floridas* (1817). See Nicolás Kanellos and Helvetia Martell, *Hispanic Periodicals in the United States, Origins to 1960: A Brief History and Comprehensive Bibliography* (Houston: Arte Publico Press, 2000): 309.

10. Cited in Félix Varela y Morales, *El Habanero: Papel Político, Científico y Literario* (Miami: Ediciones Universales, 1997): 138.

11. Esquenazi-Mayo, *El Padre Varela*: 59–62.

12. Varela's publications included *The Protestant's Abridger and Annotator* (1830), the country's first ecclesiastical review; the *New York Weekly Register and Catholic Diary* (1833); the

weekly *Catholic Observer* (1836); the *Children's Catholic Magazine* (1838); and *The Catholic Expositor and Literary Magazine* (1841).

13. Juan González, *Harvest of Empire: A History of Latinos in America* (New York: Viking, 2000): 218.

14. *La Patria* had started operating as a tri-weekly in 1846, before turning into a daily.

15. Tom Reilly, "A Spanish Language Voice of Dissent in Antebellum New Orleans," *Louisiana History* XXIII: 4 (Fall 1982): 325–7; Kirsten Silva Gruesz, "Delta *Desterrados:* Antebellum New Orleans and the New World Print Culture," in Jon Smith and Deborah Cohn, eds, *Look Away: The US South in New World Studies* (Durham: Duke University Press, 2004): 58.

16. Gruesz, "Delta *Desterrados*": 59.

17. Reilly, "A Spanish Language Voice of Dissent": 326–8; Gruesz, "Delta *Desterrados*": 58.

18. Gruesz, "Delta *Desterrados*": 62–4.

19. *La Patria*, October 13, 1848, cited and translated in Gruesz, "Delta *Desterrados*": 65.

20. *La Patria*, Aril 2nd, 1846, cited and translated in Gruesz, "Delta *Desterrados*": 69–70.

21. Reilly, "A Spanish Language Voice of Dissent": 328.

22. Ibid.: 329.

23. Keever, Martindale and Weston, *US News Coverage of Racial Minorities: A Sourcebook, 1934–96* (Westport, CT: Greenwood Press, 1997): 148; Reilly, "A Spanish Language Voice of Dissent": 330–1.

24. *La Patria*, June 4, 1846, cited in Gruesz, "Delta *Desterrados*": 61.

25. Reilly, "A Spanish Language Voice of Dissent": 330–5.

26. Ibid.: 329; Gruesz, "Delta *Desterrados*": 60.

27. Reilly, "A Spanish Language Voice of Dissent": 336–7; Gruesz, "Delta *Desterrados*": 65–6.

28. Gruesz, "Delta *Desterrados*": 61.

29. *La Patria*, July 5, 1848, cited and translated in Gruesz, "Delta *Desterrados*": 71–2.

30. For a summary of the views of Washington, Adams, Jefferson and Monroe toward Cuba, see Louis A. Pérez, Jr, *Cuba: Between Reform and Revolution* (New York: OUP, 1995): 108–9.

31. Ibid.: 86.

32. Ibid.: 110–11.

33. Louis A. Pérez, Jr, *Cuba and The United States: Ties of Singular Intimacy* (Athens: University of Georgia Press, 1990): 47; "The Attack on Cárdenas: A Reliable and Authentic Account by Officers Engaged in the Expedition," *Missouri Republican*, June 23, 1850.

34. Cited in Reilly, "A Spanish Language Voice of Dissent": 337.

35. Rodrigo Lazo, *Writing to Cuba: Filibustering and Cuban Exiles in the United States* (Chapel Hill: University of North Carolina Press, 2005): 52. We are indebted to Lazo's penetrating study of mid-nineteenth-century US Cuban newspapers for much of the information in this section.

36. Cited in Reilly, "A Spanish Language Voice of Dissent": 325.

37. MacCurdy, *A History and Bibliography*: 22–3; Reilly, "A Spanish Language Voice of Dissent": 325–6.

38. Kanellos and Martell, *Hispanic Periodicals*: 11, 167, 236.

39. Silvio Torres-Saillant, "Before the Diaspora: Early Dominican Literature in the United States," in *Recovering the US Hispanic Literary Legacy, Vol. III*, ed. Maria Herrera-Sobek and Virginia Sánchez Korrol (Houston: Arte Publico Press, 2000): 250.

40. Lazo, *Writing to Cuba*: 11–12.

41. Ibid.: 53–5; Gruesz, *Ambassadors of Culture*: 145–8.

42. Rodrigo Lazo, "Cirilo Villaverde as TransAmerican Revolutionary Writer," in Herrera-Sobek and Sanchez Korrol, *Recovering the US Hispanic Literary Legacy*: 318.

43. Lazo, *Writing to Cuba*: 12, 75.

44. *La Verdad*, April 27, 1848.

45. "The Handbook of Texas Online," at <tshaonline.org/handbook/online/articles/fcaad.html>.

46. Lazo, *Writing to Cuba*: 74–5.

47. Ibid.: 81.

48. *United States Magazine and Democratic Review* XXVI: CXL (February 1850): 112; Lazo, *Writing to Cuba*: 172–3.

49. Cited in Lazo, *Writing to Cuba*: 107.

50. Cited in ibid.: 83, 106.

51. Kanellos and Martell, *Hispanic Periodicals*: 13.

52. *El Pueblo*, August 20, 1855, cited in Lazo, *Writing to Cuba*: 95.

53. Milo Kearney, *More Studies in Brownsville History* (Brownsville: Pan American University, 1989): 47–8.

54. We are equally indebted for much of the Texas Hispanic newspaper history to Edward Lee Walraven's "Ambivalent Americans."

55. Cited in ibid.: 75.

56. Walraven, "Ambivalent Americans": 76.

57. Walraven, "Ambivalent Americans": 91–2.

58. Walraven, "Ambivalent Americans": 93–4. John Wallace's 1966 study of early Texas newspapers, *Gaceta to Gazatte*, for example, fails to mention that Bangs founded any newspapers in the Rio Grande Valley.

59. Walraven, "Ambivalent Americans": 103.

60. For a detailed analysis of the basic differences between the exile, immigrant and native Hispanic press in the US, see Kanellos and Martell, *Hispanic Periodicals*: 1–116.

61. Ralph A. Wooster, "An Analysis of the Texas Know-Nothings," *Southwestern Historical Quarterly Review* LXX: 3 (January 1967): 416.

62. Cited in Walraven, "Ambivalent Americans": 108.

63. Minetta Altgelt Goyne, *Lone Star and Double Eagle: Civil War Letters of a German-Texas Family* (Fort Worth: Texas Christian University, 1982): 231; *El Bejareño*, February 7, 1855, cited in Walraven, "Ambivalent Americans": 104.

64. Walraven, "Ambivalent Americans": 104.

65. Gruesz, *Ambassadors of Culture*: 152–3.

66. Ibid.: 156–7; Walraven, "Ambivalent Americans": 106.

67. Walraven, "Ambivalent Americans": 106–12; New Orleans *Daily Picayune*, September 8, 1885.

68. A. Gabriel Meléndez, *Spanish-Language Newspapers in New Mexico, 1834–1958* (Tucson: University of Arizona Press, 2005): 15–21.

69. Ibid.: 23.

70. Porter A. Stratton, *The Territorial Press of New Mexico, 1834–1912* (Albuquerque: University of New Mexico Press, 1984): 12–13.

71. Meléndez, *Spanish-Language Newspapers*: 6, 23.

72. Victoria Goff, "Spanish Language Newspapers in California," in Frankie Hutton, ed., *Outsiders in 19th Century Press History* (Bowling Green, Ohio: Bowling Green State University Press, 1995): 59–60, provides her list of those early California papers. See also Kanellos and Martell, *Hispanic Periodicals*: 280–3; Roberto Trevino, "Becoming Mexican-American: The Spanish-Language Press and the Biculturation of California Elites, 1852–1870," Working Paper Series no. 27 (Stanford University Department of History, October 1989).

73. Felix Gutiérrez, "Spanish-Language Media in America: Background, Resources, History," *Journalism History* 4: 2 (Summer 1977): 39.

74. Goff, "Spanish Language Newspapers": 63.

75. *El Clamor Público*, August 28, 1855, cited in Kanellos and Martell, *Hispanic Periodicals*: 89.

76. *El Clamor Público*, August 26, 1856, cited in Kanellos and Martell, *Hispanic Periodicals*: 90.

77. Leonard Pitt, *The Decline of the Californios: A Social History of the Spanish-Speaking Californians, 1846–1890* (Berkeley: University of California Press, 1966): 208.

78. *El Clamor Público*, March 21, 1857, cited in David J. Weber, ed., *Foreigners in Their Native Land: Historical Roots of the Mexican Americans* (Albuquerque: University of New Mexico Press, 1973): 174–6.

79. Ibid.: 176.

80. Gruesz, *Ambassadors of Culture*: 101–4.

81. Rudolfo Acuña, *Occupied America: A History of Chicanos* (New York: HarperCollins, 1988): 122–3.

82. Kanellos and Martell, *Hispanic Periodicals*: 91; Gutiérrez, "Spanish-Language Media in America": 41.

Chapter 6: The Indian War of Words

1. Grant Foreman, *The Five Civilized Tribes* (Norman: University of Oklahoma Press, 1934): vii.

2. Article V of the Hopewell Treaty specified that any US citizen or non-Indian who attempted to settle on Cherokee territory without the tribe's permission "shall forfeit the protection of the United States, and the Indians may punish him or not as they please." "Treaty with the Cherokee: 1785," The Avalon Project at Yale Law School, at <www.yale.edu/lawweb/avalon/ntreaty/chr1785.htm#art5>.

3. Helen Jackson, *A Century of Dishonor* (New York: Indian Head Books, 1994 [1888]): 257–71.

4. James P. Ronda, "'We Have a Country': Race, Geography, and the Invention of Indian Territory," *Journal of the Early Republic* 19: 4 (Winter 1999): 744.

5. John Ehle, *Trail of Tears: The Rise and Fall of the Cherokee Nation* (New York: Anchor Books, 1989): 116–21; Jack Weatherford, *Indian Givers: How the Indians of the Americas Transformed the World* (New York: Fawcett Columbine, 1988): 158.

6. Robert V. Remini, *Andrew Jackson and His Indian Wars* (New York: Viking, 2001): 88–93; Anthony F. C. Wallace, *The Long Bitter Trail: Andrew Jackson and the Indians* (New York: Hill & Wang, 1993): 50.

7. Ehle, *Trail of Tears*: 124–34; Wallace, *Long and Bitter Trail*: 4–13, 50–3; Robert Remini, *The Legacy of Andrew Jackson: Essays on Democracy, Indian Removal and Slavery* (Baton Rouge: Louisiana State University, 1988): 50–8. Ehle and Wallace both sketch unflattering accounts of the speculative machinations and bribery efforts by Jackson to secure control of Indian lands. Remini, however, repeatedly defends Old Hickory's actions as resulting from a higher motive. "It was not greed or racism" that motivated Jackson's land grabs, he asserts, but a desire to assure the young nation's military security by creating an American-controlled buffer against any possible European invasion along the southern coast. (See also Remini, *Andrew Jackson and His Indian Wars*: 85, 180.) While such "national security" concerns were no doubt real, it is equally true that Jackson fervently sought to open those lands up to white settlement, especially slave-based cotton-growing, even at the expense of those Indians who were loyal to the US government. Remini himself notes that, as early as 1816, Jackson declared: "Nothing can promote the wellfare of the United States, and particularly the southwestern frontier, so much as bringing into market, at an early day, the whole of this fertile country" (*Legacy of Andrew Jackson*: p. 53). In a sense, then, Jackson's career perfectly embodied the relentless greed of white Southern settlers for more and more land, no matter what prior treaties required, or who had occupied the land previously.

8. *Mississippi State Gazette*, January 8, 1820, cited in Arthur H. DeRosier, Jr., *The Removal of the Choctaw Indians* (Norman: University of Tennessee Press, 1970): 54. For Jackson's Mississippi plantation, see Wallace, *Long Bitter Trail*: 5.

9. Cited in Helen Jackson, *Century of Dishonor*: 275–6.

10. Murphy and Murphy, *Let My People Know*: 23.

11. Augusta *State-Rights' Sentinel*, July 21, 1835, cited in John M. Coward, *The Newspaper Indian: Native American Identity in the Press, 1820–90* (Urbana: University of Illinois, 1999): 51.

12. *Western Weekly Review*, October 6, 1837, cited in ibid.: 51.

13. Ibid.: 50.

14. Hershberger, "Mobilizing Women, Anticipating Abolition": 18.

15. Cited in ibid.: 20–1. Hershberger lists dozens of examples of accounts in Northern religious newspapers that defended Native Americans and exposed white abuses against them.

16. Murphy and Murphy, *Let My People Know*: 21–2.

17. Ronald N. Satz, *American Indian Policy in the Jacksonian Era* (Norman: University of Oklahoma Press, 1975): 18; Ehle, *Trail of Tears*: 157.

18. Ehle, *Trail of Tears*: 188–1.

19. Murphy and Murphy, *Let My People Know*: 23–4.

20. Cited in Barbara F. Luebke, "Elias Boudinot, Indian Editor: Editorial Columns from the *Cherokee Phoenix*," *Journalism History* 6: 2 (Summer 1979): 51.

21. Ehle, *Trail of Tears*: 224–5.

22. Murphy and Murphy, *Let My People Know*: 28.

23. Ibid.: 30.

24. Sam G. Riley, "The Indian's Own Prejudice as Mirrored in the First Native American Newspaper," *Journalism History* 6: 2 (Summer 1979): 45.

25. Ibid.: 45.

26. Coward, *Newspaper Indian*: 66–8.

27. Satz, *American Indian Policy*: 11; Wallace, *Long Bitter Trail*: 5.

28. Wallace, *Long Bitter Trail*: 7; Remini, *Legacy of Andrew Jackson*: 67; Andro Linklater, *The Fabric of America: How Our Borders and Boundaries Shaped the Country and Forged Our National Identity* (New York: Walker & Company, 2007): 194.

29. Wallace, *Long Bitter Trail*: 41–7.

30. Lewis Cass, "Removal of the Indians," *North American Review* 30: 66 (January 1830): 72–3.

31. New York *Sun*, July 19, 1837, cited in Saxton, "Problems of Class and Race": 231.

32. Hershberger, "Mobilizing Women, Anticipating Abolition," provides an excellent overview of the role women's groups and the religious press played in opposing Indian removal.

33. Ehle, *Trail of Tears*: 244.

34. *Worcester v. Georgia* 31 US (6 Pet.) 515 (1832).

35. Satz, *American Indian Policy*: 99–100.

36. Ehle, *Trail of Tears*: 259.

37. Cited in Murphy and Murphy, *Let My People Know*: 29–30.

38. Ibid.: 31; Mark Trahant, *Pictures of Our Noble Selves* (Nashville: Freedom Forum First Amendment Center, 1995): 11–12.

39. Remini, *Andrew Jackson and His Indian Wars*: 269.

40. Trahant, *Pictures of Our Noble Selves*: 12–13.

41. Murphy and Murphy, *Let My People Know*: 33–8.

42. All cited in Robert F. Heizer, ed., *The Destruction of California Indians: a collection of documents from the period 1847 to 1865 in which are described some of the things that happened to some of the Indians of California* (Lincoln: University of Nebraska Press, 1974): 249, 251, 300.

43. James W. Parins, *John Rollin Ridge: His Life and Works* (Lincoln: University of Nebraska Press, 1991 [1990]): 113–20.

44. Cited in Trahant, *Pitures of our Noble Selves*: 15–16.

45. Parins, *John Rollin Ridge*: 124–9.

46. Trahant, *Pictures of Our Noble Selves*: 16.

47. *Arkansian*, April 25, 1859, cited in Trahant, *Pictures of Our Noble Selves*: 16.

Chapter 7: To Plead Our Own Cause

1. "The men who led this movement were often also the editors and publishers of black newspapers and magazines," press historian Frankie Hutton has noted, and it was through those gatherings "that black leaders planned and plotted for their survival and success in America." See Frankie Hutton, *The Early Black Press in America, 1827 to 1860* (Westport: Greenwood Press, 1993): xiii.

2. *Freedom's Journal*, March 16, 1827.

3. Hutton, *Early Black Press*: 4.

4. *Freedom's Journal*, March 16, 1827.

5. Ibid., June 29, 1827.

6. Ibid., May 11, 1827.

7. Ibid., August 24, 1827.

8. Wilder, *In the Company of Black Men*: 149.

9. Quoted in Bacon, "History of Freedom's Journal": 8.

10. *Freedom's Journal*, May 18, 1827.

11. See Hutton, *Early Black Press*: 5; Martin E. Dann, ed., *The Black Press, 1827–1890* (New York: G.P. Putnam's Sons, 1971): 247–53.

12. Bacon, "History of Freedom's Journal": 11–16. Jacqueline Bacon, *Freedom's Journal: The First African American Newspaper* (Lanham: Lexington Books, 2007): 54–9, provides a detailed and convincing examination of the Cornish-Russwurm split. See also Lee Finkle, *Forum for Protest: The Black Press During World War II* (Cranbury, NJ: Fairleigh Dickinson University Press, 1975): 18–19, has a short summary of the split.

13. *Freedom's Journal*, March 28, 1829.

14. Dann, *Black Press*: 17.

15. *Rights of All*, May 29, 1829.

16. *Weekly Advocate*, January 7, 1837.

17. *Colored American*, March 4, 1837.

18. Ibid., September 16, 1837.

19. Ibid., August 8, 1840, cited in Hutton, *Early Black Press*: 24.

20. *Weekly Advocate*, January 14, 1837.

21. Hutton, *Early Black Press*: 18.

22. Graham Russell Hodges, "David Ruggles: The Hazards of Anti-Slavery Journalism," *Media Studies Journal* 14: 2 (Spring/Summer 2000—available at <www.freedomforum. org/publications/msj/courage.summer2000/y02.html>) provides an excellent overview of Ruggles' amazing story. On Ruggles and the kidnapping of black children into slavery, see Hutton, *Early Black Press*: 149–53.

23. *Colored American*, January 16, 1841, cited in Dann, *Black Press*: 328.

24. Frederick Douglass, *Narrative of the Life of Frederick Douglass, an American Slave,* first published 1845 (New York: Fine Creative Media, 2003): 94.

25. Hutton, *Early Black Press*: 19–21, 151–2; Hodges, "David Ruggles."

26. Mayer, *All On Fire*: 133–4.

27. Ibid.: 350.

28. Bella Gross, "The First National Negro Convention," *Journal of Negro History* 31: 4 (October 1946): 435.

29. Hutton, *Early Black Press*: 11–15.

30. Ibid.: 12.

31. Ibid.: 72, 162.

32. *North Star*, January 21, 1848.

33. Ibid., January 5, 1849.

34. Jane Rhodes, *Mary Ann Shadd Cary: The Black Press and Protest in the Nineteenth Century* (Bloomington: Indiana University Press, 1998): 2–3.

35. *North Star*, March 23, 1849.

36. Rhodes, *Mary Ann Shadd Cary*: xv, 74.

37. *Frederick Douglass' Paper*, July 4, 1856, cited in Rhodes, *Mary Ann Shadd Cary*: xi.

38. "American blood has been shed on American soil," screamed the April 26, 1846 edition of the Washington *Union*, anticipating by two weeks the words Polk would use in his war message to Congress, and both the New Orleans *Picayune* and the St. Louis *Republican* railed against Mexico's insult to American honor. See John S. D. Eisenhower, *So Far From God: The US War with Mexico 1846–1848* (New York: Anchor Books, 1989): 66.

39. "A Whig Argument for Continuing the War," *New Orleans Tropic*, quoted in the *Cincinnati Weekly Herald and Philanthropist*, September 9, 1848.

40. *Cincinnati Weekly Herald and Philanthropist*, May 27, 1846.

41. *North Star*, January 21, 1848.

42. Ibid., March 3, 1848.

43. Ibid.

Chapter 8: "The Chinese Must Go!"

1. Peter Kwong and Dusanka Miscevic, *Chinese America: The Untold Story of America's Oldest New Community* (New York: New Press, 2005): 54; Iris Chang, *The Chinese in America: A Narrative History* (New York: Penguin, 2003): 72.

2. *San Francisco Daily Alta Californian*, May 21, 1853, cited in Victor Low, *The Unimpressible Race: A Century of Educational Struggle by the Chinese in San Francisco* (San Francisco: East/West Publishing Co., 1982): 2–3.

3. Thomas W. Chinn, ed., *A History of the Chinese in California: A Syllabus* (San Francisco: Chinese Historical Society of America, 1969): 9; Kwong and Miscevic, *Chinese America*: 42–3.

4. Kwong and Miscevic, *Chinese America*: 32.

5. Ibid.: 36.

6. *Little's Living Age*, December 8, 1849, and *California Courier*, 1850 (date unknown), both cited in Chinn, *History of the Chinese in California*: 9, 10.

7. *Daily Alta Californian*, May 12, 1852.

8. Najia Aarim-Heriot, *Chinese Immigrants, African Americans, and Racial Anxiety in the United States, 1848–82* (Urbana: University of Illinois Press, 2003): 27–8.

9. Ibid.: 25.

10. Ronald Takaki, *Strangers from a Different Shore: A History of Asian Americans* (New York: Penguin, 1989): 80–4.

11. Aarim-Heriot, *Chinese Immigrants*: 44; *People v. Hall* 4 Cal. 399 (1854).

12. Chang, *Chinese in America*: 44–5.

13. Sacramento *Union*, June 6, 1853, quoted in Robert F. Heizer, *The Destruction of California Indians: a collection of documents from the period 1847 to 1865 in which are described some of the things that happened to some of the Indians of California* (Lincoln: University of Nebraska Press, 1974): 288.

14. San Francisco *Bulletin*, September 12, 1860, quoted in Heizer, *Destruction of Californian Indians*: 289–90.

15. Chang, *Chinese in America*: 41.

16. *New York Tribune*, September 29, 1854; *Harper's Weekly*, January 30, 1858, cited in Aarim-Heriot, *Chinese Immigrants*: 60–1.

17. San Francisco *Daily Morning Call*, July 12, 1864.

18. Ibid., August 23, 1864.

19. Mark Twain, *The Writings of Mark Twain*, vol. XIX (Hartford, CT: American Publishing, 1908[1899]): 304.

20. Watsonville *Pajaronian*, November 9, 1871, and November 16, 1871, cited in William E. Huntzicker, "Chinese-American Newspapers," in Hutton and Reed, *Outsiders in 19th-Century Press History*: 71–2.

21. Chang, *Chinese in America*: 53–64, provides a concise and gripping account of the Chinese role in the transcontinental railroad project.

22. San Francisco *Bulletin*, July 24, 1877; Chang, *Chinese in America*: 125–7.

23. San Francisco *Bulletin*, July 24, 1871.

24. Ibid., July 25, 1871.

25. Ibid., July 26 and 27, 1871.

26. Kwong and Miscevic, *Chinese America*: 94.

27. Gyory, *Race, Politics and the Chinese Exclusion Act*: 96.

28. Kwong and Miscevic, *Chinese America*: 72.

29. *Montana Radiator*, January 24, 1866; *Cheyenne Daily Leader*, May 6, 1879; *Frontier Index*, August 11, 1868, all cited in A. Dudley Gardner, "Chinese Emigrants in Southwest Wyoming 1868–1885," *Annals of Wyoming*, Fall 1991: 140.

30. Cited in Keever et al., *U.S. News Coverage of Racial Minorities*: 192–3.

31. John Kuo Wei Tchen, *New York Before Chinatown: Orientalism and the Shaping of American Culture, 1776–1882* (Baltimore: Johns Hopkins University Press, 1999): 189.

32. Kwong and Miscevic, *Chinese America*: 102.

33. Chang, *Chinese in America*: 132.

34. Ibid.: 133–4; Kwong, *Chinese America*: 108.

35. There was debate for years among journalism scholars about the identity of and precise founding date for the first Chinese-language newspaper, but the most detailed and convincing evidence for *Golden Hills News* and April 22nd, 1854 was uncovered by Karl Lo, "*Kim Shan Jit San Luk*: The First Chinese Paper Published in America," *Chinese Historical Society of America Bulletin* VI: 8 (October 1971). See also H. M. Lai, "The

Chinese-American Press," in Sally Miller, ed., *The Ethnic Press in the United States: A Historical Analysis and Handbook* (New York: Greenwood Press, 1987): 28.

36. Lo, "*Kim Shan Jit San Luk*": 2.

37. Quoted in Karl Lo, "Chinese Newspapers Published in North America, 1854–1975," *Center for Chinese Research Materials, Bibliographical Series: No. 16* (Washington, D.C.: Association of Research Libraries, 1976): 2.

38. *The Oriental*, January 4, 1855, quoted in H. M. Lai, "The Chinese-American Press," 28.

39. The writing style of both *Golden Hills News* and *The Oriental* was an archaic mix of colloquial and classical Cantonese, heavily sprinkled with Chinese characters that sounded like the English words they sought to convey. Its eclectic style, together with the poor quality of the hand-produced and lithographed letters with which it was printed, made it difficult for many modern Chinese scholars, even those who are native-speakers, to decipher the content of those early papers and has thus contributed to their relative obscurity. See Karl Lo, "*Kim Shan Jit San Luk*": 4; and Huntzicker, "Chinese-American Newspapers": 73–4.

40. Lo, "Chinese Newspapers Published in North America": 3.

41. Ibid.: 5.

42. Arthur Bonner, *Alas! What Brought Thee Hither? The Chinese in New York 1800–1950* (Madison: Associated University Presses, 1997): 53.

43. Ibid.: 54.

44. Ibid.: 56.

45. Ibid.

46. Ibid.: 57–8.

47. Robert E. Park, *The Immigrant Press and Its Control* (New York: Harper & Brothers, 1922): 319 (Table XVIII); Lee, *Daily Newspaper in America*: 734; Mott, *American Journalism*: 494.

Chapter 9: Wiring the News

1. Glen Porter, *The Rise of Big Business, 1860–1910* (New York, 1973): 43.

2. Starr, *Creation of the Media*: 160–1; Schwarzlose, *Nation's Newsbrokers*: 37–9.

3. *New York Herald*, May 12, 1845; *Niles' National Register*, July 4, 1846—both cited in Schwarzlose, *Nation's Newsbrokers*: 41–2.

4. Starr, *Creation of the Media*: 163–4. See also Gardiner G. Hubbard, "Government Control of the Telegraph," *North American Review* CCCXXV (December 1883): 532.

5. Richard B. Du Boff, "The Telegraph in Nineteenth-Century America: Technology and Monopoly," *Comparative Studies in Society and History* 26: 4 (October 1984): 573.

6. Smith, for example, had owned newspapers in Maine, and ended up controlling the company's New England telegraph line. Henry O'Reilly, who had edited a paper in Rochester, New York, and also served as that city's postmaster, landed a contract to build a western telegraph line for the Morse firm. William Swain, owner of Philadelphia's chief penny paper, the *Public Ledger*, was the largest investor in the Morse Company. New York publishers Horace Greeley and James Gordon Bennett became investors in Smith's telegraph line from Boston to New York. See Starr, *Creation of the Media*: 169–70.

7. Starr, *Creation of the Media*: 170–4.

8. Schwarzlose, *Nation's Newsbrokers*: 42–6; Starr, *Creation of the Media*: 170–5.

9. Frank Parsons, *The Telegraph Monopoly* (Philadelphia: C.F. Taylor, 1899): 18–24, summarizes key views of various Congressional committees and social reformers during the nineteenth century that saw telegraph as a natural extension of the federal government's power, in the words of the Supreme Court, to "facilitate the transmission of intelligence" to all Americans. See *Pensacola Telephone Company v. Western Union*, 96 U.S. 1 (1877), and James M. Herring, "Public versus Private Ownership and Operation of Communications Utilities," in "Ownership and Regulation of Public Utilities," *Annals of the American Academy of Political Science* 201 (January 1939): 96. See also Duboff, "The Telegraph in Nineteenth-Century America": 572; Parsons, *Telegraph Monopoly*: 11; Starr, *Creation of the Media*: 165–9. In Europe, the average telegraph rate toward the end of the nineteenth century was 10¢ for twenty words, while in the US it was an astonishing 25¢ for ten words. See Parsons, *Telegraph Monopoly*: 26, 29.

10. The Association of Morning Papers was formed in 1827 to jointly finance news boats to retrieve news from incoming ships. See Lee, *Daily Newspaper in America*: 209. See also Alexander Jones, *Historical Sketch of the Electric Telegraph: Including its Rise and Progress in the United States* (New York: G.P. Putnam, 1852): 122.

11. Schwarzlose, *Nation's Newsbrokers*: 56–6. For AP's official history, see <www.ap.org/pages/about/history/history_first.html>.

12. Mark Wahlgren Summers, *The Press Gang: Newspapers and Politics, 1865–1878* (Chapel Hill: University of North Carolina Press, 1994): 12–13.

13. Lloyd Breeze, editor of the Detroit *Evening Journal* and an opponent of the cartel, testified at one Senate hearing that Western Union was charging him six times as much for his news dispatches as other papers. See Parsons, *Telegraph Monopoly*: 83–5.

14. Parsons, *Telegraph Monopoly*: 88; Starr, *Creation of the Media*: 183–4.

15. Parsons, *Telegraph Monopoly*: 88.

16. Ibid.: 88.

17. Herring, "Public Versus Private Ownership": 96.

18. Coward, *Newspaper Indian*: 100.

19. Cited in Schwarzlose, *Nation's Newsbrokers*: 180–1.

20. Coward, *Newspaper Indian*: 99.

21. Elmo Scott Watson, "The Indian Wars and the Press, 1866–1867," *Journalism Quarterly* 27: 4 (December 1940): 302.

22. William Blankenburg, "The Role of the Press in an Indian Massacre," *Journalism Quarterly* 49 (1972): 61.

23. Ibid.: 65.

24. Ibid.: 66.

25. *Arizona Miner*, May 27, 1871, cited in Chip Colwell-Chanthaphong, "The 'Camp Grant Massacre' in the Historical Imagination," presented at the Arizona History Convention, April 25, 2003, available at <www.cdarc.org/pdf/camp_grant.pdf>.

26. Blankenburg, "Role of the Press in an Indian Massacre": 70.

27. Ibid.: 66.

28. "Slaughter of Indians," *New York Times*, May 12, 1871.

29. Blankenburg, "Role of the Press in an Indian Massacre": 66–8.

30. Ibid.: 68–9.

31. Ibid.: 70.

32. *Harper's Weekly*, January 30, 1892.

33. McWilliams, *North From Mexico*: 121.

34. Ibid.: 109.

35. Ibid.: 106–7.

36. US Congress, *Recommendation of the Public Land Commission for Legislation as to Private Land Claims*, 46th Congress, 2nd session, 1880, House Exec. Doc. 46: 1,116–17, cited in Weber, *Foreigners in Their Native Land*: 201.

37. *El Correo de Laredo*, July 21, 1891, cited in Walraven, "Ambivalent Americans": 179.

38. Ibid.: 201–2.

39. "Such unanimity of anti-Porfirian sentiment among Mexican journalists was not only limited to South Texas but was present along the entire border," notes Elliot Young in *Catarino Garza's Revolution on the Texas-Mexico Border* (Durham: Duke University Press, 2004): 204.

40. Walraven, "Ambivalent Americans": 165–6.

41. Young, *Catarino Garza's Revolution*": 192.

42. Ibid.: 190–208. Young deftly summarizes here how press accounts in both English- and Spanish-language US newspapers distorted or embellished the facts of the Garza War.

43. New York *Tribune*, June 30, 1855; Gronowicz, *Race and Class Politics in New York City*: 154.

44. William Barlow, *Voice Over: The Making of Black Radio* (Philadelphia: Temple University Press, 1999): 2–8; Joseph Boskin, *Sambo: The Rise and Demise of an American Jester* (New York: OUP, 1984): 14.

45. Cited in Burrows and Wallace, *Gotham*: 865; Gronowicz, *Race and Class Politics in New York City:*, 159, 165.

46. Lurton D. Ingersoll, *The Life of Horace Greeley* (Chicago: Union Publishing, 1873): 470–3.

47. R. J. M. Blackett, ed., *Thomas Morris Chester, Black Civil War Correspondent: His Dispatches from the Virginia Front* (Baton Rouge: Louisiana State University Press, 1989): 3–91, provides a detailed biography of Chester. The book also reprints a large collection of newspaper reports.

48. Philadelphia *Press*, February 3, 1865, cited in ibid.: 250.

49. Philadelphia *Press*, April 6, 1865, cited in Blackett, *Thomas Morris Chester*: 294–9.

50. Summers, *Press Gang*: 193.

51. Chicago *Tribune*, July 24 and 25, 1871, cited in Summers, *Press Gang*: 201.

52. Ibid.: 204.

53. Ibid.: 218.

54. Ibid.: 220.

55. Ibid.: 194-195.

56. Ibid.: 221. See also Emma Lou Thornburgh, "American Negro Newspapers, 1880–1914," *Business History Review* 40: 4 (Winter 1966): 486, note: "Negro papers were not

admitted to membership in the Associated Press (even if they had had the financial resources necessary, which few possessed), and consequently did not enjoy the low telegraph rates available to members of the association."

57. Summers, *Press Gang*: 221.

58. National Association for the Advancement of Colored People, *Thirty Years of Lynching in the United States,* 1889–1918 (New York: Arno Press and *New York Times,* 1969); Reed W. Smith, "Southern Journalists and Lynching: The Statesboro Case Study," *Journalism Communication Monographs* 7: 2 (Summer 2005): 53; W. Fitzhugh Brundage, *Lynching in the New South: Georgia and Virginia,* 1880–1930 (Urbana: University of Illinois Press, 1993): 8; Richard Perloff, "The Press and Lynchings of African Americans," *Journal of Black Studies*: 30: 3 (January 2000): 318, 319; *New York Times,* September 30, 1893, cited in Perloff, "The Press and Lynchings": 323.

59. Perloff, "The Press and Lynchings": 322.

60. Cited in Smith, "Southern Journalists and Lynching": 58.

61. Stewart Tolnay and E. M. Beck, *A Festival of Violence: An Analysis of Southern Lynchings,* 1882–1930 (Urbana: University of Illinois Press, 1995): 261.

62. Ibid.: 62. We are indebted to Smith's "Southern Journalists and Lynching" for his meticulous account of the events in Statesboro in 1904. While Smith appears to have made a few minor errors—one of the accused killers was named Will Cato, not Paul Cato; and the accused men received not a joint trial but separate ones, Cato's lasting for most of the day of August 15 and Reed's for half a day on August 16—his overall chronicling of the role of press coverage in stoking racial violence in this one murder case is a major contribution to a long overdue re-examination of racism within the Southern press.

63. Cited in Smith, "Southern Journalists and Lynching": 63–5.

64. Cited in ibid.: 53.

65. *Atlanta Constitution,* August 17, 1904, cited in Smith, "Southern Journalists and Lynching": 69.

66. Smith, "Southern Journalists and Lynching": 75–6.

67. New York *Herald,* December 8, 1874, cited in Summers, *Press Gang*: 223.

68. Summers, *Press Gang*: 226–9.

69. Chicago *Tribune,* December 12, 1874, cited in ibid.: 232.

70. 1898 Wilmington Race Riot Commission, 1898 *Wilmington Race Riot,* May 31, 2006, Final Report, available at <www.ah.dcr.state.nc.us/1898-wrrc>.

71. Timothy B. Tyson, "The Ghosts of 1898," *Charlotte Observer,* November 16, 2006.

72. Josephus Daniels, *Editor in Politics* (Chapel Hill: University of North Carolina Press, 1934): 307.

73. Ibid.: 295.

74. Ibid.: 295.

75. Ibid.: 285.

76. Ibid.: 308–9.

77. Ibid.: 310.

78. Harper Barnes, *Never Been a Time: The 1917 Race Riot That Sparked the Civil Rights Movement* (New York: Walker & Company, 2008): 79.

79. For a fine overview of the role played by Southern liberal editors on race issues, see Roberts and Klibanoff, *Race Beat*.

Chapter 10: The Progressive Era and the Colored Press

1. Trudier Harris, ed., *Selected Works of Ida B. Wells* (New York: OUP, 1991): 79.
2. They included poet Lola Rodríguez de Tio and Ramón Emeterio Betances, both Puerto Rican independence advocates who wrote for several Spanish-language publications; printer Sotero Figueroa, who published the revolutionary newspapers *El Porvenir* and *Borinquen*; Arturo Schomburg, the Puerto Rico–born scholar who came to New York in 1891 and became the first great archivist of African-American life; and Luis Muñoz Rivera, the founder of Puerto Rico's *La Democracia*, and later of the English-language *Puerto Rican Herald*, in Washington, DC. Rivera was the father of the man who would become the best-known Puerto Rican leader of the twentieth century, Luis Muñoz Marín. See Kanellos and Martell, *Hispanic Periodicals*: 19–20.
3. "The Indians in the United States," *La Nación* (Buenos Aires), December 4, 1885, translated and reprinted in José Martí, *Selected Writings* (New York: Penguin Books, 2002): 157–64.
4. "A Town Sets a Black Man on Fire," *El Partido Liberal* (Mexico City), March 5, 1892, translated and reprinted in Martí, *Selected Writings*: 310–13.
5. "The Brooklyn Bridge," *La América*, June 1883, translated and reprinted in Martí, *Selected Writings*: 140–4.
6. For an excellent synopsis of Martí's years in the United States, see Philip Foner's introduction to José Martí, *Our America: Writings on Latin America and the Struggle for Independence in Cuba*, ed. Philip S. Foner (New York: Monthly Review Press, 1977): 11–60. Louis A. Pérez, Jr., *Cuba: Between Reform and Revolution* (New York: OUP, 1995): 144–8.
7. Meléndez, *Spanish-Language Newspapers*: 6.
8. Ibid.: 26.
9. *El Sol de Mayo* (Las Vegas, New Mexico), March 31, 1892, cited in ibid.: 65.
10. Meléndez, *Spanish-Language Newspapers*: 65.
11. *La Voz del Pueblo* (Las Vegas, New Mexico), March 9, 1889, cited in ibid.: 44.
12. *El Independiente* (Las Vegas, New Mexico), November 9, 1895, cited in Meléndez, *Spanish-Language Newspapers*: 105.
13. Robert J. Rosenbuam, *Mexicano Resistance in the Southwest: "The Sacred Right of Self-Preservation"* (Austin: University of Texas Press, 1981): 97–118. Rosenbaum provides a fascinating and incisive analysis of both the court battles over the land and the complex evolution of ethnic and class forces during the violence.
14. Ibid.: 99–109.
15. *La Voz del Pueblo* (Santa Fe), June 7, 1890, cited in Meléndez, *Spanish-Language Newspapers*: 75.
16. *La Voz del Pueblo* (Las Vegas, New Mexico), May 16, 1891, and September 16, 1893, cited in Rosenbaum, *Mexicano Resistance*: 142.
17. Meléndez, *Spanish-Language Newspapers*: 75.
18. A. Gabriel Meléndez, "New Mexico's Spanish Language Journalists: Camilo Padilla,

Pioneer Publicist," Center for Regional Studies 105 (Spring 1994), Southwest Hispanic Research Institute, University of New Mexico: 13. We are indebted to Meléndez's fine study for our summary of Padilla's career and contributions.

19. Memphis *Free Speech*, May 21, 1892, cited in *Selected Works of Ida B. Wells*: 16–17.

20. Memphis *Commercial Appeal* and *Evening Scimitar*, May 25, 1892, cited in ibid.: 17–18.

21. Ibid.: 76–7.

22. Ibid.: 24.

23. Cyrus Field Adams, "Timothy Thomas Fortune: Journalist, Author, Lecturer, Agitator," *Colored American Magazine* IV (January–February, 1902): 225–7.

24. New York *Freeman*, May 15, 1886, cited in Martin E. Dann, *The Black Press* 1827–1890: 114–15.

25. New York *Freeman*, May 1, 1886, cited in Dann, *Black Press*: 213–14.

26. Emma Lou Thornburgh, "American Negro Newspapers, 1880–1914," *Business History Review* 40: 4 (Winter 1966): 470; Dann, *Black Press*: 25.

27. Thornburgh, "American Negro Newspapers": 468, 472; Adams, "Timothy Thomas Fortune": 228; Lee Finkle, *Forum for Protest: The Black Press During World War II* (Rutherford: Farleigh Dickinson University Press, 1975): 29.

28. Adams, "Timothy Thomas Fortune": 227–8.

29. Thornburgh, "American Negro Newspapers": 481–4; Charlotte G. O'Kelly, "Black Newspapers and the Black Protest Movement: Their Historical Relationship, 1827–1945," *Phylon* 43: 1 (First Quarter, 1982): 3; Finkle, *Forum for Protest*: 31–3.

30. Finkle, *Forum for Protest*: 33.

31. Allen W. Jones, "The Black Press in The 'New South': Jesse C. Duke's Struggle for Justice and Equality," *Journal of Negro History* 64: 3 (Summer 1979): 218.

32. Montgomery *Herald*, August 6, 1887, cited in ibid.: 221.

33. Cited in Jones, "Black Press": 219.

34. Montgomery *Daily Dispatch*, August 14, 1887, cited in Jones, "Black Press": 221.

35. Cited in Jones, "Black Press": 223–4.

36. Yunei Sun, "San Francisco's *Chung Sai Yat Po* and the Transformation of Chinese Consciousness, 1900–1920": 85–6, in James P. Danky and Wayne A. Wiegand, eds, *Print Culture in a Diverse America* (Urbana: University of Illinois Press, 1998); Kwong and Miscevic, *Chinese America*: 112.

37. Lai, "Chinese-American Press: 31.

38. *New York Eagle*, October 9, 1909, cited in Danky and Weigand, *Print Culture*: 87–8.

39. Ibid.: 87.

40. Ibid.: 89–90.

41. *Chung Sai Yat Po*, May 1, 1906, cited in Danky and Weigand, *Print Culture*: 91.

42. *Chung Sai Yat Po*, April 6, 1911, cited in Danky and Weigand, *Print Culture*: 93.

43. Charles P. Holder, "The Chinese Press in America," *Scientific American*, October 11, 1902: 241.

44. Yansheng Ma Lum and Raymond Mun Kong Lum, "Sun Yat-Sen in Hawaii: Activities and Supporters," at <www.sunyatsenhawaii.org/en/research/85-sun-yat-sen-in-hawaii-activities-and-supporters?donttouchthis=true>.

45. See Lo, "Chinese Newspapers Published in North America": 6–10; also Lai, "Chinese-American Press": 30–4.

46. Kuei Chiu, "Asian Language Newspapers in the United States Revisited": 4, at <www.cala-web.org/book/export/html/647>.

47. Ibid.: 5.

48. Erik Barnouw, *A Tower in Babel* (New York: OUP, 1966): 15. Mott, *American Journalism*: 519–45, provides an overview of the relentless Hearst and Pulitzer campaigns in 1898 for war with Spain.

49. Anthony Smith, *The Geopolitics of Information: How Western Culture Dominates The World* (New York: OUP, 1980): 69–84 provides an excellent summary of the early days of the international information cartel. See also Starr, *Creation of the Media*: 179–81.

50. Smith, *Geopolitics of Information*: 74.

51. George P. Marks, III, ed., *The Black Press Views American Imperialism (1898–1900)* (New York: Arno Press, 1971): xvii.

52. Kansas City *American Citizen*, February 24, 1898, cited in ibid.: 10–11. See also Earnestine Jenkins and Darlene Clark Hine, eds, *A Question of Manhood: A Reader in US Black Men's History and Masculinity, Vol. II: The 19th Century from Emancipation to Jim Crow* (Bloomington: Indiana University Press, 2001): 323.

53. Marks, *Black Press Views American Imperialism*: xvii.

54. Kansas City *American Citizen*, March 17, 1898, cited in ibid.: 14.

55. Cleveland *Gazette*, May 21, 1898, cited in Marks, *Black Press Views American Imperialism*: 62.

56. Coffeyville *American*, February 11, 1899, cited in Marks, *Black Press Views American Imperialism*: 115.

57. Salt Lake City *Broad Ax*, March 25, 1899, cited in Marks, *Black Press Views American Imperialism*: 118.

58. *El Regidor* (San Antonio, Texas), February 10, 1898, cited in Walraven, "Ambivalent Americans": 197.

59. Walraven, "Ambivalent Americans": 199–200.

60. Starr, *Creation of the Media*: 252.

61. Ibid.: 252; Lee, *Daily Newspaper in America*: 722–3.

62. For concise summaries of the impact of the muckrakers, see Ellen F. Fitzpatrick, ed., *Muckraking: Three Landmark Articles* (Boston: Bedford/St Martin's, 1994): 103–15; and Robert McChesney and Ben Scott's Introduction to Upton Sinclair, *The Brass Check: A Study of American Journalism* (Urbana: University of Illinois Press, 2003).

63. Michael McGerr, *A Fierce Discontent: The Rise and Fall of the Progressive Movement in America* (New York: OUP, 2005): 183.

64. Herbert Shapiro, "Muckrakers and Negroes," *Phylon*, January 1970: 76–88.

65. Ibid.: 222.

66. Mott, *American Journalism*: 725–6.

Chapter 11: Words with Wings

1. Among the best general histories are: Erick Barnouw, *A Tower in Babel* (New York: OUP, 1966); Philip T. Rosen, *The Modern Stentors: Radio Broadcasting and the Federal Government, 1920–1934* (Westport: Greenwood Press, 1980); Susan Douglass, *Inventing American Broadcasting: 1899–1922* (Baltimore: John Hopkins University Press, 1987); and Robert W. McChesney, *Telecommunications, Mass Media and Democracy: The Battle for Control of US Broadcasting, 1928–1935* (New York: OUP, 1993). For studies of early radio and race, see William Barlow's *Voice Over: The Making of Black Radio*; the early chapters of Brian Ward, *Radio and the Struggle for Civil Rights in the South* (Gainesville: University Press of Florida, 2004); Felix Gutierrez and J. R. Schement, *Spanish Language Radio in the Southwestern United States* (Austin: University of Texas Center for Mexican-American Studies, 1979); and Michael C. Keith, *Signals in the Air: Native American Broadcasting in America* (Westport: Praeger, 1995).

2. Douglas, *Inventing American Broadcasting*: 17–23. Radio "represented as powerful an assault upon sectional and parochial mentalities as any single force in American history," and thus "promoted the unity of the nation," says J. Fred Macdonald in *Don't Touch That Dial! Radio Programming in American Life, 1920–1960* (Chicago: Nelson-Hall, 1982): 298.

3. Linwood S. Howeth, USN (retired), "History of Communications-Electronics in the United States Navy, Bureau of Ships and Office of Naval History," at <www.cybertelecom.org/notes/history_wireless.htm>.

4. Douglas, *Inventing American Broadcasting*: 123–5.

5. Mark Lloyd, *Prologue to a Farce: Communication and Democracy in America* (Urbana: University of Illinois Press, 2006): 83; Douglas, *Inventing American Broadcasting*: 106–20; Barnouw, *Tower in Babel*: 17–18.

6. Jesse Walker, *Rebels on the Air: An Alternative History of Radio in America* (New York: New York University Press, 2001): 16; Alfred D. Chandler Jr. and James W. Cortada, eds, *A Nation Transformed by Information: How Information Has Shaped the United States from Colonial Times to the Present* (Oxford: OUP, 2000): 147; Susan J. Douglas, *Listening In: Radio and the American Imagination, from Amos 'n' Andy and Edward R. Murrow to Wolfman Jack and Howard Stern* (New York: Times Books, 1999): 60.

7. Clinton DeSoto, *200 Meters & Down: The Story of Amateur Radio* (West Hartford: American Radio Relay League, 1936): 26–8.

8. Douglas, *Inventing American Broadcasting*: 226–34.

9. Barnouw, *Tower in Babel*: 43.

10. Douglas, *Listening In*: 16.

11. Lloyd, *Prologue to a Farce*: 95; Douglas, *Inventing American Broadcasting*: 234–5.

12. DeSoto, *200 Meters & Down*: 34; Douglas, *Inventing American Broadcasting*: 234.

13. Barnouw, *Tower in Babel*: 34.

14. Lloyd, *Prologue to a Farce*: 97–100; DeSoto *200 Meters & Down*: 98.

15. Barnouw, *Tower in Babel*: 48.

16. Donna L. Halper, "African Americans and Radio: An Overview," at <www.coax.net/people/lwf/AAER.HTM>.

17. *Chicago Defender*, January 22, 1910.

18. "Wireless Expert Refused Position by Red Star Line," *Chicago Defender*, October 17, 1914.

19. *Chicago Defender*, October 9, 1915.

20. Baltimore *Afro-American*, March 16, 1916.

21. Baltimore *Afro-American*, February 10, 1917.

22. Baltimore *Afro-American*, May 5, 1917.

23. "Negroes for Army Singlemen," *Wireless Age*, May 18, 1918: 625.

24. "Race to Have Wireless Telegraph Operators," *Chicago Defender*, December 22, 1917. "Plans are under way for the forming of colored classes in wireless telegraphy to meet the demand being made on wireless operators by the War Department," noted *Wireless Age* in 1918.

25. Douglas, *Inventing American Broadcasting*: 268–9.

26. For a concise summary of the wartime domestic repression and its impact on the press, see Starr, *Creation of the Media*, 267–86; and Michael Emery, Edwin Emery and Nancy L. Roberts, *The Press and America: An Interpretive History*, 9 edn (Boston: Allyn and Bacon, 2000): 256–8.

27. Lee, *Daily Newspaper in America*: 452–3.

28. Park, *Immigrant Press*: 412.

29. Ibid.: 428.

30. George Creel, "The Battle in the Air Lanes," *Popular Radio*, September 1922.

31. E. David Cronon, ed., *The Cabinet Diaries of Josephus Daniels, 1913–1921* (Lincoln: University of Nebraska Press, 1963): 172–3.

32. Ibid.: 355. See also, Starr, *Creation of the Media*: 224–5; Barnouw, *Tower in Babel*: 53–4.

33. Starr, *Creation of the Media*: 225–6; Barnouw, *Tower in Babel*: 57–61; Douglas, *Inventing American Broadcasting*: 285; Lloyd, *Prologue to a Farce*: 98–9.

34. Barnouw, *Tower in Babel*, 60–1.

35. Barnouw, *Tower in Babel*: 59–60; see also Lloyd, *Prologue to a Farce*: 99–100; Chandler Cortada, *Nation Transformed*: 146.

36. Some—like George N. Gordon, *The Communications Revolution: A History of Mass Media in the United States* (New York: Communication Arts Books, 1977): 125, and Tebbel, *Media in America*: 359—claim the original Sarnoff memo was in 1916, while others say it was actually written several years later. See, for example, Louis Benjamin, "In Search of the Sarnoff 'Radio Music Box' Memo," *Journal of Broadcasting and Electronic Media* (Washington, DC), Summer 1993.

37. McChesney, *Telecommunications*: 14; Gordon, *Communications Revolution*: 126; Barnouw, *Tower in Babel*: 62–4; J. MacDonald, *Don't Touch That Dial!*: 282–5.

38. Starr, *Creation of the Media*: 328; Douglas, *Inventing American Broadcasting*: 299–300.

39. Starr, *Creation of the Media*: 334.

40. Barnouw, *Tower in Babel*: 127.

41. Douglas, *Inventing American Broadcasting*: 303.

42. Gordon, *Communications Revolution*: 129–30.

43. Barnouw, *Tower in Babel*: 88, 91.

44. See official history of WGN at <wgngold.com/timeline/1920s1930s.htm>.

45. Barnouw, *Tower in Babel*: 196–7.

46. Starr, *Creation of the Media*: 331; Edwin Emery, *The History of the American Newspaper Publishers Association* (Minneapolis: University of Minnesota Press, 1950): 198.

47. Starr, *Creation of the Media*: 333.

48. Ibid.: 333; see also Rosen, *Modern Stentors*: 21–33.

49. Douglas, *Inventing American Broadcasting*: 319.

50. "Secretary Hoover provided such admonitions—against monopoly, vested interests, excessive advertising," notes Barnouw, "but continued to give dominant groups virtually what they asked for." See Barnouw, *Tower In Babel*: 178–9.

51. Starr, *Creation of the Media*: 342.

52. *Congressional Record*, 1927, 5478.

53. Mark Goodman, "The Radio Act of 1927 as a Product of Progressivism," at <www.scripps.ohiou.edu/mediahistory/mhmjour2-2.htm>.

54. Robert L. Hilliard and Michael Keith, *The Broadcast Century and Beyond: A Biography of American Broadcasting*, 3rd edn (Woburn, MA: Focal Press, 2001): 51.

55. *Annual Report of the Federal Radio Commission to the Congress of the United States for the Fiscal Year Ended June 30, 1927*: 8, at <www.fcc.gov/ftp/Bureaus/Mass_Media/Databases/documents_collection/270701.pdf>; Starr, *Creation of the Media*: 351–2.

56. Barnouw, *Tower in Babel*: 194.

57. Ibid.: 218–19.

58. Ibid.: 251.

59. Ibid.: 140–1.

60. Ibid.: 208.

61. Ibid.: 238–9.

62. J. Emmett Winn and Susan Brinson, *Transmitting the Past: Historical and Cultural Perspectives on Broadcasting* (Tuscaloosa: University of Alabama Press, 2005): 34, 46.

63. *Second Annual Report of the Federal Radio Commission to the Congress of the United States for the Fiscal Year Ending June 30, 1928*: 2–4, at <www.fcc.gov/fcc-bin/assemble?docno=281026>.

64. *Christian Science Monitor*, August 3rd, 1927.

65. "Funeral Today for J. S. Vance, WJSV Founder," *Washington Post*, October 4, 1942.

66. *Historic Home of The Fellowship Forum* (Washington, DC: Independent Publishing Company, circa 1927): 1.

67. Nancy MacLean, *Behind the Mask of Chivalry: The Making of the Second Ku Klux Klan* (New York: OUP, 1994): xi, 5, 7.

68. *Historic Home of The Fellowship Forum*: 2.

69. David B. Woolner and Richard G. Kurial, *FDR, the Vatican, and The Roman Catholic Church in America, 1933–1945* (New York: Palgrave MacMillan, 2003): 59; David M. Chalmers, *Hooded Americanism: The History of the Ku Klux Klan* (New York: Franklin Watts, 1981): 302.

70. "Klan Radio Station Nearing Completion," *Washington Post*, August 1, 1927; "Klan Radio Station Seeks 50,000 Watts," *New York Times*, October 9, 1927.

71. Internal memo of Department of Commerce, Navigation Service, April 19, 1927. Records of the Federal Communications Commission Radio Division: Correspondence Relating to Applications for Broadcast Station Licenses 1928–1932, Reg. 173, Folder "WJMS-WJZ."

72. "Klan Radio Station Nearing Completion," *Washington Post*, August 1, 1927: 14; Chalmers, *Hooded Americanism*: 302.

73. "Station WTFF Asks Increase in Power to Enlarge Scope," *Washington Post*, October 9, 1927.

74. "Bars Fellowship Forum," *New York Times*, September 24, 1928.

75. "After All Is Said," *Time Magazine*, November 12, 1928.

76. Herbert Hoover Presidential Library, Presidential Papers, Box 210, Folder Vance A-J, 1929–1932

77. Ibid.

78. <home.earthlink.net/~hdtv/History/WTOP/WTOP-AM.html>.

Chapter 12: Trouble in the Streets

1. DeSoto, 200 *Meters & Down*: 26.

2. Geoffrey C. Ward, *Unforgivable Blackness: The Rise and Fall of Jack Johnson* (New York: Alfred A. Knopf, 2004): xi.

3. *New York Times*, May 12, 1910.

4. Ward, *Unforgivable Blackness*: 200.

5. Walker, *Rebels on the Air*: 25.

6. Ward, *Unforgivable Blackness*: 216.

7. Ibid.: 216–17; *Belleville News-Democrat*, July 5, 1910.

8. Andrew Buni, *Robert L. Vann*: 62, 72; Harper Barnes, *Never Been a Time: The 1917 Race Riot That Sparked the Civil Rights Movement* (New York: Walker & Company, 2008): 69.

9. See Claude A. Barnett, "The Role of the Press, Radio, and Motion Picture and Negro Morale," *Journal of Negro Education* 12: 3 (Summer 1943): 480.

10. Barnes, *Never Been a Time*: 84.

11. Roi Ottley, *The Lonely Warrior: The Life and Times of Robert S. Abbott* (Chicago: Henry Regnery Co., 1955): 156–60.

12. Barnes, *Never Been a Time*: 72–3.

13. Ibid.: 76–7, 87.

14. Charles M. Lumpkins, *American Pogrom: The East St. Louis Riot and Black Politics* (Athens, Ohio: University of Ohio Press, 2008): 53, 92.

15. *East St. Louis Daily Journal*, May 29, 1917, cited in Barnes, *Never Been a Time*: 104.

16. Barnes, *Never Been a Time*: 74.

17. Lumpkins, *American Pogrom*: 106.

18. Barnes, *Never Been a Time*: 121.

19. *St. Louis Argus*, July 6, 1917, cited in Barnes, *Never Been a Time*: 122.

20. *Belleville News-Democrat*, July 3, 1917.

21. *St. Louis Post-Dispatch*, July 3, 1917, cited in Barnes, *Never Been a Time*: 150.

22. *Report of the Special Committee Authorized by Congress to Investigate the East St. Louis Race Riot*, House of Representatives Document No. 1231, Sixty-fifth Congress, Second Session, July 15, 1918: 1–10.

23. *New York Times*, July 29, 1917; Barnes, *Never Been a Time*: 187–8, 199.

24. Robert V. Haynes, *A Night of Violence: The Houston Race Riot of 1917* (Baton Rouge: Louisiana State University Press, 1976).

25. Ibid.: 57–60.

26. Barnes, *Never Been a Time*: 198.

27. Patrick Washburn, *A Question of Sedition: The Federal Government's Investigation of the Black Press During World War II* (New York: OUP, 1986): 15–18.

28. Ibid.: 20–2; Chicago *Defender*, September 14, 1918.

29. Washburn, *A Question of Sedition*: 17, citing Major W. H. Loving to Chief, Military Intelligence Branch, May 10, 1918, record group 165, MID 10218-133, box 3191, National Archives.

30. Park, *Immigrant Press*: 412–47.

31. Kanellos and Martell, *Hispanic Periodicals*: 124.

32. Enrique Krautz, *Mexico, Biography of Power: A History of Modern Mexico, 1810–1996* (New York: HarperCollins, 1997): 234; Kanellos and Martell, *Hispanic Periodicals*: 21.

33. Historian Nicolás Kanellos has claimed that, by the time Flores Magón moved to Los Angeles in 1907 to launch another newspaper, *Revolución*, many of his Mexican and Mexican-American followers in this country had "rejected his extremism," especially his "openly embracing anarchism." We would argue for a more nuanced analysis. The outbreak of the Mexican revolution in 1910 dramatically affected the composition of this country's Mexican immigrant population, especially its most politicized strata. Many who favored the revolution returned home to join the fighting, while tens of thousands of conservative opponents of the uprising fled to the American southwest once Díaz was forced to resign in May 1911. See Kanellos and Martell, *Hispanic Periodicals*: 21–2.

34. Kanellos and Martell, *Hispanic Periodicals*: 23.

35. José E. Limón, "El Primer Congreso Mexicanista de 1911: A Precursor to Contemporary Chicanismo," *Aztlan* V (Spring/Fall 1974); Walraven, *Ambivalent Americans*: 229–30. Since there are no surviving copies of *La Crónica's* early issues, the exact year the paper was launched remains in dispute. Both Limón and Walraven place it in the mid 1890s, while Kanellos and Martell (*Hispanic Periodicals*: 100) place it around 1909. The few surviving copies of the paper are from the period after 1910.

36. Walraven, *Ambivalent Americans*: 226–7, 250.

37. *La Crónica*, June 25, 1910, cited in Walraven, *Ambivalent Americans*: 240.

38. *La Crónica*.

39. Walraven, *Ambivalent Americans*: 234; Idar editorial cited in "Heroes and Heroines of La Raza," *La Voz de Aztlan* I: 5 (February 27, 2000), at <www.aztlan.net/default5.htm>.

40. *La Crónica*, July 13, 1911, cited in Limón, "El Primer Congreso": 88–9.

41. William D. Carrigan and Clive Webb, "The Lynching of Persons of Mexican Origin or Descent in the United States, 1848 to 1928," *Journal of Social History* 37: 2 (Winter 2003): 411–38.

42. *Houston Post*, September 17, 1911, cited in Walraven, *Ambivalent Americans*: 235.

43. *La Crónica*, September 21, 1911, cited in Walraven, *Ambivalent Americans*: 235.

44. Cited in Limón, "El Congreso Mexicanista."

45. Vicki L. Ruíz and Virginia Sánchez Korrol, eds, *Latinas in the United States: A Historical Encyclopedia, Vol. I* (Bloomington: Indiana University Press, 2006): 337.

46. Ibid.

47. Chicago *Tribune*, July 28, 1919.

48. Chicago Commission on Race Relations, *The Negro in Chicago: A Study of Race Relations and a Race Riot* (Chicago: University of Chicago Press, 1922): 597.

49. *Chicago Defender*, August 2nd, 1919.

50. Chicago Commission on Race Relations, *Negro in Chicago*: 597.

51. *Chicago Defender*, August 2nd, 1919.

52. Ibid., September 6, 1919.

53. Carl Sandburg, *The Chicago Race Riot, July* 1919 (New York: Harcourt, Brace, 1969): 64–5.

54. *Omaha World-Herald*, September 30, 1919.

Chapter 13: Other Voices

1. J. Fred MacDonald, *Don't Touch That Dial! Radio Programming in American Life,* 1920–1960 (Belmont, CA: Wadsworth Publishing Company, 1979).

2. Susan Douglas, *Listening In*: 92–4; *New York Amsterdam News*, March 26, 1930.

3. Susan Douglas, *Listening In*: 94; Barlow, *Voice Over*: 29.

4. Douglas, *Listening In*: 92.

5. Johnnie H. Miles, Juanita J. Davis, Sharon E. Ferguson-Roberts and Rita G. Giles, *Almanac of African American Heritage* (San Francisco: Jossey-Bass, 2000): 288.

6. Baltimore *Afro-American*, September 22nd, 1922.

7. *Washington Post*, December 5, 1924: 14.

8. Barlow, *Voice Over*: 24; Buni, *Robert L. Vann*: 140.

9. *New York Amsterdam News*, April 2nd, 1930; Jannette L. Dates and William Barlow, *Split Image: African Americans in the Mass Media*, 2nd edn (Washington, DC: Howard University Press, 1993): 199.

10. *New York Amsterdam News*, January 23, 1937 and June 11, 1938; MacDonald, *Don't Touch that Dial!*: 334.

11. Adam Green, *Selling the Race: Culture, Community and Black Chicago,* 1940–1955 (Chicago: University of Chicago Press, 2006): 81–2.

12. Barlow, *Voice Over*: 51–8.

13. Ward, *Radio and the Struggle for Civil Rights*: 24.

14. Ibid.: 27–8.

15. Ibid.: 28.

16. Pamela Newkirk, *Within the Veil: Black Journalists, White Media* (New York: New York University Press, 2000): 42.

17. Jessie Carney Smith, Shirelle Phelps, *Notable Black American Women, Book II* (Farmington, MI: Thomson Gale, 1995): 400–3.

18. "Appeal for the Negro—Lester A. Walton Asks the Dignity of a Capital N for His Race," *New York Times*, April 26, 1913.

19. Mary Frances Berry and John W. Blassingame, *Long Memory: The Black Experience in America* (New York: OUP, 1982): 392.

20. Kathleen A. Hauke, *Ted Poston: Pioneer American Journalist* (Athens: University of Georgia Press, 2002): 33–4.

21. Cited in ibid, 34.

22. George Schuyler, "Negroes Reject Communism," *American Mercury*, June 1939.

23. Hauke, *Ted Poston*: 1–10. We have based much of our summary of Poston's life and career on Hauke's meticulously researched biography.

24. Ibid.: 15–16.

25. Jeffrey B. Perry, ed., *A Hubert Harrison Reader* (Middletown, Conn.: Wesleyan University Press, 2001): 6–7, 182–3.

26. Hauke, *Ted Poston*: 16–21.

27. *Pittsburgh Courier*, April 18, 1931, cited in Kathleen A. Hauke, ed., *A First Draft of History: Ted Poston* (Athens: University of Georgia Press, 2000): 3.

28. *Amsterdam News*, March 9, 1935, cited in Hauke, *Ted Poston*: 39.

29. Hauke, *Ted Poston*: 58.

30. For an excellent summary of Poston's role in the strike, see Hauke, *Ted Poston*: 61–6.

31. Ibid.: 75.

32. Ibid.: 76.

33. Mark N. Trahant, *Pictures of our Nobler Selves* (Nashville: Freedom Forum First Amendment Center, 1995): 18–20; Daniel F. Littlefield, Jr., and James W. Parins, *American Indian and Alaska Native Newspapers and Periodicals, 1826–1924*, vol. 1 (Westport: Greenwood Press, 1984): 264; Darryl Morrison, "Twin Territories: The Indian Magazine," *Chronicles of Oklahoma*, Summer 1982: 133–66.

34. Trahant, *Pictures of Our Noble Selves*: 20.

35. Marion Alisky, "Early Mexican Broadcasting," *Hispanic Historical Review* 34: 4 (November 1954): 513–14.

36. Felix F. Gutierrez and Jorge Reina Schement, "Spanish-Language Radio in the United States" (Austin: Center for Mexican American Studies, University of Texas at Austin, 1979): 6.

37. Daniel D. Arreola, "The Mexican American Cultural Capital," *Geographical Review* 77: 1 (January 1987): 26.

38. Gutierrez and Schement, "Spanish-Language Radio": 6.

39. Cecilia Rasmussen, "L.A. Then and Now: The Hard Life of a Latino Hero," *Los Angeles Times*, May 3, 1998; *San Diego Union-Tribune*, March 23, 1995.

40. Francisco E. Balderrama and Raymond Rodríguez, *Decade of Betrayal: Mexican Repatriation in the 1930s* (Albuquerque: University of the New Mexico Press, 1995): 54.

41. Ibid.: 38–9, 52–3, 121–2.

42. *Los Angeles Times*, May 3, 1988. See also Jesus Rangel, "Story of Mexican Immigrant Hero," *New York Times*, January 7, 1985; Matt Damsker, "Corrido for Don Pedro, An Unsung Hero," *Los Angeles Times*, December 9, 1984.

43. Rasmussen, *Los Angeles Times*, May 3, 1998: 3.

44. San Antonio *Express-News*, December 5, 1999, 8j; US Department of Commerce, *Radio Service Bulletin* 14 (February 1916): 2.

45. Gene Fowler and Bill Crawford, *Border Radio: Quacks, Yodelers, Pitchmen, Psychics, and Other Amazing Broadcasters of the American Airwaves*, rev. edn (Austin: University of Texas Press, 2002): 202–3.

46. Fowler and Crawford, *Border Radio*: 201–2.

47. Thomas W. Hoffer, "TNT Baker: Radio Quack," in *American Broadcasting: A Source Book on the History of Radio and Television*, ed. Lawrence Lichty and Malachi C. Topping (New York: Hastings House, 1975): 575.

48. Fowler and Crawford, *Border Radio*: 104–5.

49. Fowler and Crawford, *Border Radio*: 33–4, 98.

50. Susan Douglas, *Listening In*: 107.

51. Dates and Barlow, *Split Image*: 29, 40; Barlow, *Voice Over*: 39; J. Fred MacDonald, *Radio Programming in American Life* (Chicago: Nelson-Hall, 1982): 340–2.

52. George H. Douglas, *The Early Days of Radio Broadcasting* (Jefferson, N.C.: McFarland Company Inc.: ???): 202.

53. Douglas, *Listening In*: 107.

54. Barlow, *Voice Over*: 40.

55. "Amos 'n' Andy" (editorial), *Pittsburgh Courier*, April 25, 1931.

56. "Write in Your Views," *Pittsburgh Courier*, April, 1931; "Letters to the Editor," *Pittsburgh Courier*, May 2nd, 1931, May 16, 1931.

57. Ibid., "Letters to the Editor," May 23, 1931.

58. Ibid.: May 9, 1931.

59. Bruni, *Robert L. Vann*: 229.

60. "Courier Plans National Protest Day Against Amos 'n' Andy," *Pittsburgh Courier*, September 12, 1931.

61. Ibid.: "Amos 'n' Andy Signers Mount," August 1, 1931.

62. Ibid.: "Petitions Continue to Pour In," July 4, 1931.

63. "And Now Comes Editor Andy" (editorial), *Pittsburgh Courier*, June 13, 1931.

64. Ibid., June 13, 1931.

65. Frank Gannett letter to General Saltzman, Federal Radio Commission, November 22nd, 1930.

66. Letter from Walter S. Goodland to George Vits, February 2nd, 1931, Hoover Presidential Library, Presidential Papers, Box 148, Folder: FRC Correspondence, 1930, November–December.

Chapter 14: Uniting the Home Front

1. Federal Communications Commission, *Public Service Responsibility of Broadcast Licenses* (Washington, DC: FCC, 1946): 13–15.

2. Starr, *Creation of the Media*: 379.

3. Ward, *Radio and the Struggle for Civil Rights* (Gainesville: University Press of Florida, 2004): 7.

4. Robert McChesney has provided extensive documentation in several studies of the citizen reform movement between 1928 and 1935, among them *Rich Media, Poor Democracy* (189–225).

5. "Neither Sponsors nor Stations Heed Listeners' Grumbling," *Business Week*, February 10, 1932: 18–19.

6. McChesney, *Rich Media, Poor Democracy*: 216–17; Starr, *Creation of the Media*: 374–5; Barlow, *Voice Over*: 68.

7. "Most Conspicuously Despicable," *Time* magazine, February 4, 1935.

8. "The Control of Radio," *New York Times*, February 27, 1938.

9. Robert L. Hillard and Michael C. Keith, *The Broadcast Century and Beyond: A Biography of American Broadcasting*, 3rd edn (Boston: Focal Press, 2001): 93–4.

10. Starr, *Creation of the Media*: 379–81.

11. Starr, *Creation of the Media*: 379; Lee, *Daily Newspaper in America*: 723–7.

12. Noel P. Gist, "The Negro in the Daily Press," *Social Forces* 10: 3 (March 1932): 405–11.

13. Ira B. Bryant, Jr., "News Items About Negroes in White Urban and Rural Newspapers," *Journal of Negro Education* 4: 2 (April 1935): 173.

14. Ibid.: 174–6.

15. George E. Simpson, "Race Relations and the Philadelphia Press," *Journal of Negro Education* 6: 4 (October 1937): 628–30.

16. MacDonald, *Don't Touch That Dial!*: 304–5; Douglas, *Listening In*: 189.

17. Douglas, *Listening In*: 196–7.

18. MacDonald, *Don't Touch That Dial!*: 315–16.

19. Finkle, *Forum for Protest*: 51–4.

20. Kansas City *Call*, January 31, 1941; Boston *Guardian*, June 7, 1941; *Amsterdam News*, April 12, 1941; Atlanta *Daily World*, February 16, 1941—all cited in Daniel Kryder, *Divided Arsenal: Race and the American State During World War II* (New York: CUP, 2001): 56–9.

21. Cited in Kryder, *Divided Arsenal*: 61, 63.

22. Ibid.: 67–9.

23. Ibid.: 62.

24. Ibid.: 74.

25. Barbara Moore, Marvin R. Bensman, and Jim Van Dyke, *Prime Time Television: A Concise History* (Westport: Greenwood Press, 2006): 23; MacDonald, *Don't Touch That Dial!*: 304–6.

26. Clayton R. Koppes and Gregory D Black, "Blacks, Loyalty, and Motion Picture Propaganda in World War II," *Journal of American History* 83 (September 1986): 386.

27. Barlow, *Voice Over*: 72.

28. Ibid.: 69–70; Ward, *Radio and the Struggle for Civil Rights*: 29–30.

29. Dates and Barlow, *Split Image: African Americans in the Mass Media* (Washington, DC: Howard University Press, 1990): 205–6.

30. Ward, *Radio and the Struggle for Civil Rights*: 184.

31. Barbara Diane Savage, *Broadcasting Freedom: Radio, War and the Politics of Race 1938–1948* (Chapel Hill: University of North Carolina Press, 1999): 91.

32. Patrick Washburn, *A Question of Sedition: The Federal Government's Investigation of the Black Press During World War II* (New York: OUP, 1986): 101; Lester M. Jones, "The Editorial Policy of Negro Newspapers of 1917–18 as Compared With That of 1941–42," *Journal of Negro History* 29: 1 (January 1944): 24–31.

33. Washburn, *A Question of Sedition*: 107.

34. Richmond *Times-Dispatch*, April 26, 1942, cited in Finkle, *Forum for Protest*: 63; *New York World Telegram* April 28, 1942, cited in Washburn, *A Question of Sedition*: 85.

35. Finkle, *Forum for Protest*: 102

36. Ibid.: 55.

37. Gunnar Myrdal, *An American Dilemma, Vol. II: The Negro Problem and Modern Democracy* (New Brunswick: Transaction Publishers, 1996 [1944]): 908.

38. Kryder, *Divided Arsenal*: 143.

39. Ibid.: 12–13, 142.

40. *People's Voice*, May 22nd, 1943, and *Amsterdam News*, May 29, 1943—both cited in ibid.: 176–8.

41. For a detailed account of the Camp Stewart incident, see Kryder, *Divided Arsenal*: 168–207. See also Stephen G. N. Tuck, *Beyond Atlanta: The Struggle for Racial Equality in Georgia 1940–1980* (Athens: University of Georgia Press, 2003): 26–7.

42. Cited in Kryder, *Divided Arsenal*: 186, 188.

43. Ibid.: 146–7.

44. There have been many accounts of the Sleepy Lagoon case. See McWilliams, *North From Mexico*: 207–11. McWilliams, editor of the *Nation* for twenty years, was one of the heads of the Sleepy Lagoon Defense Committee, and thus provides a first-hand account of the events. See also Eduardo Obregón Pagán, *Murder At the Sleepy Lagoon: Zoot Suits, Race and Riot in Wartime LA* (Chapel Hill: University of North Carolina Press, 2003), which focuses more on the cultural clashes provoked and their social significance in Los Angeles history; and Frank P. Barajas, "The Defense Committees of Sleepy Lagoon: A Convergent Struggle Against Fascism, 1942–1944," *Aztlan Journal* 31: 1 (Spring 2006). Among the sensational headlines in the local papers after the Sleepy Lagoon killing were: "MEXICAN GOON SQUADS," "ZOOT SUIT GANGS," "PACHUCO KILLERS," "JUVENILE GANG WAR LAID TO YOUTHS' DESIRE TO THRILL."

45. Cited in Obregón Pagán, *Murder At the Sleepy Lagoon*: 253–4, note 96.

46. *Sensation*, December 1942, cited in Obregón Pagán, *Murder At the Sleepy Lagoon*: 91, 252 n. 82 and 83.

47. Lynell Hancock, "The Press and the Central Park Jogger," *Columbia Journalism Review*, January 1, 2003; Ron Stodghill, "True Confession of the Central Park Rapist," *Time*, December 9, 2002.

48. Cited in Obregón Pagán, *Murder at the Sleepy Lagoon*: 107.

49. Ibid.: 106.

50. Frank P. Barajas, "Defense Committees of Sleepy Lagoon": 45.

51. Ralph H. Turner and Samuel J. Surace, "Zoot-Suiters and Mexicans: Symbols in Crowd Behavior," *American Journal of Sociology* 62 (July 1956): 14–20. Riot articles from L.A. newspapers cited in McWilliams, *North From Mexico*: 220–31. Obregón Pagán

questions the claims of McWilliams that the major newspapers deliberately fomented anti-Mexican sentiment, and suggests that the biased coverage may have had little real impact on the rioting sailors. See *Murder at the Sleepy Lagoon*: 126–8.

52. *Los Angeles Times*, June 7, 1943.

53. *Los Angeles Times*, June 9, 1943, cited in Obregón Pagán, *Murder at the Sleepy Lagoon*: 134.

54. *Los Angeles Herald-Examiner*, June 10, 1943, cited in Obregón Pagán, *Murder in the Sleepy Lagoon*: 135.

55. *La Opinión*, June 6, 1943; *Eastside Journal*, cited in MacWilliams, *North From Mexico*: 224.

56. Cited in Erik Barnouw ed., *Radio Drama in Action* (New York: Farrar, Straus & Co., 1945): 70–7.

57. Barlow, *Voice Over*: 72.

58. Barlow, *Voice Over*: 73–6. CBS showed *They Call Me Joe* and *Negro in War*, both of which hailed the contributions of black soldiers; and several programs from Armed Forces Radio showcased African-American entertainers, among them the *Mildred Bailey Show* and *Jubilee*.

59. Ronald Bishop, "To Protect and Serve: The 'Guard Dog' Function of Journalism in Coverage of the Japanese-American Internment," *Journalism and Communications Monographs* 2: 2 (2000): 82.

60. Frank H. Wu, *Yellow: Race in America Beyond Black and White* (New York: Basic Books, 202): 96.

61. Bishop, "Protect and Serve": 69; "Viper" cited in Ronald Takaki, *Double Victory: A Multicultural History of America in World War II* (Boston: Little Brown & Company, 2000): 146.

62   Ibid.: 70.

63. Ibid.: 69.

64. Ibid.

65. Howard Blue, *World War II Era Radio Drama and the Postwar Broadcasting Industry Blacklist* (Lanham, Maryland: Scarecrow Press, 2002): 205.

66. Ibid.: 204. See also Gerd Horton, *Radio Goes to War: The Cultural Politics of Propaganda During World War II* (Berkeley: University of California Press, 2002): 54–5.

67. Ibid.: 66.

68. Murray Schumach, "TV Called 'Timid' on Negro Talent," *New York Times*, October 24, 1961; Barlow, *Voice Over*: 75–6.

Chapter 15: The Color Line and the Public Interest

1. Douglas, *Listening In*: 223–5.

2. David K. Wiggins, "Wendell K. Smith, the Pittsburgh *Courier-Journal* and the Campaign to Include Blacks in Organized Baseball, 1933–1945," *Journal of Sports History* 10: 2 (Summer 1983): 6–7.

3   Dave Zirin, *A People's History of Sports in the United States* (New York: The New Press, 2008): 85.

4. Wiggins, "Wendell K. Smith": 7–8.

5. Cited in Zirin, *People's History*: 86–7.

6. Pittsburgh *Courier*, February 27, 1943, cited in ibid.: 19.

7. Zirin, *People's History*: 88–9.

8. Ibid.: 72.

9. For an excellent description of this pivotal meeting and the role of the black newspaper publishers, see Wiggins, "Wendell K. Smith": 21–3.

10. *Associated Press v. US*, 326 US 1 (1945): 4, 18, 20.

11. Ibid.: 28.

12. American Newspaper Guild, "Careers for Negroes on Newspapers" (Washington, DC: American Newspaper Guild, AFl-CIO, CLC, 1964): 8.

13. Fred Blevins, "The Hutchins Commission Turns 50: Recurring Themes in Today's Public and Civic Journalism," paper presented at Third Annual Conference on Intellectual Freedom, April 1997, Montana State University—Northern. See also Mercedes Lynn de Uriarte, Cristina Bodinger de Uriarte and Jose Luis Benavides, *Diversity Disconnect: From Classroom to News Room* (New York: Ford Foundation, 2003): 23–8.

14. Federal Communications Commission, *Public Service Responsibility of Broadcast Licenses* (Washington, DC: FCC, 1946): 13–15, 48.

15. Ibid.

16. Lloyd, *Prologue to a Farce*: 137.

17. Ward, *Radio and the Struggle for Civil Rights*: 129.

18. Douglas, *Listening In*: 225.

19. Ward, *Radio and the Struggle for Civil Right*: 6, 42; MacDonald, *Don't Touch That Dial!*: 365–6; Dates and Barlow, *Split Image*: 227.

20. See Barlow, *Voice Over*: 176–85; Douglas, *Listening In*: 227–46.

21. Jorge Reina Schement and Ricardo Flores, "The Origins of Spanish-Language Radio: The Case of San Antonio, Texas," *Journalism History* 4: 2 (Summer 1977): 56.

22. Ibid.: 56.

23. Ibid.

24. Ibid.: 57.

25. Aziz Shihab, "Mateo Hears Cry of Desperate," *San Antonio Express-News*, September 10, 1974.

26. Nicolas Kanellos, *Hispanic Firsts: 500 Years of Extraordinary Achievement* (Houston: Arte Publico Press, 1977): 196.

27. National Telecommunications and Information Agency, *Changes, Challenges and Charting New Courses: Minority Ownership in the United States* (Washington, DC: US Department of Commerce, 2000): 12.

28. Ward, *Radio and the Struggle for Civil Rights*: 160–1.

29. Ward, *Radio and the Struggle for Civil Rights*: 62–3; Barlow, *Voice Over*: 136–8.

30. Quoted in Barlow, *Voice Over*: 208–9.

31. Ward, *Radio and the Struggle for Civil Rights*: 165–7.

32. Steve Penn, "Celebrating 60 years, radio station KPRS proudly remains a family-

owned business," *Kansas City Star*, August 30, 2010, at <www.kansascity.com/2010/08/30/2188746/celebrating-60-years-radio-station.html>.

33. Teresa Paloma Acosta and Ruthe Winegarten, *Las Tejanas: Three Hundred Years of History* (Austin: University of Texas Press, 2003): 192–3.

34. Ward, *Radio and the Struggle for Civil Rights*: 182–3.

35. Barlow, *Voice Over*: 207.

36. "Broadcast Tower of WUFO Felled 2nd Time by Vandals," *New York Times*, July 4, 1969: 24.

37. Federal Communications Commission, "Re-Application of Southland Television Company, Shreveport, LA" (Washington, DC: FCC, 1955): 163.

38. Kay Mills, *Changing Channels: The Civil Rights Case that Transformed Television* (Oxford: University of Mississippi Press, 2004): 247–8.

39. Geller to J. Edgar Hoover, January 1, 1967, National Archives, Records of the Federal Communications Commission. Office of the Executive Director, General Correspondence 1941–1971, Box 7, Folder "Department of Justice."

40. Ward, *Radio and the Struggle for Civil Rights*: 46. Young had embarked on the format change to reach the city's growing black consumer market, and had even allowed the local NAACP to produce a weekly show. But he had also ordered that no one on the station's staff make on-air statements opposing segregation. So when DJ Cook publicly criticized the exclusion of blacks from a city-owned golf course and from religious plays in local schools, Young immediately fired him. In response, the local NAACP branch severed its relationship with the station and filed a formal protest to the FCC about the station's racial policies—to no avail.

41. John Lash, "Educational Implications of the Negro College Radio Program," *Journal of Negro Education* 13: 2 (Spring 1944); see also *Time*, March 27, 1944. During that decade, students at Fisk University, Bennett College in Greensboro, North Carolina, Georgia's Fort Valley State College, and Atlanta University all produced shows that were broadcast on white-owned stations. In 1940/41, Bennett students co-produced *Gwen's Folks* with WBIG in Greensboro, a CBS affiliate. The much-acclaimed series dramatized a black family's efforts to overcome everyday problems. Once the war began, Bennett students produced *Americans, Too: We Have Achieved*—a series that extolled black contributions to American history. Fort Valley State even shared an Alfred Dupont award given to station WMAZ in Macon, Georgia, in 1944 for "contributing to better racial understanding."

42. See "Initial Comments of Diversity and Competition Supporters," in 2002 Biennial Regulatory Review of the Federal Communications Commission, January 2nd, 2003: 23. See also <www.thecapstone.ua.edu/index.php?page=History>.

43. Barlow, *Voice Over*: 204.

44. Ibid.: 204–5. We have largely relied here on William Barlow's excellent account of some of the major Civil Rights movement DJs.

45. <www.wwrl1600.com/history.asp>.

46. Barlow, *Voice Over*: 208–9.

47. Steven D. Classen. *Watching Jim Crow: The Struggles Over Mississippi TV, 1955–1969*

(Durham: Duke University Press, 2004): 41; Classen, *Broadcast Law and Segregation: A Social History of WLBT* (Madison: University of Wisconsin, 1995): 25.

48. Classen, *Broadcast Law*: 32.

49. Roberts and Klibanoff, *Race Beat*: 65–6.

50. Mills, *Changing Channels*: 39; Classen, *Watching Jim Crow*: 88.

51. Mills, *Changing Channels*: 25, 40; Ward, *Radio and the Struggle for Civil Rights*: 250.

52. Roberts and Klibanoff, *Race Beat*: 80–1.

53. Ibid.: 282.

54. "Negro in FCC Protest," *New York Times*, October 30, 1957.

55. Some accounts of the WLBT saga have claimed that Parker was a participant in the meetings with M. L. King, Jr., and Andy Young. But Parker has since said he did not directly participate in those meetings. See *Democracy Now!* transcript of March 6, 2008 interview with Everett Parker at <www.democracynow.org/2008/3/6/the_fcc_censorship_legendary_media_activist>.

56. Robert Horwitz, "Broadcast Reform Revisited: Reverend Everett C. Parker and the 'Standing' Case (*Office of Communications of the United Church of Christ v. Federal Communications Commission*)," *Communications Review* 2: 3 (1997): 312–15; Mills, *Changing Channels*: 65–66.

57. From the FCC's "Reply to Opposition to Petition to Intervene and to Deny Application for Renewal" [for WLBT], June 13, 1964, cited in Horwitz, "Broadcasting Reform Revisited." See also Ward, *Radio and the Struggle for Civil Rights*.

58. Henry Hampton and Steve Fayer, *Voices of Freedom: An Oral History of the Civil Rights Movement from the 1950s through the 1980s* (New York: Bantam Books, 1991): 116.

59. Roberts and Klibanoff, *Race Beat*: 273–4; Mills, *Changing Channels*: 67.

60. Mills, *Changing Channels*: 117; Taylor Branch, *Parting the Waters: America in the King years 1954–1963* (New York: Touchstone, 1989): 653; Ward, *Radio and the Struggle for Civil Rights*: 254–5.

61. Minority Media and Telecommunications Council, "Initial Comments of Diversity Competition Supporters," FCC 2002 Biennial Regulatory Review (Washington, DC: MMTC, 2003): 22.

62. "Let Negroes Give Views, FCC Says," *New York Times*, July 27, 1963.

63. Cited in Mills, *Changing Channels*: 49–50.

64. Classen, *Watching Jim Crow*: 3–4, 48.

65. Horwitz, "Broadcast Reform Revisited": 311–48; "FCC Tells Southern Stations to Halt Radio-TV Racial Bias," *New York Times*, May 21, 1965.

66. *Office of Communication of the United Church of Christ v. FCC* 359 F.2d 994 (D.C. Cir. 1966): 1,001.

67. Ibid.: 1,003.

68. Mills, *Changing Cahnnels*: 239–40.

69. Sidney A. Schapiro, *United Church of Christ v. FCC: Private Attorneys General and the Rule of Law*, Wake Forest University Legal Studies Research Paper Series, June 2006: 2.

Chapter 16: Fierce Rebellion, Furious Reaction

1. Dewey W. Grantham, *The South in Modern America: A Region At Odds* (Little Rock: University of Arkansas Press, 2001): 242.

2. Mills, *Changing Channels*: 245; Milton Muller, Brenden Kuerbis and Christiane Page, *Reinventing Media Activism: Public Interest Advocacy in the Making of US Communication-Information Policy,* 1960–2002 (Syracuse: The Convergence Center School of Information Studies at Syracuse University, 2004): 35–8.

3. "National Advisory Commission on Civil Disorders Report" (Washington, DC: US Government Printing Office, 1968): 1; Daniel J. Meyers and Beth Schaefer Caniglia, "All the Rioting That's Fit to Print: Selection Effects in National Newspaper Coverage of Civil Disorders," *American Sociological Review* 69: 4 (August 2004): 532, 526.

4. "National Advisory Commission on Civil Disorders Report": 210, 217.

5. LeRoy Collins, the agency's director, was a former president of the National Association of Broadcasters, while its deputy director Calvin Kytle was a veteran journalist and publicist. Both men were convinced that media companies were exacerbating black-white divisions; Kytle was especially critical of the newspaper industry for routinely failing to interview African-American leaders and for often running stories about civil rights alongside crime reports. See "A Pioneer in Journalism Dies," press statement from Phillip Merrill College of Journalism, University of Maryland, January 23, 2007, at www.journalism.umd.edu; Yvonne Shinhoster Lamb, "Journalist Ben. F. Holman: Advised Nixon, Ford on Racial Issues," *Washington Post,* January 27, 2009.

6. Mills, *Changing Channels*: 254–7.

7. "Editors Clash Over Slurs," *Atlanta Daily World,* April 28, 1956: 4.

8. "Sengstacke Elected to Editors' Society," *Chicago Daily Defender,* November 24, 1965: 3; "Sengstacke On Editors Assn. Board," *New Pittsburgh Courier,* May 23, 1970: 1; Alf Pratte, "But there is Miles to Go: Racial Diversity and the American Society of Newspaper Editors, 1922–2000," *Journal of Negro History* 86: 2 (Spring 2001): 167.

9. Pratte, "But there is Miles to Go": 168.

10. Ibid.: 169.

11. Vernon Stone, "Women Gain But Minorities Barely Hold Their Own in their Share of Broadcast Newsroom Jobs," *RTNDA Communicator,* April 1983: 18–19.

12. Mills, *Changing Channels*: 242–3.

13. "New Challenges from Every Side," *Broadcasting,* September 8, 1969: 25.

14. Phyl Garland, "Blacks Challenge the Airwaves," *Ebony,* November 1970: 35–42.

15. Barlow, *Voice Over*: 250–1.

16. Letter from the FCC's Broadcast Bureau to Lonnie King, January 27, 1970; letter from E. Joi Thompson to FCC's Renewal Branch, January 20, 1970—both found in FCC records at the National Archives, Office of the Executive Director, Correspondence of the Chairman, 1941 to 1971, Box 32, Folder "NAACP 1/1/67–6/11/71."

17. "Georgia Broadcasters Jittery," *Jet,* April 9, 1970: 62–3.

18. Letter from Fletcher Thompson to FCC Chairman Dean Burch, February 28, 1970, National Archives, Reg. 173, Stack 550, Row 17, Compartment 11–12, Shelf 1-N.

Record ID Officer of the Executive Director, Correspondence of the Chairman 1941–1971, Folder NAACP 11/1/67–6/11/71; Hamilton Bims, "A Southern Activist Goes to the House," *Ebony*, February 1973: 90.

19. John H. Britton, "How Blacks Won TV-Radio Fight in Atlanta," *Jet*, April 30, 1970: 14–22.

20. Author's interview with Albert Kramer, February 2009, Washington, DC; "Strike Tactics," *Broadcasting*, September 8, 1969.

21. Dates and Barlow, *Split Image*: 330–1. Because of its advocacy of the African-American community, *Black Journal* was always in danger of being dropped by local PBS stations, but local black leaders formed "Friends of Black Journal" committees to pressure stations to keep the show on the air.

22. Author's interview with Albert Kramer, February 2009, Washington, DC.

23. Mills, *Changing Channels*: 247–8.

24. Bowen was instrumental in organizing the first-ever meeting between African-American leaders and the FCC in 1973. "Black people cannot expect fair treatment in the media if they remain silent," she wrote in one of her regular columns for the *Amsterdam News* on FCC policy. See Emma Bowen, "Eye on the Media," New York *Amsterdam News*, March 3, 1973: D6. See also, "Biographical Sketch of Emma Bowmen," at emmabowenfoundation.com.

25. Author's interview with Albert Kramer, February 2009, Washington, DC.

26. Chon A. Noriega, *Shot in America: Television, the State and the Rise of Chicano Cinema*, (Minneapolis: University of Minnesota Press, 2000): 36–7; US Commission on Civil Rights, *Window Dressing on the Set: Women and Minorities in Television* (Washington, DC: GPO, August 1977): 11.

27. Noriega, *Shot in America*: 36.

28. Francisco J. Lewels, Jr., *The Uses of the Media by the Chicano Movement: A Study in Minority Access* (New York: Praeger, 1974): 64–5.

29. Mario T. García, *Ruben Salazar: Border Correspondent: Selected Writings, 1955–1970* (Berkeley: University of California Press, 1995): 232.

30. Frito-Lay initially announced in 1970 that it would stop airing the commercial, but did so only in California, Oregon and Washington. See US Commission on Civil Rights, *Window Dressing on the Set*: 58–60; Lewels, *Uses of the Media*: 59; Noriega, *Shot in America*: 35–47.

31. Domingo Nick Reyes, "Films and Broadcast Demeaning Ethnic, Racial and Gender Groups," Testimony to the US House of Representatives, Subcommittee on Communications, Power, Interstate and Foreign Commerce," September 21, 1970.

32. García, *Ruben Salazar: Border Correspondent*: 239–40.

33. Lewels, *Uses of the Media*: 86–7.

34. Noriega, *Shot in America*: 85–6.

35. The McGraw-Hill agreement established a minority advisory council for the four stations the company purchased in San Diego and Bakersfield, California, Denver, and Indianapolis. See John J. O'Connor, "Minority Groups' Significance in TV Deal," *New York Times*, May 11, 1972: 93. In 1972, NMAADC organized license challenges across the country to contest the Doubleday acquisitions in San Antonio (KITE-AM), El

Paso (KROD-TV), Odessa (KOSA-TV), and Albuquerque (KDEF-AM). Doubleday promised to hire at least one Chicano newsroom staffer who would cover the *barrio* and serve as an investigative reporter on Chicano issues at each station. It agreed to hire a Chicano anchor, conduct sensitivity training, and form an advisory board that worked directly with Doubleday executives. See "Doubleday, Chicanos Settle in Four Markets," *Broadcasting*, March 27, 1972: 10. Around the same time, the newly formed Colorado Committee on Mass Media and the Spanish Surnamed, Inc., challenged the licenses of forty-five Colorado broadcast stations. See Lewels, *Uses of the Media*: 113–14.

36. Noriega, *Shot in America*: 148–50.

37. Clara Rodríguez, *Latin Looks: Images of Latinas and Latinos in the US Media* (Boulder, Colorado: Westview Press, 1997): 190–2; Noriega, *Shot in America*: 148–52.

38. The coalition created a TV production company that produced a one-hour TV special about Mexican-Americans that aired nationwide. See Noriega, *Shot in America*: 78–9; Jorge Reina Schement and Felix Frank Gutierrez, "Citizen Action: The Anatomy of a License Challenge," *Journal of Communication*, Winter 1977: 89–94.

39 García, *Ruben Salazar*: 5, 29.

40. Enrique Hank Lopez, "Ruben Salazar Death Silences a Leading Voice of Reason," *Los Angeles Times*, September 6, 1970: C7; Lewels, *Uses of the Media*: 89–91.

41. Garcia, *Ruben Salazar*: 1; Juan Gómez Quiñones, *Chicano Politics: Reality and Promise, 1940–1990* (Albuquerque: University of New Mexico Press, 1990): 124-28; Ignacio M. García, *United We Win: The Rise and Fall of La Raza Unida Party* (Tucson: MASCRC, University of Arizona, 1989): 97.

42 García, *Ruben Salazar*: 3.

43. Henry Geller, "The Comparative Hearing Process in Television: Problems and Suggested Solutions," *Virginia Law Review* 61: 3 (April 1975): 477.

44. Dennis Lebec, "Nicholas Johnson: Maverick FCC Commissioner, 1966–1973," paper presented at the National Broadcasting Society Convention, March 1999, at uiowa.edu; Nicholas Johnson and James M Hook, Jr., "Media Concentration: Some Observations on the United States' Experience," *Iowa Law Review* 56 (1970–71): 269–70.

45. Columbia Law Review Association, "Implications of *Citizens Communication Center v. FCC*," *Columbia Law Review* 71: 8 (December 1971) 1500–1510; Geller, "Comparative Hearing Process: 482–6.

46. During World War II, the FCC froze the licensing of TV stations. Once the War ended and the freeze was lifted, the number of stations on air jumped from seventeen to forty-nine, and sales of TV sets skyrocketed. See Sydney W. Head and Christopher H. Sterling, *Broadcasting in America: A Survey of Electronic Media*, 5th edn (Boston: Houghton Milton Company, 1987): 84–5; Thomas R. Eisenmann, "The US Cable Television Industry, 1948–1995: Managerial Capitalism in Eclipse," *Business History Review* 74: 1 (Spring 2001): 4–5.

47. Eisenmann, "The US Cable Television Industry": 5; Joseph R. Dominick, Barry L. Sherman, and Gary Copeland, *Broadcasting/Cable and Beyond: An Introduction to Modern Electronic Media* (New York: McGraw-Hill, 1990): 253–4.

48. Eisenmann, "The US Cable Television Industry": 5–6.

49. Phyl Garland, "Blacks Challenge the Airwaves," *Ebony*, November 1970: 42–3.

50. Charles Tate, *Cable Television in the Cities: Community Control, Public Access and Minority Ownership* (Washington, DC: Urban Institute, 1971): 16–19.

51. Jennifer S. Light, *From Warfare to Welfare: Defense Intellectuals and Urban Problems in Cold War America* (Baltimore: John Hopkins University Press, 2003): 170–2.

52. The Sloan Foundation commission called for local governments to build the cable system as common carriers or for municipal information centers operated by private companies that provided social services. Several federal agencies jointly sponsored the National Academy of Engineering study. See Light, *From Warfare to Welfare*: 179–81.

53. Light, *From Warfare to Welfare*: 178.

54. Patrick Parson, *Blue Skies: A History of Cable Television* (Philadelphia: Temple University Press, 2008): 265.

55. Mark Robichaux, *Cable Cowboy: John Malone and the Rise of the Modern Cable Business* (Hoboken: John Wiley & Sons, 2002): 65–6; Parson, *Blue Skies*: 289.

56. Stephen Keating, *Cutthroat: High Stakes and Killer Moves on the Electronic Frontier* (Boulder: Johnson Books, 1999): 55–6; Robichaux, *Cable Cowboy*: 75–6; Parson, *Blue Skies*: 514.

57. Keating, *Cutthroat*: 53

58. Robichaux, *Cable Cowboy*: 66.

59. Keating, *Cutthroat*: 54; Parson, *Blue Skies*: 408.

60. "Business," *Ebony*, August 1983: 180.

61. Derek T. Dingle, *Black Enterprise: Lessons from the Top: Success Strategies from America's Leading Black CEOs* (New York: John Wiley & Sons, 1999): 206; Parson, *Blue Skies*: 484. James W. Roman, *Cablemania: The Cable Television Sourcebook* (Englewood Cliffs: Prentice-Hall, 1983): 180.

62. Barbara Hagenbaugh and Sue Kirchhoff, "From BET to Hotels to Banking, Johnson Keeps Moving Forward," *USA Today*, February 12, 2006.

63. Dingle, *Black Enterprise*: 223, 226; Alan Hughes, "Architects of Growth Black Enterprise," *New York* 37: 11 (June 2007): 88.

64. Dingle, *Black Enterprise*: 205–9.

65. Robichaux, *Cable Cowboy*: 73–4; Parson, *Blue Skies*: 478, 626.

66. "Comcast + NBC = Bad Deal for the Public," Free Press Fact Sheet, at www.freepress.net/files/Comcast-NBC_Bad_Deal_for_the_Public.pdf.

67. Coauthor Juan González, then a reporter at the Philadelphia *Daily News*, was also one of NAHJ's founding members, serving on its board of directors in 1984 and 1985 and as president of the association from 2002 to 2004.

68. Stanford Chen, *Counting on Each Other: A History of the Asian American Journalists Association from 1981 to 1996* (San Francisco: AAJA, 1996): 1–6.

69. Native American Journalists Association website, "About Us," at www.naja.com.

70. Clinton C. Wilson II and Félix Gutiérrez, *Race, Multiculturalism, and the Media: From Mass to Class Communication*, 2nd edn (Thousand Oaks: Sage Publications, 1995): 224.

71. Kanellos, *Hispanic Firsts*: 197.

72. Minority journalists, the report found, were usually assigned to cover stories about race. In addition, only sixteen of 141 newsmakers who appeared in the stories analyzed by

the report were people of color. See US Commission on Civil Rights, *Window Dressing on the Set*: 49–52.

73. Pamela Newkirk, *Within the Veil: Black Journalists, White Media* (New York: New York University Press, 2000): 110–15. We based much of the information for this section on Newkirk's superb recounting of the racial discrimination complaints at the *Washington Post*, *New York Times*, Associated Press, and *Daily News*.

74. Newkirk, *Within the Veil*: 113.

75. Ibid.: 114–15.

76. Ibid.: 114.

77. Richard Prince, "David Hardy, Leader of the 'Daily News 4,' Dies," at mije.org/richardprince/david-hardy-leader-daily-news-4-dies; US Commission on Civil Disorders Report: 300.

78. Newkirk, *Within the Veil*: 117.

79. Ibid.: 98.

80. Ibid.: 104–5.

81. Ibid.: 104, 110–11.

82. Ibid.: 122.

83. Ibid.: 125.

84. See the 2000 Annual Newsroom Survey of the American Society of News Editors, at asne.org/key_initiatives/diversity/newsroom_census/table_a.aspx.

85. National Telecommunications and Information Administration, *Changes, Challenges and Charting New Courses: Minority Commercial Ownership in the United States* (Washington, DC: US Department of Commerce, 2000): 14; Barlow, *Voice Over*: 249–50.

86. Christine Bache and Stephanie Craft, *Diversity Programming in the Broadcast Spectrum: Is There a Link Between Owners' Race or Ethnicity and News and Public Affairs Programming?* (Washington, DC: Federal Communications Commission, 1999): 3–20.

87. Barlow, *Voice Over*: 265–6.

88. Armistead S. Pride and Clint C. Wilson II, *A History of the Black Press* (Washington, DC, Howard University Press, 1999): 258–9.

89. See Maynard Institute for Journalism Education, at www.mije.org/minoritiesinmedia.

90. Barlow, *Voice Over*: 267–8.

91. National Telecommunications and Information Administration, *Changes, Challenges*: 14; Kofi Asiedu Ofori and Mark Lloyd, "The Value of the Tax Certificate Program," *Federal Communications Law Journal* 51: 3 (May 1999): 694–7.

92. National Telecommunications and Information Administration, *Changes, Challenges*: 1.

93. Ofori and Lloyd, "Value of the Tax Certificate Program": 700.

94. Barlow, *Voice Over*: 272–7; Kevin L. Carter, "Radio Powerhouse Cathy Hughes has Expanded Her Empire to Philadelphia's WDRE-FM," *Philadelphia Inquirer*, April 8, 1997: D1. See also Radio One's website at radio-one.com/properties.

95. Matthew Lasar, *Pacifica Radio: The Rise of an Alternative Network* (Philadelphia: Temple University Press, 2000).

96. Kristin C. Moran, "The Development of Spanish-Language Television in San Diego: A Contemporary History," *Journal of San Diego History* 50: 1 (2003): 47–8.

97.　Ibid.: 44; Federico A. Subervi-Velez, "Mass Communication and Hispanics," in Nicolás Kanellos and Félix Padilla, eds, *A Handbook on Hispanic Cultures in the United States* (Houston: Arte Público Press, 1994): 335; John Sinclair, *Latin American Television: A Global View* (New York: OUP, 1999): 99.

98.　Moran, "Development of Spanish-Language Television": 44; Subervi-Velez, "Mass Communication and Hispanics": 337.

99.　*Los Angeles Times*, September 21, 1986.

100.　Sinclair, *Latin American Television*: 339.

101.　"FCC Probing Spanish-Language TV Programming Service," *Los Angeles Times*, September 5, 1980.

102.　Nancy Rivera, "KMEX-TV, Other Stations to be Sold to Non-Latinos," *Los Angeles Times*, July 22nd, 1986: A1; Subervi-Velez, "Mass Communications and Hispanics": 338–9.

103.　Victor Valle, "The SIN Sale: Will It make Any Difference?" *Los Angeles Times*, September 21, 1986: Q3; Subervi-Velez, "Mass Communication and Hispanics": 335–6.

104.　Alex Avila, "Trading Punches," *Hispanic*, January/February 1997: 38–44; Richard Stevenson, "Hallmark to Sell Univisión to Television Groups," *New York Times*, April 9, 1992.

105.　NAHJ Press Release, "NAHJ Board Statement on NBC's Plans for Telemundo," October 23, 2006, at nahj.org/nahjnews/articles/2006/october/telemundo.shtml.

106.　Moran, "Development of Spanish-Language Television": 52.

107.　John Wilke, "Has the FCC Gone Too Far?" *Business Week*, August 5, 1985: 48; Tom Shales, "Fowler's Way: Foul is Fair, The Lowly Legacy of the Former FCC Head," *Washington Post*, April 20, 1987: B1.

108.　Caroline E. Mayer and Elizabeth Tucker, "The FCC According to Mark Fowler; Chairman's Tenure Characterized by Distrust of Most Regulation," *Washington Post*, April 19, 1987: H1; John Wilke, "Has the FCC Gone Too Far?"

109.　Veteran journalist and media historian Ben Bagdikian blasted the FCC in 1987 for relaxing industry ownership rules:

> The FCC is not bailing out a sick industry. The three networks, even with their takeover debts, are still making money. Affiliated television stations are earning annual pre-tax profits of 40 percent or more. As a result, stations that used to sell for tens of millions now sell for prices in the half-billion-dollar range. Where else can you get a business based on a license issued and protected by the US government, make 40 percent profit or more a year, and not be expected to be held to some standard of public service?

See Ben Bagdikan, "The 50, 26, 20… Corporations That Own Our Media," *Extra!* June 1987, at www.fair.org/index.php?page=1498.

110.　Mayer and Tucker, "FCC According to Mark Fowler."

111.　Reginald Stuart, "FCC Accused on Minority Issue," *New York Times*, May 23, 1985: C25.

112.　Kleiman, *Content Diversity*: 418.

113. *Metro Broadcasting, Inc. v. FCC,* 1990, at www.law.cornell.edu/supct/html/89-453. ZO.html.

114. Helen Dewar, "Senate Rejects Minority Radio, TV Tax Break," *Washington Post,* April 4, 1995: 7.

115. Bill Holland and Chuck Taylor, "FCC May Challenge EEO Ruling—Decision Could Affect Minority Recruitment," *Billboard,* April 25, 1998; Bob Papper, *Women and Minorities in the Newsroom,* RTNDA Communicator, July/August 2007: 20–5, at www.rtnda. org/media/pdfs/communicator/2007/julaug/20-25_Survey_Communicator.pdf.

116. Common Cause Education Fund, "The Fallout from the Communications Act of 1996: Unintended Consequences and Lessons Learned," May 9, 2005: 3–5.

117. Jeff Chester, *Digital Destiny* (New York: New Press, 2007): 21; Andrew Jay Schwartzman, Harold Feld and Parul Desai, "Section 202(h) of the Telecommunications Act of 1996: Beware of Intended Consequences," *Federal Communications Law Journal* 58: 3 (June 2006): 582–3, at www.law.indiana.edu/fclj/pubs/v58/no3/q-schwartzman.pdf.

118 Ofori and Lloyd, "The Value of the Tax Certificate," *Federal Communications Law Journal* 51: 3 (May 1999): 703; George Williams, "Review of the Radio Industry, 2007," Federal Communications Commission (August 2007) at <http://hraunfoss.fcc.gov/edocs_ public/attachmatch/DA-07-3470A7.pdf>

119. Kevin L Carter, "A Radio Powerhouse Cathy Hughes Has Expanded Her Empire," *Philadelphia Inquirer,* April 8, 1997: D1. Singer Stevie Wonder warned at an FCC hearing that independent stations like his KJLH in Compton, California, needed protection from conglomerates. See Christopher Stern, "Song in the Key of FCC: Wonder Wonders Why Feds Would Dereg Stations," *Daily Variety,* February 16, 1999: 14.

120. Gail Mitchell, "Q&A: Cathy Hughes," Billboard.com, December 3, 2005.

121. Federal Communications Commission, "Whose Spectrum is It Anyway? Historical Study of Market Entry Barriers, Discrimination and Changes in Broadcast and Wireless Licensing 1950 to Present," December 2000: 143. Lobbyists for Rupert Murdoch were able to keep the pressure on the FCC to deregulate further by securing a provision in the Telecommunications Act, Section 202(h), that required Congress to examine its rules every two years and repeal or modify any regulation it determined no longer served the public interest. See Christopher Stern, "FCC's new Chair Toes Clinton Line," *Daily Variety,* November 4, 1997: 1. See also Seth Schiesel, "Opposition Delay's Clinton's FCC selection," *New York Times,* August 3, 1997: A26.

122. Chester, *Digital Destiny:* 92.

123. Ben Scott, "The Politics and Policy of Media Ownership," *American University Law Review* 53: 3, February 2004: 645–6.

124. "PTC Links Indecent Programming to Media Consolidation," Parents Television Council press release, October 4, 2006, at www.parentstv.org/PTC/news/release/2006/ 1004.asp.

125. Fairness and Accuracy in Reporting, "Networks Pick Up on FCC Story," May 30, 2003, at www.fair.org/index.php?page=1608.

126. "NAHJ and NABJ Call On FCC to Delay Issuing New Broadcast Ownership Rules," NAHJ and NABJ joint press statement on May 27, 2003, at www.nahj.org/

release/2003/pr052703.html. The authors spearheaded NAHJ's media policy efforts in 2003. Juan González was NAHJ president at the time, and Joseph Torres was the association's deputy director.

127. Frank Ahrens, "Court Rejects Rules On Media Ownership," *Washington Post*, June 25, 2004: E01; "Major Victory for Localism and Diversity, Federal Court Overturns FCC Decision on Media Ownership," Free Press statement, Washington, DC, June 24, 2004. See also "Statement of Media Access Project Reacting to the US Court of Appeals Media Ownership Decision," June 24, 2004, at mediaaccess.org. The court's decision did not affect a White House–negotiated deal to lift the national broadcast audience cap from 35 percent to 39 percent. That measure passed as part of a spending bill that Congress passed in 2004.

128. Statement of FCC Chairman Kevin J. Martin, "In the Matter of 2006 Quadrennial Regulatory Review, February 4, 2008," at hraunfoss.fcc.gov/edocs_public/attachmatch/FCC-07-216A2.pdf. See also Ryan Blethen, "Time to End the Cross-Ownership Debate and Ensure Media Diversity," *Seattle Times*, May 21, 2010.

Chapter 17: Controlling the Means of Transmission

1. Coauthor Juan González, then a reporter at the *Philadelphia Daily News* and a member of the paper's Third World caucus, attended that meeting. Harris acknowledged to his guests that while he was certainly qualified to be the paper's executive editor, he believed Knight Ridder appointed him at that time because of persistent pressure from the caucus for the hiring of an African-American in top management.

2. David Laventhol, "Profit Pressures: A Question of Margins," *Columbia Journalism Review*, May–June 2001: 18–19; Shawn Hubler, "Regarding Media; Bottom Line: It's Not Just About the Bottom Line," *Los Angeles Times*, April 20, 2001: E1.

3. In addition to Harris, Frank Blethen, publisher of the *Seattle Times*, and Eugene Roberts, former publisher of the *Philadelphia Inquirer*, had warned their colleagues for years that corporate newspaper chains, with their emphasis on maximum short-term profits, were decimating newsroom staffs. See Gene Roberts, Thomas Kunkel and Charles Layton, eds, *Leaving Readers Behind: The Age of Corporate Newspapering* (Little Rock: University of Arkansas Press, 2001).

4. Roberts et al., *Leaving Readers Behind*: 51.

5. Howard Witt, "Blogs Help Drive Jena Protest," *Chicago Tribune*, September 18, 2007; Glen Ford, "Blacks Need Radio News, Not Michael Baisden Slanders," Alternet, November 21, 2007, at www.alternet.org/story/68398; ColorOfChange website: colorofchange.org/jena.

6. Project for Excellence in Journalism, "State of the Media 2004," at www.stateofthemedia.org/2004/narrative_newspapers_audience.asp?cat=3&media=2; Robert McChesney and John Nichols, *The Death and Life of American Journalism: The Media Revolution That Will Begin the World Again* (Philadelphia: Nation Books, 2010): 26.

7. David Laventhol, "Profit Pressures: A Question of Margins," *Columbia Journalism Review*, May/June 2001: 18–19; Paul Farhi, "The 'Takeover,' *American Journalism Review*, July/

August 2001: 32–3; McChesney and Nichols, *Death and Life of American Journalism*: 12; interview with John Sokolski, coauthor, along with Gilbert Cranberg and Randall Bezanson, of *Taking Stock: Journalism and the Publicly Traded Newspaper Company* (Iowa State University, 2001), March 2009.

8. Jennifer Saba, "NEW FAS-FAX OUT: Most Major Papers Continue Circ Decline," *Editor & Publisher*, October 28, 2008; Richard Perez-Pena, "US Newspaper Circulation Falls 10%," *New York Times*, October 26, 2009.

9. Project for Excellence in Journalism, "State of the News Media 2010: Newspapers, March 2010," at www.stateofthemedia.org/2010/printable_newspaper_chapter.htm.

10. Greg Bensinger, "San Francisco May Be Largest City to Lose Main Paper," Bloomberg News, at www.bloomberg.com/apps/news?pid=20601103&sid=a7W3v10uIRr0&refer =us#; Project for Excellence in Journalism, "State of the News Media 2010: Newspapers, March 2010."

11. Victor Pickard, Josh Stearns and Craig Arron, *Changing Media: Public Interest Policies for the Digital Age* (Free Press, 2009): 190–2; also Project for Excellence in Journalism, "The State of the News Media 2009," at www.stateofthemedia.org/2009/narrative_ newspapers_newsinvestment.php?media=4&cat=4#9jobs; McChesney and Nichols, *Death and Life of American Journalism*: 17–18; American Society of News Editors, "Decline in Newsroom Jobs Slows," April 11, 2010, at www.asne.org/article_view/articleid/763/ decline-in-newsroom-jobs-slows-763.aspx; Project for Excellence in Journalism, "State of the News Media 2010: Newspapers, March 2010."

12. Elizabeth MacIver Neiva, "Chain Building: The Consolidation of the American Newspaper Industry, 1953–1980," *Business and Economic History*, Fall 1995: 22–6; Bagdikian, *Media Monopoly*: 68–74.

13. MacIver Neiva, "Chain Building": 22–6.

14. Frank A. Blethen, "It's Going to Get Worse," *Columbia Journalism Review*, May/June 2001: 23.

15. Leonard Downie, Jr., and Robert G. Kasier, *The News About the News: American Journalism in Peril* (New York: Alfred A. Knopf, 2002): 79.

16. McChesney and Nichols, *Death and Life of American Journalism*: 15. See also Brian Stetler and Bill Carter, "ABC News Plans to Trim 300 to 400 from Staff," *New York Times*, February 24, 2010: B5; Project for Excellence in Journalism, "State of the News Media 2010: Introduction, March 2010."

17. National Association of Black Journalists, "Black Journalists Slashed from Newsrooms at Alarming Rate," April 20, 2009, at www.nabj.org/newsroom/news_releases/2009/ newsrel042009layoffs.php; American Society of Newspaper Editors, "Newsrooms Shrink; Minority Percentage Increases Slightly," April 13, 2008, at 204.8.120.192/files/ 08Census.pdf; Kathy Times, "How will Journalism be Transformed by the Internet?" National Association of Black Journalists, December 2, 2009, at www.nabj.org/pres_ corner/2009/prezcorner120309.php; American Society of News Editors, "Minority Employment in Daily Newspapers," April 11, 2010, at www.asne.org/key_initiatives/ diversity/newsroom_census/table_a.aspx.

18. The authors were involved from the start as leaders of NAHJ in creating the Parity

Project with Phillips, Temple and the E. W. Scripps Company. The project continues to operate at a reduced level at several smaller Scripps subsidiaries.

19. The report reviewed news coverage in thirteen newspapers, fifteen cable programs, the seven broadcast network news programs, twelve major news websites, and nine news radio and talk programs. See "Hispanics in the News: Events Drive the Narrative," Pew Research Center's Project for Excellence in Journalism, December 7, 2009, at www.journalism.org/node/18531.

20. "Media, Race, and Obama's First Year," Pew Research Center's Project for Excellence in Journalism, July 26, 2010, at www.journalism.org/node/21403.

21. "'*Waco Tribune-Herald*' Apologizes For Coverage Of 1916 Lynching," *Editor & Publisher*, May 15, 2006, at www.allbusiness.com/services/business-services-miscellaneous-business/4695426-1.html.

22. *Meridan Star*, "We Honor and We Apologize," January 17, 2009, at meridianstar.com/editorials/x681147654/We-honor-and-we-apologize.

23. Edward B. Colby, "So It Begins: Outsourcing the Newsroom," *Columbia Journalism Review*, October 25, 2005, at www.cjr.org/behind_the_news/so_it_begins_outsourcing_the_n.php.

24. See "ACON News," at www.aconinvestments.com/news/040821.html.

25. Our summary here is largely based on Janet Abate, *Inventing the Internet* (Cambirdge, MA: MIT Press, 2000), and Lawrence Lessig, *The Future of Ideas: The Fate of the Commons in a Connected World* (New York: Vintage Books, 2002).

26. Judy O'Neill, "An Interview with Paul Baran, March 5, 1990, at www.cbi.umn.edu/oh/pdf.phtml?id=295: 10, 19.

27. The network Baran envisioned contained no single path that was critical to the delivery of packets. UCLA's Leonard Kleinroch and Donald Davies of the United Kingdom's National Physical Laboratory developed and perfected the same packet-switching approach around the same time, though none of the men were initially aware of the others' work. Lessig, *Future of Ideas*: 26–7, 30–1; Lloyd, *Prologue to a Farce*: 198–9.

28. Lessig, *Future of Ideas*: 198–9.

29. Starr, *Creation of the Media*: 201–5; Lessig, *Future of Ideas*: 30.

30. Nicholas Johnson, "Carterfone: My Story," *Santa Clara Computer and High Technology Law Journal* 25: 3 (2009): 686–7.

31. Johnson, "Carterfone": 684–5.

32. Tim Wu, "Wireless Network Neutrality: Cellular Carterfone and Consumer Choice in Mobile Broadband," New America Foundation, February 15, 2007, at www.newamerica.net/files/WorkingPaper17_WirelessNetNeutrality_Wu.pdf: 5–6. See also Jonathan E. Nuechterlein and Phillip J. Weiser, *Digital Crossroads: American Telecommunications Policy in the Internet Age* (Cambridge: Massachusetts Institute of Technology Press, 2007): 58–9; Lessig, *Future of Ideas*: 26–30; Matthew Lasar, "Any Lawful Device: 40 Years After the Carterfone Decision," *Ars Technica*, June 26, 2008, at arstechnica.com/articles/culture/carterfone-40-years.ars/2; "Carterfone Changes Our World," *Communications News*, September 1984, at findarticles.com/p/articles/mi_m0CMN/is_n9_v21/ai_569360/pg_1?tag=artBody;col1.

33. Robert Cannon, "The Legacy of the Federal Communications Commission's Computer Inquiries," *Federal Communications Law Journal* 55 (2003): 173.

34. Cannon, "Legacy": 174–80.

35. Ibid.: 181.

36. Ibid.: 188.

37. Ibid.: 194.

38. Ibid.: 199–204.

39. J. K. MacKei-Mason and Hal R. Varian, "Some Economics of the Internet," paper presented at Tenth Michigan Public Utility Conference, Western Michigan University, 1993: 1–2, at 129.3.20.41/eps/comp/papers/9401/9401001.pdf. See also Rajiv C. Shah and Jay P. Kesan "The Privatization of the Internet's Backbone Network," (March 2007) at http://www.governingwithcode.org/journal_articles/pdf/Backbone.pdf.

40. *The Federal High Performance Computing Program* (Washington, DC: White House Office of Science and Technology Policy, 1989).

41. Shah and Kesan, "Privatization of the Internet's Backbone Network": 11–13.

42. Derek Turner, *Changing Media: Public Interest Policies for the Digital Age* (Washington, DC: Free Press, 2009): 51–2.

43. Ibid.: 62–3; Nuechterlein and Weiser, *Digital Crossroads*: 165–6; "Bush to Big Cable: We Love You Time Warner, Comcast, Cox! A Pre-GOP Convention Gift to Media Monopoly for Broadband," Center for Digital Democracy, August 30, 2004, at www.democraticmedia.org/brandx/doj_reverse_court.

44. Interview with Jim Pickrell, president of Brand X, December 26, 2005, at www.youtube.com/watch?v=FnA24RixIAs.

45. Turner, *Changing Media*: 64; Yuki Noguchi, "Cable Firms Don't Have to Share Networks, Court Rules," *Washington Post*, June 28, 2005, at www.washingtonpost.com/wp dyn/content/article/2005/06/27/AR2005062700415.html.

46. Turner, *Changing Media*: 25–6, 31.

47. "At SBC, It's All About 'Scale and Scope,'" *Business Week*, November 7, 2005.

48. Free Press release, "Free Press Organizes Nationwide Opposition to Time Warner Cable Metering," April 10, 2009, at www.freepress.net/node/56030; S. Derek Turner, "Blocking or Metering: A False Choice," Free Press, August 2008, at www.freepress.net/files/Blocking_or_Metering_A_False_Choice.pdf.

49. Stephen Lawson, "Time Warner to Try Tiered Cable Pricing," *IDG News Service* (PC World), January 18, 2008. See also stopthecap.com/2009/04/16/we-won-time-warner-killing-usage-caps-in-all-markets.

50. Cited in Mark Cooper, "Expanding the Digital Divide &Falling Behind on Broadband: Why a Telecommunications Policy of Neglect is Not Benign," Consumer Federation of America briefing paper, October 2004: 5, at http://www.consumerfed.org/elements/www.consumerfed.org/file/digitaldivide.pdf.

51. Federal Communications Commission, "Connecting America: The National Broadband Plan" (Washington, DC, March 2010): 23. See also John B. Horrigan, "Broadband Adoption and Use in America," Federal Communications Commission, OBI Working Paper Series 1, February 14, 2010, at online.wsj.com/public/resources/documents/FCCSurvey.pdf.

52. Nate Anderson, "National Broadband Plan Arrives, Quoting Shakespeare," *Ars Techinica*, March 16, 2010, at arstechnica.com/tech-policy/news/2010/03/national-broadband-plan-arrives-quoting-shakespeare.ars.

53. Berkman Center for Internet and Society, "The Next Generation Connectivity: A Review of Broadband Internet Transactions and Policy from Around the World," Federal Communications Commission, March 2010, at cyber.law.harvard.edu/sites/cyber.law.harvard.edu/files/Berkman_Center_Broadband_Final_Report_15Feb2010.pdf.

54. John Horrigan, "America Unwired," Pew Internet and American Life Project, July 22, 2009, at pewresearch.org/pubs/1287/wireless-internet-use-mobile-access.

55. Steven Hill, "The World Wide Webbed: The Obama Campaign's Masterful Use of the Internet," *Social Europe Journal*, April 8, 2009.

56. John Eggerton, "President Plugs Network Neutrality in China, Broadcasting and Cable," November 16, 2009, at www.broadcastingcable.com/article/389137-President_Plugs_Network_Neutrality_in_China.php.

57. Federal Communications Commission, "In the Matter of Preserving the Open Internet, WC 09-191," (Washington, DC, 2009); "FCC Adopts Internet Policy statement," FCC press release, August 5, 2005; Free Press, *Changing Media: Public Interest Policies for the Digital Age* (Washington, DC: Free Press, 2009): 21, 200; hraunfoss.fcc.gov/edocs_public/attachmatch/FCC-09-93A1.doc. See also Tim Karr, "Washington's Astroturf Economy," Savetheinternet.org, November 18, 2009, at www.savetheinternet.com/blog/09/11/18/washington%E2%80%99s-astroturf-economy.

58. Nilki Benitez, "Marisa Trevino: She's one Blogging Latina Lista to be Reckoned With!" *La Presena*, San Diego, November 6, 2009, at laprensa-sandiego.org/stories/marisa-trevino-she%E2%80%99s-one-blogging-latina-lista-to-be-reckoned-with.

59. James Rucker, "Fox News Doesn't Care About Black People, Does the Congressional Black Caucus?" *Sentinel*, April 12–18, 2007; ColorOfChange press release, "Black Activists Praise Barack Obama For Rejecting FOX/Congressional Black Caucus Institute Debate," April 9, 2007.

60. "Lou Dobbs to Quit CNN," *New York Times*, November 11, 2009.

61. Netroots Nation, at www.netrootsnation.org/about. See also H. W. Wilson Company website, at www.hwwilson.com/_home/bios/2006109895.htm; Amy Alexander, "Minority Bloggers Fight Inequality" *Nation*, July 16, 2008, at www.thenation.com/article/minority-bloggers-fight-inequality.

62. American Society of News Editors press release, "Decline in Newsroom Jobs Slows," April 11, 2010, at www.asne.org/article_view/articleid/763/decline-in-newsroom-jobs-slows-763.aspx; American Society of News Editors press release, "ASNE Newsroom Employment Declines," April 4, 2009, at www.asne.org/article_view/articleid/12/u-s-newsroom-employment-declines-12.aspx.

63. "McGruder Award Winner: Online News Sites Need to Feel 'Heat' on Diversity," *Editor and Publisher*, April 9, 2010, at www.editorandpublisher.com/eandp/news/article_display.jsp?vnu_content_id=1004082128.

64. See Cable Communications Act of 1984, 47USC531, Sec. 611, at www.publicaccess.org/cableact.html.

65. See *Time Warner Cable of New York City v Bloomberg LP*, US 118 F.3d 917.

66. Phillip Dampler, "Intended Consequences: Missouri Subscribers Can't Find Their Public/Educational/Government Channels," Stop the Cap website, February 25, 2010, at stopthecap.com.

67. David Greising "AT&T's U-verse gives short shrift to public-access programming," *Chicago Tribune*, February 3rd, 2009.

68. Mike Rosen-Molina, "Public Access TV Fights for Relevance in the YouTube Age," *MeidaShift: Your Guide to the Digital Revolution*, December 17, 2008, at www.pbs.org/mediashift/2008/12/public-access-tv-fights-for-relevance-in-the-youtube-age352.html.

69. The telecom and cable companies have been major financial supporters of Civil Rights groups. The following are a few examples of the support Civil Rights groups have received from telecom companies: SBC press release, "SBC Foundation Makes $1 Million Technology Grant To League Of United Latin American Citizens," July 4, 2004, at www.att.com/gen/press-room?pid=4800&cdvn=news&newsarticleid=21 220; LULAC press release, "AT&T and League of United Latin American Citizens Empower Low-Income Hispanic Communities With Technology," April 17, 2007, at lulac.org/programs/technology/att/index.html (LULAC was awarded $1.5 million); PR Newsire, "LULAC Receives $1 Million Grant From AT&T: Grant Will Help Improve High School Dropout Rate Among At-Risk Latino Youth," July 11, 2008; PR Newire, "AT&T Foundation Provides $1.5 Million Technology Access Grant to League of United Latin American Citizens; Grant Builds on Success of LULAC Empower Hispanic America with Technology Initiative," June 20, 2006; AT&T press release, "NAACP Near Fund-Raising Goal with AT&T Campaign Leadership," July 26, 2009, at www.att.com/gen/press-room?pid=4800&cdvn=news&newsarticleid=26949. AT&T Chairman Randall Stephenson was the chair of the NAACP's Centennial Corporate Campaign mentioned in this release. The goal of the campaign is to raise $5 million for the NAACP. AT&T has donated at least $500,000 to the campaign. In addition, the release states that AT&T has also awarded the NAACP more than $11 million over the past twenty-five years to support the organization's initiatives; National Council of La Raza press release, "Verizon Foundation Invests $2.2 million in Partnership with National Council of La Raza and Urban League to Create After School Education Program Thinkfinity.org," October 7, 2008, at www.nclr.org/content/news/detail/54262.

Mickey Ibarra, who served as director of intergovernmental affairs for the White House during the Clinton administration, is the president of Ibarra Strategy Group in Washington, a government relations and public relations firm. Verizon is one of his clients: see lists of clients on company's website, at www.ibarrastrategy.com/index.php?p_resource=clients. In addition, Ibarra's company has for years lobbied against net neutrality with Congressional members. See Ibarra's January 2010 Senate disclosure form, at http://soprweb.senate.gov/index.cfm?event=getFilingDetails&filingID=8191af2c-e19c-4ac4-bf74-984d0ffce2d4http://soprweb.senate.gov/index.cfm?event=getFilingDetails&filingID=8191af2c-e19c-4ac4-bf74-984d0ffce2d4; For a list of NCLR's corporate advisory board, visits the groups' Web site (accessed on May 6, 2010 at www.nclr.org/section/about/board/corporate_board_of_advisors.

70. Some staff members of the groups have privately admitted as much in conversations with the authors.

71. Letter from LULAC President Rosa Rosales to FCC Chairman Kevin Martin, October 24, 2006, at fjallfoss.fcc.gov/ecfs/document/view?id=6518537265.

72. Information on international broadband penetration can be found on Free Press's website, at www.freepress.net/international-broadband.

73. In the Matter of the Petition of Free Press for Declaratory Ruling that Degrading an Internet Application Violates the FCC's Internet Policy Statement and Does Not Meet an Exception for "Reasonable Network Management," WC Docket No. 07-52, November 1, 2007, at fjallfoss.fcc.gov/ecfs/document/view?id=6519825121.

74. Reply Comments filed February 28, 2008, to the Federal Communications Commission by the National Black Chamber of Commerce, Labor Council for Latin American Advancement, Latinos in Information Sciences and Technology Association, League of Rural Voters, National Black Justice Coalition, National Council of Women's Organizations, and National Congress of Black Women In the Matter of: Broadband Industry Practices, WC Docket No. 07-52.

75. *Washington Post*, letters to the editor, February 21, 2008: A14, at www.washingtonpost.com/wp-dyn/content/article/2008/02/20/AR2008022002661.html.

76. Alex Chasick, "AT&T Asks Employees To Oppose Net Neutrality," *Consumerist*, October 20, 2010, at consumerist.com/2009/10/att-asks-employees-to-oppose-net-neutrality.html; www.att.com/gen/investor-relations?pid=7818.

77. Letter from 72 House Democrats to FCC Chairman, October 15, 2009, at coloradoindependent.com/wp-content/uploads/2009/10/telcoletter.pdf.

78. Anti-Network Neutrality Letter to the FCC signed by 20 Civil Rights Groups, October 19, 2009, at fjallfoss.fcc.gov/ecfs/document/view?id=7020141807; Letter from Asian American Justice Center, National Council of La Raza, League of United Latin American Citizens and the National Urban League to FCC Chairman Julius Genachowski, October 19, 2009.

79. Reply Comments by ColorOfChange.org in the Matter of Preserving an Open Internet GN Doc. No 191 and Broadband Industry Practices, WC Doc. No 07–52, April 26, 2010, at fjallfoss.fcc.gov/ecfs/document/view?id=7020441624.

80. James Rucker, "Why Are Some Civil Rights Leaders on the Wrong Side of Net Neutrality?" Huffington Post, January 28, 2010, at www.huffingtonpost.com/james-rucker/why-are-some-civil-rights_b_440926.html.

81. Media Justice Commentators to the FCC in Matter Preserving an Open Internet and Broadband Industry Practices, April 26, 2010, at fjallfoss.fcc.gov/ecfs/document/view?id=7020437168; Malkia Cyril, "A New Civil Rights Mandate: Champion Open Networks to Close Digital Divide, Huffington Post, February 16, 2010, at www.huffingtonpost.com/malkia-a-cyril/a-new-civil-rights-mandat_b_462110.html.

Index